Alanna Nash is a feature writer for the *New York Times* and *Entertainment Weekly*, who has written five books, including *Elvis: From Memphis to Hollywood* and *The Colonel*, her biography of Colonel Tom Parker, also published by Aurum. She lives in Louisville, Kentucky.

Praise for *The Colonel*

'Perhaps the most thoroughly researched music book ever written.'
Observer

'The year's most meticulously researched and widely discussed music book ... a gripping psychological drama full of astounding hubris and needless tragedy.'
Independent on Sunday

'Horrible man. Bloody good read ... Nash doesn't ask us to forgive Parker, or even like the man, but rather to understand him ... She succeeds brilliantly.' *Uncut*

'Extraordinary is the word.' *Sunday Times*

'Nash has a marvellous story to tell ... No one will ever know whether the Colonel was the devil or the angel in Elvis's private hell; but anyone who is interested in their entwined stories – an age-old morality tale of innocence and experience – should read this book.'
Daily Telegraph

In December 1970, on the night of Sonny West's wedding, Elvis poses with his newly deputised entourage. Back row, from left, Billy Smith, former Shelby County Sheriff Bill Morris, Lamar Fike, Jerry Schilling, Sheriff Roy Nixon, Vernon Presley, Charlie Hodge, Sonny West, George Klein, Marty Lacker. Front row, from left, Dr George Nichopoulos, Elvis, Red West

l–r Billy Smith, Marty Lacker and Lamar Fike in 1996 (Tim Porco)

ELVIS

and the Memphis Mafia

Alanna Nash

with Billy Smith, Marty Lacker and Lamar Fike

Aurum

First published in Great Britain
2005 by Aurum Press Ltd
7 Greenland Street, London NW1 0ND
www.aurumpress.co.uk

First published by HarperCollins Publishers, New York 1995

A catalogue record for this book is available from the British Library.

ISBN-13: 978 1 84513 128 9

7 9 10 8
2011 2010

This book is printed on paper certified by the Forest Stewardship Council as
coming from a forest that is well managed according to strict environmental,
social and economic standards.

Text design by Nancy Singer
Printed by CPI Bookmarque, Croydon, Surrey

To the memory of Alan E. Fortas
(1936–1992)
"My boy, my boy"

"Had I but serv'd my God with half the zeal
I serv'd my king, he would not in mine age
Have left me naked to mine enemies."

—Shakespeare, *Henry VIII*

CONTENTS

ACKNOWLEDGMENTS

From Alanna Nash

Although this book is an oral history of three people, many more contributed to it in important and significant ways.

First, I wish to express my profound gratitude to Sam Hughes and Bob Solinger of The Dickens Group literary agency, who performed Herculean feats in both selling the book and helping prepare it for publication. Without them, I wouldn't have made my deadline, and this book might not exist, or certainly not in this form.

I'd also like to thank Rick Horgan, our editor at HarperCollins, who instantly recognized the merit of the project.

In its long path from inception to publication, the book took unforeseen twists and turns. In the early stages, Joyce Engelson was the most helpful with advice and support. I thank her for the many hours she generously gave me.

And while the bulk of the photographs came from the personal collection of the Memphis Mafia, we are extremely thankful to Jimmy Velvet, who contributed many more out of friendship, and to Richard Morelli, who came up with some never-before-published photos from Elvis's army days. Equal thanks go to Tim Porco, who copied hundreds of these photographs for posterity.

In addition, I am deeply indebted to the following individuals: to Blanchard Tual for sharing his extensive findings on the financial relationship between Presley and Colonel Tom Parker; to Warder Harrison for research and records regarding the divorce of J. D. and Minnie Mae Presley and for compiling geneaological information; to Sheri Lacker for hours of newspaper library research; to Susan Nadler for midwifing fate and assisting in my meeting one of the book's principal characters; to Ted Bridis and Ed Staats of the Associated Press for helping in the search for certain of Elvis's military records; to Jennifer Page of KYGO Radio, Denver, for an important tip; to Butch Hause of the *Denver Post* for researching the Elvis churches; to Barbara Rice Thompson of *Penthouse* for digging out an old interview; to Milton Metz for the gift of an important resource book; to Jo Smith for unlocking a lot of memories in Billy's head and, along with Patsy Lacker, reliving what was in many ways a painful experience; to Jim Higgins for comforting legal advice; to Judy F. May for lending her out-of-print Elvis albums and for her keen observations about Presley's acting techniques and film career; to Betty Williams, who kept the faith for nearly forty years; and to Paul Schmitt, who knows how to pull things into shape at the last minute.

Additionally, I am grateful to Brian Arnold for adapting my word processor to handle literally thousands of extra pages of transcript and text; to Diane McCall, who transcribed dozens of cassettes of taped conversation between the author and the Memphis Mafia; to Judy Harvey, who transcribed the first batch of interviews that led to a successful proposal; and to Shirley Jackson for care and feeding of the author.

I also wish to thank my parents, Allan and Emily Kay Nash, for their unyielding love and support through the years, as well as my sister, Gale Nash Snyder, and Hugh C. Wright, Jr., and Vin Morreale, Jr., all of whom helped in immeasurable personal ways.

Finally, I would like to thank the late Alan E. Fortas for suggesting me for this project and Elvis himself for being an endlessly fascinating biographical subject.

During the course of my research, I had three visits with Colonel Tom Parker in Las Vegas, where he currently lives. While Colonel made it clear he would not sit for an interview, I was journalistically concerned that he have a chance to respond to the charges leveled against him of "overreaching" in his handling of Elvis's career.

Our visits, which included his personable wife, Loanne, were extremely cordial and enjoyable. But over eight hours of rambling conversation, Colonel conveyed what appears to be his genuine belief that he served Elvis well—that he had nothing but affection for his client and never meant to hurt him. What he did in the line of business was just that—"business." Today, at eighty-five, Colonel sleeps well, he says. And he repeated what Vernon Presley publicly insisted after Elvis died: the Colonel is an honest man. He refused to comment for the book, he explained, simply because he feels no need.

From Billy Smith, Marty Lacker, and Lamar Fike

Much has been written and said about Elvis, and with the exception of a couple of books, most of it has been untrue, half-true, and confusing. Throughout the years, we have had so many people ask us what the truth was and to give them a sense of what his life was really like.

In this oral history, we hope we offer those two elements in a tasteful, balanced way. We could not have found anyone more perfect to take our words and present them to you in a more real and understanding fashion than Alanna Nash. Not only is she an accomplished author and experienced writer in the music field, she understands the entertainment industry. We thank her for the years she has spent making this book come to life. We would also like to thank Sam Hughes and Bob Solinger of The Dickens Group.

Too, we want to acknowledge the truly wonderful life experience we were fortunate to share with Elvis. The good times far outweigh the bad. This book is for the guys, especially those who were there from the early years.

Finally, we would like to acknowledge our families for their love and understanding and dedicate our portions of the book to them.

BILLY SMITH: My lovely wife, Jo; my sons, Danny and Joey; daughter-in-law, Ginger; my granddaughters, Danielle, Eden, and Stormie; and my grandsons, Rivers and Paris. And, in memory of my parents, Travis and Lorraine, and my brother, Bobby. Also, to Sarah and Woodrow Norris.

MARTY LACKER: Sheri, Angie, Marc, Brenda, Brandon, and Cody. And to Patsy for her contribution to the book and for putting up with me all those years. Also, my sister, Anne Grenadier, and in memory of my brother-in-law, Bernie Grenadier.

LAMAR FIKE: To my darling wife, Mary, and to the memory of my beloved mother, Margaret.

PROLOGUE

The flickering television images of Elvis Presley—the rough-and-ready Hillbilly Cat swiveling provocatively on *The Ed Sullivan Show* in the 1950s, the lean-and-leathered god of *The Singer Special* of the '60s, and the grotesquely puffy, jumpsuited caricature from his last live concerts of the '70s—are so ingrained in the American consciousness as almost to be snapshots from the family album.

Indeed, it is hard to find a more perfect symbol of all that is glorious and horrific about America—about the American dream turned nightmare—than Elvis Aaron Presley, who rose from wrenching Mississippi poverty to nearly unfathomable wealth as the high priest of pop. For his trouble, this American original changed not only the course of popular music, but American *thought,* only to die at forty-two, discouraged, disillusioned, and all tubbed out on drugs, cheeseburgers, and deep-fried peanut butter sandwiches. To some, it seemed a dramatic comeuppance, a tawdry end to a tacky life.

Yet perhaps no other great American has been as fully exploited and least understood. For while Elvis was the most significant folk hero of the twentieth century, he rarely spoke about himself and certainly not to the public—never, in the twenty-one years of his professional career, granting even one in-depth interview. A fascinating enigma—a mystery that will never be completely solved—he is, as critic Steve Simels dubbed him in a reference to the classic film *Citizen Kane,* "The 'Rosebud' of our popular culture."

There is the notion that Elvis Presley, infinitely complex, yet simple, was unknowable because he didn't know himself, that there was no real Elvis, only a mythological figure he invented when he sang. The man himself, the theory goes, was little more than an empty vessel into which his detractors poured their fears and his loyal flock their fondest hopes and dreams. Maybe so.

But the people who came closest to knowing Elvis Presley, the man, were his inner circle of friends and employees—the Memphis Mafia, as the press called them, the rock 'n' roll version of Frank Sinatra's Rat Pack, the young men who traveled everywhere with him as both companions and quasi-bodyguards.

Only they knew that within Elvis Presley, who survived his twin brother at birth, two beings existed—codependent but incompatible and worlds apart. One, a virtual innocent, wore black lace shirts, strummed a guitar, and sang, as writer Lucian Truscott IV once put it, "an elegant hybrid of nigger and 'neck." This Elvis, while a shy mama's boy, challenged every show business convention, operated from a position of supreme confidence, sang gospel music in his quiet moments, and addressed his elders as sir or ma'am.

But the other Elvis, a man's man who courted danger, inevitably got him into trouble. Never rising above the self-destructive ways of his luckless family, he was insecure, restless, paranoid, menacing, and eternally suspicious, a fan of the worst kind of show business excess, both personally and musically. Eventually, his public persona, draped in outlandish stage costumes and capes, became a cartoon.

As one, Elvis became one of the highest-grossing motion picture stars and the unequivocal King of Rock 'n' Roll. He holed up in a mansion of a prison called Graceland, a vampire who came alive at night and sucked at the nectar of whatever, and whoever, caught his fancy. He gave away Cadillacs to his cohorts and to strangers. He was a hero. Yet as the other, he patrolled the red velvet tombs of Las Vegas at dawn, held pistols to the heads of his friends, and allowed his wife, Priscilla, and his manager, Colonel Tom Parker, to orchestrate his life and violate his career. In retaliation, he fed his self-loathing a continuous flow of pills and too soon died, sprawled on the floor of his bathroom, purple under his own weight.

The job of keeping the dark Elvis under wraps fell to Colonel Parker. But on a day-to-day basis, it landed squarely in the lap of the Memphis Mafia. They did their job, and usually did it well. Just how well comes across in the *New York Times* review of the documentary *Elvis on Tour*: "The film strips away the storybook myth to find underneath a private person who is indistinguishable from the public one, except for the fact he dresses with somewhat less flamboyance."

Rock writer Dave Marsh, in his 1982 book, *Elvis*, called the Memphis Mafia "toadies and stooges . . . buffoons, yes-men, gold-diggers and dull thugs . . . the most small-time sidekicks that any great man has known."

Certainly the twenty or so men who filtered through Elvis's entourage were not hired for their business acumen or for their ability to advise him on matters public or private. Nor did Presley invite it, and to ensure that, he picked companions who came from, as one of them puts it, "the same little world." He saw in them, more than anything, a buffer zone—the one group of people with whom he could be himself, free from the pressures of being Elvis Presley.

"There were some dumb asses in the group," one of them concedes, and the dimmer ones didn't last long in Presley's employ. But the majority of the core group of the Mafia were never as simple-headed as the press assumed—surely not the reliable, take-charge Marty Lacker, the Mafia's foreman, who handled many of Presley's daily business demands; the frequently disruptive Lamar Fike, head of Elvis's transportation (and also Presley's premier whipping boy), later an advance man with Colonel Parker on the road; or Billy Smith, Elvis's first cousin, embittered about the way Presley's outrageous fame forever changed his family, but who served as a stabilizing factor in Elvis's volatile life and became the singer's confidant in his last days. If ever Elvis Presley had a best friend, it was Billy.

That they remained loyal to him, despite Presley's verbal and physical abuse, speaks more about their love for him than it does about their paychecks. Without them, Presley surely would have died years earlier. "We literally kept him alive," says Fike, who remembers too many close calls.

The recollections of Smith, Lacker, and Fike, presented here in oral history form, are more than just memories of their glory days with the King. They are unscheduled stops, to borrow a metaphor from rock chronicler Timothy White, on Elvis's runaway "Mystery Train." And as primary testimonies about every personal and professional turn of events in the Presley saga for thirty years—from 1947, when Smith was first able to form important impressions of his older cousin, until the day Presley died in 1977—they also forge their own form of illumination, especially since Smith speaks candidly here for the first time about their remarkable relationship.

As such, these often poignant vignettes amount to as close a psychological profile as anyone will ever get of Elvis Presley and present a serious look at the phenomenal and tragic evolution of a supremely gifted and equally troubled native genius. Never was so influential a man so poorly prepared for his fate—nor so ineptly schooled for its consequences.

This book, however, is as much about the Memphis Mafia— about what it was like to be in the shadow of the King, enjoying a vicarious, shared identity—as it is about Presley. In some ways, they were like the Italian Mafia, adhering to a veil of secrecy in hiding the truth; serving twenty-four-hour-a-day allegiance to their employer rather than to their wives and families; collecting tiny salaries; enduring personal slights and belittlement; and expected to do anything to show their devotion, including stopping bullets, if necessary.

Why did they stay? The answer is long and complicated, but also short and obvious: Elvis was their drug of choice.

While many people who spend their lives in the service of famous people eventually come to despise them, that never happened with the Memphis Mafia, who even after decades still believed that being in Elvis's presence somehow protected them from the evils of the world. "It never entered my mind that he would die," says Lacker. "That's just the way he affected us. I thought we'd all die before he would."

When he did die on August 16, 1977, it changed their world forever. Many of them discovered they'd been handicapped by their years of living a fantasy—that they had no knowledge of how to exist in the workaday world, so insulated had they been behind the gates of Graceland. Some of them found that without Presley's reflected glory, their status—and their relationships with others—quickly changed. It was a frightful awakening.

"The hardest thing I've had to do since he died is to develop another life," admits Fike. "None of us was equipped for his death. You can look at every one of us, and we all have the same problems. We all fight the business world. We try to survive with him not around, and it's not easy. We all sit down and just look at each other. And we miss him very much."

In some ways, talking for this book was cathartic. By looking back on how Elvis lived his life and trying to explain why he made the choices he did—what motivated him to produce his art, as well as the ultimate horror of his end—they also explored the unraveling of the Mafia itself. This is a story about what it's like to be a witness to history and about the toll that it takes on the psyche, especially when history ends tragically. Not surprisingly, their perceptions of events that led to that end do not always agree.

Their hope in discussing their extraordinary experience—how Presley acted within the group, how the group survived as other members of Presley's camp tried to break it up, and how it was torn asunder after he died—is to shed new light into the few remaining dark corners of the Presley saga. To those who question their right to expose this information, they correctly reply it was as much their lives as it was his.

My own affinity with Elvis Presley goes back almost as far as theirs. I had just turned six when Elvis made his first appearance on *The Ed Sullivan Show,* and, like all of America, I sat transfixed in front of my family's television set, astonished by the urgency of this human comet who was just passing through. As a child shackled to two weekly drudgeries—classical violin lessons and Saturday morning allergy shots—the high point of my young existence was listening to Top 40 radio and buying 45 rpm singles at the hi-fi shop after my Saturday appointment.

Most of my records were by Elvis (though others such as Fats Domino also made the grade), and as I listened to them—to a kind of Southern experience that was far more deeply rooted than my middle-class Kentucky upbringing—I wanted to know everything there was to know about a man who sent up such an electrifying cry and shuddering moan. Eventually, this fascination set me on a lifelong path of writing about popular music and its culture.

On August 16, 1977, I was celebrating my twenty-seventh birthday when the Louisville *Courier-Journal,* for which I free-lanced as the pop music critic, telephoned to say that Elvis Presley was dead. Could I find his stepgrandmother, who lived in town?

I struck out with Mrs. Presley, but the next day the paper sent two reporters to Memphis to cover the outpouring of grief that attended Presley's funeral. I was one of them and John Filiatreau the other. John and I were standing in the press pool in front of Graceland when Presley's head of security, Dick Grob, came out with a bullhorn, stood directly in front of us, and announced, "Any members of the press who want to view the body line up behind these two."

And in we went. No, the body, dressed in a white business suit, a blue shirt, and a silver tie, did not look like Elvis Presley. And yes, it held a waxy hue. But it was still Elvis Presley in that casket, with the roots of his sideburns—as white as an undisturbed snowbank—badly in need of dyeing.

So many times as a child, I thumbed through the pages of fan magazines, staring at the voodoo sensuality etched on Elvis's face and at the ordinary faces of the young men who formed the knot of his friendships. I wondered then what it was like behind the gates at Graceland. How had they lived their lives there? How had Elvis—and his parents—borne up under the crushing weight of fame? And what about the Memphis Mafia? Was a life of running errands for the King really so grand?

I began to learn the answers that week in Memphis as my paper decided to publish a rotogravure extra on Elvis and asked me to interview anyone who knew him. I had never been to Memphis before and had no contacts. Bill E. Burk, who had written dozens of Presley columns through the years for the Memphis *Press-Scimitar*, took pity on me and introduced me to a number of people, including Alan Fortas, a core member of the Mafia for twelve years. It was Alan who, in time, brought me to this project.

The interviews for this book took place over a three-year period and were conducted in hotel rooms, homes, offices, and restaurants in Memphis, Nashville, and Louisville. I interviewed each person separately, many times, and we had several joint sessions, events that always sparked high emotion and often differing opinions and recollections of the same event. The transcripts of these interviews formed a four-thousand-page mountain.

In the course of this book, the astute reader may find that the principals sometimes talk authoritatively about events that happened before they joined the group. A neat trick, to be sure. But since Presley's death, they have spent their lives in search of the

"Rosebud," doing genealogical research in libraries, with each other, and with other members of the Smith and Presley families.

Like the survivors of a bad car wreck in which only the driver was killed, Billy Smith, Marty Lacker, and Lamar Fike are in some ways closer than blood relatives, bound by a singular shared experience, by pride and shame, and by remorse. Today, eighteen years after Elvis's death, not a week goes by when they don't see him in their dreams. A way of righting old wrongs, of saying things that never got said?

More likely a specter on the lam—Presley's own way of letting them know he's still around. Prone to long religious diatribes in the last half of his life, Elvis once lectured the group about the hereafter. He told them that if he went first, they'd better be good, because he'd be watching everything they did. "I'll haunt your asses!" he warned.

And so he does.

Alanna Nash

CHAPTER 1

THE FAMILY

LAMAR FIKE: I've been thinking about the Meditation Garden. Have you ever noticed the way the graves are laid out? You'd think Elvis would be between his mama and daddy. But he's between Grandma and his daddy. I figure that's so he can keep an eye on Vernon—see what he's up to—and not be distracted. Otherwise, those graves would be spinning like a circle saw. Because while Gladys was alive, they got into it pretty good. You had a wife who dominated the whole thing, a husband who didn't like to work, and an only child who was doted on by his mother. A child who listened to his mother and father argue all their lives. That's what molded Elvis into what he was. It was one of the most dysfunctional families I've ever seen.

BILLY SMITH: In 1981, Albert Goldman wrote a book called *Elvis*. The man's dead now, and you're not supposed to speak ill of the dead. But he had a way of writing that made me mad as hell. The book was degrading. By the time he finished talking about my family, I'm sure everybody thought, "That's white trash." But I'll tell you what—that four-eyed son of a bitch should have walked down that road one time. Just because you're poor doesn't mean you're white trash. Goldman thought if you come from Tupelo, Mississippi, and you're a sharecropper, you couldn't be too damn good, especially if there's talk of incest in your family. I understand where people would think that. But Goldman just took it to the extreme.

My daddy, Travis, who was Gladys's brother . . . well, I guess you couldn't be the son of a bootlegger and not drink. Because that's what my granddaddy, Robert, was, a bootlegger, even though he farmed, too. But Goldman said Elvis's great-grandfather on the Presley side was a horse thief. I've done some research on my own. And there's a question whether that was him or somebody else.

LAMAR FIKE: There was nobody in the world who could research like Albert Goldman. I deplored the hateful tone of that book, but even though I was one of his main sources, and shared in the royalties, I couldn't control Albert. What I liked best about that book was the research because I learned so much about what caused Elvis to be what he was. I went into the libraries and the Tennessee Museum and tracked his family all the way back to Ireland. His name was originally "Pressley."

BILLY SMITH: This stuff about Elvis being Irish, and that funny spelling of the name, that's all bunk. Elvis was Scottish.

LAMAR FIKE: If you look in Elaine Dundy's book, *Elvis and Gladys,* you'll see that John Mansell, Elvis's great-great-grandfather on the Smith side, was half Scots-Irish, half Indian. She says he grew up "wholly 'wild Injun'" One thing that made Elvis so interesting is this interplay of Irish genes and Indian genes. Gladys's side of the family were Indians. Elvis's great-great-great grandmother was Morning Dove White. She was Cherokee. Full-blooded. Born about 1800, died 1835. Buried in Alabama. She was married to William Mansell.

BILLY SMITH: Elvis knew that he had Indian blood in him. He liked that. He said that's where he got his high cheekbones.

LAMAR FIKE: Gladys was just like her father. She was more like a man with those big, wide shoulders. That's where Elvis got them, not from Vernon. And, of course, Elvis got his temper from her, too.

BILLY SMITH: Aunt Gladys is the biggest key to Elvis.

LAMAR FIKE: The Dundy book says that Gladys had some Jewish blood on her side. Ever hear of White Mansell? He was the son of John Mansell, Elvis's great-great-grandfather, who had a couple of wives simultaneously and kids by both, and a girlfriend, too. White married a woman named Martha Tackett, in

1870. Dundy says that Martha's mother, Nancy J. Burdine Tackett, was Jewish. She credits Elvis's third cousin, Oscar Tackett, with this information. Anyway, White and Nancy had a bunch of kids. One of the girls was Lucy, otherwise known as Octavia Luvenia, or Doll. Doll was Gladys's mother. Since, by Jewish orthodoxy, the mother continues the heritage, Elvis was Jewish. If you want to believe that.

BILLY SMITH: That's totally untrue. My grandmother Mansell was French. My ancestors were French and Indian. *Elvis and Gladys* has some good research. But there's no Jewish there. Never has been.

MARTY LACKER: Maybe she was a Jewish Indian. No, really. Billy could be forgetting there's such a thing as a French Jew. Jews are everywhere.

BILLY SMITH: I'm not forgetting nothin'. She's just not. I wouldn't be ashamed of it. There just wasn't any Jewish blood in our family.

LAMAR FIKE: This Jewish rumor got perpetuated when a reporter named John Heilpern at the *New York Observer* went down to Memphis. He may have been tongue-in-cheek about it, but he came to the conclusion that Elvis was Jewish, for three reasons. One, [Presley friend] George Klein told him Elvis's grandmother was Jewish and said there was a Star of David on the left side of Gladys's original memorial stone, that Elvis had gone back years after her death and had the Star added. Well, that stuff about the stone is true, but there's also a cross on the right. Two, he thought Elvis was Jewish because the Dundy book seemed to back George up. And three, he thought Elvis was Jewish because Elvis sometimes wore a Hebrew *chai* pendant—the symbol of life—with his cross.

MARTY LACKER: Elvis wore the *chai* because he liked to cover all the bases. He said he didn't want to be kept out of heaven on a technicality. But I can tell you the whole story of the footstone because I'm the one who had it made. Elvis was just hung up on all the religions. And he believed Jews were God's chosen people.

I'm Jewish, and we were talking one day, and he said, "I'd like to change the footstone on my mother's grave." And he told me he wanted the cross and the Star of David.

So I went to White Monument, over on Bellevue and South Parkway, and I had it made, and he and I went out there to look at it. He stood in front of it, and tears came to his eyes. Then he turned and looked at me and said, "I want you to call Harry Levitch," the jeweler, who was Jewish. It was like he was wanting to show Jewish people, "I'm not prejudiced" or "I care." I don't know where the stone is now. Knowing Vernon, who was anti-Semitic as hell, he probably destroyed it.

BILLY SMITH: That footstone's up at Graceland, in the garage, best I remember.

LAMAR FIKE: It was a very strong matriarchal family. On both sides and way on down the line. All the Smith women were domineering, and they all married weak husbands. Doll, Gladys's mother, was tubercular and never left her bed, but she ruled that family with her sickness.

BILLY SMITH: Doll was definitely the focus of that family. Robert, her husband, was a go-getter, and he bought her everything she wanted. He catered to her like a baby, and so did the kids. Elvis saw it in the Presleys, too. Maybe it goes back to Rosella Wesson. She was Elvis's great-grandmother, Vernon's father's mother. That's Jessie's, or J.D.'s, mother. She supposedly had all these children by a couple of different guys. One was part Cherokee Indian. She was definitely an "I'll do what I want to do" kind of woman. Her father, Dunnan Presley, Jr., run off when she was little, and she never knew him. So when she had ten kids, she never told any of them who *their* daddy was. She was a sharecropper. One of these Presley women ended up in the insane asylum. I don't know which one.

LAMAR FIKE: Minnie Mae, Vernon's mother, was a tough old bird. Tall, skinny, and peppery. Elvis called her "Dodger" because he threw a ball once and it missed her face by a fraction of an inch. She was certainly more dominant than Jessie. He up and deserted her ass in 1942. Went to Mobile, Alabama, and then

Louisville. He filed for divorce in 1946, claiming Minnie deserted *him,* after he begged her to leave Tupelo and come to Louisville. Whether he asked and she wouldn't or he never told her, he was shacked up with some woman up there in Louisville, a retired schoolteacher named Vera K. Leftwich.

Jessie's legal file has some interesting stuff in it. Like the deposition where he insists he tried to get Minnie Mae to come to Louisville. He claims she "abandoned me October 19, 1942." There's also two letters in it, both written in longhand, which support Minnie's desertion claim.

> Dear Sirs,
> I am writing to you about the letter I received from you last week concerning a divorce. I didn't desert my husband. As a matter of fact, he deserted me, and has been living with another woman and he hasn't sent me any money in over a year, and I am not able to make a living. We have five children and they are all married and have families of their own and I have to depend on them for a living. I want you to send me the papers to fill out and if you want my husband's record you can write to the Chief of Police Elsie Carr of Tupelo, Miss.
>
> *Sincerely yours,*
> *Mrs. Jessie Presley*

LAMAR FIKE: Two months after Grandma wrote that letter, her daughter, Delta Mae Biggs, took exception with Jessie's petition in equity.

> Dear Sir:
> I am writing in behalf of Mrs. Minnie Mae Pressely [*sic*], which is also my mother. Tell Pressley [*sic*] he can have a divorce if he will give Mama $200 cash. She won't ask for alimony. If he doesn't want to do that she will not give him a divorce. He told a falsehood about several matters to you. He has (5) children not (3). He also deserted Mama.
>
> *Thanks*
> *Delta Mae Biggs*

LAMAR FIKE: After that, the attorney wrote Grandma that her husband refused to pay anything for settlement or for alimony, even though Jessie made $30 a week as a cabinet maker. Jessie told his attorney to go ahead with the divorce, and he got it in 1948.

MARTY LACKER: Jessie just didn't give a damn. Minnie was two years older than he was, and I don't think he ever did much except father children. When he got married, he was slim and handsome and about six feet tall. He was known as a hellraiser. He liked nice clothes and he liked to cat around. Somebody in the family said that's where Elvis got it. Except Jessie liked his booze, too. He'd buy the house a round of drinks to get everybody to think he was a good guy. Meanwhile, his kids did without the things they needed.

LAMAR FIKE: Jessie remarried as soon as his divorce came through. On all of his affidavits and depositions, and on his second marriage certificate, Jessie signed his last name "Pressley." If you look at Grandma's letter in the divorce file, though, she used "Presley." I don't think anybody knows exactly when the family changed the spelling, but Vernon used the double "S" on his Social Security card.

Jessie died of heart disease in 1973, and he's buried in Louisville. His tombstone says "Presley."

MARTY LACKER: In 1958, after Elvis got famous, Jessie cut a record called "The Roots of Elvis" for some fly-by-night company there in Louisville called Legacy Records. He called himself Grandpa Jessie Pressley. That year, he went on *I've Got a Secret*. His secret, of course, was that he was Elvis's grandfather. He was sixty-two years old. He sat in a rocking chair and sang, and the show's emcee, Garry Moore, backed him on the drums.

Jessie told a Toronto newspaper that he specialized in "religious and working songs" that he learned as a cotton picker in Mississippi. He also said he didn't like rock 'n' roll and that he didn't want Elvis to help him. He said, "I want to make it on my own."

LAMAR FIKE: Jessie came out to a show we did in Louisville once, in 1971. I met him backstage. He was real country, quiet.

Elvis wasn't close to him at all, although when he played Louisville in '56, he went out to Jessie's little bungalow and had lunch with him and gave him a Ford Fairlane, and a TV, and a hundred-dollar bill. But on the whole, it was a rather frosty relationship. Grandma called him a son of a bitch. The South has a tradition of being matriarchal. Historically, there were always great women in the South. There were great men, too, but the women held the family together while the men were more concerned with providing. I've always thought that women were much stronger than men in the long run, that when the world ended, the women would be standing long after the men hit the ground. Elvis and I used to talk about this, and he didn't agree. He always had that macho thing, that he was the man of the house and ruled. But maybe a strong woman was what he was really searching for. Because Gladys ruled her house when she married. But when Elvis came along, he and Gladys ruled that roost together.

BILLY SMITH: Aunt Gladys was a strong-willed individual. If you scared her real bad or made her mad, she'd lash out at you. In Tupelo, they still talk about when she was sharecropping with her family. The guy who owned the farm come by on a horse with his high-topped leather boots and a whip. And he jumped on her parents and her sisters with it. Gladys was ten or eleven years old, but she ripped a plowshare off and took the point and hit him in the head with it. Damn near killed him.

LAMAR FIKE: Everybody in that family was scared of Gladys and her temper. There were nine boys and girls, and she ran 'em all, even her eldest sister, Lillian. Everybody knew not to mess with her much.

Except for Billy, and maybe one or two others, the Smith family was just wilder than goats. By God, they were tough! Tougher even than the Presleys, and they were violent people.

BILLY SMITH: I took more from my mama's side of the family when it come to fighting. I don't like it. But my daddy went through the worst that any man can go through, and he wasn't scared to fly in there and hang with it. He and Uncle Johnny come close to death after they moved to Memphis. Five guys jumped 'em, and they cut Daddy down the side of his face and stabbed at his back. They stabbed Uncle Johnny all the way down his chest and just did miss his heart. Daddy was bleeding and laid open, but he was running across the street after them as best he could, and then he collapsed. He laid in the middle of the street yelling, "You sons of bitches! I know who you are! Goddamn, you better kill me! If you leave me alive, you're going to know it!"

About a year and a half later, Daddy saw one of them, Doyle Pruitt, coming down the street. We had just come from a movie. Mama said, "Travis, don't do it!" But Daddy said, "Go on in front of me. And don't look back."

When Pruitt crossed the alley, Daddy stepped out and knocked that son of a bitch down and stomped his face. I thought he never was going to stop. He disfigured that guy like you wouldn't believe. Broke his ribs, his cheekbones, knocked his teeth out, and put out one of his eyes. Aunt Gladys hid him out. Later, he got two more of those guys. Daddy was easygoing, but he would kill you if he had to.

LAMAR FIKE: Travis was very funny and benevolent. You just didn't want to cross him, especially when he was drinking.

BILLY SMITH: Our family has always been a little unusual. My grandfather and grandmother, Bob and Doll, were cousins. *Elvis and Gladys* says they were first cousins. But I think they were second or third. Gladys had Mansells on both sides of her family.

And you've got this double first cousin thing. A set of brothers—Daddy and Uncle Johnny—married sisters, Lorraine and Lois. So their kids and my brother, Bobby, and me were double first cousins.

You've got double first cousins on the Presley side, too. Vernon and Vester were brothers, and they married sisters, Gladys and Clettes.

LAMAR FIKE: In some ways, Gladys and Vernon were a good match, but in other ways, they were terrible. Vernon had a hell of a time keeping a job because he just didn't like to work, and he wouldn't get up early. Gladys got things done. She put her age back four years when they married. He was seventeen, and she was twenty-one, but claimed to be seventeen. I don't think Elvis ever realized that. He always thought she was younger.

BILLY SMITH: Vernon might have been lazy and uneducated, but he wasn't stupid. He was real handsome when they married. Vernon was flashy in his dress, and he carried himself well. And he acted like he had good manners, especially around women. Back then, a lot of people married to get away from home. By the time Gladys was a teenager, her father had died, and the kids had to carry the load. Aunt Gladys had done moved out and was running a sewing machine at the Tupelo Garment Center when she met Vernon. But she still felt responsible for the rest of the family. They eloped two months after they met, in 1933.

LAMAR FIKE: Vernon thought he was a stud. Elvis used to say that Vernon knew when Elvis was conceived, because afterwards, he blacked out.

BILLY SMITH: Elvis had a story about his birth, too—that the sky had this strange blue light or a blue ring around the moon. But I don't guess that morning was really any different from any other.

MARTY LACKER: Elvis felt he was put on earth for a specific purpose. He didn't know what the purpose was, unless he had a lot of pills in him.

BILLY SMITH: Elvis was born at home on January 8, 1935, at 4:35 A.M., according to the records. Jessie, named for Vernon's father, was born first, around four. Dr. William Robert Hunt delivered the babies. Gladys went into labor, and the family had some concern because Gladys was having problems.

Dr. Hunt had no idea it was twins, although Gladys knew because she'd picked out the rhyming names—Jessie Garon and Elvis Aaron. "Elvis" is Vernon's middle name. I don't know where the "Garon" come from, but they give Elvis the "Aaron" for Aaron Kennedy, one of Vernon's friends there in Tupelo.

Vernon's father, Jessie, come in about the time Gladys was in labor, and he was drunk out of his mind. Jessie Garon had just been delivered, and he was dead. They brought him out to another room, and Vernon was just coming out as Jessie was going in. Vernon was crying, but Jessie thought he was laughing. He went in and said, "Gitchy, gitchy, goo!" and "Oh, ain't it a beautiful baby!"

The baby didn't respond, of course. So Jessie just kept going, "Gitchy, gitchy, goo!" Vernon was hurt to the bone, so, finally, he yelled out, "Oh, goddamn, Daddy! The baby is dead!" The story goes that Jessie got this funny look on his face and just said, "Oh, oh!" About the time all that was happening, Elvis was born.

CHAPTER 2

TUPELO

MARTY LACKER: Dr. Hunt must have misunderstood Vernon's accent when Elvis was born. Which is understandable because when Vernon pronounced "Elvis," he always left out the "l." Not too long ago, Dr. Hunt's daughter found his physician's record. And he'd written down the name as "Evis [sic] Aaron." That's "Aaron" with two "A's."

I hope all those people who see "Aaron" on Elvis's gravestone and interpret it to mean he's not really dead—people such as Gail Brewer-Giorgio [author of *Is Elvis Alive?*]—will take note of that. It ended up "Aron" on a lot of things through the years, but "Aaron" was right.

One day in late '66, I was talking to Elvis about religion, and he brought up Aaron. I said, "That's something I've always wondered, Elvis. How come you spell 'Aaron' with one 'A' when it's two 'A's' in the Bible?" Because Elvis might have been named for Vernon's friend Aaron Kennedy, but he always referred to it as a Hebrew name and how Aaron was the brother of Moses. And he said, "Well, back when I was growing up, a lot of people around Tupelo didn't spell right."

Elvis looked over at Vernon and said, "As a matter of fact, Daddy, from now on, I want my name written with two 'A's,' especially on legal documents." That's why it has two "A's" on the gravestone.

BILLY SMITH: Dr. Hunt charged $15 for his delivery fee. Vernon couldn't pay it, so welfare did. Elvis was Dr. Hunt's nine hundred and twentieth delivery. He was sixty-eight when Elvis was born, and he died in '52, without ever knowing that baby was somebody special.

MARTY LACKER: There are two things people always talk about in trying to sum up Elvis from a psychological point of view. One is his relationship with his mother. The other is an obsession he supposedly had with his dead twin.

LAMAR FIKE: Dick Clark produced the first TV Elvis biopic, *Elvis*, in 1979. He had Kurt Russell talking to this shadow, which was supposed to be Elvis's twin. That was fucking hilarious. Where the shit did that come from? I never heard Elvis talk to Jessie Garon. And he wasn't twin obsessed. I was with Elvis about three years before I learned he had a twin.

He did tell me he had a twin toe, on his right foot. I said, "What do you mean, a twin toe?" He said, "Well, some twins have toes that are webbed, or there's a little bit of extra skin between the second and third toes. And from that, I must have been an identical twin." But other than that, he never talked about his twin. Gladys didn't either. I saw these toes, though. Elvis had real long feet. Ugly, too.

BILLY SMITH: Lamar believed that twin toe stuff, huh? That's funny. I did, too, for a long time. But Elvis never had any webbed toe. He just told that about him and Jessie Garon. He did have ingrown toenails a lot and three big warts on his hand. I guess if we sat down long enough, we might come up with some mystical bullshit for that, too.

LAMAR FIKE: That lying dog! He'd tell me something, and I'd believe it.

MARTY LACKER: Elvis had the greatest imagination. He'd tell a lie with a straight face.

BILLY SMITH: Albert Goldman wrote that Elvis heard Jessie Garon's voice all the time from the age of four or five, telling him to do good deeds. He says this gave Elvis a split personality, so that there was a "good" Elvis and an "evil" Elvis. Hell, that's the biggest bunch of bull that ever was! When people read that Elvis had a twin, they'd come up and ask about him, and Elvis would say, "He was born dead, I never knew him."

On the other hand, Elvis thought there was a reason why Jessie was born dead, and he was the one who lived. He did say one time, "If my twin brother had lived, do you reckon the world could have handled two?" Elvis was much too vain to share anything.

LAMAR FIKE: Albert said that Gladys used to take Elvis to Jessie's grave when he was a kid. That's another crock of shit. I don't think they knew where the grave was.

BILLY SMITH: Oh, hell. They all knew exactly where it was. They just didn't want somebody digging it up and holding the remains for ransom. The grave was never marked because they didn't have the money to buy a headstone. By the way, Goldman says Jessie's buried in Priceville Cemetery. Actually, he's in another cemetery. I don't know the name, but it's out towards Saltillo.

There's a little plaque for Jessie there in the Meditation Garden. And you'll see they spelled it "Jessie," not "Jesse," although people always write it that way and Dr. Hunt spelled it "Jesse" on the birth record. He put an "i" in "Garon," instead of "Jessie."

MARTY LACKER: I always wondered why the Presleys didn't have more children. Especially since Vernon was such a lover boy. We used to call him "Hair Trigger."

BILLY SMITH: The best I can remember, Aunt Gladys couldn't have any more. *Elvis and Gladys* says that she miscarried when Elvis was seven. I don't think so. I never heard anybody in the family talk about it, or Elvis either. Aunt Clettes and Uncle Vester didn't know about it, and it's hard to keep something like that quiet. Dr. Hunt made no record of it, and he attended her until she moved to Memphis. Aunt Gladys supposedly went to the Tupelo Hospital, but people in our family didn't go to the hospital in those days.

LAMAR FIKE: I think it scared the heck out of Gladys when the twin died at birth. I don't think she ever got over it. That's why she was so protective of Elvis. She doted on him constantly. A smothering kind of affection. But he would also do it to her. He loved to pat on her, and he talked baby talk to her. Called her

Satnin'. He would rip through a paragraph, and I couldn't make heads or tails of it. But she could. And Vernon could, and Elvis would baby-talk him, too. I used to sit at that breakfast bar and wouldn't understand a damn word they said, especially since Elvis had that little stutter. It was like a foreign language.

BILLY SMITH: Gladys talked that way until she died. "Satnin'" meant a real condensed round of fattening, and Aunt Gladys was always heavy. Elvis would pat her on the stomach and say, "Baby's going to bring you something to eat, Satnin'."

She called him "Elvie," by the way, when he was little. He hated that when he got to be a teenager, so she stopped. She also called him "Naughty," like "You're a naughty boy."

LAMAR FIKE: In a lot of ways, Elvis treated his father like he wasn't his father. And that has to go back to Elvis's formative years and what he went through while his father was in Parchman Penitentiary, the Mississippi state prison, and the shame and the stigma that followed after Vernon got out. Elvis never forgot it, even though he was only three and just barely four while his daddy was gone. But Elvis and Gladys would go see him. You're talking about something like 125 miles, from Tupelo to Parchman. Friends or family had to take them—Gladys couldn't drive. A kid as sensitive as Elvis would remember that, and the charity of it.

Vernon had forged a check he'd gotten from Orville Bean for a hog. He either traced a new one on a blank or altered the existing one for a lot more than it originally was—changed it from $4 to $40, I think—because he felt cheated on what he'd gotten for the hog.

Bean was a dairy farmer there in Tupelo. Vernon had worked for him before Elvis was born. Orville loaned Vernon $180 to build that little shotgun house on Saltillo Road where Elvis was born, and then he rented the house to the Presleys. It was Bean's property until he got his money back, with interest. But Vernon's father owned the lot, and lived next door. It's incredible that Vernon would try to pull that on Orville. But Elvis said, "Daddy was really sort of roped into the situation." He and Travis, Gladys's brother, and a guy named Lether Gable.

BILLY SMITH: Vernon always wanted more of things, and they got this bright idea. All I remember is my daddy telling me how they done it. They added the zero and changed the writing. And Vernon done most of that. Because my daddy couldn't read or write, except to sign his name.

It was enough money that my daddy and Lether went to Texas. Vernon stayed in Tupelo and maybe bought stuff for his family. Maybe not, too. Vernon wasn't as committed to his family as he should have been as far as providing. He might go out and buy something for himself first. But Gladys was the opposite. She thought of Elvis and him first.

LAMAR FIKE: One reason Vernon wouldn't have anything much to do with his father was he wouldn't bail him out. But when Travis went to jail, J.D. and some other fella paid his bail. Lether got bailed out, too. Vernon could carry a grudge to his grave.

BILLY SMITH: Maybe J.D. thought he was going to teach Vernon a lesson. But I think he just liked Daddy better than Vernon. You couldn't help but like my daddy. He was a whole lot like Aunt Gladys. Always ready to do any and everything. But he was also easily persuaded by certain people. That's probably how the whole thing happened. They were drinking and just did it on a whim. Vernon got to thinking about that little check, and the more he thought, the madder he got. And they said, "We'll fix that Orville!" And they lived high, for a time.

From what my mama told me, Daddy and Lether thought they'd find a job down in Texas. But all they come back with was a new shirt, a new pair of pants, and a big hat. She said Daddy thought he was really going to be "Mr. It." But as soon as he stepped off the train, they were waiting for him, and they just hauled him right on off. So he changed his new duds for jail rags. They'd gotten Vernon first, of course. Daddy was twenty-two. Just old enough to realize he'd made a drastic mistake.

When my mama told that story, it was a comical thing. But Parchman always had the reputation as being one of the toughest prisons in the South. Of course, Parchman had that famous chain gang. The story went around that Vernon got bullwhipped, and that's why he never went shirtless after that.

They got three years, but they only had to serve eight months—June 1, 1938, to February 6, 1939. Aunt Gladys got a petition up, I believe, and they got out on what they called "a hardship case." When Vernon come out, he had the attitude that "I've done my time, so people should give me some slack now." But they didn't, and it changed him. Even his friends thought, "No, he's gone to jail. It's best not to socialize because people might think I'll get into trouble with him." It made it very difficult for both him and my daddy. By the time I was born in '43, Daddy was sharecropping again.

LAMAR FIKE: The Presleys were so poor that all three of them had to sleep in the same bed. And, of course, while Vernon was gone, Elvis slept with his mother. He slept with her until he was thirteen, when they moved to Memphis. But this stuff that Dee Presley [Vernon's second wife] told the *National Enquirer* about Elvis and Gladys being lovers is just totally nuts. I don't care what Vernon supposedly said. I knew Gladys very well, and that never happened.

MARTY LACKER: I was interviewed by *Entertainment Tonight* on that, and I said, right on camera, "That just can't be true." Many young boys sleep with their mother, especially when they're scared. Elvis's father was in prison for a long time, and I'm sure that was a frightening situation. And don't forget there was only one bed in the whole damn house. To say that Elvis got off on sleeping with his mother, or that she molested Elvis, is a lie. There is no way in the world that happened.

BILLY SMITH: When Vernon was in prison, Elvis and Gladys got extremely close. They were each other's only world. And Gladys wanted to make Elvis feel special. She'd buy him treats, like ice cream, or maybe something a little out of the ordinary, if she could.

LAMAR FIKE: Elvis had his own knife and fork and plate when he was a child. His own cup and glass, too. You know how you'll sometimes be sitting at a table, and you'll reach over and get something off of somebody's plate and eat it? If you reached over to Elvis's plate, he would cut your arm off. That was one of his idiosyncrasies. He was a pretty complicated dude.

BILLY SMITH: The only thing I can remember about tableware is that Elvis used to carry a knife and fork in his back pocket because he didn't like to eat with anybody else's. He'd eat from your dishes, but not with your silverware. He didn't break that habit until he went into the army. Used to take that knife and fork to school with him. He didn't eat or drink after anybody, and he didn't want you to drink after him.

Elvis was a pretty resourceful kid, even at a real early age. Mama used to tell this story about him, from when he was about four. He wanted to go downtown. So Aunt Gladys and Mama took him. Back then, you could get a sack of bananas for about ten cents. Elvis loved bananas, so he wanted to carry them. And the sack was as big as he was. When he got tired, he had Aunt Gladys and Mama take turns carrying *him* instead of the sack. He held on to it the whole time.

After a while, Aunt Gladys tried to talk Elvis into giving them a banana. But he wouldn't do it. Then she tried to shame him into it. Finally, he reached down and pulled one out. He thought about it for a while, and then he broke the banana in two and gave each one of them half.

LAMAR FIKE: Elvis once told me all his friends were girls when he was growing up, from the earliest age.

BILLY SMITH: Elvis related to women more than he did men. He had very few male friends in early childhood. He was just with women more.

Elaine Dundy wrote that Elvis patterned his personality after Captain Marvel, the comic book hero. She said that's where he got this "humble and humorous" side and this notion to save his family. And she says he patterned his look after him, too—the hair, the stance, and the costumes he wore in the seventies, with the capes and even the TCB lightning bolt. Maybe so. He started reading those about the time he started first grade. So he might have absorbed all that and not really have known it.

You know that story about how Elvis liked to watch girls wrestle in white cotton panties? That was supposed to be his biggest turn-on—that, and two women together. Well, when he was four or five, my mama and Aunt Clettes were dancing together to some music. They were up on a trunk, waving their skirts around so they were flying up.

Elvis was in the room. And the more they danced, the more excited he got. He grabbed my mama by the leg. And he said, "Oh, my peter!" Well, Gladys went wild. She yanked him up and yelled out, "You all quit that damn dancing!" She pointed at Elvis and said, "Look what you're doing to him!" When my mama told me that, I liked to died.

LAMAR FIKE: It was about this age—five or six—that Elvis said his nightmares started. I'm not sure when the sleepwalking started.

BILLY SMITH: In 1940, a year after Uncle Vernon got out of Parchman, him and Aunt Gladys and Elvis moved down to Pascagoula, Mississippi, so Vernon could work at the shipyards in the Works Progress Administration.

When Vernon went to prison, either J.D. sold their lot on Saltillo Road or Orville Bean evicted them. So Aunt Gladys had been making the rounds, staying at different people's houses— her cousin, Frank Richards, and his family, I know—earning some money doing seamstress work and taking in laundry. They stayed in Pascagoula only about eight months. I think Uncle Vernon sharecropped for a while when they got back.

MARTY LACKER: It's funny. I was down in Tupelo recently, and I met some people who told me that none of Elvis's relatives want to talk about him. I said to one woman, "I hear you're Elvis's cousin." And she said, "Yeah, big deal." The fact is, once he left Tupelo, those people never saw him again.

BILLY SMITH: You hear a lot of different stories about how Elvis got interested in music. In the beginning, it came from Shake Rag, which was an area in Tupelo you didn't go into. It was black. We lived in Saltillo, which is real close to Shake Rag, and in order to go a lot of places we had to walk right by it. You're talking about only maybe three or four blocks down. Some people say Elvis never heard black music, but he sure did. You couldn't *not* hear it. The walls were so thin you'd hear 'em inside. Or they'd be out there singing. That's where he picked up on a lot of it.

MARTY LACKER: Elvis always liked to make things more dramatic than they were. He took a bunch of us down to Tupelo one time to get a police badge. And he made a point of driving through what was left of Shake Rag. He said, "This is where I come from. This is where I lived." Shake Rag was nothing but shacks—places that had big holes in the walls and cracks in the boards, where people put newspapers up to keep the wind out. It took us a while to figure out that he hadn't actually lived there at all, just on the edge.

BILLY SMITH: The Pentecostal church was a big influence on Elvis's music, too. But Elvis listened to black music, to gospel music, and to whatever was on the radio. And he liked this local country musician, Mississippi Slim, and Jimmie Rodgers, who had also come from Mississippi. But he was around gospel music more. That stuff about Elvis learning to shake his leg and move onstage because Brother Frank [W.] Smith, the Assembly of God preacher there in Tupelo, done it is bunk. The preacher didn't move like that, and neither did Elvis. When he was in church, he'd just stand there, almost mystified by the music. Of course, later, Elvis had intentions of getting into a gospel group.

Even when he was real little, music just done something to him. Of course, it's well known about the talent contest at the Mississippi-Alabama Fair and Dairy Show, where he come in second. Actually, Elvis said it was more like fourth or fifth place, so I guess he didn't win at all. He sung "Old Shep," without any musical accompaniment. That was in 1945, when he was ten.

Elvis got a guitar for his eleventh birthday, even though he wanted a bicycle. It was cheaper than a bike—he got a $7.75 model that Gladys bought from Mr. Forrest Bobo at the Tupelo Hardware Company. He was disappointed. But he got the bike, too, later on, and then he wrecked it and broke his arm, so he couldn't play the guitar for a while.

Elvis learned to play guitar from various people. Brother Smith, the pastor, supposedly showed him a few runs. He used to sing "Old Shep," too. And several members of the family took credit for it—Uncle Vester and Uncle Johnny. But that's not true. My uncle by marriage, Hubert Tipton, was the first one to teach Elvis the chords and all. He played a pretty fair guitar. To be honest, Hubert and his brother taught Elvis more than anybody else.

MARTY LACKER: I think Shake Rag was still the biggest influence. Elvis said, "I loved that music. Sometimes I'd just sit there in Shake Rag and listen and talk to people." They had juke joints there that must have looked pretty exciting.

BILLY SMITH: Shake Rag was definitely important, but it's a myth that Elvis spent a lot of time there and was befriended by a lot of people. I think you have to look at both Gladys and Vernon, too, when you're figuring out Elvis's musical influences. He got his talent from both sides. Gladys had a pretty good voice, and so did Vernon. Every once in a while, they'd all sit down and sing gospel songs together. We rarely went to church with them, but on occasions we did, and Vernon sang some there. Of course, Elvis got his flashiness from Vernon, both in his behavior and the way he dressed. Like I said, Vernon always wanted more. Of everything. Except responsibility.

LAMAR FIKE: Vernon had been a deacon in the church, but after Parchman, people looked at him as a criminal. And when he did find a job, he wouldn't show up. One time, Elvis said, "Lamar, Daddy's had a backache for thirty years. He wouldn't work if you held a gun to his head."

BILLY SMITH: I don't know where Vernon worked during the time before we moved to Memphis. Now, I've read that he worked in a defense plant in Memphis for a while during the war and that he come back to Tupelo in '46 and drove a truck for a wholesale grocery company. I think he made $22.50 a week. Which wasn't enough. There's a story that he got pretty much kicked out of Tupelo for moonshining. I don't know.

They lived in a lot of different rental houses. The last one was at 1010 North Green Street, in Tupelo. It was a four-room house near the slaughter yard. We lived on North Green, too, but we didn't live with them. Minnie Mae moved in because J.D. run off and left her.

They stayed there until we all moved to Memphis. But we moved to the Mitchell place in Tupelo because my daddy was sharecropping for him. I was real small, and there's very little I can remember until about three or four years of age. Aunt Gladys and Grandma used to keep [baby-sit] me. I used to drive

Grandma crazy. I was so small, she put me in a number-three washtub. She thought that would hold me, but I would rock that tub until I turned it over. One time I climbed out and run out in the middle of the street buck naked.

I remember the cows and the hogs that we had on the Mitchell place. And I remember the fireplace because I backed up too close to it and my nightgown caught on fire. Mama yelled, and Daddy jerked it off and put the fire out. It burnt me, but not so's it left a bad scar. But it was a cotton nightgown, and, boy, they go up quick.

My daddy said that he wasn't any better off than when he first got out of prison, 'cause he was still sharecropping. He and Uncle Vernon thought if they moved to a bigger city, things would be better. Vernon said, "There's got to be more than this."

So we ended up moving to Memphis. Vernon and Daddy had gone there together before. Stayed three weeks and couldn't find anything. This time, Daddy sold two cows and killed our hog to get some money, about $105. They had their cooked-out lard and salted-down pork, and that money, which was enough to get by on 'til somebody got a job. I think Vernon sold something, too. I'm pretty sure we come in Daddy's car—a '37 or '39 green Plymouth. There were seven of us in that one car—Daddy and Mama, me and my older brother, Bobby, and Gladys, Vernon, and Elvis. And all our belongings. This was September of '48. I was five years old, but I remember every dang mile.

CHAPTER 3

MEMPHIS

BILLY SMITH: When we got to Memphis, we all moved into the same place, an old renovated house at 370 Washington Street. It had one apartment upstairs, and one downstairs, and a community bath. We lived up and them down. Elvis's mama and my daddy were closer than a lot of brothers and sisters. So the living together worked out okay. This was in North Memphis, which isn't the best part of town.

At first, it was real tough. We ate turnip greens, it seemed, like night and day. For a while, it looked like it was back to Tupelo for us. Then Aunt Gladys found a job in a drapery factory, Fashion Curtains, and Mama followed a few days later, at a laundry. Daddy and Vernon spent weeks looking for work. They had to put cardboard in their shoes to cover the holes. Then Daddy found a job. Eventually he worked at Precision Tool, where Elvis later worked. And Uncle Vernon hired on at United Paint in early '49. He stayed there longer than anywhere. Usually, he'd get a couple of paychecks, and that would be about it. Anyway, at that time, the two families made a grand total of $120 a week. After a while, some of the other family come on up.

On Washington Street, we lived next to a vegetable stand. I still remember the name "Magolio." What produce they couldn't sell, they threw out in the trash cans. I remember going through there and finding bruised bananas to eat. When you're that poor, you scavenge for what you can get. Elvis loved to tell about the time I fell into one of the fifty-five-gallon trash cans. I was so little that he had to pick me up by my legs and pull me out. But I wasn't turning a-loose of them damn bananas.

Elvis was eight years older than me, and he kind of looked after me and my older brother, Bobby. There was this guy, Frankie, who was the son of the owner. He used to shoot Bobby and me in the back with a damn BB gun, pop us pretty good. And of course, Elvis confronted him about it. He took up for us.

LAMAR FIKE: Of all those Smith cousins, Billy's the only one that came out worth a damn. Elvis felt like he raised him.

BILLY SMITH: We lived on Washington Street for only a few months. Then the Presleys lived on Adams Street for a while. All those streets are real close together, Jefferson, Washington, Adams. Well, the Presleys just moved over from Washington to Adams. And then a very short time after, Aunt Gladys applied for welfare assistance. They got into that Lauderdale Courts complex, at 185 Winchester, and we moved to Poplar Street, which was about a block away. Some books say they lived on Poplar Street, too, but that's wrong. Anyway, I could go around the block and visit. And if I remember, we moved to Third Street, which is across the way. Then when they moved to 462 Alabama Street, we lived on High Street. We always lived right around the same area, until Elvis got into music in a big way and bought the Audubon Drive house in '56.

Gladys was so thrilled with the Lauderdale Courts place. This was a pretty big housing project, like four hundred apartments. The Presleys' apartment had two bedrooms on the ground floor. They paid $35 a month for it. They moved there in the fall of '49 and stayed until early '53. Because Gladys was photographed a lot in the last year or so of her life, when she was sick and sad about Elvis going to the army, people have the idea she was a down kind of person. But I remember her as very outgoing and high-strung. Fun-loving would be a better way of saying it. She could make you feel great just by being there.

I have this vivid memory of going over to Lauderdale Courts one summer when Elvis was at Humes [High School]. They were playing music, and Gladys was dancing around. And Elvis was dancing with her. They were having a ball. And Vernon and my mom were over there, and my brother, too. Of course, I was kind of small. And Gladys said, "Well, it don't look like they're having too much fun." So she went in there and got all Elvis's toys for us to play with while they played cards. She was always jolly. Always laughing and carrying on.

When they were getting ready to move to Alabama Street,

Elvis give me all his toys. I've got about four or five of 'em left—a little metal dump truck, a car, a little wrecker truck, and a tractor, I know. Both Elvis and Gladys were pack rats. They kept everything. So I think she was surprised he give 'em to me. But she didn't seem to mind. I guess they felt sorry for me. Or maybe they were just trying to keep me occupied because I was a little hellion.

LAMAR FIKE: Gladys always wanted the best for Elvis. And if there was a way to get it, she was going to find it.

BILLY SMITH: Aunt Gladys was a mover and shaker. I think that's where Elvis got it. She told him, "Whatever you do, go after it hard, and grasp onto it." And so Elvis started working at seventeen as an usher at Loews State Theater. That's where he got fired for punching another usher. He told the manager that Elvis was getting free candy from the concession girl. Even back then, Elvis bought some of his own clothes. He didn't have a lot, but what he had was nice and up-to-date.

In a little while, his tastes changed. He started going down to Lansky Brothers on Beale Street where the blacks hung out. I remember his first pink-and-black outfit. I thought, "My God Almighty!" But it also excited me, like, "Hell, let *me* do it!" I read that he wore clear plastic shoes, but I only remember some black-and-white ones. They had pointed toes, with the white laid in across the black. A lot of blacks still wear 'em nowadays.

My family thought, "Goddurn, why don't he just go down there on Beale Street and live with 'em?" They said, "Somebody's going to beat the hell out of him and peel them nigger outfits right off his hide!" Back then, "nigger" was a real loose term. And it was a complete switch for a white man to dress like that.

But the families remained close in Memphis. My daddy and Elvis's mama both thought, "If I've got it, and you need it, you can have it."

I remember when Elvis got his driver's license. My daddy was working for Precision Tool. He was making fairly good money, and he had just bought a '51 Chevrolet, with a sun visor and all. Elvis wanted to borrow it to take his driver's test, and my daddy let him have it.

When he went to take his test, we all went. Elvis was sitting in the front with Daddy and Vernon. Very seldom did he ever say anything dirty in front of them. But a guy pulled out in front of Daddy, and Elvis yelled, "Watch where you're going, you son of a bitch!" We were all shocked, you know. The car got real quiet. That year, Elvis won the Safe Driving Award at school.

By the way, the story about Aunt Gladys walking Elvis to high school until he got a car is the honest truth. Until Elvis was a senior, Vernon and Gladys just had only one car, a '39 Lincoln. So like most kids, Elvis had to walk more than he got to ride. And Aunt Gladys didn't walk him all the time. But if there was something bothering him, or if he come in and confided to her that "so-and-so at school is picking on me," she would walk him to school. And a lot of times, she would hide behind a bush and follow him home without him seeing her.

Actually, Aunt Gladys looked after all of us. I was riding a horse one day, and it bucked and kicked. And she flew mad, and she said, "Get the hell off that horse, you big-eyed rascal!"

Both Bobby and me got treated good, but especially me. It wasn't just because I was the youngest because there were other cousins my age.

Now, Elvis and Gene Smith got pretty close after Gene moved up to Memphis. Gene was another first cousin, and he was Elvis's age. His mama was Levalle Smith, Gladys's sister. She was a Smith, and she married a Smith, Edward Smith. Which I don't think was any relation, but who knows? Hell, back then, cousins married cousins. Maybe that's why we're all warped. Anyway, Elvis and Gene worked together at Precision Tool until they threatened to cut Elvis's hair. Actually, I've heard that's a myth. They just found out he was younger than they thought.

There's a picture of Gene and Elvis with their prom dates. Gene is with a girl named Bessie Wolverton, and Elvis is with Dixie Locke. He has on a white tuxedo jacket. Somehow the story got started that Elvis wouldn't dance in high school. That's not so. He went to several proms. One with a fourteen-year-old girl named Regis Wilson. Well, now, I take part of that back. She give an interview to *People* magazine once in which she said they *went* to Elvis's senior prom, but Elvis told her he didn't know how to dance, so they sat and drank Cokes all night. Maybe he just couldn't dance very well, which is funny, considering what he did onstage later on. But I remember him dancing with a lot of girls in high school.

Dixie was his serious interest. He went with her about two years, from about '53 to '55. She was three or four years younger than Elvis. You always hear that he wanted to marry her, and expected to, but that she dumped him when he went on the road 'cause he was gone all the time. But Dixie just thought he was too possessive. And Elvis was always jealous of what she might be doing while he was away. I don't know that they would have married because everything did a 180-degree turn when Elvis realized the effect he had on women.

LAMAR FIKE: Elvis said his social life in high school was practically nonexistent. Kids made fun of him—an only child, very poor background. He had a lot of girls around him, but as pals. He could relate to them in some way. And he had younger friends that he liked and trusted because he could direct them and have more fun. He was a person who got intimidated very easily by somebody with more intelligence or ability. As a result, a situation developed where he had to have people around him all the time. That's why he later assembled the entourage, the Memphis Mafia.

BILLY SMITH: When Elvis got to Lauderdale Courts, he made friends with Buzzy Forbess, and Paul Dougher, and Farley Guy. But even though they hung out together, they probably weren't all that close. Even in high school, Elvis had mostly female friends. George Klein was a friend, but they really got closer after they graduated and Elvis went into music and George went into radio.

MARTY LACKER: Elvis liked George because in school George was one of the very few people who were supposedly "in." George was senior class president, and he paid attention to Elvis. Elvis didn't forget stuff like that.

BILLY SMITH: One reason Elvis didn't have a lot of male friends in high school was because of his ducktail hairdo. And then, of course, he had those sideburns. Before the ducktail, I think he had a permanent. There are pictures of him, age seventeen or eighteen, with his hair real curly. Aunt Gladys would have given it to him. She used to give herself those Toni home permanents back then.

LAMAR FIKE: Elvis's main friend in those days was Red West. Red protected him one time in school. A bunch of guys had Elvis cornered in the restroom and were going to cut his hair, and Red stepped in and took care of them. Red was a big football player, the badass. He'd just drop you. Elvis never forgot favors.

The hair-cutting incident had to be real traumatic. You're talking about a guy who'd been having vivid nightmares on a regular basis since he was a tiny kid. Mostly they were about people attacking him, trying to kill him. Elvis told us that when he was three, Vernon dreamed that the house was on fire, and he tried to throw Elvis out the window to save his life. But he missed, and he threw him ass-first against the wall.

The most amazing thing to me was that Elvis and his mother and father all had the same nightmare one night when Elvis was little. They thought the house was flooded. So they got up out of bed and took the mattress and put it out on the roof.

Elvis had nightmares almost every night until he died. That's why he wouldn't sleep. And that's one reason he did so many pills.

MARTY LACKER: Red ended up protecting Elvis most of his life. He was pretty tough, but he also had a lot of sensitivity. Red was poorer than most of the kids. He didn't have many clothes, or much of anything else. And Harry Levitch, this Jewish jeweler, helped a lot of kids, including Red. Red was always thankful, and so was Elvis. That's why he started trading at Mr. Levitch's store. The first thing he bought was an electric mixer for his mother. Two days later, he walked back in and said, "Mr. Levitch, can you get me another electric mixer?" Harry said, "Certainly, who will this be for?" And Elvis said, "This is for Mama, too. I'm going to put one at each end of the kitchen so she won't have to walk so much." He bought jewelry from Harry for years.

BILLY SMITH: Elvis had just turned eighteen when they moved to Alabama Street. A rabbi, Alfred Fruchter, lived upstairs. I remember he had a little beard and goatee, and kind of gray hair, and he was bald on top. The Presleys didn't know anything about the Jewish religion, especially about Orthodox Jews and about not turning on anything electrical or driving a car on the Sabbath. And the first Friday night they were there, the rabbi came to the door the same time Vernon did. It was dark, so the rabbi asked Vernon if he would turn on the light for him.

Vernon said, "The string's hanging right there." He said, "Reach up there and turn it on yourself." The rabbi said, "I'd rather you turn it on." So Vernon finally did it, but he was real suspicious.

This happened two or three times, and Vernon kept saying, "That guy's strange." He mentioned it to another neighbor, and the neighbor said, "Well, he's Jewish." And Vernon said, "I don't care what he is. He's not helpless."

MARTY LACKER: George Klein tells a story about when the Presleys lived with the rabbi. Except he didn't get it quite right. He says that Elvis was the one who turned on the light, and the rabbi scolded him, and that's how Elvis learned about Judaism. He also says that when the Presleys first came to Memphis, they didn't have any place to live and no money, and a rabbi let them live in his basement rent free. That's supposedly why Elvis hired so many Jews.

That's bull. The Presleys paid $50 a month rent, plus utilities, on Alabama Street. And they didn't live in the basement—Minnie Mae slept on a cot in the dining room. And Elvis never talked about it.

I think he just happened to like us personally. There were actually only two of us—me and Alan Fortas—for any length of time. Larry Geller was there for a little while in the sixties, but Geller wasn't a practicing Jew. And of course, George Klein. But he wasn't around that much after the early years. Then there's Lamar. Lamar's Jewish depending on what day it is.

BILLY SMITH: When he was a kid, Elvis wouldn't sing on the porch unless it was dark. But I read that he played little clubs and dances in town before his first record came out, like basement parties at the Hotel Chisca. I remember we got a piano for Christmas when Elvis was in high school. He came over one day and just started playing. I thought, "Well, boy, he can play the piano." I don't know how he learned. It was some piece of music that was fairly fast, and he got to moving around a lot. He only done it just for a few minutes, and then he upped and quit. I thought, "Wow, that's weird to see him jump around like that while he's singing!" If there were a lot of people around, he was too shy to do it.

LAMAR FIKE: Here was this bashful guy who stuttered a little, and yet he could get onstage and do all sorts of things. Well, Elvis was a gunslinger. You meet a gunslinger without his guns on, and he's just as normal as everybody else. But when he puts his guns on, you better watch your ass! You've got to be schizophrenic to be in this business. In the early days, Elvis used to say he wasn't aware his leg was shaking to the music, that it just happened. But he was no fool. He found out what worked and made it work again.

BILLY SMITH: Elvis always liked to sing. But I don't remember him saying, "I want to be a singer." Except after he got his guitar, it might have crossed his mind. But it wasn't anything that he harped on or totally devoted his life to. In his teenage years, he would go listen to the gospel groups. But he also thought about becoming a policeman.

LAMAR FIKE: He tried to be an electrician's apprentice for Crown Electric. Started work there in November of '53, after going back to Precision Tool for two months, in September. When he got famous, everybody said he was a truck driver. But he was studying to be an electrician—pulling wire and hauling it to a job site in a Dodge panel truck. There's a difference. Before that—right after he graduated high school, that summer of '53—he worked at M. B. Parker Machinist's Shop. That's where he was working when he cut his first record—not Crown Electric as everybody says.

BILLY SMITH: June 13, '53 is when Elvis walked into the Memphis Recording Service on a Saturday afternoon and plunked down his money to make a record. It was a ten-inch acetate. He recorded "My Happiness" and "That's When Your Heartaches Begin."

Elvis told me he was saving it for Gladys's Christmas present. But then Marion Keisker [Sam Phillips's studio manager] contacted him about coming back and all, and it wasn't like he could keep it a secret. Gladys said, "What were you doing down there?" So he had to confess. I don't think Elvis had any thoughts of it going any further than that one record. If he did, he sure never talked about it.

CHAPTER 4

MARTY

MARTY LACKER: This term "Memphis Mafia" is kind of funny. You know how it started, don't you? Somebody yelled it out in a crowd one time—said we looked like the Mafia because we wore black mohair suits.

Some people have thought we were part of the real Mafia. I wasn't, but my father worked for them as a bookie in New York. They used to come to my house to collect money. In a way, I'm thankful for that childhood because it's allowed me to survive.

My socioeconomic situation wasn't that different from Elvis's. Contrary to the belief that all Jewish people are wealthy, we'd always been poor. We never wanted for food, but we lived in a tenement in the South Bronx, which is a pretty rough area.

We moved to Memphis in 1952, when I was fifteen, because my sister, Anne, married and moved there. My mother and father wanted to be near her, and they also wanted to get me out of New York before I ended up in jail or dead. Of the six thousand kids in Morris High School, I had the fourth-highest average. But I didn't have the patience to sit in class. So I started hanging out with the gangs.

Actually, I didn't have that much time to get in trouble. I delivered papers when I was twelve years old. At fourteen, I was working in the New York garment district, pushing racks and loading trucks. That's no easy thing, but I liked working better than going to school. It gave me a sense of responsibility. My parents still worried about me. They thought the move to Memphis would be a good thing.

In the fall of '52, I enrolled at Central High School. Of course, I still had my New York ways about me. I dressed the way I had at home—loud pants and shirts, my shirt collar turned up, and my hair piled up in the front. Kids didn't dress that way in

Memphis. Guys wore T-shirts and jeans and had crew cuts.

I really wanted to play football. Rufner Murray was a heck of a football coach, but he was a total redneck. He hated "Yankees." And he wouldn't let me go out for the team.

I'd go watch them play, and I'd see this guy just walking around by himself. He stood out like a sore thumb because he dressed like I did, in flashy pegged pants with saddle stitching and pistol pockets. His hair was slicked back, and he had side-burns. Nobody knew him—he didn't go to Central. Everybody used to point at him and sort of laugh.

You'd never see him talk to anybody. He'd just walk around and look up in the stands. It was like he was parading, looking for girls. And he'd watch Alan Fortas, who was an All-Memphis football player.

I never did get to play football, so I started getting in a lot of trouble. Finally, I was sent to the principal's office for probably the fifth or sixth time. He told me to bend over because he was going to paddle me. Well, I wasn't going to let anybody hit me. And I certainly wasn't going to voluntarily bend over so he could do it.

The next day, my father came to school. He looked at this guy and said, "If you ever lay a hand on my son, we're going to have a problem." And the principal got upset and said, "Your son can no longer go to school here." So I transferred to Humes. I was in the tenth grade.

About a month after I got to Humes, spring practice started, so I went out for the team. The coach's name was Rube Boyce. He called me "The Brooklyn Demon," even though I was from the Bronx.

One day, I saw this kid who dressed like I did. He'd wear a pair of black pants with chartreuse pistol pockets and chartreuse saddle stitching down the sides of his legs. And he'd wear a shiny black shirt or a pink shirt. The first time I saw him, I knew he was the same guy who used to come over to the games at Central. Somebody told me his name was Elvis Presley. He was a senior.

Pretty soon, everybody at school started kidding us. They'd say, "Who's going to outdress who tomorrow?" But the honest fact is that Elvis and I probably never had a fifteen-minute con-versation. But every time we passed in the halls, we acknowledged each other. He was a library worker, by the way. That's probably the last thing you'd think he'd be.

Every once in a while I'd see Elvis on the sidelines, watching. He wanted to play so bad. But his mother didn't want him to play, and Coach Boyce told Elvis that the only way he would let him come out for the team was if he would cut his hair. And Elvis wouldn't do it. Coach Boyce always denied that, by the way. He said Elvis did go to practice, for two weeks, and they moved him around because he wasn't worth a shit in any position.

There was one other place I used to see him. Shortly after I moved to Memphis, I got to be friends with Terry Shainberg, whose family owned a big department store. Terry was Jewish, like me, but he liked to go to these black Baptist churches.

One Sunday night, he asked me to go to East Trigg Baptist to listen to the gospel music. The music was fantastic. It didn't matter what religion you were—it really moved you when the choir started singing and the people in the audience jumped up and danced in the aisles. The preacher, Reverend W. Herbert Brewster, was well known for his broadcasts over WHBQ, and he could really talk that talk.

A couple of times, I saw Elvis sitting alone, riveted by it all. Because on Sunday nights, they got more into the singing than the preaching. Years later, I talked to Dr. Brewster, and he told me Elvis had come back and said how much he enjoyed the services.

I don't remember much else about Elvis in high school, except the talent contest that April. Red West played the trumpet. And Elvis sang "Keep Them Cold Icy Fingers Off of Me" and encored with "Till I Waltz Again with You," that Teresa Brewer song. The girls went nuts.

If you looked at Elvis back then, you never would have thought he'd amount to anything. He was not what you'd call "book smart." You could have put five guys in a lineup and said, "Which one do you think is going to be successful?" and Elvis would have been the last one picked.

In July '54, a year after Elvis graduated, I was driving down Vollintine Avenue one night with my buddy, Monte Wener. We had the radio on, and we heard Dewey Phillips [disc jockey] say, "We have a young man here from Humes High School," and he played "That's All Right (Mama)."

Monte and I looked at each other, wondering who the hell it was. When Dewey said "Elvis Presley," it shocked us, even though Monte's mother put shows together for the veterans at Kennedy Hospital and used Elvis on some of them. But this was a totally different style.

Three months later, I was in a manager's training program at Shainberg's Department Store in the Lamar-Airways Shopping Center. Katz Drugs opened up their first Memphis store there, with a big cat's face on the front that swayed back and forth and blinked. The shopping center promoted the opening with "Fun on a Grand Scale." I went out to the back parking lot, and there was Elvis on a flatbed truck, jumping around and singing. I walked up to the stage, and he looked at me and smiled and made a little pistol with his fingers and pointed in my direction.

After that, he came out with record after record. I'd go to see him perform until I went into the army in December of '54. I didn't really get to know him until I got out of the service, in '57, right after he moved to Graceland.

A couple of years ago, Sonny West told me that when I started running around with Elvis, they were talking about all the guys one day. Somebody asked him, "How come you took Marty on?"

Elvis said he remembered that I was always alone in school, that I didn't have any close friends. He said I kept to myself. I never knew he saw that, but it was true.

CHAPTER 5

STAR TIME

Once Elvis became a national phenomenon, countless of the great blues musicians of the period came forward to say they knew he would make it: They'd seen him around the Beale Street clubs—the Paradise, and Club Handy, and the Palms Club on Summer Avenue—or sat in with him in long jam sessions. The blues singer Roy Brown said in a 1977 article in *Blues Unlimited* that Elvis would come see him whenever he played Tupelo. Another story has a teenage Elvis buying wine for Brown's band at several Memphis clubs.

But while Elvis was certainly a fan of Brown's, and of Howlin' Wolf, Sonny Boy Williamson, Lowell Fulson, and Junior Parker, who cowrote "Mystery Train" with Sam Phillips and first recorded the song, most of those earliest Elvis sightings are likely spurious, for a variety of reasons—Elvis was too shy to approach such performers for jam sessions, most clubs in the area were not integrated, and Elvis, a teetotaler, was underage to be buying alcohol, even for someone else.

A classmate, Fred Fredrick, told the editors of *Elvis Up Close* that Elvis and other white teenagers got their blues education across the bridge in West Memphis, Arkansas, at the Plantation Inn—where a white clientele listened to R & B—and at Danny's, where black trumpet player Willie Mitchell led the house band.

"Elvis went to Danny's because of Willie . . . because of the music. It was different. It wasn't white hillbilly and it wasn't the black blues. It was a danceable music deal . . . Those clubs gave Elvis an awful lot of his music."

It is certainly true, however, that while Elvis was enchanted by the gospel singers at Ellis Auditorium, and at one point had difficulty deciding whether to channel his talent into gospel or secular music, deep down, he also wanted to be a great blues singer himself. When a reporter for the *Charlotte Observer* asked Elvis in 1956 how he came upon his style, Elvis answered, "The colored folks played it like that in the shanties and in their juke joints, and nobody paid it any mind until I goosed it up . . . down in Tupelo, I used to hear Arthur ["Big Boy"] Crudup [the writer of "That's All Right (Mama)"] bang his box the way I do now. And I said that if I ever got to the place where I could feel all old Arthur felt, I'd be a music man like nobody ever saw."

BILLY SMITH: Man, to say what it was like when Elvis first hit in 1954 . . . well, to actually hear "That's All Right (Mama)" on the radio was unbelievable. Then it was, "Boom, boom, boom!" Things happened quick.

Dewey Phillips was the first disc jockey to play Elvis. And the first to interview him, too. Dewey was a pioneer. He took some of the first steps toward getting white stations to play black music. His station, WHBQ, had broken into the black market a few years before, but they were still playing a lot of white singers, like Dean Martin. The night he had Elvis on, Dewey played "That's All Right (Mama)" just over and over, like six times. He asked Elvis what high school he went to so people would know he wasn't black.

I understood why he did that because when I first heard Elvis on the radio, even I thought, "God, that ain't Elvis. This guy sounds like a Negro." I was confused because in high school he just did basic singing. Same way when he went to do that record for his mama. "My Happiness" is more like trying to be the Ink Spots. But Elvis just turned loose on "That's All Right (Mama)." It was just so upbeat and different from what few songs he sang around the family that I thought they were playing the wrong record.

MARTY LACKER: Once you get out of the white gospel, like with Jake Hess and the Imperials, and the Blackwood Brothers, most of the singers Elvis really loved through the years were black— Roy Brown, Jackie Wilson, Brook Benton, Billy Eckstine, Arthur Prysock, the Ink Spots, Roy Hamilton. And he absolutely loved black gospel. You always read that Dean Martin was a big influence and that Elvis sang that kind of music ["That's Amore"] at the Eagle's Nest when he was eighteen or so. But I never personally heard Elvis say anything about trying to sound like Dean Martin. It was mostly obscure black guys.

BILLY SMITH: People ask me why Elvis sounded black, and I tell 'em about Shake Rag. And about how he would listen to WDIA, which was the first black radio station. He used to go to Pop Tunes [also known as Poplar Tunes, a record store on Poplar Avenue] a lot in high school, and listen to black singers. Then, who knows what he heard down on Beale Street? Even if he was just down there shopping at Lansky Brothers or having his picture made at the Blue Light Studio. I don't think anybody really knows, not even Sam Phillips.

It was always strange to me how Elvis and [guitarist] Scotty [Moore] and [bassist] Bill [Black] came up with that sound. There have been so many stories. It wasn't like Elvis said, "I invented this upbeat music." It just happened to be in the process then, from blacks *and* whites. It was what he was looking for—it tore the cover off. He had a long hard battle trying to find the right sound, and when he did, it just broke loose. It released that energy inside him.

But to say, "Elvis invented rock 'n' roll," well, he didn't really. Everybody lays claim to it . . . Bill Haley, and on back to 1951 and Jackie Brenston with "Rocket 88." Sam Phillips says that was the first rock 'n' roll record. But you got to hand it to Elvis. You associate rock 'n' roll with Elvis Presley because he brought it to the forefront. It took a white boy to bring it to a white audience, and that was Elvis.

MARTY LACKER: Who invented rock 'n' roll? It sort of evolved after World War II, from black people like Wynonie Harris, Fats Domino, and Amos Milburn. But a lot of black people loved Elvis's music. And then, some black people think he plagiarized all of the old Negro artists.

I got into a heated discussion one time in an interview I did on a radio show in Atlanta. A black guy called in and said Elvis just ripped off all these old black singers. I tried to explain that Elvis admitted he got a lot from them. I said, "There was a time, and I remember it, when it was called 'race music,' when parents of white kids and older white people in general did not want black records even sold in white record shops. Didn't want their kids listening to black music on the radio. Then along came Elvis and changed everything." We used to listen to Clyde McPhatter and Hank Ballard and the Midnighters here in Memphis, and even back in New York. But most white kids didn't. If anything, Elvis opened up the doors for black artists.

BILLY SMITH: From all I can gather, Sam Phillips was looking for a certain sound. Everybody knows what he supposedly said before he found Elvis: "If I could only find a white boy who could sing like a Negro, I could make me a million dollars." Well, Sam was really looking for a white boy who could bring the *feel* of black music to a white audience.

It was almost like it was destined to happen. Because when they first got the inkling of it, things weren't going too well, so they took a break. Elvis and them were goofing off. And Elvis started singing "That's All Right (Mama)" kind of like "Big Boy" Crudup, but real fresh like. And Sam heard what was pretty close to what he'd been looking for. Then, Elvis was doing [Bill Monroe's bluegrass waltz] "Blue Moon of Kentucky" in almost a quick, rhythmic way, clowning with it. It was more country when he started doing it. Sam recognized he was getting closer to the sound, though, and he added that slapback echo, and said, "That's what I'm talking about! We're just about on it, now!" And when Elvis really got it, he said, "Hell, that's different! That's a pop song now, nearly about."

So they just experimented for several weeks. That sound didn't happen overnight. They worked until they got what they wanted.

MARTY LACKER: I knew Scotty and Bill briefly. Scotty was always very quiet and calm. And Bill was a happy-go-lucky guy. Later on, he got a little abrasive. Of course, Bill always played the old-fashioned stand-up slap bass. Really whacked that thing. He was a ball of energy. He bounced up and down and from side to side, and he was always cracking jokes. Initially, Bill didn't think Elvis had much talent, by the way. And a lot of people thought the same of Bill.

Scotty I knew better. Scotty worked in a dry cleaner's for a while. He was a hat specialist. I think he and Bill first met when they joined a band called Doug Poindexter and the Starlite

Wranglers. I never heard Scotty say a cross word to anybody. He keeps a fairly low Elvis profile. He was smart enough to know you can't live on that forever.

Scotty is a talented guitar player—his guitar licks set the mood and put that rockabilly sound together, although I don't think he influenced Elvis's style particularly. They just sort of did jam sessions and got the whole thing rocking.

I remember Elvis saying that Sam Phillips was the one who put him with Scotty and Bill, but there's some confusion about whether Elvis knew Bill before that. I think he just knew Bill's brother, Johnny. And Bill's mother, Ruth, lived in Lauderdale Courts when the Presleys were there, and then she moved to Alabama Street when the Presleys lived there. She used to see Elvis occasionally.

BILLY SMITH: They didn't live on Alabama Street but maybe sixteen months at the most. Then Elvis started traveling, and in late '54, they found a house on Lamar Street. A real short time later, in about the middle of '55, they moved from Lamar to Getwell Street.

MARTY LACKER: In July of '54, right before Elvis's first record came out, Elvis and his parents signed a one-year contract with Scotty Moore. Scotty was Elvis's first manager.

BILLY SMITH: At that point, Sam Phillips was a record producer, and he really didn't have any experience in getting anybody bookings. But Scotty did. He got Elvis local gigs.

LAMAR FIKE: Elvis got to be making $500 a night when Scotty was booking. Scotty's still got a copy of the contract. Elvis didn't know shit about business. He just wanted to sing. He didn't give a damn about anything else.

CHAPTER 6

THE "OPRY"
AND THE "HAYRIDE"

On October 2, 1954, Elvis made his first and only appearance on "The Grand Ole Opry," the revered country radio program out of Nashville's Ryman Auditorium, where a talent manager named Colonel Tom Parker often did his booking from the free phones in the hallway. The facts of that historic performance have clouded into myth. But according to most of the witnesses, the truth is as follows: Elvis was booked on the program by Jim Denny, the "Opry" manager, after a conversation with Sam Phillips. They agreed that Elvis should perform on the 10:15 to 10:30 segment of the "Prince Albert Show," hosted by Hank Snow.

Denny, who was almost as famous for his terrible toupee as he was for his position with the "Opry," met with Elvis before the show. Someone—probably Denny—made the decision that Elvis's single, "That's All Right (Mama)," wasn't country enough for the "Opry" audience, so Elvis offered to sing the B side, "Blue Moon of Kentucky," even though he worried that Bill Monroe, one of the "Opry"'s Old Guard, would take offense at Elvis's revved-up rendition of his bluegrass classic. At the time, Monroe seemed less than pleased. Later, Elvis was thrilled to learn that the stern-jawed patriarch liked it after all.

The "Opry" audience, however, was not that enthusiastic. Elvis inspired a complimentary round of applause, but there was no encore. Just what conversation Elvis had with Denny after his appearance has been the source of much debate. Legend has it that Denny, disgusted by Elvis's wild movements and hepcat beat, told the young singer to "go back to Memphis and drive a truck." Other witnesses, including Chet Atkins, say that Denny spoke politely with Elvis, using the deep, slow voice he'd manufactured to disguise his lifelong stutter, but didn't make any reference to future appearances. Elvis was so heartsick, and so afraid the failure signaled the end of his career, that he cried all the way home, leaving his stage costume in a gas station bathroom when he stopped to change clothes.

MARTY LACKER: Even before the disastrous "Grand Ole Opry" audition, Sam Phillips had set up Elvis's first "Louisiana Hayride" appearance with Pappy Covington, who was the "Hayride"'s talent booker. They agreed on a date two weeks after the "Opry" [October 16, 1954], and Sam sent Elvis's record to Pappy, and wrote him a letter to make sure everybody understood Elvis was white. The "Hayride" was over KWKH, out of Shreveport, Louisiana, and it reached pretty much all over the South—they had 190 stations on CBS. It was sort of a junior "Grand Ole Opry," second in prestige and broadcast coverage. But Hank Williams had started there, so it wasn't anything to turn your nose up at. Elvis's appearance led to all kinds of things, including becoming a regular—he was headlining after a month—and bookings on the road. When he started on the radio show, Elvis got $18 and Scotty and Bill $12 each. The tours paid better, of course, or Elvis couldn't have quit his job at Crown Electric and Scotty and Bill couldn't have quit their band, the Starlite Wranglers.

BILLY SMITH: When Elvis went on the road, Gene and Red went with him. That was the start of the entourage. Aunt Gladys was glad Elvis had 'em because he had those nightmares and walked in his sleep sometimes. When you say Elvis had a strong link with his mother, it's true, boy. She had ESP about him. When he was on the road with Scotty and Bill, he had an old Cadillac, and it had a bad wheel bearing and caught fire. And Gladys sensed that. She was asleep and bolted upright. She didn't know exactly what was wrong, but she was tuned in.

MARTY LACKER: Elvis probably took his first pills in those very early days to stay awake when he was traveling long distances. Gladys always had this obsession about her weight. So the doctor gave her diet pills—uppers. And Elvis would see those and hear about them, and he would try them.

BILLY SMITH: Elvis took No Doz back when he was traveling for "The Louisiana Hayride." And yeah, I think he got some of his pills from Aunt Gladys. But there's a theory that Dewey Phillips give Elvis some of his first amphetamines, or at least Benzedrine. I don't know it for a fact, but it might have been. Dewey, at times, was real wild. On the radio, he had this country way of talking, and he'd go on this tear, sort of squawking, even while the record was playing. He'd say crazy things, like, "Get yasself a wheelbarrow load of mad hogs, run 'em through the front door, and tell 'em Phillips sentcha!" And he'd talk a mile a minute. Somebody said he was on drugs because of some old war injury. I do know he went to the VA hospital a lot to get straightened out. That Colin Escott book, *Good Rockin' Tonight,* says that on the air he was "wired from his usual combination of uppers and corn liquor." He sure sounded like it. I remember him coming around in '57 and '58, and even in '56, over on Audubon Drive.

Elvis liked Dewey. He went to his funeral in '68—one of the few funerals he went to. Marty says he stood up against the wall back where the family was and cracked jokes with one of the other guys. I can see Elvis doing that. Death made him uncomfortable.

MARTY LACKER: Elvis and Scotty and Bill were basically playing in school auditoriums and gymnasiums. Lots of country acts did that until well into the sixties. But Elvis started getting too big. Scotty couldn't handle the music and the management and booking, too.

BILLY SMITH: They decided they needed a real manager and booking agent. And Sam Phillips got in touch with Bob Neal. Scotty let Elvis out of his contract on January 1, 1955, and Bob came on board.

LAMAR FIKE: Bob Neal was a disc jockey on WMPS, which was the biggest radio station in Memphis and one of the first Top 40 radio stations in the country. Sam knew Bob because he always wanted him to plug his records. Bob also did some promoting, and on July 30, '54, he'd put Elvis on a country show with Slim Whitman and Billy Walker at the Overton Park Shell. And Elvis walked away with it, with "Blue Moon of Kentucky," standing out there shaking his leg.

Later, Bob became the booking agent for the Sun Records group. He was booking everybody from Johnny Cash and Carl Perkins to Jerry Lee Lewis, after Jerry Lee came up from Louisiana in '56. At one point in '55, Elvis played a high school in Lubbock, Texas, and he shared the bill with Carl Perkins, Johnny Cash, and local boy Buddy Holly, who hadn't put together the Crickets yet.

MARTY LACKER: I think Elvis always thought that Cash and Perkins resented him for making it as big as he did. One night in 1969 or '70, we were sitting in the den at Graceland and Johnny Cash's television show came on. Carl Perkins was the guest. And when Johnny introduced Carl, he said, "Here's the guy who *really* should get the credit for 'Blue Suede Shoes.'" [Perkins wrote it and also had his own record of the song out.] And Elvis really got upset. He said, "Well, that no-good, jealous son of a bitch." And he got up and walked out.

It's funny how Elvis's and Johnny Cash's lives were connected. But also not connected. In early '55, Elvis played some dates with the Carter Family. You know how country people are. After the last one, June Carter—now June Carter Cash, Johnny's wife—told Elvis if he was ever in Nashville to come by and see her.

So not too long after that, Elvis and Red went to Nashville for a lark. Red says they were totally broke, so sure enough, they went to June's house. Except June wasn't home. She was out on tour. So they just broke a window, went in, fixed themselves something to eat, and then went to sleep in the big double bed in the master bedroom.

June was married to country singer Carl Smith at the time. The next morning, Smith came home and saw the broken window and the mess in the kitchen, and headed for the bedroom. Elvis heard him coming, and when Carl opened the door, Elvis just kind of sat up in bed and rubbed his eyes and said, "Hi, Carl." Then Red woke up and realized that he was just a lump under the covers and that Carl might think Elvis had his wife in bed and go get a shotgun. Red said he slowly peeled back the covers and stuck his face out and said, "How you doin', Carl?" And Carl broke out in a big laugh.

Red said when they got up, Carl showed them all around the house. And when June came home that night, they all had a big supper and sat around and sang together 'til morning.

You've got to give Carl Smith credit for being a good sport. But then he probably knew that June wouldn't cheat on him. And, of course, Anita Carter was the one Elvis was really interested in. Poor Elvis. Anita couldn't have cared less about him. Not that way

LAMAR FIKE: Bob signed Elvis about the same time Elvis got signed to the "Hayride." He'd made a couple calls to try to get Elvis on the show himself. But they'd already heard of Elvis through Slim Whitman and [talent manager] Tillman Franks. Bob set up Elvis Presley Enterprises in the Sterick Building at Madison and Third. Everything was pink and black then, from Elvis's stage costumes to the song folios and the stationery Bob used in the office.

A couple of weeks later, Oscar Davis came out to see Elvis at the Eagle's Nest, a little club out at Rainbow Park. Oscar was an independent promoter. He'd been Hank Williams's manager, and he later managed Jerry Lee [Lewis]. He was no rube. He'd come out of vaudeville, and he'd worked with a lot of big stars, like Ernest Tubb and Roy Acuff. And he'd worked with Eddy Arnold and Hank Snow, largely through Tom Parker. He did "advance" work for Colonel sometimes, even though Oscar was a bigger promoter than Colonel at the time. He was top-drawer. Nicknamed "The Baron." Oscar was the one who first mentioned this new singing sensation to Parker. Bob Neal arranged it. He wanted to get Elvis on those big package shows.

BILLY SMITH: Bob Neal was a real nice man. He just didn't know exactly what to do. He got Elvis some good exposure, and he made him some pretty good money—like $1,500 or $2,000 a night—before he ever got famous outside of Memphis. I sometimes wonder how different things might have been if Bob had stayed Elvis's manager. But after Elvis got going real good, Bob realized he was getting too big for him to handle. He said, "He's growing faster than I am." Bob always said the first time Colonel actually became involved with Elvis was in February '55, when he helped Bob book Elvis into Carlsbad, New Mexico. But now Hank

Snow says Colonel is the one who had Hank put Elvis on his segment of "The Grand Ole Opry." So maybe Colonel was way ahead of everybody else, and they just didn't know it.

LAMAR FIKE: Colonel was essentially a one-star manager. He didn't have a group of stars because he didn't think he could give them enough individual attention. He'd managed Eddy Arnold in the late forties up 'til '51, and now he managed Hank Snow. In addition, he was an equal partner with Snow in Hank Snow Enterprises–Jamboree Attractions, which packaged tours. And now he needed somebody to open the Hank Snow Jamboree tour of '55. So he put Elvis on. Hank was supposed to be the headliner, but it didn't turn out that way. Elvis was the second or third act on the show. But the girls screamed so loud, Elvis had to come back onstage. Hank couldn't even do his show. About ten dates into the tour, Hank said, "Either take Elvis off the damn show, or put him on before intermission." Bill Black did Elvis's merchandising, by the way. He was out there selling pictures up a storm.

MARTY LACKER: Elvis used to tell me about playing Jacksonville, Florida, in May of '55. It was the Gator Bowl, a stadium, and he said they had 14,000 people in front of the stage. They were held back by a big chain-link fence, but the crowd got so wild that they rushed that fence and down it came. They started toward the stage, and the police tried to erect some kind of barricade, but they just kept coming. The band was getting shook. Scotty yelled, "Come on, Elvis, let's go!" But Elvis kept right on singing. Finally, they had to grab him and pull him off the stage. They followed him into the dressing area and tore most of his clothes off. He asked for it, though. Because at the end of his act, he said, "Girls, I'll see you all backstage." A similar thing happened in Vancouver, in '57. But Jacksonville was his first real riot. When he went to get in his car, it was covered with names and phone numbers. Girls had scrawled 'em with lipstick or scratched 'em in the paint with safety pins.

LAMAR FIKE: Colonel started doing business with Bob Neal, and when he saw what those contracts were bringing in, he started sabotaging Bob's relationship with Elvis. Elvis was paying Bob

Neal 15 percent and Colonel was hoping to get 25 percent. So every night, Colonel would come back and peel off, say, $100 to $250 extra.

Elvis said, "Why didn't I get this from Bob?" And Colonel said, "Look, I'm giving this to you. This is what you should be making, and with me, you will make that."

On August 15, 1955, Elvis signed a contract with Colonel Parker that named Colonel as "special adviser" to Elvis and Bob Neal. But when you read it, you see Colonel's clear intent is to wrestle Elvis away from Bob, under the guise of negotiating and assisting "in any way possible the build-up of Elvis Presley as an artist."

You know the little exchange Elvis and Colonel supposedly had when they signed one of their contracts, don't you? Elvis, always respectful to his elders, said, "Sir, you put a lump in my throat." And Colonel shot back, "Elvis, you put a lump in my wallet."

BILLY SMITH: When Elvis died, Bob gave some interviews where he said he wasn't bitter about losing Elvis. He basically just let Elvis go, partly because he was tired of the traveling. He'd been in it more for the fun than the money, and he'd just spread himself too thin. See, Bob told Elvis at the beginning, "I'll do what I can." Out of all of them, he's the guy who really put himself out.

LAMAR FIKE: When Elvis came home after one of those tours with Colonel, he talked to Sam Phillips. They were riding around in Sam's '54 Fleetwood Cadillac, and Elvis was trying to figure out what to do. Sam said, "There are two people in this business I would trust to manage you. One of them is my brother, Jud, and the other one is Tom Parker." Jud did a little of everything. He'd been an army chaplain, a gospel promoter, and a production assistant for Jimmy Durante. He'd worked as a front guy for Roy Acuff when he had his tent show, and he'd supposedly worked for Colonel for a spell. Jud did promotion for Sun for a while, and then Sam and Jud had a falling-out because Jud could match anybody drink for drink. In a way, Sam was telling Elvis, "I don't know a lot about Tom Parker, and I'm not sure if I like him that well. But he could do a hell of a job for you."

MARTY LACKER: Colonel could have just conned Bob Neal out of Elvis's contract, but he decided to take a different tack. He saw that Elvis's family was poor country people and easy marks. And he put on this act of being God-fearing and all, but he thought he might need more. Gladys didn't like him at all. Colonel was a carny type, but the Presleys saw him as Big City, and they weren't used to Big City people. Gladys asked him what church he went to, and he had to dance around that one, boy! I never knew him to go to church, and I never heard him mention God or religion, period. I don't think he put a lot of stock in it.

Anyway, he knew that Vernon and Gladys, like most rural people, were big country music fans. So he figured he'd send Hank Snow, this big country star, down there to spend a couple of hours with them and impress them.

BILLY SMITH: Aunt Gladys was a hard person to win over. She saw what Colonel was doing by bringing Hank Snow down here. Colonel hooked Vernon so quick it was unreal. He told him he was going to get Elvis out of his "Louisiana Hayride" contract because it wasn't enough money, even though Elvis was now getting $200 a night. And Colonel did get him out of it, but it cost 'em $10,000. Vernon saw dollar signs tumbling one after the other, and he said, "Hey! Hey! Hey! Let's get this thing going!"

MARTY LACKER: All Vernon was looking at was the money, because he still didn't want to work. So that's how Colonel got Elvis's management contract. It was a case of convincing Vernon and Gladys that "I'm going to do everything for your boy and I love him." I don't think Gladys ever bought it, but Vernon and Elvis overruled her.

LAMAR FIKE: The second thing Colonel did was go to Jean and Julian Aberbach. They were music publishers—smart Viennese Jews. Jean had worked in music publishing in Paris and Berlin during the days of cabaret. He came over here about 1940. He worked for Chappell Music when he first got here, and then in '45 he and his brother Julian founded Hill and Range Music. They built it up into a major independent publisher. Had offices in sixteen countries.

Hill and Range was another way of saying country and western, although they published all styles of music, including

"Frosty the Snowman" and "Arrivederci, Roma." Through the years they had some great writers, too. Like Burt Bacharach, Hal David, and a list of guys who figure real heavy in the Elvis saga— Doc Pomus and Mort Shuman, Ben Weisman, and Jerry Leiber and Mike Stoller. In the forties and fifties, when New York publishers didn't give a shit about country music, they handled Ernest Tubb. And they also had a joint publishing venture with Eddy Arnold and Hank Snow through Colonel Parker.

Colonel always liked Jean and Julian. And he figured with their help, he could easily get Elvis's record contract away from Sam Phillips and Sun Records. Sam couldn't get his distributors to pay him on time, and he owed a lot of money to Chess Records on another deal and also to his brother, Jud, as part of a buyout agreement. He just couldn't make anything, and he owed Elvis, and probably other artists, back royalties.

In January of '55, Sun's liabilities were three times their assets. Sam was doing everything he could to keep out of bankruptcy. He'd already tried to sell Elvis's contract to Paul Cohen, at Decca Records in New York, through Webb Pierce and Jim Denny. He wanted $20,000 for it, although some people say he asked considerably less. Then other folks say Decca offered $8,000 and got turned down. Either way, it didn't fly. And it didn't fly at Columbia or MGM or Dot, either. And Columbia supposedly offered $40,000.

When Colonel came into the picture, he went back to Decca, this time to Owen Bradley in the Nashville office. Actually, he ran into him at the dog track at Daytona Beach. Bradley coordinated Decca's Nashville recording sessions, as assistant to Paul Cohen. He'd been a staff pianist and bandleader at WSM, and he opened the first recording studio in Nashville. He was already becoming famous, although he'd become a lot more famous producing Patsy Cline and Conway Twitty and Loretta Lynn in the sixties and seventies. Owen was a country music producer, and he didn't much like rockabilly or rock 'n' roll. But he was interested in Elvis, because he heard he was stopping the show wherever he played. So he tried to get Decca to take him. But Decca was very conservative. Part of that was probably because Colonel wanted too much money. The price had gone up since the last offer. Colonel thought Elvis's contract was worth $50,000. Some people say he got it.

BILLY SMITH: That's when Colonel set up the deal with RCA. He already knew Steve Sholes [head of RCA Victor's Nashville operations]. RCA was Hank Snow's and Eddy Arnold's label. Mr. Sholes had seen Elvis perform either at the Disc Jockey Convention in Nashville, or on another showcase, and he told people he hadn't seen anything that weird in a long time. Colonel told Bob Neal there was a good chance that he was going to get a lot of money from RCA, and when he pulled it off, he'd give him a commission. That's probably another reason Bob gave up without a fight.

MARTY LACKER: Atlantic Records had just started up as a black label with Ray Charles, Big Joe Turner, and the Drifters. And [founders] Ahmet Ertegun and his partner Jerry Wexler wanted to buy Elvis. Ertegun was passionate about black music—R & B and blues and jazz. He had an honest love for it, and he was trying to get black artists and the black sound into mainstream America.

So he had a special interest in Elvis. He thought that Elvis, unlike Bill Haley, who'd covered Big Joe Turner's "Shake, Rattle and Roll," understood what the music was all about. And that Elvis conveyed the same feeling the black artists did, that they came from the same roots. I think he saw what Sam Phillips did—that Elvis had the same insecurity as black people, that he identified with their oppression, and that it came out in his music. So he went after Elvis's contract.

But RCA won out. Because Atlantic stopped at $25,000. They just didn't have any more money. Then Colonel went to Jean and Julian Aberbach and said, "I need money to get Elvis on RCA." So Elvis's Sun contract was bought by both RCA and Hill and Range. You sometimes hear there was $50,000 in this deal altogether, but I think it was really $40,000, at least some of it against royalties. RCA gave Sam Phillips $20,000 and gave Elvis a $5,000 bonus to cover the future royalties he would have gotten from Sun. And Hill and Range came up with $15,000 for a copublishing deal on Sam Phillips's Hi-Lo Music publishing company. And there was one important stipulation—the Aberbachs insisted on having the publishing rights to one side of every Presley single. In other words, when Elvis went to record, he had to pick from songs that they gave him. For the rest of his life.

This is where you see how shrewd Parker is. He worked a deal with Hill and Range to set up several publishing companies for Elvis under the Hill and Range umbrella. He named them "Elvis Presley Music" and "Gladys Music." The Aberbachs would get to administer the publishing companies for the money that they put in.

The ownership of Elvis Presley Music was split up with Jean owning 25 percent, Julian owning 25 percent, and Elvis owning 50 percent. But later there were other companies—Mr. Songman Music, Aaron Music, Elvis Music, Inc., and Whitehaven Music. Colonel structured some of those for his own benefit, so there was more for him than Elvis. Colonel owned 40 percent of Mr. Songman Music, for instance, while Elvis owned only 15 percent. Then Freddy Bienstock, who worked for the Aberbachs, owned 15 percent, George Parkhill at RCA owned 15 percent, and Tom Diskin, Colonel's right-hand man, also owned 15 percent. And that was the same for Aaron Music. So Colonel was getting money that had nothing to do with Elvis's split and nothing to do with his merchandising and managing Elvis. The publishing royalties should not have been part of it.

In other words, he was double dipping. In fact, in some of these arrangements, *everybody* got at least as much or more than Elvis did. And these were people like Parkhill and Diskin, who were part of it for no reason other than Colonel wanted to reward them for being in his camp.

LAMAR FIKE: When Elvis signed with Colonel, and they put that deal together with RCA, son, it broke wide open. Steve Sholes had to personally guarantee that the advance would be made back during that first year, and boy, it was. RCA sold 12.5 million singles and 2.75 million albums during Elvis's first year with the label. What happened was, in pop music, except for Pat Boone and Bill Haley, the business had been controlled by older singers—Tony Martin, Frank Sinatra, Perry Como, Tony Bennett. Elvis kicked the door open, and for the first time, young people had their own music. Elvis was the musical counterpart to James Dean—he gave that generation a voice. Then Chuck Berry and Jerry Lee [Lewis], who had been regional acts, broke loose nationally, and the Everly Brothers, and Ricky Nelson, and Bobby Darin followed. Rock 'n' roll was in full swing. Later, all the imitators started, the teen idols like Fabian and Bobby Rydell.

This was great for just about everybody but the folks in

Nashville. Because in two years, Elvis single-handedly wiped country music off the face of the earth! The country artists couldn't get booked. And yet Elvis was raised on it. It took country music five years to recuperate, with that countrypolitan "Nashville Sound" that Chet Atkins and Boots [Randolph] and Floyd [Cramer] came up with. Elvis separated the pop music charts and then put them all together again. He combined all these different types of music. Of course, what Elvis did to country music then, country's doing to rock now.

MARTY LACKER: Sam always says he's not resentful about selling Elvis's contract. It got him out of a jam, although he finally had to sell the whole Sun label later on. The interesting thing is what happened to his relationship with Elvis. In 1969, Elvis invited him to his opening in Vegas, but that's about the only time he saw him. I was shocked he invited him then, because of the things Elvis had been saying about Sam. He still called him "Mr. Phillips," you know. But he really didn't want to go back and relive that time.

In the late fifties, when people like Rockin' Ray Smith and Jerry Lee Lewis were still at Sun, Elvis used to go over there for late-night jam sessions. Him and Jerry Lee on the piano. But once Elvis came home from the army, he never went back to see Sam again. In fact, on a couple of occasions, he said, "I don't *want* to see him."

One time, one of the music organizations put on a dinner to honor Sam. And Sam's son, Knox, asked me if I would talk to Elvis to get him to come. Elvis was out in L.A., and I was in Memphis. I called him, and he said, "Hell, no, I don't want to do that." And I said, "Well, let me make a suggestion. Send a telegram saying, 'I'm sorry, I'm in Vegas doing a show.'" So he told me, have one of the guys send it from Las Vegas so it would have the Vegas postmark.

The night of the dinner, Knox asked me to read the telegram to everybody. Sam was sitting right next to the speaker's platform, and as I got up to read the telegram, he looked at me and said sarcastically, "Why the hell isn't Elvis here?" But Elvis certainly didn't feel any allegiance.

LAMAR FIKE: I don't think there's a particular reason. Probably it's because Sam was a drinker. Elvis didn't like people who drank. Sam was part of Elvis's past, and he wanted to blow it off.

MARTY LACKER: One time in the seventies, after Elvis's Memphis Sessions, when he began to cut bad songs again after that brief blaze of glory, I was over at Sam's recording studio. Sam said, "Where in the hell is Elvis getting these shitty songs? Why doesn't somebody do something?" That was the only other time Sam brought up Elvis's name to me.

LAMAR FIKE: Sam lost big with Elvis in the long run. But there were other losers, too. Oscar Davis and Hank Snow, for instance. Oscar should have had part of the action for alerting Colonel to Elvis. And Colonel absolutely screwed Hank out of his percentage because they owned Hank Snow Enterprises–Jamboree Attractions together. Colonel's first contract with Elvis identifies the "Party of the Second Part" as "Col. Thomas A. Parker and/or Hank Snow Attractions." Hank probably knew Colonel was a con man, but he had no idea what a sham artist he actually was. No one did, really.

CHAPTER 7

THE COLONEL

A cross between P. T. Barnum and W. C. Fields, Colonel Tom
Parker was like his most famous client—bigger than life. As such,
much of Colonel's personal history is half fabrication, half colorful fact. The basic biography Parker handed out in the fifties had
him born of carny parents in West Virginia on June 26, 1909,
orphaned at age ten, and soon after going to work for his uncle's
Great Parker Pony Circus.

From there, the trail gets easier to trace. After army duty,
Parker joined the Royal American Shows, a higher-class outfit
than most carnivals since it traveled by rail rather than by truck.
Parker worked the "pie car" with the organization, feeding the
carny crew between towns. When the train pulled into Tampa,
the carnival's headquarters, Parker threw up a "mitt camp" to
teach the palm readers their trade.

Parker was still living in Tampa in the early forties, working
for the humane society and doing a little promoting on the side,
often bringing in country music stars from Nashville. One of the
shows he booked was Pee Wee King and the Golden West
Cowboys, with Minnie Pearl and Eddy Arnold. Parker signed on
as King's road manager for four years, but he especially liked the
smooth-voiced Arnold, and when "The Tennessee Plowboy" left
King's show, Parker became his personal manager.

"Colonel was one of the most energetic men I've ever seen,"
remembers King. "Regardless of how big the crowds or advance
sales were, he always tried to get bigger crowds. He was always
very considerate and good to the entertainers, and no matter who
he managed, he did a tremendous job. He knew what he wanted,
he had his own way of getting there, and if he made any mistakes, they were well covered. Everything he got credit for, he did
on his own."

While Parker was easygoing and conscientious, King also remembers that Colonel would bargain for radio time and newspaper ads, and even with the auditorium managers. "Besides getting the ticket money," says King, "he'd ask for a cut in the concessions. So Tom had a way."

Part of Parker's "way" was to indulge in some of the most outrageous stunts in show business history. One of the most ingenious revolved around a pair of dancing chickens. As recounted in Jerry Hopkins's *Elvis: A Biography*:

"Country singers long have performed at rodeos and livestock shows, and in those days there was a $20 entertainment tax charged per performance unless you had a livestock exhibit, so the Colonel would carry a hog or a couple of chickens in the back of his car, put them in a box outside where Eddy sang and mark it 'Livestock Exhibit,' thereby saving the 20 bucks.

"The Colonel was traveling with two chickens when Eddy was too sick to appear, and so he went to the stock show's producer and said he had a substitute act, Colonel Parker's Dancing Chickens. As the Colonel tells the story, he sent his assistant to the nearest general store to buy a two-dollar hot plate and an extension cord, which he placed in the chicken cage and covered with straw.

"The hot plate was plugged in, Bob Wills and the Texas Playboys went into 'Turkey in the Straw,' the curtain went up, and a bewildered audience saw two chickens high-stepping around the cage, trying to keep from burning their feet. The Colonel says he got away with this for two days, two shows per day, until Eddy was able to sing again."

Parker and Arnold split up in the early fifties, and although Parker had previously promoted the pop crooner Gene Austin ("My Blue Heaven") and managed several other acts besides Arnold (including the Dickens Sisters—relatives of a Parker employee—who toured and recorded with King), he devoted most of his energies to one performer at a time. In 1954, after a short stint managing country/bluegrass performer Mac Wiseman, he signed Canada's Hank Snow, already a star and a member of "The Grand Ole Opry" for four years. Soon after, Parker met Elvis Presley.

When Parker and Presley first signed their contract, Colonel promised Elvis he'd turn his $1 million worth of talent into $1 million. Within thirteen months, Colonel made good on his pledge.

BILLY SMITH: Colonel's relationship with Elvis . . . Boy, that's a complicated tale. Elvis was doing fairly good from '54 to '55. But when the Colonel came along, bang! Instant success! Elvis had money, he had women running after him, he had mass popularity, he was on television and signing movie deals. And he had his picture everywhere you looked.

Colonel did that for him, and they got along fine. He lived up to his word to Elvis's mama and daddy. And just about all the things he accomplished were unheard of at the time. Colonel vowed to keep it going, and, in return, he was saying, "You've got my loyalty. Now I want yours." Elvis was easily swayed by the Colonel, and his loyalty continued right to the end. But Colonel was cunning, and he knew how to manipulate Elvis, too.

LAMAR FIKE: Elvis's greatest flaw, and his fatal flaw, was his loyalty.

MARTY LACKER: Sometimes, in the early days, Colonel would say to Elvis, "You are like a son to me, and I love you." I think everybody believed it at the time. Arnold and Snow got wise to him in a way that Elvis never did. But for decades, neither one of them would talk about him and then only Snow did, in his book, *The Hank Snow Story*. Fear of retaliation, maybe. That was Colonel's deal—control.

LAMAR FIKE: What happened to Colonel was a unique situation. In our business, when a manager and artist click it's phenomenal. Like Erv Woolsey with George Strait, who've been together for more than ten years. The Colonel looked at the gold mine he had, and went, "Uh-*huh*," and tied up all the loose ends. He was fortunate in that Elvis was so malleable. Colonel was one lucky manager. His favorite saying was "If you can't operate from a position of strength, do not operate."

MARTY LACKER: From the beginning, Colonel instilled in Elvis the importance of being a nice, polite person. Colonel said, "You don't make waves, and you don't make promoters mad." And later on, when they got into the movies, he told Elvis not to rile the Hollywood people. He said, "You do everything they say. If you're going to sign a contract, you do exactly what they want, no matter what they do to you. If you do anything wrong, they'll ruin your career and you'll go back to being just a poor kid again."

Of course, because of his carnival background, Colonel viewed most people as suckers. He didn't really give a damn about anybody. Basically, he looked at people for what they could do for him.

LAMAR FIKE: What happened to Tom Parker is what every manager wants—one big superstar. And it made him a very wealthy man. Elvis made an average of $7 to $15 million a year in sixties and seventies monies. Colonel had 25 to 50 percent of it. That's not bad. And, of course, after Elvis died, he made a lot more money. A *lot*. But then he gambled a lot of it away, too. Carnies are also gamblers—they can't resist their own shell game.

MARTY LACKER: Once a carny, always a carny. Do you remember the Elvis Presley Midget Fan Club? Right after Colonel took over as Elvis's manager, he pulled this publicity stunt to advertise one of Elvis's concerts. He hired a bunch of midgets to parade around the streets wearing little suits and carrying banners that promoted the fan club and the concert. He did that with elephants, too. He loved elephants, of course. That comes from his carnival time. He collected them. If Elvis was going to buy the Colonel a gift, he'd get him something with an elephant on it. But Colonel always liked midgets.

One time . . . what the hell was the occasion? It was in Hawaii. He went on the radio, or advertised, that the first authentic, full-blooded Hawaiian midget who showed up at the radio station would get free tickets to the show. Well, there are very few full-blooded Hawaiians left, and there sure as hell aren't many midgets. Colonel never gave anything away.

LAMAR FIKE: The con started a long time ago, and it's never stopped. Even the military title. Colonel was stationed in Hawaii in the army. As a private, he served two years in an antiaircraft section of the coastal artillery at Fort Shafter, Hawaii, which is right outside Honolulu. I think that's why he had Elvis make *Blue Hawaii*. Anyway, when he couldn't get a hotel room, he'd get on the phone and say, "Colonel Parker's coming." Because army personnel would get a hotel room before civilians. That's how the "Colonel" bit started. Later on, in '48, I think, he got an honorary Colonel certification from Governor Jimmie Davis and the State of Louisiana. Davis, of course, had been a country music singer.

BILLY SMITH: Colonel could snow anybody. That's what he called himself, you know. "The Snowman." During the movie years, Hal Wallis called him "America's Number One Snow Man." Colonel even had a bigger-than-life-size snowman in his office out at the sound lot at Paramount. And he had little certificates printed up that said "Snowmens [sic] League of America," a take off on the Showman's League of America, with a drawing of himself as a snowman, with the hat and the gloves and the cigar.

MARTY LACKER: Oh, yeah, I remember that. All the original Memphis Mafia got membership cards and a rule book. It had blank pages.

LAMAR FIKE: Never before or since has anybody ever been put together the way Colonel put Elvis together. Colonel is a genius. He would go in and buy thirty-second radio spots on Elvis to advertise his show. They'd go, "Elvis, Elvis, Elvis," with an echo, a three-second delay. That's all it was. Then the voice-over would say, "Appearing in such-and-such city. Tickets—" Very effective.

BILLY SMITH: Once Colonel had Elvis established, he didn't want to overexpose him.

LAMAR FIKE: "You give a kid a candy bar every day, and he gets tired of it." That's the way Colonel thought.

MARTY LACKER: Even though you saw Elvis's picture every-where, in some ways he was underexposed. For example, Colonel wouldn't allow him to play New York City at the height of his early fame. He kept him playing small towns because Colonel wanted sellout crowds. He thought if he didn't have a sellout, it would be an embarrassment. The act wouldn't live up to the image. Which is ridiculous. Because if they liked Elvis in L.A., and they liked him in Oshkosh, why wouldn't they like him in

New York? But Colonel also thought he couldn't get the same cooperation from the police in New York for security.

BILLY SMITH: People always want to know whether Colonel told Elvis to hide himself away from the public. In the beginning, at least, he said, "Remain a mystery." And rationing Elvis worked out at first. The press would want an interview, and Colonel would quote some outlandish price and say, "You pay this much money, you get an interview." So people wanted it all that much more.

But then when Elvis's fame became pressure and the fans became so rowdy—which was right from the start, almost—Elvis built a shell around himself with the guys who were the forerunners of the Memphis Mafia. And he stayed in that shell because he was afraid to get out and walk the street by himself. Colonel encouraged it. I just don't think anybody knew how unhealthy it could get.

LAMAR FIKE: When you're a manager, and you have an artist like Elvis, you do what you can to keep him at a premium. And to hold on to him.

BILLY SMITH: Elvis respected Colonel, especially in the early days. He looked up to him and to his mama—not his daddy. He thought, "They're teaching me things, and they're watching out for me." But he couldn't talk to the Colonel about his personal life because they kept business as business, and that was it. Except the Colonel told him not to get married. He said, "In due time, if you want to get married, fine. But right now, don't get serious with anybody because your career is taking off. You need to dedicate yourself to that." I'm sure Colonel didn't want to risk disappointing all those teenage girls who dreamed about Elvis.

LAMAR FIKE: Colonel was a personal manager, not a business manager. There was no real business manager, although Vernon would pretend to be one after a while. The checks would come in to the Colonel, he would take his percentage out, and he would send the money on to Elvis. That's the way they did it, and that's the way managers do it today.

BILLY SMITH: Let me give you a little something here. Elvis looked at Colonel like he was a mentor. And the teacher is always the smartest and is always right. So consequently, Elvis trusted Colonel with the money and the ability to make the right business decisions for him. And Elvis didn't want to be a businessman, and he didn't think he had to be, because he respected Colonel. Now we know he should have learned more about the business. Not until his final few years did Elvis really break down and realize what was happening. But even then, he had such a loyalty to Colonel that he let it go on just like it was.

MARTY LACKER: The student/teacher comparison is pretty apt. The thing is, there are good teachers who really have the benefit of the student at heart, and then there are those who take advantage.

BILLY SMITH: In the beginning, Colonel had Elvis's benefit at heart. But just like Elvis, the Colonel changed. People get greedy.

LAMAR FIKE: When the Colonel signed deals, he would discuss them with Elvis first. Well, in a fashion he would discuss things with Elvis. But he would never ask Elvis's permission. He would just say, "Do you want to do it?" Elvis would say, "Yeah." And then Colonel would go make the deal. The important thing is that Colonel had total freedom to make any deal he wanted. Elvis would say, "Take care of it. Bring me the paper, I'll sign it and go do the show." Elvis signed the contracts blind. He didn't know what they were. He just signed them. But Elvis signed too many contracts without looking at them. Then, too, early on, I don't think the Colonel did anything to cause Elvis to distrust him. Colonel's flamboyance was probably a problem at times, though. Because the Colonel was as big a character as Elvis.

BILLY SMITH: The Colonel was putting on a show in his own way. He had an ego, too. And he fed it, in the things he said, the people he kept around him, and the way he looked. He was always a contradiction and a mystery. I thought it was funny that he would sometimes wear an undershirt in public. He didn't do it all that much. Once in a great, great while and then mostly in the office. Because Colonel was a showman. He played that promoter image to the fullest, and he dressed the part. He loved it. Power and authority were his whole life. He was married, but she was usually in Nashville or Palm Springs, and he was in Los Angeles or on the road for Elvis. They didn't have any kids, except for her son by a previous marriage. His name was Bobby. He had multiple sclerosis. Died the same year as Elvis.

LAMAR FIKE: Colonel's wife was named Marie, so he called her "Miz Rie," you know, "misery."

MARTY LACKER: Mrs. Parker didn't go along on trips very often. She hated everything. Colonel would do his little duty and call her every day and ask about the cats. They had cats at the Palm Springs house, and she had her favorite, Midnight. In the early years, especially, Colonel would go back to Palm Springs on the weekends.

LAMAR FIKE: Colonel met Marie and fell in love with her while they were working the pie car on the carnival train. He knew every trick in the book. When they'd set up the stands to sell foot-long hot dogs at the carnival, Colonel would stick about an inch of wiener in each end, and then fill the middle with slaw. Then he put a whole wiener—minus the ends—down on the ground in front of the stand. If anybody came back and complained that Colonel had cheated him, Colonel would puff up and say he hadn't done anything of the sort. Then he'd point down at the ground and say, "There! You must have dropped it."

Colonel might have had a soft spot for elephants, but he didn't give a shit about this cat of Marie's, Midnight. And Marie just doted on it. I was at the house one day, and Colonel and I were sitting in the den, talking. Marie came in all distraught and said, "Midnight's on the roof! Midnight's on the roof!" Colonel said, "He'll come down."

She came back in a little while and said, "Midnight's still on the roof! Do something!" So Colonel went out with a hose about as big as a fireman's, with tremendous pressure, and aimed it at that cat, and blew it over the garage and the porte cochere, and out into the street. It landed on its feet, but boy, was it surprised! Colonel came back in, and he said, "Now, *that's* how you get a cat off a roof."

After a while, Elvis found it hard to get along with the Colonel. They were friends, but at arm's length. Elvis always called him "the Admiral," just to be different. And Colonel always called him Elvis, except when he was discussing him with somebody else. Then he referred to him as "Mr. Presley." Or sometimes as "My Boy." But Elvis had his world, and the Colonel had his.

Managers usually subjugate themselves to the artist. But Colonel never did that. He always considered himself an equal. Consequently, both Colonel and Elvis had their own entourage. Elvis eventually had a thick wall of people around him who were terribly loyal, but the same thing existed in Colonel's camp. They were just older in Colonel's camp. And both camps operated from the simple premise that one was the star and the others were the underlings.

Colonel established this pattern from way back. The camps lived and traveled the same way, with the private jets, the hotel rooms, and people waiting on them hand and foot. That was one of the most amazing things to me. Elvis would get pissed off about Colonel and his camp. It was hilarious.

MARTY LACKER: Colonel's camp was an interesting crew. For years, his whole office was men, even the secretary. While I knew him, he didn't have a woman around him until the seventies, and then only one, Miss Miller. Loanne Miller. He always gave the impression that he didn't like women around, as far as business was concerned. He didn't like them meddling in the business or into anybody's affairs.

I saw a woman with a heavy Viennese accent named Trude Forsher in one documentary [*Elvis in Hollywood*], identified as Colonel's assistant. She was related to the Aberbachs in some way. She's supposed to have been Colonel's West Coast secretary. But I think she was really only there in Elvis's prearmy days, from *Love Me Tender* through *King Creole*.

LAMAR FIKE: Colonel had a core group, just as Elvis would come to have one. Tom Diskin was the Colonel's right-hand man, his Best Boy, or whatever you want to call it. He did everything. Colonel had a male secretary named Jim O'Brien. George Parkhill, from RCA, was part of this outfit, too. Then there was Bitsy Mott, who was Colonel's brother-in-law. Bitsy had been an infielder for the Philadelphia Phillies. He would be in and out, back in the mid- to late fifties. His real first name was Elisha.

MARTY LACKER: Bitsy Mott was almost the forerunner of the Memphis Mafia. Some of the books even say he was a member. But he wasn't, really. He traveled as a bodyguard, up until the time Elvis went into the army. Back in the early years, the Colonel was always at Elvis's side when they went anywhere. And so was Bitsy. But Bitsy worked for the Colonel. He didn't work for Elvis. He ended up with bit parts in some of the movies—played a soldier in *G.I. Blues* and a state trooper in *Wild in the Country*.

Somebody asked me the other day if these guys who worked for Colonel saw him as a father figure. I don't know. Because quite honestly, we weren't around Colonel that much. Personally, I don't understand how anybody could feel any warmth for him. And I don't know what those guys thought or why they were there. Or what they did when they weren't with Colonel. Most of them weren't married. At least, not at the time.

LAMAR FIKE: Colonel ran his camp with military decorum. Sometimes it got a little like *Dr. Strangelove*.

MARTY LACKER: Colonel would tell these guys what to do, and then he'd say, "That's an order!" He and Tom Diskin had been together a long time. Yet if Colonel wanted him, he wouldn't say, "Tom." He'd bark, "Diskin!" It made no difference who was in the office. A lot of times, Parker would say something to somebody, and then he'd say, "Isn't that right, Diskin?" And Diskin would parrot, "That's right, Colonel!"

LAMAR FIKE: The way Colonel's men barked these silly replies to him on cue . . . it was comical, but pathetic.

MARTY LACKER: I don't know why these guys put up with his bullshit. Maybe they didn't have any other place to go. Tom Diskin was a smart man, especially in financial matters. I don't know if he's the guy who worked out all the percentages with the Hill and Range publishing companies and all of Colonel's other deals. But even though Diskin had a lot of money put away from his investments, he still hung in there with Colonel. Jim O'Brien, the secretary, seemed to be very intelligent. And he would take all this crap from the Colonel. He was very quiet. Now these other guys who were around him, they were like carnies. They were all there for a hustle.

Later on, when the Memphis Mafia was in full swing, Colonel tried to get Elvis's crew to answer to him like that. Alan Fortas used to, and Joe Esposito would at times. Red West never would, but sometimes Sonny West would, because Sonny used to go along with the Colonel's stuff just to be going along with it. But Sonny wasn't fooled by him.

LAMAR FIKE: I guess I knew Colonel as well as anybody who's ever known him. And he was always a very odd duck. We would be in a restaurant, and if a waitress tried to put her hand on him, or accidentally hit his arm, he'd snap, "Don't touch me."

MARTY LACKER: He didn't like anybody touching him. Period. On one or two occasions, I saw the Colonel and Elvis hug, but that was Elvis's doing. Parker was odd in a lot of ways. He'd talk out of the side of his mouth, for example. I mean, literally. He'd twist it and turn it into a little pocket of a mouth. Probably because he always had a cigar in it.

LAMAR FIKE: Parker had a bad back and used a cane a lot. But it became so much a part of him that whether his back hurt or not, he used it. He always wore an elastic brace around his waist and the upper part of his back. Of course, Colonel was very over-weight. God, he could eat. Ate like a moose. Jesus. Except when he got free food off of people, everything he ate was a boiled din-ner. A circus dinner. He always wanted to teach me how to do it. In the carnival, they used to take everything and put it in a big pot. Slumgullion. Boiled. And he liked to barbecue stuff. He had a cookhouse out in the back of his house in Palm Springs. It was a barbecue pit with a house built around it, and it had a big walk-in freezer in the back.

When we'd stay in hotels, he'd get a bunch of free dinners and put them on the jet back to Palm Springs. When we got off the plane, he'd say to the luggage handlers, "Would you rather have a ten-dollar tip or a nice meal from a hotel?" They'd take the meal, thinking they were going to get a big feast. And he'd hand them this tray. That way, he wouldn't have to tip them and the meal didn't cost him anything. He loved to do stuff like that. Just to see if he could get away with it.

MARTY LACKER: Colonel used the cane as a prop, to get sympathy, like "Oh, poor old Colonel. He can't lift this. He can't lift that." I don't think he needed that cane, except to raise it and threaten people when he got mad. He did that to me one time, but after I told him off, he never did it again.

LAMAR FIKE: We always thought Colonel was the classic eccentric. There was something uniquely American about him, you know, the self-made millionaire iconoclast. In 1978, when I was doing the book with Albert Goldman, [publisher] Kevin Eggers called me and said a guy in New York had told him about an obscure book called *The Hillbilly Cat.* Kevin alerted Albert to it. Kevin told me, "Lamar, this book is by a guy named Hans Langbroek. And it says that the Colonel is a Dutch citizen." I said, "You're kidding." He said, "No, he's from Breda, Holland." I said, "I'll track it down." So he sent the book to me. And he wrote to Breda and got some articles by a reporter named Dirk Vellenga. The articles also said Colonel was Dutch. Dirk eventually wrote a book called *Elvis and the Colonel,* based on his research.

I was managing a country singer named Billie Jo Spears, and we were going to Europe. So I caught the train to Amsterdam, and I changed trains and went to Breda. That was the strangest feeling, being on that train, going to meet some guy that I didn't know was for real or not, but feeling like I was about to discover something kind of monumental. Because at first I thought this was probably bullshit. I never suspected Colonel was a foreigner. But the more I thought about it, the more I began to believe it. Because I never understood his accent. Colonel would speak in what I thought was a little German that he'd learned somewhere. And all he was doing was speaking his native tongue. He would rip it out at me. But when he spoke English, he couldn't pronounce his "R's," which is typical of Dutch or German pronunciation problems. I just thought he had a speech impediment. So I told Kevin Eggers and Albert, "You know, I think there's something here."

I got to Breda, and Dirk met me at the train and took me over to Colonel Parker's sister's house. She walked into the room, and I went into absolute shock. I couldn't believe it. She looked just like Tom Parker. She showed me pictures of the Colonel when he was a kid and showed pictures of one of his brothers.

When you're sitting there talking to a guy's sister who looks just like him and she's Dutch, and she doesn't speak a word of English, it just blows you away. I sat there looking at her and the pictures, and I went, "Holy shit, this is another man!" It's like finding out that your all-American father is really Latvian and has three wives in the old country. I said, "What in God's name? Where did Tom Parker come from?"

His real name is Andreas Cornelis van Kuijk, which is pronounced "von Kick." They called him Dries, for short. He was born June 26, 1909, like he said, but that's about all that's the truth. He jumped ship, not once, but twice. He came over here the first time at age seventeen or so, and then again maybe a year later, and enlisted in the U.S. Army in 1929. You wouldn't think he'd want to be in the army, but his father had been in the military for a while, before he became a livery man and tended horses. In Breda, military officers were highly respected because Breda had been a fortress town for centuries. And Colonel's family didn't command much of anything—they lived over a stable. Colonel served in the U.S. Army until he was discharged in about '31.

Most people think Colonel took the name of Tom Parker from a guy who had a pony show. Dirk Vellenga says that when Colonel enlisted in the army—claiming to be an orphan—the captain who interviewed him was named Thomas Parker. Apparently, Colonel, who was still going by Andreas van Kuijk, or Dries, just stole Parker's name and put an "Andrew" in the middle to represent his past.

The carnival stuff was after the army, too. He worked as an advance man, drumming up publicity in all these little towns in the South. He joined the Johnny J. Jones Exposition and then the Royal American shows in about '35. In the forties, he settled down some. He ran the animal shelter in Tampa—he was the dogcatcher. And he'd hire elephants and all these exotic animals whenever a new department store opened in town. He knew how to draw out the customers. Somewhere along the line—probably during this same time—he worked as a department-store Santa Claus. That's why he later liked to dress up as Santa on Elvis's Christmas cards.

Discovering a man I had known almost all my life was not who he said he was just astounded me. It has to be one of the most shocking things in my existence. The only thing that could have been more shocking was to find out that Elvis didn't really die, that he's alive somewhere, like some of these idiots want to believe. It totally freaked me out.

I got back to Amsterdam that night, and I called Albert. I said, "You won't believe this." Then I took the Concorde and flew back to New York to meet with him. Albert said, "Why don't you call the Colonel?" So I called him, and he answered. I said, "Why didn't you tell me you were Andreas van Kuijk?" And he said, "You never asked me." I said, "You lived your life as a sham!" He said, "Lamar, I'm a carny."

But then he tried to smooth it over. He said, "Well, my brother, Ad, came over here to visit me. He met Elvis in Hollywood. Elvis knew." I said, "Bullshit, Colonel." I said, "He never met your brother." So he hung up on me. But I'm certain Elvis didn't know. If he'd known, we would have found out. Because Elvis could rarely keep a secret. He would ask you to keep a secret so he could tell everybody first. And he couldn't have waited to tell us that the Colonel was Dutch.

After that phone call, I really started tracking him. I got into the army files through the Freedom of Information Act and traced his records to a warehouse in Tampa, Florida. But his file was missing. Whether it had been stolen, I don't know. But it was gone.

The Goldman book was the first to really expose Colonel's citizenship. But it came in handy for him when the estate got on his ass in the eighties. He filed legal papers that said since he served in the U.S. Army without the permission of the Dutch government, he automatically forfeited his Dutch citizenship. So since he wasn't a citizen of the U.S., and never became a naturalized citizen, he was a man without a country. Try suing a man in a federal court that has no jurisdiction over him!

MARTY LACKER: The real question is why he kept it quiet so long. After he had been here for decades.

LAMAR FIKE: I don't know what Colonel was afraid of. He paid his taxes on time, and after the IRS got on his ass once in the early years, he took hardly any deductions. He had Elvis do the same thing. Their tax policy was just horrible. I guess he was afraid they'd ship him back to Holland. I don't imagine he wanted to go.

MARTY LACKER: I was told that before Colonel's mother died in Holland, one of his brothers contacted him and said, "Your mother is dying." He never sent a get-well card, or flowers, or made a call or anything. He totally turned his back on that situation, from about 1932 on. And why not? He wasn't that guy anymore. He had reinvented himself. The old shell game again.

LAMAR FIKE: Colonel is one of the real legends. Not only of show business, but of international hucksterism. But most of the guys who worked for Elvis couldn't stand him. Couldn't stand his pettiness and the way he loved to play head games. Alan Fortas loved him. He thought Colonel was magic. Thought he hung the moon, especially with what he did for Elvis. And in the early days, the Colonel did do a hell of a job. But then, time passes, and the old shit doesn't work anymore. Some of the guys still talk to him. But we don't talk. Everybody says, "The Colonel this, the Colonel that." The Colonel's full of shit. He's an asshole. He really is. To me, he's a miserable old bastard.

CHAPTER 8

1956—RUNAWAY
SUCCESS

On June 5, 1956, Elvis sang "Hound Dog" on *The Milton Berle Show* and the country went into outrageous uproar. It was Elvis's second appearance for Berle, following six provocative performances on "Stage Show." But to a certain segment of the public, Elvis's stage mannerisms during "Hound Dog"—the way he staggered his legs, pivoted his hips, and thrust his pelvis—went beyond suggestive, to border on the pornographic striptease.

Suddenly, Elvis Presley, whose first RCA single, "Heartbreak Hotel," was a million-seller in eight weeks, and whose eponymous first album sold 362,000 copies within a month (RCA's first $1 million album by a solo artist), was on everybody's lips. The mayor of Jersey City, New Jersey, exercised by his mission, was filmed banning rock 'n' roll from the city limits. A young Southern preacher, lathered from emotion, stood before his flock and a newsreel camera to decry, "I believe rock 'n' roll is a contributing factor to our juvenile delinquency . . . I know the evil feeling that you feel when you sing it! I know the lust position that you get into, the beat!"

And shortly, in San Francisco, California, two high school girls would be suspended after winning a "Why I Love Elvis" contest and collecting a kiss from their idol. "We don't need this kind of publicity," their principal said, close on the heels of his counterpart in Wichita Falls, Texas, who declared, "We do not tolerate Elvis Presley's records at our dances, or blue jeans, or ducktail haircuts."

But if "the Nation's Only Atomic Powered Singer," as Elvis was billed, was considered a threat by conservative adults, in concert he generated such hysterical fan reaction from teenagers that his guitarist, Scotty Moore, remembers the screams canceled out all the sound onstage. Unable to hear either themselves or the singing, the musicians kept their place by watching Elvis's body movements. "We're probably the only band," Moore says today, "that was literally directed by an ass."

For his next television appearance, on *The Steve Allen Show*, where he once again sang "Hound Dog," Elvis was outfitted in tails and directed to sing to a top-hatted basset hound. "It's not too often that I get to wear the, uh . . . suit and tails," he told his host. It was a humiliating put-down, a sliver of fun for Allen at Elvis's expense. But it also helped the young singer secure his hold on America's collective id.

Now a national curiosity, earning $5,000 to $10,000 a night, Elvis began attracting attention from such disparate camps as the friends and entourage of the late James Dean and the jealous boyfriends of his own fans. Quick to join a scuffle, he shattered his horseshoe ring in an altercation with a smart-talking detractor in Ohio and that fall would once again make the newsreels for a fight with a Memphis gas station attendant.

Such notoriety only fed the public interest. In September '56, Colonel demanded—and got—$50,000 for Elvis's three appearances on *The Ed Sullivan Show*. Even as the granite-faced impresario was at first so concerned by the reaction to the first two performances—and annoyed by what he erroneously thought was a "device" in the front of Elvis's pants ("It looks like his own personal organ")—that he insisted Elvis be shown from only the waist up on the third. Soon Colonel signed a deal to license Elvis's image on everything from charm bracelets, to lipsticks ("Hound Dog Orange"), to cologne.

In their astonishing collections of Elvis photographs taken during this time, Alfred Wertheimer (*Elvis '56*) and Jay Leviton (*Elvis Close Up*) capture the innocence of a young prince, unprepared to assume the throne, and unaware of its consequences.

Just after completing work on *Love Me Tender*, his first feature film, Elvis bought his mother a pink Cadillac, actually a blue one, repainted to its cheery hue. Soon, there were three more Cadillacs in the drive. "Four Cadillacs?" a radio reporter asked him. "I do have four Cadillacs," Elvis replied. "But I haven't got use for four. Maybe some day I'll go broke and I can sell a couple of 'em."

BILLY SMITH: The first time I saw Elvis perform after he became a big star was in Russwood Park, in Memphis, in July of '56. They had 14,000 people there. Elvis got seats for the family right down in the front row. Jack Clement, who engineered for Sam Phillips, and who later became a big producer for Johnny Cash, was on that show. He was a singer, too, and a songwriter. He come out first, and the audience, mostly females, started booing and yelling, "We want Elvis! We want Elvis!"

I thought, "God, what in the world?" They kept hollering, and Jack Clement said, "Folks, if you'll just let me finish this one damn song, I'll let you have Elvis." And when Elvis come out, hell, you couldn't hear him for all the screaming. And if you were in the path, boy, you were in trouble because all those women were trying to get close to him. That was a real shocker. I was thirteen, just at the age to really be impressed by what I saw. I thought, "Lord, have mercy! What is it that he's got? Give it to me quick!" This was my cousin, you know. 'Course, we knew he was doin' good because two months earlier he'd bought that house on Audubon Drive and put a swimming pool in. But I had no idea what really went on at the shows. Or how big he was getting.

MARTY LACKER: When things started breaking loose, the first thing Elvis did was go out and buy his parents and Grandma a new house at 1034 Audubon Drive. A modern, one-story ranch with green siding in a good part of town. It was a typical fifties dream home, except it had a game room and a double carport, which was pretty snazzy, I guess. That was in May of '56. Paid $40,000 for it, cash.

BILLY SMITH: When they first moved to Audubon Drive, Elvis didn't see any reason why the fans couldn't come around the house. A lot of times, he opened the door, and said, "Yeah, come on in." Then he changed his mind right quick. He'd glance up at the window, and they'd be there with their noses pressed against the glass. He put up a wall, with a little-bitty wrought-iron fence with music notes on it, and a gate. But the gate, hell, they could jump over that. You could understand the neighbors getting agitated. They'd come home, and their drive would be blocked, and there'd be kids in their yard, trampling down the grass.

MARTY LACKER: The whole street was pissed. They complained to the police, who put up signs that said, "No standing, no loitering." Finally, the neighbors had a meeting. And they went to Vernon and said, "We'd like to buy your house. Elvis has ruined the neighborhood."

Vernon went back and told Elvis, and it was like hitting him with a brick. He felt rejected, and it hurt him. He got so mad that he said, "You go back to those sons of bitches, and you ask them how much they want for all *their* fuckin' houses. I'll buy 'em, and they can get the hell out of here." But then they came with a petition.

BILLY SMITH: When the petition started, Elvis hired my daddy as gate guard. He could trust him, and he needed somebody to control the crowd as much as possible. It had to be pretty damn trying for Aunt Gladys and Vernon. The fans didn't know when Elvis was on tour and when he was at home, so even when Elvis wasn't there, they were knocking on the door. Being gate guard at that house was hard work for my daddy. I can remember going over there almost every other weekend. That's when me and Elvis got really close, closer than we were when I was little. And I remember that Aunt Gladys started getting sad. I don't think she could take all those people. Or Elvis's fame, either. It put 'em in different worlds, separated 'em. I think Gladys enjoyed having my daddy close by. It was like she had somebody extra to talk to.

MARTY LACKER: People would knock on the door, and sometimes Mrs. Presley would let them come in and just talk. They'd want to see Elvis's room. You've seen the pictures of it. A lot of people think that pink bedroom of his looked like a teenage girl's room. It had a pink dust ruffle on the bed, sort of taffeta. Actually, it was borderline fuschia, not pink. And he had a pink-and-white flowered bedspread and pink-and-white flowered wallpaper. And a dark pink telephone and pink stuffed animals everywhere. And pictures of like, angels, on the wall. Back then, even the clothes he wore were pink—shiny-pink satin shiny shirts, or pink-trimmed black shirts. Actually, his room looked like something his fans would have wanted themselves. Audubon Drive—that's when those three girls, Heidi, Gloria, and Frances started coming.

BILLY SMITH: Heidi Heissen, Gloria Mowel, and Frances Forbes. I remember them quite well. They used to come over for slumber parties with Elvis. Just with Elvis, not anybody else. They were in junior high. They stayed until about three or four in the morning, holed up with Elvis in his room. Then somebody, usually Lamar, would take them home.

I've seen them interviewed on TV the last couple of years. They always say nothing sexual happened. Elvis would put makeup on them, and they would put makeup on him. He would do their hair, and they would do his hair. Like he was their age. I guess he could pretty well relate to them. Like when he first colored his hair. Things like that fascinated him.

So I can see how they based a friendship on it. And they've talked about dating Elvis. I don't think he ever had sex with them. But I do know that they were with him alone by themselves for four or five hours at a time and that they'd lie on the bed together, and have pillow fights, and he'd tickle 'em until they couldn't take it anymore. In other words, they'd do things that might ordinarily lead to sexual situations. He enjoyed giving thrills, you might say. At times, he maybe didn't have a date or hadn't particularly chosen anybody for the night. And of course, they would be some of the last ones to leave. Maybe they just got to talking. I really don't know what he got out of it. But before Gladys got up, the girls were out and gone.

LAMAR FIKE: Phew! I'll tell you what. Elvis always said, "Fourteen or sixteen will get you twenty." Meaning, having sex with fourteen- or sixteen-year-old girls will get you twenty years in jail. But later he was the worst! He got in the middle of everything. From what I've heard, he had three or four young girls in his room at once from the "Louisiana Hayride" days on. One time he told Vernon it was six. He used to come up with ideas that would just make me shake my head.

Heidi, Gloria, and Frances were fanatical fans. And he got interested in them to start with because they showed up everywhere. He felt like he could talk to them, ask, "What's going on? What are the kids saying?" And he would find out through them how the fans were reacting. Frances, Heidi, and Gloria were just as nutty as fruitcakes, but they were fun. He got irritated with them sometimes, but very seldom. I'd drive them home at two, three, or four o'clock in the morning. And the amazing thing is that I never had one problem with any of the parents. I never thought anything about it.

BILLY SMITH: Heidi, Gloria, and Frances went roller-skating with us and became a part of the group that went to the fairgrounds. That lasted from late '56, until about '61, maybe '62. When Elvis went into the army, they even went down to Texas to see him during basic training. And a lot of times, they came down to the gate, even while he was gone. I think he cared about them. He wrote one of them a letter when he went overseas.

But Elvis knew durn well he could get away with having sex with a minor. Jerry Lee Lewis stepped in a pretty deep pile when it came out in '58 that he'd married his thirteen-year-old cousin. It ruined his career for ten years. But that didn't phase Elvis. He believed in getting them young. How did he put it? He said, "You get 'em young, and you can mold 'em and raise them the way you want 'em to be."

MARTY LACKER: The same thing happened later on, out in California.

BILLY SMITH: Elvis had peculiar sexual fetishes. He told me he got a big kick when he cut loose in a girl's hair. They'd masturbate him, and he'd ejaculate in their hair. He loved it.

LAMAR FIKE: Hey, listen, Elvis was the King of Kink. He really was. He pushed the edge of the envelope all the time because he could get away with it. He was continually testing the limits of acceptable behavior. And he could talk his way into, or out of, anything.

CHAPTER 9

HOLLYWOOD

When Colonel Parker took Elvis to Hollywood in the spring of '56 fresh from his *Stage Show* appearances ("He can't last," proclaimed Jackie Gleason, the producer. "I tell you flatly, he can't last."), he was the hottest unproven actor in the world. Still, every movie producer instinctively realized that as the new emotional target of the youth generation, Elvis could inherit the audience James Dean left behind when he died in a car crash in late '55. All they had to do was get him on the screen.

On April 6, Colonel sat down with producer Hal Wallis at Paramount and hammered out a deal for three pictures at $450,000, later to swell to $2.3 million for seven movies in seven years.

"People asked me if I'm going to sing in the movies," Elvis, who hoped to separate his music and acting careers, told a reporter. "I'm not, as far as I know. 'Cause I took strictly an acting test. Actually, I wouldn't care too much about singing in the movies. . . . I want to be the kind of actor that stays around for a long time."

The test had been for *The Rainmaker,* which Wallis planned to make with Burt Lancaster and Katharine Hepburn. Elvis had believed that the N. Richard Nash classic would be his first picture. But the role of Jimmy Curry went to Earl Holliman, instead.

Immediately, Wallis loaned Elvis out to Twentieth Century-Fox for a post–Civil War drama to be called *The Reno Brothers,* starring Richard Egan and Debra Paget. The third-billed Elvis was upset to learn that he would be singing in one scene, after all.

Yet when advance orders for the single of "Love Me Tender" rolled in at more than a million copies, the film itself was retitled and the producer added three more songs to take advantage of the singer's popularity. Elvis, dubbed a "howling hillbilly" by *Life* magazine, was inconsolable. The movie made back its cost within three days, which told Wallis that Elvis could carry a picture—as long as he toted a guitar.

Before his second movie, *Loving You*, went into production, the star met with writer/director Hal Kanter and immediately got to the point. "He said, 'Do I have to smile very much in the picture?'" Kanter recalls. "He said, 'I've been watching Bogart, and Dean, and Brando, and they don't smile very much. I don't want to do that, either. If I don't smile, I'm gonna get 'em.'" But since *Loving You* was written around Elvis's perceived persona—a country boy finds overnight success in the music business—he had little choice.

After his first two films, Elvis told the press, "I went to Hollywood [because] that's how it works. You get a record, and then you get on television, and then they take you to Hollywood to make a picture. . . . I wasn't ready for that town, and it wasn't ready for me."

Yet both were fairly prepared for *Jailhouse Rock*. Like *Loving You*, Elvis's third picture was a semiautobiographical story, chosen purely as Presley product, to sell tickets and records and not to a build his profile as an actor—even as Elvis worked on his technique to make sure it did. Colonel wangled $250,000 plus a piece of the profits from MGM for Elvis's time, but the star took it all in stride: "Tomorrow I may not be worth a nickel."

Such modesty placed Elvis in good stead with his fellow cast and crew members, who noticed that he arrived on the set focused and prepared and that he brought them coffee in the mornings himself, even before he got his own.

They also appreciated his humor. When a hair-cutting scene called for a barber to shear a specially fitted wig, and not Elvis's real hair underneath, a hush came over the room as locks began to fall on Elvis's shoulders. Suddenly, the whirring of the shears stopped short. "Oh, God, I think I cut his hair," came the barber's shaken voice. Elvis quickly spoke up: "Man, there's Frankie Avalon fans everywhere!"

Afterward, Elvis would make *King Creole*, a gritty picture set in the New Orleans underworld, based on Harold Robbins's novel *A Stone for Danny Fisher*. Here, Elvis, who had begun to show a natural ease before the camera, would do the finest acting of his career. But for the most part, the direction of Elvis's films had already been set. "He was just too famous, too fast," says screen-writer Allan Weiss (*Girls! Girls! Girls!* and *Fun in Acapulco*). "The snowball was already rolling, and there was no way for it not to continue down the hill."

LAMAR FIKE: Hal Wallis had the biggest role in shaping Elvis's movie career. Of course, as soon as he bought him, he loaned him out to Twentieth Century-Fox for *Love Me Tender.* But that was to test the waters, I think. Wallis made Elvis in Hollywood. And Wallis eventually ruined him. Wallis and Colonel had a kind of strange relationship. They were next-door neighbors in Palm Springs. But the Colonel wore Wallis out. Just beat him up, day and night. The Colonel was rough on everybody. He had "the property."

MARTY LACKER: Parker got Wallis to do what he wanted. And the reason Parker kept the house close to where Wallis lived is he wanted to know what was going on. Colonel committed Elvis to a long-term agreement at essentially fixed prices. That was basically to get his foot in the door. But who knows what kind of deal he had with Wallis? We know Colonel got credit as "technical adviser" on all of the movies. That must have been a salaried perk.

BILLY SMITH: When Elvis first went out to Hollywood, he was green as a gourd. I don't think he'd ever even been in a class play. So he was uncomfortable being around his costars. It's obvious in Elvis's *Love Me Tender* that he overacted. But he didn't have much direction. And he was distracted a lot because he fell in love with Debra Paget.

Elvis would always be bad about romancing his costars, and it started on the very first movie. Before he got real famous and went to Hollywood, he'd pull all kinds of tricks to get a woman he was interested in to pay attention to him. He even faked a faint-ing spell with Anita Carter [of the Carter Family] when they were on the road together in '55. He went so far as to go to the hospital on that deal. Elvis was totally captivated by her singing and by her looks. And now he really had this desire to be with Debra Paget. But she was a mama's girl, and striving to be a big star, and to her, Elvis was just another actor. He thought she was beautiful, and he searched for that look in almost every woman after that. Even Priscilla was a variation on Debra Paget. Look at the strong jawline and the eyes.

I heard that he proposed to Debra Paget, and she turned him down. I don't think he ever proposed to her, but hell, he may have.

LAMAR FIKE: Elvis proposed to a lot of girls in the early years, but I think he thought that was what he was supposed to do. We were taught as kids that you grow up, smoke cigarettes, and get married. But he didn't really want to get married. He chased everything in skirts. Especially in California.

MARTY LACKER: You've got to remember that this was Elvis's first picture. All of a sudden, he was looking at this movie star, who was so much different than the girls he had known. But she wouldn't have anything to do with him romantically off the set. Supposedly, she was going out with Howard Hughes.

LAMAR FIKE: Elvis would go over to Debbie's house. She lived with her family. And there would always be some car out there following Elvis and Debbie around. The assumption was that it was Hughes's people. And later on, we found out it was. Elvis was fascinated by Hughes, but contrary to what you might read elsewhere, Elvis never met him and he never talked to Hughes on the telephone, especially not on a regular basis.

BILLY SMITH: Elvis wasn't big on talking on the phone to begin with. People thought he just picked up the phone and called whoever he wanted. He didn't. The guys in the group kept numbers for him. If Elvis wanted to make a phone call, the guys made it, and then when they got the party he wanted, Elvis got on the phone.

MARTY LACKER: About Elvis falling for his costars . . . there's some guy making the rounds of the tabloid TV shows saying he's the love child of Elvis and Dolores Hart, who played his girlfriend in Loving You and King Creole. She left show business in 1963 and became a nun, and this guy claims she dropped out because she was pregnant and that she kept quiet about it for the love of

Elvis and his career. All of us were around all the time then, and if something like that had happened, Elvis would have talked about it. He would have been scared as hell. This guy calls himself Elvis Aaron Presley, Jr. And get this—he's an Elvis impersonator, cape and all.

BILLY SMITH: Elvis was bound and determined that Hollywood wasn't going to change him. But it started in little ways. He had his teeth capped in '56, I believe. Some of the Alfred Wertheimer pictures of his early RCA recording sessions show him with his natural teeth. But somebody decided he had to have new ones. Nobody teased him about getting all dandified because his teeth looked so good before that it was hard to tell the difference, except for the whiteness. And for a little gap he had. He also had the warts removed from his hands. You can see them in that piece of film where he's on the phone doing an interview with Hy Gardner for his TV show [*Hy Gardner Calling!*].

MARTY LACKER: When he was a kid, Elvis liked Tony Curtis a lot. He saw him on the screen in *Son of Ali Baba,* when he worked as an usher at Loews in '52. Elvis thought he had the ideal masculine look. He had that shiny black hair and blue eyes. Some people say Elvis copied his ducktail haircut. I don't know, because he liked Rudolph Valentino, too. But from then on, Elvis wanted the black hair.

BILLY SMITH: Right after *Love Me Tender,* Elvis made the most dramatic change in his looks. That's when he realized what makeup and color could do. For *Loving You,* he dyed his hair black, like his mama colored hers. She did that because she was getting gray. But as best I remember, it was Aunt Gladys's idea for him to dye his. She said, "I think it would bring out the blue in your eyes." His natural hair was blond to brown, but he dyed it bright blond for a real short spell. There's an early publicity picture of that. When he dyed it black, Gladys said, "You got that Tony Curtis look now."

MARTY LACKER: Elvis started dyeing his hair for the movies, but he'd worn makeup from time to time on his little shows around the Memphis area. A little eye shadow, maybe some mascara.

There were times during the movie years when he went home and never bothered to wash it off. He just wore it the rest of the day. He liked the look it gave him. He even wore it to the recording sessions. Ray Walker, of the Jordanaires, tells a story about how Elvis got tickled about something and laughed until he cried. And then he said, "Man, I can't afford to shed any tears or my mascara will run."

Of course, in the seventies, when he went to visit President Nixon, he had on enough mascara for the Avon Lady. But he'd worn it some before the movie days, in the early fifties.

BILLY SMITH: I don't remember right off when that started. I think seeing his mama try new things might have had something to do with it. Back when he started doing the movies, he got a makeup kit. He kept eyeliner and pancake makeup in it so that when he wasn't at the studio, he could touch up if he wanted. He kept a lot of little things in it. He just liked the looks of it, and he liked saying, "This is my makeup kit." It was a little black bag with drawers, and it had a little key, so all the drawers locked. It was a little-bitty thing, about six to eight inches wide and about ten inches high.

I remember he bought several containers of pancake makeup, different shades of it. Actually, he tried some on me. He wanted everybody to wear it. I thought he was doing some "guinea-pigging," trying it on other people to see how it looked. And, yeah, he would use mascara on his lashes, especially after he dyed his hair. Then he dyed his eyebrows and eyelashes, so he wouldn't need mascara anymore.

It was funny. When he had it all together, Elvis was proud of the way he looked. He'd tell you in a minute, "I'm the best-looking son of a bitch you've ever seen!"

MARTY LACKER: On those first two movies, Elvis stayed at the Hollywood Knickerbocker, on Ivar Avenue. His parents went, too. Elvis rented the whole eleventh floor. He'd sit up there and write his name in lighter fluid on the glass-top coffee table, and then set it on fire, watch it blaze. Girls remember stuff like that. Then, for *Loving You*, he moved to the Beverly Wilshire. That was his home in Hollywood until he started renting houses in the sixties.

BILLY SMITH: Vernon and Gladys ended up being extras in *Loving You*. They're in the audience during the TV broadcast. Aunt Gladys is in the aisle seat in the fourth row. You can see her if you look real quick. Uncle Vernon is sitting next to her. She went out there not because she wanted to go to Hollywood but because she was afraid something would happen to Elvis. Eventually, when he started taking sleeping pills, it decreased his sleepwalking. But Gladys wanted somebody with him all the time. When he was making *Loving You*, he almost walked out the eleventh-floor window of the Beverly Wilshire. He got up one night, and the window was open, and Gene caught him just in time.

In '57, he had this recurring dream that guys were trying to kill him. He'd get in a fight, and they'd have knives, and they'd try to stab him. Sometimes, he'd jump up and grab something and break it and gesture real wild with his fists clenched up.

Elvis had a lot of nightmares where somebody was trying to hurt him. The one about the knives started when him and Gene went down to Mexico after some shows in '56. Elvis dreamed that these guys were trying to jump him and cut him up. In the dream, they were on a big rock and trying to back him up and surround him. Elvis was acting it out and fighting like mad. He jumped up in the bed, and he started swinging the pillow around, and then he started throwing glasses and pitchers of water all over Gene, who didn't appreciate it too much.

One time I didn't know he had been asleep, and I come up to the door, and he was just crazy. I got him calmed down, and he said, "I thought I got rid of you." I said, "Got rid of me? What do you mean? I didn't go nowhere." And he said, "I thought I killed you. I had this dream that you were trying to stab me. I got the knife away and cut you, and you were dying. And you kept saying, 'I'm not going to die,' and I kept saying, 'Hell, yes, you're going to die.'" We laughed about it, but it was kind of disturbing, you might say.

Anyway, that, plus the sleepwalking, is why Aunt Gladys encouraged the first guys to hang around Elvis. Junior Smith, another of the cousins, went along in the early days. But Aunt Gladys always liked Red and Gene, especially. She thought Red could protect him and Gene could kind of watch him.

CHAPTER 10

MOVIE STARS AND EVERYTHING

MARTY LACKER: The core group of the Memphis Mafia started as a buffer zone.

LAMAR FIKE: You could see how the cousins were obvious choices for the entourage. They had the same background, the same kinds of references. And they were family. With Red, it was a little different. Elvis never ran around with a lot of people his age, and he always felt like an outsider. Red had taken up for him in high school, and Elvis was extremely loyal to him. And with his fame, Elvis found there were other guys who wanted to be around him and who would be loyal, too. After a while, it just sort of turned into an entourage.

MARTY LACKER: Red was also involved with Elvis's music. He played trumpet, and he could read music, and he wrote some pretty good songs. Elvis would talk to him about music, and do warm-up vocals with him, and he'd bounce ideas off him during the recording sessions. As tough as Red was, though, he was also concerned about what people thought about him. He was sensitive, but bad. He would hit you, then talk, whereas his cousin, Sonny, who met Elvis in '58, would talk to you and then hit you. But both of them have been good friends to me. And to Billy and Lamar, too.

LAMAR FIKE: Red would have done anything for Elvis, including kill somebody, if they threatened Elvis. Red had a very fast temper. Bad motherfucker. Boy, he could whip some ass. In the latter years, he caused Elvis a lot of problems with lawsuits because he beat up on so many people—guys who were harassing Elvis or wanting to. But Elvis loved him like a brother. The press always called us Elvis's bodyguards. Most of us were more like companions. Nobody was ever brought into the group to be a bodyguard, for example. If any of us were really bodyguards, it was Red and Sonny West.

MARTY LACKER: On the opposite end of the scale, you had a personality like Gene Smith. Gene was the first person to travel with Elvis. Gene was crazy, but he made Elvis laugh. He talked funny, first of all. Instead of "truck," he'd say "cruck." And he'd call a "light bulb" a "light bud." Not on purpose, but because he thought that's what it was. In high school, Gene was the closest thing Elvis had to a brother. Later on, Billy was. But in the beginning, Elvis would have given Gene anything he wanted.

LAMAR FIKE: Out in Hollywood, Gene got on this kick where he was going to be an actor. He came in one day in '57 and said he was changing his name to "El Gino Stone." We fell on the floor laughing. Because Gene being an actor was tantamount to me flying a rocket. He was pretty homely, for one thing. We all played extras in Elvis's movies, and Gene would come up and say, "You should emote *this* way."

   Elvis got mad at Gene one time out in California. There were four of us in the car and Gene was just making Elvis crazy. Elvis said, "Listen, you motherfucker, I pay you $150 a week to be funny, and I ain't cracked a smile in a solid year. You're fired." The three of us fell clean out of the car laughing. And Gene just sat there and said, "Durn it!"

MARTY LACKER: A lot of people thought Gene wasn't too swift. I don't think that's true. But Elvis was protective of him.

LAMAR FIKE: When it came to picking guys for the group, Elvis looked for spirit, as opposed to outward appearance and personality. That's why he liked Cliff Gleaves. Cliff was his own traveling show. He'd been a disc jockey, and a little bit of everything, but he'd really never worked a day in his life. Cliff would finger-pop, and snap his fingers, and talk real fast, in a patter that was unreal. He drifted in and out of the group for years. But he fit because he could get in anywhere, and he got along with everybody.

Cliff was also the consummate con man. He started hanging out with Elvis real early, before most of the rest of us. He was amazing. He lost a nut—a testicle—in the Korean War. And he screwed everything that moved. When Elvis got mad at him, he'd call him a "one-codded bastard." Charlie Copper-Cod. That was Cliff Gleaves.

MARTY LACKER: The last time I saw him, Cliff looked like a total bum. But in the early years, he was a smooth operator. He didn't have a penny in his pocket, but he always had on a coat and tie.

In the late fifties, there was a restaurant in downtown Memphis called Jim's Place. It was across from the Peabody Hotel, and it was known for steaks and veal. Cliff and I went there to dinner one night. I didn't have much money, so I ordered a veal cutlet. But Cliff had his suit on, so he ordered the biggest steak on the menu. And appetizers and soup and salad. He was acting like John D. Rockefeller, telling the waitress how good his steak was, saying, "My compliments to the chef."

I knew he didn't have any money. So I said, "Cliff, I can't cover your meal, man." He said, "Don't worry about it." I said, "What the hell are you going to do?" He said, "Don't worry about it!"

We got up to leave, and I paid my check. Then Cliff walked up to the cashier, who happened to be a woman. He said, "Boy, you sure look nice tonight." And he talked to her for thirty minutes. By the time he was finished, he'd conned her so well she completely forgot about his check.

Finally, he said, "Hey, it was good talking to you again." And he turned around, walked out, lit up a cigarette, and nonchalantly strolled down the street. That was Cliff.

BILLY SMITH: Once the Mafia began to build up, I asked Elvis why he had all these guys around him and if he really cared about 'em. I guess to understand it, you have to go back and imagine a kid who's kind of a loner. He's real shy, and he's a little different from everybody else in the way he is inside. He doesn't know how to get close to people, especially males. It was just easier for him to get affection from women. As a teenager, it was still the same thing, very few male friends. Then all at once, bam! Success hits. And he can't have females around him without getting into trouble, but he can have males. So he figures, "I'll get this group of guys, and we'll build a strong bond. They'll do what I tell them to because they'll work for me, plus they'll be my friends. They'll trust me and I'll trust them."

LAMAR FIKE: At first, nobody got paid. We just got our expenses, but we would have paid him just to tag along. When we'd go to California, we'd stay in this fancy hotel and eat the best of everything and rub shoulders with famous people. And we didn't have a dime in our pockets. Elvis took care of everything.

MARTY LACKER: Elvis didn't like Hollywood. He didn't like the people. He didn't like the phoniness. And he never really changed his opinion. Although he became more polished as the years went on, and more educated in people in general, he was still a country boy at heart, with simple tastes. He didn't want to go to parties. He didn't want to go out and be seen. It made him uncomfortable. What we used to do was sit up all night and watch TV or talk or listen to music. In California, if we needed something, we had it brought to us.

BILLY SMITH: Elvis wanted friends who were in touch with that Southern world that he came from, not actors and producers from the Hollywood scene. He wanted this little group that talked the same way he did and ate the same kind of food. He also had a tough time being alone. He didn't handle it too good.

Of course, he also needed somebody for protection, and he needed somebody to do odd jobs and to look after his schedule, and take care of everyday things. Like getting him places on time, or taking care of his wardrobe, or helping him learn his lines. He needed somebody to do things that he really didn't want to do. Later on, in the sixties, we all had specific jobs and titles. At first, we were like Robin Hood's Merry Men.

LAMAR FIKE: In the beginning, Colonel liked the idea because he wanted to keep Elvis isolated. At first, it was because of the fans. But after a while, it got to be a habit. And Elvis was a lone wolf by nature—a Capricorn—and Capricorns like to get off by themselves sometimes, even though Elvis had difficulty being totally alone. Jesus was also a Capricorn, you know. And he had twelve disciples. Elvis liked that analogy.

BILLY SMITH: I think Elvis felt shut off because of his popularity. But if he wanted to go out, he went. He wasn't a prisoner. He just didn't want to go out that much. And Colonel didn't want Hollywood to see him too much. Colonel thought, "The less they know about you, the more they want you." That went for everybody.

MARTY LACKER: Colonel also figured that Elvis could rant and rave to us and vent the frustration he couldn't show to the rest of the world. That way, he never had the bad press that Frank Sinatra got.

Then, too, Colonel feared that if Elvis got out more, and was exposed to more people, especially people in the entertainment field, he would start learning more about the business.

The rule was: Anything that had to do with business was Colonel's territory. Colonel said, "You take care of the entertaining, and I'll take care of the business. If someone approaches you about any kind of business, don't talk to them, just tell them to see me." And the same thing was told to all the guys. What we didn't know then was that Colonel didn't want Elvis to find out how other managers worked or what percentage they had of their acts and their side deals.

LAMAR FIKE: Any good manager protects himself and his artist. But Colonel may have taken it to the extreme. He didn't even want Elvis fraternizing with other actors. And that was fine with Elvis. One night in '57, Cliff Gleaves finally talked him into going to a party given by a guy who had a famous clothing store out there. It was a masquerade party, and Elvis went with a mask, the old French-type mask with the handle on it. Nat King Cole and every star in the business was there. We lasted maybe about an hour, and Elvis said, "I gotta get out of here." That was one of the few times he ever went to a celebrity party. He just didn't do it.

MARTY LACKER: For a while, Elvis saw Nick Adams out there. That was really his only actor friend. He liked him a lot. In fact, when Nick was more or less blacklisted in Hollywood, Elvis took him on the road as an opening act. He was a great imitator. He was a little guy, very short. And he was self-conscious about it. Some of the guys went over to Nick's house one day, and Nick was in the steam bath. He yelled out, "Don't come in here! Don't come in here! I don't have my boots on!" And he wouldn't let the guys come in until he did.

This stuff that Earl Greenwood came out with in his book [*The Boy Who Would Be King: An Intimate Portrait of Elvis Presley by His Cousin*] about Elvis having homosexual encounters with Nick doesn't sit right with me, to put it mildly. First of all, I don't know that Nick was homosexual, even though some of the James Dean books hint at it, and Goldman comes right out with it. But, if he had ever approached Elvis, he wouldn't have been around as long as he was. Because Elvis didn't put up with that.

Jailhouse Rock might have had an underlying homosexual theme, but that doesn't mean it carried over into Elvis's life. Nobody in the group was homosexual. Nobody. Not Lamar, not Charlie Hodge, who came into the entourage after Elvis got out of the army, nobody. Somebody got the rumor up after Elvis's death that he and I had been lovers and that I was writing a book about it. That's a sick lie, and I wish I knew the son of a bitch who said it.

And as for Earl Greenwood, first of all, he claims to be a second cousin. Billy says he isn't. And I've seen the entire family tree, and there's no Earl Greenwood on it. He was a guy who hung around the gate. Every once in a while, he was allowed up to the house with all these other people who came up, and maybe he had his picture taken with Elvis at the skating rink. So what? There's no way that he knows anything about Elvis. He's a squirrel. I've seen him on a couple of TV shows, where they've introduced him as Elvis's cousin. One of them was a game show, where you had to guess which celebrity people were related to. They didn't get it.

BILLY SMITH: Nick was a real nice guy. He'd been James Dean's friend, and there were some similarities between Elvis and James Dean, and Nick was drawn to that. After he met Elvis, it grew into a pretty strong friendship. He used to visit him in Memphis, and his mother would come with him sometimes.

Because he was attached to his mother the way Elvis was to Aunt Gladys. There's a picture of Gladys and Nick's mama together at Graceland. Now, Nick might have been homosexual. I don't know. But Elvis didn't talk about that. He would have been torn about it because he liked Nick, but he didn't like homosexuals. Eventually, their friendship sort of fell off, although Nick still came around from time to time in the sixties. But Nick's acting career took off pretty good again, and, of course, there were so many demands on Elvis. And then Nick was having personal problems, too. He ended up killing himself with an overdose of drugs in the late sixties, on the day Lisa Marie was born. Elvis thought Nick was a really fine actor. I think he tried to learn things from him.

LAMAR FIKE: Elvis mentioned wanting to go to acting school one time. He never did do it, though. He wanted to be a great actor, but Elvis was always Elvis. He couldn't be anything else.

BILLY SMITH: As an actor, Elvis got a little better in *Loving You.* He looked more at ease, but he overacted a little even there. *Jailhouse Rock* seemed to be a big improvement. Then, *King Creole* was fairly dagum good. Actually, that was his best movie, I think. He thought so, too. If he'd been allowed to carry on with more dramatic pictures like *King Creole*, I think the entire Elvis Presley story would have turned out different.

I read somewhere the other day that Elvis went to Actors Studio in New York and studied with Lee Strasberg before he went out to California. That never happened. Somebody just got that up, probably because they knew Elvis wanted to be a serious actor like James Dean. But Elvis copied certain traits from several actors. He liked Dean's rebel attitude and his intensity. And he liked that brooding of Marlon Brando's and the way Rudolph Valentino projected a lot out of his eyes. Elvis tried to do the same thing.

MARTY LACKER: When Elvis first went out to Hollywood, he was tremendously excited about being an actor. He wanted it more than anything. More than being a singer.

BILLY SMITH: No, no. Elvis would have settled for being a *good* actor. But music was his number one thing.

LAMAR FIKE: One of the surprises of *Jailhouse Rock* was the flair Elvis showed for rock choreography in the big production number. Alex Romero was the choreographer, but he talked to Elvis and he watched the way he moved, and then he translated what Elvis wanted into the dance steps—like strutting and grabbing the pole. He showed Elvis what he had in mind, and then the two of them tied it all together. And Elvis was brilliant at it. That's one of the best things in the picture.

When the filming was over, Elvis was really proud of what he'd done. Then three weeks later, Judy Tyler, the dark-haired girl who played opposite him, got killed in an automobile wreck near Billy the Kid, Wyoming. It really, really upset him. He broke down and cried.

Her real name was Judith Hess. Her father was Julian Hess, who played trumpet for both Benny Goodman and Paul Whiteman. Cute girl. This was only her second movie. She started in the business at seventeen as the original Princess Summerfall Winterspring on *Howdy Doody*. When she did *Jailhouse Rock*, she was a newlywed, but she and Elvis had a thing going. The wreck cut her in half. And Elvis couldn't get over it. He gave an interview to the *Commercial Appeal*, saying he didn't think he could stand to ever watch the movie. And he meant it at the time. But in thirty-six hours he was over it.

LAMAR

LAMAR FIKE: The first time I met Elvis, I'd never seen anything like him in my life. I was raised in a Southern middle-class family. And we were taught that you didn't fool around with people with sideburns, because they were bad, or at least they came from the other side of the tracks. It didn't bother me, but it would have bothered my mother.

I had a Christian upbringing. We lived in Cleveland, Mississippi, when I was little, and I was a Presbyterian there. Then we moved to Memphis, and my whole family, with the exception of my father, became Episcopalian. Everybody always thought I was Jewish. I might be. Depends on how you look at it. My mother is Jewish. But Mother liked the Episcopal religion, so we went to the Episcopalian church. I sang in the St. John's Boys' Choir. I was a soprano for three years. We made some recordings, and I loved that because that was show business.

My dad made $75 to $80 a week back in the thirties and forties, as a farm implement salesman. A traveling salesman. I didn't want to do that. See, I'm a character. It's not a case of being proud of it, or not being proud. I just believe that people expected me to be a character, so I became one. I've never been a normal person.

I was just always fooling around with some part of the business. I took singing lessons when I was a kid. Did little recitals. Sang "Stardust." But I was more interested in the behind-the-scenes, where the maneuvering is. I figured you lasted longer if you were in the back. One of my uncles, a dentist, called me "Promoter" because I was always getting something going—booking bands when I was fourteen years old. One summer, I told everybody I represented Lamar Fike because I didn't want anybody to know how young I was. And I made more money in one summer than my dad did all year. I always enjoyed stirring things up, and I was always very independent.

Basically, I'm a loner. I have a sister who's five years younger. I've never forgiven her for being born because she cut into my loner territory. I've had to learn how to share things, and that's difficult. Part of my personality has to do with my size. Obesity runs on both sides of my family. And I was self-conscious of it. But I believe you could parachute me out in the middle of the Mojave Desert naked, and I would come out with a suit of clothes and a Cadillac.

I first met Elvis in 1954. George Klein was teaching me how to be a disc jockey, and he and Sam Phillips showed me how to run a board. He introduced me to Elvis over at Sun Records. Elvis was just a kid, nineteen. He was ten months older than I was. I said, "Are you going to be country or what?" He said, "I'm just singing." I didn't know what he was. But I said, "This is going to be different." And when it started happening for him, I'd see him different places and we'd talk. I still couldn't get over the way he looked.

My father died that same year. We took him down to Texas and buried him in Mart, a town eighteen miles southeast of Waco. All my life, I'd spent every other summer and Christmas in Mart with my cousin. So when Dad died, the insurance paid the house off, and we moved to Texas.

I went to Texas Christian University for about a semester. They asked me to leave. I was just so bad—cut English five times. I set all kind of records. We lived in Austin for a while. Then Mother decided she wanted to move back to Waco. And I got tired of the whole thing.

The summer of 1956, I was at loose ends, so I went back to Memphis and stayed at the YMCA. That's where I met Cliff Gleaves.

Cliff was just an unbelievable character. He was a disc jockey, of sorts. He had a little fright while we were living there. He knew the guy who lived next door, and he hadn't seen him in a few days, so he went over to check it out. Cliff knocked on the door, and nobody answered. So Cliff went downstairs and got a key. And the guy was dead.

I heard this shouting, and I said, "What is it?" Cliff was out in the middle of the hall, and he yelled, "That son of a bitch has been dead for twelve hours, and nobody cares! He could have laid there 'til he stunk the building up, and still nobody would care!" He was an unusual cat.

Cliff had gone to California with Elvis on *Love Me Tender.* Now he was going to New York for *The Ed Sullivan Show.* He would knock on my door and say, "Come on, let's go out to Elvis's house," which was on Audubon Drive. I went out three or four times and spent the afternoon. And Elvis and I would talk.

The heat really started out there on Audubon Drive. I mean, it started rolling, back in '56. Elvis started picking up steam, and pretty soon, holy moley! Everybody wanted him. He had that whole James Dean crowd—Rafael Campos, Nick Adams, Jack Simmons, Natalie Wood—courting him, which he loved, because Dean was his favorite actor after Tony Curtis. Pretty soon, Nick Adams and Natalie Wood, who'd both been in *Rebel Without a Cause,* were following him home to Memphis. An amateur photographer, a guy named Robert Dye, took some terrific pictures of Elvis riding around on his Harley-Davidson at the Mid-South Fair with Nick Adams on the back. That was in September of '56, when Elvis came home to do the Tupelo homecoming concert—the Mississippi-Alabama Fair show. Adams was an odd guy. But Elvis really liked him.

Natalie Wood was another story. Elvis was dating Natalie about the time he was doing *Love Me Tender.* Nick introduced them. And when Elvis did a screen test for the film version of the Broadway play *Girls of Summer,* Natalie did the test with him. She came out and stayed at the house in October '56. Nick Adams was there, too. They just hung out in Memphis for a few days. Elvis had this spider monkey named Jayhew. Elvis would play the piano, and the monkey would sit there, screeching. Elvis laughed like hell. Natalie hated it.

God Almighty, I was in love with Natalie Wood. I thought she was the most beautiful thing I'd ever seen. I just stared at her, she got me so. Finally, after she'd been at the house a while I just couldn't stand it. I went up to Elvis and said, "What's it like with her?" And he smiled and made an extremely graphic and very funny remark about her feminine hygiene. I thought, "Oh, God." I was crushed. He ruined it for me. Years later, her sister, Lana, wrote a book [*Natalie: A Memoir by Her Sister*]. She quoted Natalie as saying, "Elvis can sing, but he can't do much else." He would have died.

When you get down to it, I guess you could say I went after him. I wanted to be around him. It was one of those situations where we just liked each other. I have a very left-handed sort of humor, and Elvis always thought I was funny, even when I didn't mean to be. I got that from my mother. She just died in '94. She always used to say, "Have me cremated, Lamar. Just don't let me get close to a vacuum cleaner." So I look at things with a pretty jaundiced eye. Elvis and I laughed a lot.

One day in early '57, he said, "Hey, what's going on with you?" I said, "Nothing much." He said, "I'm going to the coast to do *Jailhouse Rock* soon. Give me a call sometime."

I said okay and went on back to Texas and bluffed my way into a radio station, KEBE, in Jacksonville. I told them that I'd been a disc jockey before. It was a total lie, but I did an aircheck and got on. I used the name of "Don Lamar" because Lamar Fike has no rhythm at all. And I found out I didn't want to be a disc jockey. The Teletype machine ran paper all over the floor, and I'd go in and try to clear that damn thing, and go back and change the record, and run out and read the barometer. I had preset turntables, and I'd put the wrong commercials on. It was like an Abbott and Costello picture.

After about three or four months, I said, "Fuck this, man. I don't want to do this shit anymore." I had a Sunday afternoon show, and one day I just put an LP on, locked the doors, and got in the car. I heard the record going "chick, chick, chick" on my way out of town. That was my way of signing off.

I went back to Waco and read in the paper that Elvis had just started *Jailhouse Rock*, and that he'd swallowed a cap off his tooth. The cap lodged close to his lung, and the doctors were afraid it would cause an abscess or pneumonia, so they put him in Cedars of Lebanon Hospital. I called him and just by sheer luck got straight into the room. He picked up the phone.

I said, "How you doing?" He said, "Lamar? Where are you?"

I said, "I'm in Waco." I told him about my little exit from the radio station. He laughed and said, "What are you going to do?" I told him I didn't know, and he said, "Get your ass out here." He had Suite 850 at the Beverly Wilshire Hotel. It was one whole wing of the hotel. It was four bedrooms, a living room, a big dining room, and a den. It was enormous. To this day I can still draw that suite because it left such an impression on me. The dining room was on the left, and I'd say the hall was twenty-five or thirty feet long. A suite like that today would cost you $1,500 to $2,000 a day.

I came lumbering in, all three hundred pounds of me, in a pair of yellow cowboy boots, which is what I always wore. And George Klein was there. He'd been there about a week. He'd just had his nose done by Dr. Maury Parks. He had a nose that, well, you could write a book about his nose. And probably put the book *in* his nose. It was an abominable nose, and Elvis felt sorry for him. He said, "George, I think this operation will change your life." And Elvis paid for it.

I stayed out there for the rest of the picture, which was about two and a half months. That was one of the few movies Elvis enjoyed. He got me a little job as an extra and just let me hang out. He paid for everything. Bought me clothes. And whenever I needed money, he'd just hand it to me.

It was an incredible experience. In '57, everybody wanted to see Elvis because he was a total, outright phenomenon—I guess the biggest thing since Sinatra. He was even a curiosity in Hollywood. All these big stars were coming around. I'd open the door and people like Robert Mitchum would be standing there with a fifth of scotch, asking Elvis to be in his next picture, *Thunder Road.* He wanted him to play his son, a guy who ran moonshine.

Mitchum was the type of guy who'd just say to the star, "Here's the fuckin' script. Let's get together and do it." Elvis told him he had to talk to his manager. And Mitchum said, "Fuck, I'm talking to you. I don't need to talk to your manager. Let's do the picture." And Elvis said, "Well, I can't. Not unless the Colonel says I can."

Elvis didn't like being around other stars, but I loved it. I was crazy about being able to meet all these people I'd seen only in the movies, like Clark Gable and Robert Taylor. I thought their heads were ten feet tall and eight feet wide because I'd sat in the theater and watched them. So when they came around, it made a wreck of me. I said, "Jesus God, man!" Elvis just fell out laughing.

One time on *Jailhouse Rock* we were in what they call the permanent dressing room at MGM. We were having lunch. That was when the star system was dissipating, and it was doing the same thing at Twentieth Century-Fox and at Paramount, too. But MGM still had as many stars under contract as there were stars in heaven. Gable was on the last part of his contract. And Yul Brynner was there. Richard Thorpe, who was a legend, as far as I was concerned, since he'd done *The Student Prince* and *The Prisoner of Zenda*, was the director on that picture, and Pandro S. Berman produced it.

We were sitting there eating, and there was a knock on the door. I answered it, and there stood Glenn Ford. I was just dumbfounded. I didn't know what to do, so I slammed the door in his face. I turned around to Elvis and I said, "Glenn Ford's at the door." And Elvis said, "Why did you slam the door?" I said, "I didn't know what to say to him." I was in shock. He said, "Ask him in."

Things like that happened constantly. When I met John Wayne, I told him, "I thought you won World War II single-handedly." And I saw Mike Todd and Elizabeth Taylor one day. I said, "Holy Jesus!" I broke out in a run to get to her. I said, "My name is . . . " And I forgot my name, I was so knocked out to see her. She was just a raving beauty.

I also saw some strange shit. Natalie Wood came over to the suite a couple of times. We started calling her the Mad Nat. By now I knew that Natalie was a good person, but she was nuttier than a fruitcake. She wasn't very sure of herself, and you never knew what she was going to do. One day, she got out on the window ledge at the Beverly Wilshire. Apparently, she'd decided she liked Elvis better than she did in Memphis because she said she was going to commit suicide over him.

I came running in to Elvis, and I said, "Elvis, she's out on that thing! She's going to jump!" And he said, "Fuck it, she won't jump." I said, "I'm telling you, she's going to do it!" She crouched out there about half an hour—promising, swearing—she was going to jump. We finally talked her back in. I just collapsed in a chair. But Elvis was real nonchalant. He said, "I told you she wouldn't do it."

He finished the picture, and he and his cousins Junior and Gene Smith, and George and Arthur Hooten, who was an early member of the entourage, came back to Memphis on the train. Back then, Elvis was afraid to fly. He'd had a near crash in '56, and he promised Gladys he'd take a train or a car or a bus after that. I didn't take the train. I climbed in my Chevrolet, and made it back to Memphis in thirty-some hours.

He'd just moved into Graceland, only bought it a few months before. I drove up and parked my car back in the back because he'd said, "Just come on home with me." I thought he meant permanently. After a little while, he said, "Lamar, you're going to have to go." I said, "Why is that?" He didn't have an answer, so I just stayed. I was the first member of the group to live there. I had the brown bedroom, upstairs. I was twenty-one years old.

CHAPTER 12

GRACELAND

In March '57, Elvis and his parents moved into Graceland, a Southern colonial with a stone facade, situated on thirteen and three-quarter acres at 3764 South Bellevue Boulevard (U.S. Highway 51 South), in the working-class section of Whitehaven. The suburb was still so rural that when Elvis got off the train there after appearing on *The Steve Allen Show*, Gregory Martinelli wrote in *Elvis '56*, the railroad stop—just a flag stop, really— "wasn't much more than a grass field turning yellow, and a sign-post that read 'White' . . . Elvis, still dressed in his suit and white knit tie, drifted through the burrs and foxtails, wondering which way to go."

The original Graceland property was some five hundred acres, named after Grace Toof, the daughter of the owner, S. E. Toof, who'd founded a Memphis printing company. Upon her death, Grace left the property to a niece and two nephews, the boys, Toof and Bates Brown, selling their share to their sister, Ruth Brown Moore, and her husband, Dr. Thomas Moore. In 1938, the Moores had the mansion built as a country house, to indulge the doctor's hobby of raising purebred Hereford cattle. They drained a lake on the property and sold it to a developer, selling other acreage behind the home for what became the Graceland subdivision.

When Elvis bought the property from Mrs. Moore—for about $100,000—she stipulated that a portion of the land adjacent to the north fence go to the nearby Christian church, which would adopt the Graceland name. Elvis complied and then immediately began tailoring the property to his needs, ordering construction of a swimming pool where Mrs. Moore cultivated her roses.

Although a prominent doctor had made an offer on the house, Mrs. Moore said she was pleased to sell to the Presleys because she knew they weren't "drinking people" and that they would respect Graceland's elegant history. In short order, Elvis began celebrating his splendid home and his increasing fame with a new collection of friends—staging fireworks fights and water-melon-seed spitting contests in the yard.

BILLY SMITH: One of the reasons Elvis bought Graceland was he felt he needed the acreage. That way neighbors wouldn't complain about his fans and all. And he wanted his parents to be able to get some rest. On Audubon Drive, the fans stole the wash right off the line.

They moved to Graceland in the spring of '57, between *Loving You* and *Jailhouse Rock.* And they hired a professional decorator, George Golden, who liked to run Vernon crazy. Because Elvis had left his plans on how he wanted things to be done and Gladys wanted it all finished by the time he got home at the end of June. When Elvis come back from making *Jailhouse Rock* four weeks later, Vernon looked like he didn't have a hair left on his head. Pretty soon, they put that limestone wall and the music gates up. Put it around everything.

LAMAR FIKE: Elvis told us that damn fence cost $35,000, which was almost as much as what he paid for the whole house on Audubon Drive! That might have been an exaggeration, though. I think the newspaper said the fence was $13,000.

BILLY SMITH: When Elvis first moved to Graceland, he kept three or four donkeys somebody had given him in the swimming pool. He didn't have any other place to put them because they hadn't finished the fence. Oh, they had all kinds of animals out there. A couple of horses, I remember. And Vernon had two hogs, so he could kill 'em for ham, bacon, and sausage throughout the winter. He kept the pork out back in the old pumphouse, which he used as a smokehouse.

Elvis had peacocks and ducks and a turkey he called "Bow-Tie," because he was solid white except for three black feathers right under his neck on his breast. The feathers made the turkey look like he was dressed formal all the time, 'cause one hung straight down and the other two went out on each side. Maybe it was Aunt Gladys who give him that name Bow-Tie. The turkey was a pisser—he was always floggin' somebody in the rear end.

One time, Daddy got ticked off at him and threw a rock and hit him in the head. Bow-Tie laid there for a long time, and Daddy thought he was dead. He felt terrible about it and he was going to go tell Vernon he'd killed the ol' turkey. Just as he turned around to get in the Jeep, Bow-Tie struck again. That bird didn't hold a grudge—he got even.

LAMAR FIKE: Elvis had this blue '54 Fleetwood limousine, which he'd painted yellow. He used it to stock the grounds. This time, he was hauling fowl—twenty chickens, six guineas, two peacocks, eight ducks, and a turkey.

We got into the limo, Vernon and Elvis and I, and we went out to Germantown, which was a long drive back then. We told the farmer we wanted all these birds, and Elvis said, "Could you put them in the backseat of my car?" The farmer looked at the limo, and back at Elvis, and kind of shook his head in disbelief.

Well, we were driving, and all the birds started to fight. They were flapping around like crazy, flying into the front seat, going nuts. Feathers were floating around like a snowstorm. We were laughing and trying to beat the damn things off. Elvis could barely drive. Finally, he said to me, "You got to get back there with them."

I got in the backseat, and these things started shittin' like they'd never get the chance again. The shit stuck to me, and the feathers stuck to the shit. And when Elvis and Vernon drove in back at Graceland, they just got out and left me. Elvis was calling, "Come here, Mama, and see what I got for you!" Meanwhile, I was locked in the back screaming, "Get me out of this damn car!"

Elvis thought it was hysterical. But that car had so much shit in it that even after he sent it to the Cadillac dealer to be cleaned and fumigated, it was never the same. Elvis told his daddy it was time to buy a new car. That's when he got that 1958 black Cadillac limousine.

MARTY LACKER: What I remember best about the menagerie there was the mynah bird. Talked its head off. You'd walk by and that bird would curse a blue streak: "Fuck you!" and "Son of a bitch!"

BILLY SMITH: Oh, it could say a lot of things. Like "Get out of here!" and "Go to the devil!" The mynah finally kicked the bucket, and I don't think anybody was real sorry.

MARTY LACKER: Elvis probably choked his ass.

LAMAR FIKE: When we came back from making *Jailhouse Rock* in the summer of '57, we were home for several months. Elvis had made so much money in the first two or three months, and his taxes were so screwed up that he couldn't work for a while. Apart from the movies, he was selling records like nobody had ever seen. When the single for "Loving You/Teddy Bear" came out, it sold 1.25 million copies in a week.

Colonel couldn't resist putting the needle to all those people who didn't think Elvis would make it. So in '57, he took him back to "The Grand Ole Opry." We went backstage, and Elvis was photographed with Brenda Lee, and with Johnny Cash, and a bunch of others. Elvis had on a tuxedo. He stood backstage a while, and then he walked out front and somebody introduced him to the audience. But that was it. The only time he ever performed on the "Opry" was for that audition in '54.

Afterwards, we went over to the governor's mansion to see Governor Frank Clement. We stayed up there until one o'clock in the morning playing the piano. The Prisonaires, who recorded for Sun, sang for us. They were real convicts, from the Tennessee State Penitentiary, in Nashville. They sang "Just Walkin' in the Rain."

BILLY SMITH: Elvis used to tell everybody how close we were. He'd tell people, "I actually raised him." And in a sense, he did, because I was with Elvis damn near as much as I was with my mother and father. Really, over the years, more so.

I remember one time we were playing touch football on Alabama Street. I looked up to him even then. I used to go get him Pepsis. Then after he became famous, he used to ask me to do stuff all the time.

My parents trusted the fact that I was well taken care of. That's why they let me go to "The Grand Ole Opry" with him in the summer of '57, when I was fourteen. Elvis bought me a new suit so I would have something nice to wear. First new suit I had in, God, years. We went to that party at the governor's house later on, and I got tired, and Governor Clement's wife told me to go on in the bedroom and go to sleep. She told Elvis, "Just leave him here. I'll put him on the bus tomorrow." And Elvis said, "No, I'll wake him up when we get ready to go." But I never did go to sleep. I was afraid I'd miss something. I always followed Elvis around like a little puppy dog. I was totally captivated by him.

When Elvis had that time off in '57, he loved being able to spend it at Graceland. The place was like something out of a fairy tale to us. We didn't even know anybody who *knew* anybody who had a house like that. In our family, owning a car was a big deal. You know why Elvis really bought it? He wanted something grand for his mama. Once, Gladys saw some big house somewhere, and she made a comment about how pretty it was. Elvis was still little, and he said, "Mama, someday I'm going to buy you a house just like that."

LAMAR FIKE: Gladys was like my second mother. I think I got along with her better than anybody in the group. She was an unusual woman. She had only a third-grade education. But goddurn, she was smart as a whip. And a very kind woman. But she had a temper like you could not believe. And she could scream, boy. When she exploded it was like, "Holy shit!" And Elvis and his mother fought like cats and dogs. The fights always started at the dinner table. I mean to tell you, they'd get to arguing with each other, and it would scare the crap out of me.

Her worrying would just drive him to distraction. They'd argue about that. And he'd argue that she drank too much. She was a beer drinker. And it would just get rough-and-tumble. She'd be cranky, and then Elvis would get cranky. And, boy, they'd crank in together.

Elvis loved purple hull peas—crowder peas—and sliced tomatoes and bacon and mashed potatoes. She would fix that for him, and we would have it for dinner, along with some hot peppers that Vernon and I liked. One night, Gladys was sitting at one end of the table, and Elvis was sitting at the other. I was in the middle, and Vernon was across from me. And they started arguing. Elvis said, "Mom, you worry too much about me. Don't worry about me, I'll be okay."

And Gladys started. She said, "Don't tell me to not worry

about you!" Then it got worse. Elvis stood up and picked up the plate of tomatoes and just slung 'em. They bounced off the wall and went all over the room. Then he picked up the bowl of purple hulls, and I ducked. I thought, "Man, I'll never survive this!" I ran out of the room.

I had never seen fights like that in my life because I wasn't raised like that. When my mom and dad would argue they'd close the door, and we never knew anything about it. When Elvis and Gladys got it on, they put on a show. And they didn't seem to mind lighting into each other while I was at the table. God Almighty! They would say words to each other that I had never heard. But they would hug right afterwards.

After I moved in, Cliff Gleaves moved in. He'd stay a while, then go tearing off somewhere. I don't think he ever had a real address, other than Graceland. The last time I saw him in Memphis, he told me he was sleeping at the cemetery. He's just the weirdest guy. That's why Elvis liked him.

MARTY LACKER: Lamar was fairly weird, too, you know. I think Elvis liked him for a variety of reasons. One is that he needed somebody to pick on. Lamar is also brilliant. I don't think that's why Elvis picked him for the group, though. I think he thought Lamar would give him a colorful life. But he teased him relentlessly, usually about his size. Elvis called him "The Great Speckled Bird." Or "Buddha."

LAMAR FIKE: I could take a lot of abuse and not pay too much attention to it. But with Elvis, I have to admit it hurt sometimes. He called me all kinds of names. Sometimes as a term of affection, he'd call me "Birdy." I guess it was because my eyes were big, like an owl's.

I can't remember the actual instances, but they hurt so bad sometimes I really cried. Afterwards, he'd come and hug me and say, "I didn't mean that. I was just feeling bad." And I'd say, "Okay, no problem." It was so hard for him to say, "I'm sorry." And I'd just kind of go off and swallow my Adam's apple and hope to God I could put up with it again next time.

I think everybody was a whipping boy for Elvis. And it got worse as the years wore on.

BILLY SMITH: I think there were a lot of reasons Elvis picked Lamar. What did he say one time? "I need somebody I can laugh at."

LAMAR FIKE: Down deep, I knew Elvis really cared for me. I stayed because of that and because he was fun to be around. We were in such a sheltered environment. It never rained on us. It never got cold. It was like big wings over us. We were sort of in a fishbowl, but protected. When I moved into Graceland, it was the greatest feeling because we could close the gates and we were so isolated that nobody could get to us. Nobody. Not even bill collectors. The people who did come up were there because we let them up. We lived such a fantasy that it was hard to judge reality. We didn't care about the outside world. It was like an addiction. We had to stay there in order to think.

BILLY SMITH: When they moved into Graceland, Vernon asked my daddy to be the head gate guard, just as he'd been on Audubon Drive. My parents and Bobby and me moved into a three-bedroom house in the back of the property.

Vernon's brother, Vester, worked as the groundskeeper at the time. Later, about '60 or '61, he started working on the gate, too. One day, Daddy and Vernon got into it. You couldn't have took Vernon at his best day and thrown him in my daddy's direction. Because Daddy would have beat his damn brains out. Daddy cared about Vernon. But here's the difference between 'em. One time, Vernon told Daddy, "You're going to have to get them damn people outside the gate." And that embarrassed Daddy to death.

Well, before Daddy knew it—and I guess this is partly where I get my temper—Daddy said, "Let me tell you something, you white-haired son of a bitch!" He said, "As long as you live, don't never come down here at this gate and embarrass me in front of a bunch of people like you just did." He said, "You call me up to Graceland and tear me up if you want to. But you do it in privacy. Don't you do it in front of a bunch of people." And from that day on, Daddy never had any problems.

MARTY LACKER: Vernon resented everybody because he thought they were taking his place with Elvis. He also thought we were all after his money, so he hated everybody who came around.

LAMAR FIKE: We'd been back [from California] only a couple of weeks, or maybe less, when Alan Fortas first came up. I'd known him in high school, played football against him.

MARTY LACKER: Alan came into the group in 1957. He's the guy who found out Elvis got a "C" in music in high school. The Board of Education dumped all their old transcripts at Alan's father's scrap paper yard. And Alan just happened to find Elvis's. Elvis wanted him in the entourage because he was like Gene—he made Elvis laugh. But Alan wasn't dim like Gene. He was a class clown kind of guy. He was sort of big, and despite the fact that he was a high school football star—he was an All-Memphis player and got a bunch of college scholarships and had his picture in the paper all the time—he always felt a little on the fringe of things. He was Jewish, and unlike a lot of guys who came in and out of the group, Alan was from a solidly middle-class family. His uncle, Abe Fortas, became a Supreme Court justice for four years during the Lyndon Johnson administration. He was Johnson's friend and confidant, but he was the only high court justice forced to resign. He quit when it came out that he was on a $20,000-a-year retainer from a foundation funded by a guy who went to prison for stock manipulation.

Alan had a sad aspect about him. He hid a lot of pain. And he had an absolutely huge heart—would do anything for you if the chips were down. He had this older brother who was a genius at school, and teachers were always comparing the two. Unfavorably, of course. So Alan became a comic. He was only happy when he was stirring something up. The other times, he was bored with everything. What really attracted Elvis was that Alan was this football star, which is what Elvis wanted to be. He called him "Hog Ears." For pretty obvious reasons.

BILLY SMITH: Alan fit like a glove. He just won everybody's heart. And if he didn't win it, he'd con your heart.

Alan was driving Elvis's black limo home to Memphis from California one time, and he had the corduroy drapes pulled around the windows. He was speeding, and a cop pulled him over. The cop said, "What kind of car is this?" And Alan said, "Can't you tell? It's a hearse." The guy said, "A hearse?" And Alan said, "Yeah." The cop asked him where he was going, and Alan told him he was going to Memphis. He said, "I've got a body in here that needs to be buried very shortly." Then he said, "Do you want to get in and smell the embalming fluid?" And the cop said, "No thanks. Just keep on going."

MARTY LACKER: I'll give you an example about Alan that happened in the sixties. Elvis called me "Moon." I had a bald spot, which was getting bigger. It bothered Elvis, so he volunteered to get me a Hollywood hairpiece. I said, "I don't want it." You know why? Because I knew Alan would pull it off my head in front of people.

BILLY SMITH: Two more guys came into the group at the same time as Alan—Louis Harris and Tommy Young. They didn't last long. Tommy stayed only about eight or nine months. Louis lasted a while longer. He was real quiet, a nice guy. Sort of studious. And respectful.

MARTY LACKER: George Klein brought Louis in. George didn't drive, and he was always asking guys to carry him out to the house. That's how Alan got into the group.

LAMAR FIKE: Louis was a little nerdy, bless his heart. You almost felt sorry for him. He would get in a taxi, and they wouldn't put the meter up. That kind of guy.

Tommy didn't fit because we never did let him fit. He was a bit of a smartass, thought he was a "pretty boy." He knew the market was there because all the girls wanted to hang around Elvis.

MARTY LACKER: We had two or three guys who were there for what they could get. But Elvis was hip to that. He used to test people every now and then.

LAMAR FIKE: We could be pretty rough on guys we didn't like. If a guy was getting ready to step off a cliff, we just let him step.

That wasn't the case with Alan. Everybody liked his wit and the sort of dogged loyalty he had about him. Not too long after Alan came into the group, he went down to New Orleans with us to do *King Creole*. He was like me—loved being around movie people. And he usually ended up making friends with Elvis's costars. They liked him because he had a childlike quality about him.

In a way, Alan was a misfit. But then most of us were misfits. In some ways, that's our story. Elvis looked for oddballs. Some people might theorize that he picked guys like that to make sure they'd be faithful to him. I don't think he had any rhyme or reason for it. But he did like underdogs, except George Klein had been class president. Elvis almost always liked the guy they treated worst.

MARTY LACKER: George really wasn't part of the group, no matter what he says. He traveled on a couple of trips in the late fifties, and went on one to Hawaii. And he spent some vacations with the group. But he wasn't there for the nitty-gritty, even though when you hear him on TV or at some of these Elvis fests, where he gets up and speaks, you'd think he was Jiminy Cricket, in Elvis's pocket twenty-four hours a day.

LAMAR FIKE: George was never an intimate member of the Memphis Mafia, as he claimed to be. When we came back from *Jailhouse Rock,* and we left to go make the next picture, George stayed home to do radio. He was Elvis's connection to the radio and record business, to let him know what was going on.

MARTY LACKER: When I came out of the army in '57, I was twenty years old. Elvis had just moved up to Graceland. One weekend, George called me and said, "How would you like to go up to Graceland?" Basically, he needed a ride.

It's like a picture in my mind. We drove up the driveway to the back of the house, and at that time, there was no Jungle Room. It was just an open patio. And just as we got out of the car and started walking towards the back, Elvis came out from the barn with Anita Wood. Anita was cohost of a local television show with Wink Martindale called *Top Ten Dance Party.* She was real petite, real blond, and real cute—a beauty contest winner. She was nineteen.

This was the first time I had seen Elvis since the Katz Drug Store opening, and by now he was this big star. I even remember what he wore. He had on this big blousy shirt—black with white polka dots on it. We got up to the fence and Elvis said, "Hey,

George, how you doin'?" And George said, "Elvis, you remember Marty, don't you, from school?"

Elvis really surprised me because he said, "Yeah, man, you just got out of the army, didn't you?" I looked at him, and I said, "Wait a minute. I know where you've been, but how would you know where I've been?" He said, "I just know. People tell me things."

We talked for a while, and then we went in the house and shot pool and stayed up all night. Some of the other guys were there. I got to see Red again, who had also been at Humes.

Just as I was leaving, Elvis said, "Hey, I'm glad you came. Anytime you want to come back, just come out."

LAMAR FIKE: What Elvis liked about Marty was the Humes High School connection. And Marty came up through the same sort of impoverished background Elvis did.

BILLY SMITH: I think Elvis knew that Marty had ways of getting things done, in a business sense. Marty is a take-charge kind of guy.

MARTY LACKER: After that, I went out to Graceland almost every night. I loved show business. When I was in school, I played the saxophone, and when I got out of the army, a couple of friends talked me into going to Keegan's School of Broadcasting. So I went to school and hung out at Graceland.

LAMAR FIKE: Elvis just reversed day for night. That started after he got in the business. Most entertainers sleep 'til eleven or twelve o'clock in the afternoon or later. It's a habit on the road. You work a show and you get through at twelve or one o'clock in the morning. Then you don't get back to your motel until two or three, and you're partying or whatever. You get to bed by maybe three-thirty or four. And you've got to get eight hours sleep, so you sleep 'til noon. So at Graceland, Elvis got up around noon, or maybe two o'clock, had breakfast, took care of whatever needed taking care of, and then about four or five o'clock, guys like Alan would start coming around. Things started shifting into full gear about seven or eight o'clock. Vester would be at the gate, and he'd start calling up to say who was there and ask should he let 'em in. Then we went to the skating rink, or the movies or the fairgrounds, or whatever.

MARTY LACKER: Back then, we used to do a lot of roller-skating. We'd go to the Rainbow Skating Rink, out on Lamar Avenue. Elvis would get the guys together and rent it out for $65 a night. They'd close to the public around midnight, and then Elvis and his friends would take it over until daylight. The guys would bring dates, and Elvis even let a bunch of kids who hung around the gate at Graceland come along. We'd have about 100 or 150 people.

We didn't roller-skate like most people. We'd make up games, like "War," where we'd choose up sides, the teams would line up at each end of the roller rink. Then at the count of three, we'd all skate towards each other and just knock the hell out of our opponents.

Elvis loved it. We'd have a big box of elbow pads and kneepads, and every hour we'd go in the bathroom and see who got hit the hardest. This one girl who used to come, Barbara Glidewell, told Rose Clayton and Dick Heard [Elvis Up Close] that Elvis didn't care how rough it got because he'd take these "happy pills" he got from the dentist. So I guess he wasn't feeling any pain.

I remember Elvis would have this guy, Bemis Atkins, who invented Pronto Pups, the corn dogs, come out there with his machine. We really had a ball.

BILLY SMITH: There was this real tough girl named Melinda who used to skate with us. She could hang in there with the best of them. When Sonny West came around in '58, she hit him and hurt his collarbone real bad. And Sonny was 6'2", about two hundred thirty pounds.

On skates it didn't matter. You could bust their ass just as quick, them being three hundred pounds and you one hundred pounds. It depended on how good they could skate. And Melinda was a good skater, and rough! Elvis dated her for a while.

We had this other game called "Pop the Whip." You'd get a lot of people and make a chain by having 'em hold each other around the waist. Then you'd make this real sharp turn. Well, the front of the line was hard to hold on to, and the middle, too. But the end of the line was hell. Because by the time it whipped around, the last person got snapped in two. One girl ran into the wall and hit her cheek. It laid her out pretty good.

The first time Elvis took me out there, I was about fifteen. I'd never been on a pair of skates in my life, but he showed me no mercy. Just when I was going pretty good, he'd knock my legs right out from under me and laugh like crazy.

The skating years lasted from about '57 until about '61. Then it was more the fairgrounds time. He'd rent out the whole Mid-South Fairgrounds, there on Parkway, starting around eleven or twelve at night, and go strong until about seven in the morning. He loved the roller coaster and the Dodgem cars. It was nothing for him to ride the roller coaster seventeen times straight, without it ever stopping. Everything to excess.

LAMAR FIKE: Elvis was always pushing the limit. I don't think he was trying to be macho. I think it was letting off steam. When he moved into Graceland, he got out there on a big tractor with a bush-hog on it and cleaned the back acreage. Then he decided he'd tear down the old back fence. He hooked a chain around the fence posts and then to the tractor and pulled them out of the ground.

Finally, he hooked the chain around the corner post and began to pull. He didn't realize it was set in concrete. The tractor bucked and almost turned over on him. He was just teetering there for a second. You knew when something scared the crap out of him because he'd start laughing. Gladys ran out, screaming, "Elvis, get off that damn tractor and put it up right now!" He was white as goose down. He climbed off and put his arms around Gladys and said, "I'm okay, Satnin'. I'm okay." He never thought anything would happen to him.

BILLY SMITH: One of the most dangerous things Elvis liked to do was shoot off fireworks. I'm not talking about a couple of Roman candles. I'm talking about artillery. Hell, we could have put somebody's eye out or burnt the house down.

Lamar got hit between the eyes one time, and he thought he'd lost his sight. He went to hollering, "I'm blind! I'm blind!" Of course, it was just for a second. But, hell, we had burns all over us. Even one of the horses got hit in the rear end.

There was one night we made the whole sky light up. Thousands of dollars of fireworks, set off by fifteen or twenty guys. I'm talking about six-inch bombs that shot several hundred feet in the damn air and spread out. And rockets and these helicopter spinning things. When they hit, they hurt, boy!

MARTY LACKER: We did other things, too, like go to the movies. At first, we'd go downtown to a regular theater and sneak in the side door after the movie started so no one would see who it was. We'd go up and sit in the balcony. Elvis had a rule that a member of the group had to sit behind him to keep people away from him. Because when people recognized him, they'd get up and come over and ask him for his autograph.

Only rarely would Elvis want to be alone. But sometimes in the fifties, he'd get in the old, beat-up, Chevrolet panel truck and go out by himself. He'd take a jar of ice water and a bunch of bananas. That was usually when he had a problem he wanted to mull over. He would ride around with a motorcycle hat pulled down over his head. He could get through the gate because nobody thought he'd be in that truck.

We never knew where he was. Later, he told Sonny that he'd go down to this park and watch girls playing ball. Sometimes he took Anita with him. That was unusual for him to do that with a woman. But they'd ride around in the afternoons through the different subdivisions. And he'd take her over to Lauderdale Courts and show her where he used to live. He trusted her more than he did most women, I think.

BILLY SMITH: Anita was usually Elvis's date for the skating rink and the movies. She was around for a long time in the early years. They started going out in July of '57, when he invited her to go with him to watch 'em put up a special front for [the Memphis premiere of] *Loving You.* The very next month, he give her a diamond and sapphire ring. A lot of people thought he was going to marry her.

LAMAR FIKE: George Klein set up their first date. He was always kind of a glorified pimp when it came to Elvis meeting girls. I called her, and we went by and picked her up. She lived in a rooming house, of sorts, with this old lady named Miss Patty. We drove around, and Elvis brought her to the house. Anita was very innocent. But that got to be a strong and heavy relationship, I'll tell you.

MARTY LACKER: Elvis used to call Anita "Lil' Bit" or "Little" because of the size of her feet. He was very affectionate with her. But that doesn't mean he didn't fool around when she wasn't there. She started staying at Graceland, but everybody believes that was a chaste relationship.

BILLY SMITH: Once in a while, Anita spent the night at Graceland, and I think Gladys knew it, even though she had a strict policy about that. It was Elvis's house, but Gladys made the rules. And she didn't allow the opposite sex to sleep over, but she made an exception because she liked Anita a lot, and she hoped they'd get married and have kids.

LAMAR FIKE: The term "chaste" is sort of nebulous with Elvis and a lot of his girls. His sexual appetites were very, very strange. It wasn't a case of just jumping a girl. He liked for them to keep their panties on, but he liked to see a little pubic hair creeping around the edges. Really, the touching and the feeling and the patting and everything else meant more to Elvis than the actual act. Intercourse was never that big of a thrill to him. He liked everything that led up to it better.

I guess Elvis was the King of Foreplay. This was all from the patting he exchanged with his mother growing up. You've got to understand this was an only child, whose mother still walked to school with him when he was fifteen, sixteen years old to make sure nothing happened. He slept with both parents up 'til God knows when. That was not a thread that ran through that family. It was a cable.

So I can imagine that Anita was a virgin and that their relationship was "chaste," in the strictest sense. Elvis respected virginity. He used to tell Alan, "I'll never break a virgin. There are too many whores around." By the way, Elvis gave Anita that ring. But he didn't want to get married. Never did.

MARTY LACKER: I remember one time that was kind of funny. Anita went out shopping, and while she was gone, Elvis brought another girl upstairs. He was fooling around with her in the bedroom, when all of a sudden, one of the guys called up and said, "Hey, Elvis, Anita's coming through the gate."

If you looked out his window, it was a straight drop to the ground. So we put a ladder up to the window. He let the girl climb down first, and he waited about five minutes, and then he went down. Anita came in and went upstairs and, of course, he wasn't there. He walked around the back of the house to the front and came upstairs behind her. And he said, "Oh, you're home. Great." He would do stuff like that all the time. But he liked Anita a lot. He did a lot of stuff for her that he wouldn't do in the latter years, like go on *Top Ten Dance Party.*

BILLY SMITH: It was Anita who turned him on to those tanning pills, those pills that turned your skin brown.

LAMAR FIKE: I remember when he got on that tanning kick. He'd come in and say, "Do you see this right here?" And his palm would be yellow, and he'd be thrilled. That's because he liked pills of any kind. It was already starting.

CHAPTER 13

"DAMN'D TO EVERLASTING FAME!"

MARTY LACKER: I didn't see any of the drug taking back then. I have more innocent memories of those years. I remember coming back from the movies or the skating rink at daylight and eating watermelon in what is now the Meditation Garden. Every once in a while, we'd have a watermelon fight, where we'd throw hunks of the stuff at each other.

One night, I said, "Hey, I'm going up to Union City [Tennessee] to live for a while." I'd landed a job at WTUC Radio. Elvis said, "Good luck. I hope you'll come back when I'm home."

LAMAR FIKE: Because I lived at Graceland, I saw a lot more than some of the guys. Gladys was drinking, but she was also taking amphetamines. Elvis got his first uppers from his mother, in '57. Gladys had a tremendous problem with the change of life. It was squirreling her out. Her doctor had given her these things, and Elvis would swipe them out of the bottle and never let her know. She couldn't figure out how she was taking so many of them, and she would have to go get her prescription refilled. This was Dexedrine. And sometimes Desbutals.

Well, Elvis and I got hold of that damn bottle, and I took two or three of them. I said, "Boy, I want to stay on this elevator for a while!" We used to get so damn ripped, our teeth would chatter. I got to the point where I couldn't even swallow one because it would stick in my throat.

Elvis just loved the shit out of pills. He loved what they did. Any pills. He would open a box of Bayer aspirin and chew the whole damn bottle. He thought that pills were the answer for everything. If anybody believed that medicine would shape the world, it was Elvis.

BILLY SMITH: I never heard anyone in the family say Gladys had a difficult time with menopause. The only thing I remember about her acting strange was once when she had a nightmare at Graceland. She got up, and went to the kitchen, and sat down in there for the longest time. She talked to the maid, Alberta [Holman], about it.

About the pills, I think Elvis's biggest introduction to drugs was during the army days. But I'm sure Aunt Gladys, at times, probably said, "If you got a headache, why don't you take this? This is a pain pill."

LAMAR FIKE: He slacked off on the Dexedrine for a while. But only for a while. Because Elvis had such an addictive personality that he would just lock onto these things. When this first started, we would be driving home from a movie, and he'd take a different route. I'd say, "Where are we going?" And he'd say, "We're going to Florida" and just drive straight on out the highway. Finally, he'd stop at a service station and I'd call Gladys and tell her. But you never knew what he'd do when he got hopped up. And, of course, the amphetamines didn't help his nightmares any.

MARTY LACKER: Some of the guys used to sleep in the bedroom with him because of his nightmares. You just couldn't leave him alone.

LAMAR FIKE: I had to go in there and sleep with him on a regular basis, and I went through a couple of those nightmares. They scared me to death. He hit me in the jaw one night and never knew it, and I said, "That's enough of this shit." So I put a sleeping bag down at the end of the bed and slept down there.

One night, I woke up and found him standing at the end of his bed. God, the bed was enormous. It had to be nine feet square. And he had this cover, and he was slinging it around and yelling, "Get away from me! Everybody, just get away!" So I got on my hands and knees and crawled around and flipped the light on and he woke up. Usually, when this happened and he came out of it, he'd just crack up laughing.

When girls stayed over, I would have to stay up and take them home afterwards. Elvis wouldn't go to bed 'til I got back. When I got home, I would either get in bed with him or in my sleeping bag. I didn't think anything about it because, hell, my cousin and I used to sleep together all the time. That's what you do in the South. Elvis rarely had a good night's sleep. That's why it took so much shit [drugs] to knock him out.

BILLY SMITH: When he was sleepwalking, you couldn't just full-fledged shake him or run and scream, "Hey, wake up. You're having a nightmare." Because he'd punch you out. The best thing to do was to just call his name and barely touch him. Mama told me once that when the Presleys lived in Lauderdale Courts, Elvis got to sleepwalking and went outside in his underwear. This boy and girl that he knew had just come home from a date. The girl saw him and went over and woke him up. He was so embarrassed because he was practically naked, you know. So Gladys started taking the knobs off the doors so he couldn't get out and roam around at night.

LAMAR FIKE: Somebody said to me the other day, "This must have been a tortured guy." Well, Elvis was the kind of guy who made mountains out of molehills. He'd kill a fly with a sledgehammer.

One reason, I guess, is by '57, he was already feeling like his life was not his own. He wanted to be a big star, but he hadn't counted on a lot of things. One time, back then even, he said to me, "Lamar, I'm a robot. Somebody just tell me what to do and move me around."

When he went on stage was the only time he could control who he was. But already by '57, Elvis would lose his temper and blow up. In the time I was with him, he fired me probably 100 times and I quit probably 150 times.

In '57, '58, we got into violent arguments. He'd ask me how I liked something he was doing, and I'd say, "Well . . . " But from the beginning, we had that sort of relationship. And when Elvis would run you off, or you'd quit, you'd get out there in the world and find it was pretty rough. But usually, after he fired you, he'd change his mind. Gladys would always tell me, "Lamar, anything Elvis says is from the mouth out. It's not from the heart."

BILLY SMITH: One thing that really hurt Elvis was when Scotty and Bill left. It was right after *Jailhouse Rock*, in '57, just before Elvis's second Tupelo Fair Show. He played a benefit for the Elvis Presley Youth Recreation Center, and he was expecting them to do it with him.

LAMAR FIKE: Bill Black talked Scotty into quitting. But [drummer] D.J. [Fontana], who joined him during the "Hayride" days, wouldn't do it. He was the only one who stayed. He always called Elvis "Chief." He said, "Chief, I'm still here."

I remember this because the scene was really terrific. We were at the Beverly Wilshire Hotel in Los Angeles. I was sitting in the living room, and Elvis walked in and said, "I think Scotty and Bill are fixin' to quit." I said, "Well, you better call Colonel."

Elvis got on the phone, and he said, "Colonel, Scotty, and Bill are quitting. What am I going to do?" And Colonel said, "You're going to get another band. That's what you're going to do."

Elvis hung up and said, "What am I going to do without them?" I said, "You're going to do a show. They're just musicians." Elvis thought it was the end of the world.

It came down in an interesting way. Elvis and I got in the car, and we drove over to the old Knickerbocker Hotel. That's where Scotty and Bill and D.J. were staying. We drove by, and there was Bill in the lobby of the hotel, walking back and forth, just preaching to Scotty and D.J. Elvis turned around and looked at me, and he said, "What do you think?" I said, "It looks to me like Bill's running the shooting match."

We were going to Hawaii in November, and we knew they didn't want to go. Bill didn't want to fly. So we said we'd go over on [the ship] the *Matsonia*.

But that wasn't the real reason. They didn't think they were getting enough money. Because while Elvis was making this fabulous fortune, they were getting a salary of $100 a week at home and $200 a week on the road, plus a $1,000 Christmas bonus. They wanted recognition, and they wanted a percentage of the profits, same as they got when they first started out. And Colonel said, "Fuck you. You're not going to get it. That's the way it is, boys, cut-and-dried."

MARTY LACKER: They were also tired of sitting around. They'd done this little five-day tour of the Pacific Northwest, but that was the first time they'd worked with Elvis since March or April, and they wanted to be paid while they weren't on the road.

LAMAR FIKE: I don't blame Scotty, Bill, and D.J. for trying, but they could be replaced. You could have put them in the Seattle Fair and they wouldn't have drawn twenty people. Musicians have a tendency to forget that.

It finally came down on September 21. Bill called and said it was over. Elvis sat down with me and he said, "It's happened." He was lower than a snake's belly. The Colonel said, "That's no problem." And he put that Nashville group together for the Tupelo Fair—Floyd Cramer on piano, Hank "Sugarfoot" Garland on guitar, and Bob Moore on bass.

They blew everybody away. Elvis turned around to me after the fair with this big grin on his face. He said, "Shit, I didn't need Scotty and Bill anyway, did I?" But Scotty never completely went away. He was around, off and on, 'til '69.

BILLY SMITH: When Elvis first started, Gladys and Vernon were—God, I don't think you could describe the feeling. It was like "Here's a son that made it." And they relayed that to most of the family. My daddy was different, but a lot of the relatives were resentful. When Elvis started making those appearances on TV, like on The Milton Berle Show, we realized he was big-time. And there was a lot of envy.

I remember in '57, a lot of the family came around to Graceland. I was just damn proud to be there. I never asked for anything. I never thought about it. First of all, there wasn't a lot of need because Elvis bought a lot of stuff for Bobby and me when we first moved there.

When it got close to Christmas, Elvis asked his daddy to get $15,000 in one-thousand-dollar bills. He carried them around with him for days. On Christmas Eve, he laid all fifteen bills across his bed. Then he invited some of the family up one by one. When they got up there, and they saw that money, he'd go to the bathroom, or find some excuse to leave the room, to see if they'd take any. And somebody did. Years later, Elvis told me he knew exactly who it was, his cousin Billy Mann. Elvis never said a word about it. He let Billy think he'd pulled a good one on him, but Elvis never had any use for him after that.

MARTY LACKER: Elvis told everybody, "Don't even let him come anywhere near the gate." And Billy Mann was the one who ended up taking that picture of Elvis in the casket for the *National Enquirer.* So that tells you even more about those people.

BILLY SMITH: When it came time for Elvis to invite me up, I saw those bills and said, "Gosh, Elvis, you shouldn't leave that laying around. Anybody could come in here and take it."

I was just a teenager. And I'm not saying I never stole nothing. I did, as a kid. But I got my ass whipped for it, and I knew the difference.

From then on, Elvis always kept me right with him and not just at little stuff like the skating rink. I mean, day in and day out. And there were other little tests. You had to prove yourself to him.

That same Christmas, he had several members of the family on both sides working for him. And he give 'em all a thousand dollars. Back then, that was a hell of a lot of money. Some of 'em up and quit working, and at the time Elvis needed twenty-four-hour security the most. It made it a hardship on those who stayed. My daddy worked around the clock 'til Elvis could get somebody to replace him. And then, after the money was blown, the others come back and begged for their jobs. Elvis took 'em back, but he didn't feel the same.

One time, Vester kept asking Vernon for a raise, and Vernon wouldn't give him one. So he came up and asked Elvis. There were two or three of us in the den, and Elvis was ticked off because Vernon had told him Vester had threatened to quit. So Vester came into the den, and he said, "Ever since you've been here, Elvis, I've been down there buckin' that gate." And Elvis said, "I'll tell you what, Uncle Vester. If you don't like it, you can buck that fuckin' gate in another direction." And Vester shut up and left. He never did quit. He didn't have any other place to go.

Christmas of '57 is the most memorable one because it was

my first Christmas at Graceland. If I remember right, Elvis give me and my brother $200 for Christmas. Maybe it was $200 in all, a hundred-dollar bill for each of us. I was used to getting a dollar-a-week allowance, so it was like having Santa Claus for a first cousin.

That whole Christmas was like a kid's dream. Elvis had a white nylon tree with red Christmas balls on the white carpet. And he'd put the red velvet drapes up. And he had holly hanging around, and berries. Aunt Gladys always had all kinds of good things to eat during the holidays. A couple of Christmases before, Bobby and me and some of the other cousins went to the Goodfellows dinner for underprivileged kids. I'd damn near choked to death on turkey, trying to get finished so I could go back for seconds.

I remember that Elvis asked Bobby and me to go with him to get presents for his mama and daddy. We went to Whitehaven Plaza, this new little shopping center. That must have been for some smaller gifts. Because I was thinking he give his mama a mink coat that year, but that might have been Christmas of '56. And it seems like he give his daddy a diamond ring.

Sometime around there, Elvis got his draft notice. He knew it was coming because Colonel talked him into going to get his physical long before the draft board called him up. Maybe he thought it made Elvis look real patriotic. Anyway, when the draft notice come, Colonel said to ignore it, that he'd get him a deferment until March, when *King Creole* was finished. Elvis was real happy, you know, although later on, I think he might have thought Colonel tricked him into enlisting.

Elvis gave Colonel an $1,800 Isetta sports car that Christmas. And he was in such a good mood that he let photographers come up and take pictures of him with his draft notice under the Christmas tree.

That night, he set off almost $2,000 worth of fireworks behind Graceland. Me and Bobby helped him. That was probably the best Christmas I ever had.

CHAPTER 14

GLADYS

LAMAR FIKE: I've never seen anybody connected like Elvis and Gladys were. It was just amazing.

BILLY SMITH: Aunt Gladys could always tell when something was wrong, especially with Elvis. Like when Elvis swallowed that tooth cap on *Jailhouse Rock*. She was in Memphis, and he was in California. And she kept telling Vernon, "Something ain't right. I can feel it." It wasn't an hour later until she got the phone call. She even knew when he was upset about something. She would say, "I feel uneasy about Elvis. Maybe we ought to call him." And she was almost always right.

LAMAR FIKE: Gladys had more common sense than anybody I've ever known, but she also had these old-fashioned superstitions. When Elvis closed the garage in and made it into a big bedroom, she made him keep the doors on it because it was bad luck to close up windows and doors.

BILLY SMITH: Elvis wasn't all that superstitious, himself. If a black cat ran in front of the car, he didn't turn around and go back the other way. And he didn't believe in "lucky" shirts or good-luck charms.

LAMAR FIKE: Gladys was not the dour person that everybody thinks she was. I guess maybe that's why she and I got along. Because we'd both just start laughing. When she laughed, every square inch of her laughed—her stomach, her feet, everything. We'd be in absolute hysterics. Elvis would come out of his bedroom, walk down the servants' steps and hit the kitchen, and say, "What are you two up to?" And we wouldn't even be able to tell him.

BILLY SMITH: Aunt Gladys could find humor in small things. That was a gift both she and Elvis had. And believe it or not, Uncle Vernon could laugh about things, too. Socially, Gladys liked the old ways, the Southern ways. In other words, when Elvis would have a party late at night, she wasn't crazy about that. But she never said much because it was his house. She might say something like "I hope we don't have no slut parties going on here." Because that's how she'd been raised. But she tried to be up for Elvis most of the time. His time at home was very limited, especially when he became famous.

LAMAR FIKE: Vernon, man, she kept him running. I watched her jump on him one day and lock him down so quick it was unreal. He was scared to death of her.

BILLY SMITH: I think a lot of their arguing was because Vernon was flirty with the women who hung out down at the gate. And probably other things occurred. I don't know. But I remember Aunt Gladys saying, "Maybe you ought to stay away from that damn gate so much."

LAMAR FIKE: One time, Vernon had screwed around or something. I think it happened way back. And Gladys said some horrible things. She could get to the nitty-gritty real fast. She had these country sayings where I'd just go, "My God!" And Elvis had them, too. But she had this way about her that was very upfront. Gladys said this girl had "piss-burned hair." Now that's as hard as you can get. Elvis would smolder, and smolder, and all of a sudden, he'd blow. That's the way Gladys was. And they'd both get it over with, and that would be the end of it.

MARTY LACKER: Vernon always thought he was a stud, see? He'd dye his hair blond, and later he grew that mustache.

LAMAR FIKE: Gladys drank Schlitz Tall-Boys. She'd drink 'em out of a sack to cover 'em up. That's an old country thing. She'd sit by the window and drink about two or three of them, and she'd be on the wall.

When she and Vernon would get in an argument, you'd hear Gladys, but you wouldn't hear Vernon. Gladys was a screamer.

Her voice could penetrate a steel vault. And Vernon would talk under his breath real low. So when they argued, all you could hear was Gladys's screaming.

One time, Gladys hit Vernon with a goddamn pot of beans and knocked him clean off the chair. This was in Texas, in 1958, when Elvis was in basic training for the army. Elvis and I were sitting in the living room. Vernon apparently said something under his breath, and Gladys had a pot of beans on the stove and just grabbed 'em off and hit him in the head with the damn stew pot.

Elvis and I both broke out in a run when we heard it, and when we rounded that corner, Vernon was lying on the floor with navy beans all over him and a big welt on the side of his head. He was out cold. She just dropped him where he sat. I said, "Holy shit!" She was slinging pots and pans, and beans were all over the kitchen. It scared the shit out of Elvis. He thought Vernon was dead.

BILLY SMITH: Vernon got his revenge from time to time. He got mean as a snake when he got drunk. That's the times he whipped up on Aunt Gladys. That's what really tore Elvis up. It didn't take much to get Vernon drunk—half a pint of whiskey maybe. He'd just go crazy.

LAMAR FIKE: Vernon beat the shit out of Gladys a bunch of times.

BILLY SMITH: He'd maybe slap her or something like that. I don't think it happened all the time, so I don't want to make it sound like it was a constant thing. Maybe half a dozen times at Graceland. One time, Gladys had a mark on her face, right this side of her eye, on the left temple. That's a dangerous place to hit somebody.

Elvis saw it, and he said, "Daddy, you lay a hand on her again, and I'll kill you!" Now that's a pretty harsh thing to say to your daddy. My daddy heard it, and I know he was concerned, afraid Elvis might actually kill Vernon. God, Elvis would have went stark-raving wild if he'd have known about some of those other times. I think it started when Elvis went on the road.

LAMAR FIKE: Nobody's ever talked about this before, and I think it explains why Elvis called home so much. A lot of times, he called not so much so Gladys would know how he was, but to make sure Vernon wasn't abusing her.

Elvis sat down with me one afternoon and he said, "You think I call Mama all the time because I miss her." He said, "Well, that's number one. But number two, if I ever catch Daddy again, I'll fuckin' kill him."

BILLY SMITH: Vernon would not have done it, I don't think, had Gladys been sober. He picked the times when she was drinking, and towards the end of her life, when she was ill. I don't think he was going to try her when she was sober. Vernon was a big man, about two hundred ten or two hundred twenty pounds, 6'1" or 6'2". Taller than Elvis. Elvis wore lifts in his shoes—even his house shoes—to make him look over six feet. But Vernon was pretty good size, and Gladys was maybe 5'6" or 5'7". She was fiery, though, and she could lower him. So Vernon took advantage of her when she was at a weak point. That's what made Elvis really mad. Instead of helping her when she needed it, Vernon got angry with her.

LAMAR FIKE: Elvis and Gladys would gang up on Vernon in a New York second. They perceived him to be weaker than they were. It was always more of a mother-son than a father-son relationship. And from the time Vernon went to prison, it became an Elvis-and-Gladys-against-Vernon situation. But she did things that bugged Elvis, too. I mean, she wouldn't go to bed 'til we came home from a movie. If it was two o'clock in the morning, she'd still be sitting up, and she wouldn't go to bed until Elvis and I went upstairs. They fought about that, but then they'd hug and pet. Elvis would always pat her shoulders.

I'll tell you a classic about Gladys. Elvis gave me a motorcycle, a Harley K-model, shovel-head K. And he bought himself another big Harley, and we were going to drag-race in the drive. The drive was blacktopped all around the back. This was in '57, at Graceland. I popped the clutch loose, and it reared up in the air and did a wheelie, and I couldn't control it. So it went over on me. And when it went over, it knocked Elvis's motorcycle over on me, too. He was able to get off, but I was trapped under both of them, and they were both running and spinning around, knocking the hide off of me and everything else.

Gladys was in the side yard, in the garage, and she came out and stepped in the middle of those motorcycles and pulled both of those damn things off of me—six hundred, eight hundred pounds. Lifted them both up running, and told Elvis to shut 'em off. She said, "Now get up and put those damn things in the garage! I don't want to see 'em anymore." And walked in the house. Elvis looked at me, and I looked at him, and I said, "God Almighty!" He said, "I'll tell you, Lamar, she's as strong as an elephant."

BILLY SMITH: I remember that. Lamar and Elvis got to arguing about which bike was the fastest, and they took off real fast, and in just a few seconds, Lamar lost control, and he went over and hit Elvis's motorcycle. Elvis went over and said, "You big, clumsy, lumbering ox! Hell, I thought you could ride!" It was kind of funny. But Elvis was all the time doing something crazy. And a lot of it was dangerous.

LAMAR FIKE: That same year, '57, Elvis and I were riding down Highway 51, the road in front of Graceland that's now Elvis Presley Boulevard. We would top that hill doing 100 to 110 miles an hour, and we'd reach out and hold hands to see which one would let go first. We'd hit that curve going into the house, and sparks would fly.

This one time, we were out there at one o'clock in the afternoon. We were slowing down to sixty or seventy miles per hour because a mist was falling. And a city bus was about to stop. Elvis turned left, and I tried to turn, and I went down. And the motorcycle slid sideways up under the bus, past the rear end, and buckled the back of the bus. Well, I got hung up, and I couldn't get out. And the bus couldn't move. The wheels were clearing the ground.

Elvis came back around and stopped the motorcycle, and he kicked the stand down. He got down on his knees and he said, "Are you okay?" I said, "Jesus, what do you mean am I okay? I'm pinned under a city bus!" It scared the daylights out of me because I couldn't move. But I was trying not to act scared. I said, "For Christ's sake. Sure I'm all right. Can you get me out of here?"

Well, he started to laugh, and he couldn't quit. I said, "This is not funny. I'm really under here, and this thing could blow up or something." Well, the madder I'd get the more he'd laugh. And when Elvis started laughing, he would just come apart.

A crowd started to gather, and the crowd got around *him*. I'd call out, "Have you got a minute? I'm under a bus here." They called a wrecker to lift the back of the bus, and they pulled me out. The incredible thing is that I really was all right. It only tore the leather off my jacket. When we got home, Gladys just shook her head.

BILLY SMITH: Aunt Gladys's whole life was family. But then, Aunt Gladys had a lot of family to take care of. She seemed to be able to handle most any situation. One time, Gladys and Vernon had given my daddy $200. And Uncle Johnny, who was my daddy's and Gladys's brother, was there. And he got real upset about the $200. He left, and he got to drinking, and he come back pretty well lit. He confronted Aunt Gladys about it, and she said, "Well, Johnny, it was a loan, not a gift. We've loaned you money before, so don't take it personal."

And Uncle Johnny said, in this low, whiny voice, "Yeah, but goddamn, I want my share, too. You all done got big-time money." Aunt Gladys was getting uptight about the whole thing. She said, "Well, I'm not going to give you any right now. You need to go home. You're drinking." Uncle Johnny said, "That's my goddamn right if I want to drink." And he said, "If you want to be like that, you bitch—" And when he called her a bitch, boy, she slapped the fool out of him. Vernon got on the phone and called my daddy. By the time Daddy got there, Uncle Johnny was gone. Aunt Gladys had told him to hit the road. She said, "You come back when you're sober, and if you can't act no better than that, don't you come back at all!"

LAMAR FIKE: Johnny came to the back of the house one time and said he was going to kill everybody in the house. He was drunk, and had a gun, and gave his solemn word he was going to shoot everybody. When Johnny drank, he wouldn't even know where he was.

BILLY SMITH: Aunt Clettes was the same way. When she got drunk, she got mean. That's probably why Elvis didn't want any of the guys to drink. He said that when he went over to his relatives' houses when he was a kid, all he'd see was beer cans. I guess that's right.

LAMAR FIKE: Elvis's whole family were drinkers. They weren't what I call heavy drinkers, but they'd take two drinks and they'd be drunk.

BILLY SMITH: Elvis's relationship with his parents is complicated. He would talk back with his daddy, but never with his mother. It doesn't mean he didn't love his daddy. He certainly did. But his mother was the key figure in the family. In other words, Elvis would listen to her when he would not listen to anybody else. Especially after he became famous.

If she said "no" on something, very seldom would Elvis go against her. For example, Elvis done a little water-skiing. Gladys didn't like it, but she tolerated it. But when he wanted to buy a boat, she said, "Oh, hell, no, you're not going to do that!" They talked and talked. Finally, he said, "I'm old enough, Mama, you can't worry about me constantly!" But he didn't buy one until after she passed away.

MARTY LACKER: On the other hand, Elvis saw his parents as his babies. He called his mother his baby.

BILLY SMITH: "Baby" is a word he liked to use. Elvis was the provider, but Gladys was the protector.

MARTY LACKER: As time went by, Elvis and Vernon reversed roles. Vernon would just strut around like he was king of the hill when Elvis wasn't at home. Whatever he said went, unless you could reach Elvis. And sometimes Elvis would override him, even from California. Vernon was more worried about Elvis losing money and being poor again than anything else. Not for Elvis's sake, you understand. He was afraid he might have to go back to work.

Vernon disliked three quarters of his family because he thought, "You're getting stuff, and you shouldn't be getting it. I should be the only one. Maybe you're even getting something that

I should have." Most of the family was that way. If somebody got a dollar more than the other, they hated his guts.

LAMAR FIKE: Elvis kept that family in line.

MARTY LACKER: One of the main problems between Vernon and Elvis was Vernon's laziness, the fact that he wouldn't work and that Gladys really had to support the family in the early years, in the drapery factory in Memphis and later at St. Joseph's Hospital, as a nurse's aide. Elvis never really forgave Vernon for that.

BILLY SMITH: Elvis set both his parents up in a position where they could receive some money. Gladys got money off of Gladys Music. And Vernon had ten percent of two of the other music publishing companies, Elvis Music, Inc., and Whitehaven Music.

We're getting into business things now, and I don't know all that much about it. I do know that Gladys and Vernon had a separate bank account from Elvis. I'm sure Elvis gave Gladys money. I don't know how much. I just know that she had her own money and that Vernon and Gladys had their own money apart from Elvis. Because aside from the publishing income, Vernon got money from Elvis for taking care of Graceland. That started when they moved in there, in '57. I also know that Vernon had ways of going to the bank and getting money for Elvis, maybe without Elvis knowing.

MARTY LACKER: They had an accountant, of course, but Vernon took care of some of the business himself. After a while, he even became Elvis's business manager. God, that was a joke.

BILLY SMITH: Vernon was the cause of a lot of anger and frustration for Aunt Gladys, but in a way, they were pretty much like any married couple. She still didn't drive, even though Elvis had gone out and bought her a pink Cadillac. So Vernon took her places. Places that didn't cost much money. He was stingy as hell. And she was just the opposite. She was generous, so she would tell him, "Don't be so stingy." And sometimes he would give in. Or she'd say, "Don't be so harsh," because Vernon could be if he wanted to be. But she would do it in a real light way so as not to embarrass him.

LAMAR FIKE: I've often thought about what Vernon and Gladys wanted. Vernon didn't want a whole lot. He wanted what he had—being able to buy his cars, piddling around the house, and not working.

And Gladys wanted, well, not material things, certainly. Elvis was always trying to give her furs and jewelry, and she thought it was foolish. Gladys wanted everything to be simple. She wanted her and Elvis and Vernon to be able to live their lives by themselves. And she wanted Elvis to get married. Wanted him to have children.

MARTY LACKER: I only saw Gladys a few times at Graceland because by the time I started coming back up after the army, she was starting to get sick. She would take a lot of pills and drink some. She stayed in her room mostly. Or she'd stare out the window and dip snuff.

BILLY SMITH: I don't think Aunt Gladys had a best friend, or at least not when she lived at Graceland. She took up with Alberta, the maid, for company. Because Vernon was out a lot. Grandma was there, but she was Vernon's mother. Vernon always struck me as wanting a lot of people around, even though he hated everybody that was around Elvis. But I can never remember Aunt Gladys and Uncle Vernon having that many close friends, even before Elvis became famous. I'm not real sure Vernon would have wanted her to have friends.

LAMAR FIKE: To say that Vernon was "suspicious" of people is a gross understatement. It was practically branded on his cheeks. He didn't trust anybody, and he didn't have any real friends. Everybody called him "Mr. Presley." I was the only one in the group who called him "Vernon."

In Vernon, I saw a man who was bewildered by everything. Deep down, I think he was a good person, and funny. Vernon and I got along, although I don't know if he resented my living there in the house and eating their food. He would always bitch about the damn grocery bills.

BILLY SMITH: After they got Alberta, Gladys continued to cook, but just a little bit. Cooking was a bond she had with Elvis. They loved the same kind of food. Maybe food *was* love in that house.

LAMAR FIKE: Elvis had very strange eating habits. In '56 and '57, he would eat sauerkraut, mashed potatoes and gravy, very crisp bacon, and sliced tomatoes. He would eat the tomatoes with his hands, and then he would crumble up the bacon and put it in the mashed potatoes and take the sauerkraut and gravy and make a mixture of it.

He loved it. He ate it for two or three years—the same meal every day for two or three years. Do you understand what I'm saying? Not the same thing three times a day. The menu for the day had three different meals on it, but he would eat those same three meals every day for months on end. In the mornings, he'd have eggs that were fried so hard you couldn't drive a nail through the yoke. Or he'd have an omelet. But he would eat the same thing over and over again. He'd eat it 'til he couldn't stand to see it. Then he'd quit eating it for a long time. About eight months before he died, I looked up one day and he was eating mashed potatoes and gravy, sliced tomatoes, and he was crumbling up burnt bacon. He said, "I had a taste for it."

He used to like peanut butter and toast with butter on it. It was so goddarn rich, it would just kill you. I see the recipe in these Elvis books now, and it says he fried 'em in two table-spoons of butter. Heck, he'd have Gladys fry 'em in a whole stick of butter. Or he'd want mashed banana on it and sometimes three or four strips of crisp bacon. God, he loved bacon. He could eat a pound or a pound and a half at a time. But it had to be burned almost beyond recognition. He loved burnt bacon and mustard on rye toast.

And he loved cheeseburgers and hamburgers, of course. But mainly he just liked typical Southern cooking. Everything had to be fried. Or he'd eat vegetables cooked in animal fat. He'd eat enough field peas to fill this room up. And corn bread and milk. Vernon and I used to fight over the corn bread. We'd put it in our milk. Or we'd cut up onions and put the onions and the corn bread in buttermilk. That's just how you're supposed to eat in the country, especially in the South. No wonder they took my gallbladder out.

MARTY LACKER:· That may be Southern food. But Albert Goldman wrote stuff that perpetuates that stereotypical thinking about Southern people. He said that Elvis sat in bed and grabbed a hunk of mashed potatoes—gravy and all—and stuck it in his mouth and used no utensils.

That made me furious. Because he didn't write it in a way that suggested this happened once. There might have been one time when he was blown out of his skull [on drugs], sitting in the middle of his bed, when he just stuck his hand in and grabbed some mashed potatoes and put 'em in his mouth. But Goldman wrote it as if that's the way he ate all the time. That's the biggest piece of junk I've ever read in my life.

LAMAR FIKE: I don't know where Albert got that. Elvis did eat tomatoes with his hands, but he didn't regularly eat mashed potatoes that way. And he ate a lot of other stuff with all five fingers and a thumb on it. He didn't cut a sandwich, for example. He picked it up and held it in both hands. Like you were going to try to wrestle it away from him.

And he had a thing about drinking coffee from a cup. Most people would drink from, say, the middle of the cup, with the handle on the far right. He would put his mouth right next to the handle. You can see him do it in *King Creole*, in that kitchen scene with Jan Shepard, the actress who plays his sister. He holds his toast with both hands in that scene, too.

I asked him about the cup, and he told me, "I've always had a thing about people putting their hands on stuff." I guess he figured nobody had drunk on that part of it. It probably goes back to him having his own silverware when he was a kid, silverware that nobody touched.

That's the reason Elvis wouldn't go out and eat—because he had atrocious table manners. I mean, we used to cut his steak up for him.

MARTY LACKER: Any meat that Elvis ate had to be almost burnt. He didn't like to see any red or any blood. He'd gag at the sight of a pink hamburger. Or he'd throw it away or throw it at somebody.

We were doing a movie one time—I forget which one—and one of the crew members was a big muscular guy who always shaved his head. He used to eat raw steaks. When the catering truck came around, he'd order a steak and say, "Throw it on the grill." And as soon as it hit the grill he'd say, "Okay, turn it over." Then he'd say, "Pick it up," and he'd eat it. We showed that to Elvis one time, and he got the shivers.

LAMAR FIKE: You could wear it for shoes, his meat would be so tough. I'd eat a steak medium rare, and he'd see me, and he'd say, "Damn you." I said, "I can't eat it like you, for Christ's sake. It's just horrible." And I'd have my eggs over easy, and I'd break the yellow, and he'd go nuts. He hated fish, by the way. When Gladys was pregnant, the smell of fish made her sick. I guess she told him that, so Elvis hated fish all his life.

BILLY SMITH: Aunt Gladys worried that Elvis didn't eat right on the road or even in Hollywood. But then she worried about everything. It got worse as he got more famous. She missed him, and she resented that he was gone so much. She felt robbed— thought she was losing him, to the fans, to Colonel. But she also loved it that he had done something with his life.

LAMAR FIKE: Gladys always said she couldn't stand to see Elvis in the grave before Vernon. She wanted to die before both of them. She used to say, "You know, Lamar, I never can see Elvis in a casket." She said, "I couldn't stand to see him die." So she said, "I want to go before him." She was very proud of Elvis, but his stardom scared her. The fans drove her to distraction, beating on the doors and crowding around him, tearing his clothes off. She thought they were trying to hurt him. It drove her over the edge.

I think Elvis's fame killed her. No doubt in my mind. If it didn't kill her, it sure as heck hastened her death.

CHAPTER 15

THE TILT

On March 24, 1958, Elvis arrived at the Memphis draft board modeling a wan smile and a loud plaid sports jacket over a striped shirt. In his possession was precisely what the induction notice said to bring—a razor, a comb, a toothbrush, and enough money to last two weeks. Vernon, Gladys, Lamar, Cliff, Anita, and Colonel Parker, who handed out balloons stamped "King Creole," went along, for moral support as much as company.

Once inside, Elvis stepped forward to take his place with the country boys, rednecks, poor whites, luckless blacks, urban trash, and down-on-their-luck hopefuls who typically made up the army of the fifties. Even in the equalizing regime of the service, Elvis stood out: He was placed in charge of the other fourteen recruits for the bus trip to Fort Chaffee, Arkansas. Before departing, Elvis kissed his weeping mother and gazed fondly at the '58 Cadillac limousine he'd also leave behind. "Goodbye, you long, black son of a bitch," he said with a wave, and then climbed aboard the bus to begin life as Private Presley.

At a press conference on the afternoon of March 26, the army announced that Elvis would be stationed at Fort Hood, Texas, for his eight weeks of basic training.

As with every other of Elvis's press conferences, the questions were more like softball tosses, which Elvis sometimes ignored and other times knocked over the back fence. What if rock 'n' roll should die out while he was in the service? "I'll starve to death," Elvis quipped. But the question struck a nerve—that was precisely what troubled him, even as he proudly reported that he'd now sold 25 million singles.

How did Elvis feel about being sent to Europe? "I'd like to go to Paris. And look up Brigitte Bardot." And maybe record an Italian song? "I don't know if I could cut the mustard."

Elvis hoped to go to school in the army, he said, in case something "happened to the entertainment business." Or maybe he'd go to college when he returned stateside, "but it's according to what the future holds for me." He wanted to keep busy, he said. "I don't like to sit alone too much and think."

Once he arrived at Fort Hood, the new recruit received 15,000 letters a week, all from fans pledging not to forget him during his tour of duty. And all forwarded to Colonel's office in Madison, Tennessee, for reply. "The people never stopped coming to Graceland, thousands of 'em, all the time Elvis was in the service," Vester remembered. "Travis was on the gate, and he walked them up around the house all day long."

In Killeen, Texas, Elvis rented a house rather than live on the base, claiming he needed to care for his parents, who would soon arrive. "On the weekends, he'd come to our home in Waco," recalled Eddie Fadal, a disc jockey friend from Elvis's early touring days. "We even went to the expense of building a room similar to Elvis's own suite at Graceland onto our house for Elvis to relax in.

"On the surface, he was happy. But behind the facade of a soldier, Elvis was very sad . . . about so many things—giving up a career which he loved so dearly . . . and sad simply because of the added anxiety and stress overseas duty would cause his beloved mother. The first time he called her from Texas, he did it from our house. He'd been at Fort Hood for two weeks, and he hadn't had a chance to phone. When he got her on the line, all he said was, 'Mama . . .' And, apparently, she said, 'Elvis . . .' And from then on, for a whole hour, they were crying and moaning on the telephone—hardly a word was spoken."

BILLY SMITH: As soon as Elvis got the draft notice, God, Aunt Gladys got real upset. She was sure her baby was going to get killed, even though there was no war going on. To her, Germany was enemy territory. And it would stay that way, even though everybody told her how American the base was.

LAMAR FIKE: The 2nd Armored Division unit went straight to Germany after basic training to replace the 3rd Armored Division that was serving in Europe. Elvis was already planning on taking the family with him, even Grandma. But Gladys said, "I'm not going with him to a foreign country. I can't do it." You're talking about a woman who had a third-grade education. I remember she said, "Lamar, I can't see myself away from Sonny Boy that long. But I just can't go with him."

BILLY SMITH: She was taking diet pills, and she was drinking. She tried to hide it from Elvis, but she couldn't.

MARTY LACKER: Elvis knew his mother drank. He knew everything she did. Even if he wasn't with her.

BILLY SMITH: As a teenager, I could tell when she was inebriated. But she usually stayed in her room. She was not one to openly drink, not even with family. I guess because she didn't want to be like the rest of them. I wouldn't necessarily call her an alcoholic. Now, my daddy was closer to being an alcoholic than she was. The biggest majority of the time she would go without it, but it seemed like when she got worried, she clung to that real quick.

LAMAR FIKE: Right before we left for the service, Gladys was getting bloated. The menopause was driving her absolutely screwloose, and she'd take those amphetamines, and she'd wash 'em down with beer. One minute she'd be happy, and the next minute she'd be a raving maniac. And she would be hot one minute, cold the next.

BILLY SMITH: One reason Aunt Gladys took the diet pills was because she wanted to look good for Elvis in her pictures. She didn't want Elvis to be embarrassed by her size. And Colonel was all the time telling her how to dress, and how to act in public.

LAMAR FIKE: When it came time for Elvis to go to basic training in Texas, Elvis wanted Alan to go with him and then just go on to Germany with him, too. But Alan's mother wouldn't let him go because she didn't want him over in Germany. It was that Jewish thing. So Elvis said, "Lamar, I want you to go with me." I said, "Okay, fine."

When Elvis went down for his physical, I tried to get in the army, too. Because of my weight—I guess I was still about three hundred pounds then—they tried to get me clearance through the surgeon general. But the surgeon general wouldn't give it. So I just went along with Elvis anyway. I brought the [Lincoln] Mark II to Killeen, checked into a motel, and hid in that son of a bitch for a week. I was scared to go out because the Colonel had called me and said, "Don't talk to anybody. He's not supposed to have any of his guys with him." The press was all over us, trying to find out who I was. I was the only one with him in Texas 'til Red came back from the Marine Corp.

BILLY SMITH: I think there was a lot about Gladys's health we didn't know. She was like Elvis. Regardless of how bad she might be hurting, she never let him know. She'd say, "I'm all right. I'll be fine." But just before she went out there to Fort Hood, and they got the trailer and all, she just seemed withdrawn. And worried.

LAMAR FIKE: It started when Gladys came to Killeen in mid-June. At first, we lived in a three-bedroom trailer parked outside of Fort Hood. But people wouldn't leave us alone. So we rented the mayor's house. And Gladys started getting sick. One day, I looked at her, and she was getting a yellow tinge to her eyes and her skin. And I went to Elvis and I said, "You need to call a doctor. Something's wrong, and I mean it." But he didn't want to hear about it.

BILLY SMITH: She had yellow jaundice. Whether it was just from the drinking, I don't know. But her liver was giving out.

LAMAR FIKE: Gladys and Vernon started fighting as soon as they got down there. Fights usually happened early in the morning, in the kitchen. One morning she jumped on him, and she said, "You steercotted [castrated] bastard!" I turned around to Elvis and I said, "That's the funniest line I've heard this year."

Not everything was unpleasant for her down there, though. We took her to Eddie Fadal's house in Waco for the Fourth of July to eat hamburgers. She seemed to enjoy that. Elvis met Eddie in '55 or early '56, back when he was real hot in Texas, before he broke nationally. Eddie had a theater, and he was a big fan. And he would come and take Elvis to eat and stuff like that. Then, when Elvis was in the army, and we were at Fort Hood, Eddie would come up and bring pies and stuff. We would go over to his house and stay overnight or the weekends because it was close to Killeen.

Alan said Colonel told him he thought Eddie was a homosexual and wanted Elvis to watch out for him. Elvis thought that was nuts. Eddie didn't require anything of Elvis. He'd been a disc jockey at one time, and he was real nice to him. He was older and had a family, and we would go visit them on Lasker Street there in Waco. It was his old family home, and it was like a home away from home for us. Later on, I ended up marrying Eddie's daughter, Janice, and living in that house.

Eddie used to come up to Graceland once in a while. But Eddie was never really a strong member of the group. He was an outsider we let in every once in a while. He was a good person. He just died in '94, of a heart attack.

BILLY SMITH: I remember Anita Wood went down to Texas a couple of times. I was jealous. Because everybody seemed to be going except me.

LAMAR FIKE: Elvis thought Gladys would get better. But she just kept getting worse. I kept telling him, "We've got to get her back home." We got in a big fight about it. I said, "If you don't let her go to the hospital, buddy, she's going to die right here on you." But Elvis wouldn't let her go.

Red was down there then, and he and I sat there and preached to him. It was like trying to peel a Band-Aid off a potato. You just couldn't get it off. Then she got so yellow that they finally called a doctor. He told 'em what he thought was going on, and after that, Elvis begged her to go to the hospital. The doctor thought she ought to go back to Memphis. We took her to Temple, Texas, and put her on the train. This was on August 8. She didn't want to go. She knew she was dying. She started that stuff again about wanting to die before Elvis and Vernon.

Right after they got back to Memphis, Vernon called me and said, "Lamar, you need to tell Elvis to get up here as quick as possible—tomorrow if he can." I said, "He's out in the field." So I got in the jeep and went out in the field and got him. We came back in, and he went in to get an emergency leave. I went with him. This captain was sitting behind the desk. Elvis said, "I need an emergency leave, sir, my mother is dying." And the captain said, "Is she actually dead yet?"

Elvis stopped, and his jaw tightened up, and he said, "I want you to understand who I am and what I'm getting ready to do." He said, "My name is Elvis Presley. I sell a lot of records, and I'm a star." He said, "I've played your little army games. I've shot your guns, and I've rolled your tanks. But that's my mother."

He said, "If I don't get a pass in my hand in the next five minutes, you can stick all this stuff up your ass. I'm going AWOL, and it's not going to look good for you when I call a press conference and say, 'The reason I went AWOL is because they wouldn't give me emergency leave to see my mother.' Now, how does that grab you?"

It sounded like movie dialogue, but he actually said it. And son, there was some fast moving. That captain jumped up from behind that desk and went to the major's office, and he was white as a sheet.

Elvis turned around, and I said, "Are you serious about that?" He said, "I'm going AWOL. Get the car ready, charter a plane, and come back and pick me up. We're going to Memphis." And that captain came back in with the pass in his hand, and he said, "You can go ahead and go." That was August 11 or 12.

BILLY SMITH: Aunt Gladys had acute, severe hepatitis, but a heart attack actually killed her. Elvis didn't want an autopsy, so I guess we'll never know what brought it on. She didn't seem to be in that bad a shape. Because the night before she died, we had gone up to Methodist Hospital to see her. Elvis said, "Mama, do you want me to stay the night?" And she said, "No, son, everything's okay." He said, "Well, I might go to the movie, and then I'll come back by here." She said, "No, just go on to the movie now, and come back up here tomorrow. If I need anything, Daddy will call you." So he kissed her and left. She would never worry him. That's how strong a mother's love is. I don't think Elvis had any idea she would die. He really thought she'd get better.

LAMAR FIKE: Gladys was going fast. They drained something like a gallon and a half of fluid off of her two days before she died. August 13 was a Wednesday. God, what a day and night that was! That day, I carried Grandma, or Miss Minnie, home, and I came back to the hospital and Gladys was deathly ill. I didn't get to see her. And Elvis said, "Lamar, she's asked about you two or three times." I said, "Elvis, you've got me running my brains out here." He said, "Come with me in the morning and we'll go see her, 'cause she's going to be all right." I'd already talked to the doctor. I said to Billy or somebody, "She's not going to make it through the night."

BILLY SMITH: Gladys always had that ESP about Elvis. Well, the night before she died, he had it about her. He didn't want to be alone, and he asked me to spend the night in his room. I told him I had to go home and ask my mama. He said, "Well, run on out and ask her and come back."

Elvis didn't like for men to sleep in the same bed with him. So I made a pallet at the foot of his bed with a couple of blankets and a pillow. For just a few minutes, we watched TV. And then he thought he could go to sleep. So we turned the TV off, and we talked a minute, and then we both drifted off.

He never really went to sleep, but I think he dozed off a bit. Then he raised up and said, "Something's wrong." I said, "What do you mean?" He said, "I don't know. All of a sudden I got an eerie feeling."

Nothing else was said, and he laid back down. And it wasn't too long after that when the phone rang downstairs. This was a little after three A.M. Everybody had gone home. And Lamar was out somewhere. Elvis said, "It's late. Maybe you might ought to go down there and get it." And I said, "All right."

When I answered, I could hear Vernon. He said, "Oh, God—" He was just sobbing. He said, "Tell Elvis . . . " Then he really broke up. I don't know if the nurse took the phone from him or if he handed it to her, but she got on, and I could hear him crying in the background.

She told me her name, and then she said, "Tell Elvis he needs to get up here quick as he can. His mother has taken a turn for the worse."

I run upstairs, and all the while I was choosing not to believe that Gladys was dead. I didn't know how to tell Elvis. I got up there, and I said, "That was the nurse at the hospital." And he jumped up real quick. I said, "She said to tell you that you might ought to get up there, that your mom is starting to slip."

And he said, "Oh, my God! No, Mama, no!" I think he knew. But he didn't want to believe it. And he put on his white shoes. He had on a pair of white pants, and a white ruffled shirt, and no socks.

We run downstairs, and we jumped into the Lincoln Mark II, and we tore out of there like all hell had broke loose. The whole time we were driving, he said, "Oh, God, I'm scared! I'm afraid I've lost my mama!" When we got to Methodist Hospital, he didn't even stop the car. He just left the son of a bitch running. In drive now. And he jumped out. The car just went right on over the breaker. That's the only thing that stopped it. He didn't care.

I shoved it into park real quick and got out. I just left the keys in it, with the motor still running and the lights on and both doors open. Elvis wasn't waiting for shit. I was just a kid—fifteen, I guess—and I was going at almost a dead run to keep up with him.

We got upstairs, and as Elvis turned the corner, Vernon and a nurse were coming up the hall from Gladys's room. Vernon reached out his arms and said, "Oh, God, son!" And he broke up. When he did, Elvis just run towards him, and they met in the middle.

Vernon said, "God, son, she's gone!" And all the color drained out of Elvis's face. He was white as a sheet. He started to sob this kind of unearthly sound. I can't really tell you what it was like. But it just went through me.

It was a sad thing to see them hurt that way. Even as a teenager, I felt their hurt. They cried for a little while, and then Elvis said, "I want to see her. Where is she?" And they didn't want him to. Vernon kept saying, "No, son, don't go in there." And the nurse said, "She's still in her room. But it might not be a good idea to see her." Elvis said, "No, I've got to see my mama!" I guess he had to see that she was really gone before he would accept it. So he went in, and I went with him.

I remember Gladys still had on her little pink nightgown. She'd had an oxygen tent pulled over her, but they had it turned back. She had a restful look about her.

Elvis leaned over and put his hand under the back of her head and pressed his cheek to hers. He was crying and stroking her head, and he was patting her on the stomach. I didn't understand everything he was saying to her. But I heard him say, "Oh, God, Satnin', not now. Not when I can give you everything in the world."

I backed up, and I thought, "Oh, God! Man, this is not happening." I'd look at him for a minute, and then I'd look at Vernon, and then at Aunt Gladys. I can still see his face, and I can see hers. Elvis was just steadily petting and talking to her. Finally, Uncle Vernon and the nurse got him and said, "Come on out." We went down the hall to the waiting room. By that time, other people had got up there. Every time somebody new would walk in, Elvis would just break up all over again. His world had just been snatched from him.

LAMAR FIKE: In the wee hours of the fourteenth, I drove up the drive to the house in that '58 black Cadillac limousine. The wind was blowing, and I saw the doors were open. Grandma came out, and she said, "Gladys is dead, we need to go to the hospital." We shot over there and that elevator opened, and I've never heard such crying and screaming and hollering in my life. It was unbelievable. This wailing. Almost like wolves. It made me shudder. I came around the corner and Elvis was walking towards me, and he said, "Lamar, Satnin' isn't here." And I said, "I know, Elvis, I know."

BILLY SMITH: I read someplace that the night she died, the last time Elvis was up to the room, she said, "Son, when you come back tomorrow, make sure the other patients have these flowers." That's probably the truth because that sounds like her. But Elvis probably took it to mean, "Just make sure these flowers are distributed to some of the other patients," because she'd gotten so many, you know. She was talking good, and he thought she was getting better, and it wouldn't be long 'til she was out of the hospital. Then all of a sudden, BANG! It was just such a shocker.

LAMAR FIKE: Vernon said he was asleep there in the room with her, and she woke him up, struggling for breath. He got to her as quick as he could, and raised her head, and called a nurse to get the doctor. They put her in an oxygen tent, but it was too late. She'd gone into cardiac arrest.

Elvis and I sat down and talked before we left the hospital. And as we were going out the door to get in the limousine, the ambulance was pulling out with Gladys's body. That was another trauma. He wouldn't let her go for the longest time. He was sobbing, saying, "She's all we ever lived for." And, "She was always my best girl."

When we got home, Elvis went to the telephone and made a few calls, so people would know about the funeral. He told Eddie Fadal, "I've lost the only person I ever really loved."

MARTY LACKER: You know what was weird? Red's daddy passed away the same day. Red had two funerals to go to when he got home.

BILLY SMITH: Elvis wanted Aunt Gladys to lie in state there at Graceland, right between the music room and the living room. That son of a bitch Goldman wrote that when they brought her home, Elvis whipped out his comb and fooled with her hair and massaged her feet in the casket. That's not true. Or I never saw it. Let me put it that way. I heard him say things like, "Baby, I'm going to miss you." And, "Wake up now, Mama, and talk to Elvis." He petted her, even in the casket. That's true. And he might have arranged her hair or maybe felt her hands and all. Because in a way death fascinated him. And yet it scared him, too. But most of the time, he just sat up on the couch and looked at her. He sat up almost all night and just stared.

I don't think he even said anything, not even to his daddy. The times they did talk, they tried not to talk about Gladys being dead. They talked around it—about what they needed to do or how she would want something. The night before they actually brought her home, they talked about what she was going to be buried in, which was a crepelike lavender blue dress.

LAMAR FIKE: It just killed me when she died. It broke my heart. But, God, Elvis . . . they brought her back to Graceland, and he got nearly hysterical. Started that wailing again. It made my skin crawl. When people came to pay their respects, he'd take 'em over to the casket and talk. Like, "Here's Eddie, Mama. You remember him. You met him down in Texas."

BILLY SMITH: There was no wailing out that I heard. If there was, Elvis done it in private. He was pretty tore up. At one point, he got up from the couch and went out on the porch, and he sat on the steps there, next to one of the marble lions, and put his arm on his knee, and his face kind of on his arm, and just cried something awful. I followed him out there, but I didn't know what to say or do. I wanted to go over and hug him and say, "God, it will be all right." But I felt like it would only make things worse, so I just let him be.

I can never get that out of my mind. I remember it so vividly because Elvis was my idol. Just being with him was such a thrill. I wanted to protect him, and make sure nothing like that ever happened to him. I hated to see him hurt.

LAMAR FIKE: They had the service for her, where the Blackwood Brothers sang and Reverend [James] Hamill officiated, and then they took her over to the cemetery. And when it came time to lower the casket into the ground, Elvis jumped up and hung on to the coffin. He was saying stuff like "Everything I have is gone!" And then he got totally hysterical. He said, "Goodbye, darling. I love you so much. I lived my whole life just for you!" And he went on and on about how he couldn't be without her. I had to pull him off the casket. It took two or three of us to get him off. That was a pretty bad scene, God. He screamed, "Please don't take my baby away! She's not dead. She's just sleeping."

BILLY SMITH: He broke down crying, but he didn't drape and cling to the casket. Elvis had more class than that. Even though he was hurting the worst in his life, he wouldn't have done that. But he did say things, and put his arm around the casket, and then they lowered it down. There just wasn't no hangin' on.

LAMAR FIKE: All in all, it was a pretty civilized affair. I mean, the fans had crowded around the Memphis Funeral Home like it was some kind of circus opening. Vernon wanted to let 'em all parade by to see the body. But, thank God, I talked him out of that.

BILLY SMITH: The shock of Aunt Gladys's death was bad enough, but then we got another one when her will was read. Uncle Vernon had altered it. I'm almost sure of that. Because Aunt Gladys had told two or three people that they'd be taken care of if she died. She said, "If anything ever happens to me, there's a provision in the will for my brothers and my sisters." And she told Vernon what she wanted to leave them. And it was left up to the executor of her estate, who, I know, was Vernon.

But as soon as she passed away, you didn't hear no more about it. I'm sure Vernon told Elvis, "We'll take care of the family. There's no need to put out the money." So either it was never done or Vernon changed the will. And Elvis was too out of it when she died to pay attention to stuff like that.

LAMAR FIKE: Four weeks after Gladys died, Elvis was shipped overseas. He never had time to get over her death. He carried her damn nightgown around for weeks. Wouldn't put it down for anything. Slept with it in the chair. And cried all the time. All the time. He probably needed grief counseling, although nobody talked about that back then. When we got over to Germany, he was still reeling, still trying to put it together.

When you chronicle the demise of Elvis Presley, you have to realize that the tilt started when Gladys died. That was the most devastating thing that ever happened to him. He would never be the same.

CHAPTER 16

GERMANY

BILLY SMITH: Right before Elvis left Memphis to rejoin his unit at Fort Hood, he went to Gladys's bedroom door and said, "I got to go, Mama," and broke down right there. Of course, Gladys had been dead and in the ground for ten days or so. It like to killed him.

The troop train that carried him to the Military Ocean Terminal in Brooklyn, New York, had to stop on a spur track in Memphis. I went to the train to see him with my mama and daddy. The sergeant wouldn't let Elvis get off the train, but he let him come to the door. Some of the guys came, like George and Alan. Elvis was really glad to see us. We told him we'd be waiting for him to get home because we were trying to act jolly. I climbed up on the train and told him how much I was going to miss him, and he leaned down and hugged me and said, "Take care, little fella, and stay in touch. I'll be talking to you." We both got tears in our eyes, and then he said, "Don't forget me while I'm gone."

He was somewhat scared. He knew he had an obligation to go, but he didn't know how the other troops were going to act towards him. He felt he had to live up to an image and be this certain person. In the real early days of his career, guys wanted to jump him and fight because of who he was, and he thought that might happen in the army.

We talked about it a little bit, but I was fifteen, and I couldn't exactly give him advice. I know he worried about how his absence was going to affect his popularity. That June, he'd gone to Nashville and cut "I Got Stung," and "A Big Hunk O' Love," and "A Fool Such as I," and some other songs, so he could have records out while he was gone.

LAMAR FIKE: Before he went in the service, Elvis told the press he was looking forward to being in the army. That wasn't true. He put it off as long as he could. He hated it because it took away everything he had going for him, including being a star.

MARTY LACKER: Elvis was a very promilitary guy, a guy who was in ROTC in high school. But when he came back from Germany, he told me, "Man, that was one of the worst things I've ever done." But I think he liked the fact that he made a name for himself because he didn't shirk any responsibility. But he didn't like the army at all. He could have taken the easy way out and gone into Special Services, which is what the army wanted him to do. But Colonel Parker said, "No, you go in there, and you do your service exactly like everybody else."

LAMAR FIKE: Colonel always acted like he didn't want Elvis singled out, so the public would think he was the patriotic boy-next-door. But the real reason Colonel kept him from entertaining the troops was because Elvis didn't get paid and Colonel didn't want people to see Elvis free. Not even on a USO show, although he and Charlie Hodge did a serviceman's variety show onboard the *U.S.S. General Randall.* That's where he first hooked up with Charlie, you know. Charlie was his bunkmate. They hit it off because Charlie was a musician, too. Charlie sang with the Foggy River Boys on "The Red Foley Show." On that USO show, Elvis played piano and Charlie emceed and did a little comedy.

I remember Bob Hope sent people to Elvis to try to get him to do his Christmas tour. And Elvis turned it down. He was in Grafenwöhr, near the Czechoslovakian border, up to his armpits in snow with the 32nd Tank Battalion, but he had to turn it down because Colonel thought, "Why should he work for the army for nothing when he gets $50,000 a night?" That's like when the White House wanted Elvis to come sing for President Nixon. Colonel asked if it paid. Somebody told him, "The performance is compensated by the honor of being asked." So Colonel said, "Let 'em pay like everybody else or Elvis doesn't go."

MARTY LACKER: I didn't have much contact with Elvis while he was in the army. I saw him just before he went in and then again after basic training in June of '58, after his Nashville recording session. I wrote him one letter in Germany and sent him a magazine, *Modern Screen,* because they did a story on me as program director of this radio station in Knoxville. When I went up there, the radio station was ninth or tenth in the market, and six months after we took it over, we were number one.

When Elvis went over to Germany, he took some of the guys with him. He didn't ask me to go, maybe because he knew I'd already been over there.

LAMAR FIKE: Elvis docked at Bremerhaven, West Germany, and all these screaming fans were waiting, trying to see him while he boarded the troop train. He was going to Ray Caserne, Friedberg, which was the home of the U.S. 7th Army. Just as soon as he got there, they had a press conference and told everybody they assigned him to Company D, 1st Battalion, 32nd Armor, 3rd Armored Division of the 7th Army. He was going to be a jeep driver for Master Sergeant Ira Jones, the platoon leader. He couldn't drive a jeep for an officer. Just an average soldier, you know. He made it to private first class by the end of November and then specialist fourth class the following June. When he got discharged in March 1960, he was a buck sergeant, but somebody put an extra stripe on his uniform to make him a staff sergeant. I think that uniform was custom-made. I'll lay you money Colonel was behind that.

Elvis was at loose ends the whole time he was in the service, so when he went to Germany, he took Grandma and Vernon and myself and Red. A little later, Cliff came over. Elvis went ahead of us, and we caught up with him the day after he got there.

At first, we moved into Ritter's Park Hotel in Bad Homburg, a resort spa where folks with bad hearts, and respiratory ailments, and other afflictions would come for the thermal baths.

Elvis hadn't been there but about twenty-four hours when we went for a walk in the park—Elvis, Vernon, Red, and I. All these German photographers descended on us like a horde of locusts. They wanted to photograph him with this little sixteen-year-old girl, Margrit Buergin. She couldn't speak English. Elvis would try to talk to her and it was basically impossible. Margrit was a pretty girl, blond. Elvis dated her on and off the whole time he was in Germany, but the heavy stuff lasted about two months. Then he got tired of her and went to somebody else.

BILLY SMITH: Elvis never did write to me from Germany, and in all the time he was over there—nearly two years—I talked to him only twice on the phone. He wrote to George once, and to Alan once, and he wrote to Anita several times. Elvis wrote maybe a dozen letters his whole life.

MARTY LACKER: One of the best-known stories about Elvis in the seventies is about the time he shot out the television when Robert Goulet came on. Everybody thought it was because he didn't like Goulet's style of singing and couldn't stand his voice. But the real reason has to do with Anita.

Anita was a local singer when Elvis met her, but she was hoping to become a bigger singer, maybe an actress. I know she went out to Hollywood to visit Elvis once or twice, and I don't think it was just to see him—I think she was hoping it would lead to something else. When she won her beauty contest, she also won a seven-year recording contract with ABC-Paramount Records, and she made some records for other people.

And when Elvis was over in Germany, she did a number of shows around Memphis, and she also traveled. In fact, she went on tour with Robert Goulet. And she wrote Elvis a letter, and Goulet put a P.S. on it that said in effect, "Hey, Elvis, don't worry! I'm taking pretty good care of Anita!" Understand, there was nothing going on between Anita and Goulet, but Goulet probably figured it would really annoy Elvis to suggest that there was. I remember Elvis telling me this story, and it was obvious that it burnt the shit out of him. And that's the reason that in 1974, when he saw Goulet on television, he pulled a .357 Magnum pistol out and blew the fuckin' TV up. It ate at him all those years.

LAMAR FIKE: We didn't stay at Ritter's Park Hotel more than a day or so. Then we moved into the Hilbert's Park Hotel in Bad Nauheim. While we were there, Ibn Saud, the king of Saudi Arabia, arrived with his thirty-two wives and twenty-five or thirty sons and entourage. Took over the whole hotel. I've got a picture of myself in all that Bedouin gear. Elvis didn't like it that the king attracted all that attention.

We weren't there very long either. Four days. Then we rented the top floor of the Hotel Gruenwald, also in Bad Nauheim. Everybody had his own room. We put in a kitchen and everything. And Elvis rented a separate room downstairs, just for the bags of mail.

The Gruenwald is where I had a little altercation with the old lady downstairs, who was a heart patient, there for the health cure. We'd pretty much roar up there. Red and I broke the bed in Elvis's room by wrestling on it. So we quit that. But Red used to come over to my room, and we'd sit in there and talk and carry on. And the old lady would take her cane and beat it on the ceiling to tell us to be quiet. So I bought a damn cane and started beating it on the floor. It like to drove her crazy. She'd pound on that ceiling like there was no tomorrow, and I'd get the cane and beat it back on the floor like there was no tonight. It was hilarious.

We were still there at Christmas. God, that was dismal. It was Elvis's first Christmas without Gladys. We had a tree set up, but Elvis couldn't get the spirit. We tried to make the best of it. We gave presents to each other, and went through the motions, but it didn't seem like Christmas. We talked about Gladys all the time. He'd say, "Remember when Mama did this?" I'd say, "Yeah," and we'd both start laughing about it. We'd remember how she'd get mad and how she loved to go out and feed the chickens. Really sad.

BILLY SMITH: Elvis told me about being in that hotel for the first Christmas. The guys bought some fireworks to cheer him up. Without really thinking, Elvis blasted the German civilians from the balcony of the hotel. The hotel manager didn't like that too much, and Elvis and the guys had already been reprimanded for doing other crazy things, like having water fights in the halls.

Finally, one day, they were having a shaving cream fight, and Elvis locked himself in his room. Well, Red put a paper under the door and set it on fire to smoke him out. The smoke came out in the hallway, and some of the older people there thought the whole building was on fire. After that, they were asked to get the heck out.

LAMAR FIKE: We moved out of the Gruenwald Hotel into Frau Pieper's house at Goethestrasse 14. This was a five-bedroom, three-story, white stucco place, with a white picket fence. That's where Elvis lived the rest of the time he was in Germany. He never did actually stay on the base. So nobody really knew what we did. Germany was like the lost years of Elvis. Had Jesus lived in a later time, and the twelve disciples been around, they would have been rocking just like we were.

On a typical day, Elvis would get up at four-thirty in the morning. Red and I would get up, and we'd go downstairs. Grandma would be up cooking breakfast. We'd make sure Elvis got dressed on time. He always looked the ideal soldier because Red and I kept his brass and his boots spit-shined. He had about eight or ten pairs of boots and probably a hundred uniforms, a hundred shirts, a hundred pants. He'd go to the PX and buy them—hell, he was making $400,000 a month when he went in there, and basic soldier pay was $83 a month, up from $78 at Fort Hood. I think he was up to $122 a month when he was discharged.

He would win "Best-Dressed Soldier" all the time. I told him, "You ought to give that medal to Red and me." He loved that. He'd come in for lunch and go back out in the field in fresh-pressed fatigues. And boy, it would drive them crazy.

In the mornings, Elvis would have somebody come by in a jeep and pick him up and carry him over to the post, which was about fifteen kilometers away. And he usually stayed gone during the day and came back during the evening. We put a sign out in front of the house that translated to AUTOGRAPHS BETWEEN 7:30 AND 8:00 P.M. ONLY.

We'd go into town, walk around and see the sights, or whatever. And at night, if Elvis would be on maneuvers, Red and I would go down to the beer halls and drink. And Red would beat the shit out of four or five Germans on a regular night.

Frau Pieper was a bitch and a half. She lived in a room off the kitchen. She wouldn't get out of the house, so we rented the whole place for $800 a month, which was about five times the going rate. She was an absolute maniac. She used to run us crazy, and we drove her crazy right back. I threw a firecracker under her bed one night. We just did everything to try to get rid of her, but we never could. Actually, I think she had the hots for Vernon. God, she was horrible. She's got to be dead now because she was sixty-something then. I'd say she's dead or turned into something good to eat, one of the two.

She and Grandma would get in these arguments. Grandma

was speaking English, and Frau Pieper was speaking German, and they acted like they understood each other. Grandma cussed all the time. Here was this old woman cussing a blue streak, and Elvis and I would just lose our breath laughing because it was hilarious. She put Frau Pieper down, and cussed her out, and called her every name in the book. Every other word was a cuss word. Grandma would get cantankerous as hell. Frau Pieper mouthed off to her one day, and Grandma threw a skillet at her. She missed her that time, but later on she decked her.

BILLY SMITH: I hear Grandma worked her over pretty good. And when Elvis came in, Grandma got to him first. Since Frau Pieper didn't speak English, she didn't know what Grandma had told him. She tried to tell him what Grandma had done to her, and Elvis pretended to sympathize. He was petting her, saying, "Well, it'll be all right. You got your butt beat, didn't you?" Frau Pieper thought he was taking up for her. She was nodding and smiling, and he kept on petting her, and all the while he was saying, "That's right, you old bag, Grandma knocked the shit out of you, and you probably deserved it."

LAMAR FIKE: Ordinarily, Grandma was a very quiet woman. She basically just dipped snuff and stayed in her room. Elvis would give her a $10 bill and she'd keep it for five years. Back in Memphis, she decorated her room with all the stuffed animals the fans sent. Looked like a toy store. In the latter years, she moved into Gladys and Vernon's old bedroom.

Grandma was a funny person. Tall and skinny. Wore sunglasses night and day. The light hurt her eyes. I liked her. I called her "Miss Minnie" at first, and then I started calling her "Grandma." Elvis would kid her. He'd cuss, and she'd cuss back at him.

Vernon acted sort of indifferent to her. There was no reverence there. It was "Mama this and Mama that," but no affection or respect. So Elvis was her world, and she adored him. After Gladys, she was the only person who could cook Elvis's breakfast. She'd get sick, and she'd still get up and cook. Grandma became his mother. That's why he brought her to Germany, because he had to have a connection. He used to sit by her bed over there in Germany by the hours.

One time, Grandma was sick for a week. So Elvis would come
in my room at three o'clock in the morning and lie down on the bed
and say, "How you doin'?" I'd say, "Elvis, you've got to be out of
here at six A.M.!" It didn't matter. He had to have somebody to talk
to. He just wanted you to listen. I'd make two or three comments,
and he'd say, "I'm tired of this shit!" and get up and go to bed.

MARTY LACKER: This stuff about Elvis being a regular soldier
. . . he was like everybody else during the daytime and when he
was out on field trips. But at the other times, he wasn't like
everybody else. He lived in a house off the base. There were
women all over the place. Cars—he bought a used BMW 507, a
sport coupe. Of course, he totaled it on the Autobahn on New
Year's Day. The rumor got out that he was killed, so he donated a
pint of blood to the Red Cross to show he was still alive. But he
was not a deprived soldier, by any means.

LAMAR FIKE: I think BMW lent him that car. He thought he was
buying it, but it turned out he signed a leasing agreement. They
let him have it cheap because he went to the factory and they
took pictures of him there.

We got another car after that. It was a 300 Mercedes sedan,
four-door. Vernon wrecked it. Elvis had dated this little girl,
Elisabeth Stefaniak. She was eighteen, a German by birth, but
her stepfather was an army sergeant named Raymond
McCormick. Elisabeth was a companion to Elvis. That wasn't a
real romance. She took care of all the fan mail, and she could
speak German and write it. She was very fluent. And she would
translate for everybody. She was more like a secretary.

Anyway, Vernon and Elisabeth were coming back from
Frankfurt. Vernon would go to the PX there and buy groceries
because you could get them so cheap. And somehow the right
front tire went off the Autobahn, and the car went clean across it
and flipped over on its top. Elvis and I rushed out there, and
Vernon and Elisabeth both were all right, but the car was gone.
Elvis ended up bringing Elisabeth back to Memphis with him to
work in the office. But she married a guy named Rex Mansfield,
who was in Elvis's unit and who was the closest friend Elvis had
at that time. That was before he got so tight with Charlie Hodge
and Joe Esposito.

MARTY LACKER: Joe met Elvis in the army in '59. He wasn't in Elvis's outfit, but they were stationed at the same place. Joe was a clerk, a bookkeeper, I think. Lamar and Red met him at a bar. And then they introduced him to Elvis. Joe was a bit of a loan shark. He'd loan all these soldiers money at 100 percent premium. Joe was an operator. He's not a stupid guy. He's a pretty good hustler.

Everybody called him "Diamond Joe." He's Italian, of course. Joe's from Chicago. And there were a lot of Mafia people in the neighborhood where he grew up. Matter of fact, he told me he dated the daughter of a Mafia figure for a while. I'm talking about the Italian Mafia now, not the Memphis Mafia. Joe had a nutty sense of humor. Elvis liked that.

LAMAR FIKE: Red and I both liked Joe. I thought maybe he had something that our group could use. I talked to him, and I told Elvis, "You ought to consider hiring this guy Joe Esposito when you get back." And Elvis said, "Well, make sure I meet him." So Joe started coming over to the house a lot when we were in Germany, the same way Charlie would come back and forth.

Joe would crack Elvis up real quick. But nothing, really, made Elvis happy in Germany. He vacillated between "What the shit am I doing here?" to "I'm an American" to "This is the army, Mrs. Jones." At one point, he said, "I'm about ready to go back home. They can stick this army up their ass. I'm fed up with it."

Elvis was not a person who liked to take orders. If you asked him to pick up an anvil, he'd carry it on his back for twenty years. But if you *told* him to do it, he'd tell you where to put it.

They drafted me while I was over there. I had to go to the 3rd Armored headquarters and let them flunk me. I was about one hundred pounds overweight, even though I was down to 265 or 270, something like that.

BILLY SMITH: One time Elvis was on maneuvers, and they'd gone up in the mountains and it was cold and snowing like mad. This was probably in Grafenwöhr. Elvis said they would do anything to stay warm. They couldn't build fires, so they would get on the tanks to keep warm.

Elvis was a scout in the tank corps, and he drove a jeep for this master sergeant. They had this direct heating system rigged up from the motor. One day, they pulled a canvas up over their themselves, and when it got warm, they got sleepy. Elvis said next thing he knew, he woke up in the hospital with carbon monoxide poisoning—they got exhaust fumes coming up from a hole in the floorboard. Having a heater in the jeep was against regulations. The army covered for him, though, because they didn't want it to get out that he almost died in one of their vehicles. They said he was in the hospital for tonsillitis.

LAMAR FIKE: Elvis got in trouble over there one other time. He was on maneuvers, and he took a wrong turn, and before he knew it, he was practically in East Germany. Because they were up near the eastern border. Grafenwöhr is where [Germany's General Erwin] Rommel trained his troops. Anyway, Elvis caught on to it—it wasn't a very guarded border—and he wheeled around real quick and got out of there. He didn't actually go into East Germany, but he got real close. It scared the shit out of everybody.

One of the reasons Elvis didn't like to go out in the field or on maneuvers was because he had a big fear of snakes. I think he always thought he'd jump in a foxhole and one would be waiting on him.

BILLY SMITH: 'Course, the strange thing about that is that he had a lot of books about snakes. He was fascinated by them. And he used to go snake hunting. He liked killing them with a shotgun.

MARTY LACKER: Elvis had a number of obsessions, and one was karate. That started when he was in Germany. He took instruction from Jürgen Seydel, a champion karate expert. That's who he first trained with. Then he met a guy named Hank Slemansky, who was a paratrooper and ranger for Special Services, the equivalent of a Green Beret. He was a martial arts instructor, too. He taught Elvis karate in '59 over there. Elvis was intrigued with it because nobody much had ever heard of karate in the States. Slemansky told him he jumped from a plane one time and his chute didn't open, and he broke his back. But because of the martial arts discipline, he'd learned not to feel pain, and he got up and walked away. That seems far-fetched, but I think Elvis believed it. Slemansky got killed in Vietnam in the sixties. Elvis was real upset.

When Elvis got back to the States, he was talking karate all the time. That's when he got his first-degree black belt. In a way, he helped popularize it here because the magazines wrote stories about him learning martial arts, and a lot of kids became aware of it. He'd buy up a bunch of lumber, and he and the guys would go downtown in the middle of Main Street in Memphis and start breaking boards with karate chops.

LAMAR FIKE: Elvis always pictured himself as a badass, but he never was, and karate gave him permission to be that.

MARTY LACKER: When Elvis was in the tank corps, he had a sergeant who gave him Benzedrine because he had to stay up all night and watch during maneuvers. Elvis saw that it helped him stay awake and alert.

LAMAR FIKE: He liked that Benzedrine. So he went looking for some more, and some stronger stuff, too. He found a pharmacy mate over there who'd give him anything he wanted as long as he got paid. We'd get all kinds of stuff—buy it by the jugs, boy. He'd taken those pills of Gladys's before, but that slacked off. But when he found the pharmacy mate, that's when he started back again.

Responsibility was not one of Elvis's things. Here was a guy who made money like an Arab oil sheik, for Christ sake, back when money was money. He had it all—his closest buddies around him, Cadillacs, a beautiful home, and adulation. The only thing he didn't walk on was rose petals. And so this army stuff didn't set too well with him, and he'd take pills so he could sort of be someplace else. We didn't think anything about it at the time.

BILLY SMITH: Actually, for a soldier, Elvis had a pretty good time over there. I remember him telling me about the day him and Lamar and Red started throwing snowballs at some of the civilians. The civilians didn't take it as a game after a while, and they started chasing 'em. And Lamar was running behind Elvis and Red. Elvis and Red made the corner, but Lamar missed the turn. He was still going straight ahead. There was this picket fence in front of a house there, and Lamar didn't slow up in time. His feet flew out from under him, and he slid for half a block—went right through the fence. Elvis and Red went back and helped him to his feet. I think they had to help carry him home.

LAMAR FIKE: Red and I didn't have any money at all, and every day Vernon would give us two marks a piece. Back then, a mark was about a quarter. If we wanted to go out and drink, or have fun while Elvis was out in the field, we'd have a tough time.

One day Elvis came back from maneuvers and said, "How much is Daddy giving you?" I said, "Two marks a night." See, Elvis didn't pay attention to what people were paid. Elvis didn't know what a loaf of bread cost, not even in America. But now this got his attention.

Elvis said, "What! Fifty cents? You can only buy a couple of beers with fifty cents!" And he went in and said, "Daddy, what the hell are you doing?" Vernon said, "Well, everything else is paid for. Let them go out and try to get some money on their own."

Elvis said, "They're living with me. What do you want them to do, get a job?" So Elvis had him give us two hundred marks a week, and we would go on trips and stuff. Later on, Elvis decided we should have a little salary. He'd give us a couple hundred dollars occasionally.

Vernon liked me, but he would turn on me in a second. One of the biggest fights that Elvis and I got into was in Germany in '59. Vernon kept mouthing off to me. And I said, "I'm sick of hearing your mouth. Damnit, you're driving me crazy. Fuck you!" Well, Elvis picked up a three-layer chocolate cake that somebody had sent him and hit me with that son of a bitch. It was as hard as a brick bat. Elvis said, "I know Daddy was wrong, but you just can't fight with him." And I said, "Well, I'm sure as hell not going to let him run over me. I won't even let you do that." Then he apologized. It was one of the few times Elvis ever said "I'm sorry" to me.

MARTY LACKER: When Elvis came out of the army, a lot of his rough edges were gone. He was exposed to a whole lot of different things. He spent time in Paris, and he saw how other people lived. Of course, the Colonel would have liked him to stay dumb and unpolished because he could control him a lot easier.

Parker may have gone to Elvis's induction, playing ringmaster to all the reporters and photographers, but he couldn't go to Germany with him because as an illegal alien he didn't have a passport. Of course, we didn't know that then. At that press conference they gave before he shipped out, Elvis said they'd already been talking about a tour of Europe before the army. That never could have happened because Colonel wouldn't let any of his seconds in command play advance man.

BILLY SMITH: Just because Colonel kept Elvis from entertaining the troops doesn't mean he never sang any music over there. He'd go to these nightclubs, like the Moulin Rouge in Munich or the Lido in Paris, and play some. And he made some home recordings, too. They came out on record in 1984, in that *Elvis: A Golden Celebration* set. He had a piano, and Charlie Hodge would go over, and they'd sing together. It's kind of funny—on one of those home recordings, on "The Fool," Elvis stops and calls out to his daddy in the other room. He says, "Hey, Daddy, would you mind getting these kids out of the window? They're yelling, and I can't hear what I'm doing." Fans, I guess. You really get the feel of that whole scene—you can almost see it. When you listen to those today, you feel a little bit like you're eavesdropping.

LAMAR FIKE: Those eighteen months over there were really rough. Elvis lost fifteen pounds, from 185 to 170. He was miserable. And he was scared to death his career was going to dry up. In February of '60, right before he went home, *Billboard* reported that he'd sold $50,000,000 worth of records. But in December of that first year, '58, his decline on the charts was pretty obvious.

BILLY SMITH: Colonel had told him, "Look, son, I will keep you on top." The whole time Elvis was in Germany, there were records released right on schedule. And Colonel kept promoting him. He had movie deals waiting on him when he come out. And he had the Frank Sinatra TV special set up for as soon as he got back.

But inside, Elvis was wondering if the public was going to see him the same. And he was afraid of how much the music had changed. Because he said, "While I was over there in Germany, things seemed like they were at a standstill." He said, "It's almost like I stepped backward into the music world rather than forward."

That's why when he came out of the army he wanted to record "It's Now or Never." I can tell you he was proud of that song. Because all during the fifties, people said, "He's a fly-by-night singer. He doesn't have that good a voice." He liked that challenge, and he worked on his voice the whole time he was in Germany. He was thinking about what he was going to do and sound like when he come out. Before, his music had a kind of playful innocence. But in the early sixties, Elvis felt like "I've got this force, and I'm going to use it."

MARTY LACKER: While Elvis was in Germany, RCA had a press conference where an executive said that Elvis would probably change his style of music when he came back. Well, Colonel's office got thousands of calls from fans who didn't want anything changed. But Elvis himself was changed. All of a sudden, he wanted to be a crooner. You've got to remember what he was exposed to over there. He was listening to European music. And they came up with "It's Now or Never," which was a takeoff on "O Sole Mio."

Elvis loved opera, and he especially liked Mario Lanza. He would watch *The Student Prince*, which was set in Heidelberg, over and over again. He loved the power of the big voices. And he loved big orchestras. He liked real dramatic things. He'd see these maestros conducting, and he would get up and imitate them, standing in front of the television.

BILLY SMITH: Elvis had a range of about two octaves and a third. Most pop singers have about a one-octave range. He was a high baritone. He could nail high G's and A's full-voiced. That was just his natural ability. But in the army, practicing with Charlie, he made his voice stronger. He sang more from the diaphragm, and with some power, rather than just from the throat. He'd say, "It's the same music, just with more balls."

LAMAR FIKE: He sang every night in the living room. Charlie had gone to the Stamps School of Music, and he and Elvis talked a lot about how to improve the range, how to sustain notes at the top of the register.

One reason Elvis was real concerned about range and pitch and making his voice stronger was because he started having a little trouble with his hearing. He had a perforated eardrum, or at least some kind of trouble, from being around a big cannon. He came home at Fort Hood one afternoon and I said, "How did it go today?" And he walked right by me. They immediately pulled him out of tanks and put him into the scouts. Some of these books say his hearing deteriorated more through the years and caused him trouble onstage. I don't think so.

MARTY LACKER: If Elvis had trouble with his hearing, it was temporary because he could hear a pin drop on a two-inch-thick carpet. He'd sure as hell hear what you were whispering across the room, especially if you didn't want him to.

BILLY SMITH: His hearing cleared up, and it certainly didn't deteriorate over the years. There's some story about when he was a kid, he had ear trouble, and Aunt Gladys supposedly poured urine in his ears. That's a bunch of shit. We used "sweet oil" that you heated up and dropped into the ear. But urine . . . God! We were country, but we weren't completely ignorant.

LAMAR FIKE: There are a lot of misconceptions about Elvis, some big, some small. For example, Albert Goldman wrote that Elvis kept me a virtual prisoner over in Germany. We had an argument about it. I said, "Albert, it wasn't a case of being a prisoner. I went everywhere with him. I did everything I wanted to do. I traveled all over Europe." When Elvis went to Grafenwöhr for the winter maneuvers, Cliff and I would get on a train to go to Italy and Switzerland. We'd stay gone for three or four weeks. So I wasn't a prisoner. I told Albert, "You can't say that." But again, what are you going to tell Albert?

Cliff decided he wasn't going to come straight to Germany. He flew to Paris and stayed with a couple friends for about a week. Then he flew to Munich and stayed there for a couple weeks. Elvis said, "Where is the son of a bitch?" So Cliff came and stayed two weeks, and then he took the Volkswagen and stayed gone for a month.

MARTY LACKER: Actually, that probably worked out for the best. Elvis could only take Cliff for two or three days at a time.

LAMAR FIKE: After a while, Cliff moved in with Currie Grant over in Wiesbaden. I tried to tell him that wasn't really the cool thing to do, that Elvis had brought him over there and Elvis wanted him around him. He spoke very fast, and he said, "Wait a minute, man. Don't you tell me what I can do now. I'm not going to stay around and shine some fuckin' shoes. I'm going to Wiesbaden." And he packed up and took the 220 Mercedes. Stayed gone three months that time.

That's how Elvis met Priscilla—through Cliff. Her stepfather, Captain Joseph Beaulieu, was a career officer. He'd been transferred to Wiesbaden Air Force Base, which was near Friedberg. Priscilla was born in Brooklyn and moved to Connecticut for a while, but she'd lived in various places—the last was Austin, Texas. Her real father, Lieutenant James Wagner, was a navy fighter pilot who'd been killed in a plane crash coming home on leave. Her mother remarried two years later and had four more kids. So Priscilla was the eldest. Apparently, her stepfather was pretty strict. She says he wouldn't let her wear a tight skirt when she was a cheerleader, so at thirteen she joined the Girl Scouts so she could wear a tight uniform.

Cliff met Currie Grant in Wiesbaden. Currie was a clerk for Air Force Intelligence at Schierstein, near Wiesbaden. His wife's brother was Tony Bennett, the singer. Currie ran a weekly variety show for the air force, and he was also a photographer. Cliff and Currie would go up to this pool, and that's where they met Priscilla. She'd been in Germany about a week and a half. Currie was taking pictures of her. Cliff described her to Elvis, and Elvis told Cliff to have Currie bring her over.

There are all these different stories about how Elvis and Priscilla met—Priscilla says that Currie approached her at the Eagle's Club in Wiesbaden, which was a place American service families went for dinner and to see shows. Priscilla says he asked her if she'd like to meet Elvis Presley. And Currie at one point was saying that Priscilla sought *him* out at the Eagle's Club and said, "Hi, I understand you know Elvis Presley." That might be true because she says in her book [*Elvis and Me*] that before she left Texas, she told her girlfriend, "I'm going over there to meet Elvis." But the meeting with Cliff is what really set the wheels in motion.

When Cliff described her to Elvis, I went over to take a look at her. I told Elvis, "She's as cute as she can be. But God Almighty, she's fourteen years old. We'll end up in prison for life." He had Currie and his wife bring her over to the house anyway. I remember she wore a little blue-and-white sailor suit, and white socks. I watched that from the very beginning with abject fear.

CHAPTER 17

FUN AND FRAULEINS

LAMAR FIKE: One thing people always ask me is, "What did you think of Priscilla?" And I say, "I think she was a very lucky fourteen-year-old." Very ambitious. Very aggressive. Typical young teenage girl, looking around for some trouble to get into. She loved the idea of being with Elvis, being away from her mother and stepfather.

I was there the day they brought her over from Wiesbaden. In fact, when Elvis came down to the living room, I introduced them. Joe Esposito was the only other person there, I think. One thing led to the other. Elvis was smitten with her from the start.

BILLY SMITH: In the beginning, Priscilla was like every other woman—Elvis thought she was pretty, and her coloring was a lot like his mother's. And he realized she looked like Debra Paget.

MARTY LACKER: Everybody thinks that Elvis's meeting Priscilla was the main event of his going to Germany. That's not true. There were several main events. Vernon's romance with Dee Stanley, for instance.

LAMAR FIKE: One day, Elvis got this phone call from an American serviceman's wife, inviting him to come to their home for dinner. She was an older woman, with three little boys. She said she was from Tennessee, and she wanted to welcome a fellow Southerner to Germany. Elvis didn't want to go, so he told her to call back, that he'd have to talk with his father. When she did, he countered with an offer for coffee at the Hotel Gruenwald. Then he sent his father to meet Devada Elliott—Dee Stanley.

I remember the day. It was the winter of '58–'59. Vernon and I were having breakfast in the restaurant, and this blonde came up in a white coat. Vernon introduced himself and said Elvis had been called away. So she made her moves on Vernon. Boy, she stalked him like prize game.

It got so bad that I called Elvis in Grafenwöhr. I said, "You've got a bad problem here. Your dad is involved with a first sergeant's wife." I said, "Her husband is a big bad guy. He's a heavily decorated lifer—George Patton's personal bodyguard. I don't know if we can take him [in a fight]."

At first, Vernon and Bill and Dee were all great friends. Bill was even glad to have somebody to keep her company while he went out on maneuvers. But pretty soon, Red and I started carrying Vernon out of Bill and Dee's apartment on a semiregular basis because he'd get drunk and pass out. We'd get him in the car and bring him back. One night, we were walking through the parking lot of the hotel, carrying him. I had his legs, and Red had his head. And the MPs came up and put all three of us in the jeep, and we talked them out of arresting us. Next day, Vernon swore up and down it never happened.

MARTY LACKER: Elvis didn't like Dee from the start. He questioned her sincerity, you might say. Dee was real hyper, nervous.

BILLY SMITH: The "Dee thing" turned Elvis away from his daddy. Vernon had been seeing younger women, and it was too damn quick after Gladys's death. Elvis resented the hell out of it.

LAMAR FIKE: Vernon started jumping everything that moved the day after Gladys died. We went back to Fort Hood, and I was doing something in the bedroom, and Elvis came in and said, "Where's Daddy?" I knew where he was. Vernon had picked up this blonde who came over to the house, and he was banging the hell out of her. I said, "He went somewhere with somebody." Elvis said, "What do you mean 'with somebody'? Who's 'somebody'?" I said, "Just somebody."

Well, it hadn't been out of my mouth twenty minutes when Vernon drove in the driveway. It was night, and he got out of the car with her and started walking towards the house. Elvis said, "Who is that?" I said, "I don't know. It's just somebody that Vernon said he knew." Well, Elvis started questioning me and accused me of protecting his daddy.

I said, "I'm not protecting your daddy. She came up here, and he picked her up, and he probably got laid. What the hell?" Elvis said, "You son of a bitch!" And I said, "You asked me, didn't you?"

Vernon came in, and Elvis said, "Daddy, I want to talk to you." They got back in the bedroom, and you never heard such hemming and hawing in your life. Elvis said, "Now look! Mama ain't been in the ground a week! We're going to have some changes here!"

Then Vernon got over to Europe, and it got worse. When he first started dating Dee, Elvis fought with him about it. Then he thought, "Daddy's lonely. He needs somebody." So he finally said, "Okay, bring her over to the house."

There was a little bedroom right off the living room where Vernon stayed. Vernon would take Dee in there, and when they started banging, Dee would start screaming [with pleasure]. God Almighty, she'd scream so loud you could hear her all over the house. Elvis would turn sixteen shades of red. We'd be in the living room, and he would look at me and say, "I can't stand this. It's driving me crazy!" Sometimes he'd just go upstairs. Or Vernon would come out of the room about twenty minutes later, and he'd be real cocky, and he'd sit there.

One time Elvis said, "Daddy, you need to take her in a car or take her out somewhere. Don't do it in here." He said, "Everybody in the house is hearing this."

But it got worse and worse. One time, they spent over an hour in there, and Elvis had about fifteen people in the house. When Dee started to holler, Elvis got up and started playing the piano so damn loud it made Liberace sound like a paraplegic. He beat that piano to death, man.

BILLY SMITH: Months before Elvis came back to the States, he sent his daddy home, supposedly on business, but he was really just disgusted by all Vernon's carrying on with Dee. But Dee flew back to the U.S. with Vernon. She took her boys back to Virginia and parked 'em with their Aunt Peggy. She said she was trying to get everything straight in her mind. She couldn't decide whether she wanted to stay with Bill, who she said drank too much, or go with Vernon.

Well, they hadn't been back anytime when Vernon invited her to come to Memphis to see Graceland. This was in April of '59.

She come over, and Vernon tried to convince her to leave her husband. Word got back to Elvis, and, boy, he turned [on him]. Vernon went back to Germany the next month, and Bill Stanley went home to Virginia to fight for his marriage. Nobody seemed to be on his side, though. [Their son] Billy Stanley says that even his commanding officer told him, "If you raise any hell about this, you can forget your pension."

Vernon couldn't stand being away from her. So he sent Dee a telegram which said, "Will be arriving soon, can't live without you," or words to that effect. But it arrived while Dee was gone, and Bill read it.

So Vernon arrived in Virginia, and they had a showdown. That's when Dee put her kids in a kind of fancy orphanage, a private home–school, called Breezy Point Farms. The boys spent the Christmas of '59 there, and Vernon and Dee went back to Germany.

LAMAR FIKE: Elvis was very comfortable while they were gone. That's when we started going to Munich and different places. Because Vernon's affair with Dee really bothered him. And I think he felt a little guilty that he'd sent his daddy to have coffee with Dee instead of going himself.

BILLY SMITH: A couple of years ago, Dee wrote a book about her life with Elvis and Vernon. This was her second book. It was never published as a book, but parts of it run in the *National Enquirer.* That's where she said that Elvis and Gladys were lovers. Another thing she said was that Elvis had a "secret gay life." I don't see how she could know much about Elvis, because she really wasn't around him that much.

But let's give her the benefit of the doubt for a minute. Elvis said some harsh things to his daddy about her, things that made Vernon extremely angry. It wouldn't surprise me to know that Vernon had said some things to her about *him* when he was mad.

MARTY LACKER: Dee alleges a lot of things she has no way of knowing. She was kept away from Elvis, on his orders. Whatever she heard, she got from Vernon. Or she heard it from her three wonderful boys, Billy, Ricky, and David, who didn't know diddly. I tell you again, Elvis Presley was not gay.

LAMAR FIKE: Everybody's got a story, and the tabloids are always willing to print it. In 1991, there was a story in the *Globe* about a woman named Kim Tracy who claimed that she dated Elvis for five months in Germany, and that she got pregnant by him, and had a miscarriage. She said Elvis called out Gladys's name during lovemaking and that he would climax and say, "Mama, Mama," and then, "Sorry, Mama, sorry."

She also said that Elvis rented a house for her about an hour's drive from Hamburg and that he kept her locked away in a suite of rooms because he was so jealous of her seeing other men. In typical tabloid style, they had her saying, "I was a prisoner of love."

I've got the article here. She says, "He used to hide under the bedclothes and play a game in which he would say, 'The snake is coming to get you, the snake is coming to get you.'" Christ. She should hope. I was in Germany the whole time he was there, and I never heard about this woman.

If Elvis had jumped as many girls as it was rumored, he would have had blood running out of his nose all the time. He wouldn't have weighed thirty pounds. He'd have been nothing but hair, teeth, and eyes. But actually, he damn near was at one time. I watched it change from '57 on. In '57, he was after everything he could get. And in Germany, he was fascinated with the idea of real young teenage girls, which scared the crap out of all of us.

After his mother died, he just let loose sexually. We went to Paris for two weeks in the summer of '59. Everybody thought Elvis went there on vacation. But he went to study karate. And while we were there, we went through the whole Lido chorus line. Same thing at the 4 O'Clock Club. We were staying at the Hotel Prince de Galles. And it got so bad that the club would have to call us at the hotel to get the girls back over for the show. We'd have as many as thirty or thirty-five girls there. You'd get up in the morning and just step over bodies. There were wall-to-wall women everywhere. But that was part of his thing—several in the bedroom at a time.

Elvis liked Paris, so we went back twice more. He liked the Folies Bergère, and the Lido show and the Blue Bell girls, who spoke English, not French. We had three limousines just picking them up and taking them back to the club. That first time, Elvis flew over and Jean Aberbach and an attorney named Ben Starr came along. And Jean showed us around, took us up to the Louvre and the palace. Going back to Germany, Elvis hired a Cadillac limousine for $800 so he could get back in time for the last night of his leave. Those two weeks cost about $10,000.

There was another reason Elvis liked Paris. He'd get in a funk and worry about whether he was still hot. And when we arrived in Paris that first day—you've seen those pictures of Elvis walking down the street there—we didn't make it a block. The crowd got so bad that the gendarmes had to get us back into the hotel. That made him feel like he was still on top.

BILLY SMITH: When all that was happening, I was back in Memphis going to school. I didn't know anything about what Elvis was really doing. I'd see Anita Wood sometimes, and I just assumed Elvis would marry her when he got home.

LAMAR FIKE: Elvis was still talking to Anita for an hour or two at a time. But he just kind of outgrew her.

Do you know the book *Private Elvis* by Diego Cortez? It's got a lot of pictures of Elvis, and some of Red and me, taken at the Moulin Rouge, the nightclub in Munich. He's with all these German dancers, and maybe some B-girls, call girls. Listen, German girls are not innocent. German girls are extremely aggressive. But they weren't whores. Somebody said the other day that those photos are horrifying, that the girls look so bad. Hey, they looked good to us at the time.

My hair is solid black in those pictures. But then I saw some movie with the great German actor Peter von Eyck, who had solid white hair. I told Elvis I loved Von Eyck's hair, and he said, "You ought to have that done." So I dyed my hair white. Man, my head smoked for three days.

Elvis was dating Vera Tschechowa then. He met her when they gave Elvis that BMW. She was an actress who lived in Munich, and Red, myself, and Elvis would go there to see her. We had a driver named Joseph Wehrheim, who drove our big 300 Mercedes four-door sedan to Munich, where Vera would take us to the clubs.

The Moulin Rouge was owned by a retired army sergeant who married a German girl. We would go up there and fool around with the girls, and then Elvis would stay over with Vera and her mother, who was Olga Tschechowa. She was one of the great German actresses, and a favorite of Adolf Hitler. She always called him "The Führer," never Adolf. I used to talk to her. Tough lady.

In one of the books, *Private Presley* by Andreas Schroer, Vera says nothing happened between her and Elvis. She says he was more interested in one of the Moulin Rouge girls. Shit, Elvis was after her, all right. That's why he stayed at her house.

In some of these pictures, he looks like a guy who's been having nonstop sex for six months. But it wasn't easy to bring women to the Hotel Edelweiss, where we were staying. It would close. They'd lock the doors at nine o'clock at night. So we raised the window, and we'd bring women in that way. And we got caught. Man, the proprietors raised holy hell with us and kicked us out. It's amazing that nobody ever got a social disease from these little escapades. But nobody did.

Elvis had no compunction about that kind of stuff. To him, it was just banging. He had absolutely no guilt and no trouble balancing his behavior with his religious beliefs.

BILLY SMITH: When I got a little older, Elvis told me some of those stories. Right before he left for the army—seems like it was about '57 or '58—he wanted to fix me up with a girl for my "initiation to manhood." That's what he called it. A much older girl. I was about fifteen. I didn't go along with it. I was embarrassed to death. I told the girl, "You're too old for me. I wouldn't know what to do." I told Elvis, "I'll find my own girl in time."

He was always doing stuff like that, like when he hired a prostitute for Lamar because he thought Lamar was too heavy to get a woman on his own.

When Elvis got back from Germany, he kidded me about still being "untried," you know. And he told me this other story about Lamar, about how he fell in love in Europe. And he would *laugh*, boy. That was one of Elvis's favorite stories on Lamar. He brought it up every chance he got.

LAMAR FIKE: Oh, dear God. I was planning a white wedding.

We used to hang out at a club called Le Bantu, which was behind the Lido arcade in Paris. And we'd stay there 'til six or seven o'clock in the morning because everybody in show business would come there and hang out after they got through. Elvis liked that.

We'd talk to that whole group from the Moulin Rouge. I fell in love with a girl who was in the show. I kept telling Elvis, "I'm in love, I'm in love," and I went on and on about how pretty she was.

Well, after the show, Elvis went back and talked to some of the girls, including the one I fancied. Elvis asked her to come out and meet me, and next thing you know, I had her out in the car about five o'clock in the morning. We had a sunroof on that car, and it was open. And, boy, I made a move on her and let out a bloodcurdling scream. My "she" was a "he." In a flash, I was standing up with my head through that sunroof, screaming and laughing. You couldn't tell a guy from a girl there. Elvis admitted it himself. He said, "Man, if someone hadn't told me, I never would have known."

BILLY SMITH: Elvis would say, "Yeah, Lamar fell in love over there. And when it was all said and done, she had one [penis] bigger than he did."

LAMAR FIKE: It scared the crap out of me. After that, one of the "girls" would sit down by Elvis, and Elvis would look at me, and I would look at him. One time, he said, "What do you think?" I said, "I have no earthly idea [whether it's a man or a woman]. But I wouldn't tell you if I knew." They looked just like women. Their gestures were absolutely perfect.

One night, this girl was sitting two tables over, eating French onion soup. Part of the cheese was in her mouth, and the rest of it dribbled down her chin to the bowl. She sat there sucking that cheese for a lifetime. Elvis said, "Are you looking at that?" I said, "Yeah. Have you ever seen anybody who could suck cheese out of a bowl that good?" And Elvis said, "What do you think it is, a he or a she?" I said, "I don't know. I'm too nervous to find out."

We got in there one time, and [the American newspaper columnist] Dorothy Kilgallen was there, trying to get a story on Elvis hanging out with all those girls, or guys, or whatever they were. Elvis sat down, and I looked over to the left, and I saw her. And I turned around and said, "Hey, we got to get out of here.

Dorothy Kilgallen's over there." And man, we cleared that place so fast.

Finally, we quit going because we got so uneasy. Elvis never got fooled, but he got really anxious about it. He did date a female contortionist one night, at a club in Frankfurt. He stayed in that dressing room five or six hours—came out of there wringing wet.

BILLY SMITH: Elvis never wanted to talk about one of the weirdest things that happened when he was over there in Germany. It gave him the willies.

LAMAR FIKE: In November of '59, Elvis started taking skin treatments from a guy who called himself Dr. Laurenz Landau. He was a South African, and he said he was a dermatologist. He had this magic formula to keep your face young, and he claimed he was ninety-eight years old, or some ridiculous figure. He bragged about how tight his face was and what a good complexion he had.

At first, he just wrote Elvis letters telling him about his method, which he called Aroma Therapy Treatments. He said he ground up roses, and carnations, and orange blossoms, and all these other flowers, and mixed 'em with yogurt and resins and crap, and put this "elixir" on your face. And he said that after ten weeks of treatments—a "cure" was like twenty treatments a week, two and a half hours a session—his method would reduce your enlarged pores and minimize your acne scares and wrinkles. He told Elvis he advertised in a magazine called *Show Biz*, and he claimed to have four references. He was pretty upfront about wanting to come to the States and build up a clientele of American movie stars.

Elvis was a sucker for shit like that because he was terrified of getting old and because his skin was pretty rough in places. He had pores big enough to hide a tank in. So he had Elisabeth Stefaniak answer Landau's letters. Landau gushed over Elvis and acted like a big fan. He said he'd treat Elvis free until they got results if Elvis would send him the money for passage and put him up while he was in Germany.

There were a lot of letters back and forth about this, with Landau asking exactly when he should come. One of the last letters he sent from South Africa said, "Elvis, please don't disappoint me, as I won't be able to get over it easily." And when Elisabeth didn't answer soon enough for him, he just showed up at the gate.

We brought him in, and every day he would do these yogurt and honey treatments, putting this junk on Elvis's face and getting him to eat it, too. I remember thinking, "Great God!" Elvis, of course, thought he was getting younger. Here's a guy twenty-four years old, worrying about his face. I said, "For Christ's sake! Give yourself a break! Bring this bastard in when you're about forty." But he always worried about his skin because he had such a bad complexion when he was a kid.

Little by little, Laurenz got to be part of the regiment. He was an odd duck, very, very different. He was probably about forty, and he had thin, translucent skin. He was extremely aggressive and bossy. And he was snoopy, just watching too much and seeing too much.

As it turned out, Laurenz did himself in. He was always looking at a couple of the guys like he wanted to get 'em alone. And then one day right before Christmas, he was giving Elvis a massage on his face and his shoulders. And all of a sudden, he eased his hand down between Elvis's legs and gave him a good squeeze. And, boy, Elvis jumped thirty feet up in the air.

Red and I heard all this commotion, and we practically knocked the door down. I grabbed Elvis by the waist and pinned him up against the wall to keep him from killing that guy. And Red got Laurenz out of the house. Elvis beat me in the head, and on my back, and everywhere else, saying, "I'm going to kill the son of a bitch!" And I said, "Look, we don't need this right now."

The amazing thing is that on Christmas Eve, Laurenz came over and acted like nothing happened. He wished everybody Merry Christmas and asked Elvis when he wanted his next appointment. Elvis told him to get the hell out, and Laurenz went bananas. He started screaming and picked up a photo album from the table and ripped it right in half. And he said he had all kinds of compromising tape recordings and pictures of Elvis and "a young, young girl" in intimate moments, and he threatened to expose them.

Vernon was practically apoplectic, thinking Laurenz actually had something. I don't know if that stuff existed or not. I never saw them.

From there, it escalated. Elvis told Laurenz he'd give him a couple hundred dollars for the treatments and enough money for a plane ticket to London. And I think Laurenz agreed to that, but then he called and said he'd given up his entire practice in South Africa for Elvis, and he wanted a bunch more money—serious money—and if he didn't get it, he'd go to the papers. He was blackmailing Elvis.

It alarmed Vernon because Elvis had told Laurenz that if his treatments worked, he'd help him become a big skin specialist in America. Now Elvis wasn't following through, and Laurenz was upset. I'm surprised Laurenz didn't stir up any more than he did because he threatened to tell everybody Elvis had gone back on his word, and that he had a fourteen-year-old girl in his room every night, and that he was a pervert to boot.

Vernon was so worried that he made Elvis go to his commanding officer and tell the army everything that happened. The MPs came over and Elvis sat there and rolled out all the details, except he said that Laurenz had made homosexual advances to several of his friends. He never mentioned he'd copped a feel on him. He probably thought if it got out people would say he'd invited it. Because he knew a little bit about Laurenz's past in that area— that he was an admitted bisexual and that he'd had his first homosexual experiences growing up in an orphanage. All this made it into the FBI file that J. Edgar Hoover started on Elvis in the fifties.

Later, we found out that Laurenz wasn't a doctor at all. I don't know what happened to him. But given Elvis's later photographic escapades with Priscilla and a couple of other women, I've always wondered if Laurenz gave him that idea.

MARTY LACKER: Priscilla says in her book that she and Elvis never had sex until they were married. Personally, I don't buy it.

BILLY SMITH: When Elvis latched onto Priscilla, it wasn't much different than being with Heidi, Gloria, and Frances.

LAMAR FIKE: Elvis molded Priscilla. And the way she is today is the result of what he did with her when she was fourteen years old. He may not have done a great job, but at one time, she was a lot of fun. The important thing to remember is that Elvis did a great job *for himself.* That's all he cared about. He taught her everything about sex, for example. She was what he wanted her to be.

Of course, they slept together before marriage. He never had intercourse with her, but he did everything else there was to do, for Christ's sake. When it comes to sex, you've got to remember that Elvis was more interested in titillation than anything else. He didn't like penetration that much because he was uncircumcised, and sometimes intercourse tore his foreskin and he'd bleed. But he was a stone freak, and don't ever think different. He had every fetish there was. He had her going through hoops right from the start.

BILLY SMITH: Oh yeah, he had sex with Priscilla before marriage. Priscilla told my wife, Jo, because they were pretty close when Priscilla first come over from Germany. She told Jo that Elvis entered her one night when they went up to his room in Bad Nauheim. But see, Elvis's thing was virginity. He told her, "Around the guys, you are a virgin."

MARTY LACKER: Elvis didn't think virginity was really all that important. He just wanted everybody to think that the girl he was with was special.

BILLY SMITH: Years after this, in 1966, we all got horses. One day, Priscilla got on her horse, Domino. She was riding it bareback. And Elvis said, "'Cilla, you'd better get off before you lose your virginity." Perfectly straight-faced, you know. We thought, "Oh, hell."

LAMAR FIKE: One night in Germany, I had taken Priscilla home to Wiesbaden at three o'clock in the morning, and I came back, and Elvis said, "She's a virgin." And I said, "Well, I would hope so. She's only fourteen years old."

And he said, "No, I know for sure. I found out tonight." I said, "Are you saying what I think you're saying?" And he said, "Yeah." I went, "Okay, that's interesting. Now, what prison are we going to?" He said, "Nothing will ever happen. I've got this whole thing in control." And I said, "I hope to God you do. Otherwise, they'll ship us home in a goddamn cage." And Elvis just laughed.

MARTY LACKER: There was a guy who used to bring Priscilla around to Elvis's house some, over there in Germany. He would take her home to her parents' place, and then he'd go back to the barracks. Well, he was a scumbag. He was using cute little girls to get into the house, to be around Elvis. And he tried to put the make on Priscilla one night when he took her home. She says in her book that he tried to rape her. But he didn't succeed. Elvis told us about it, himself.

BILLY SMITH: This guy—she calls him "Kurt" in her book—definitely had something on Priscilla. Do you think that Elvis Presley would have tolerated somebody who had made a threat on a woman he cared about? Do you think he would have allowed that person to come around? Well, this guy come around several times in California when we got home.

LAMAR FIKE: Elvis thought Priscilla was telling the truth. The guy dummied up, probably because somebody paid him or threatened him with death.

MARTY LACKER: Two days before Elvis left Germany, Vernon and Grandma and Lamar flew back to New York. Vernon and Grandma flew on to Memphis, and Lamar and Colonel went to Fort Dix, New Jersey, to meet Elvis when he got off the military transport plane at McGuire Air Force Base. He landed in a blinding snowstorm, and Lamar said Elvis had taken some pills for the flight because he was scared to fly in that kind of weather. A lot of the reporters stayed away, it was so bad.

Elvis had a welcome-home press conference at Fort Dix, and then they drove to New York and got on a private train car and came back to Memphis, stopping in strategic cities for the fans. Somehow, through his friends, Colonel had Senator Estes Kefauver read a tribute to Elvis into the *Congressional Record.* Elvis had that extra, bogus stripe on his dress uniform, and the whole idea was to make him look like a war hero come home.

LAMAR FIKE: I'm sure Elvis counted every click of that train track, and I'm equally sure he thought about Dee and Priscilla. Both of them would make his life hell, boy. It just took Priscilla a while longer to do it.

CHAPTER 18

HOME

When Elvis returned to the States on March 2, 1960, he was a different man, although at the time he tried not to show it. During a press conference, a reporter asked him if two years of sobering army life had changed his mind about rock 'n' roll. "Sobering army life?" Elvis answered. "No, it hasn't. Because I was in tanks for a long time, you see, and they rock and roll quite a bit."

Later, Elvis made it clear that his taste in music hadn't really altered because "I appreciate all types of music really. But I have to do what I can do best, so I do the rock stuff." Yet in short order, Elvis would show that, indeed, his taste had matured, both in his music and in his dress ("Well, you get a little older, you know. It's like the sideburns. They were okay for a while, but you outgrow it . . . The army took care of those . . . Even though they were worth $1 million apiece.")

In the postarmy era, Elvis's image was no longer that of an unschooled ruffian, but of a middle-class hero. Yet politically and culturally, the sixties would be as foreign to him as the fifties were familiar. With his mother dead and his innocence gone, the prearmy Elvis was merely a memory.

LAMAR FIKE: We came home, and Elvis was lost like a duck in a snowstorm. About a week before we left Germany, we were sitting in the living room, talking. He said, "What am I going to do? I'm going back, and Mama's not there." I said, "Elvis, you've been wanting to go home forever." He said, "Now that I'm going, I don't want to."

BILLY SMITH: When Elvis come out of the army, my family moved from Graceland to an apartment on Fairly Road in Memphis. I was still around Elvis as much as ever, though. He found out that I was singing, imitating him, while he was in the army, and he ragged the shit out of me about that. He always said, "Hell, he tries to be just like me." I guess it boosted his ego.

Once Elvis was back home, it was almost, "Man, let me get right back to work! I got to get away from here."

He changed Graceland a lot. He did away with most of his mother's pictures. Albert Goldman said Elvis had a picture of Aunt Gladys on an easel near his bed, so he could stare at it for hours on end. That's totally untrue. I'd like to know who concocted that, Goldman or Lamar. Sounds like a Lamar special to me.

LAMAR FIKE: No, he didn't have a picture of his mother on an easel by his bed. Or a picture of Jesus on another one. Give me a break.

MARTY LACKER: The stuff about the Jesus picture . . . I don't know about one on an easel near his bed. But later on, he kept a picture of Jesus on top of a console tape recorder by the door of his bedroom.

BILLY SMITH: Not long after Elvis got back, he said, "If Mama were here, my life would probably be a lot different." He said, "Maybe I should have married Anita and had kids like Mama wanted me to. I regret that. Because she would have been wild about grandkids."

He had a lot of guilt that she worried about him so much. He said, "If she hadn't worried, she might still be alive." After I got married and had kids, he told my wife, "You ought to quit worrying so much about your boys. That's what Mama done. She worried herself to death."

He also regretted that medicine hadn't progressed enough to save her. And he kind of resented the fact that she held back telling how sick she was. For a while there, he was just reliving it all over again. So it was good that he went right back to work.

MARTY LACKER: What's interesting about the prearmy Elvis and the postarmy Elvis is that before he went in, he looked kind of sexually "dangerous." But he wasn't all that wild then, really. There was a kind of playfulness about him. After the army, sexually, he was basically a predator. But he started looking like the boy-next-door, and he was practically deemed safe for all America.

He started cutting his sideburns up higher and higher. And his manner of speaking was different, and so was the way he dressed. He started wearing tuxedo coats, and colored shirts, and cummerbunds. Almost every day. And sometimes, he'd wear an ascot instead of a tie. He was just different. He wasn't that raw, unsophisticated person, uneducated in the ways of the world.

LAMAR FIKE: The first real work Elvis did when he came back was that TV special, in late March, in Miami. They called it *Frank Sinatra's Welcome Home Party for Elvis Presley.* Timex sponsored it. Frank's whole Rat Pack was there—Sammy Davis, Jr., Peter Lawford, Joey Bishop. And Colonel called out three hundred members of Elvis's fan club, just to make sure he had an enthusiastic audience.

Elvis was pretty nervous about it. Afterwards, he said, "I wasn't nervous. I was petrified. That's why I was moving and shaking—not from the music."

We went to Florida by train. And we had to go to the outskirts of Miami to get off because so many people surrounded the station. But Elvis didn't like doing the show. He didn't like Frank back then. Frank had made a lot of derogatory comments about Elvis when he was starting out—said his music was "deplorable, a rancid-smelling aphrodisiac." Said it was "the most brutal, ugly, degenerate, vicious form of expression it has been my displeasure to hear."

How about that? But when having Elvis on a show worked to his advantage, he sucked right up to him.

MARTY LACKER: Sinatra was still putting Elvis's music down when Elvis was in the service. That's one reason Colonel charged Frank $125,000 for that show. That amount of money was unheard of at the time. Elvis didn't like the thrust of the show. At one point, he sang "Witchcraft" and Sinatra did "Love Me Tender." I think Elvis thought they were making fun of him, the way Steve Allen did when he had him on in '56 and made him sing to a basset hound.

But when he came back from doing the show in Florida, he said, "Man, to my face, they couldn't do enough for me. They were totally different from what I heard." But knowing those people, I'm sure they were different behind his back. Mia Farrow told

Elvis one time that Frank couldn't stand to be in the same room with him. That's what Lamar says.

LAMAR FIKE: Gladys's death did a lot of things to Elvis. It hardened him in one sense and made him more self-confident in another. He turned into another person. He was never again what he was in '55, '56, '57. At the time, I couldn't detect it because I was in the eye of the storm. But I see it now. I've heard people say he was at his best before he went into the army. I think after Elvis came out of the service, the biggest change, other than becoming harder, was that he became much more what people thought he should be.

You could see that on the Sinatra special. And you could see it with *G.I. Blues*. That's the first movie we did after we got back. And that's the first of a jillion pictures where they stuffed him into an army uniform, or some variation. You can thank Hal Wallis for that.

G.I. Blues was where Elvis got involved with [South African actress/dancer] Juliet Prowse. J.P. His costar. She was an older lady, and she was just a little too smart for him, so he dumped her ass. Sexually, though, Elvis's story with every girl was basically the same. He said Juliet Prowse liked to grab her ankles and spread her legs real wide. But then he said it about another girl, too. I said, "I thought that was Juliet." And he said, "Well, a lot of 'em do different things like that." And I said, "Oh, okay."

Part of the attraction with Juliet was that she was Sinatra's girlfriend. Frank visited her on the set one day. Then he came by Elvis's dressing room to say hello. That was interesting. But Elvis was never paranoid about Frank, or afraid of him either.

BILLY SMITH: When Elvis got back from the army, he didn't know exactly what was happening with his career. He wanted to make serious movies, and the first thing Colonel lined up for him was this lightweight piece of junk that played on his army experience.

Musically, things were changing, too, because he cut "It's Now or Never" and "Are You Lonesome Tonight"—the bigger, more mainstream pop sound—a month after he got back, and "Surrender," which was a kind of operatic Italian love song, a couple of months later.

LAMAR FIKE: Elvis liked very dramatic singers and dramatic recitations. He had a record of Charles Boyer doing recitations, and he absolutely loved it. And he liked the way those Pentecostal ministers preach, with all that fanfare. And how gospel singers recite things while all that humming's going on in the background. That's probably why he liked "Are You Lonesome Tonight," because it had that recitation.

BILLY SMITH: Elvis loved the resonance of Charles Boyer's voice, but he also loved the way he talked songs out more than sang them. I remember one song he liked was "I Saw Venice Turn Blue," and another was "Where Does Love Go?" That was a very romantic album, with "Hello, Young Lovers," and all. Elvis liked that romance. And he always liked a manly voice, even when it was being soft.

MARTY LACKER: Actually, "It's Now or Never," which was his favorite record up to that point, became his second-biggest-selling single. By early '61, it had sold a little over four million, and "Don't Be Cruel" had sold around six million. But he didn't know how it was going to do, and the less control he felt he had elsewhere, the more he wanted at home.

BILLY SMITH: After Gladys died, Elvis took her place. He became the dominant figure in the family. His daddy could try to talk to him, but nobody could tell him what to do.

LAMAR FIKE: One time in '60, when we had just come back from Germany, we were upstairs, and Elvis was raking me over about something. He was madder than a hornet. He said, "You're fired! Get your ass out of here!" So I went downstairs, and Vernon went up, and then Elvis called me back up. I met Vernon coming down the steps and I said, "What's going on?" And he said, "Well, hell, Elvis just fired me." I said, "How does a son fire his father?" And Vernon said, "I've got to go out to the office and figure that one out myself."

But you've got to remember that Elvis lost more than just his mother when Gladys died. He lost his confidante. They used to talk about stuff for hours on end. He sure didn't want any of the guys giving him advice. If one of us had tried, boy, he'd have been on us like white on rice.

BILLY SMITH: At times, like when he was hurt, he did talk to the guys. But I'm not sure he wanted anybody to know him that well.

LAMAR FIKE: I think when Dee came over here, she thought she was going to get close to him in some way. But she was only ten years older than Elvis and not particularly motherly.

MARTY LACKER: Dee used to follow Elvis from room to room. And leave him these notes addressed to "My Little Prince." He came down the steps with one of those one day, and he said, "I've got her little prince, and you know where it is."

LAMAR FIKE: Elvis's biggest worry about the Vernon and Dee situation was that Vernon was going to move Dee into Gladys's room. So he just shut that room off. That's the reason Dee and Vernon went to Panama City, Florida, for a while. That whole deal was very uncomfortable for Elvis.

BILLY SMITH: Elvis reacted to that the same way he reacted to the stress of previous situations. One, he played a lot. And two, he thought, "Well, let's just pop a few pills here, and then we'll be happy."

MARTY LACKER: When he first came back, we partied like hell. And not just skating parties. Things were a lot wilder.

LAMAR FIKE: I think you can break the serious drug use into three stages. The first stage came in the sixties, when Elvis came back from Germany. That's when he started real heavy on uppers. And that's when he wanted to buy a drugstore. I said, "Elvis, you can't just go dispense pills. You've got to go to school to be a pharmacist." He said, "No, I'll own the son of a bitch. I can do what I want." He believed the laws were written for him.

Elvis had a very addictive personality. He loved pills, even vitamins. Whatever you had, he wanted it. He just liked to get fucked up. There is no other way to say it. He loved it! It wasn't to escape any kind of reality, either. Shit, there was no reality in that group in the first place, so how can you escape it? Jesus Christ! Some of the guys think he took stuff whenever the pressure was on. But if that was the reason, Dee must have sent him running to his best stash.

MARTY LACKER: Dee stuck her nose in everybody's business. When Elvis was traveling, she acted like the lady of the house. The maids laughed at her, even though she ordered them around. The Smith side of the family resented her, too, and resented Vernon for moving her into Graceland.

BILLY SMITH: Elvis said to Dee, "You care about Daddy, and Daddy cares about you. That's all fine." He said, "But as far as you ever being anything other than Daddy's wife, that's never going to happen. You'll never take my mother's place. Let's get that out in front." And he said, "You two can stay out in the garage apartment back of Graceland, but not in Mama's room."

MARTY LACKER: Not very long after Vernon got home from Europe, Bill Stanley came to Memphis and signed all the legal papers, which effectively gave Dee custody of the kids. Dee says in her first book, *Elvis: We Love You Tender,* that Vernon poured him a couple of drinks, and Bill said, "I'm going to tell you something. You have her now, you took her from me, but if it wasn't for this"—holding up his glass and meaning the liquor—"you or any other man couldn't have taken her from me." But Bill had some consolation—he got $250,000 and a new car every year for keeping quiet. And that saved his pension, too. He got his full retirement.

LAMAR FIKE: They literally had to buy Bill out. According to his son, David, he flat nailed 'em. Got a bunch of money upfront and then additional money and the cars. Bill was a highly decorated soldier—won the Congressional Medal of Honor. He was a hell of a soldier. So it wasn't hard for him to keep his mouth shut. He died a few years ago.

MARTY LACKER: Elvis couldn't stand it that Dee and Vernon were right out back. Finally, he told his father, "I think you need to find somewhere else to live. I don't want her here." So they found that house on Dolan Street. It was around the corner, but it was at the end of the property. Elvis bought it for them.

One day, we were sitting in the den—what people now call the Jungle Room—in front of those big picture windows, and Elvis saw Dee walking up the backyard from her house. Vernon was sitting there with us. And Elvis said, "Lock the goddamn doors! If she comes in I want her to come around the front! I don't want her in this room!"

It never did get much better. Dee came around at Christmas, but only because Elvis wanted his father there.

LAMAR FIKE: Dee and Vernon were in that house, but they still weren't married. One day in July of '60, Colonel Parker called and said, "Get Dee out of there, *today*. Either get her out of there, or I'm gone." Because reporters had their cameras set up and were shooting across the street [from the house]. So Vernon and Dee went down to Huntsville, Alabama, and got married at her brother's house. Elvis refused to attend.

BILLY SMITH: That's when Elvis told Anita Wood to stay away from Graceland. She wasn't exactly living there, but it was her *being* there at any time that seemed to maybe create a problem.

LAMAR FIKE: Oh, yeah. Morality became an issue. Colonel never let Elvis off the hook. He said, "There's a morals clause in every one of your movie contracts, so keep your nose clean."

You'd think after his army experience that Elvis could have stood up to Colonel, but he relied on him even more heavily. And Hollywood provided the quickest way of making big money, so he started Elvis on a grind of three pictures a year.

BILLY SMITH: After the first one, *G.I. Blues*, Elvis went to Las Vegas to cool down. He took Lamar, Red, and Gene and these new guys, Charlie Hodge and Joe Esposito. And he took Sonny West, who was Red's cousin.

MARTY LACKER: In the early years, when Elvis wasn't playing Vegas, we'd go out there just to have a good time. That was when Dean Martin and Frank Sinatra and all those guys were really swinging. Frank and Dean used to like to be around Elvis because of the girls. They would go into the lounges, and sometimes we'd be in a lounge to see a show. And these girls would start coming over to try to meet Elvis. And all of a sudden the waiter would come over with bottles of champagne or drinks.

Elvis didn't drink much. So we'd say to the waiter, "We didn't order this." And he'd say, "Oh, it's compliments of Mr. Sinatra and Mr. Martin." Then he'd point to their table and say, "They would like for you to join them." And Elvis would always say, "Tell them thank you very much, but I'm getting ready to leave." And when the waiter walked away, he'd say, "Those sons of bitches. I know what they want. They want me sitting with them so the women will come over."

LAMAR FIKE: Sonny didn't actually join the group until '60, but he hung around a little starting about '58. His real name is Delbert. Sonny was dating Patsy Presley, Vester's daughter. He started coming up to the house, and that's how he worked his way into the organization.

At first, Sonny was very humble. He wanted everybody to like him. Later on, he became more sure of himself and turned into a good security person. Sonny was the type guy who would talk forever on different subjects. We used to call him "The Great Explainer." He could explain water. He'd tell you a story, and if it took five minutes, he'd stretch it out to an hour. He was a dreamer. Like all of us.

BILLY SMITH: Now we had Charlie, Joe, and Sonny. I thought, "Why all the guys?" But the entourage was really coming into being. Elvis took Charlie with him to Nashville to sing on his first religious album, *His Hand in Mine*. And he made Joe Esposito foreman of the group. I later saw that he needed these guys. Now people had real jobs. And Elvis paid a salary.

LAMAR FIKE: The highest I ever made with Elvis was $365 a week, and that was just before he died. In 1960, he started us off at $37.50 a week. He didn't pay us much because that was the chain that held you—he didn't want to give you too much independence. We were sort of like ranch hands. We lived on the premises and ate the food and got our bunks, like a cowboy.

Elvis was never big on salaries. He paid Joe more, but that's because he was foreman. The fact that he actually made more money was kept very secret because if the guys had known, they'd have killed both him and Elvis.

Joe pretty much left me alone. Colonel told him to. He said, "Let Lamar do what he does," which at that time was heading up transportation—and not just taking people home at three o'clock in the morning and chauffeuring Elvis around when he needed it. I mean coordinating the trips to California, too. So Joe never really threw orders at me. I have a thing to this day about somebody popping orders at me. Elvis could do it to me, but anybody else, I'd tear their head off.

MARTY LACKER: Elvis thought Joe could do a lot of the paperwork—pay the personal bills, keep the books. He answered to Colonel about as much as he did to Elvis, coordinating activities between Elvis and the Colonel's office.

BILLY SMITH: When Elvis started paying the guys a salary, Vernon got furious. Maybe Joe Esposito was about the only one he liked, but he didn't really trust him.

LAMAR FIKE: We had sort of a code within our group that was sometimes unrealistic, but basically we all lived by it. We were cohesive on account of Elvis. And Joe would be the first to break that code.

When he first came in, he was reticent, like everybody else was when they first began working for Elvis. Kind of like being a cat in a new house. You know how a cat walks with his tail down, slouching around checking everything out? After about two or three weeks, the tail's straight up in the air and the son of a bitch is running through a brick wall. That was Joe.

Joe was the third one to move in. We shared the brown bedroom upstairs.

MARTY LACKER: Elvis hadn't closed Graceland off upstairs yet. Grandma lived across the hall in what would later become Lisa Marie's room.

Charlie Hodge lived at Graceland, too, but not really until the later years. For most of the sixties, Charlie wasn't a real part of the group. It was just their common interest in music that kept him and Elvis together. Charlie would be out on the road with Red Foley or Jimmy Wakely. But when he didn't have any work, he would come by and say, "Can I stay here 'til I go back on the road again?" And Elvis would say, "Yeah, okay." So every once in a while, you'd see Charlie bringing his little clothes bag with his little clothes in them because Charlie was a little guy—about 5'5". And he'd stay for a while. Charlie got on most people's nerves when he drank too much.

BILLY SMITH: By the time Elvis came out of the army, I was almost eighteen years old. That's when I went to work for him. And that's when our relationship changed. At times, I could talk with him and say things, but I knew not to blurt things out like I did when I was a kid. Not to him, at least. It was real odd to work for a member of your family, especially a person you loved, that you'd known all your life and looked up to.

I was still real hot-tempered, and in some ways, working for Elvis made it worse. I resented people with power trying to manipulate me, and yet I let Elvis do it. But even with him, I would rebel. I would get angry and say, "The hell with this," and leave.

MARTY LACKER: Billy used his mouth as a weapon. When somebody said something that he didn't like, like if Joe gave him an order, he'd say, "Well, goddamn, I ain't going to put up with this. I'll quit!" Then, when he did, Elvis would get upset and say, "Well, goddamnit, why did you let him quit?"

BILLY SMITH: Elvis called me "Mighty Mouth," but my mouth was my only defense. When Elvis got famous, I thought, "Hey, Elvis is my cousin." I was still living in tough North Memphis. And I'd run my mouth, and I usually ended up in a fight. And because I was small, I usually ended up getting the crap beat out of me.

When I got to Graceland, I was very rebellious. School only made it worse for me. Because I thought everybody ought to love Elvis like I did. And if somebody said something against him, I'd light into 'em.

Pretty soon, I got a reputation. My classmates thought,

"Because you're Elvis Presley's cousin, you think you're some-thing." So then, I got to living up to that smartass attitude. And it wasn't until I got on up to eighteen, nineteen years old that I real-ized I'd better cool it.

Elvis and Anita Wood come to pick me up at school one time in the limousine. The principal's secretary called out on the loud-speaker for me to come to the office, so I played that up real big. I knew a whole bunch of people had to be watching us, see. I thought it was serious, you know. But not as serious as my brother, Bobby. With Bobby, it was serious as a hog shitting.

See, I was confused about a lot of things. The Elvis of the fifties was different from the Elvis of the sixties. For instance, in the beginning, family was important to him. He'd been taught, "Keep your family because they're the most loyal. They're the ones you can trust." But in the sixties, Colonel influenced him a whole lot more than people ever knew. A lot of what Elvis said and did was the Colonel's dictate. And his guidance was some-what distorted, in my view. He told Elvis it was okay to keep his family around him, but he told him never to let them get too close. He said, in effect, "Always keep them beneath you."

The way Elvis changed towards me was part of his hardening after the army, I think. Elvis wanted you to realize that he had made it, and you were just an average person, and that's all you were ever going to be. He let you know that he was the boss, and he was the one with the money and the popularity. It was strange. I was hurt by it.

Now, too, after he became famous, and after he'd been hurt by some of his family, I still felt I had to prove myself to him. And I needed for him to prove himself to me in some ways. I just hoped that we both understood each other.

LAMAR FIKE: I've known Billy since he was fourteen years old, and the way he's changed through the years is phenomenal. He's gone from being just a totally insane kid to somebody who's very down-to-earth, with a good grasp of things. Had Billy been left alone, he would have either killed somebody by now, or been in prison, or ended up like his brother, Bobby. God only knows what he'd have been like. I don't think he'd have lived to be twenty-five. Because he was crazier than a barn owl.

Elvis worked with Billy, and he literally raised him. And we just practically beat him up to get him to pay attention. We used to lay up at night and figure ways to kill him the next day. I told Elvis, "I can take care of this little son of a bitch for you tomorrow!" I mean, I had drawn out plans! Billy was just evil.

MARTY LACKER: Billy was like a pesky mosquito. For instance, he was little for his age, and when we'd go skating, he'd get down real low and blindside you. He'd grab your legs and squeeze so damn tight, or he'd knock your legs out from under you and then just skate off. He'd say things that would make you want to knock his block off.

BILLY SMITH: You can't put that many guys together and have them get along 100 percent of the time. But we had what we called "burning sessions." We would slur one another pretty heavy.

MARTY LACKER: If there were a bunch of us guys sitting around, we'd likely rip into the guys who weren't. We talked about Elvis when he wasn't there—and we hoped to God he wasn't eavesdropping because he liked to do that.

LAMAR FIKE: Elvis was a real gossipmonger. And he was two-faced, especially about other guys in the group. He'd put them down real bad. He'd put down the Colonel real bad, too.

MARTY LACKER: If we had a real gripe, we'd usually confront the guy. Through the years, I think there were only about three guys that the rest of us totally disliked.

LAMAR FIKE: We had to suppress our anger. Except for Red. Red didn't know how to suppress anger.

BILLY SMITH: In the early days, I always thought the guys were conning me. And it cost me. Like with Red.
    I had gotten my job with Elvis, which was cleaning up his dressing room. Well, one day Red cut his hair in there. And Elvis had said he didn't want anybody in his dressing room. I wasn't the brightest teenager. So I told Red, "You're going to have to clean up your damn mess." He said, "What do you mean?" I said, "Your hair and all."

I should have said, "Look, Red, when you get through . . . " I could have done it in a nice way. But I didn't. And Red mouthed back, and I called him a son of a bitch. A little later, Red come in the dressing room and we got into another argument, and he rapped the shit out of me. That got my attention.

LAMAR FIKE: The amazing thing is that in one year, Billy changed to a whole other person. That was in '62, when he married his childhood sweetheart, Jo Norris. We thought Jo was the prettiest thing that ever breathed and hated him because he got her. Everybody just loved Jo and couldn't stand Billy. We'd say, "How in the shit did he get her, man?" We couldn't believe it.

But I can never remember Elvis really, sincerely, ever getting mad at Billy. And I've had Elvis so mad at me he was ready to kill me.

BILLY SMITH: Sure he got mad at me. But when you think about it, only somebody like Elvis with a strong personality could bring a group of guys like that together. You had an Italian Catholic, you had a couple of Jews, and later on you had an Eastern religion zealot. But we blended together. Elvis was the glue.

CHAPTER 19

MANCHILD IN THE PROMISED LAND

LAMAR FIKE: In August of '60, we were out on the set of *Flaming Star,* and Elvis and this big wrangler named Jim—you know the kind, tight jeans and a big belly—went riding over in the back streets where the western set was. That's Century City now. Elvis was getting acquainted with the horse he was going to ride in the movie, when the horse decided he wanted to go back to the barn.

We were sitting there, when out of the blue, here came Elvis. His horse was just wide-open. And the wrangler was nowhere in sight.

There was a road there with asphalt pavement, and a gate and a fence and a lot of things you could run into and get hurt pretty bad if you were on top of a runaway horse. And the horse turned to go down this road. His legs went one way, and Elvis, hanging on, was pretty much leaning the other. And we couldn't do a damn thing about it.

Well, that horse came running in underneath that gate. If Elvis hadn't ducked, he would have decapitated himself. And then right after Elvis ducked, the horse got to his stall and stopped on a dime. Elvis sat there a minute, just white as a sheet, and then he climbed off. He never let go of the reins. He reared back like he was going to hit the horse, and he hollered, "You son of a bitch!"

Just then, Jim, the wrangler, showed up. Jim said, "Mr. Presley, I am so sorry about this. I don't know what happened." And he got up on that poor animal and spurred him for about fifteen minutes, until a bloody froth came out of his mouth. He said, "I got to tender that mouth up."

When he finished, he said, "Mr. Presley, I'll have another

horse out here for you tomorrow." And Elvis said, "No, no, I want him." And that's the horse that Elvis rode in *Flaming Star.*

BILLY SMITH: Elvis liked *Flaming Star* because it was a more serious movie than *G.I. Blues.* He had a real dramatic role, and one that touched home a little bit because he played an Indian— his mother was Kiowa, and his father was white. Which went back to the Cherokee heritage on Gladys's side. And in the movie, the mother dies suddenly, and Elvis could certainly relate to that.

LAMAR FIKE: Slowly, but surely, the pictures Elvis made after the army gently ushered him from being a rock 'n' roller to a leading man. And you never knew who was going to be drawn in by him. I got surprised on *Flaming Star.* Carl Sandburg was downstairs at Twentieth Century-Fox one day with Eleanor Parker. I saw him, and I was so impressed because I'd read his works on Lincoln.

I went over and introduced myself and told him I worked for Elvis. He said, "How is that young man?" I said, "He's doing fine." He said, "He's a fine young man, isn't he?" I said, "Yes, he is." I guess I shouldn't have been surprised. He collected and sang American folk songs and ballads. Sandburg was very tall, very gentle. His hair was solid white. He must have been in his early eighties then. I had my picture made with him. It was one of the thrills of my life. I went back and told Elvis, and he said, "Who the fuck is Carl Sandburg?"

BILLY SMITH: Elvis sang only two songs in *Flaming Star,* and that was fine with him because he wanted to take the focus off singing and concentrate on acting. Colonel wanted him to sing four songs, and he fought for 'em. The director was Don Siegel, who made *Dirty Harry* with Clint Eastwood years later. He was sympathetic to Elvis. He said a lot of nice things about him as an actor. Siegel shot the singing scenes like Colonel wanted, but he cut the songs down to the two Elvis wanted.

I remember Elvis wore dark makeup and brown contact lenses to make him look more Indian-like. They gave up on the lenses, though, because they made his eyes look too dark. But by gosh, if he didn't really look like an Indian. It was almost spooky.

LAMAR FIKE: Red had a small part in *Flaming Star*. He played an Indian brave. Almost every one of the guys worked as extras in one picture or another. You have to look pretty quick to see any of us, but we're there. We made some extra money. After Elvis found out that Marty wasn't doing any acting because he was taking care of business, he made us pool the money and split it up.

BILLY SMITH: Elvis had that kind of mumble and stutter way of talking. He didn't like to look at himself on screen because he'd say, "God, listen to that fast-talking Southern boy! You can't understand a word he's saying!" After *Flaming Star*, he tried to slow himself down.

LAMAR FIKE: Elvis got wild as a goat in '60. The guys had already gotten thrown out of the Knickerbocker Hotel because they were having water fights in the halls. We'd stayed at the Beverly Wilshire, and things had gotten kind of touchy a time or two. Like the time Sammy Davis, Jr., came over and we were throwing whole pizzas at each other. Then during *G.I. Blues*, things got a little rowdier, and Elvis and the hotel management mutually agreed that we'd get another place.

BILLY SMITH: They were essentially asked to leave. I wasn't there. I was still in high school. But I heard about it. They were horsing around in a play fight. It was Joe and Red and Sonny, teasing Elvis, holding him down and tickling his nose.

They took it too far, and Elvis got superagitated. And then Elvis got loose and jumped up and started chasing them around. He threw a guitar and a few other things down the hall after them. It got out of hand, and one of the other guests reported them. Colonel decided he didn't need that kind of publicity. He wanted to get 'em in a house where nobody would hear 'em.

LAMAR FIKE: In September of '60, Elvis rented 525 Perugia Way, in Bel Air. This was an Oriental-style house. Frank Lloyd Wright designed it, and at one time the Ali Khan and Rita Hayworth owned it. So did the Shah of Iran. Fast company, huh? It was very modern, which Elvis liked, with modern furnishings. He

hated antiques of any kind. He said, "I grew up with antiques."
Meaning everything they had was old and worn-out. We stayed
there about a year, and then we moved to Bellagio Road.

MARTY LACKER: Joe and I found the houses. And not everybody
wanted to rent to Elvis Presley and five or six guys. I remember
one time in the mid-sixties we saw a house that we liked a lot,
and we were thinking about renting it. It was owned by Nanette
Fabray, who was Shelley Fabares's aunt. Shelley really liked
Elvis, and Elvis liked her. But when Nanette Fabray found it was
for us, she refused to rent it.

We had a husband and wife, Jimmy and Lillian Jackson, who
took care of us. He was the maintenance man, or butler,
although he wasn't really a butler. And she was a cook. We had a
maid, too.

Elvis didn't want to buy a place because he didn't want to call
California home. He could take the people for a few months—to
do the movies—but then he wanted to go home. There were tax
reasons, too.

LAMAR FIKE: It's unbelievable, but Elvis paid 91 percent in
taxes. He had this accountant, and he had taken some deductions, and the Internal Revenue Service came back on him.
They were able to settle for about $80,000, but after that, Elvis
didn't want the IRS to say, "You owe this from years past." So
he always paid what he owed ahead of time and had the IRS go
over his books periodically to make sure he hadn't missed anything. That was Colonel's idea, although we couldn't figure it
out at the time.

MARTY LACKER: Colonel was afraid of the government finding
out that he wasn't a U.S. citizen. So instead of getting Elvis with
financial people or tax attorneys who could show him how to
invest his money, Colonel said, "When it comes to paying taxes,
don't fool with the government. Don't end up like [boxer] Joe
Louis" [who had a celebrated run-in with the IRS]. He said, "I
want you to pay 90 percent, because that's what I'm paying."
That's basically why Elvis never did anything with his wealth, not
even invest it in tax-free bonds.

When it came to the end of the year, and they told him how

much he made, he was proud of it. He used to brag. Because a lot of times the press would say, "Elvis Presley is slipping in popularity." So he'd say, "Yeah, I'm really slipping. I made $7 million this year."

LAMAR FIKE: Elvis made Vernon his business manager, and even though Elvis hated talking on the phone, he and his father would have long conversations between California and Memphis.

Vernon was hardly the most knowledgeable guy, but the reason Elvis made him business manager was because Vernon said they couldn't trust anybody. That was one reason the estate and Elvis's finances were in such a shambles when he died. Neither one of them trusted anybody. They didn't want anybody to know what they were doing or how much they had.

MARTY LACKER: Actually, there was one investment, in a coal mine, I believe. Vernon made and lost something like two-and-a-half million dollars.

Any lawyers, bankers, and accountants Elvis hired were of Vernon's choosing. Vernon would say, "I'd like you to do this and this and that." And if it wasn't good for Elvis, they wouldn't tell him otherwise. They'd just go ahead and do it. Vernon made something like $84,000 a year, for which he did almost nothing. He only listened to what Parker and the rest of them told him.

Vernon couldn't teach himself about money management because he read like a kid. He'd run his finger under the lines on the page, trying to figure out the words. It's about all he could do to sign his name.

BILLY SMITH: I don't know where Marty got that. Vernon could read and write and understand things. If somebody wrote a contract, there might be a lot of big words in there Vernon didn't understand, but he could basically read it. He didn't have a great education, but Vernon could read and write fairly well.

LAMAR FIKE: People say, "If Elvis had been a more astute businessman or taken more interest in the workings of his career, he would have been a much bigger star." But God Almighty, he made more money than anybody I know of. And next to Jesus and Coca-Cola, nothing's any better known than Elvis Presley.

BILLY SMITH: Elvis never discussed business with any of the guys. I wish to God I could have broke him of that. But see, that was Colonel's influence. He told Elvis, "Don't talk about business. They don't need to know nothing. In fact, your daddy needs to know as little as possible. That's just between me and you. The old Colonel will take care of that."

Not until his final few years did Elvis realize what was happening. And then, he didn't do anything about it. Why? Because a poor kid made it big. The Colonel had told him, "I'll see to it that you'll always be able to write a check for a million dollars." That's staggering to somebody who come out of Tupelo and North Memphis.

MARTY LACKER: Elvis used to brag to me and some of the other guys. He'd say, "Oh, man, I get a nickel a record!" Colonel would con him so much that he would convince him that he'd gotten the best deal possible. They initially had a twenty-year contract with RCA. And every time, the Colonel would re-sign with RCA and say, "They're putting so much faith in you that they're going to put you under contract for another year." So there was always a perpetual twenty-year contract, but no increase in royalties. And it really got me because Elvis always said, "Hey, I did great! RCA is going to sign me for another year." It was like Colonel had worked a miracle. There were a hundred managers out there who could have handled Elvis's career a whole lot better. And protected his money, too. Plus there were other record companies and other movie companies who would put up all the money in the world to get him. He really had no idea what was going on outside of his own little world. And none of us knew enough about how the industry worked to be able to advise him.

Years later, when I got out from under his shadow and got out in the real world, I went to work in the music business, and I found out what other artists were getting and how deals were made.

When I'd talk to Elvis and he'd tell me about his paltry royalty and about being signed again for another year, I'd look at him and I'd say, "Yeah, Elvis, that's nice. But you know, they ain't doing you a favor." And he never asked me why.

The real question is what was RCA doing for the Colonel? He had an office in the RCA building on Sunset Boulevard for a good while. It remained empty, but it was all part of his wheeling and dealing. He had it even after Elvis died, until the estate made him give up all of his rights to Elvis. But Colonel was big on perks. He refused to close a movie deal one time 'til the studio threw in the ashtray on the table. They thought he was nuts. But that's why Colonel called himself The Snowman. He got all kinds of things free. Except a lot of the time, Elvis was the one who paid the price.

LAMAR FIKE: Colonel also got a lot of perks from the William Morris Agency, which represented Elvis for all of his professional life. Colonel had three residences. One was this house in Palm Springs. Colonel said William Morris bought that house, and he rented it from them. No wonder. He provided them with their biggest star.

MARTY LACKER: The William Morris Agency also gave him an office. He used to get these guys, "his trainees" he'd call them. He was supposedly breaking them in for William Morris. But by the time they got through working for the Colonel, a lot of them didn't want to work in the business anymore.

LAMAR FIKE: Colonel told everybody in the office that if somebody came in, they had to look like they were totally consumed with work. So if Colonel heard footsteps, he immediately had everybody start dialing phones and sending telegrams—all kinds of shit just to look busy.

MARTY LACKER: Colonel was always putting on a show. He told us these stories about when they signed the movie contracts. He'd start negotiating with these people, and he'd let them draw up everything, and he'd change half of it. Just to change it. What started out as a contract maybe about an inch high would end up being ten inches.

Finally, they'd get it all done. And then he'd say, "Okay, bring it down here, and I'll sign it." They'd send a studio courier, and Colonel would say, "What is this?" The messenger would say, "This is the contract that came from So-and-so at MGM." And Colonel would say, "Who are you?" And he'd say, "I'm the messenger from the studio." And Colonel would say, "No, no, no. Take this back. Tell 'em if they want me to sign this, the president has to bring it down to me himself."

LAMAR FIKE: There wasn't anything Colonel didn't ask for. His office was called the "cookhouse." It's an old carny expression. He'd turn part of a soundstage into a kitchen and have somebody come in and cook.

MARTY LACKER: Colonel would have these William Morris kids do the cooking, and he'd have them clean the tables—all kinds of stuff that didn't have anything to do with being an agent.

Lunchtime was the only time the Colonel really stopped. He'd have a big wooden table from the movie studio, and he'd cover it with this old oilcloth. And he'd have all kinds of food. He always had a refrigerator full of stuff. Most of the food was "appropriated" from somebody. He would get the studio to buy him something, or William Morris.

He loved to eat. And he liked to go over to Vegas to gamble and to see his good friend Milton Prell, who ran the Sahara Hotel. The restaurant at the Sahara was called "The House of Lords." And everybody in the hotel was afraid of Colonel because of his association with Milton Prell and because of Elvis. So he'd go in and order the waiters and the maître d's around. And he'd have banquets full of food and sit there and eat it all.

I went with him and Joe one time. He had food all over the table. You could have fed fifty people, and it was just the three of us. But, of course, it was free, so he ordered everything there was.

LAMAR FIKE: Colonel enjoyed lording it over people. That's one of the reasons he called himself "Colonel." And insisted that everybody else did, too.

MARTY LACKER: On the movie sets, he would have the top brass from William Morris come over. Colonel had a special chair made for [Chairman of the Board] Abe Lastfogel. It had "The Admiral" on it.

Elvis might have been William Morris's biggest client, but the fact of the matter is the Colonel did the booking. He might have used them for advice on the movies, and later Las Vegas, or for contacts. And he might have had them put him together with people. But it's a little bit of a puzzle as to exactly what they did for Elvis to earn their 10 percent.

LAMAR FIKE: Here's an interesting riddle for you. According to Goldman, the agency never had a documented representation agreement with Elvis. And nobody at William Morris will tell you. But legal papers filed after Elvis's death say the same thing.

MARTY LACKER: It may not be far-fetched if Colonel didn't have a contract with William Morris. Colonel didn't like signing anything, so that could have been a handshake deal between him and Lastfogel. Then, again, it could have been another of Colonel's side deals.

LAMAR FIKE: When we weren't actually on the movie set, we didn't see Colonel all that much. For one thing, Colonel lived in Palm Springs. Alan [Fortas] was usually the one who drove Colonel back and forth. And too, Elvis didn't invite Colonel to the house because he didn't want Colonel to know too much about what went on there.

That Perugia Way house—that was the first one with the two-way mirror, so we could spy on guys making out with their girlfriends. Sonny was the one who got it.

BILLY SMITH: The two-way mirror was there, and we used it. But that was just a short-lived thing. The way Albert Goldman described it, you'd think we used it all the time, and that's not true. It started with one little mirror, maybe three-by-two, in a kind of a closet, to watch the guys and their dates in the den. Later, when we moved to Bellagio Road, we graduated to a bigger one, like five-by-five feet. Elvis had one put in the dressing area out by the swimming pool, which had a men's and women's dressing room. And I think he might have used that sucker maybe twice. You had to crawl under the cabana to use it.

LAMAR FIKE: Elvis was a voyeur. Always was. There's nothing wrong with being a voyeur.

MARTY LACKER: In the early years in Hollywood, a lot of people thought we were all gay. There used to be parties almost every night in Hollywood, and we didn't socialize a lot.

In the beginning, the invitations came through the Colonel because nobody could get to Elvis. And Elvis would never go to the parties. His excuse was usually: "I have to get up too early in the morning." But Elvis just didn't like the people. He knew they weren't really interested in him as a person, that they just wanted to be around Elvis Presley. And they made him uncomfortable. Because he was still a country boy with simple tastes. So, all in all, he just figured we didn't have to go out and be seen.

That, coupled with the fact that he had an entourage of anywhere from seven to thirteen guys, and we were all living in this house together and didn't go anywhere, led to the rumor, "Oh, they must be gay." Little did they know that the house was packed with women.

BILLY SMITH: When we got out to California, I was going with Jo, who's now my wife, and we were real serious. But Elvis said, "You ought to date out here, so it doesn't look like you're gay." I said, "You date. I don't want to." I guess he couldn't understand commitment.

MARTY LACKER: The gay rumors first got going when Elvis started hanging out with Nick Adams. And you can see why gay men would be attracted to Elvis. His cousin Gene Smith was looking at him one time, and he said, in that funny way he talks, "Elvis, you know I ain't no damn queer, but you're the prettiest thing I've ever seen." And it was true.

Elvis didn't like a man to put his hands on him unless you were joking around. Even though we all loved each other and were almost as close as brothers, you couldn't go over and put your arm around Elvis's shoulder. He almost always flinched.

LAMAR FIKE: I've never seen that trait. Elvis and I would hug. And I never noticed he didn't want to be touched. I used to put my hand on his shoulder and talk to him.

BILLY SMITH: I hate to say it, but Elvis was prejudiced about homosexuals. He wouldn't mistreat them for anything. But if one of them had made a pass at him, all hell would have broke loose.

On *Fun in Acapulco*, which was set at a resort hotel, the script called for Elvis to make this dive and for a bunch of guys in swim trunks to carry him up the steps. One actually grabbed him, or at least Elvis said he did. And he cussed and raved about that. He wanted us to find out who it was and get him thrown off the set.

MARTY LACKER: During the week when we were doing movies, we had to get up at four-thirty A.M., so Elvis would go to bed early. But the fans rang the doorbell all night. I'd get up at two, or three, or even four in the morning and answer it. They'd say, "Can we see Elvis?" I'd say, "I'm sorry. He's asleep." And sometimes they'd say, "Could we just go to his door and look in at him? We won't wake him up." A couple of times, I had to threaten to throw them off the property.

On the weeknights, Elvis wouldn't let any of the girls up from the gate. Or if Elvis had a date, one of the guys would have to take her home about one o'clock in the morning. But on Friday and Saturday nights, he would let all the girls in, even if he had a date with somebody.

They'd come in droves. Because the word got around that on Friday and Saturday nights, if you were fairly good looking, you could get in. Every five minutes there would be a knock on the door.

The parties at Elvis's house weren't really parties. There was a bar back there where he used to keep liquor for the guests. He didn't drink at the house, and most of us didn't drink, either. Essentially, we'd watch television, except there would be all of these women. One night I counted 152 girls and us six guys. They were all trying to figure out a way to get Elvis to notice them.

We had this big console TV in the middle of the main den, and there were long couches up against the wall with two chairs on each side. So we'd all sit there and watch television or talk. A lot of times, the picture on the television would be on, but the sound wouldn't. That's the way Elvis liked it. And he'd have music playing on the phonograph.

So that's basically what we did. And people would go out by the pool, which was downstairs and out in the back. Then, after a while, some of the guys would walk off with a girl and go towards their rooms.

But primarily, Elvis and some of us would sit up there on the couch and talk all night long. When the sun started to come up,

Elvis would say, "I'm going to bed." He always took one or two, or sometimes three or four girls with him. And then the rest of the girls would leave.

BILLY SMITH: One time, on Perugia Way, there was five girls come up there together. And Elvis just took all five of them into his room.

LAMAR FIKE: Everybody was trying to fuck Elvis. We had girls all over. We'd meet them at the studios and invite them up there. It was kind of like owning a candy store.

MARTY LACKER: Maybe some of the girls came because they were actresses who hoped Elvis would advance their careers. But he wasn't the kind of guy who made promises like that.

BILLY SMITH: Elvis didn't really brag about his sexual exploits, except later on when he didn't have as much sexual activity.

MARTY LACKER: He was funny about that. Sometimes he'd tell us about what he did, and sometimes he wouldn't. Nothing real freaky. But you never knew if Elvis was telling you the truth because he would make up a lot of stuff. Just to get you excited, I guess. He loved to manipulate people. Like about keeping a secret. He'd tell us things and say, "Now, don't tell anybody about this, or your ass is fired." The very next day, or maybe that same night, we'd hear it back from a stranger. We'd say, "Where did you hear that?" "Oh, Elvis told me."

LAMAR FIKE: Elvis had very specific ideas about what kind of women he liked. He went after weak, subservient women as a rule. Physically, he liked 'em dark-haired and petite, about 5'2" and 110 pounds. He was an ass and legs kind of guy.

He didn't like smart women. There were a couple of exceptions, but usually, if they were intelligent, they were out. He went from cute girls, like Anita Wood, to just astoundingly beautiful women. But mental capacity wasn't his thing. He didn't like women speaking out, either. That's one reason he liked teenage girls. They weren't a threat.

Elvis's thing with women was they had to baby him and take

care of him. Because his mother raised him that way. I've never seen anybody who could bring out the basic instincts in a woman like he could. They'd get around him, and they'd immediately turn into nurses. They waited on him hand and foot. Even the real young girls would do that.

You need to understand that Elvis had a lot of personalities. Around us, he was a dominant badass. Around the public, he was "Captain America, apple pie, and Mama." But Elvis was also a person who did not like to have a real conversation with a woman. Except Gladys.

BILLY SMITH: Yeah, he enjoyed being babied. But he could be the nurturer, too. But once he had done it for a little while, he thought, "That shit's over now. Let's get on with it."

I'm not sure he wanted his girlfriends to be stupid, though. I think that's unfair to both Elvis and the women. I'd say Elvis liked a woman with a good wit, who was fairly intelligent. He wasn't looking for total beauty, either. Most of them *were* good-looking women, but then, he went with a lot of women who weren't beautiful. I'll tell you what, though—he didn't hit it off with a lot of women because something would turn him off.

MARTY LACKER: Dirty fingernails, or dirty toenails, were a total turn off. He didn't even like to go to bed with a girl who had *ugly* toes.

LAMAR FIKE: I guess some people would think we shouldn't be talking about this. But my God, the man was probably the biggest sex symbol, other than Marilyn Monroe, ever. How can you not examine what motivated him in that area?

BILLY SMITH: Elvis liked that mystique about courting. If women came after him, he wasn't interested. Always, in the early years and in the later years, too, unless Elvis already had a date, the guys pretty well let him have first pick of the girls before they made a move on anybody. That was standard.

LAMAR FIKE: There were very few men who were allowed to visit the house. If somebody came over to see him that he liked, they had to get past us first. Like Johnny Rivers used to come over some in the early sixties. If Elvis wanted to see him, he would tell one of us to let him in. But Elvis would never take him somewhere alone. Never, ever. He wanted at least one of us with him at all times. For company and for protection. Elvis was more confident onstage than he was off. Onstage, he knew what he could do.

People thought we kept Elvis cocooned. The fact is, he didn't want to be left alone with a guy. And nobody outside of our circle knew what he was like. Absolutely nobody. He didn't trust anybody. He was safe only with us. And even though we were a veil of secrecy—that was one of our unwritten rules and one of our functions—he didn't have intimate conversations all that much with us.

I've had people say, "Didn't you think that was odd?" Well, I didn't have anything to judge it by. It was normal to us. And what's normal to us is not normal to anybody else. I think you could say that about our entire lives.

MARTY LACKER: Only the guys in the group really knew Elvis Presley. I mean, *really* knew him. And there were things we didn't know. In the last years of his life, Billy was closer to him than anyone. He was his best friend. And more than that, really. He was more like a brother or a son.

I read these things where certain entertainers like Mac Davis or Wayne Newton or Bill Bixby said they were friends of his. That's a joke, man. He was never close to those people. And as the years went on—which is when most of these guys say they buddied up to him—he became less and less in touch with the outside world. He was certainly beyond calling up Bill Bixby or any of them and inviting them over for a Pepsi, let's put it that way. He just didn't want them around. He'd say, "Get them away from me."

People would get in so far, and we'd shut 'em down. We wouldn't let them in all the way. Nobody ever got in. And we just kept it that way. Because that's the way he wanted it. Understand, now, that's not what we thought he wanted, but what he told us he wanted. He could always be what he wanted to be around us. But he couldn't be that way around anybody else.

LAMAR FIKE: I think it's fair to say that Elvis demanded special attention. And you had to guard yourself because you'd find yourself treating him like one of the guys, and all of a sudden, he'd throw it up to you. Elvis would say, "No, that shit stops there." He had to be the center of attention.

We would have birthday parties among the group, and after a while we got to where we would never invite him because he would come in and expect everything to revolve around him. He found out we stopped inviting him, and it made him madder than a hornet.

MARTY LACKER: Elvis was the one in charge, and he never let you forget it. We used to sit around the house and play cards some. And Elvis always had to be the banker, the house. We played blackjack, and he'd always put Sonny on his right-hand side. That way, he would take, or not take, the last card to help his hand.

Billy and the others were aware of what was going on because everybody owed Elvis money. He didn't owe anybody anything. And everybody would complain about it, and he'd say, "Well, that's how those big hotels in Vegas were built, guys. The house is always the winner. You can't beat the house."

BILLY SMITH: Goldman wrote about how Elvis would humiliate us in front of the guests if we didn't light his cigar quick enough. Well, we had a job, and he was the boss. If he picked up a cigar— he smoked those little Hav-a-Tampa Jewels and Rum Crooks or the bigger Villiger Kiels—we knew to light it for him. He almost demanded that. Maybe some of the guys thought that was humiliating, but I never did. Now, he might have said, "All right, you need to pop to it." In other words, "Get it quick." If he was mad, he was liable to say something harsh.

Christina Crawford, who had a bit part in *Wild in the Country,* came up to the house one night to see Joe Esposito. She's Joan Crawford's adopted daughter, the one who later wrote *Mommie Dearest.*

Elvis was smoking cigars that night, and every time he'd take one out, Joe would start to light it for him. And Christina would reach out and grab it and break it. And Elvis said, "Don't do that. That's not funny." So he picked up another one, and Joe went to light it again. And she broke it again. And Elvis said, "I've asked you nicely." She said, "Well, he shouldn't have to light your cigars."

And Elvis said, "Look, he works for me, goddamnit. And he knows when I get a cigar to light it for me."

But she did it a third time, and boy, Elvis got mad. They got into just a barrage of words. Elvis said, "Look, you bitch —" and Christina threw a drink in his face. He stopped a minute, and then he said, "I'm going to eliminate this problem." He got up and stepped on top of this five-by-six marble coffee table we had and grabbed her by her ponytail and dragged her across the damn table out of the room. Then he kicked her right in the rear as she was going out the door.

It wasn't but a short time later that she came back up and apologized. She said the reason she done it was because she resented seeing her mother treat everybody who worked for her the same way.

LAMAR FIKE: Yeah, the guests who came to the house sometimes got onerous. The women *and* the men. Johnny Rivers got barred from the house for cutting the song "Memphis" after Elvis played him his demo.

MARTY LACKER: That happened in '64. Johnny was up at the Perugia Way house one day, and Elvis played him a dub of his cut on the song. Not too long after that, we were coming home from the studio in the Rolls, and we were listening to the radio, and they started playing "Memphis" by Johnny Rivers. Naturally, we all got upset. I turned around to Elvis and I said, "If you put yours out real quick, that'll kill his." And Elvis said, "No, let the little bastard have his hit record. I wish him luck, but I never want to see him again."

About two Saturdays later, Johnny came up on his motorcycle because he used to go riding with the guys on the weekends. Alan and I happened to be in the courtyard out front, and we both started calling him a no-good thief. He acted real innocent. He said, "What did I do?" I said, "Johnny, if you don't realize what you did, that's your problem. But you've got five seconds to get off this property, or we're going to throw you over the wall." He never came around again. But Elvis could get cruel. And he'd burn into you.

LAMAR FIKE: The biggest fights that we all ever had with Elvis was over girls. I had a girl one time, and he took her away. I protested, and he said, "If you don't shut up about it, it's going to cost you." And I said, "Well, fuck you! You take my girl, and you tell me it's going to cost me?" And he said, "I'll tell you what. That just cost you a trip."

BILLY SMITH: When Elvis made *Wild in the Country*, with Hope Lange and Tuesday Weld, Hope got him drinking a little vodka and stocking the bar with it. Before that, he didn't allow liquor in the house. Hope came over one time and asked for some, and Elvis was embarrassed not to have any.

Elvis didn't drink that much, but there were times when he tried it. For a while there, probably '63, he got on it hot and heavy. It was almost like Elvis needed to see what the big thrill was. That went on for maybe four or five months, mostly when we went to Vegas. There were times, but not every day, when we'd just get totally drunk. He'd drink mostly vodka and tonic. And then, it was over, and he hardly touched it again.

MARTY LACKER: He could hold his alcohol pretty well, though. It might be affecting him, but he'd still walk a straight line. He would get up and go to the bathroom, and nobody would be the wiser.

In the early days, he was that way with pills, too. The average person couldn't tell. We knew what to look for because speed, or uppers, make your pupils get a little bigger. But Elvis didn't see that doing pain pills was just as harmful as drinking alcohol.

BILLY SMITH: With pills, Elvis said he wanted to get the same feeling that an alcoholic gets with booze, except not be totally out of control.

MARTY LACKER: On *Wild in the Country*, he got a boil on his rear end. He didn't bathe a lot. Every time we'd leave a motel room on the road, me or Joe or Billy would check the room and the bathroom to see if he left anything, and we'd never see any used towels. And the soap on the tub wasn't unwrapped, either. He didn't smell, though, because he loaded up on deodorant and cologne— Brut. But he had a lot of blackheads on his back.

The studio doctor lanced this boil, but it still hurt like hell. He couldn't sit down—he had to just sort of pivot on his hip.

This was when he was on location in Napa, California. One weekend, when he wasn't shooting the movie, the guys went to San Francisco. Elvis was in so much pain he couldn't handle the trip in the car. So he stocked up on a bunch of pain pills. At one point, they were stopped for some reason, when a car full of kids pulled up beside the Cadillac limo and started mouthing off. Elvis had begun carrying this little four-shot derringer. He kept it in his boot, and he kept another one in his pocket. It made an interesting effect with his little cigars—he thought it made him look like a real bad guy. He rolled down the window and stuck the gun out, and those kids took off like ninety carrying the mail.

Of course, he had some fights through the years. He even got into a fight with a Marine.

BILLY SMITH: This was real early on. The way Elvis told it, he had this play gun on him from one of the movies, a starter's pistol that fired blanks. Somehow, these Marines got to following him and Gene. They kind of cornered him in a park. Elvis told us the one guy jumped him and started beating him up. Elvis said, "There were two of them, and I was a little scared." He said, "I had this little ole gun that would shoot blanks, and I just jerked it out and stuck it right under his chin and said, 'You son of a bitch. You're not going to bother nobody. I'll blow your damn head off.'" And the cops arrested him for assault and battery. And the other guys, too. I think the police got him for carrying a concealed weapon, but he got off that.

Now, about the fight Elvis had with the service station attendant in '56 . . . Elvis pulled in there to get gas and a Pepsi. And some girls recognized him and asked for his autograph. The guy, whose name was Edd Hopper, got jealous, and he come over to Elvis and said, "Look, you're going to have to move this car." And Elvis said, in a real nice way, "I'll sign these autographs, and then I'll move it."

Hopper kept on, and Elvis kept signing. So Hopper said, "Look, I done told you to move this damn car." And I guess from Elvis's looks, Hopper just took him as being weak. And he reached over and kind of slapped Elvis on the back of the head and said, "I told you to move this—" And he never got the rest out of his mouth. To hear Elvis tell it, he almost beat the guy to death. But Hopper was the one who got fined in court. Elvis was exonerated.

Elvis had a lot of incidents happen like that, so he became like a cat, constantly watching. He had a gun even back in '56, a little .22 that he kept in his room.

You've got to remember, too, that starting in '56, Elvis routinely got death threats. The first one come on a postcard, from Niagara Falls, New York. It was written in pencil, and it said, "If you don't stop this shit, we're going to kill you."

LAMAR FIKE: While we were over in Germany, in '59, some woman in Canton, Ohio, sent a handwritten letter to RCA Records. She said a relative of hers in West Germany wrote her to say that a Communist soldier from East Germany was going to kill Elvis, even if he had to blow up the house and everybody in it. She said he'd wear an American army uniform to throw everybody off, and she gave the dates he'd try to do it. That ended up in the FBI file.

Stuff like that made Elvis really nervous and uncomfortable because it played into his nightmares. The first hard-line death threat came in '57. The FBI caught the woman who did that. She said she'd bomb us from an airplane. I had to go out and crank up those damn cars every morning, expecting them to blow up. It scared us good, boy. We'd be playing badminton in the backyard, and a plane would come over, and we'd all run inside the house.

That's how Elvis became friends with Captain [W. W.] Woodward of the Memphis Police Department. He was always taking care of Elvis. Big guy, about 6'4". He used to travel with us some in the early years. If I remember right, he was assigned to Elvis in the security detail, particularly when Elvis did shows around Memphis, like at Russwood Park. He shepherded a lot of situations for Elvis, and Elvis was pretty close to him.

Just why, I don't know. I guess you could make all kinds of psychological cases for it, but we never talked about stuff like that.

Woodward is like an unknown character in all of this. But he always had a car around us. Whenever we'd go somewhere, a car would be nearby. Vester or whoever was on duty would say Elvis had left the gate, and it would go out on the radio, and all the cops would know he was out, and they would track us. A car would pick us up in different areas of town. But that wasn't just in '57. That was all the time, whenever he was in Memphis.

MARTY LACKER: All that stuff put together made Elvis think more and more about somebody shooting him. And as the years went by, he started carrying guns. One time, he went out to Kerr's Sporting Goods Store in Beverly Hills. He was looking around at the guns, and he spotted Paul Newman in the store. He went over, and they said hello to each other. And Elvis, as crazy as he was, said, "Hey, Paul, I want to show you something." And he opened up his coat, and he had two guns in his belt, one on each side. Then he took another little gun out of his pocket. Paul said, "Hey, it was nice seeing you," and he turned around and left.

Later, Elvis started getting badges from law enforcement agencies. Not honorary, but real ones.

Lamar and some of the others started calling him "Crazy." They'd say, "What's Crazy doing today?"

LAMAR FIKE: Tuesday Weld came over to the house a few times on *Wild in the Country*. She was only seventeen then, and very smart, but she had an edge to her. I never got good vibrations from her, and neither did anybody else in the group, except Alan. He was crazy about Tuesday, and they became friends. In fact, she gave him a white German shepherd.

Elvis dated her a little. She had the ass and legs, and Elvis liked that, and she'd baby-talk with him, but that was about it. She used to come over to the house with the girl who later married Frankie Avalon. Tuesday came in and looked through the two-way mirror one time and called us all a bunch of adolescents. I saw her in New York two years later, and I spoke to her, and she high-hatted me.

Wild in the Country was a terrific picture. It had a beautiful look about it, partly because we shot some of it on location in Napa Valley. And Philip Dunne, the director, was brilliant. This was another one of those dramatic roles that Elvis liked.

Colonel hated it because Elvis sang only four songs in the picture. It made money—all of his movies did because they were so low-budget—but in comparison to a lot of the others, it flopped miserably. So Colonel used that as leverage for the formula pictures he laid on him from there on out. He'd already had *Flaming Star* stiff at the box office. So Colonel pointed at *Wild in the Country* and said, "That's what I'm talking about. You want to do the serious stuff? We won't make any money!"

MARTY LACKER: In those days, we traveled by car a lot, and we pulled some good pranks on the road. We'd stay in these motels and order room service. We always had more than one room. And sometimes the rooms were connected. So right after we hung up the phone, we'd start taking all the furniture out and put it in the other room and close the door.

The guy with room service would come up and knock on the door. And he'd wheel the cart in, and see that he'd come into an empty room. We'd be standing there. And everybody would act normal and keep a straight face. Nobody would laugh. And we'd watch the guy, and he'd look around. But he wouldn't know what to say because he didn't want to get in trouble with Elvis.

He didn't question it while he was in the room. He'd park the cart, and we'd sign the check, give him a tip, and he'd leave. Then he would go back and tell either the desk clerk or the manager. And about fifteen minutes later, there would be a knock on the door. But between the time the waiter left and the manager came up, we'd put all the furniture back in the room.

So the manager would knock on the door, and he'd start off with, "Mr. Presley, we have a problem. The waiter just came down and said all the furniture was missing from this room."

We'd look at him like he was nuts. And then Elvis would say, "What are you talking about? Come have a look." And the manager would step in and see that everything was in place. And the guy's face would turn beet red. He'd make some excuse and say he was terribly sorry. And then, when he closed the door, we'd just fall on the floor laughing.

We used to have a great time. The camaraderie then was really great.

LAMAR FIKE: God, back in those early days, we were thicker than molasses. Most of us, anyway. You have to understand that Elvis was a true chameleon. I promise you, they couldn't put up a maze in a fourteenth-century castle like what was in his mind. He was such a dichotomy. Different personalities would emerge at different times, and he would use them to his advantage.

The biggest problem in dealing with these personalities was trying to outthink him. Oftentimes, you would know what to expect, but if he caught you figuring him out, he would do just the opposite to throw you off or prove you wrong. He just didn't want you to know him. That was rough to be around. You were addicted to it, but God, it was rough.

MARTY LACKER: The sad thing is, as good a time as we had back then, I think there were always doubts in Elvis's mind about why we were there. All of us really cared about him. Sure it was glamorous, to a point. But it got pretty damn old—sitting around all the time, doing nothing, being on-call twenty-four hours a day, and having to listen to him rant and rave. We weren't there for the money because there wasn't any.

I guess you get that way when you reach that level of fame and fortune. You have to wonder sometimes why those people are around you and ask yourself, "Are they here because they care about me? Or are they here because of what they can get or what I can do for them?" There were times I sensed that Elvis really didn't know.

BILLY SMITH: I think Elvis looked at all of us and saw things that other people teased us about—like when Red was teased about his red hair in high school. We were outcasts, in a way. And Elvis knew what he went through himself as he come up.

I don't think he ever planned to collect "outsiders." But "outsiders" collected him. And if he took a strong liking to you, like he did Lamar, and Red, and George, he'd do almost anything for you. He was as loyal to you as you were to him. Just as long as it fit his needs.

LAMAR FIKE: Elvis had a couple of really great personal traits. And one was, if you got in a big argument with him, he would settle it that night. He would not let it go another day. He'd say, "Okay, I love you," and it would be over. Of course, he didn't actually say, "I'm sorry."

BILLY SMITH: Elvis didn't really know how to tell you he loved you. He showed you, like by sticking up for you or buying you things. Like once, when Elvis decided to go to Wilshire Motors in California. At the time, my wardrobe was real limited. I think I had on a T-shirt and a pair of blue jeans.

Everybody was looking at something different, and I happened to go over to this BMW. I was leaning on it, and the salesman came over. He said, "Look, you're not going to buy anything. Why don't you get off the car? You're going to scratch it."

Elvis had real keen ears, and he turned around and said, "Sir, who are you?" And he said, "I'm So-and-so. I'm a salesman here." And Elvis said, "I don't want to talk to you, goddamnit. Get the manager out here." The salesman recognized him then, and he said, "Oh, Mr. Presley!" And Elvis said, "Mr. Presley, hell! Get the manager out here. That's the person I want to see."

The manager came out. And Elvis said, "How much you want for this goddamn car?" The manager told him. And Elvis said, "I'll take it." And he said, "You have this son-of-a-bitch salesman drive it up to my house." Then he added, "And the next time, tell him to be a little more respectful to his customers."

He bought that damn BMW. That's the one we drove back and forth across country. And that's how he bought that Rolls-Royce. He brought it back to Memphis, and one of the maids, Alberta, said, "Oh, Mr. Elvis, I want to see that new car you've got. Everybody's telling me you brought a Rolls-Royce home from California!" And Elvis said, "It's setting out front there, Alberta."

She kind of screwed up her face, and she said, "All I saw out there was some old black car, a '38 Buick maybe." Elvis looked like he'd been slapped, and he said, "That old black car you're talking about—that's the damn Rolls-Royce!" For a while, he wouldn't bring it back to Memphis. She put him down bad.

🕺 🕺 🕺

LAMAR FIKE: Christmas of '60 . . . That was some Christmas. Dee didn't rescue her kids from boarding school and move 'em in until after she and Vernon were married, and this was their first Christmas in Memphis. I think it was fun for Elvis. He went out and bought all this stuff for them, but he would just keep them at arm's length.

MARTY LACKER: That first Christmas, when Vernon asked Elvis to be nice to the Stanley boys, he bought 'em drum sets and bicycles. I remember a couple of us were standing in the dining room, going into the hallway, when he came in and handed us these boxes. He just sort of said, "Here, set this shit up for them boys." Elvis looked at me and said, "That ought to hold the little bastards for a while."

LAMAR FIKE: Billy, Ricky, and David Stanley would stay with Vernon and Dee over at their house, which was connected to the back of the fourteen acres. And Vernon treated them very well. Then later on, Elvis worked them into the group.

In defense of the Stanley boys, it's well to remember that they didn't ask to be there. And Elvis was stuck with having stepbrothers, so he made the best of it.

MARTY LACKER: The Stanley boys—all three of them—always claimed that Elvis was like their brother. The fact is, Elvis always referred to them as "Dee's boys" or "Dee's brats." The only reason he did things for them is because his father asked him to.

BILLY SMITH: Later on, Elvis kept them around for one reason and one reason only. And I hate to say this, but it's true. To get drugs for him. Ricky and David were on the street. And Elvis, in essence, put them there.

LAMAR FIKE: I'm very partial toward David because I raised him from the time he was three years old. Or I feel like I did. Those boys have had it hard. What you have to remember is that they were corrupted by Elvis Presley. All of them were. Absolutely. No doubt about it.

CHAPTER 20

JUNIOR

BILLY SMITH: If you look at a lot of those pictures of Elvis in the fifties, you'll see Junior Smith. Junior was Gene's brother and Elvis's and my first cousin. His mama was my daddy and Gladys's sister, Levalle. Junior's real name was Carroll. He's in a lot of those Alfred Wertheimer pictures because he went on some of the New York trips. He was part of the whole traveling show. More to the point, he was in the core group of the Memphis Mafia, with Red and Gene. Of course, nobody called it the Memphis Mafia then. You'll know Junior in these pictures. He always reminded me of Jack Elam, the actor. He looked like him. His expressions. The way he did things, the way he talked. Even had a bad eye like Elam. Elam always looked like he was about to do something really painful to you. So did Junior.

LAMAR FIKE: Junior was a really fucked-up individual. He got a Section 8 over in Korea. He was in the Big 8 stockade [military psychiatric ward].

BILLY SMITH: Junior was always sullen, but what done him in was the fact that he couldn't get over what happened over there. He went in a village and opened fire on a woman and some kids with a Browning automatic rifle and killed them. And it drove him crazy. He saw that all the time.

LAMAR FIKE: We'd say, "Oh, oh, he's remembering stuff again." I used to see him sit there and hold a cigarette until it burnt through his fingers. I'm going to tell you something. If anybody was ever a killer, it was Junior Smith.

BILLY SMITH: Almost as soon as he got back from Korea, he started staying on drunks, and he couldn't hold a job for any length of time. But in some ways, Junior was a happy-go-lucky guy. He was a lot of fun to be around, but even when he was funny, it was a solemn type of humor. It took you a second to realize, "Hey, he's cracked a joke, here."

LAMAR FIKE: Junior had a very sardonic wit. Everything was bullshit to him.

BILLY SMITH: Both Elvis and Vernon were crazy about him. Lee Edward, Junior's oldest brother, had just drowned in '56. That had a whole lot to do with the way Junior was, too, along with everything else. Anyway, Elvis wanted him around.

LAMAR FIKE: The way he could look at you. God! It would make your bladder weak. We were out in California doing *Jailhouse Rock*, and he was sitting there looking at me across the room. He said, "You know what I'm going to do to you?" I thought, "Oh, shit." He said, "I'm going to kill you." I said, "Why?" He said, "Because I just don't fuckin' like you." I told Elvis, "That son of a bitch is planning on killing me!" He said, "Aw, Junior's just talking." I said, "Bullshit!" He unnerved me no end.

BILLY SMITH: Junior was just as softhearted as he could be. But when he got to drinking, he might hurt you, or even kill you, and not realize what he was doing. Junior was a fun-loving guy, boy.

LAMAR FIKE: Red West was really wired around him. Because Junior would just lay up and wait for you outside the door. You'd walk by, and he'd slip a blade in your ribs if he felt like it. I think Gene was capable of it, too. So Red never fucked with them. Junior was six foot tall, but I don't think he weighed ninety pounds.

MARTY LACKER: I think Junior might have been into drugs. On top of everything else.

BILLY SMITH: Up until '58, Junior hung out with Elvis. And then Elvis went in the army, and Junior just stayed drunk. And, 'course, my daddy, too, could pitch a bender in a minute. One

night in '60—I'm thinking it was in the fall, or maybe the winter—
Junior and Daddy were drinking. They got just all sloppy drunk.
Finally, Daddy went to his bedroom and passed out. And Junior
went to my room and laid down on the bed.

I came home probably around eleven or eleven-thirty and
went in my room. I realized Junior was there, and I started to
crawl over, when I saw there was something on the bed. I could
smell the alcohol, so I thought, "Well, he's done thrown up on the
bed." So I went into the living room and laid down on the couch.

The next morning, I got up before everybody else. And something just told me to go in there. It was almost eerie. And maybe
it was my imagination, but it seemed cold to me, like something
was wrong. I looked at Junior, and my heart liked to stop. He had
thrown up, but the stuff on the bed had some blood mixed with
it, and it seemed it had come out of his nose. Oh, God, it was
horrible. I stared at him for a minute or two, and I didn't see any
movement at all. I walked over and touched him, and he was
stiff. Rigor mortis had set in.

I thought, "God Almighty! He's dead!" To find somebody like
that, believe me, it's scary. I ran in to where Mama and Daddy
were, and I said, "Daddy! I think Junior's dead!" He said, "No,
he's all right." Then he went in, and I heard him say, "Oh, my
God, he is!" He'd had a cerebral hemorrhage or maybe an alcoholic seizure.

Elvis was extremely hurt by Junior's dying. He took a lot of
the blame on himself for not providing more for the family or giving them more opportunities. But the most peculiar part about
this is that when Junior died, Elvis became obsessed with knowing what death was like.

Junior was at the Memphis Funeral Home, and Elvis wanted
to go see the body. So we went up there about three or four A.M.
The door was locked, but a guy let us in the back way. We went
on up and viewed the body and all, and Elvis started talking
about death in general. And then he said, "Let's ease on back and
see how they do this."

We went on back through the little hallways. It was dark as
hell, except for a little green light in the very back corner. I couldn't
see my hand in front of me because we weren't close enough to
the light. We went around, and then we saw a lot of lights, and
when we passed through there, we heard this noise. It was hard

to tell what it was. We were in the room where they display the caskets. Elvis looked at me, and I looked at him, and we both had our eyes wide open, with these scared looks on our faces. It was kind of comical.

This sound was a good little ways down the hall, and it was a heck of a noise. When we got down there, it got darker. And the noise got louder. Finally, Elvis stopped. I was so glad he did, man. I just froze. He looked at me and he said, "You hear that?" I said, "Yeah, and I don't want to hear it no more. Let's get the hell out of here." Elvis said, "Let's don't go yet. Let's see on around."

We went on back, and we saw this mortician. There were two on duty that night—one was working, and the other one was laying there in one of the caskets snoring. That's what the noise was. And the other guy back there had rock 'n' roll music on.

We thought it would be real cold in there, and this wild-eyed person would come out. But he was just a normal guy. And when he saw Elvis, he stepped out and said, "Can I help you?" Elvis said, "I'm Elvis Presley. You've got my cousin up there, and I was just fascinated about all this." And the mortician said, "Y'all are not supposed to be here." But he was also just beside himself that Elvis was there. And, of course, we talked a while.

I looked around and saw a couple of bodies with sheets over 'em. I was kind of spooked. I started to back up, and damn if I didn't back up into one of the carts that had a body on it. When them cold feet hit me, man, I damn near jumped through the ceiling. I said, "Holy mackerel!" I was ready to run, boy. Because I wasn't quite as brave or fascinated as Elvis was. It just didn't set well with me. But they talked for a few minutes more, and Elvis asked the mortician all kinds of questions.

He did that about three times through the years, usually when somebody he knew had passed away. He seemed to want to know a little bit more about it each time.

When it come out in Red and Sonny's book [*Elvis, What Happened?*] that he liked to go to morgues, people thought he was a damn freak. And I can see that—it's creepy. But part of it is just a Southern upbringing, and part of it is being curious about what in the hell happens when you die. He had a fear of it, and he wanted to face that fear. And I think he was just trying to bridge the gap and hold on a little longer.

CHAPTER 21

BOBBY

BILLY SMITH: My brother, Bobby, was similar to Junior in a way. They were both kind of troubled.

Bobby was sixteen and I was fourteen when we moved to Graceland. Neither one of us had really gotten into trouble before that. We were just going to school. Then in a heartbeat, we were living at Graceland, surrounded by all this big to-do over Elvis. We thought, "Gosh, we got it made." Believe it or not, Bobby's situation was a prime example of a good kid going bad by someone else's success. Bobby went that way *because* of Elvis's fame.

MARTY LACKER: Bobby used to get in a lot of scrapes, but he was a nice kid. Some of the guys thought he wasn't worth anything. But Bobby and I always got along. Back in the fifties, when Elvis first started making movies, he'd take Gene and Bobby to California with him.

BILLY SMITH: Bobby had a heart murmur, but I don't think that's what turned him. I think what happened to Bobby is that he grew up hearing about his daddy going to prison, and then, all of a sudden, his first cousin is this movie star. And Bobby thought, "This is a strange family. How do I fit in here?" He had a real hard time dealing with the shame on one side and the pride and the envy on the other.

MARTY LACKER: On *Jailhouse Rock*, they were staying at the Beverly Wilshire, and Bobby went down to the drugstore and bought a $500 hairbrush and charged it to the room.

LAMAR FIKE: Elvis got the bill and he said, "What the hell is this?"

BILLY SMITH: I've always believed Bobby thought the hairbrush was $5, not $500. But it hacked Elvis off. And Bobby was quick-tempered.

LAMAR FIKE: From there, it seemed to go downhill.

BILLY SMITH: When Elvis went into the army, Bobby thought, "He's in there. It can't be that bad." So he joined the National Guard. Pretty soon, he started thinking of ways to get the hell out. So he swallowed safety pins. He swallowed them closed, but one of them come open and punctured his intestine. And they give him, what do they call it? A Section 8.

MARTY LACKER: From there, Bobby turned into a con man.

BILLY SMITH: It started right away. He conned a cabdriver into bringing him three hundred miles home from Fort Campbell, Kentucky. He told him Elvis would pay the bill and give him a big tip. When they got to Memphis, Bobby got the driver to take him to the shopping center up the road. He said he wanted to get a gift for Elvis, and then they'd go to Graceland and get the money for the cab.

Well, hell, Bobby cut out. The driver went down to the gate, and he found out that Daddy was the gate guard and that it was his son in the cab. Boy, he got real hostile with Daddy and Daddy with him. 'Cause the fare was something like $300. And Daddy wouldn't pay it.

LAMAR FIKE: In some of those Alfred Wertheimer pictures, you can just see the hunger in Bobby's eyes.

BILLY SMITH: Things got worse and worse. He started writing bad checks on Elvis. I don't think he had any of his personal checks. He'd just take a blank check and fill it out and sign Elvis's name. He'd give 'em to people he knew at the stores. He pulled it off for a while, and then he got caught. Didn't stop him, though. He was in and out of jail for it. Daddy said, "Look, son, you've got to quit this stuff." And Elvis got angry. But Bobby thought, "He's got it all. He can afford it." And then he started with the cars.

MARTY LACKER: Bobby would go down to all the car dealers and say, "I'm here to buy one for Elvis. He wanted me to pick one out for him."

BILLY SMITH: He'd drive it until he got bored with it and then tell them to come get it.

LAMAR FIKE: I went down there one day, and he had five different Cadillacs. I said, "God Almighty, Bobby, what are you doing?"

BILLY SMITH: Elvis tried to help him somewhat, but he was just too busy.

LAMAR FIKE: I want you to know something. Elvis had more talks with Bobby than anybody could ever imagine. He really worked with him. But it was one thing after another.

MARTY LACKER: I think Bobby had an unlucky streak in him.

BILLY SMITH: The really incredible thing is that after all of that, he got run over, down in front of Graceland. That was in '61. I guess Bobby was about nineteen or twenty. He was running across the road. He'd been talking to some friends, and he was coming back across, and a kid who wasn't much older than Bobby came out of the side road and down Highway 51. He'd been drinking, and he claimed he didn't see him. He hit Bobby dead-on. The bumper caught him and threw him up over the hood, and then he rolled on across. It crushed both of his legs, and broke his cheekbone, and cut him up a little. He had some internal bleeding, but it was mostly his legs.

Somebody took a picture of him on the stretcher. It looks like a slab. My daddy was there, right behind his head. And Elvis was there with a real funny look on his face, sort of a mixture of pity and disgust. My brother looks dead in that picture. It tore him up pretty bad.

After that, he tried working a couple places, but his legs were so brittle he couldn't stand long. Then he started taking advantage of the situation. If he broke his leg, or hurt it at a store, say, he'd sue the hell out of them. His attitude was, "I don't care. The world owes me something."

MARTY LACKER: Bobby got pretty pathetic then.

BILLY SMITH: Things just kept occurring. He was always getting disappointed with women, for example. He even got married a bunch of times. He loved a family, loved kids. But somehow or other, it just didn't work. He couldn't hold a job, and the women, naturally, resented that. Finally, he got all wrapped up with a girl named Bonnie Allen. She ditched him for somebody else. And that messed him up even more. He decided that life had just turned against him.

LAMAR FIKE: Bobby's last eight years were hell for everybody.

BILLY SMITH: He'd been living with my parents. On September 13, 1968, I got a call. Bobby had taken rat poison. I had a hard time believing he had actually done that because I can think of a lot of other ways to go. But when I got over there, I realized he really had done it. I just didn't think he'd taken enough to kill himself.

Bobby and me were always pretty close, but now I got angry, and we had some pretty harsh words. I pushed him up against a wall, and I said, "Why are you doing this to Mama and Daddy? Think about them! Don't just always think about yourself." I still didn't think he had taken that much poison. But Mama said, "I saw him! He took the whole box."

I got him to drink mineral oil, to throw up. And then I said, "You need to go to the hospital right now." At first, he refused to go. Finally, we talked him into it. They pumped his stomach, and they wanted to keep him overnight, but he wouldn't stay. So he went back home, and sometime during that night, he passed away. He was twenty-seven, almost twenty-eight. It was so sad. Just pitiful. That was a rough time, boy. You just don't know.

Bobby's whole story is tragic to me. I still find myself thinking, "I could have had an older brother. What would it have been like with the two of us?"

MARTY LACKER: When Bobby died, I was with Billy. He asked me to make a tape of Elvis's songs for the funeral.

BILLY SMITH: Elvis called me at the funeral home. He wanted to come home, but he couldn't. He was making *Charro!*, and he'd been gone for something like seven months. We talked for just a few minutes, and not until later did we really get into a deep discussion about it. He said, "I hope everybody understood. I was just so preoccupied with so many other things." He regretted that he hadn't taken more time with a lot of people, not just Bobby.

So many of the relatives—I'd say ten or so—died pretty young, especially on the Smith side of the family. One cousin, Robert, who was Junior and Gene's brother, worked for a chrome-plating company, and he fell in a vat of hot liquid chrome, up to his waist. It cooked him. But a blood clot actually killed him, just when he was getting better.

All those deaths . . . A lot of times, I'll say, "Well, maybe it was their choosing. They could have changed it." That's what we're supposed to be able to do in life. Other times, it just feels like somebody threw a hex on us.

CHAPTER 22

HACK TIME

In January of '61, Elvis signed a new, five-year, nonexclusive contract with Hal Wallis. Like their previous pact, it demanded a movie a year. That March, Elvis, Colonel, and the entourage flew to Honolulu to begin shooting *Blue Hawaii*, the movie that would become the biggest-grossing picture of Elvis's career—$30 million—and sell some five million soundtrack albums, two million in just six months, more than any other Elvis album to date.

While Elvis continued to harbor dreams of being a serious actor, the success of *Blue Hawaii* cost him whatever slim opportunity still remained. Although Colonel insists that Elvis picked his own movies from scripts sent directly to his house, others say that after *G.I. Blues* and *Blue Hawaii*, Colonel saw what worked—a musical-comedy framework for fourteen mostly mediocre songs, a romantic backdrop, and lots of girls—and vowed to repeat the formula for the remainder of his client's years on the screen. Wallis wholeheartedly supported Colonel's decision, declaring, "A Presley picture is the only sure thing in show business."

Two days before the start of production, Elvis gave a benefit concert in Honolulu to raise money for a memorial to the *U.S.S. Arizona*, the first ship downed in the bombing of Pearl Harbor twenty years earlier. The idea was Colonel's. The previous December, he'd read an article in the *Los Angeles Herald-Examiner* that mentioned the project would be funded entirely by donations. Such generosity with Elvis's time was highly uncharacteristic of Colonel (when *Time* wanted to put Elvis on the cover, Colonel said, "That will be $25,000") and seems to speak nostalgically about his days in Hawaii in the service.

Elvis, who wore plain black slacks and the jacket to his famous $10,000 gold lamé Nudie suit (he claimed the heavy pants restricted his movements), was anxious and apprehensive about the performance. Aside from two shows at Memphis's Ellis Auditorium the previous month, four years had passed since he'd last been onstage.

Presley would have been far more shaken had he known that this would be his last concert for seven years, until his 1968 *Comeback Special* freed him from grinding out mass-production hack movies that stifled his acting ability and smothered his spirit.

MARTY LACKER: Colonel was really in his glory on *Blue Hawaii*. He took a liking to Tom Moffett, who was the general manager of KPOI Radio there, and he had Elvis doing all sorts of promotional shit for him. It was only a twenty-thousand-watt station, so broadcast range was limited to Hawaii. But Colonel gave Moffett an interview with Elvis every time he went over there. Which he never did anyplace else.

LAMAR FIKE: Colonel's timing was phenomenal. Elvis was filming one day when Colonel ran in front of the camera and yelled, "Cut! Cut!" Then he turned to Norman Taurog, the director, and barked, "Taurog! Elvis is wearing his own watch!" Colonel had it written into the contract that if Elvis wore any of his own clothes or jewelry in the movie, Paramount had to pay him an additional $25,000. So Colonel said, "If you use any part of that shot, we want our money." Norman asked Elvis to take his watch off, and they redid the scene.

MARTY LACKER: All of these big-time agents and managers and producers would dress real nice. But what would Colonel wear? A big smock that said, "Elvis, Elvis, Elvis." He looked like a clown. But he didn't care. If somebody asked him about it, he'd say, "You remember whose name is on there, don't you?"

Colonel started this thing where he'd put the guys through stupid little antics in front of other people. He'd tell the guys he had these mystic powers that would make them do anything. He'd swing a pocket watch in front of their faces, and then he'd say, "When I pull my ear, you quack like a duck. Or if I scratch my nose, you squat down and bark like a dog." He made one of the guys actually get down on all fours and nip at people's legs. It was really degrading stuff.

LAMAR FIKE: Colonel believed in mind over matter. He must be doing pretty good—he's still alive.

BILLY SMITH: Colonel would play his little silly-ass games. He talked one guy into going over on his hands and knees and raise his leg like he was pissing on the chair. He'd pull his ear when he wanted me to do something. He liked for me to quack like a duck. And I did it. I played right along like a lot of the others. Finally, it got old. If he pulled his ear, I let him jerk that son of a bitch about off.

LAMAR FIKE: Elvis might let Colonel make us look stupid, but he didn't let anybody yell at us. That was *his* privilege. After *Blue Hawaii*, we did *Follow That Dream*, for United Artists. We did it down at Crystal River, Florida. And we took that '60 Cadillac limousine—the white one—that's in the Country Music Hall of Fame.

There was a scene where I was supposed to drive the limo on the beach. The camera truck was out in front of me, and I was supposed to pull out and circle back around and come back in. I pulled off, and I got stuck in the sand, and the damn limo sank all the way up to the axles. The director, Gordon Douglas, and everybody on that camera truck jumped off and started cussing at me.

In a flash, Elvis came off that truck. He turned to Douglas, and he said, "If you open your mouth again, I'll tear your head off!"

Then he turned to the crew, and he said, "Any of you motherfuckers think you can pop off at one of my people, you're mistaken. If this happens again, I'm walking off the set." And everybody got real nice.

That year was really bad for me and cars. I tried to talk Elvis into buying a Ferrari. He wasn't sure he wanted one, so he borrowed a 4.9 Ghia coupe from the dealer. I said, "Shit, I'm going to drive this Ferrari." I crossed Sunset out of Bel Air and turned to the left. Bing Crosby's place was over there. And I came wheeling around that corner and caught a damn wet place in the road, and I lost it.

The Ferrari went clean up into Bing's fence, and I couldn't move. I broke two of the chrome wheels, for starters. I had to get out of the car and pull the damn fence back to get the car loose, with these fucking Great Danes snapping at me and threatening to eat me up.

I came back to the house, and Elvis was up in the bathroom. I said, "I need to talk to you." He said, "What is it?" I said, "Boy, I have fucked that Ferrari up bad." He said, "Are you kidding me?" I said, "No." He said, "Are you finally learning your sports cars now?" Elvis had to pay for it, and he got mad as hell.

BILLY SMITH: Elvis could spot a hit instantly. On *Blue Hawaii*, he sang "Can't Help Falling in Love," and that was a monster. And he had a couple more good songs on that soundtrack. But then with *Follow That Dream*, he only sang six songs, and the title song was about the only decent one. RCA only put out an EP [extended play, four songs on a 45] from that movie and from the next one, *Kid Galahad*.

He was still recording most of his singles in Nashville. He cut the majority of the movie stuff in California, at Radio Recorders. But as a rule, his singles weren't coming entirely from the movies yet. He went to Nashville three times in '61, to cut an album called *Something for Everybody*, and singles like "Little Sister" and "(Marie's the Name) His Latest Flame," and "Good Luck Charm."

MARTY LACKER: Elvis could always recognize good lyrics. Especially with the slow songs. He would attach himself to them on a personal level. And he could memorize a song after hearing it only twice.

BILLY SMITH: In the earlier days, God, everything was hot and good. You could see his energy flowing. He'd listen to a few demos, and then he'd say, "Let's go out and try this." Then, when he got out in the studio, he might say, "The mood's not right. Let's cut the lights off," or, "Give me some blue lights." Or he'd listen to what he did, and then he might say, "It needs more sax-ophone . . . more drums." Elvis knew what he wanted out of himself and out of his records. He kept going until it sounded right to him. He did eighty-some takes on "My Wish Came True" and still wasn't really happy with it. But other times, he could whip 'em out just bang, bang, bang.

For a long period of time during the movie days, that was lost because of the damn songs. At first, when they give him material he didn't think was up to par, he'd go in his room and think, "What can I do to make this better?" He always tried his best, even with the worst song.

MARTY LACKER: When Elvis recorded in Nashville, the songs were picked beforehand. Freddy Bienstock, from Hill and Range, would find the songs, and Lamar and sometimes Joe would help Elvis cull 'em out. He'd listen to the demos, and then he'd go into the studio and record 'em. At that time, he was still doing the old way of recording, where everybody was in the room together, the band and Elvis. And they'd just do the songs over and over again.

RCA always assigned one of their producers to an artist to oversee the session. But with Elvis, the producer really didn't have that much to say. It was Elvis's decision.

Nobody from RCA ever really did say much after Steve Sholes got out of the picture. In the late fifties, when Elvis started recording in Nashville, Chet Atkins produced Elvis's sessions. But Atkins didn't do anything but sit around.

One night at a session in RCA's Studio B, Elvis looked over and Chet Atkins was at the console with his head down, asleep. Elvis watched him through the whole damn take, and he never woke up. Elvis waited 'til the session was over, and then he told either Colonel Parker or Tom Diskin, "I don't want that son of a bitch here anymore."

LAMAR FIKE: About the sleeping, well, Chet is a very laconic person. He'll be talking to you and almost lie down and fall asleep. Elvis didn't understand that. I was the one who had to tell Chet to leave. I said, "Hey, Chet, Elvis would feel more comfortable if you didn't come to the sessions anymore." And Chet said, "That's all right, Lamar."

MARTY LACKER: In the late fifties and early sixties, Bobby Darin used to do a lot of Elvis's demos. It shocked me the first time I heard him. I said, "Man, that voice sounds familiar." Back then, there really was no "sweetening," or overdubs—replacing a bad note with a good one or putting an instrumental track on later. Everybody would play on the take, and you'd hear the same old licks on almost every song. It was basically the same musicians, like Buddy Harmon on drums and Bob Moore on bass. And, of course, the Jordanaires were the backup singers. Elvis insisted on them.

LAMAR FIKE: *Follow that Dream* was in '61. We started doing really crazy things around that time. One reason is because we were getting more and more into pills. Not all of us, but Elvis was, and I was, and to a degree, Sonny and Alan. Alan had just started back up with us the year before. Elvis had him handle a lot of the travel arrangements and take care of the cars, and since I helped with transportation, we spent a fair amount of time together.

When we did *Follow that Dream,* Alan and I took Elvis's big Chris-Craft Coronado speedboat down to Florida. Beautiful boat. Had gull-wing doors that opened at the top and a Cadillac engine. Those boats are collector's items now. When we got it down there, we docked it at the back of Elvis's motel suite.

Going down there, Alan was in the Cadillac limousine and I was in the Chrysler station wagon. I had the boat behind me. We had these walkie-talkies and we'd stick the aerials out the window and talk driving down the highway.

At one point, Alan was in front of me. He passed this car and whenever I tried to pass it, the driver would speed up. I couldn't get the boat and the car around him. I'd get the car but I wouldn't have room to pull the boat around. I got the walkie-talkie and told Alan, "This son of a bitch is about to run me crazy." Alan said, "What are you going to do?" I said, "Watch."

I started to pass that guy, and when I got the boat right beside him, I pulled into his lane. The boat just shoved him clean off the road across a flat field. Boy, he went through fence rows! Fence was flying everywhere, man, and grass. Tore his car all to pieces. I said, "That'll teach that son of a bitch never to do that again."

🏃 🏃 🏃

MARTY LACKER: In the early sixties, when the guys came home from California, Elvis wanted to start going to the movies again, and he got the idea of renting the Memphian Theatre in Overton Square to show midnight movies. That way, he could have his own party and invite who he wanted.

BILLY SMITH: Just as Elvis had a certain protocol at the skating rink, he had one at the Memphian. At times, he would let a lot of people in, and other times, nobody but the inner group could come in.

Elvis always sat in the same place. I think it was row E. I don't remember exactly what seat, but he basically sat right down in the middle, in the center of the rows, where you could see real good. Most times, his date was on his left side. Then his drink table, where he kept his water, and his Pepsi, and his cigars, was on his right. And right over from that would be one of the guys, usually Joe.

Elvis didn't want you to sit next to him. And most of the time, not directly behind him. You had to sit on either side. He had this thing about somebody being directly behind him, or to the side of him, maybe just because we had this big theater all to ourselves, and he didn't want to be cramped. But he also didn't allow anybody much to sit down in front of him.

Sometimes we'd have water fights in the theater. I don't imagine the owner appreciated that too much.

MARTY LACKER: One of the things I remember about going to the Memphian was keeping guys out of the men's room when Elvis was in there. If he started walking up the aisle to go to the bathroom, one or two of us would get up and go right behind him. And then one of us went in ahead of him to see if somebody was already there.

He was really particular about that. I understand it because you'd get people who'd go to the bathroom just to see how big his dick was.

BILLY SMITH: Elvis didn't want you to see him. He always went into the stall rather than use the urinal.

MARTY LACKER: Elvis was a little ashamed of being uncircumcised. Maybe he thought it was old-fashioned or kind of country. When he mentioned once that sex was a little painful sometimes because the foreskin tore, some of the guys suggested he could get that fixed. And he cringed and said, "No, no. It would hurt too much."

MARTY LACKER: I spent all of '61 working for WHHM Radio in Memphis. But that September, I decided to get out of radio. And at the same time, Elvis asked me to go to work for him for real. By this time, I had a wife and a child, my daughter, Sheri. Elvis paid me forty-five dollars a week. Of course, he paid all my expenses, but that didn't really help my wife and baby. Fortunately, they lived with my parents.

Red was married now, too, to Pat Boyd, who worked in the office at Graceland. We complained a few times about the terrible salaries, but it didn't do any good. Because Elvis had no conception of what it cost to live—the price of a dozen eggs or the average telephone bill.

That's not to say he wasn't generous. Because he did understand how it felt to have certain things. You hear about all these cars that he bought for strangers. He used to tell me that when he was a kid in Lauderdale Courts, he'd sit on the curb and watch all these nice cars go by. And he said to himself that someday he would have a car like that. Big, shiny car. He understood that better than salaries.

BILLY SMITH: Elvis actually thought he was paying us *beaucoup*s of money. He had no idea.

LAMAR FIKE: On occasion, the subject of money would come up, and Elvis would say, "I pay you all enough. You can buy all this shit yourselves."

MARTY LACKER: *Kid Galahad* was my first movie and my first trip with him. I'd never been to California before. That was when Elvis introduced me to drugs. I had never taken anything until I started traveling with him. He was kind of seductive about it. We were getting ready to drive all the way out there.

Elvis came over to me, and he was holding this dark blue felt box. He slowly opened the lid, and there was a rainbow of pills inside. He said, "I'm going to give you some stuff to help you stay awake."

They were all uppers—Dexedrine, Dexemyl, Desbutal. But he had downers, too. He used to get these huge plastic jars from doctors, and they were just full of sleeping pills. He kept them in a safe up in the bathroom at Graceland. Then we had another safe that we carried with us. And before each trip, we'd transfer pills from those big jars into small ones. We were already doing that by '61.

He got them from everywhere. He got them from the studio, for example. Elvis also had a dentist in California who supplied him. His name was Max Shapiro. Shapiro's been indicted. His nickname was "Dr. Feelgood." He worked on my teeth, and he worked on Elvis's teeth a couple of times. But primarily, we used him because he gave us pills.

One of the guys told me he went to Dr. Shapiro's office one day, and in the elevator, he ran into Mack Gray, who was Dean Martin's right-hand man. You know those huge, plastic see-through jars that wholesale pickles or mayonnaise comes in? Mack Gray got on the elevator, and he had one of those, just filled with brightly colored Tuinals and Placidyls that he got from Dr. Shapiro.

LAMAR FIKE: Max was the connection for morphine and Demerol. He was sort of like one of the Three Stooges. Really inept. He liked to be around the stars. The Feds called Max up on some other stuff, but he managed to stay out of the Elvis investigation. I guess the other stuff he got into was bigger. Not too long after Elvis died, Max sued the estate for something like $14,000. Said he'd performed dental services for all of Elvis's friends, and he wanted his money.

MARTY LACKER: Somewhere around '64, Shapiro called me one night when we were out in California doing a movie. He said, "Come over here, I want to show you something." I went over to his house, and he showed me a box filled with bottles of liquid Demerol, which is synthetic morphine. By that time, I was taking a lot of stuff, and so was Elvis. But this was just a little too much for me. The bottles were about six inches tall and about three inches in diameter, packed the way they're shipped from a pharmaceutical company. Labeled and everything.

He threw me one, and he said, "Here, take this back up to the house with you." I said, "There is no way I'm going to give this to Elvis." Shapiro never charged anything for the prescriptions. He would just give them to you. But he wanted to get in good. He liked to tell people that he was friends with all these entertainers.

I had a thirty-six-inch waist the day Elvis first offered me pills. After I started taking 'em, I was down to twenty-nine inches.

LAMAR FIKE: By *Kid Galahad,* we'd moved to 10539 Bellagio Road. The address is wrong in a lot of books. Elvis was tired of the Perugia Way house, and he needed more room.

MARTY LACKER: The Bellagio Road house was like a Mediterranean villa. Lots of marble, huge ceilings and columns.

LAMAR FIKE: Elvis lived like a star of the twenties or thirties, like Valentino or Francis X. Bushman. All the trappings and an endless supply of money. He loved it.

MARTY LACKER: One of the reasons Elvis needed more room was because he was bringing more guys into the group. Like Ray Sitton. We called him "Chief." He wasn't a bad-hearted guy, but he'd get on your nerves a lot. He was just this big ol' goofy guy.

Lamar hated his guts because he used to have to room with him. He was huge—bigger than Lamar, even. And he was taller than Lamar, probably 6'3", and weighed about 380. He and Lamar used to get in bad arguments.

Sitton used to come to the gate at Graceland before Elvis hired him. Elvis sometimes stopped to talk with the fans when he was going in and out of the gates, and he got used to seeing Ray. He'd say, "Hi, Chief, how's it going today?" Well, Elvis used that name pretty loosely, but Ray didn't know that.

One evening, the guys were in the den and somebody came in and said, "Chief asked if he could come up to the house." Elvis said, "Chief? Who the hell is that?" And the guy said, "I don't know. He said you knew him." Elvis said, "Man, I call everybody

Chief." He thought it was funny, so he said, "Okay, bring him up." I think Elvis felt sorry for him. That's how he got on the team.

Chief worked as an extra on *Follow that Dream*, in Florida, and then he went out to California for *Kid Galahad*. He always had a smile on his face. Unfortunately, it was like a simpleton's smile. He got kidded a lot because of his size. I don't know if that drove him to drink, but Chief drank too much, and when he did, he'd do stupid things. He'd get drunk and take the cars out and get in trouble. Elvis finally told him, "If you drink anything, you will not drive any of my cars." And Chief did it again the very next night.

There's an Italian Restaurant out there called Miceli's. We used to go there for pizza. We were standing out on the street, just talking, about eleven-thirty P.M. Elvis had gone to bed, and we left Chief there in case Elvis wanted anything. All of a sudden, here came Elvis's black Chrysler station wagon with Chief in the driver's seat. He passed us, all waving and smiling, like "Hey, there's nothing wrong with me being out here." Chief wasn't too bright.

Finally, he had a couple of car accidents while he was drinking. And Elvis said, "Chief, I don't want you driving my cars anymore." But it didn't stop him. He'd get in the station wagon and go cruising around Hollywood after Elvis went to sleep. He'd come in smelling of liquor and stumble into everything. And it just went on and on. He'd get drunk and start cornering women. Most of the girls found him very unappealing. And while he was generally harmless, he tried to force himself on one. That's when Sonny hit him. Sonny or Red. And Elvis got upset. Chief was out of there.

LAMAR FIKE: Chief was the proverbial square peg. And if we didn't want somebody to fit, they never fit. We'd close ranks and that son of a bitch would lie out there and die before we'd let him in. Elvis hired Chief because he made me mad on *Follow that Dream.* He's dead now, and I'm sorry, but I hated the son of a bitch.

MARTY LACKER: We had another big fat guy in the group, Arthur Hooton. He goes all the way back to the mid-fifties. His mother had worked with Gladys at Britling's cafeteria. Arthur was a funny guy—used to do funny stuff. He went on a few trips with Elvis, traveling to Mississippi to do all these little shows. Then, in the late fifties, Elvis just let him go. Arthur was a nice guy, but he was a little strange. Whenever you talked to him, he'd go, "Yeah," no matter what you said.

LAMAR FIKE: Arthur Hooton was another very loyal person. We used to call him "Arturo van Hooton." He got a regular job, and got married, and that was it. He's so obscure, he's like the answer to an Elvis trivia question.

BILLY SMITH: When a new guy come in, he had to work his way in. It was an interesting mix. You had two Jewish guys, Marty and Alan, who were stingy with Elvis's money. And you had an Italian Catholic, Joe, who loved to spend it. Joe would say, "Oh, hell, it doesn't matter what it costs. Elvis has plenty of money." Joe was flashy. They didn't call him Diamond Joe for nothing. His idea of "accounting" was keeping up with everything Elvis spent, gathering receipts, and then sending them back to Vernon.

About how some of the guys seemed like losers or underdogs . . . There's another factor here. When you first met Elvis, and you were around him a little while, he looked to see if you were in awe of him. And if you were really spellbound, he liked you even better. He didn't think, say, "He's a good businessman. I could use him in the group." He looked for people who would put him on a pedestal and look up to him.

LAMAR FIKE: Elvis was the most insecure human being I've ever been around in my life. He took the cake. He was destiny's child, but he was never prepared to be what he was. That's one reason he didn't like us to like other stars. You had to be very cool. Bob Conrad, the actor, became a dear friend of mine. And Elvis used to get really pissed off when Bob and I were together. He would get madder than a hornet. He'd say, "Hey, let *him* pay you."

Kid Galahad was that picture with Gig Young. Boy, what a hopeless alcoholic. And he had psoriasis real bad. He was married to Elizabeth Montgomery, and when she'd come up on the set, Elvis would just go bananas. God, she was beautiful. This was the boxing picture, and Elvis would get up in the ring and dance up and down on the ropes, just cooing over her.

Charles Bronson was on that movie, too. Charlie was real quiet, but real strong. He and Elvis sort of circled each other for a while. After they got to know each other, they got along real well. Elvis decided he wasn't a threat.

BILLY SMITH: Most show people made Elvis uncomfortable. He thought they were judging him.

MARTY LACKER: Elvis was the first star to have a Rolls-Royce sedan limousine, a huge Phantom V. He had it shipped over in '61. We used it a lot to go to the studio, and one day Elvis got a message from Colonel. Jerry Lewis had called him and said, "Tell Elvis if you're going to have a Rolls-Royce like that, and you're going to ride around town, you should dress in proper attire, not in casual clothes. And don't let those guys around you wear jeans." Jerry had a reputation as a natty dresser. Whether he was jealous of Elvis, I don't know. There were certainly a number of people out there who were.

When Colonel told Elvis what Jerry said, he hit the roof. It really upset him and hurt his feelings because Elvis always loved Jerry's movies. Norman Taurog, who directed a lot of Elvis's pictures, also directed Martin and Lewis, and Elvis liked that. Elvis had Lewis's dressing room at Paramount, the main dressing room in a long row of buildings. It had a bright red door, and it was nicely appointed. He really enjoyed it.

I had to go to the Colonel's office from the soundstage one day. And walking back, I passed that dressing room. We weren't using it then, because Jerry was making a movie. And just as I got in front of the door, it opened. Now, when a door opens, you expect to see somebody standing up, either coming or looking out. But as the door opened, I saw Jerry Lewis's head down on the floor, his face turned so he was looking up and smiling at me.

He was doing it as a joke. And it was funny because it totally shocked me. I laughed, but I kept walking. I went maybe five or ten feet, and I turned around to see if he was still there. Now his head was midlevel, and he was looking out the door. I laughed again and turned and kept walking. But something made me turn around a second time, and when I did, his head was up on top of the door, and he was laughing and sticking his tongue out.

The guy's timing was perfect. How did he know I was going to turn around when I did?

Of all those guys out there, and certainly of the entertainers who claimed to be one of Elvis's close buddies, only Sammy Davis, Jr., was really a friend. He never wanted anything except to have a good time. That went on through the seventies. We didn't see him that often, but maybe once every two or three years, we'd get together with him for the day.

LAMAR FIKE: Elvis started dating Connie Stevens on *Kid Galahad.* He met her at the end of '60. Somebody introduced them—I don't know who. Connie was a very nice person. She was a lot of fun—always bouncy and giggly. But that was no big romance. It was more or less a flirtatious thing. It just lasted about a year.

MARTY LACKER: Connie came and visited Elvis in Idyllwild while we were doing the movie. We were staying at this big lodge. Elvis wanted her to come have dinner there, but he didn't want all the guys around.

I was new to the traveling, but from the beginning, Elvis treated me like I was Joe's assistant. And he said to Joe, "Give Marty some expense money." He told me to take all the guys to the one restaurant in town, while he and Connie and Joe had dinner at the lodge. And Lamar popped up. He said, "What's this fuckin' shit? He's just started traveling with us, and you're giving him the money to pay for us?" I was kind of shocked, you know. And Elvis said, "Don't worry, Lard-ass. You're going to get something to eat." The next morning, Elvis asked me to take Connie and her cousin and her agent to breakfast. Lamar probably didn't like that, either.

The relationship with Connie ended when she got ticked off at Elvis for sending Joe to pick her up for a date one time. She thought she and Elvis were going to have a romantic dinner by themselves. But when she got to the house, Elvis had his usual six or eight guys and 150 girls.

LAMAR FIKE: The fact that we kept Elvis so isolated drove Colonel nuts. He thought he had to know what was going on inside the organization. And on *Kid Galahad*, we began to suspect that Joe was his inside man. Joe would report back stuff to Colonel about Elvis's personal habits and how he felt about the way Colonel was handling his career. Joe didn't get paid for it, but Colonel would do favors for him and make sure he got in good positions.

The Colonel tried to get me to do it one time. I said, "Man, I can't keep up with everything that's going on. Get somebody else."

MARTY LACKER: Since Joe was the foreman, he was dealing with the Colonel a lot. If Parker wanted to talk to somebody other than Elvis, it was always Joe.

BILLY SMITH: I'd say that 1961 was the real start of my difficulties with Elvis. He had a lot on his mind, I know. But Elvis also had a way of making you feel you were nothing without him. Sometimes it was subtle, and sometimes it was outright. A lot of times, out of anger, he'd cut loose on you.

For example, I wanted to go home for Thanksgiving that year. I'd never been gone for the holidays before, and I wanted to see my family and Jo. I'd threaten to quit if things weren't just the way I wanted 'em. And Elvis said, "If you leave me, you're not going to find another job where you can make this kind of money."

One time he said family didn't mean a damn to him. And, boy, that cut deep. I don't know if he meant it or not. I'm like Marty. I never knew if he cared as much about the guys as we cared about him. But I was constantly trying to prove myself to him. I wanted him to know, "Hey, I'm not here just because of your money and your fame. I love you, and I'm glad you made it. Whatever you need, we'll do it. In return, all we ask is that you show us the same respect."

LAMAR FIKE: Elvis always had a tremendous temper, but the pills made it worse. On *Follow that Dream*, he fired us all, one by one. I think I was first, and then Alan, and on down the line. When you got fired, you had nowhere to go. And when you realized, "I'm going to have to get a regular job," it put the fear of God in you. But he rarely meant it. Guys were already starting to leave when he said, "We need to talk this over." And he got every-body back together.

MARTY LACKER: We were doing *Kid Galahad* when I first noticed what Elvis called his makeup case. It was a professional, Hollywood makeup case with little drawers in it. He carried it with him wherever he went or had one of us carry it. It wasn't for makeup anymore. He used it to carry pills.

The whole top layer of that kit was nothing but prescription bottles. All legal. He had all kinds of stuff. Uppers and downers. Pain pills. You name it: Empirin [with] codeine number 3, the strongest there is. Demerol. Percodan. Tuinal. Placidyl. He had a pharmacy in that box. We could always tell when he was taking something by the way he acted. And if we didn't see him, we'd hear him, even in the dressing room on the set. We'd hear the bottles rattling.

That's how I got used to taking stuff in the daytime. We all had our own prescriptions by this time. But sometimes we ran out, and we'd take his.

BILLY SMITH: Over the years, I'd heard Elvis was allergic to codeine. It didn't stop him, though. He'd take that Empirin [with] codeine and codeine tablets mixed with other things, too.

LAMAR FIKE: Elvis wasn't big on reality when he was clean, and when he had pills in him, reality was a Popsicle—you licked on it and threw it away. When we were doing *Kid Galahad*, the Bel Air fire started. A lot of those big mansions burned. It was a dry sea-son, and the fire kept creeping up the hills. And it started getting close to the house on Bellagio Road. We were up in Idyllwild, watching it on television.

Elvis said, "Lamar, drive back to the house, get all my clothes and the Rolls-Royce, and fuck everything else." And he made me go all the way back to Bel Air, about a three-and-a-half-hour drive, and load the station wagon with his stuff, and then drive back to Idyllwild. I got down to Bel Air, and I couldn't get up to the house for the fire trucks. Finally, I worked my way through and loaded up and came back. The fire was already up the street, but not around his house. He didn't give a shit whether the house burned or not—he didn't own it. And I don't think the

issue of my safety ever came to his mind. He was thinking about
the Rolls-Royce and the clothes.

MARTY LACKER: Elvis could be so insensitive. Patsy, my wife,
remembers that when Elvis was in a bad mood, and Lamar would
laugh at something, he'd turn to him and say, "Cool it, fatty,
you're nothing but a joke."

LAMAR FIKE: If you didn't like it, you didn't have to stay.
Working for Elvis was kind of like being in a velvet cage.

MARTY LACKER: When production on *Kid Galahad* wrapped in
December, Elvis decided to go to Las Vegas for a week or two
before going home for Christmas. Billy and I decided to skip
Vegas because we wanted to see our families. Well, Elvis got over
to Vegas and had such a good time that he extended his vacation
another week.

Elvis really liked this bellhop at the Sahara, Johnny Joseph.
When Elvis got ready to leave, the guys packed everything up and
Johnny and the other bellhops brought everything down and
loaded the cars. But when the guys got almost to Arizona, they
discovered the road was closed because of snow. On the way
back, they stopped and called Johnny and told him to get some
guys ready to unpack the cars, and make sure the rooms were
available.

Well, the funny thing was, it happened three times. Elvis
would hear the road was open, and he'd say, "Okay, we'll leave in
the morning," and they'd get out of town, and the snow would lock
'em in again. So finally, the last time they called Johnny, he said,
"Bullshit, you guys ain't comin' back here." He said, "We've been
loading and unloading, and loading and unloading, so you just
stay where you are." Elvis thought it was funny. They went back
anyway, and they didn't get out of there until January of '62. They
were there six weeks. And after the third time, Johnny said, "Man,
if you're leaving this time, leave. Don't come back again this trip."

During that six weeks, I worked in the office at Graceland,
going through the fan mail. Elvis also got letters from people suffering from every conceivable disease, who swore they'd be cured
if Elvis would just see them or send 'em money. Other people
asked him to invest in their business, or their invention, or what-

ever, and promised him a million-dollar return on his money. He got some unbelievable letters. We had one guy who called himself a cousin, "Tony Presley." I can still quote his letter.

He wrote, "Dear Cousin Elvis, I went by the furniture store yesterday like you told me to, and I picked out the living room and bedroom suites. The store just needs to know how you want to pay for this. I sure do appreciate you buying me all this furniture. And I hope to talk to you again next week. Your cousin, Tony Presley." Then, once or twice a week, we'd get these nude pictures of a woman named Ruby. There were a lot of nude pictures from women who wanted a date. Vernon had a special drawer for them. I don't know what he did with them, but every once in a while, when he'd get a really funny one, he'd show it to Elvis.

Elvis didn't really read the fan mail. And, of course, most of the answers that people got were written by people in the office, not Elvis. Vernon and Patsy Presley used to handle it. They'd mimeograph letters and send 'em out. And then Sonny signed a lot of the pictures, and so did Red. All of us used to sign, actually. Elvis signed every once in a while.

Sometimes we made bonfires of the fan mail, out back of Graceland.

CHAPTER 23

SCATTER

In the early sixties, the entourage took on its most problematic and entertaining member, a forty-pound chimpanzee named Scatter. His trainer, Bill Killebrew, who featured both Scatter and his brother, Chatter, on a Memphis children's show, wanted to pare down the act and approached Elvis about buying the chimp as a companion. "I guess he figured Graceland was the kind of untamed place where a monkey would feel at home," remembered Alan Fortas.

Elvis, who'd adored Scatter's earlier incarnation, Jayhew, was an easy mark. But no one in the group foresaw the inevitable trouble that comes with mixing eight guys, 150 girls, and a chimpanzee eager to make his reputation as rock 'n' roll's ultimate party animal.

BILLY SMITH: Alan was the one who talked to Killebrew about showing him to Elvis—he was responsible, somehow. Alan was crazy about Scatter.

LAMAR FIKE: Alan was crazy, period. He loved to get things going with people, stuff they wouldn't normally do. He and I were the ones who had to put up with Scatter and drive him back and forth to California.

MARTY LACKER: Scatter was with us on my first trip cross-country. We had him in a cage in the back of the Chrysler station wagon. One night, we checked into a motel in Flagstaff, Arizona. The chimp stayed in Alan and Lamar's room. All night long, we heard Scatter going, "Ba-dum, Ba-dum!" just running back and forth in the room.

The next morning, Lamar said, in this real quiet voice, "You need to come in here and see this." Scatter had gotten up on the drapes and started swinging on them, and they were partially pulled down. And he'd shit all over them. Oh, God, it was a mess. Lamar said Scatter was just throwing everything he could find. He'd even shit in his hands and thrown it on the walls.

I said, "How do you think we're going to get out of here without paying for this?" Lamar said, "Don't worry about it." So we closed the door and went and had breakfast at the restaurant across the way.

LAMAR FIKE: Just about the time our food came, I looked out the window, and I said, "Oh, my God!" The Mexican maid was knocking on the door. We all jumped up at the same time and tried to yell at her, but it was too late. Before we could even get out of our chairs, she'd walked in and closed the door to start making up the room. It was early in the morning, and the room was dark.

Well, you can picture what it was like for a Mexican maid to open a motel room door in Flagstaff, Arizona, and find a chimp inside. Scatter ran across the room and latched onto her, and she went bananas. She started screaming the most blood-curdling yell I have ever heard. We ran over there, and God, that was the funniest sight. That maid came flying out of that room with Scatter wrapped around her like a damn boa constrictor. He'd jumped on her back, and fastened his legs around her waist, and put his hands over her eyes so she couldn't see.

We peeled Scatter off of her, but then he bolted out the door and went tearing out across the porte cochere which ran over the shed in front of the hotel. He went right up the drainpipe and over the top. The maid was still screeching. And Scatter was on the damn roof, just dancing up a storm—laughing at us.

Alan said, "What are we going to do?" I said, "Go get in your car, and I'll go get the station wagon. I'll leave the back door open and the window down, and the door to the cage ajar. Just slowly drive off."

Well, that car hadn't rolled ten feet when Scatter was on that sucker. He thought we were going to leave him. He stuck so tight he looked like adhesive tape.

MARTY LACKER: We'd paid when we checked in, so we took the keys and threw them on the front desk, and just took off before anybody discovered how bad it was.

LAMAR FIKE: As much of a terror as he was, Scatter was also capable of behaving like a gentleman. Alan used to love to take him for a drive in the Rolls-Royce. He'd buy little suits for him, and sometimes he'd stick a chauffeur's cap on him and balance him on his lap. When they'd meet a car, Alan would duck down to make it look like Scatter was driving. One guy drove right off the road.

MARTY LACKER: We came home one night on Bellagio Road and found out that Scatter had bitten Jimmy, the butler, real bad. Elvis was furious. Jimmy and Lillian were all upset and yelling and threatening to quit if Elvis didn't get rid of him.

Scatter was upset, too. We kept him in the basement, underneath the steps, and Alan tried to get him to go downstairs to his cage, and he wouldn't.

Elvis finally calmed down, and he walked up to Scatter, and he stood over him. Scatter was on top of his cabinet, and he looked up at Elvis with these innocent eyes, and all Elvis did was stare at him, trying to keep a straight face.

Finally, Elvis said, "You coconut-headed little motherfucker, you'd better get downstairs in your cage. And you'd better not ever bite anybody anymore, either."

Scatter hopped off the cabinet, and he slowly walked downstairs like a man going to the electric chair, with his hands folded in front of him. We all followed him. Alan put his hand out for Scatter to hold it, but he wouldn't do it. He had too much pride. He just marched down to the basement and right into that cage. We came upstairs, and Elvis fell on the floor laughing.

LAMAR FIKE: Elvis hit him with a cue stick one night. He hit him so damn hard that chimp just saw stars. And then he ran up the curtain. I said, "God Almighty!" I came down with a gun. I said, "Elvis, if you'll lead him about two yards, I'll shoot him."

BILLY SMITH: We had a huge 35mm projection screen on the wall in the basement den, and it was covered by drapes. Scatter would always run up the side of that damn thing. Or get up on the drapes and start swinging. One time, he miscalculated a little and went right through the screen. Punched a hole in it with his foot. He was cute, but he was just so destructive. He pulled out the phone lines once or twice.

LAMAR FIKE: Another time, the damn monkey had bitten me, and caused me a lot of problems, and tried my patience every which way but loose. So I just went out and got a Hot Shot, a kind of cattle prod. I knew chimps hate water, so I ran a tub full and forced him into it. And he landed in that water, and he started going, "Ruuuuuh!" I said, "Okay, you little bastard," and I jammed that cattle prod into him, and I promise you, every hair on his body stood straight up.

Everybody came in, and Elvis said, "You're trying to kill him!" And I said, "Yes, I'm going to kill the son of a bitch right here!" I hated that damn chimp.

MARTY LACKER: Elvis used to wait until the den was filled with girls, and everybody was real comfortable and having a nice time. Then he'd whisper, "Okay, boys, let him out!" We'd open the door from under the steps, and Scatter would come out whooping like crazy and scaring a couple of people so bad they almost had a heart attack. Because he could make some noise. He was about three-and-a-half or four feet tall, and he made an impression. And he would just naturally gravitate towards the girls.

BILLY SMITH: Alan taught him a lot of things, but he learned some on his own. When a woman got up to go to the bathroom, for example, he'd run and hide behind the bathroom door. And in a minute, we'd hear this godawful scream and this frantic grabbing of the doorknob. It was like jerking the door off the hinges. The girl would bolt out of there screaming her head off, and Scatter would come waddling after her.

One time, this big, tall girl named Pat Parry was over at the house. Well, she didn't know about Scatter, and this sucker made his entrance. He come in with that screeching and with his hands up, and she thought he was going to attack her. He didn't, but then he kept trying to look up her skirt. She told him to stop, and then when he wouldn't, she said, "You do that one more time, and I'm going to knock the hell out of you." They were both in front of a couch by the bar. Well, naturally, Scatter did it again. And Pat came off the floor and hit that monkey under the chin, and he did a back flip and landed on the couch, dazed. He looked at her like he couldn't believe it. He had a head like a bowling ball, but she put a dent in it.

MARTY LACKER: One of Scatter's favorite pranks was to lie on his back on the edge of the couch, so he would be half on the couch, and half off. And when a girl walked by, he'd crook his finger under the hem of her skirt and stick his head up there. He really had a thing about that. You can imagine how it went over. And sometimes he'd masturbate in front of everybody. Believe it or not, we did not teach him to do that. But Sonny and Alan would put him in a bedroom with a couple who was making love, and he'd get excited and jump on the guy's back. Scatter was the real life of the party.

BILLY SMITH: We knew a woman named Brandy Marlow who'd come to the parties. She made her living as a stripper, but she didn't come to the party as one. She was just a guest. But she liked to play around with the chimp. She thought he was fascinating.

One night, the monkey got in her lap, and she had on a low-cut blouse. And Scatter kept running his finger down her cleavage. Elvis said, "Is he bothering you?" She said no. So Elvis said, "Well, if you don't mind, see how far he'll go." And the monkey went to unbuttoning with both hands.

Scatter started off with somebody's drink one night. Turned out, he was a damn suds-head. He liked beer, but he could down a fifth of liquor before you knew it. He'd get so damn drunk that he would fall off the couch onto the floor and just slide.

He got loose in Bel Air once, and the next-door neighbors were real upset. The final straw came when he went over there again. They were having a fancy cocktail party, and Scatter went roaring through their house with his hands up and all the hair standing up on his back. He went, "Whoo-whoo-whoo!" Loud as a freight train, you 'know.

When he screamed, God, it would just send chills down your spine. And it scared the hell out of the party guests, especially when he ran towards 'em. He just wanted attention, really. They didn't know that once you saw him, he'd let down and go on about his business. But, man, they went nuts! They said people went up on the back of couches and on the tables. He cleared the house.

So that did it. Scatter was banned from Bel Air. We had to take him back to Memphis.

LAMAR FIKE: Scatter met a sad end. We put him outside behind Graceland. He couldn't stand being left alone after all the attention he'd gotten. He died out there by himself, hanging on to the side of the cage.

BILLY SMITH: When we took Scatter back to Graceland, the maids had to feed him because we were gone so much. One day, a maid named Daisy went out there, and she had her wig on, and that damn chimp grabbed that wig right off her head. It scared a couple of years off her life. We always thought she poisoned him. And it wouldn't surprise me. Because not long after that, the monkey come up dead.

MARTY LACKER: I happened to be out in the backyard when they took him off. He was hard as a brickbat, just frozen dead. Two guys came from the animal shelter, and each guy had one arm, supporting him, because he was upright, with his long arms out and his legs bowed. It was eerie. It kind of shocked me. They just carried him out to their truck and hauled him off. Poor old Scatter. Alan cried and cried.

CHAPTER 24

CHANGES

MARTY LACKER: When I got home after that first trip, my wife, Patsy, didn't want me to go back out again. So in February of '62, I quit traveling with Elvis and went back into radio. I got a job at WHBQ, the number one station in Memphis.

I didn't really mind dropping out of the group, partly because I couldn't stand Colonel. I still got to see Elvis when he was home. Boy, there were all kinds of changes going on in the group that year, or there would be.

BILLY SMITH: Early '62, or maybe the last part of '61, was when Elvis made a final break with Anita Wood. Elvis was corresponding with Priscilla, and talking about her a lot, even though he hadn't seen her in two years. Elvis was somewhat fickle. He'd be madly in love for a little while, and then somebody else would come along, and he'd think, "Here's someone who understands me a little more." And Anita wanted to get married, and they argued about that a lot.

LAMAR FIKE: I think Anita saw his personality changing, and she didn't know what to think or how to handle it. She thought the army made him sad and pensive, which it did. But how much she knew about his drug use, I don't know. The changes that came with bigger and bigger fame were hard enough for her.

BILLY SMITH: In '62, Elvis went out and bought a Dodge motor home for us to travel in because this traveling in cars was getting kind of old. We were cramped, and we needed more room for the stuff, too. The motor home was only twenty-five feet long, but we thought it was huge. It was like a Winnebago. Lamar took it down to Florida to a guy named Jimmy Sanders, who'd painted a Cadillac purple for us. Jimmy turned it into a bus. It had a breakfast nook up front, and a couch on the other side, and a bedroom in the back.

LAMAR FIKE: Elvis traveled in that motor home for three years. I talked him into buying it, but I cursed the day. It was uncomfortable, and it would break down. God, we had some times in that thing.

MARTY LACKER: When we started traveling in the home, we got tired of losing radio stations, so we rigged up a big reel-to-reel tape recorder to play tapes. Elvis liked Andy Williams at the time. And up came "Moon River." Joe sang out, "Mooo-oon Lacker," because my face is round and I had lost most of my hair. Elvis looked back at me, and he said, "Moon Lacker, you poor old bald-headed son of a bitch." And he started laughing and almost crashed the bus. From that moment on, they started calling me "Moon."

BILLY SMITH: You didn't ever want Elvis to drive. He couldn't keep his mind on what he was doing. He'd leave the turn signal on half the time.

LAMAR FIKE: Elvis would get behind the wheel and start talking, and he'd be doing eighty one minute and ten the next. We were going across the desert one time, and I said, "Can I ask you a question?" He said, "What?" I said, "Why are we going so slow?" He said, "What do you mean?" I said, "Elvis, we're going twenty-five or thirty miles an hour here." He said, "Oh," and he ran it back up again. And he started talking, and he let it run back down again.

BILLY SMITH: There were times when Elvis liked to leave you totally in limbo, just for the hell of it. Sometimes he'd do it to punish you. He did it to me when I wanted to go home in '62. I was getting married in November, and I said, "Look, I got to go home, man. I got to see my family and my fiancée."

One day, after a week of promises, Elvis said, "Okay, we're going to leave tomorrow." We sat in the den, waiting. Well, tomorrow came, and again, he had something else planned. He just didn't want to go.

LAMAR FIKE: We'd come out and get on the bus, thinking we were actually leaving. We stayed on the bus for five goddamn days! I said, "Fuck this shit, boy." Elvis liked to run us crazy.

BILLY SMITH: Finally, I said, "Either we're leaving tomorrow, or I'm taking a flight out of here, and you can stay!" And Elvis just blew up. He said, "Well, goddamn, we'll just go then!" Seven days later, we made it to Memphis. He punished me the whole way.

LAMAR FIKE: That's exactly right. Elvis drove. And he stopped every fifty miles.

MARTY LACKER: Elvis drove 250 miles a day, max. All the way from California.

BILLY SMITH: Sometimes it was less. One day, we drove one hundred miles.

LAMAR FIKE: That was the trip from hell. Finally, Elvis got tired and went in the back. That was our window of opportunity. Joe or Red would get behind the wheel, and we'd gain one hundred miles, just like that. They took turns and floorboarded that son of a bitch. Actually, Elvis pulled that stunt several times.

BILLY SMITH: That was Elvis's way of never letting you forget who was in charge.

LAMAR FIKE: The motor home lived a hard life. Marty broke a side mirror off it one time, but I ripped the top off. When we went to Vegas, we'd stay at the Sahara Hotel because of Colonel's friend, Milton Prell. I was driving, and I was just worn-out. We'd been there for a while, and we'd gambled and lost a lot of money.

Elvis and his dad were sitting at the breakfast nook behind the driver's seat. And I said, "This is Lamar Fike, your safe and courteous driver." And I took a left under the covered walkway in front of the Sahara. It had maybe a ten-foot clearance. And the motor home had a twelve-foot clearance. I heard this "Crrrrrr!" And the bus came to a jarring halt. I peeled the top back about fifteen feet on that son of a bitch. It looked like an open sardine can, just rippled.

The worst part was that all that gunite poured down on Elvis and Vernon. I glanced back at Elvis, and he looked like a wolf. All I could see was his eyes. And he was blinking. The bus was just silent for a minute. Only thing you could hear was this gunite sprinkling down. And then Elvis said, "Lamar!" And I said, "Oh, God!"

Elvis pulled me out of the seat, sat down, and started driving down the highway. That damn gunite was just flying out the top, leaving this trail. And then I remembered something.

I said, "Elvis, I was going to stop and get gas." He said, "You didn't fuel it up?" I said, "I figured we would stop at a station." And do you know, for spite, Elvis drove it 'til it went to empty. In the middle of the Mojave Desert. He said, "Now, Lamar, you get out and find some fuel." And I went, "Jesus Christ!" I got out, and there were all these dead cow skulls everywhere. And I hitch-hiked and got some gas, and thank God, I got a policeman to bring me back. It was hot out there, boy.

🏃 🏃 🏃

MARTY LACKER: Elvis was an impulsive guy. And when you mix impulse, temper, and pills, you're going to have some interesting situations.

In '61, Harold Loyd went to work at Graceland, on the front gates, on the night shift. Harold was Elvis's first cousin on his mother's side. His mother was Rhetha Smith Loyd. She and Gladys were sisters. Rhetha died when Harold was about nine and Elvis was five. She burned to death in a house fire in Tupelo. Harold grew up living with various relatives, moving from one family to another.

Elvis liked Harold because when Elvis was a kid, Harold used to bring him candy bars, PayDays. Harold lived with the Presleys for a while in North Tupelo when he got out of the service. And every month when he got his government check, he'd cash it at a little store there and buy a box of Baby Ruths and PayDays. Elvis used to talk about that a lot. So much so that Harold wrapped up half a dozen PayDays and put them under the Christmas tree for Elvis just a couple of years before he died.

Harold never had the nerve to ask Elvis for anything. One time, he needed a pickup truck because his was falling apart, and he asked Sonny to ask Elvis because he didn't want to do it. Elvis was funny. If you needed something, and you went to him and asked him for it, more than likely he'd say no. But if a third party came to him and said, "Elvis, So-and-so needs something," he'd do it. So Harold got his truck, because Elvis remembered the PayDays.

Even though Harold never intentionally gave Elvis any trouble, in '62, they got into it. Elvis came home to Memphis after *Girls! Girls! Girls!* He went out to the midnight movie, and when he came back about three or four in the morning, he pulled up to the gate and Harold wasn't there—he was up checking on things around the house. Elvis was in a brand-new '63 Buick Riviera, and he blew the horn about three times. And Harold still didn't open the gate. Elvis had a lot of people with him—probably about fifteen cars—and he was embarrassed not to be able to get in his own driveway.

The lights were off at the gatehouse, so he thought Harold was messing around or sleeping. And he got pissed off, and he said, "Fuck you, Harold! I ain't waiting for you." And he backed across the highway and drove full speed through the gates— busted them open and drove up the driveway. Tore the hell out of the gates. And did about $800 damage to the car because as the gates swung open and hit the curb, they flew back and slapped the side of the Buick.

Harold heard this awful commotion, and he didn't know what the hell had happened. He started running down from the house, and he met Elvis about halfway down the driveway. Elvis stuck his head out the window and said, "Goddamnit, I don't know what the hell you were doing, but you better be alert! And from now on, those gates better pop open when I get there!"

For years after that, we'd be sitting out in California or some-where, and about three or four A.M., Elvis would look at his watch and say, "I wonder what Harold is doing about now? I'll bet he's not sleeping on the job."

LAMAR FIKE: Of all the group, I was the one who really got into Elvis's shit, so to speak. But I would do it when nobody else heard me. I'd tell him what was really going on. And he'd get mad and fire me, or I'd get so disgruntled I'd quit because I couldn't take it. It was making me nuts. Sometimes he'd punish me. Like in May of '62. He'd just finished *Girls! Girls! Girls!* and we got in one of our slam-bang arguments.

By then, I'd been with Elvis five years. And I was itching to get on with my life. I wanted to work in some other aspect of the business, and it was difficult because people didn't look at us as having any training. When Elvis and I were in Germany, we used to go over the songs he got from Hill and Range. I would help winnow them down to some reasonable amount.

As a consequence, I got pretty close with Jean Aberbach and Freddy Bienstock at Hill and Range. I first met Freddy when we were doing all the background stuff for *Jailhouse Rock*. So when we came back from Germany in 1960 and did *G.I. Blues*, Elvis set it up where I would be his liaison to Hill and Range. I did the same thing Freddy did, which was present songs to him, but Freddy couldn't get as tight into Elvis as I could.

So in '62, when we started arguing, I came back at him with something he didn't expect. The month before, Dub Albritten, who was Brenda Lee's manager, had a heart attack. Dub called me and said he couldn't go on the road anymore and asked if I'd be Brenda's road manager. I told him I'd have to think about it. I'd helped Brenda on a motion picture she'd done at Twentieth Century-Fox called *The Two Little Bears*, and I got to know Dub real well. We got along.

I didn't really think I was going to accept. But then I had this argument with Elvis. It happened in the dining room on Bellagio Road. Elvis stormed out and went halfway up the steps, and then he turned around and said, "You're fired!" I said, "You can't fire me. I've already quit." We parted on pretty bitter terms.

I road-managed Brenda about a year. Then she got married, and pretty soon she got pregnant, so she came off the road, and that took care of my job. But I stayed in Nashville, and took over the Hill and Range office there, and became a tighter liaison between Hill and Range and Elvis from 1963 all the way up to 1970. I learned the music business as a result of Elvis because Jean and Julian Aberbach taught me everything about publishing. I was happy doing that because I'd found my niche.

BILLY SMITH: If somebody wanted to leave Elvis's employment and go somewhere else, that really bothered him, and he'd have to talk. If somebody quit, boy, he couldn't take that.

LAMAR FIKE: The first year I was gone, Elvis wouldn't contact me directly because he was still mad. But the funny thing is, after that, I was with him just as much as before. He'd do a picture, and I'd go out to California. Elvis never really let go.

🕺 🕺 🕺

BILLY SMITH: That year, 1962, was the first really chaotic year. Marty left, then Lamar left, and there were just a lot of changes. That's when Gene come back to work for Elvis, after being gone a couple years.

When he first come back, we drove out to California in the motor home. And about Texas or Arizona, Gene started getting real hyper. He'd been up for several days on speed, and he couldn't go to sleep. We were taking so many uppers and downers. Gene had these little pills, these uppers, which he called "go-go pills." I guess they were Dexedrine. God, there were so many of them, I can't remember them all.

Gene was trying to fix everything on the bus, even stuff that didn't need fixing. He'd get a damn screwdriver, or something in his hand, and not know what in the world he was doing. He had a habit of licking his lower lip with his tongue when he was working on something, and he'd have that screwdriver and that tongue going at the same time. At one point, Elvis was driving, and Gene was trying to fix the accelerator right under his foot, with the bus going seventy-five miles an hour.

Elvis started getting annoyed because Gene was flying pretty high and being a pest. So Elvis give him five hundred milligrams of Demerol—which is a pain pill—to relax him and help him nod off. But half an hour later, Gene was still wide-awake, so Elvis give him another five hundred milligrams and told him to go back in the bedroom and lie down.

Later on, Elvis told me, "Go check on him." It was kind of dark in back, but I saw that Gene's eyes were about half open, which was the way he usually slept. But he was breathing odd. Then, I didn't think he was breathing at all. So I shook him, and he felt cold.

It scared me because I'd found his brother, Junior, dead in my bed. So I thought, "Oh, God, no, Gene's dead!" I came running back up front of the motor home and I yelled, "Elvis, pull over! I think Gene's dead!"

Elvis slammed on those brakes, boy, and run back there and shook him. I know it scared him pretty bad, too, or he would have just said, "Aw, hell, let the son of a bitch sleep." It took Elvis a while to wake him up, and when Gene did come around, it was slow.

At first, Elvis said, "C'mon, Gene, stay awake! Hang in there with us!" And then he wanted to kill him. He said, "Hell, you don't know what you're doing! You mix all this stuff up, and you don't know what counteracts what." Which was true. He was taking downers along with sleeping pills to counteract the uppers he'd taken earlier in the day. Elvis had started memorizing the *Physician's Desk Reference,* so he knew what he could mix with what. He knew enough to tell a doctor where he hurt—make up stuff, you know—to get a certain kind of pill.

When we finally got Gene awake, Elvis dragged him out of the motor home and we walked him alongside the highway for a while to make sure he was all right. Finally, we saw he was going to make it. We got back on the bus, and Elvis climbed behind the wheel. About a minute passed, and Elvis turned around and said, "Goddamnit, Gene. I ought to kill your ass!"

MARTY LACKER: Gene Smith made the most foolish mistake of all because Elvis would have done anything for him. I guess the best way to put it is that he and Elvis had a misunderstanding about some missing jewelry. And Elvis said he didn't ever want to see Gene again. That was late '62. Every once in a while, Gene would come up to Graceland. But every time he came up, he wanted something. And Elvis was always hurt.

BILLY SMITH: Sometimes I think Elvis give things away more for effect than out of wanting to help somebody. For example, he had a habit of picking up hitchhikers. He'd stop, and they'd get in not knowing who it was, and he'd turn around and say, "How you doing?" Gosh, they'd just freak out. Sometimes they'd say, "Elvis Presley! And on his bus!" But a lot of times they were just too dumbfounded to say anything. They'd be in total shock.

One time he picked up two boys who were in the service. They got to talking, and he asked them where they were from and why they were hitchhiking. One of them said he was trying to get home, and he didn't have much money. So Elvis carried them to the next city and bought 'em plane tickets. Now, he didn't always do that. It depended on his mood. And if you hit him at the wrong time, he wouldn't help you for nothing.

In late '62, I was getting married, and I asked Elvis to sign a note for me at the bank. It was for $1,600, and I was in bad need of it. I told him what I needed, and he said, "Goddamnit, I can't even walk in the house that some son of a bitch don't want me to sign a note or give him a handout!" And I thought, "God!" It flew all over me. I know my heart sunk to my damn feet. Because I was desperate, and I thought, "My gosh, it wasn't like I wasn't going to pay it back." And hell, I'd just seen him buy an expensive shotgun for some sailor in a sporting goods shop in Beverly Hills—just because Elvis overheard him talking to his wife about saving enough money to buy it.

I finally said, "The bank won't let me have it. I'm only nineteen years old. You've got to be twenty-one to sign by yourself." He didn't say a damn word. So I said, "Well, you don't have to sign anything. I appreciate it, but I'll handle it myself." I tore the note up, and I started to walk out. And then I turned and said, "I quit."

Boy, he got mad! He got mad at himself because he knew damn well he was wrong and that he'd hurt my feelings. He couldn't stand to hurt anyone's feelings.

Little by little, he worked his way back around to make up with me. But I never did pursue the note no further. I worked my way out of that money mess all by myself.

MARTY LACKER: When I was back working in radio in Memphis, I used to go over to Graceland to play touch football with Elvis and the guys. And two new guys started coming around—Richard Davis and Jimmy Kingsley. They were friends. I think Richard had known Alan and Sonny, although he was a little younger, like twenty-two.

One day, Jimmy told Elvis he liked this expensive jeweled watch he had on, and Elvis just slipped it off his wrist and said, "It's yours."

Elvis really liked Richard better because he had a hell of a sense of humor. Jimmy was basically a nice guy, but he was a little bit of a wiseass. Sarcastic.

In August of '62, Elvis went out to California to do *It Happened at the World's Fair.* Jimmy and Richard hopped in the car and followed him out there—just showed up in L.A. and said they were on vacation.

Elvis was getting ready to go to Seattle to do the location shooting, and after he talked to them a little while, he and Joe disappeared in the bathroom. In a minute, Joe stuck his head out and asked Richard and Jimmy to come in. Elvis said, "I'm going to Seattle to do a movie. How would you like to come work for me?" Richard says they were probably the only two guys Elvis hired in a bathroom.

Richard left the group periodically and came back in. He worked as a valet with Elvis's movie wardrobe. Jimmy didn't do much of anything for Elvis.

BILLY SMITH: Elvis called Richard "Broom" because he was so skinny. He was a lot of fun. Whatever you wanted to do, he was in for it, regardless of how rough it got.

Jimmy would have been shunned out of the group had he not pulled the wool over everybody's eyes. He conned us all, and he eventually let his true colors show. He started pushing Elvis to get us into the Screen Extras Guild so he could get into the Hollywood scene. He wasn't really interested in Elvis. I could tell by the way Jimmy talked that he wasn't going to last long. He bitched about everything that went on, and he bad-mouthed Elvis.

MARTY LACKER: About the third time Jimmy pulled that crap, I said, "You know, Jimmy, if you don't really like the man, you shouldn't be here taking his damn money." Jimmy's dead now. Shot himself, in '89.

BILLY SMITH: The parties we had on Bellagio Road were a little different from the parties we had earlier on Perugia Way. One reason was a lot of the guys were married now, like Red, and Marty, and Joe. Or they were almost married, like me, and like Lamar. So their priorities were a little different.

MARTY LACKER: Even though at times there were so many women around, most of the married guys didn't cheat on their wives. It was awfully tempting, but there was always a fear of somebody getting pissed off and blabbing. Two or three of the wives, by the way, married the guys just because they wanted to be around Elvis. But we never talked to anybody about what went on in the group. There's a lot of stuff I never told my wife, and everybody else was the same way. It was an unwritten rule. In that sense, we really were a Mafia.

BILLY SMITH: Elvis had very strict rules where the girlfriends and wives were concerned. Number one was, "Don't fool with my girlfriend, and I won't fool with your girlfriend or your wife." And number two, he expected the women who came to the parties to mind their manners, and when they didn't, like Christina Crawford, he'd get angered into doing something he'd regret. He got so mad at an actress one time that he picked up a watermelon and threw it at her and hit her in the rear.

The most famous incident like that happened on Bellagio Road in '62. A girl was there at a party, and she was trying to get Elvis's attention any way she could. She wasn't getting anywhere with him, and after a while, she followed him downstairs where he was playing pool. And she got real abusive.

Women to him were a dime a dozen, let's face it. And she demanded his attention to the point where he finally had to say, "Look, I'm shooting pool, and I'm going to finish this game before I do anything else." And she took the cue ball off the table. Elvis said, "If you do that again, they'll have to surgically remove it." And she said, "You're a smartass son of a bitch, aren't you?"

That's all it took. The first thing that went through his mind was, "You don't call me that—my mother's dead!" And he harpooned the hell out of her—launched that cue stick before he even knew what he had done.

He hit her in the shoulder, almost on the collarbone—not in the breast, as some people say. And he went right over to see about her. Of course, he wasn't going to apologize. But he felt bad about it. He told one of the guys, "Take her to the doctor and make sure she's all right, but get her away from me." Later, he broke down and cried because he done it. That was Elvis, though. Just for that brief moment, he would hurt you, but he wouldn't really mean to do it.

LAMAR FIKE: I think Elvis just did what he wanted to do. He had no parameters. There was no line of demarcation. He moved the lines of behavior wherever he wanted them, and if he went too far, he moved them out farther. His discipline was nonexistent. And the more insulated he got, the stranger he got. You have to understand that you're not dealing with a normal person. But then normal people don't go into this business to start with. Or if they do, they aren't normal when they get out of it.

MARTY LACKER: Elvis was never big on going to restaurants because he'd have everybody coming up to him, wanting to shake his hand or get an autograph. I never saw him refuse an autograph to someone's face.

A couple of times, Joe talked him into going to the Luau in Beverly Hills. We used to go through the backdoor and sit in a private room in the rear. No one ever knew he was there.

We got him to go out some to the Red Velvet nightclub on Sunset Boulevard near Cahuenga. It was owned by a friend of ours, the father of a girl named Sandy Ferra who Elvis dated on *G.I. Blues*. She's married to Wink Martindale now. The Red Velvet was one of our favorite hangouts.

We used to have a lot of good times. Sandy's father, Tony, always had two booths reserved for us. He wouldn't allow anybody else to sit there, even when he knew Elvis wasn't coming with us.

Monday night was Talent Night. Some of the guys who came out of there were pretty good—the Righteous Brothers and the Checkmates [,Ltd.]. A lot of black groups.

BILLY SMITH: Basically, Elvis liked blacks. He liked black music, of course. But he also liked black artists in the business. And black sports heroes.

MARTY LACKER: Jim Brown, the former football star, was doing a movie out in California one time when we were out there, and he came over to the set. A number of football players used to come over and see Elvis—Rosey Grier, and Mike Henry, and a lot of guys from the [L.A.] Rams.

We always watched the Cleveland Browns because Elvis really liked Jim Brown. He liked to watch him bust tackles because Brown was the greatest runner of all time. So when these football players came to visit, Elvis would always say, "What kind of guy is Jim Brown? Do you know him?"

Everybody told us what a cold person Brown was. They said he never talked to anybody, that he never gave anybody any tips on breaking tackles, and that he was the same on the movie sets—he just didn't share much.

Well, we found out that Brown sort of liked Elvis, and since it was mutual, Elvis invited him to come on the soundstage to meet him. We started talking to him, and he seemed real friendly. Finally, the conversation got around to "Man, how in the world did you break those tackles? You'd have four guys on you, and you'd run right through them." And he told us how he did it. We didn't find him reticent at all.

He came to Memphis one time for something, and Elvis said he'd like to have him out to the house. Richard and I took the limo and brought him over. We all sat in the living room, and somehow the conversation got on karate. And of course, Elvis had to get up and start doing a demonstration.

For some reason, Jim thought that was childish, or it didn't set well with him. So he said, "Well, I'm late for an appointment. I gotta go." And I made some stupid remark, like "What's the matter? Can't handle karate?" And he looked at me like "I can handle whatever you got." And that was it. Elvis was happy to see him, but they never spoke again.

LAMAR FIKE: People ask me how Elvis felt about blacks. He had a Mississippi upbringing, so I think he had a certain amount of prejudice. But in the entertainment business, I've never seen a color line drawn. You're judged on what you can do, how fast you can draw your gun. They don't care if you're black or white. If you can outdraw them, you're a gunslinger.

I heard Elvis use the term "nigger" maybe once or twice, but never directly to anybody. And as a rule, he didn't use it. Alan was on a call-in radio show out of Louisville a few years ago, and a black waiter from Chattanooga called in. His name was Willie, and he said he was standing about three people away from Elvis at the Patton Hotel in the fifties, and he overheard Elvis say, "All a nigger can do for me is buy my records and shine my shoes."

But it wasn't like him to make racist remarks like that.

MARTY LACKER: Sometime in the seventies, we were in Baltimore, and a guy who's now a football coach with a major team came backstage with a couple other players. And he used the word "nigger." Elvis didn't say anything while he was there. But then Elvis made an excuse to get them out of there, like "Well, I got to get ready." And when the coach left the dressing room, Elvis had a fit because he'd used that word. He said, "That no-good, prejudiced bastard." With Elvis, it was always "Do as I say, not as I do." He was prejudiced, but he didn't want anyone else to be.

BILLY SMITH: Elvis tried not to be prejudiced, but at times he come off that way. It's really hard to get that completely out of you when you're brought up that way. I'm the first to admit that I still am, to a certain degree. And that's how Elvis was.

MARTY LACKER: Every Christmas, or anytime someone asked, Elvis gave a lot of money to black charities. When he met black people, he always showed them the same respect he gave anybody else. He'd say, "Yes, sir," and, "Yes, ma'am," and talked to them like they were old friends.

But Elvis was prejudiced about blacks, sure he was. Because of the way he grew up. His family hated blacks, hated Jews, hated everybody. And that only came from ignorance.

You also have to consider the times. When his daughter was little, we were talking about this one time and he said he'd be damned if Lisa Marie married a black man. Which is kind of ironic now. He gave blacks all the credit in the world when it came to music. But he thought the races should be separate in love and marriage.

He had a couple of dates with Joan Blackman when he first went to Hollywood. She costarred in two of his movies, *Blue Hawaii* and *Kid Galahad.* And she used to come over to the house some. Alan asked Elvis what happened to that romance, and Elvis said Joan had dated a black guy and it turned him off.

One night at the Memphian—much later, now—Elvis was out of his mind on drugs. Me and Red were up in the lobby with him while the movie was on. Elvis started screaming and raving because this girl he had dated in California called him all upset. He said she'd told him she'd gone on a date with a famous football player who happens to be black. This guy thinks he's a badass. He has a reputation for beating up women, especially white girls.

Well, Elvis had taken too many pills, and he was talking about shooting him or having somebody kill him. And Red and I were trying to calm him down. But he just kept on. He always thought that I was good friends with a couple of guys in the real Mafia because of my father. And he remembered that I had met some guys from what he called the Black Mafia at a music business function, so I played on that.

I said, "Elvis, do me a favor. Let me take care of it. I'll put a stop to it." I had no intentions of doing that, but I wanted to quiet his ass down and get him to forget about it.

He looked at me and he said, "You will?" I said, "Yeah." He said, "Okay. Let me know what happens." I think he forgot about it by the time he got home.

BILLY SMITH: Elvis went at everything in a big way. He'd do it 'til he wore it out, and then it would just die off. In the early sixties, Elvis got on this suit kick. He went through a Louis Roth phase because he went through the factory one time. Then he sent Alan down to Julius Lewis in Memphis to buy a couple dozen suits and shirts and the whole works. Everything except underwear because he didn't wear any. Later on, he decided we should all wear suits, and he bought 'em for us—hauled us all down to some store in Beverly Hills for suits and ties.

He said, "We're going to dress accordingly." Well, some of us groaned, but we knew it wouldn't do no good. For a few days, we all dressed in these new suits, uncomfortable as hell. Then one morning, Elvis showed up without his tie. Alan said, "Hey, Elvis, if you're not wearing a tie, how come we have to?" Elvis thought a minute, and then he said, "In the mornings, if I come down in a suit, you all dress in a suit. If I come down in casual clothes, you wear casual clothes."

Well, God, it got to looking like a Keystone Kops comedy—guys constantly going back in their bedrooms to change. Colonel saw us in the suits one day and told us they made us look like old men. Boy, Elvis didn't like that! That was the last time he made us wear suits.

MARTY LACKER: Just before *It Happened at the World's Fair,* Elvis had everybody get black jumpsuits. He got a white jumpsuit for himself. Then they all got in the Dodge motor home—which was also black and white—and took off across country.

They'd pile out at the service stations to stretch, and the attendants and the other customers would take one look at 'em and get uneasy. Some people just got back in their cars without getting their gas—I guess they thought they were about to get robbed.

When they went to Seattle for the location shooting, Elvis told the guys to keep wearing the jumpsuits so he could pick them out in the crowd because the World's Fair drew eighty thousand to one hundred thousand people a day.

After they finished up there, they went to Vegas to relax. We did wear our suits in Vegas because it was stylish. And in Vegas, the sun bothered us, so we all wore dark sunglasses.

Elvis had Joe make reservations to see Johnnie Ray at the Hacienda Hotel, and when twelve guys who all looked alike arrived in black limousines and black mohair suits and sunglasses, people started to stare. The guys just automatically surrounded Elvis to protect him from the crowd, and somebody yelled out, "Who the hell are they, the Mafia?"

A Las Vegas newspaper reporter happened to be there, and he put "Memphis" in front of "Mafia." And when it came out in the newspaper the next day, it just stuck. Elvis thought it was funny, and since it made him sound like a bad dude, he decided it was all right. He even used it sometimes. We'd been called "flunkies," and "leeches," and worse, you know. So Elvis told us we finally had a respectable title.

CHAPTER 25

PRISCILLA

In 1962, after months of transatlantic phone calls, Elvis persuaded Captain and Mrs. Joseph Beaulieu to allow Priscilla to visit him in California for a two-week vacation that summer. For two years, Priscilla had been writing to Elvis on special pink stationery—per Elvis's instruction—so Joe could pick her letters out of the mountains of fan mail. She was now sixteen years old.

BILLY SMITH: When Priscilla flew into L.A., Elvis sent Joe to the airport to get her and bring her back to Bellagio Road. He threw a party so he could show her off, although I'm not sure she knew it was for her. She seemed so young in comparison to everybody else. I don't know that I have too many impressions of Priscilla when she first come over. I didn't spend that much time around her. She didn't stay at the house—Elvis thought it would look better if she slept at George and Shirley Barris's. George is the car customizer who did Elvis's Solid Gold Cadillac that's in the Country Music Hall of Fame.

Alan took her shopping one day and bought her all these sexy, sophisticated clothes that made her look a whole lot older than she was. And then Elvis took her someplace and had her hair darkened and fixed the way he liked it—which was piled high. And he had her makeup done so she looked kind of painted, you know. He thought it made her look more womanly, I guess you'd say.

Actually, Alan said all the changes made her look like a Vegas hooker. We were going to Vegas while she was there, so maybe Elvis wanted her to have the right look.

LAMAR FIKE: I talked to Alan after Priscilla's visit. I said, "What did you think of her?" Alan said, "Well, she's a nice girl. A little *young* maybe." I laughed. He said he told Elvis there were a lot of pretty girls who were legal age but that Elvis said, "Alan, a sixteen-year-old girl is a lot more advanced than a sixteen-year-old boy in every way." And Alan told him, "Yeah, but they're still jailbait."

BILLY SMITH: I thought Priscilla was beautiful and that she had a fairly good personality, although to a certain extent she was false. I'm about three years older than she is, so I would have been closer to her in age than any of the other guys. But there wasn't any special feeling between us because you never got real close to any of the girls that Elvis was with, out of fear of how he might take it. So I just treated her with as much respect as I could.

After that first visit, she went back to Germany. She really didn't want to go, but Elvis didn't want any problems with her parents. I've wondered what they thought when they saw her get off the plane with her new look.

Apparently, they weren't upset about it because after we got back to Memphis, Elvis got on the phone and called her daddy and talked him into letting her come for Christmas. She flew to New York, and Vernon and Dee met her at the plane and brought her back to Memphis.

MARTY LACKER: That early winter of '62, I was still at WHBQ Radio, and I went over to Graceland one afternoon. Elvis was up kind of early, which was unusual. When I got there, he was sitting out on the front steps, which was also unusual for him. We sat and talked for about an hour, and then I said, "Well, I'll see you later. I've got to go." And Elvis said, "No, no, wait a minute. I want to show you something." We talked on a while, and then all of a sudden, the front door opened, and out came this girl, all primped up. She had her hair dyed black and in a beehive, and she was made-up like a painted doll, with all this mascara and bright eye shadow. She was pretty for 1962, but even then, just way overdone.

Elvis said, "This is Priscilla, from Germany." I looked at him, and smiled, and gave him a nod, like "Yeah, she's really pretty." He showed her off like he was showing off a new car. She was his trophy, his new toy.

BILLY SMITH: When Elvis first met Priscilla over in Germany, he give her some Dexedrine to help her stay awake for those late-night parties. And when she come over for Christmas, he give her something else. She was so excited about coming to the States that she hadn't slept in a couple of days, and then Elvis kept her up until about four A.M., and she was wore out.

They were getting ready to go to bed, and Elvis told her he was going to give her something to help her sleep, even though she said she didn't need it. He popped out two five-hundred-milligram Placidyls. She took them, and she didn't wake up for two days. It scared the hell out of Vernon and Grandma, I remember. They wanted to get a doctor in there. Elvis said no, he'd just walk her around. But that didn't do any good, either. She finally woke up on her own. You'd think Elvis would have learned his lesson with Gene in the motor home, but I guess he didn't.

She went back to Germany again right after Christmas, and Elvis immediately started trying to persuade her parents to let her come there to live. Elvis had to do a lot of talking, boy. He said she'd get a better education here than in Germany, that he'd put her in Catholic school at Immaculate Conception. And he promised that she'd live with Vernon and Dee in their house, not in Graceland, so she'd be properly chaperoned.

I don't know how he sold them that bill of goods, but he did. She came back over while we were making *Fun in Acapulco*, in either February or March '63. Her dad come with her, first to California and then to Memphis. It's always puzzled me just why they allowed that.

MARTY LACKER: Let's get right to the meat of it. Say you're the parent of a sixteen-year-old girl, and a grown man, a millionaire, came to you and said, "I really care about your daughter, and I want her to come live with me." What would your answer be, unless you had an ulterior motive? I know what my answer would be: "Get the hell out of here!"

LAMAR FIKE: Well, that's an absurd question. I mean, nobody in their right mind would let that happen. I'd have castrated him, buddy, I promise you that. It's obvious that Elvis was *very* persuasive. But it might have been more than that.

MARTY LACKER: There are all kinds of theories about what made these parents turn a sixteen-year-old girl loose in another country with a twenty-eight-year-old bachelor who was doing everything there was to do in Hollywood and Vegas.

In 1976, Elvis dated a woman named Minde Miller. This was, I believe, a two-night romance. Minde did a TV interview a couple of years ago. She said that she and Elvis talked more than they did anything else, and she asked him about Priscilla and how he convinced her parents to let her come over here and live with him.

She says Elvis told Priscilla's parents that he would marry her. And I'm sure that's true. I can hear him say it: "I really love her and when she gets a little older, after she finishes school, I'm gonna marry her." And he may have meant it at the time. But like a good liar and a good hustler, he would tell anybody anything to get what he wanted.

After he was with her a couple of years, though, the bloom went off the rose. As Minde puts it, he said, "Hey, I had her, so what was new anymore?" Some people wonder if Captain Beaulieu had a contract with Elvis or a written promise to marry Priscilla.

LAMAR FIKE: There's been speculation that Elvis made a deal. "If you'll bring her over here, I'll marry her."

BILLY SMITH: Sometimes Elvis seemed like he couldn't give much to anybody, that he didn't have much warmth. But he did. When he cared about somebody, he cared deeply. He just might not have shown it in the ways most people do.

When Priscilla first come over here, he liked to show off for her. One night, Elvis and Priscilla, and Richard Davis and his date, and my wife, Jo, and me went to the fairgrounds. We got on the roller coaster, and when we started up the first long hill, Elvis said to me and Richard, "Let's get out on the top and wait for it to come back around." He wanted to play a trick, see.

Well, we did it, and the girls finished the ride alone. They got back down to where the operator was, and he started stretching his neck, looking for Elvis. When he saw that Elvis wasn't anywhere in those cars, he nearly had a heart attack. He got all agitated and called for the manager, whose name was Malcolm Adams. We called him "Wimpy." But before Wimpy got there,

Priscilla told the operator, "Go again!" And when they got back to the top, we all got back in. Elvis liked to run red lights and jump intersections—anything to give everybody a thrill.

I'd say Elvis was crazy about Priscilla, at least at first. He was always telling her how pretty she was. And when the guys were around, he'd say, "Here she comes. Isn't she beautiful?" He tried to show that he cared for her. He just wanted total control of her. But he didn't want to give up anything to keep her.

MARTY LACKER: When Elvis went out to California, he didn't want Priscilla around because of all the women out there. We left Bellagio Road in late '62 and moved back to the old house on Perugia Way. And Priscilla was hardly ever in that house. He insisted that she stay at home. He always said he wouldn't have time to take her anyplace or do anything with her. He said, "You'll have more fun staying in Memphis and going shopping.". But he called her every night.

LAMAR FIKE: At one point, Elvis thought she was screwing around on him. Now, this was right after she got there and was going to Catholic school.

BILLY SMITH: It was always all right for Elvis to do pretty much what he wanted to do, but it was never all right for the woman. If Priscilla had slept with somebody else, that would have been it. She would have been gone. It's the old double standard. Maybe that's the way we were brought up. Elvis expected her to be totally loyal. He thought, "I'm in California, and I can fool around and it won't mean anything because it's going to be over and done with. But when I get back home, I know I'll have somebody there because she's loyal." He had that old Southern belief—"A woman's place is in the home."

MARTY LACKER: At first, it was easy for him to keep Priscilla in Memphis because she was going to school. That next year, '64, my family moved to Graceland and my wife and daughter sort of baby-sat her until late '65, when we moved into our house. Because only Grandma was there with her all the time. I say "baby-sat," but she was seventeen. So she and my wife were keeping each other company, although my wife didn't put up with any of her nonsense. In a lot of ways, she was still a kid. And she was spiteful. She'd get in arguments with my daughter, Sheri, over her toys or what television show they were going to watch. It was kind of ridiculous. Sheri was four or five years old.

There really wasn't a lot for her to do at Graceland but just sit around and talk to Grandma or Vernon and Dee when they came over. She also went out with the girls, mostly shopping, and to lunch. And sometimes they went to a movie at night. But Priscilla began to take advantage of that situation right away. At first, she and Elvis's cousin, Patsy Presley, were just shopping buddies. Then they became pretty good friends—more like Patsy was following Priscilla, or working for her, really. And Priscilla was no better than Patsy. If Patsy had said no to Priscilla, Elvis wouldn't have said anything. Because Elvis really cared a lot about Patsy.

BILLY SMITH: Priscilla liked the other wives to cater to her. Some did, but most of them didn't. My wife was one of the worst. Priscilla would say, "Why don't you get my coat?" My wife would say, "Why don't you get it yourself?"

LAMAR FIKE: Priscilla brought out a litany of unfriendly feelings in a lot of people, and still does. But basically, Priscilla was not a cold person. There's a difference between being cold and [being] defensive. Priscilla is extremely defensive. And she's very, very greedy.

I'll give you Elvis's relationship with her in a nutshell: You create a statue. And then you get tired of looking at it.

MARTY LACKER: Elvis's infatuation with Priscilla started wearing off early, right after she first came. But he put up with her because he didn't want to hurt her and because she was convenient. His running time with women, if he got halfway serious, was about four or five years, if that long. So he put up with her. I think you have to look at what he wanted in Priscilla and what he didn't. First of all, he didn't look at her as an adult. So he didn't think of her as a partner at all.

LAMAR FIKE: Elvis was rearing her. That was obvious. The only time he'd really talk to her was when he'd go on a sympathy trip. She'd soothe him with baby talk, and she'd pet him the way he loved to be petted. And they'd baby-talk back and forth. He called her "Nungen," which was Elvis for "young one." But he also started calling her "Satnin'" since Gladys was gone. Priscilla waited on him hand and foot. Every woman that ever went with him waited on him hand and foot. Other than that, he didn't feel the need of talking to her. They'd have a conversation, but it would be so one-sided in his direction.

MARTY LACKER: Priscilla was his geisha girl. They'd sit on the couch, and she'd be patting his face, and his hair, and they'd talk that baby talk. That was his trip.

BILLY SMITH: Elvis wanted a woman who liked what he liked. But for her to give advice, well, it just didn't happen. He was more likely to confide in Grandma.

MARTY LACKER: The fact that he played around on Priscilla in itself isn't startling. But the fact that he started playing around on her four months after she got there is something altogether different.

CHAPTER 26

"ALL GUNS POOLSIDE!"

By April of '63, RCA boasted that Elvis had sold more than 100 million records worldwide. While that made Elvis the undisputed King of Rock 'n' Roll, in his film roles the transformation from rough rocker to passive leading man was complete—and the movie songs more flaccid than ever. In a 1961 press conference, Elvis tried to put the best spin on everything, declaring, "I would like to play a dramatic role, but . . . I'm not ready for that, really. I haven't had enough experience in acting, and until I'm ready for it, it would be foolish to undertake something very dramatic . . . You can rest assured that there will be music in almost all of them . . . There has to be."

On-screen, and before the public, Elvis was handsome and debonair, laying his perfect manners out like a sterling silver place setting—the personification of a desirable bachelor-at-large. At home, he was becoming increasingly something else.

MARTY LACKER: All the time I was in radio, I liked to write and be creative, and most of the spots I did were humorous. We did good production work at WHBQ. A guy from WNOE in New Orleans heard about me and offered me a job there as production director and weekend on-air talent. It paid a lot more, so I went down there in October of '62. And for the first time, WNOE became the number one station.

My personal life wasn't going as smoothly. Patsy hadn't really wanted to move to New Orleans. I found a house for us out near Lake Pontchartrain, and the first two days we were there, it was so hot we had lizards crawling on the walls. The mosquitoes were unbearable. Sheri was two or three years old, and as soon as she went out the door, she'd come back in with her whole face a mass of mosquito bites. That really shook Patsy up. Quite frankly, she had a nervous breakdown while we were there. It was hard for me to see her like that. And it was rough in other ways. Especially financially. Even though I was making more, it seemed like I was always broke.

My son, Marc, was born on January 8, '63. He had the same birthday as Elvis and my sister, Anne. My bills were so high that I didn't know how I was going to get him out of the hospital. I mentioned it to either Alan or George Klein during a phone conversation, and one of them told Elvis. About three days later, I opened up the mail and there was a check from Elvis for $300. I was so surprised. I wrote him a thank-you note and told him I'd pay him back as soon as I could.

That spring, we were back in Memphis. The year before, Joe had married a Vegas showgirl named Joanie, and his daughter, Debbie, had been born. We went back for the christening.

While we were home, I went over to Graceland. Little by little, I'd saved $50 in cash—I remember it was two twenties and a ten—and I put it in a white envelope. Patsy was with me, and the three of us talked for a while. Then when Elvis was getting ready to go upstairs, I asked him if I could see him in private for a minute.

That's the way most of the guys would start when they wanted to borrow money, and he knew it. He didn't like to be asked for money unless you had a really good reason. So he said, "Yeah, what is it?" I pulled the envelope out of my back pocket, and I handed it to him. I said, "That's part of the money you sent me when my son was born. I'll pay the rest back as soon as I can." He looked so surprised. We were in the dining room at the time, and he left and went up the hall stairs. And as he got halfway up, he turned to me and said, "You don't know what this means to me. You're the first one who's ever paid me back." And he had tears in his eyes.

Fifteen minutes later, he came back downstairs. I was sitting at a table on the patio. And he handed me the envelope and said for me to take it back, that I needed it more than he did, and the fact that I tried to pay it back made him happier than he could say. Then he said he'd burn the damn money if I didn't. So I put it in my pocket.

LAMAR FIKE: In May of '63, Elvis came to Nashville for a recording session at RCA's Studio B. I hadn't seen him since I quit the year before. I went over to the studio, and we hugged and made up.

After that, I was back and forth with him, going out and doing pictures with him and heading up the Nashville office of Hill and Range. I spent most of my time finding songs for him. That year—1963—was also the year I met Kevin Eggers. Kevin had a company with Hill and Range, and we became friends. After Elvis died, Kevin put the whole deal together for the Goldman book and published it under his imprint at McGraw-Hill.

When I was talking to Elvis at the recording session, I told him I was getting married. I'd met a woman named Nora at the Copacabana while I was working for Brenda Lee. She was a Copa girl, a dancer. I said, "My name is Lamar Fike, and I'm going to marry you." I was twenty-eight at the time.

When I started back traveling with Elvis, I got right back into that cocoon, to where the outside world was very strange to me. I had a phone in my car because I was in the business, and I got used to having one with Elvis.

One day, I had to pick up Freddy Bienstock at the airport. It was about seven-thirty in the morning. I was driving, and here was all this traffic. I didn't know what to do. I got on the phone and called Nora. I said, "Is there some sort of bomb scare, or attack or fire somewhere?"

She said, "What are you talking about?" I said, "There are all kind of cars out here on the road at seven-thirty in the morning! They're everywhere! What are they doing?" She said, "Lamar, it's rush hour. They're going to work." I had totally forgotten that people did that at that hour. Because I'd go to work at ten or ten-thirty.

I also discovered real quick that being away so much didn't help the marriage. I was married to Elvis, really. Hell, we all were. There was never any question where my allegiance was. My wife was secondary. And most of the guys felt that way. Not because Elvis made us feel that way. Because we chose to be that way.

I'm just now, in my late fifties, getting to know my children, for Christ's sake. I mean, you're talking eternal devotion to Elvis. The Catholic Church would hope to God it has monks and nuns as dedicated as we were. Seriously. Hitler never had the kind of loyalty Elvis had around him.

BILLY SMITH: Elvis expected us to be married to him. He didn't want you to put anybody before him. My wife's greatest struggle was with Elvis. She thought she was in a battle with him over me. And she was.

A lot of times I thought, "God, what in the hell am I doing? I've got a family here." I regret it now. But I wanted to be loyal, and I also liked that lifestyle—the excitement, the pictures, Hollywood. It gets in your blood.

It made me feel special. Yet I wanted to be home with my family, too. It was hell. But it had to be even worse for Jo because the guys were constantly doing things, and she was alone. And it took me a while to see that she was going through sheer misery. Jo still sees Elvis as a threat, and he's not even here.

MARTY LACKER: My family and I stayed in New Orleans almost a year, and then we went back to Knoxville, where all of Patsy's relatives lived. I didn't have a job, but my reputation was still good enough in radio to get me a shot at the morning show.

Patsy was ecstatic because she wanted to stay in Knoxville with her family. But that afternoon, Alan called. He said, "Elvis wants to know if you want to come back." That was September of '63. I thought about it a little while, and then I gave him my decision. My wife wasn't pleased.

Once I started back to work, I told Vernon to take $25 a week out of my paycheck until I'd paid back the whole $300 Elvis had loaned me. I said, "I'd appreciate it if you didn't tell Elvis." I don't think he ever did.

BILLY SMITH: About '63, I think, is when Elvis started realizing that the movies weren't ever going to get much better. He called them his "travelogues." The story almost always stayed the same—boy, girl, romance, trouble, lots of songs, happy ending. Only the locations changed. *Fun in Acapulco* was maybe a little more forgettable than some of the others. Hell, most of 'em after *Wild in the Country* are pretty forgettable.

He done *Fun in Acapulco* with Ursula Andress. She scared him a little, I think. She wasn't his kind of woman because she wasn't petite and she wasn't dark-haired. Alan had the hots for her. He always liked blondes. But Elvis was more fascinated by her than anything. She had those big shoulders, you know. He was laughing about it one day. He said, "I was embarrassed to take off my damn shirt next to her!"

But they flirted with each other some. She was married to John Derek, but she used to call Graceland a lot. She wouldn't ask for Elvis because she knew Priscilla was there. So she'd ask for Alan. And then the secretaries would tell Alan that Ursula called, and Alan would call her back, and Elvis would get on the phone.

MARTY LACKER: There's a picture of Elvis and Ursula in the booklet for RCA's *From Nashville to Memphis* boxed set, where they're gazing at each other on the movie set, like they're ready to gobble each other up. But that wasn't any real big romance. He just enjoyed being with her. She came to visit him on the *Roustabout* set later on and maybe on another picture, too. Her nickname was "Ooshie."

BILLY SMITH: Elvis didn't actually go down to Mexico for *Fun in Acapulco*. He done it all at Paramount, except for a camera crew who went down there and shot the backgrounds and stuff. Elvis was kind of touchy about Mexico, anyway.

Back in '57, a Mexico City newspaper said Elvis had eloped and come down there to get married and that they had a hotel suite reserved for him. Well, he didn't even know the girl he was supposed to be married to. So he said it wasn't true, and the rumor went around that he'd gone on the radio in Texas and said he'd kiss three black girls before he'd kiss a Mexican girl. I'm sure he never said any such thing in public. Or it would have been in a joking way. He loved the Spanish look a whole lot and copied some of that. And he had Mexican friends through the years.

That statement about Mexican girls like to start a war down in Mexico City. They said this was further proof that Elvis was ruining the morals of America, and now he was starting on Mexico. Radio stations down there wouldn't play his records, and a bunch of people got together in a downtown square and piled up his pictures and his albums and set 'em on fire. Somebody even took out a big newspaper ad that said, "Death to Elvis Presley!" It ended up in his FBI file. Stuff like that hurt him.

MARTY LACKER: Altogether, Elvis probably gave away a hundred cars and trucks. And each year at Christmas, he gave $105,000 to Memphis charities. He did a lot of other nice things for people, too, that you never heard about. He bought a house for one of his maids, for example. You might expect that. But he did things you wouldn't expect. Like when he first got famous, he bought ROTC uniforms for Humes High. And then later on, he anonymously gave a lot of stuff to the Los Angeles Police Department, like money for toys for kids at Christmas. And then kind of offbeat things, like uniforms for the police marching band and flak jackets for the dogs that sniffed out bombs. Actually, they probably also sniffed out drugs.

A lot of people hit him up for things, and he could have said no a lot more than he did. For example, when we moved back to the Perugia Way house, there were two English girls who used to come to the house on weekends. They were sisters. They lived in Redondo Beach, south of L.A., and they'd come up and sit and talk to Elvis.

The schedule back on Perugia Way was no different from anywhere else. On the weekends, we'd stay up all night. When the sun started coming up, Elvis went to bed. He was like Dracula.

One morning, we all went to bed, and I was in my room, and the phone rang. I answered it, and it was the English girls, just sobbing. I kept saying, "What's wrong? What's wrong?" Finally, they said, "We got home and found our mother dead on the floor." I talked to them for a while, and they said they didn't know what to do. They didn't have any money to take her to a funeral home.

I asked them where they wanted to have her buried, and one of them said, "I know Mother would want to be buried back in England." But she said none of their relatives over there had any money. And then she said, "To be honest with you, you're really the only people we know over here." So I said, "Give me your number, and I'll call you back."

Elvis hadn't gone to sleep yet, so I told him about the call. And he said, "Do whatever has to be done." I took care of the arrangements, telling the funeral home to prepare the mother any way that the girls wanted and ship her home to England. Elvis paid for everything. And then he flew the girls to England with the body. That's the last we heard of them. Except to get a very nice letter.

I could give you a lot of examples where Elvis showed he cared about people that he didn't even know—people he heard about whose situations touched him. But other times, he just didn't give a shit.

BILLY SMITH: Elvis started getting into class separation. If he got ticked off at somebody in the group, it might be weeks before he'd speak to them again. He'd turn to somebody else and say, "That cocksucker, I'm ready to fire him." He'd pal up with that guy for a while, and then it wouldn't be long 'til he'd go to the next one.

A lot of times, if he was hacked at somebody, he'd start thinking there was a Judas among us, and he'd start telling things to just one person, and he'd play one of us against the other. This always happened when he'd heard that one of the guys had said something about him. And we were all guilty of that.

To some degree, Elvis was paranoid. When everybody thought he wasn't around, he'd stand at the top of the stairs at Graceland, or in the doorway coming down to the den, where we couldn't see him, and listen to our conversation. He did this in California, too. And if somebody said something, he'd bring somebody else up and say, "I understand that So-and-so thinks such-and-such." Then you almost knew that either somebody had said something to him or he had overheard you.

Same way with the Colonel. The Colonel picked the hell out of every one of us to find out what Elvis done.

MARTY LACKER: By the early to middle sixties, anytime Elvis saw two of the guys talking by themselves, he thought they were talking about him. He'd say, "What the hell are you whispering about?" That's what happened the time he hit Sonny at a party on Perugia Way, which shocked the life out of us. That's when we knew he had really changed.

BILLY SMITH: Sonny had a date. He brought her up there, and he thought she was making eyes at Elvis and Elvis was making eyes at her. One thing led to another, and Elvis supposedly put a move on her, and Sonny resented it. The rules were that if you brought your own date, she was off limits to everybody else.

Sonny said, "Hey, man, this is my date. You know I can't compete with you." And Elvis said, "Well, Sonny, the girl come on to me." From there, Sonny got real agitated, and they got into a cuss fight, and Sonny started backing Elvis up 'til he backed him into a wall. He got right up in Elvis's face. And he should never have done that because Elvis thought he had no choice but to fight back. Because Elvis was like a caged animal. He was scared, and he was probably a little bit leery of Sonny, and he was leery of Red.

In a plain old fistfight, either one of them could have whipped Elvis, but he was a funny person. He would kill you in a minute, boy, because when you got him cornered, he didn't know no better, and he'd urge you on. And he picked up a Coke bottle first. But thank goodness he hit Sonny with his fist.

Sonny didn't hit him back because he couldn't believe it. He was stunned. He felt like it shouldn't have come to blows, and he was shocked because Elvis had never hit one of the guys before. Sonny thought they were just arguing and cussing each other. Sonny yelled, "I quit!" And Elvis yelled something like, "You can't quit, you mother-you-know-what, because I've fired your ass!" Then Elvis pretty well kicked him out of the house. Although when Sonny was packing, Elvis had one of the guys make sure he had some money. And it was a good while after that until Sonny come back.

One time in '63, Elvis had been upset about something, and he took it out on all of us. Then he realized what he'd done. And he broke down and cried. He said, "You guys know how I am. Don't take it personal. You know I don't mean it." We knew he had a lot of fears. And he had to maintain a certain image. Like he once said in a press conference, "An image is one thing, and a human being is another." He had to live up to that image.

MARTY LACKER: The difference in Elvis and the image of Elvis was never greater than in the TV movies they've made about him. Nothing has been done that even comes close to capturing his personal power or the strength of his personality. He had a great deal of intensity, magnetism. That's the reason most of us stayed with him for so long.

BILLY SMITH: The thing about Elvis was that you never knew where you stood with him. All he had to do was get mad and start taking it out on the guys, and I'd get angry and say, "The hell with this," and leave. I was fired numerous times, but it didn't last more than a hour or maybe a day at the most. But I actually quit about three times.

I quit one time in late '63 because of Vernon. We were in California, on Perugia Way. In '63, my first son, Danny, was born. We'd been out in California two or three months, and by now this was really getting old to me. No wives were allowed out there at the house. And it was putting a heck of a strain on my marriage, and I'm sure on Esposito's, too.

I talked to Elvis about it, and he said, "Well, call her every night if you want to—I don't care." He was making *Viva Las Vegas,* I think. And he said, "Tell Jo it won't be much longer. As soon as I get through with the movie, we'll come home."

We went home, like he said. We were home about three or four weeks. Then two days before we were fixin' to go back to California for *Kissin' Cousins,* Vernon come up to me and said, "Before you leave, I want to know how you plan to pay this phone bill." I said, "What phone bill?" He said, "The one for all those calls you made back to Memphis from California." He said, "You run up a bill close to $600."

My first thought was, "God Almighty!" Because that was an awful lot of money back then. And then I thought a second, and I said, "What do you mean? Elvis is going to pay it." And Vernon said, "Uh-uh, this is too much. It's going to have to come out of your check." And I flew mad.

I was making seventy-five dollars a week. I said, "I'll tell you what. As of today, you can quit paying me. That way you'll get it paid a hell of a lot quicker. Tell Elvis I quit." And I got in my car and went home.

Vernon may have been my uncle, but my relationship with him had gone downhill years before that. You could tell he resented all the guys around Elvis. He didn't show it as much when Aunt Gladys was alive. But after Elvis come back from Germany, and he had more guys around him, Vernon let that resentment show. Maybe it was because Elvis spent more. Vernon was always watching that money, boy.

Elvis didn't see me that night. And the next night, when they were getting ready to go back to California, Esposito called me and said, "Where are you? We're packing already." I said, "I'm not going. You tell Elvis that I quit." He asked me why, and I said, "You tell Elvis to ask his damn daddy why."

Later, one of the guys told me Elvis threw a fit and tore the kitchen all to hell and back. And then he started in cussing his daddy. He told Vernon, "Goddamn, Daddy, I'm rich! There are some things you don't do!" But he never once called me or said he was sorry about it. He went on to California, and I stayed here in Memphis. I went to work for a little old lumber company.

I didn't have any contact with Elvis for probably three or four months. And if I hadn't made the first move, I might never have had any more. But it got around Christmastime, and I missed him real bad. So I bought him a box of candy, and put a Christmas card with it, and wrote down my name. I said, "I wish you the best."

My daddy was still working for him as gate guard. And Elvis sent word to my daddy that just because I'd quit didn't mean I wasn't allowed to come up there. So I went on up because I knew he wouldn't come to me.

I got up at the house, and Elvis asked me what happened, and I told him exactly what it was. He said everything was forgiven. And then he said, "But don't ever do that again." He said, "Come to me. My daddy works for me just like you do." And I thought, "Yeah, right. I'm going to put myself above your daddy and put him in the middle." I'm kind of dumb about a lot of things, but I was never that dumb.

From then on things were pretty much cleared up. Vernon never told me to do anything again. And I didn't have to pay the phone bill. I wasn't about to pay the damn thing.

LAMAR FIKE: From '63 to '64 on, Elvis got squirrelier then a yard dog. The pictures started declining, and he got tired of doing the same thing. He'd have to be damn near drugged to do a singing scene. And when I was out in California with him, I saw that things got weirder at the house, too.

BILLY SMITH: One day on Perugia Way, we were all in the den watching a war movie on TV. Elvis started talking about how stuff like that was done in the studio—how the special effects guys did such a great job making a tub of water look like a real ocean and toy ships look like real ones. Then he got this sort of mischievous grin on his face, and he said, "Let's set up our own ocean in the pool."

He sent Richard and me down to the toy store to buy all the boats they had, and about twelve BB guns. We went back to the house and put all the little boats in the pool and loaded the guns. Then we lined up, and Elvis said, "Ready, aim, fire!" And we blasted the hell out of those little boats. Plastic flew all over the place.

After about an hour of this, we started getting bored and we kind of eased up. Nobody said anything—just started putting the rifles down. And then Elvis said, "You know what's wrong? It's too easy. We need moving targets." So he sent us back to the store for those little windup boats and some with batteries. And he said, "Get some more BB guns so we won't have to stop and reload."

We got home and put the boats in the water, and Elvis yelled, "All guns poolside!" Then he set a time limit, and whoever sank the most ships would be declared the best shot. Of course, Elvis bragged that he was the best shot because he'd won some sharp-shooter medal in the army. Well, the battle began, and this went on for the rest of the day. We even had snacks brought down to the pool so we wouldn't have to stop to eat. The neighbors must have . . . well, they thought we were lunatics anyway.

At some point, somebody tried to take a picture—Joe, maybe—and the flashbulb didn't go off. He picked it off the top of the camera and threw it in the pool, and somebody took a shot at it. Well, when the BB hit it, it flashed. So Elvis told us to go to the camera shop and buy all the flash bulbs they had. We were standing at the cash register, and the salesman said, "What kind of film do you need to go with these?" And Richard said, "Oh, we don't use film with them." And the guy said, "I see." He watched us all the way out the door.

By the time we got back to the house, it was getting sort of dark. We dumped all the bulbs in the pool and lined up with the rifles and cut loose. And man, that pool lit up like the Fourth of July. It never hit us that the flashbulbs were made of glass, you know. And next morning, we come out there and seen what a mess we'd made. We had this Mexican gardener, and when he seen all this glass and broken plastic in the bottom of the pool and all over the yard, he about keeled over. He couldn't speak English, but we got his message loud and clear. Some of the guys cleaned up the yard, and the rest of us took the pool.

We never did it again, but not because of the mess—because Elvis lost interest. It was fun while it lasted, and it helped him release tension. If he'd just stuck to BB guns from then on out, it would have cut down on a whole lot more tension later on.

MARTY LACKER: The day John F. Kennedy was shot, I'd been up two or three days doing pills. I was always taking pills. Sometimes I stayed up four or five days on them. I'd have to take a lot of sleeping pills just to counteract the uppers so I could finally get some rest.

Anyway, that morning, I'd gone to my room to go to bed, and I'd turned on the TV to relax. And the bulletin came on saying President Kennedy had been assassinated in Dallas.

Elvis had gone to bed an hour or so earlier, and I figured he was probably asleep. But I knew he really liked Kennedy. So I went in the hallway and knocked on his door. I didn't get an answer, and I knocked harder. And I heard him say, "Get away from the door! Go on! I don't want to be bothered now."

I said, "Elvis, you need to get up. President Kennedy was just assassinated in Dallas." There was this long pause. And then he said, "What?" I said, "President Kennedy was just assassinated, and it's on TV." I thought he would turn on the television in his room and watch it from bed. Instead he yelled, "Have them bring some coffee into the den." And he got up and put his robe on and came on in there. By that time, I got some of the other guys up, and we all gathered around the TV.

Most of us were just silent, but Elvis started screaming and hollering. He said, "What kind of no-good motherfucker would do that? Kennedy's a good man!" He had his coffee cup in his hand. And all of a sudden, he slammed his cup down on the big marble-topped table in front of the television. It broke in his hand, and the pieces just shot everywhere.

I'm sure Kennedy's death reminded him of his own mortality, which always made him uneasy. But it was more than that. Elvis thought of himself in the same context as the president. He said, "Goddamnit, if anybody ever assassinates me, I want you guys to get to him before the police do. I want you to pull his eyes out, rip his throat apart, and kill that son of a bitch!" He said, "I want you to make him suffer! I don't want some mealymouthed bastard going on television and telling the world, 'I took out Elvis Presley.'" He was just screaming. He said, "I don't want him to be able to sit there and smirk about it."

We were kind of shocked, you know, even though we knew he got in a terrible mood whenever somebody he liked or admired died. This one had more behind it, though, because he'd gotten these death threats through the years, and in fact, he'd get another one about six weeks later, on a postcard from Huntsville, Alabama. It was handwritten, and addressed to "President Elvis Presley, Memphis, Tennessee." It said, "You will be next on my list," and it had his name on the top, and then Johnny Cash, and some name we couldn't really make out, and then an attempt at writing President Lyndon Johnson, and then George Wallace. Vernon took it seriously because Huntsville was where Dee's family lived, and he thought some of her wacko relatives might have sent it.

With the Kennedy assassination, Elvis stayed glued to the TV for two days. And when they led Lee Harvey Oswald through the jail on his way to the sheriff's office, Elvis started ranting again. He said, "I mean it! If somebody kills me, I want you to get to that son of a bitch and torture him!" And he was talking to Oswald on TV, saying, "You no-good wimpy bastard! You rotten son of a bitch!" And again, he looked around and said, "You remember what I told you, guys!" And his eyes were almost glowing, he was so hot. Then when Jack Ruby shot Oswald, it set Elvis off again. He started screaming, "That's right! Kill that little bastard! Don't let him sit up there and tell everybody how he killed the president!"

I think that's when his fondness for guns began to turn into an obsession. He realized that if somebody could bring down President Kennedy, they could take him out just as easily. His obsession didn't really take hold for a couple of years, though. He had another obsession at the time—Ann-Margret.

CHAPTER 27

THE FEMALE ELVIS

In July '63, Elvis began filming *Viva Las Vegas* with a Swedish-born actress-singer-dancer the press dubbed "the female Elvis." Discovered by comedian George Burns in Las Vegas in 1960, twenty-two-year-old Ann-Margret [Olsson] had made only three other films, *State Fair*, *A Pocketful of Miracles*, and *Bye, Bye Birdie*, the latter loosely based on the Elvis saga. But her combination of personal magnetism, hyperfemininity, flirtatious sensuality, and wholesome reserve had already made her the quintessential Hollywood sex kitten. Men would have died for her.

One night before principal photography began, Elvis invited the red-haired actress to the Perugia Way house to get acquainted. The night before, he informed the guys that he wanted no one to accompany him when he went to pick her up. Furthermore, he expected the house to be empty when he returned.

Yet this was different from Elvis's usual trysts with Hollywood starlets. In a photograph taken of the two of them at a birthday party for Ann-Margret's landlady, Elvis looks more emotionally vulnerable than in any other picture with a woman since those taken with his mother. Whether Elvis was intrigued with Ann-Margret simply because she was his female counterpart, their obvious chemistry made *Viva Las Vegas*, another formulaic musical with a simple-minded plot, one of Presley's most memorable vehicles.

LAMAR FIKE: Elvis's affair with Ann-Margret was not just an affair. He was really in love with her. It got hot and heavy. Phew!

MARTY LACKER: They started shooting the picture in Hollywood first, and then they went to Vegas for location shots. Elvis stayed in Milton Prell's suite at the Sahara, and he and Ann holed up in there for the whole weekend. No one ever saw them.

That drove Red and Lamar absolutely crazy. They tried to get them to come out, but nothing doing. Elvis wouldn't even answer the door for room service. They had to leave the food tray outside. Then when Elvis made sure everybody was away, he'd pull it in. So to play a trick on them, Red and Lamar stuffed newspaper under the door and lit it. They just aggravated the shit out of them. This is pretty childlike, but they even shined butter knives 'til they looked like mirrors. And then they slipped 'em under the door to see if they could see Ann without her clothes on. They tried everything. But Elvis and Ann would not come out of that suite.

I think their episodes were a lot different from the kind Elvis had with other girls. And so what? Neither one of them was married, and they really cared a lot about each other. She was a pretty strong person, and she was the first girl in a good while that he felt really connected with. Ann's as smart as a whip. And she adored him. And Priscilla was back at Graceland.

BILLY SMITH: Once you met Ann, you didn't forget her. She had the same effect on men that Elvis did on women.

LAMAR FIKE: Everybody was in love with Ann. Even the director of the picture, George Sidney. Ann didn't want his attention, and she started telling Elvis, "He won't leave me alone." So Elvis got pissed off at Sidney, and one thing led to the other. Colonel went to see the dailies, and he sat there with his mouth open—Sidney had the cameraman shoot four minutes of Ann's butt moving. In close-up. And even in their two-shots, there was more of Ann than there was of the two of them. Colonel went bananas. He said, "I'm not going to put up with this!" There was a lot of shit flying around during the editing of that picture.

BILLY SMITH: Elvis and Ann had a lot in common. For example, she could ride a motorcycle, and she enjoyed being out on one. She was in the music business to a certain degree, and she was an actor with a hot career. She also had an ego like he did.

MARTY LACKER: I think the fact that they were so similar is why they understood each other. They were also very sensual people.

LAMAR FIKE: Very seldom would Elvis ever go anywhere by himself, but he'd go out alone with Ann. It used to rattle all of us. We would give him a bunch of money, and he'd jump in that Rolls-Royce and stay gone. Nobody knew where he was, except that he was with her. It blew our minds.

MARTY LACKER: Ann genuinely liked people, and she liked every one of us. She wasn't intimidated or threatened by us. I think she also respected us. We used to have a lot of fun with her. She had a terrific sense of humor. We called her "Rusty" because that was her name in the movie and because of her red hair.

A couple of years after *Viva Las Vegas,* she was doing *The Cincinnati Kid* on the same lot where we were doing a movie. Alan and I went over to her dressing-room trailer one day. The door was open, and the director was there. But when she saw us, she asked the director to give us some time together. In other words, Ann was a very gracious person, and she was like that with everyone.

BILLY SMITH: Alan was in love with her, plain and simple. One time, Elvis and Ann and Alan and I went to Vegas in the Rolls. Alan and I were in the back. And it got a little cool back there. Ann had this white fur coat, and she threw it in the back for us to cover up with. And, boy, Alan just had a fit. He was intoxicated by that perfume in her coat and by her smell. He just went wild. Ann practically had to wrestle him to get it back.

MARTY LACKER: Elvis tolerated us saying things to Ann because she took it in the right spirit. One night, Elvis and Ann and Alan and I were outside in the courtyard at Perugia Way. She was going on location the next day, and we'd all walked out to her car. She'd just bought a pink Cadillac.

Everything about this woman, everything she wore, smelled fantastic. Elvis was standing next to her. And I had my hand hooked into her arm, with my head resting against the sleeve of her coat. Elvis didn't seem to mind because he knew that she was totally involved with him and that none of us had a snowball's chance in hell of ever dating her, anyway.

I said, "Ann, what is it you wear that smells so wonderful?" And she started to laugh. She had a funny little laugh, almost like a giggle. Her face would light up. She didn't really answer me because Alan kept trying to get her to tell him what kind of perfume she wore, too, and she never would.

I remember she had on these tight white pants—really tight against her legs. Alan kept staring at them, staring at her body, and finally he said, "Ann, would you do me a favor?" And she started to giggle because of the way Alan said it. She said, "What is it, Alan?" He got this little impish look on his face, and he said, "Would you run around the block about four times and let me have your pants?" About a second passed, and then both Ann and Elvis just fell on the ground, laughing.

LAMAR FIKE: The only other person Elvis ever costarred with who had that same kind of personality was Shelley Fabares. Both she and Ann were fun people to be around. Ann took everything with a laugh. She didn't give Elvis any problems. And she was never threatened by another woman.

MARTY LACKER: I don't think Ann ever questioned Elvis about Priscilla. She was too sure of herself. None of us knows whether she ever brought up the idea of marriage. After a while, Roger Smith came into the picture, but I think she cared so much about Elvis that she put Roger off for a time. Every once in a while, Elvis would say, "Roger Smith calls her, and she goes out to dinner with him, but there ain't nothing there." But even though I think Ann and Elvis were really, truly in love, I still don't think he would have married her. He bought her a round, pink bed. Had somebody make it for her. But that wasn't a proposal of marriage. That was a proposal of something else. This idea that Ann was the love of his life . . . if you ask me, Elvis didn't have one. I'm not sure he was capable of it.

LAMAR FIKE: I think Elvis would have married her in a New York second. But he made it clear he'd do it only if Ann quit the business. Elvis believed in the old Southern idea of the wife stays home and cooks dinner and has it on the table when the husband gets home. And Ann was very career-oriented. She wouldn't do it. She'd worked all her life to get where she was, and she wasn't going to let anybody stand in her way.

BILLY SMITH: There's no doubt that Elvis was in love with Ann-Margret. But he would have remembered the advice his mama give him. Which was, "Don't marry anybody in the business. Your careers will clash."

MARTY LACKER: There's a simpler explanation for this. He didn't want to look up on a movie screen and see her in bed, kissing somebody. He couldn't have handled it.

BILLY SMITH: Priscilla was so scared that Elvis would marry Ann-Margret that she even tried to be like Ann. Jo spent a lot of time with her, and she says Priscilla watched Ann's movies and learned some of her dance moves, and tried to dress like her, and had her hair done like hers. She'd stand in front of a full-length mirror just cussing Ann, all the time trying to be as much like her as possible. It was pitiful. How could she compete? She'd just graduated from Catholic school, where she wore those little uniforms, and now she'd enrolled in the Patricia Stevens Finishing School there in Memphis.

MARTY LACKER: Priscilla heard the rumors about Ann-Margret. The fan magazines even said they were going to get married. But Elvis told her that the romance was just publicity generated by the studio.

BILLY SMITH: They had plenty of arguments about Ann. I don't know to what extent because usually those took place up in his room, away from everybody else.

MARTY LACKER: This story of Elvis and Ann-Margret has an ironic twist. They used to have these gospel shows at what was then Ellis Auditorium, in Memphis. Priscilla got Patsy to go with her once, and Mylon Lefevre, of the Lefevre Family, was on the show. And Priscilla went nuts over him. He's a wild-looking guy, or he was back then, with long hair flying everywhere. He was the black sheep of the family because he sang more modern music—he eventually became a Southern rocker—and because of the way he looked and lived.

After the show, they went backstage to meet him, and according to Patsy, Priscilla openly flirted with him. And when he came back in town, she wanted to go see him again. She tried to get Patsy, and then Jo, to go with her. But Patsy and Jo had already talked about it, and they said no. So Priscilla went on her own. She went down to the auditorium every time Mylon came to town, and she didn't always have a companion.

I don't know if Elvis knew about Priscilla's flirtation with Mylon or not. I don't think so. It's not something you tell a guy like Elvis Presley.

BILLY SMITH: Elvis never knew. He would have beat the shit out of Mylon, or tried to. And he certainly wouldn't have recorded one of his songs ["Without Him"] a few years later.

The funny thing about this is that Elvis was too good a teacher because real quick-like, Priscilla grew to be just like him. When he said he wanted to get these girls at a young age so he could mold them and bring them up, he didn't count on Priscilla being just as flirty as he was.

CHAPTER 28

MILLION-DOLLAR SHROUD

The Movies and the Music

After *Viva Las Vegas*, Elvis became increasingly chagrined at the quality of both his movies and his records. Although his pictures are sometimes kindly referred to as "the last great series of Hollywood star vehicles," as critic Dave Marsh put it, nearly all the movies made after 1960 were assembled around Elvis's personality—or the Hollywood moguls' perception of it—the way larger movies were once fashioned around female stars such as Shirley Temple or Mae West. Presley pictures were guaranteed to pull a certain bankable gross just because he was in them.

Therefore, Colonel and the studios figured it wasn't important who the costars were or how transparent the plot. Elvis always played a "man's man," such as a crop duster or a stock car racer—an honest, do-right fellow saddled with a troublemaking sidekick. In the end, the two are routinely pulled out of their jam by Elvis's take-charge gumption and the goodwill of a beautiful woman somehow involved in their predicament. With story lines like those, it didn't much matter the quality of director, cameraman, or film editor—everything was going to look dated, anyway. As such, the budgets got skimpier ($800,000 for *Kissin' Cousins*, compared with $4 million for *Blue Hawaii*) to allow a bigger profit.

The songs in these movies were equally formulaic, as was their use. One—usually sung over the opening credits—was always up-tempo and full of optimistic attitude. The remainder can be found sprinkled throughout the film every ten or fifteen minutes. Almost without exception, these supplementary tunes are instantly forgettable. If the sixties movies boasted a couple of worthwhile songs ("Can't Help Falling in Love" from *Blue Hawaii*, "Return to Sender" from *Girls! Girls! Girls!*), the raw rock 'n' roll—the guttural sound of a class of people never granted even the slightest privilege—was long gone.

Instead, the bland pop songs that made up the soundtracks were too often along the pathetic lines of "Song of the Shrimp" (*Girls! Girls! Girls!*), "Cotton Candy Land" (*It Happened at the World's Fair*), "(There's) No Room to Rumba in a Sports Car" (*Fun in Acapulco*), and "Petunia, the Gardener's Daughter" (*Frankie and Johnny*). Elvis's singles, for the most part, also came from the movies, and the soundtracks were often recorded in one day, with minimal retakes.

On *Girl Happy*, director Boris Sagal, who'd sensed Elvis's disillusionment, heard him complaining about the manure he was asked to turn into music. The director allegedly took Elvis aside and encouraged him to give up the hackneyed pictures and to go east to study the craft of acting at Actors Studio or the Neighborhood Playhouse in New York.

Elvis supposedly said he'd love to do that, but he didn't see how, given his schedule. "I'm looking forward to finally doing a picture where I can just act and not have to sing," he told Sagal. But that day was a long time coming.

"I wish I could make just one good picture," Elvis confided to a leading lady of the era. "I know people in this town laugh at me."

LAMAR FIKE: Elvis had heard this suggestion about going to acting school before. He said in one of those early press conferences that he was sure school wouldn't hurt him any, but he never did too well in school. He certainly knew enough to be embarrassed by most of the pictures he did because they were just empty-headed star vehicles. He did a movie called *Stay Away, Joe*, which actually was a little bit better than most. But in one scene, he'd been sleeping under a house, and he came up from under it with his hair combed, every hair in place.

MARTY LACKER: Elvis was ruined by the Colonel and by Hal Wallis. They didn't let him develop. If they had only let him continue in the same vein as *King Creole*—the way he delivered that scene where he broke that bottle and said, "Now, you know what I do for an encore . . . " But they kept putting him in crap.

Hal Wallis made a statement in that documentary *Elvis: The Echo Will Never Die,* that really upset me. A film critic and author from England, Stephen Phillips, said that Parker and Wallis and the other movie producers were to blame for castrating Elvis's acting career. He said Elvis could have been in the same league as James Dean or Marlon Brando. And Wallis said, "The idea of tailoring Elvis for dramatic roles is something that we never attempted. Because we didn't sign Elvis as a second Jimmy Dean. We signed him as a number one Elvis Presley." In other words, to sing his songs.

When you hear stuff like that, you see it's no wonder Elvis died at forty-two. He has to bear some responsibility for what he got involved in. But the people who ruined his career should have been made to pay for it—in particular Colonel Parker. They just killed him.

BILLY SMITH: The producers of these movies would say to Elvis, "Let me put you in a boat! You'll be a boat pilot who moonlights as a singer. Next, you'll be a race car driver. Then you're going to fly a plane at the World's Fair." And all this silly shit.

LAMAR FIKE: Some of Elvis's pictures are so camp they're considered classics today. They're like a kaleidoscope. One picture changes into another, and sometimes you barely notice it.

I think all the guys agree that Elvis died of terminal apathy. He got bored with being Elvis, and he became a parody of himself. He wanted to be who he was so bad, but he was locked into this shroud that he had to put on like a damn suit, and he couldn't get out of it. He tried his best to get out of it. Except when it came to bucking Colonel.

BILLY SMITH: It wasn't until about '64, when the movies and the songs got really terrible, that Elvis started to question what the old Colonel was doing for him. Colonel said, "You're getting paid a million dollars! As long as the pictures make money, why worry about it?" So for several years, Elvis didn't try to buck him again. Colonel always said, "Don't make waves!" And I heard Vernon say to Elvis one time, "Don't offend the Colonel. Just remember how much the Colonel's done for you." Hell, if the Colonel had hollered "Boo!" Vernon would have jumped through the wall.

MARTY LACKER: The only thing that kept Elvis going after the early years was a new challenge. But Parker kept running everything into the ground. He couldn't see the forest for the trees because he was a hustler and a con artist. He was only interested in "now money"—get the buck and get gone.

About '64 or '65, Elvis started saying, "Colonel, I'm tired of doing the same old damn movies." The turning point was *Girl Happy*, when the script was so lame and the songs, like "Do the Clam," were so obnoxious. When he had to film the scene where he sings "Fort Lauderdale Chamber of Commerce," he went around the whole day ranting.

LAMAR FIKE: It isn't fair to say Elvis hated all the pictures. He liked *Roustabout* because he got to work with Barbara Stanwyck. She helped him as an actor.

MARTY LACKER: Even though most of the later pictures hurt his reputation as an actor, they hadn't tarnished his star quality. Everybody still wanted to meet him and be around him, and that included other stars. On *Girl Happy*, he had all kinds of visitors, starting with President Johnson's daughter, Lynda Bird, and her friend, George Hamilton, the actor, who was from Memphis. Probably Colonel set that up. Because Hamilton somehow knew the Colonel and Colonel had known Johnson when he was running for the Senate, down in Texas. Colonel was also a friend of one of Johnson's staff members—Walter W. Jenkins, the one who got arrested for making a pass at a guy in a men's room. The point is, Colonel had friends in high places in both the Kennedy and the Johnson administrations. He was real tight with all of their assistants. The chief of staff and all these other people. Which may explain why he was never deported.

Lynda Bird and Hamilton wanted to come over to MGM, where we were filming, and Elvis agreed to meet them in this big green field just behind the swimming pool. They started walking towards us, and they were flanked by all these Secret Service agents with these real serious looks on their faces. And when Elvis saw them marching across this field to come see him, he said, "Okay, you guys are my security team. Let's meet 'em halfway." He had us flank him just like the Secret Service flanked Lynda Bird and Hamilton. And he said, "Keep your eyes on them and stare them down." So we did. And it looked like some big summit meeting, with all this formality. The Secret Service agents looked a little confused. They thought they were there to protect Lynda Bird from us, and we were standing ready to protect Elvis from them. Elvis talked to 'em for a couple of minutes, and then we all turned in formation and walked away. We stood it as long as we could, and then we broke up and laughed like hell.

Elvis was in the small portable dressing room on the set one day, before he had his big trailer. I stepped out for a minute to smoke a cigarette, and behind these stacks of boxes I saw a figure walking from one stack to the other.

I couldn't make out who it was. And then finally, out came a young Paul Anka. He was about twenty-three then. I think he was wanting to see Elvis, but he didn't have the nerve to knock on the door.

LAMAR FIKE: As far as the movie years were concerned—and by that I mean the sixties—they might have been years of incredible frustration, on the whole, but they were also years of incredible money. And when you've already been paid for the pictures, and you've already spent half the money, you've got to do them. All of those pictures were presigned. So Elvis had no choice.

This isn't a very popular view, but Colonel's formula was correct. The serious stuff—the movies that didn't have many songs in them—flopped. That's a pretty good argument. On the other hand, by the time Elvis figured out he was being screwed around, it was too late. He signed too many contracts. If the Colonel handed him a contract, he'd sign it and never look at it. That's what you get for signing contracts that you don't read.

MARTY LACKER: The thing Parker harped on about the movies was the money. He always used to brag, "They never lost one penny." Well, big deal. Each film after *Blue Hawaii* made less and less money. Towards the end, Elvis really just gave up.

BILLY SMITH: Elvis wanted to get back to doing live concerts and personal appearances, but Colonel wouldn't listen. One time during the movie days, Elvis said, "Damn if it don't seem like Colonel is trying to hold me back!" I think Colonel was a little bit scared of what might happen, too—that he might have to do some heavy-duty promoting in case Elvis bombed out on the road. That, and the fact that the money was still coming in from the movies, meant that Colonel was going to ride that horse until it dropped.

One of those times when Elvis was really agitated at Colonel, he said, "I hate that old man. I wish he'd just go on and quit." I said, "You really want that?" And he said, "It would be nice."

MARTY LACKER: When Elvis would go to Colonel and say, "I don't want to do any more of these crappy movies," Colonel would say, "I deal with these executives all day long, and they'll ruin your career if you don't go along with them." And then he pulled that stuff again about Elvis having to go back and drive a truck. I think Elvis realized that wasn't true, but he understood that he had a hell of a lot to lose.

The tension and the stress of all this got so bad that Elvis started having severe nosebleeds. We'd be on the movie set, and he'd just start gushing blood. Sometimes the director would have to hold up a shot because he'd be in the dressing room and we'd be putting ice on his nose and stuffing it with cotton to get it to quit bleeding. And, of course, when the tension got bad he'd dig deeper in his makeup case of pain pills—Empirin [with] codeine, Demerol, Percodan, all in pill form. That was his way of coping.

As time went on, he started stepping up the dosage. Because where two work for you today, next week you may need three to get the same effect. And then you need something stronger, or a combination of things. So it kept going that way. And when someone put pressure on him, whether it was the Colonel or his father or Priscilla, he took more.

LAMAR FIKE: I think the nosebleeds could have been from drugs. Either way, they were nosebleeds like you would not believe. Shit, they'd last an eternity. We'd run and get towels and everything else.

BILLY SMITH: I'd love to know exactly what Colonel hung over Elvis to get him to do what he wanted. Colonel inspired fear in him. He built that over the years, and now it was paying off.

Maybe it was the drugs, although Elvis never said this. You'd have to have been deaf, dumb, and blind not to see what was going on. And Colonel was quite capable of exposing that. Or of exposing Priscilla living at Graceland. Elvis might have thought, "If I piss Colonel off, would he use something against me?" Colonel had Elvis and Vernon both believing, "Without me, you won't get the benefits you're getting now. You'll never get the kind of deals I get for you." It was a kind of blackmail, really.

MARTY LACKER: We sit around and wonder just exactly what Colonel had on Elvis. Maybe he held Vernon's prison record over him. A couple of years ago, a story came out in the *Star*, the tabloid, that said that when Elvis was in the army, he met some English guy, a reporter named Derek Johnson, in Germany. The story said Elvis and Johnson became friends and that Elvis told him he'd been involved in a hit-and-run accident in the fifties while he was working at Crown Electric—that he'd killed a man and panicked and left the scene in his truck. I don't think that's true. But say it was true and Elvis had told Colonel?

LAMAR FIKE: Elvis's main problem was that he hated confrontation. He'd say, "I'm going to take care of this shit!" And he never would. Not with Colonel. Elvis was scared to rip into Colonel. He had the hammer.

BILLY SMITH: Right around '66, Elvis mentioned that Colonel said the studio was complaining about Elvis slurring his words a lot and speeding up his speech so much that they weren't catching a lot of what he said. They were having to do a lot of looping—redoing the dialogue after the shooting was finished. Colonel got on him bad about that.

MARTY LACKER: The uppers Elvis took had a lot of undesirable side effects. They made him grind his teeth, for example. I've lost a couple of teeth myself that way. In Elvis's case, it was a real shame because otherwise, he took perfect care of his teeth. If he ate a cracker, he'd go up and brush. And he was constantly going to the dentist. Both to have his teeth worked on and to get pills. But his teeth were beautiful. When he smiled, he lit up a room.

LAMAR FIKE: Colonel got on Elvis about a lot of things besides talking too fast. Like about what he was eating. For the two or three months between movies, Elvis would eat whatever he wanted. Then about three or four weeks before he had to be back in California to go into wardrobe, he'd start a crash diet. That made him irritable as hell. And he was already irritable from the diet pills—the uppers. After we'd finish the movie, he'd eat his ass off again. He'd go up in his room for four days to a week and never come down. He didn't want to see anybody. He'd have his food sent up, and he wouldn't do anything but stay in bed.

MARTY LACKER: Colonel knew Elvis's vulnerable spot. He'd couch everything in terms of Elvis losing his career.

For example, Colonel used to check Elvis out before the movies. Not only for the drugs but for his weight. And, boy, that used to aggravate him. Elvis would get so mad he'd sputter. He'd say, "Goddamn, two pounds overweight! Who gives a shit?" But Colonel would come back and say that the camera picks up every ounce. He'd tell Elvis, "If you look fat, your fans aren't going to love you, and neither are the producers." And Colonel and Hal Wallis were not above using little tricks on him.

One day we were finishing up a picture at Samuel Goldwyn Studios, and we were standing outside the soundstage in the studio street. There were about four or five of us. Elvis was in that perennial army uniform, and we were talking. Just then Mina Wallis walked up. She was Hal Wallis's sister. She said, "Oh, Elvis, honey, how are you? I was at the studio today and I just thought I'd come over because I knew you were shooting." Elvis greeted her warmly, and everything was nice and cordial. And in the course of this, Mina put her arm around Elvis's back and his waist, the way people put their arm around your shoulder. Well, she kept it around his waist, and she was saying things like "We can't wait for you to do this next picture." And we just stood there for what seemed like a nice conversation.

Finally, she left, and as soon as she got out of earshot, Elvis started calling her every name in the book. He said, "That goddamn old fucking bitch! That Colonel cocksucker!" We were all bewildered because she'd been so nice. Somebody finally said, "What's wrong with you?" And Elvis said, "You know why that bitch had her damn arm around me? She was feeling to see how much fat I had around my waist!" Colonel used to do that all the time. Elvis said, "Hal Wallis and that fucking Colonel sent her over here to find out."

BILLY SMITH: Elvis liked sweets, and he loved to eat, period. In the final years, his weight gain was more from illness than it was from food. But in the sixties, he gained because he liked to eat too much, and the wrong things, like a pound of bacon and a six-egg omelet. Away from Hollywood, man, he ate like a stevedore.

MARTY LACKER: One night, we went to Radio Recorders, the recording studio Elvis used in Hollywood for the movie sound-tracks. He was in no mood to do anything that night, but he was trying. Colonel was there, sitting in a glass booth with a table and some chairs, and he had the two producers of the movie with him. We hadn't been there very long, when Colonel called me in and said, "What the hell has Elvis been eating?"

We'd just come from Memphis a couple of weeks before, so I knew what he meant, but I pretended not to. I said, "What are you talking about, Colonel?" And Parker banged his cane down on the floor, and he said, "Goddamnit, he's gained weight!" The two producers were hearing every word of this. So I said, "Well, he's just been eating what he always eats." And Colonel raised his cane in the air and started yelling at the top of his voice. He said, "Goddamnit, don't lie to me! Tell me!" It made me mad, and I flew off the handle. I said, "Look, if you want to know what Elvis has been eating, get your fat ass in there and ask him."

BILLY SMITH: The guys were the heavy for Elvis at times. If he was late to the studio—and some mornings, you couldn't stir him with a flamethrower—Colonel would be mad as hell. And Elvis would turn to us and say, "You goddamn guys didn't wake me up!"

MARTY LACKER: Elvis got along pretty well with all of his direc-tors. He liked Norman Taurog, and he respected Fred De Cordova, who directed *Frankie and Johnny*, and later became producer of the *Tonight* show.

One of the few times Elvis really clashed with one of his direc-tors was on *Roustabout*. Elvis had some kind of virus and a 104-degree fever. He didn't feel like sitting up, much less make a movie. But the director, John Rich, was a no-good bastard, and the fact that Elvis was sick didn't cut any ice with him. He kept making him do one particular scene over and over. Actually, it seemed like he was just pushing Elvis to see how far he could go. Elvis resented the hell out of it, but he'd just smile and do what Rich said.

Usually, when stuff like that happened, we'd play practical jokes on each other and on the cast and crew to make Elvis feel better. On *Roustabout*, we started doing stuff, and John Rich piped up, yelling, not at Elvis, but at the guys. He said, "If you don't stop that and shut up, you're going to have to leave the soundstage." And, boy, Elvis came to life. He said, "Let me tell you something, Mr. Rich. When these fucking movies cease to be fun, I'll stop doing them. And if my guys go, goddamnit, so do I."

BILLY SMITH: It was bad enough that the movies were horrible. But the majority of the songs were, too. It just seemed like Elvis couldn't find any satisfaction, and he didn't know what to do about it.

MARTY LACKER: In about '65, we were at Radio Recorders working on a soundtrack for a movie, and Elvis was just fed up with everything. That meant he was taking more pills.

I forget what the picture was, but it was like all the rest of them. He had this big damn orchestra in there. And he started singing, and he didn't settle for the first take. They were getting ready to do it again, and in the middle of the session, Elvis reached his breaking point, and he started ranting. He said, "Goddamnit, I'm tired of all these fucking songs, and I'm tired of these damn movies! I get in a fight with somebody in one scene, and in the next one I'm kissing the dog. And these songs suck like donkeys." He said, "What difference does it make how many times we do it? The song is a piece of shit!"

Somebody tried to calm him down, but nothing was right. And Elvis said, "I'll tell you what. You just cut the tracks of the songs in this next movie, and I'll come in later and put my voice on."

BILLY SMITH: To really understand Elvis's frustration during this time, you have to see what else was going on in music and in the movies. In '64, the Beatles had hit in a big way over here, and that whole British invasion had started. The music was exciting, and it was different. It made Elvis look out of touch. Because he wasn't having big hit records anymore and his records weren't filled with new ways of doing the old stuff, like the Beatles' records were. And pretty soon the Beatles started making movies, too. *A Hard Day's Night* and *Help!* had a lot of wit to 'em. And here's Elvis doing *Girl Happy* and *Tickle Me*. Elvis's pictures were pretty old hat in comparison.

MARTY LACKER: Elvis used to get the Memphian to run the Beatles' movies for us. They were a lot hipper than Elvis's. Maybe secretly, he felt threatened by the Beatles. But he never talked about that, not even in unguarded moments.

BILLY SMITH: Elvis was very threatened by the Beatles, but he tried to hide it. When the Beatles were on *The Ed Sullivan Show,* the Colonel sent a telegram that Sullivan read on the air, a kind of "Welcome to America" thing. It made it seem like Elvis was a fan, but also like he wasn't worried about their success and what it might do to his. Colonel wanted them to get together, and the Beatles did, too. Elvis was one of their idols. They wanted him to come to England. But Elvis said, "If they want to see me, they can come over here." That's why when they finally did get together, the Beatles had to come to the house in California. Elvis wanted to prove a point. It was pure ego.

The guys and I protected that ego. We hated to see Elvis hurt. Maybe we protected him too much. But we tried to warn him about things in a low-key way.

LAMAR FIKE: I went over to England in '63 with Brenda Lee. The Beatles were her opening act. I took one look at them and went, "Jesus Christ!" I said, "The only time I've seen anything like this is with Elvis." They just blew me away. Right after that, Elvis came to Nashville for that recording session where we made up. And I said, "Elvis, there's a group coming out of England that's going to be so hot. They're getting ready to break wide open." He couldn't have cared less.

BILLY SMITH: Brian Epstein, the Beatles' manager, was talking to Colonel one time, and he said, "The Beatles are as big as Elvis, and they draw a bigger crowd." The Colonel told him, "I'll tell you what. You put the Beatles in one coliseum. And if I can rent the land across from you, I'll pitch a tent. We'll see who draws the most, and we'll go for broke." I'd hated to have put that to a test. The Beatles were like early Elvis in that they were rebellious, with the long hair, and they had that hard-driving rock 'n' roll going for them. And they were brand-spanking new.

LAMAR FIKE: When Elvis first came on the scene, the record-buying demographics shifted from the older generation to fifteen- to twenty-four-year-olds. But back in the mid-sixties, he started losing the demographics because the kids weren't buying single acts. All of a sudden, it was nothing but groups out there. A single act couldn't get a record deal.

MARTY LACKER: In '65, we went over to Hawaii to do *Paradise, Hawaiian Style.* Herman's Hermits were big at that time with "Mrs. Brown, You've Got a Lovely Daughter" and "I'm Henry VIII, I Am." And they were over in Hawaii, and somehow arranged a meeting with Elvis through the Colonel. They came over to the Polynesian Cultural Center where we were shooting one day.

Some of those English groups were sort of smartasses. And Peter Noone, who was Herman, certainly was. We were in this big tent, and there was a whole group of us—Billy, Richard, Charlie, I think, and Joe. And Noone started joking around. There were these poles holding up the tent, and I was leaning against one, listening and thinking, "You little son of a bitch."

Elvis talked to him for a little bit, and Noone figured he'd trap Elvis into giving him a compliment. He looked at him and he said, "Tell me, Elvis, who's your favorite group?" And Elvis said, "Well, I sort of like them all." Noone persisted, though, and he said, "But who's your *favorite* group?" And I sort of under my breath whispered, "L.A.P.D." This was long before Elvis got into collecting badges. But he thought it was funny. And without blinking an eye, he shot back, "Los Angeles Police Department." Everybody broke up, and Noone just sat there frozen. He didn't know what to say.

LAMAR FIKE: About the only single act that was happening at the time was Tom Jones. He came along in '65 with "It's Not

Unusual" and "What's New, Pussycat?" Now, Elvis was threat-ened by Tom Jones.

BILLY SMITH: Tom Jones . . . It's kind of funny. Elvis called him "Sock Dick." He thought Jones put a rolled-up sock in his pants to make himself look more well endowed. He said, "That son of a bitch come along after my fans, and he's hot."

MARTY LACKER: Elvis really liked "It's Not Unusual." He thought it was a great record. We didn't know that Tom was from Wales because of the way he sang. As a matter of fact, at first, Elvis thought Tom was black.

Tom's first two records had just come out when we were doing *Paradise Hawaiian Style*. One day we were at Paramount, and I got a call from Tom Diskin in the Colonel's office. He said that Tom Jones was going to be on the lot, and Jones wondered if he could come by and say hello to Elvis. Jones had said that Elvis was his idol. And because Elvis liked Tom's record, I went and asked him, and he said, "Okay, let him come over."

Tom came over to the set with a guy who was, I think, his agent. He was a bald-headed guy, with a big mouth. We came outside, and as they started talking, I got up on the first or sec-ond rung of a big ladder that was leaning there, and just held on, listening. Jones was telling Elvis how much he'd been influenced by his music, how much he loved what he did, and what it meant to meet him. He had this look of awe on his face, like he was talk-ing to God. He was literally shaking. And Elvis surprised him, I think, when he told him how much he liked his record. Which was the truth.

Then all of a sudden, this agent guy popped up and said, "Listen, Elvis, I can book you in England's Wembley Stadium with a guarantee of a million dollars for one show. What do you say?" Well, Elvis kind of ignored him, but the guy kept on. I guess that was his reason for being there. Finally, I turned to him and I said, "Hey, look, why don't you just let 'em talk? Elvis wanted to meet Tom because he liked his record. If you've got some offer you want to make, go call Colonel Parker. Elvis doesn't discuss business with anybody."

It still didn't deter him. He wouldn't quit. So I got a little testy, and I said, "Look, sport, don't bring this up again." And then Tom told him, "You'd better stop." Because Elvis was getting agitated. He felt like he'd been used.

LAMAR FIKE: Elvis sort of liked Tom. Because Tom was a singer who moved, and he did a lot of Elvis's moves. And Elvis liked to go see his shows. We saw him in Vegas, and then we met him over in Hawaii, when Elvis was on vacation in '68.

MARTY LACKER: Tom was a nice enough guy, but Elvis didn't think of him as some big pal. And I'm sure Tom didn't really consider himself such. Not really. One time in Vegas, in the seventies, Tom came backstage to the dressing room after one of Elvis's shows. There were a lot of other people there, some entertainers, like James Brolin, the actor, and his wife, who were nice people. Elvis was in the back changing his clothes, and Tom sat there running his loud mouth, being Mr. Macho, Mr. Cocky, Mr. Everything. He was like the Big Star.

After a little while, the doors opened and Elvis walked in. And Tom got dead silent. He wasn't Mr. Macho anymore.

Tom Jones is one of these entertainers who became Elvis's big friend after he died. You know what I'm saying? He was part of that documentary I worked on, *Elvis: The Echo Will Never Die*. We went out to Vegas to interview him for it, and his public relations guy, John Moran, told me that Jones said he could have straightened Elvis out and gotten him off pills if he'd had the opportunity. I looked at Moran and I said, "You tell Tom he's full of shit." Jones would never have opened up his mouth in front of Elvis.

During the interview, Jones had the nerve to say something like "If Elvis had had a few more friends around"—intimating himself—"he wouldn't have died when he did." I just shook my head. Elvis would have kicked Tom Jones's ass so far out the door he couldn't find it. These people talk, but they don't know what the hell they're talking about. Elvis was the same way with Tom Jones as he was with the Beatles. He liked their music. And that was about it.

LAMAR FIKE: Elvis didn't understand what the Beatles were about. He liked some of their songs, like "Hey Jude," and he loved "Yesterday." But he never understood the wave.

MARTY LACKER: Elvis couldn't stand the psychedelic stuff, like Jimi Hendrix. And he didn't particularly like Mick Jagger. He didn't like looking at him. He thought Jagger's antics were sort of fake and effeminate. And he didn't like the attitude that the Rolling Stones and a lot of these English groups had. So many of them came off as a bunch of arrogant jerks. Elvis believed that if you had talent, you just went out and demonstrated it without all this extracurricular crap.

I'm not sure Elvis understood what the sixties were about, politically and culturally. Colonel always drummed it in his head not to take sides on politics or religion because he said it was bound to offend somebody, no matter which side Elvis took. He said, "Don't speak out on anything. Half of your fans won't like you anymore." And most managers would tell their stars that. So that's why Elvis never talked politics. And he never voted.

LAMAR FIKE: I think Elvis didn't like to see any kind of injustice, but if it didn't directly affect him, he was a little bit indifferent. And in that sense, he wasn't the big humanitarian people make him out to be. He cared more about helping individuals than helping masses of people or a cause.

MARTY LACKER: Now, in private, he would express his opinion. He supported civil rights, for example. This was the time of all the uprising[s] by the blacks, especially in the South. Television news was full of the civil rights marches and demonstrations, with film of black people all over Alabama and elsewhere getting beaten to a pulp. He didn't like to see anybody beat on. But he didn't speak out about it because of what Colonel had told him. He could have been a force in that regard because Southern people, particularly, liked him. But he never tried.

He also didn't like the whole idea of "Tune in, Turn On, Drop Out," which came along later, because it was too closely related to the counterculture, to opposing the war in Vietnam. Something like the Yippie movement made no sense to him.

Elvis was gung ho on military matters. He could quote

[General Douglas] MacArthur's farewell speech verbatim. The part that really stuck in his mind was the ending. Not, "Old soldiers never die." But, "With that, I bid you a fond, affectionate farewell." When Elvis would get upset at somebody, he would change it. He'd say, "I bid you a fond, affectionate, fuckin' farewell." And with that, he would turn around and walk out of the room. He loved to shock people.

LAMAR FIKE: Elvis liked heroes. He liked people who were bigger than life. The trappings meant a lot to him. He thought [General Omar] Bradley hung the moon, for example. In the seventies, we went up to the Memphian to see the movie *Patton*. Elvis loved it. He saw the movie about four times. And we got to talking about Bradley, and somebody we knew found out where Bradley lived. And we got in the 600 Mercedes limousine and drove to his house. A full colonel, who was his aide, met us at the door. Elvis introduced himself and said he wanted to meet the general. This aide ushered us in, and we sat there and talked to the general for quite a while. Elvis went up and saw him two or three different times. Lord only knows what Bradley thought of Elvis. And why he was there.

The fascination, I think, was just that Bradley was a legendary hero. He was the last surviving five-star general. Elvis thought that was big stuff. But I don't think he cared about being a military hero himself. I think he would have been happy being the president and absolute despotic monarch of the United States. Elvis wanted to do things, but he didn't want to put up with the problems of getting there. He wanted everything Johnny-on-the-spot. With Elvis, it was instant gratification all the way.

MARTY LACKER: Somebody like Bradley would have been much more of a hero to Elvis than counterculture leaders like Jerry Rubin or Timothy Leary. He was pretty predictable there. But he could also be unpredictable. The only time Elvis stopped liking the Beatles, for example, was when they got involved with the Maharishi. Which is kind of ironic, seeing what he got into as far as religion was concerned. And this was what was funny—when the Beatles started talking publicly about smoking marijuana, Elvis thought it was terrible. He felt they were a bad influence on kids. In the meantime, he was getting blown out of his skull on pills.

BILLY SMITH: I think Elvis felt out of touch with the sixties, but not with the early Beatles. He thought the early Beatles were real similar to his early music. He loved the loud, hard-driving sound that they had. He wanted that himself. Elvis was always fighting for his records to sound some other way than how they did. Especially when he was making the movies. Not all of them because he liked that more sophisticated ballad sound, too. But occasionally, he wanted his records to sound raw.

For example, he'd ask for the bass to be brought forward a little more in places. And he wanted his voice mixed down, and the music brought up louder, even if it overrode his voice sometimes. He thought RCA was bringing his voice out too much. And it pissed Elvis off.

He'd say, "Those New York sons of bitches! They're screwing with my music!" Because a lot of times they took the tapes from the recording sessions up there to mix 'em. And he'd explain again. He'd play a Beatles record, and he'd say, "This is what I'm looking for right here. I want that drive back. And I don't want my voice to be brought out front. If it's there, I want the background singers brought out with me."

MARTY LACKER: Before RCA could release any of Elvis's records, the final mix had to be sent to the Colonel. And the Colonel would call up RCA and say, "No, I want my boy's voice up a little bit more."

The funny thing is, they used to cut these acetates for Elvis after the sessions, and we'd take 'em back and listen to 'em. The acetates sounded better than the actual records did after the Colonel finished screwing with them.

When you look at how Colonel controlled absolutely everything, you just can't believe it. I read an interview with Bones Howe, who engineered a lot of the early records, in *Musician* magazine. Bones said Colonel told him, "I designed all these album covers. People say they're in poor taste, but we're selling millions of records. These guys at RCA want to do fancy artistic stuff, but they don't know who the audience is."

Well, Lamar and I found out a few years ago that Colonel charged RCA for the pictures they used on the record jackets. Colonel denies this, I hear. But two of the top guys at RCA told us that they don't have many pictures of Elvis for that reason.

Now, most record companies would demand that their artists sit for photo sessions. But Colonel refused. Every still picture that was taken for a movie, or on a movie set or on location—even if they were taken by the studio photographers—had to be handed over to Colonel. With the negatives. He controlled them all. And he sold RCA one picture at a time. He'd say, "This is what the cover is going to be, and this is what it's going to cost you." What I don't know is how or if Elvis and the Colonel shared the proceeds. But I have a guess.

CHAPTER 29

HILL AND RANGE

MARTY LACKER: The reason Elvis was cutting so many crappy songs is that most of them came from Hill and Range. Colonel insisted on that because he got a piece of the action. That's the way he structured Elvis's publishing companies from the beginning.

LAMAR FIKE: Jean and Julian Aberbach, who owned Hill and Range, were old friends of Colonel Parker back in the Eddy Arnold days. That's the reason that they were able to get in the position they did with Elvis.

MARTY LACKER: The Aberbachs owned a publishing company called Bay Music. A lot of the demos Elvis got were from Bay, and they were crummy ol' European songs, really old-fashioned sounding. They were ten or fifteen years behind American music. And those were the songs that Elvis was handed to record because the Aberbachs wanted to get double mileage out of them.

LAMAR FIKE: Hill and Range was always a major publishing company. But I built it into a very powerful company in Nashville, and I'm proud of that. I spent nine years there, from '63 to '72, and I was making $50,000 a year, which was a lot of money then. And even though Elvis was Hill and Range's biggest source of income, I could maintain my independence from Elvis through this job.

Hill and Range gets criticized a lot for what it did with Elvis, but I think Hill and Range served Elvis well. In the late sixties, I gave him two songs that did great for him. A kid named Darrell Glenn wrote a song called "Indescribably Blue" that was a big single for Elvis in '67. And another one of my writers, Eddie

Rabbitt, came up with "Kentucky Rain," which was Elvis's last million seller and fiftieth gold record.

In the seventies, two other Elvis hits came out of that office. We had a song called "T-R-O-U-B-L-E" that Jerry Chesnut wrote, and "It's Midnight," which Jerry and Billy Edd Wheeler wrote together.

MARTY LACKER: You need to understand the scenario. Lamar was in Nashville, the Aberbachs and Freddy Bienstock, who was their nephew, were in New York, and Colonel was in L.A. If Lamar had been able to tear himself away from Bienstock and the Aberbachs and the Colonel more often, the way he did with some of those tunes that weren't strictly Hill and Range's, like Jerry Chesnut's stuff, Lamar probably could have gotten Elvis some damn good songs.

LAMAR FIKE: Freddy was the manager of Hill and Range, and he became the liaison between Hill and Range and Elvis. He would bring me a set of demos, and I'd go through songs and find the ones that I thought Elvis would like. Sometimes Charlie Hodge would do it, too.

MARTY LACKER: The Aberbachs never came to the recording sessions. It was always Bienstock. Freddy's a pretty wealthy man, so he probably doesn't give a shit what anybody thinks of him, but I didn't like him. He acted sort of like the Colonel. He was one way to your face and another way to your back. I don't think he cared about Elvis that much, either.

BILLY SMITH: Hill and Range was great in the beginning. But they became stagnant in later years. Colonel just got too greedy.

MARTY LACKER: In the early years, the Colonel was fine. But after a while, Elvis should have had things like his own record label, distributed by a major company. No other artist had that at the time. But how many other artists sold a million records?

LAMAR FIKE: Colonel could have set up deals like that, but he didn't. Because he structured the deals for his own benefit, and his friends. Colonel got away with murder. He didn't own a piece of every one of the companies, though. Elvis owned 50 percent of Gladys Music, and he owned 50 percent of Elvis Presley Music. Jean and Julian Aberbach owned the other 50 percent. Managers don't normally take a piece of the publishing, but Colonel got a piece of everything Elvis got because his contract was based on the gross. Hey, you've got to give him credit. He had a hell of a gravy train, and he kept it that way.

MARTY LACKER: The demos of those Bay Music songs were almost the only demos that Elvis would get to hear. Any new song had to be sent to Colonel Parker's office so Parker and Bienstock could listen to it. That way, they'd send Elvis only what they wanted him to hear.

LAMAR FIKE: After a while, the demos got so locked that Elvis literally became a parody of himself. Because Elvis would just ape whatever the demo singer was doing. And a lot of times, the demo singer was trying to sound like him. So Elvis would end up copying a guy who was copying him.

MARTY LACKER: In the fifties and the sixties, demos were made just the way the song was written, with the songwriter's arrangement. And a lot of times, the arrangements were fairly good. Except that didn't mean that that's the way the final product should be. Elvis would put his own final touches in there.

Then, when he was doing the stuff with these Nashville pickers, the creativity wasn't there. They would sit around and read music or do that crude numbers thing [a rough chord chart and musical shorthand known as the Nashville Numbers System], and that's the way it would come out. And because there was no real creativity, after a while, Elvis just lost his fire in the studio.

Look at all those years he didn't have a hit record! In '60 and '61, he was flying high, with five number one singles—"Stuck on You," "It's Now or Never," "Are You Lonesome To-night?" "Surrender," and "Can't Help Falling in Love." Then in '62 and '63 he had "Good Luck Charm," "Return to Sender," and "(You're the) Devil in Disguise," which went to one, two, and three, in that order, on the *Billboard* chart. Finally, in '65, he had "Crying in the Chapel." But then, it was four long years before he got up in the top five again, with "In the Ghetto." And that was like a lifetime away.

LAMAR FIKE: Marty thinks Elvis would have made more money if he'd had better songs. That's crazy. Elvis would have made more money if Colonel had taken less commission. Elvis had one of the strongest catalogs of any artist who ever recorded.

If Elvis was unhappy, you have to remember that the only person who could change that situation was Elvis. He had to sit up and say, "What the fuck are you people doing? Do something to straighten it out!" But he didn't have the balls.

About the only thing I think Hill and Range really screwed up on was failing to have Elvis affiliated with either ASCAP or BMI as a writer so that Elvis could get the money that was coming to him for airplay. That was rectified, but not until after Elvis's death. Elvis didn't really write anything, but he had those credits. In the early days, they'd ask the writer to give Elvis part of the credit, and, of course, part of the writer's royalty.

MARTY LACKER: That's another reason the songs got so shitty. In the early years, when Elvis was the surest thing going, every songwriter and publisher wanted him to cut their song. So the Aberbachs and Bienstock and the Colonel would go to that person and say, "Elvis will record your song if you give us 25 percent of your copyright." Sometimes it was a third, and sometimes it was 50 percent.

It may not have been fair to the songwriter, but in those days it was good business. Otis Blackwell, one of the greatest songwriters on the planet, gave up part of "Don't Be Cruel," "All Shook Up," and "Paralyzed." Elvis is listed as the cowriter, and they never met.

As the years went on, the Aberbachs and Colonel continued that practice. But by then, a lot of artists had come along and sold large numbers of records because Elvis opened the door for a lot of people. So all of these songwriters now had a lot more candidates to sing their songs, although there's not a one of them who wouldn't have wanted Elvis because it meant instant sales and because they wanted to be able to say, "I've really made it— Elvis Presley is cuttin' one of my songs."

But after a while a lot of them started balking at giving up 25 or 50 percent of the copyright. They didn't have to do it anymore. Lamar doesn't see anything wrong with any of this. But you've got to understand—he was working for those people, for the

Aberbachs and the Colonel. I see a lot wrong with it. It isn't even done anymore.

LAMAR FIKE: This criticism of Colonel isn't totally warranted. Every manager wants to tie a situation together where the artist does his own songs and has his own company. You want to put the wagons in a circle. And this is what we did with Elvis. When you have that amount of influence, the funnel is controlled at your end.

You always try to get deals. That's how Gladys Music and Elvis Presley Music were built. Everything was kept within the framework of the company because that's where your money is made. The most money Elvis made at any particular point is when those publishing companies were sold. Copyrights are worth a lot of money.

MARTY LACKER: Keeping everything inside of the company might have been good for Hill and Range, but it wasn't good for Elvis. It wasn't until the late sixties and early seventies that he was exposed to contemporary writers or even a good source of songs again.

LAMAR FIKE: Elvis just ignored things, hoping they would go away. That's how he was kept in control until the latter years when his sales declined. Then he got confrontational. So we had to retreat and change our tactics.

Until then, it was a locked deal. We assigned writers that we knew we could get the publishing on. And we didn't let a lot of outside people in.

MARTY LACKER: As an example, Ivory Joe Hunter wrote "My Wish Came True," which was BMI's Song of the Year in 1959. Well, years later, Ivory Joe came back with another good song and said, "I'd like to get this to Elvis." They gave him the same crap about the publishing, and Ivory Joe said, "No, I ain't gonna do it." Well, Elvis never got to hear the song.

The same thing happened later on in the early seventies with Dolly Parton. Elvis loved her "Coat of Many Colors." He saw her singing it on TV, and he put the word out that he would like to record it. Well, when they called Dolly, she said, "I'd love for Elvis to do the song, but you're not getting 25 percent of my publishing."

LAMAR FIKE: The songs declined somewhat through the years. I'll admit that. Especially the movie songs. But musicals are musicals. It's hard to come up with great songs for crap.

MARTY LACKER: Hill and Range had these people writing songs for the movies. The Aberbachs and Bienstock would send them a script and say, "We need a song in this scene, and we need a song here." And a lot of times, they came up with some of the dumbest damn songs you've ever heard. Like "(There's) No Room to Rumba in a Sports Car." After the Colonel and Bienstock picked the music from the demos, Elvis and Joe Esposito and I would go upstairs in Elvis's office next to his bedroom at Graceland and play these songs. Red would be up there a lot, too.

We'd put these demos in stacks marked "Yes," "No," or "Maybe." I'd say 99.9 percent of the time, the "Yes" stack was tiny, and even those songs were borderline. So after a while, a lot of the "Maybes" went back into the "Yes" pile. You can imagine what the "No" stack was like.

Not all the songs during the early sixties were terrible. There were exceptions. Doc Pomus and Mort Shuman wrote "(Marie's the Name) His Latest Flame," and "Little Sister," and "Surrender," and "Suspicion," and "Viva Las Vegas," although the last one was the only song used in the movies, I think.

Jerry Leiber and Mike Stoller wrote for Gladys Music in addition to their own companies, and in the fifties they did the stuff for King Creole, Jailhouse Rock, and Loving You. They wrote the whole score for Jailhouse Rock in one afternoon at the Gorham Hotel in New York. That was some of their best work, actually, aside from "Hound Dog," which they originally wrote for Big Mama Thornton.

They wrote for Elvis for years after he made "Hound Dog" a pop hit. But in the sixties, their contributions, like for Fun in Acapulco, and Viva Las Vegas, weren't as memorable, because they became less enthusiastic about writing for Elvis's pictures. Jerry said he thought they were "dopey," and they decided not to do anymore, even though it was like money in the bank. But every once in a while, they'd submit songs that got used in Elvis's films that they'd recorded with other people, but that hadn't been big commercial successes. Like "Girls! Girls! Girls!' and "Little Egypt" [from Roustabout], which the Coasters had done, and

"Bossa Nova Baby" [from *Fun in Acapulco*], which they'd done with the Clovers. They just recycled those songs for Elvis's movies.

Ben Weisman, who was a Hill and Range writer under Jean Aberbach, cowrote with several guys, particularly Fred Wise. Ben came up with a few good songs, like "Got a Lot o' Livin' to Do," and "Don't Ask Me Why," and "As Long as I Have You," and "Rock-a-Hula Baby," which is marginal, I guess. But considering he wrote fifty-seven songs that Elvis recorded—more than anybody else—he didn't exactly bring in a treasure trove of classics. He wrote a lot of the real junky movie songs, like "He's Your Uncle, Not Your Dad," and "Do the Clam," and "Change of Habit."

LAMAR FIKE: I've known Jerry Leiber and Mike Stoller since '57. Mike says it was hard enough to write songs for *Jailhouse Rock* and *Loving You*. But to find inspiration after those . . . well, that was a challenge.

MARTY LACKER: The quality of the material didn't matter to Parker and Bienstock because not only did they get money for the songs used in the movies, but then the songs were repackaged as movie soundtrack albums and some of them were released as the singles.

Part of the reason Elvis died at forty-two was the way those people fucked him around. If Elvis had gotten what he had coming to him financially, he probably wouldn't have been in the frame of mind he was in at the end. It's hard to imagine, but there were times when he was that far from being dead broke.

LAMAR FIKE: Good God! Marty blames Hill and Range for Elvis's whole demise! That's bullshit. I saw a lot of those pill bottles, let me tell you. And not a one said "Hill and Range" on it.

CHAPTER 30

FALLOUT

BILLY SMITH: The damn pill bottles might as well have said "Hill and Range," or "RCA," or "Colonel." Because Elvis started to take a really good look at the advice Colonel was giving him. Like about that yacht.

MARTY LACKER: Sometime in late '63, Colonel read in the newspaper that the *Potomac* was going to be salvaged. The *Potomac* was Franklin Delano Roosevelt's presidential yacht. He had a summit meeting with Winston Churchill and Joseph Stalin on it. And that's where he got the telegram from Albert Einstein and Edward Teller telling him the atomic bomb test was successful.

Colonel thought it would be good publicity for Elvis to save the *Potomac*. So they bought it for $55,000. The thing was a wreck, but instead of restoring it, Colonel pulled one of his carny tricks—he had only one side of the boat painted, the side that faced the cameras at the dock. But as soon as Colonel got the word out that Elvis was going to give the boat to charity, they had a rude awakening. Nobody wanted it. Including the March of Dimes, which was a crime, since FDR suffered from polio, and that was his charity. I guess they were afraid they couldn't afford to maintain it.

Finally, St. Jude, the Memphis children's hospital that Danny Thomas founded, said they'd like to have it. They were going to sell it and use the money for the hospital. But Colonel arranged this big ceremony with Elvis and Danny Thomas in Long Beach Harbor in February of '64.

There were a lot of photographers there, and Elvis was all smiles when he and Thomas signed the papers. But when we got in the car, Elvis was just spewing, he was so angry. He said,

"That ungrateful motherfucker!" Apparently, when they were sitting at the table, Thomas leaned over and whispered, "Why in the hell did you buy this piece of shit?"

LAMAR FIKE: The Colonel made more good decisions than bad, I think. In the mid-sixties, he had a lot on his mind. His wife, Marie, developed Alzheimer's disease, and she deteriorated pretty fast. She didn't actually die until the mid-eighties. The Colonel kept a nurse with her around the clock.

MARTY LACKER: By about '64, Joe and Charlie were making frequent reports to the Colonel. Joe, especially. That led to a lot of tension. I liked Joe, even though he looked down on some of the guys. Red didn't like Joe, and the feeling was mutual. Joe looked upon Red as this big ol' dumb tough guy, which was far from the truth. And Red hated Joe because of his attitude. There were a couple of times Red came close to busting Joe up pretty good.

LAMAR FIKE: I didn't have much use for Joe. After Elvis died, he popped off at me about something, and I said, "Listen to me, you little cocksucker. The only reason I put up with you was to keep some sort of harmony in this organization." I said, "Elvis is dead. You got no hold on anybody here. Nobody gives a fuck about you, and people are tired of your shit. Furthermore, you're lucky Red West hasn't killed you."

BILLY SMITH: Joe thought he was better than some of Elvis's family. He was a big college man and pretty smart. I liked him in some ways, and in other ways, I didn't. He was a perfect example of a guy who pretended to be above average, but wasn't. I'd say Joe's philosophy was, "If you can't dazzle 'em with your brilliance, then stun 'em with your bullshit."

LAMAR FIKE: Joe cared about Elvis, but he also used him. He spent tons of money on his expense account. After he got married, he lived out in California, and he couldn't have maintained his lifestyle out of what Elvis was paying him. So he supplemented his income by making sure he got the same perks Elvis got. Like from the hotels. If Elvis got a crystal set, Joe would make sure he got one, too. He pulled that leverage thing. I looked him right in the face once, and I said, "Joe, if I had my choice between you and a hernia, I'd rather have that belt on."

MARTY LACKER: Charlie was worse. Charlie was like a little puppy dog around Elvis. But when you asked Charlie to do something, Charlie's pat answer was, "I don't do that. That's not my job." Hell, he didn't have a job! Later, when Elvis went back on the road and Charlie held his scarves for him, Charlie would say, "I don't do that because my job is being onstage with Elvis."

BILLY SMITH: There was this class separation, see. It was like Joe was number one, and Charlie always thought he was second. He had this idea of him and Joe being called "Sarge" and "Lieutenant." They wanted to run the group like a military operation. I thought, "Sergeant Esposito, hell!" I didn't call him a damn thing, except maybe "son of a bitch."

Stuff like that just burnt me up. I resented the fact that I was related to Elvis, and I'd known him all my life, yet I had some guy working for him telling me what to do. So I just raised hell about it. Finally, Elvis told Joe and Charlie, "Leave him alone. I'll take care of him."

Elvis knew what Joe and Charlie were doing. And he was well aware that too many things were getting back to the Colonel. After a while, Joe began to get a little braver about how he talked to Elvis. Then one day it was all over. Elvis and Joe had words. And Elvis fired him.

MARTY LACKER: I guess you could say that Joe quit because Elvis couldn't ever fire anybody. Not directly. What happened was, we were coming home to Memphis from doing one of the pictures, and we stopped in Amarillo, Texas, at a Holiday Inn. The word got out to the press that Elvis was there. And that evening, when we woke up, there was a crowd of people and TV cameras outside the hotel. That really upset Elvis because he wanted to leave and he couldn't walk out without causing a commotion. So he started ripping into Joe, saying he let it leak out, because it was the foreman's job to check into the motel and set up the rooms.

I remember this so vividly. Joe and I were up in Elvis's room. Elvis was sitting on the bed, and Joe was leaning against the dresser, and I was right by the door. And Elvis was screaming at Joe. I said, "Wait a minute, Elvis." And he said, "You shut up! I don't want to hear it!" And he started in on Joe again. After that, neither one spoke to the other, all the way from Amarillo to Memphis. Which meant there was something else underlying all this because most of the time, Elvis stayed mad for about thirty minutes. And once we got on the road, Joe would have joked him out of it.

When we got back to Graceland, Elvis went upstairs. Usually, when we came back off a trip, he'd stay upstairs for a few days, just to unwind by himself, and we'd go off to our families, even though we'd check in every day. But when we were in Memphis, Joe lived there at Graceland in the garage apartment because his family was in California.

I'd go over every day, and I'd ask Joe, "Did you hear from Elvis?" And he'd say, "When I call up there he won't answer the phone." Well, this went on for a week. And Joe said, "I don't know what to do. I've got all these checks that need to be signed." And he said, "If he doesn't talk to me soon, I'm going back to California." I said, "You mean quit?" And he said, "Yeah, I guess so. It doesn't look like he wants me around."

LAMAR FIKE: If Elvis really wanted you gone, he'd make your life so damn miserable that you would leave. He'd shut you down. And most of the time you'd never know why.

MARTY LACKER: After about ten days, Joe said, "If he don't talk to me today, I'm leaving. I'm going to call up there and tell him." Elvis answered the phone, but he didn't want to deal with Joe. So Joe said, "If you're not going to come down and sign these checks, then I'm going home." And he waited and waited, but Elvis didn't come down. So Joe handed me the checkbook and the gas cards and the bills, and he said, "You tell him I waited as long as I could."

I tried to get him to stay, but he got somebody to drive him to the airport. And no sooner had Joe pulled out of the gate than the intercom buzzed there in the garage apartment. I answered it, and Elvis said, "Is he gone yet?" I said, "He just left." And Elvis said, "Tell Hattie I want my breakfast. I'm coming down."

I waited until he finished eating, and then I said, "Here, Elvis, Joe left these credit cards and the checks to be signed." And he turned to me and he said, "Well, it looks like we got a new fore-man." I thought he meant I was pushing myself on him. So I said, "No, Joe just asked me to give these to you." But he repeated it. Then he said, "And you got a raise." So I said, "Are you sure?" And he said, "Yeah." That's how I became foreman. I think my pay went up to $150 a week.

My family and I had been living with my parents, way over on the other side of town. But now, since I had to be with Elvis twenty-four hours a day, I said, "Elvis, if it's okay with you, we're just going to move out to the garage." And he thought he'd play with me a little bit. He said, "Goddamnit. I make you the fore-man, and the very next minute, you want to move into my fuckin' house." And he started laughing.

BILLY SMITH: In '64, we'd been out in California for two movies, which was about four months. And like before, I was real eager to get back to Memphis. There were only four of us with Elvis then—me, Richard, Marty, and Alan. The others had quit or been fired. And Red and Sonny were off working in the movies.

Elvis had a hairdresser named Sal Orifice. It turns out Sal was getting ready to start his own business, but nobody knew it. He was keeping it secret. All we knew was that he wasn't coming up to the house as frequently. One day, Elvis asked if anybody had got in touch with Sal to come up and fix his hair. We said we couldn't find him, which was true. Elvis got mad and said, "You sons of bitches tell him that if he can't make it up here, as much money as I pay him, then I don't need him."

Well, I took that personally. I didn't like being called a son of a bitch.

In a little while, we found Sal, and he come up to the house late that night. Elvis had already gone to his room, and he was still mad. So when Sal come up, I told him exactly what Elvis said. Sal said, "That's why I come up here tonight, to tell Elvis that I'm going to have to quit. I'm starting my own shop."

About two hours later, Elvis come out and said, "Did anybody get in touch with Sal?" And I piped up and said, "I told him exactly what you said, Elvis. I said, 'If you can't get up here when Elvis wants you . . . '"

And Elvis never let me finish. He thought I'd fired him. He didn't know that Sal was already quitting. All he knew was that he had movie rehearsal the next day and no hairdresser. So he threw a temper tantrum. He beat the coffee table and jumped up and said, "Since you're all in a firing mood, all you sons of bitches are fired! Get the hell out."

Boy, whew! I know my face went red. But I just said, "Okay." I went in my room, and I packed my suitcase. I think everybody else hung around a little while to see if Elvis was really serious.

When I come out, I went in the den to tell Elvis goodbye. He was sitting there with his leg propped on the coffee table and shaking his foot the way he always done when he was nervous or mad. He said, "You leaving?" And I said, "Yeah, I'm heading for Memphis. I've got to find a job." And Elvis said, "Then take all these other sons of bitches with you." So Richard and Marty took me to the airport.

Alan was the only one left at the house. And about an hour or two later, Elvis fired him, too. But Alan told Elvis he wasn't going to leave until he got somebody else to come stay with him—that he'd leave the next day. A little bit later, Alan was getting ready to go to bed and Elvis buzzed him and said, "What time does that plane to Memphis leave?" Alan said he wasn't sure. And Elvis said, "Call and have that plane stopped and get Billy back here."

Alan called the airport and had Marty paged. He told him, "Elvis wants you to bring Billy on back." Treating me like I was still a little kid, you know. He said, "Even if he's already boarded, get him off." So Marty ran like a wild man, which for Marty was pretty good. I was already in my seat, even. Marty told me what Alan wanted, and I said, "No, you tell him I'm not coming home. I've got to find a job. I don't have time for all this."

Marty went back to the phone and told Alan, and then he come back and said, "Alan wants to talk to you." Well, Alan went through the whole thing. I said, "Look, tell Elvis if he wants me back, he's got to tell me himself."

Alan said, "Hold on." And Elvis got on the phone, and boy, it liked to killed him. He said, in this real curt tone, "Yeah?" I said, "Look, if I'm fired, I've got to go home." I said, "If I'm hired, well, I'm not going to say I'm sorry. That's going to have to come from you. Because I don't think I was at fault. I just need to know one way or the other." And Elvis said, as fast as he could talk, "I'm sorry, and you're hired."

MARTY LACKER: Sal recommended a hairdresser named Larry Geller, who worked at Jay Sebring's shop. Jay ended up being one of Charles Manson's victims. Elvis was on his way back to Memphis in May of '64 and brought Larry with him. And little by little Geller just eased his way into the group.

Geller was Jewish, but he was into all this mystic stuff. He's one of the reasons Elvis's head got so screwed up. California was sort of a breeding ground for all these off-the-wall Far Eastern religions. And Geller really filled Elvis's head with all that stuff. I started calling him "The Swami." Then everybody used it.

Before Elvis met Larry Geller, the only religious book he read was the Bible. When he was young, and he'd go to his mother with a problem, she'd say, "Go in and read the Bible, son. You'll find your answers in there." So he knew the Bible. He had a deep belief in God, although he didn't have much faith in preachers. When he got famous and started making money, and especially when he moved into Graceland, he said, "Every time I go to church, they have their hand out, wanting money." Especially Reverend [James] Hamill, who'd been the Presleys' Assembly of God minister in Memphis. He's the one who preached Gladys's funeral. Elvis singled him out. He said, "I never see the guy that he doesn't ask me for money." Hamill pretty much turned Elvis off to going to church.

Geller wanted Elvis to be a preacher, but not just any preacher. He wanted him to be The Messenger, right? Geller was smart, see. Almost every time he came up to the house, he brought a new book on all these different religions. A whole slew of 'em: *The Tibetan Book of the Dead*, and Paramahansa Yogananda's *Autobiography of a Yogi*, and *The Rosicrucian Cosmo-Conception*, and *The Urantia Book*, all this spirit shit. I basically liked Geller. But little by little, I started getting that uneasy feeling.

LAMAR FIKE: Larry Geller was a hippie from the sixties, and he's a phony son of a bitch. He's like plastic. You could make toys out of that bastard.

MARTY LACKER: One time on Perugia Way, Elvis and I were sitting in the den and Geller came in and brought this book on spirituality. He was talking to Elvis about it, telling him how important it was, and emphasizing that it was a first edition, autographed by the author. The more he mentioned that it was a rare book, the more it hit me wrong. Finally, Elvis said, "What are you going to do, Larry? Are you going to let me have this book?" And Larry said, "No, no, Elvis. There's probably not another copy out there like this that I could get my hands on. Not an autographed first edition." It was like he was dangling a piece of candy in front of Elvis and pulling it back.

The guys and I had been around Elvis so long that all he had to do was just look at us, and it was a signal. When Geller said that, Elvis looked over at me with a glint in his eye. Elvis always knew that if he asked me to find something, I'd turn over every rock until I got it. So I just smiled back at him. When Larry left, Elvis said, "See if you can find the fuckin' thing."

The next afternoon, I went down to Hollywood Boulevard, to the Pickwick Book Store. I told the guy what I was looking for, and I said, "I'd really like to have a first edition, if there is one." The guy looked it up in his microfiche, and he said, "Yeah, I got that." I said, "A first edition?" He said, "I don't know." He went away for a minute, and he came back with a first edition, and it was autographed. He said, "We've got eight copies, and six of 'em are autographed."

I brought one back to the house, and I put it down on the table in front of Elvis without saying anything. He picked it up and leafed through it, and he just smiled. He said, "That's what I thought."

So Elvis was onto Geller almost from the start, but Geller suckered him anyway. The more time Geller spent with Elvis, the more Elvis got involved with these religions. And the more involved he got, the more obsessed he became.

After Elvis died, Geller went on TV shows and called himself Elvis's spiritual adviser, his guru. He was really just the guy who helped fuck up Elvis's head.

LAMAR FIKE: In '64, Elvis was out in California to do a picture, and the guys had their first brush with trouble. One day, they were at the studio, and Elvis sent Richard back to the house on Perugia Way in the Chrysler station wagon to get something, a change of clothes, I think. Richard was hurrying, trying to get the stuff and get back. And those streets in Bel Air are treacherous.

Anyway, "Broom," as we called him, was rounding a corner and he hit a Japanese gardener. The gardener was cutting a shrub or something and backed out into the street, and Broom killed him deader than hell. It shook him up bad. He withdrew for a while.

The accident wasn't his fault, but in California, if you kill a pedestrian, you're responsible. That's when Colonel brought Ed Hookstratten into the picture. Ed was this big-shot Beverly Hills attorney. Still is. He represented a lot of stars, and he was married to Patricia Crowley, the actress. Ed became Elvis's personal attorney. He settled with the gardener's estate, and the insurance company had to pay a bundle.

MARTY LACKER: Elvis couldn't be bothered with business details. That was the Colonel's job. Colonel gave Hookstratten the instructions on handling Elvis, and he followed them.

The day Elvis went to Hookstratten to discuss the settlement with the gardener's estate, I wrecked Elvis's Chrysler New Yorker. I'd taken one of Elvis's dates home about six in the morning, and on the way back to Perugia Way, I fell asleep at the wheel. I was screwed out of my head a lot during that time, and I hit the streetlight at the corner of Sunset and Carolwood, right across the street from Jayne Mansfield's house. I don't remember getting to the corner, but I took the pole with me at the front of the car. The hot wires from the light pole were just flicking toward the back bumper of the car. If they had touched the bumper, and I'd opened the door . . . well, I was just lucky.

Hookstratten handled that, too, because we had to pay the city for the pole. He must have thought Elvis had hired the world's worst drivers.

BILLY SMITH: After Joe left, Elvis decided he wanted some more people around. The organization ran real smooth with just the four of us, but Elvis missed the noise. And the action. So he told us to start looking for two or three more guys to add to the group.

I got Jerry Schilling hired. Jerry wanted to fit in bad. He would run errands for you, just do anything. He was like a shy little guy, but he had a pretty good sense of humor. I think he first met everybody when he played touch football with the guys, and he was coming to the movies and the fairgrounds. We called him "Mr. Bodybuilder" because he was athletic. Then we called him "Mr. Milk" and finally just "Milk."

LAMAR FIKE: Jerry had a good personality. But there were problems from the beginning. Jerry's a pious asshole. He claims he knew Elvis back in '53, from the projects, but I think it was Red he knew. As a kid, Jerry used to go watch Red play football. I don't think he knew Elvis then. Jerry is as full of shit as a Christmas goose.

MARTY LACKER: Jerry was about one week away from being graduated from Arkansas State University when he quit to go to work for Elvis. What he learned in those three and three-quarter years, I have no idea.

At the same time Jerry came in, Elvis hired a guy named Mike Keaton, who was Jerry's friend. Mike was a quiet, religious guy. Elvis found out that he belonged to the Assembly of God church, which the Presleys had attended when Elvis was a kid. I think Elvis liked Mike because of the conversations they had.

LAMAR FIKE: What cinched it for Mike was when Elvis found out that Mike's wife was named Gladys. Then he wanted him in the group. And Elvis made it a point to get to know Gladys.

MARTY LACKER: We were getting ready to go back out to California to make, I think, *Tickle Me*. Elvis had been made a deputy sheriff of Shelby County [Memphis] that day, and he was feeling kind of cocky. He thought that was a big deal, and he'd really wanted it. That night, which was the night before we left, we were at the Memphian, and that's when Elvis asked Mike and

Jerry to join up. Jerry knew we were going to ask him. He kept talking about it when Elvis wasn't around. Richard, I think, dropped it on him. He said, "Don't worry about it. You're going to get hired." But here it was just hours before we were supposed to leave, and Elvis hadn't said anything to Jerry, and Jerry sat there in the theater all nervous and anxious, his face getting red.

When the movies were over, we were walking up the aisle— Elvis was in front of me—and I said, "Elvis, Jerry and Mike Keaton are standing over there wondering if you're ever going to say anything to them." Because Elvis always liked to do the hiring. He didn't like to do the firing, but the hiring he liked. And he looked back at me and smiled, and he said, "Yeah, I was just lettin' 'em sweat a while." Then he walked over to them and said, "How would you like to go to L.A. tonight?" That meant they were hired.

BILLY SMITH: Even though I brought Jerry into the group, as soon as he joined, I knew he was along the same lines as Jimmy Kingsley—looking to see what he could get out of Elvis.

LAMAR FIKE: Elvis wanted to take Jerry down two or three times. He was going to do it, too. They had very different political views, and Jerry didn't see why he should keep them to himself. Jerry was very liberal, especially about the Vietnam War, and, of course, Elvis was kind of like John Wayne. And Jerry used to piss him off. We didn't know the term "liberal" back then. Elvis just called him a Communist. He said, "That Commie bastard." Nobody was ever real close to Jerry. Except Joe.

MARTY LACKER: Jerry got more outspoken, and Elvis grew to really dislike him. Another reason he didn't like him was because Jerry was Catholic. Geller had already convinced Elvis that Catholicism was dangerous.

Mike didn't fit in very well, either, but for a different reason. Mike didn't fit in because he didn't like to do the crazy stuff we did.

LAMAR FIKE: Mike was like a bubble in a nut factory. Do you know what I'm saying?

MARTY LACKER: Starting in about '64, Priscilla started scheming to change Elvis's way of life. I don't know if she ever genuinely loved him, but I think after a while it got to be a game with her. I've got to grant her—he didn't treat her very well. But if she was looking for an ideal relationship, she wasn't going to find that with Elvis. Still, she stayed on his ass all the time on the telephone. She'd say, "Why can't I come out there? Why can't you stay here?" She was putting pressure on him to marry her.

LAMAR FIKE: You know, Elvis had a terrific arrangement. He had Priscilla at home, and he had Ann-Margret in California, and whatever else there was on the road in between. And when Priscilla bitched about it, he got mad. Elvis's defense was a great offense. He'd get all over you, and you'd back off in a defensive mode to try to fight him off. It was so funny to watch him do it.

MARTY LACKER: Elvis threatened two or three times to ship Priscilla's ass back to Germany. They got in an argument one night upstairs at Graceland. Billy and Lamar and I were sitting in the kitchen, and all of a sudden we heard them arguing. The upstairs was almost soundproof, but we heard it like we were in the room.

BILLY SMITH: That was a famous argument. It wasn't a roadhouse riot, but he slapped her, and she stumbled back and hit the corner of that big television set and cut her eye. It's a wonder it didn't put that eye out.

MARTY LACKER: Elvis was just livid. He called downstairs, and I answered the phone. I said, "Yeah?" And his exact words were, "Get this fuckin' bitch a plane ticket!" He said, "I'm packin' her damn shit now, and I want the first flight out of here!" And he hung up the phone. I told everybody what he said, and everybody started going, "Oh, shit! Oh, shit!" And you could hear him yelling at her. But what he was doing was playing a game with her. She'd called his number on what he was doing out in California, but he turned the tables on her. She got scared as shit and started apologizing. Then about fifteen minutes later, he called back down and said, "Cancel the flight." In an hour or two, they came downstairs and he was just all goody-goody. She had this big gash, and he said, "She tripped and hit her head against the TV set."

BILLY SMITH: He felt bad about it. He tried to cover it up with makeup, but you could still see the cut.

LAMAR FIKE: That was a sad situation. This girl was totally out-numbered.

BILLY SMITH: If the heat got too bad, Elvis would just get on a plane, or on one of the buses, and we'd go to California. He'd just run away from the problem.

A lot of times, they would call each other on the phone and work it out. But the bloom had been off that rose for a long, long time.

MARTY LACKER: Elvis never stopped seeing other women. Even when he was dating Ann-Margret. I think he thought he had to do it, like it was expected of him.

In '64, we all went to Vegas for a few weeks and stayed at the Sahara. One night, we went to the Desert Inn to see the McGuire Sisters. And from a distance, Phyllis McGuire looked just like Anita Wood. We all saw the resemblance. Elvis said, "Man, she's as pretty as Anita." And he kept saying it throughout the show. So after the show was over, he said, "God, I've got to meet her."

We went backstage, and she was there with her sisters, Chris and Dottie. They were real nice. Phyllis was the youngest, but she was the dominant one. She did all the talking. When we got up close to her, she really didn't look like Anita. She was blond like Anita and wore her hair up, but that was about it. She and Elvis started getting to know each other, and after that, Elvis went back every night. He wouldn't go to the show, but afterwards, they'd hole up in the dressing room for something like two and a half hours.

Finally, one of the guys worked up the nerve to tell Elvis that seeing Phyllis wasn't such a good idea. Because it was pretty well known that she was the girlfriend of Sam Giancana, the mob boss. But, of course, Elvis wouldn't pay any attention to it.

One night before we went to bed, Elvis said to me, "Be sure I get up by noon, because at one o'clock you and I are going somewhere." We had the Rolls-Royce with us, and he said, "Tell the guys to have the Rolls ready." This was totally unusual, since he didn't get up until four or five o'clock. When I got to his suite at one o'clock, he was ready, but he seemed real anxious. He got behind the wheel of the Rolls, and we went back over to the Desert Inn.

We went upstairs, and Elvis knew exactly which room to go to. He knocked on the door, and Phyllis cracked it open a little because she had the chain on it. She had her hair in rollers. Elvis started talking to her, but she didn't really want to let him in. So he said to me, "Why don't you just go wait in the car?" And I thought, "Oh, shit, here we go again."

I went down to the car, and about an hour and a half later, he came down. We were driving back to the Sahara, and he was talking, and all of a sudden he started laughing. I asked him what he was laughing at, and he said, "I was up there with her, and I noticed there was a gun sticking halfway out of her purse." He said he asked her what she was doing with a gun, and she said Giancana had given it to her for protection. And Elvis said he looked at her and said, "Yeah, well, tell him I carry two of 'em."

I said, "Elvis, it's kind of foolish for you to say something like that. What if she goes back and says that to the guy in a way he doesn't like? He's a guy who plays for keeps. It wouldn't make any difference to him who you were." He just laughed it off.

Elvis's affair with Phyllis McGuire wasn't much of a romance—about two weeks' worth, I'd say. As far as I know, he never saw her again, except when he opened in Vegas in '69. She came to one of the shows with her family.

LAMAR FIKE: Elvis had all kinds of women out there in California while Priscilla was in Memphis. I'd go out there, and it was like a revolving door. He dated [singer-songwriter] Jackie DeShannon for a few months. And [costar] Mary Ann Mobley during *Harum Scarum.*

Harum Scarum—what a horrible picture, good God! Elvis in a sheik costume! That was one of Sam Katzman's specials. They called him "King of the Quickies" because he did everything fast and cheap. The sets rattled, they were so old. The temple set was left over from Cecil B. DeMille's *King of Kings*, from 1927, if you can believe that. The only good thing about that picture was that Colonel got voted down when he wanted a talking camel added to the story line.

BILLY SMITH: After Marty became foreman, we got to see a little different side of Colonel. He'd always picked us for information, but now that Joe was gone, and Charlie was off somewhere, he stepped it up. He'd say, "You know, you need to report Elvis's every move to the old Colonel." And then he'd ask, "What did Elvis do? What did he have to eat last night?"

We'd just ignore it. But then one day, we were coming back from Palm Springs in the car. Just Colonel and me. And he talked stuff all the way back to Los Angeles. He said, "Vernon doesn't really know business that well. If Elvis would let me handle his money, he'd be a whole lot better off financially." And he kept talking and talking. I knew he wanted me to go to bat for him with Elvis.

Finally, I said, "Well, maybe Elvis would be better off. But Colonel, that's his daddy. Whether he makes mistakes or not doesn't matter. That's still his daddy." And I said, "You can quit picking. Because I'm not going to get in the middle." And he never mentioned it again.

MARTY LACKER: When I became foreman, Parker would call me to talk to Elvis. One day, Colonel said to Elvis, in front of me, "Don't forget, Marty needs to call me every day in case I have to tell you something." Elvis said, "Sure, I'll remind him." Then when we left, Elvis said, with this sly smile on his face, "Don't call him."

So Colonel would call and say, "What's going on? What did Elvis do today?" I'd say, "Oh, same old stuff, Colonel." He'd say, "What do you mean?" I'd say, "Just the things we normally do." And he'd say, "No, I want to specifically know what he did."

This one day when we were in Memphis, I said, "Colonel, I'm not going to tell you everything he specifically did. We got up in the afternoon, and we went to the movies, and that was it." I never, ever saw any need to tell the Colonel what Elvis was doing.

I had a number of run-ins with Parker. I knew that he wasn't to be trusted. When I became foreman, Alan was coforeman for a while. Well, maybe ten minutes or so. Just a very brief time. Colonel had always talked to Alan, and Alan was crazy about him.

One day, Colonel and I and one of the other guys were standing around talking at the studio and Alan came by. Colonel said, "How you doing, Alan?" And he turned to us and said, "I love him like a son." They talked on, and as Alan was getting ready to go back to the set, Colonel said, "Tell Uncle Abe hello for me." Because Alan's uncle was a Supreme Court justice. Alan said he would. And Colonel put his arm around him and said, "You're a good guy, Alan." And when Alan got out of earshot, the Colonel looked at me and said, "He's a no-good son of a bitch. He just sits around. He don't do anything for Elvis."

BILLY SMITH: Colonel wasn't crazy about Marty. Neither was Vernon, especially when Marty became foreman.

MARTY LACKER: The foreman had very specific duties. In the recording sessions, I'd organize all the guys. And I was more or less the buffer between Elvis and the people from the studio. I was the one who got the call for the next day's shooting, and I made sure everybody knew about it. I also got the pages for his script and outlined them. Elvis's memory was fantastic, by the way. He hardly ever flubbed his lines. And he would learn everybody's part. In between takes, he'd sit in the dressing room and read his script.

In addition to handling all the bills, I wrote all the checks. Elvis signed them, of course, but I was the one who wrote them for daily expenses and expenses for the group.

There were times when I'd write checks for $50,000 or maybe $100,000. One day, Colonel called, and he said, "I want you to write a $50,000 check to the Motion Picture Relief Fund, as a charity donation, for Elvis. I've already cleared this with him. I'm donating another $50,000," which I doubted. And he said, "This afternoon, Frank Sinatra is coming over to the set, and we'll have photographers there showing Elvis handing over the check to Sinatra." I asked him why they were doing this, and he said, "Because Bob Hope asked us to." And I said, "Okay."

Back then, $50,000 was a hell of a lot of money. And because I knew the way the Colonel was, I started thinking. Of course, when you take so many pills, you get paranoid, and you worry about everything. But I thought that since this check was in my handwriting, Colonel might someday accuse me of stealing $50,000. So on the little line for the explanation of the check, I wrote, "Given to Frank Sinatra on the set, as per request of Bob Hope." I thought that would also be good for the accountant.

After that, I continued to make out the checks that way. I didn't know it at the time, but the fact that I went into such detailed explanation grated on Colonel's nerves. A few years later, during the biggest showdown Elvis and Colonel ever had, Colonel declared that somebody else would write the checks. And when he did it, he said, "Now maybe the explanation portion of the check won't be so full."

BILLY SMITH: Money, or rather the control of money, was power in that camp. Even for Elvis. Sometimes he would go out and spend a lot of money just to aggravate Vernon. Then Vernon would confront Elvis. But he never understood Elvis to the fullest because he picked the most inopportune times to say something to him. You'd think a father would know better. He would catch him right after he'd bought something and say, "We've got to cut back!" Well, the next thing you knew, Elvis would go out and buy more.

MARTY LACKER: Elvis would say, "Look, goddamnit, I make the fucking money, and I'll spend it the way I want!" And Vernon would turn around and leave, mad as hell. On a number of occasions, Elvis would say to me or Billy, "Goddamnit, he thinks *that's* spending? Wait 'til he gets the bill for the shit I'm going to do today!" And he would purposely go out and spend some enormous amount of money. Like that time in the mid-sixties out in Hollywood. Elvis bought eleven Harley-Davidson motorcycles for all of us. Except I didn't want one. The press loved it. Said to watch out for "El's Angels."

I had a grudging respect for Vernon. He did the best he could, you know? The amazing thing about him was that for a long time, he never looked his age. The skin on his face was like a baby's, even when he was fifty years old. He gave me a tip about that once. He said, "I use only cold water on my face and no soap. It dries you out, gives you wrinkles." Maybe out in the country they didn't have a lot of hot water. Maybe that's where Elvis got this idea that he didn't need to bathe.

LAMAR FIKE: You know what it was with him? Elvis never knew how to bathe. He thought a whore's bath was the real thing.

BILLY SMITH: I want to clear up about this idea about Elvis not bathing. That didn't happen until later, starting about '74, when he wouldn't shower for maybe two or three days. But I didn't always take a damn shower every day when I first started working for Elvis. Because you don't take a bath every day in the country. When Elvis was real little, everybody in the area had to tote their water from two or three wells there in East Tupelo.

But Elvis wasn't always dirty. He was a clean person in the earlier years. The Jordanaires say that Elvis was always semi-dirty. That's not true. What do they know about Elvis Presley? The only time the Jordanaires got to see him was when they made a record. In the sixties, Elvis would go upstairs and take a shower and put on clean clothes sometimes three or four times a night. You never smelled him until the later years. And I blame the drugs for that.

MARTY LACKER: Billy's sensitive about this topic. But the truth is that there were times even in the sixties when Elvis didn't bathe, either.

LAMAR FIKE: When you're doping, man, it's a drag to bathe. Elvis just got so fucked up he didn't care about it.

MARTY LACKER: When I became foreman, we were living on Perugia Way. About once or twice a month, I would have to do the expense reports to send back to the accountant in Memphis. I'd stay up two or three days at a time. And one night, after I'd probably been up three days—I was sitting in the middle of the bed, writing. I had all the books and receipts around me. And I was so screwed up on pills that the last thing I remember, I looked at the clock and it was like two-thirty or three o'clock. The next morning I woke up and I was still in that same position, right in the middle of the bed. The books had been moved, though. And when I went in to eat breakfast, everybody started laughing. Especially Elvis.

He said, "Man, you've got to start getting some fuckin' sleep." I said, "Why?" Red was there at the time. And Elvis said, "Me and Red opened up the door, and there you were, sittin' in the middle of the bed, with your head down on your chest, fast asleep." He said, "You had a pen in your hand, and when you fell asleep, the pen dragged right across the paper." He said they just touched me with a finger, and I fell backwards on the pillow. But you couldn't help stuff like that when you were doing as many uppers as I was.

When Christmas rolled around that year, I found out that the foreman had a couple of extra duties that nobody had told me about. One was to buy the Christmas gifts that Elvis gave out. Elvis liked my taste. I guess it goes back to the flashy days at Humes High School. So when it came time to buy these Christmas gifts, Elvis and I went into the small conference room upstairs at Graceland and made out a list. He told me what to buy for a few people—his father, his grandmother, Priscilla, or whatever girl he was going out with at the time—but for the other people, he'd leave it up to me. And the guys did, too. That Christmas we gave Elvis a white Bible, and I designed this tree of life with all our names, and Hebrew and English and Latin phrases, and I had it stamped on the Bible in gold. For his birthday a couple of weeks later, I had a gold medallion engraved with the same design.

I was kind of amazed that Elvis wanted to give gifts to the guys he'd fired or who had left. Like Esposito. And Gene Smith. Elvis said, "Send them a hundred-dollar money order." I'd talked to Joe a few times since he left, and he'd mentioned his oldest daughter, Debbie. Just before Christmas, he said, "Remind Elvis that he's Debbie's godfather, and she needs new furniture." That kind of took me back, you know? But when Elvis said to send him the money order for Christmas, I brought this up. And Elvis said, "Well, that's nice that she needs new furniture." But he didn't buy it for her. The next night, Elvis said, "I want to buy Debbie a real nice cross on a chain." He wouldn't let anybody dictate to him.

Joe wasn't the only one who did stuff like this by the way. I'm sure George Klein doesn't want people to know this, but he used to give me his Christmas wish list every year. He'd say, "I need this, and I'd like to have this and this." Hoping I'd tell Elvis.

LAMAR FIKE: You know how Colonel liked to pose as Santa Claus on those Christmas cards he'd send out for Elvis? That speaks volumes, really. And yet Colonel could be sincerely benevolent, and he's done a lot of things that he never wanted people to know about. He took pride in that. He used to give Alan big hunks of meat. Alan would drive him back and forth to Palm Springs, and a lot of times he'd have Alan stop at a meat market, and Colonel would buy $500 worth of steaks and tell Alan to divide them with Elvis.

He gave me money one time when I was on the wall, man— just literally broke. Elvis was finishing up a picture at Twentieth Century-Fox, and I had come by, and Colonel was with [producer] Jerry Wald. I was over in the dressing room, and Colonel came in and said, "Lamar, how you doing?" He stuck his arm out to shake my hand, and he put five one-hundred-dollar bills in my palm and walked away. I said, "Thank you." And he said, "What for?" But on the whole, Colonel was the cheapest son of a bitch who ever walked the earth. And you'd really see that at Christmas.

MARTY LACKER: Colonel always had the guys do a lot of things for him. And some of the things he did in return were so petty and cheap. At Christmas, that first year I was foreman, Colonel sent two big boxes to Graceland for the guys. We opened them up, and they were filled with stuffed animals. Now, I'm sure those stuffed animals came from one of two places—the supply house Colonel used when he was in the carnival, because they looked like the kind you win at those games, or they were the teddy bears that Elvis's fans sent him. And Colonel said to me three times, "Now, you be sure that all the boys get some of these. And be sure they know they came from the old Colonel."

One Christmas, he sent us, like, eighty bucks. He wrote me a note that said, "This is my Christmas gift to the guys. I want you to take this money and divide it up among them." I mean, we're talking probably seven or eight guys at the time. And he had the audacity to add, "P.S. I'm going to check with Mr. Presley to make sure that's what you did. Merry Christmas."

Then one year, he gave each of us all a very valuable gift—a foot massager. A foot massager! And the stuff he sent always looked like it came from some surplus store, real crummy quality.

But that was Colonel. Each June, when it was time for his birthday, he would call and say, "Be sure to remind Elvis and the boys that tomorrow is the old Colonel's birthday." Elvis would send him an elephant statue or something, but I don't think the rest of us ever sent him anything.

LAMAR FIKE: In late '64, a couple of days after Christmas, Alan got married to a cute little blonde named Jo Tuneberg. Jo was from Mississippi. Right after the ceremony, they were driving over to tell Elvis they'd gotten hitched and somebody ran into Alan's '59 Caddy and totaled it. Alan showed up at Graceland in a rental car.

When he told Elvis about it, Elvis walked them outside and asked Alan for a dollar. Alan took out his wallet, and Elvis said, "Congratulations, you just bought *this* car." And he handed Alan the keys to Priscilla's little red Corvair. She'd just gotten it as a graduation present the year before. He didn't care. Elvis loved to play Santa Claus. Loved to spend money. Especially when he was high.

CHAPTER 31

THE GURU

LAMAR FIKE: From '64 on, things started getting really strange. Geller turned Elvis upside down.

MARTY LACKER: Geller used to talk to Elvis about words. Elvis was always a little self-conscious about his education, so he went along with it. He and Geller would dissect words, and Geller would break them up into syllables, like a teacher. Pretty soon, Elvis said, "This could be a good learning experience for all of us."

BILLY SMITH: The difference between me and Elvis was he'd find the word in the dictionary and learn it, and I'd just say, "What the hell does it mean?" He had a hunger to learn. He read constantly, and he was self-educated. If you said something about a subject he'd read about, he might have fifty books, but he'd pick up the right one and turn right to the page. He remembered things word for word.

MARTY LACKER: One day, at Graceland, Elvis looked at me and said, "I want you to go out and buy ten dictionaries and ten yellow legal pads. And get some pencils." He said, "We need to have a session on words for an hour or two in the evenings." I said, "Are you serious?" He said, "Yeah, don't argue with me. Go get 'em."

Well, we did this for a while. The whole group would sit around in what is now the Jungle Room. None of that jungle stuff was there then. Vernon decorated that room from Sears, with these big round tables like you'd see in a restaurant, with high chrome bottoms and big round black tops. Elvis would open the dictionary, find a word, and cut it up into syllables. And then we'd all say it out loud.

LAMAR FIKE: Elvis would get hung up on phonetics. He heard the word "condominium" one time. And he walked around going, "Con-do-MIN-i-um." Over and over, like a mantra. I said, "If I hear 'condominium' one more time, I'm going to scream."

MARTY LACKER: He wouldn't just say the word. He'd go into this whole explanation. He'd say, "Let's break it into 'condo' and 'minium' and see what it really means." We lost our minds. We changed it to, "Conned a many of 'em." Those classes lasted three or four weeks. By then, Elvis had gotten tired of them.

BILLY SMITH: You know how Larry would bring these religious books up to show Elvis? Well, pretty soon, Elvis started giving out these books to people. One was *The Impersonal Life.* And he gave away Kahlil Gibran's *The Prophet.* And Madame Blavatsky's *The Voice of Silence.*

MARTY LACKER: He got on this tear about reincarnation. But he thought only strong people got to come back. If you were weak, you were finished. He was pretty certain Gladys would be reborn. He didn't get into séances or say he was going to communicate from the grave. But in a way he did. He said, "When I'm gone, I'll haunt your asses! I'll know everything you're doing."

LAMAR FIKE: The Scientologists tried to get Elvis involved later on, mostly to get money out of him. He wanted no part of it. And he nailed them pretty hard. Priscilla and Lisa Marie are into it big-time. They say they're not a cult, that it teaches you to confront issues, talk things out, and get straight with yourself.

MARTY LACKER: When Alan married Jo Tuneberg, I was sort of surprised. I'd known Jo a long time, from back when I was a teenager. She liked to have a good time. And that meant she wanted Alan thinking about her 100 percent of the time. But Alan wanted to hang out with Elvis. She'd get real mad at him, and they'd fight. So he'd escape all of that by taking pills and by drinking.

When they were getting ready to take their honeymoon, we

happened to be going out to California, so Alan thought he'd combine the trips. Elvis said okay, as long as Alan took his own car because he didn't want any women on the bus.

I was on the bus almost all the time, and so was Geller and a couple of the other guys. Elvis and Geller started getting into these conversations about religion. And I knew he was feeding Elvis all this shit for a reason.

Pretty soon, Geller told Elvis he ought to think about becoming what we'd now call a New Age evangelist. He said, "As big a celebrity as you are, if you started saying these things publicly, you'd be one hell of a religious leader because so many people would follow you." And Elvis was getting a little embarrassed. Geller got so worked up that he was shaking.

Well, I'd heard enough. I said, "Larry, why don't you shut your fuckin' mouth? He's not a religious messenger. He's not a holy man, and I don't think he wants to be one."

Larry started arguing with me. But Elvis said, "Marty's right, Larry. I don't want to hear any more about it." And Geller shut up for a while. But the religious talk continued, to the point where Elvis was just weirded out. I said, "I'm going to ride in the Cadillac."

One night, we checked in a motel somewhere. The next day, Alan and Jo and I stayed back to pay the bill. Elvis had pulled out in the bus first, and we were behind him, just speeding like the devil to catch up. We went about three miles down the road, and we couldn't find him. We figured that he'd just speeded up, too, and that he was way ahead of us.

We never saw him the whole day. The next morning, we were having breakfast, sitting by the window in the restaurant, and looking out at the cars on Route 66. And here came Elvis in the bus. He'd been behind us all the time. At the last stop, he and Geller went around the corner from the hotel and hid from us. I'm sure Geller was working on Elvis, trying to get him to be a cult leader. Because things got weirder after that.

BILLY SMITH: It was like Elvis was searching for something. He'd listen to what Larry told him, and he'd think, "Don't rule out this because this might be it." He was looking for fulfillment. He starved for it, and he was willing to experiment with a whole lot of things to find it. Which led him to try other kinds of drugs. In the mid-sixties, for example, Elvis had marijuana around the house and LSD. Just to see what it was like. He'd heard that LSD would give him a kind of altered consciousness, so that maybe he'd see the light of God. I heard he smoked pot, but he didn't like it because it burnt his throat. I never actually saw him do it, but I saw him eat brownies that supposedly had marijuana in them. I'm not sure how it affected him. I don't know if he acted especially goofy. We ate 'em, too, so we might have been just as goofy as he was.

LAMAR FIKE: I usually had some grass, and so did some of the other guys. We got some and took it back to the house on Perugia Way one day and made a bunch of fudge brownies with it. We all ate 'em, except Elvis wasn't there at the time, and nobody told him.

Elvis was very nocturnal, of course, and he would get up at night and go to the refrigerator. And he found this tray of brownies. And hell, he loved those. Priscilla was visiting at the time—she'd finally managed to get out there—and Elvis took the tray back to the bedroom. And they didn't come out for four days. They just stayed ripped the whole time. And they didn't know what had caused it.

I went to get some of 'em, and I realized what had happened. I said, "Oh, my God, they've got the fudge brownies!" I went in there and told Elvis what had happened, and I said, "Are you loaded?" Elvis held out the tray, and he said, "Lamar, put another ounce in there." He was ripped to the skies.

MARTY LACKER: Somebody asked me once, "How did Elvis reconcile his drug use with his religion?" He didn't. Elvis didn't consider himself a drug addict. A drug addict was somebody who stuck a needle in his arm or snorted coke or did all the street drugs. He abhorred those people.

LAMAR FIKE: I don't think that ever crossed his mind. Does the Bible tell you not to take Placidyl? Does it say, "Thou shalt not pop a Seconal"? None of us had any guilt. Elvis had his own religion.

MARTY LACKER: One day on Perugia Way, Geller brought some LSD. Elvis thought it would enhance his spiritual experiences. Priscilla was there, and Jerry and Charlie and Red and Sonny.

They were all in Elvis's bedroom. And Elvis was asking who wanted to try it, telling Red it would help him be more creative, write better songs. I don't know if Elvis tried it or not. Red says in his book that Elvis had them test it out for him.

BILLY SMITH: At the time, they said Elvis tried it. He liked you to be a guinea pig before he tried something like that—to see how it affected you. LSD was a street drug, see, and he was afraid of it.

LAMAR FIKE: We tried hallucinogens for a while. We just didn't like them. This was late '64, or early '65, when all the Hollywood types like Cary Grant were trying it. One time, Alan brought some LSD back to Graceland. I went over there, and Jerry and I dropped some at the same time. Elvis gave me a 750-milligram tab, and he walked me through the whole process. He'd read this book, so he thought he knew what to do.

That was my first time. God. I went upstairs, into what was then a conference room, and had my LSD trip. I had two big plastic jars of dates because we were just hung up on them. I walked in and Jerry was sitting in the middle of the floor in the closet, eating dates hand over fist.

It fucked us both up pretty good. I tried to dive into the hood of a car. We had a black '64 Cadillac limousine, with the side windows filled in. Elvis had taken me outside and walked me around, and I couldn't get over the car—the black was so deep. He said, "You can't touch the car, Lamar." But I thought it was a swimming pool. Just everything seemed surreal. Even the texture of the leaves. Boy. I had flashbacks of that for two or three years afterwards.

BILLY SMITH: Larry Geller is also the one who got Elvis into Self-Realization. It teaches that we are all a part of God, but we are gods, ourselves, in a way. People who follow that think you can have this aura, like Christ, by being pure, like Mahatma Gandhi. In other words, you can't believe that Christ was the only one. And they teach you to believe that you can heal a plant or make the wind do what you want if you believe strong enough.

Elvis was taken by it. But deep back in his mind, what he learned as a child in the Assembly of God church stood out more. He was thinking, "Who's right and who's wrong?" He got into a turmoil about it, so he tried to combine the religions. He'd say, "This new stuff sounds a little easier, so maybe it's right. After all, we're all part of God."

MARTY LACKER: The Self-Realization teachings were based on the beliefs of the yogi Paramahansa Yogananda. I always read that his disciples, I guess you'd say, had a fellowship center, a sort of a spiritual retreat, on Mount Washington, in the Hollywood Hills. But all I remember is the Self-Realization Park at the end of Sunset Boulevard, near the Pacific Coast Highway. It was a block away from the ocean in Santa Monica. The woman who ran it called herself Sri Daya Mata. Her real name was Fay Wright.

Geller used to tell Elvis about this place, and he gave him a brochure for it, which said that when the yogi died in the early fifties, his body refused to deteriorate. Three weeks after his death, his body was still perfectly preserved—no mold, no odor, no decay. It quoted the Forest Lawn people as saying this was unparalleled—they'd never seen anything like it or read about it in any of their mortuary books. Elvis thought that was great, you know, because he liked to visit morgues and look at dead bodies. So he was totally fascinated.

One day, Geller asked him if he'd like to meet Daya Mata. Pretty soon, he started going over there all the time. Daya Mata was supposed to help him realize self-control and the highest form of spiritual existence through meditation. I thought it was just a waste of time and money.

I'll say one thing, though. This meditation park was very, very peaceful. If you had things on your mind, and really wanted to get away, it was a great place to go and just sit.

BILLY SMITH: Daya Mata wrote a book called *Only Love,* which Elvis read and kept around him all the time. He called her "Ma," which I guess was short for "Maya." But Priscilla used to say she looked like Gladys. So maybe that's part of why he called her that. When Vernon found out Elvis was giving her money, he went haywire. If her letters came to Graceland, Vernon tore 'em up.

In a little while, Larry started telling Elvis he should go on television and preach about Self-Realization. They had at least one heated discussion about it. Larry said, "That's why you were put here on this earth." And Elvis said, "No, my music is why I was put here. I think I'll hang with that."

MARTY LACKER: Long before Geller, Elvis used to say that he felt he was put on earth for a specific purpose. He didn't know what the purpose was, except to entertain people, and make them feel good through his music. So he fulfilled his destiny. Most of the millions of people who were affected by Elvis never saw him perform live. And I can tell you there are scores of people whose lives he changed. Lots of people have written letters about how listening to Elvis's music kept them from committing suicide or made them well when they were sick. Now, you and I might not claim stuff like that, but these people are very serious about it.

LAMAR FIKE: The wacko part of this is that Elvis is becoming a religion unto himself. In 1990, there were two Elvis churches in Denver. One was The Church of the Risen Elvis, started by two women, and the other was The First Presleyterian Church, which was begun by two men. Martin Rush, one of the founders, said, "Elvis died so we could get fat and use drugs . . . It's the way he would have wanted it."

In 1993, there was an Elvis convention in England and some guy got up onstage and said, "Gimme an 'E'! Gimme an 'L'!" You know, the whole trip. "Who's going to live forever? ELVIS!"

Fans pay huge prices for his scarves and clippings from his toenails—all this shit, like they're pieces of the cross. They say Red and Sonny betrayed him like Judas with [their book] *Elvis: What Happened?* and that I did the same thing in helping Goldman. And they say that Elvis has been "resurrected" because of all these phantom sightings. This one piece on the Gannett wire said that "groups of female fans have given up marriage to live near Elvis's grave." They might as well just build the Graceland convent, and run around in little nun costumes like Mary Tyler Moore in *Change of Habit.*

BILLY SMITH: Elvis never really bought Geller's idea to be a messenger. But he did get on these preaching sprees. He liked to call them "conversations." He'd jump up on the coffee table and deliver this sort of Sermon on the Mount. Most of the time, what he said was real funny because of the pills. He'd get into this big, loud preacher's voice, and he'd carry on about Jesus and Mary gettin' it on at the well. Or he'd say something like, "Moses was this white-haired son of a bitch who came down from the mountain. The burning bushes directed his ass on down."

If it made him happy, what the heck? Most of the time, he did it just with the group. Although he'd do it when we had girls over. They didn't know whether to laugh or not.

LAMAR FIKE: Elvis had one of the most extraordinary egos of any human I've ever seen. I'd go in to see him in the morning, and I'd say, "You got a minute?" He'd say, "Yeah." I'd say, "What lake are we walking across today?" He'd say, "You son of a bitch!" He used to get so mad. I said, "You're getting really bad about this."

MARTY LACKER: This religion thing lasted from '64 until he died. And I got to where I just couldn't stomach it. Goldman, by the way, says Elvis believed he was a divine messenger. I never heard him say that.

LAMAR FIKE: I think Elvis thought he was a prodigal son, not the Messiah. But I think he thought he would become omnipotent. Because the combination of Geller and the drugs really expanded his mind. After a while, it got to where he halfway believed he had superhuman powers. Like in the seventies, he got into healing, the laying on of hands. He wanted to really help people, but he wanted to be thought of as above mere mortals, too. He would bounce back and forth.

When Elvis would give us a bunch of money, Charlie and I would harmonize and sing, "What a Friend We Have in Elvis." It used to get him so damn mad! He would just go crazy! Then, after a time, he'd sing it himself. He'd laugh about it and call us his "disciples."

One night, he and I were sitting in the middle of the bed at Graceland, and he said, "You know, Lamar, there'll always be a star in your crown." I'm not a great student of the Bible, so I said, "What the hell are you talking about?" He said, "You're kind, you always look out for people, and you're not self-centered." I said, "Yeah. So?" He said, "Lamar, I'm self-centered, you're not. I think about myself and what and who I am all the time. And I don't like it. Being self-centered is a really bad situation."

I said, "Well, I always thought self-centered meant being ego-tistical and arrogant." And he said, "I'm not either one of those, am I?" And I said, "I question that." And he started laughing. That was a rare episode of reality with him. And he got off it real fast.

Right after that, he got into this thing of parting the clouds. When he started that, I went, "Holy moley!"

MARTY LACKER: He'd have two or three guys go out in the back-yard on Perugia Way with him, and he'd have them look up at the sky. Then he'd say he'd parted the clouds or made the stars move. And he'd say, "Did you see that?" He was testing us. Of course, you get enough pills in you, you can see anything.

We'd be in the bus, traveling in the early daylight hours or in the evening. We'd look up at the clouds, and Elvis would say they looked like people. Everybody who was dead. He'd say, "Oh, look, Joseph Stalin." Or, "John F. Kennedy." Then, one time, real softly, he said, "Oh, my God!" Red and I said, "What's wrong?" And he said, "Look, there I am. In the clouds."

BILLY SMITH: Elvis used to stop the bus in New Mexico, where it's just wide-open spaces and the sky is so expansive. He'd get out and say, "Look, man! All those UFOs!" It would be a shooting star or something. But he'd say, "Can you see them?" I think he had a need to believe in mystic stuff.

Every once in a while a weird incident would take place. One time, we were driving across the Arizona desert, and it was cool out. This was the wee hours of the morning. And here come this white-haired man with a white beard. Walking from out of nowhere and going way off to the side of the road. He was proba-bly just a hitchhiker, but he didn't look interested in a ride.

He had on a white shirt and dark-colored pants. We started to pass him, and he just kept walking. We all looked at each other like "God, what was that?" And somebody said, "That's Jesus." We were into this Self-Realization thing by now, so it started us thinking.

Another night, we come over the mountains close to Albuquerque, and we seen these blinding lights shining to oncoming traffic. Elvis slowed down, and we come to a stop and got out. It was a damn car, turned upside down, on its top. Not a soul around. It scared the hell out of us. We looked all over for somebody because we thought they might be hurt or dead. But we never found anybody.

It kind of gave us the creeps. Just miles and miles of desert darkness. And this weird light.

MARTY LACKER: About this same time, when Elvis was really into his spiritual self, he woke up on Perugia Way one day, and he looked out this big picture window to the right of his bed. There was a lot of shrubbery by the window, and Elvis said he was lying in his bed, and he looked out and he saw a bird sitting on the bush. And the head of the bird was Jesus. It really shook him up.

BILLY SMITH: Once Larry came into the picture, Elvis studied the Jewish religion quite a lot. I remember he kept asking, "What is it about Jews, man?" He was fascinated by how most Jews seem to make good. I think that burnt Vernon up, actually.

MARTY LACKER: Some of what Elvis grew up with was still in him, as far as Jews were concerned. It was drummed into him that Jews were trying to take over the world, so he believed that crap. He was still around his father, who was full of hatred for everybody, and Colonel Parker. I've heard Parker make anti-Semitic comments.

Red got in a conversation with Elvis and some of the other guys one time, and Elvis evidently said something derogatory about Jews. Red popped up and said, "Now wait a minute, Elvis. Marty's Jewish." And Elvis looked at him and said, "Well, Marty's one of the good ones."

There are a lot of good—and bad—people in all the religions. But Elvis was never taught that growing up. Vernon was a vicious person, and totally anti-Semitic, as was most of his family.

Vernon had this kind of odd way of talking. He also had a nasty habit of puckering up his top lip while he was talking, and he'd get this smartass, know-it-all look on his face. He had an attitude. And he was really upset when Elvis hired Geller. For one, it was another guy to pay—taking money out of Vernon's pocket, the way he looked at it. And two, Geller was Jewish. And Vernon didn't want any more Jews around. He would have keeled over if he'd known I got Elvis eating food from a kosher delicatessen.

LAMAR FIKE: Vernon was very prejudiced, but I don't know that Elvis ever really was.

MARTY LACKER: Elvis liked a lot of Jewish opera singers, and he liked some Jewish music. On Perugia Way, my room was in the back, next to his, and it overlooked the backyard. When you're under the influence of drugs, you get obsessed with stuff, whether it's food or music. I happened to like the Jewish prayer for the annulment of vows, Kol Nidre. And I had an album of Johnny Mathis singing it, of all people, and I used to play the hell out of that at night. I'd get in a trance, more or less. I'd play it louder than hell. And sometimes Elvis would be sitting out in the backyard, and I'd play it over and over, loud as I could, and he never said anything. He must have liked it because usually if he didn't like to hear something, he'd scream, "Turn that fuckin' thing off!"

He used to do this Hebrew thing with Alan. They were watching *The Greatest Story Ever Told,* and somebody in there said in Hebrew, "Ali Ali loma sabat." I think it was supposed to be Jesus Christ on the cross, saying, "My God, My God, why hast thou forsaken me?" And Elvis and Alan used to say that to each other all the time. It became a catchphrase. Elvis thought it was hipper to say it in Hebrew than in English.

Geller claims in his book [*If I Can Dream: Elvis' Own Story*] that Gladys told Elvis she had Jewish ancestors, starting with her maternal grandmother, Martha Tackett Mansell. Which is pretty close to what Elaine Dundy says in her book. Dundy just has it going back a step farther. Geller says Gladys told Elvis this when he was young and warned him not to tell any of the relatives, including his daddy. Geller said Elvis was fascinated by this, and by Jews, and by their culture.

I know that when Geller first came to Memphis, Elvis took

him out to the cemetery to show him Gladys's footstone with the Star of David. But the thing is, Elvis would say anything. He might have told Geller that Gladys was Jewish to make him think he wasn't prejudiced. But if Elvis *was* Jewish . . . boy, that would be a kick, wouldn't it?

CHAPTER 32

HEADACHES AND HALLUCINATIONS

The Middle Sixties

In January '65, Elvis's soundtrack for *Roustabout* beat out albums by the Beach Boys, the Beatles, and all the other British invasion groups for the top spot on the *Billboard* "Hot LPs" chart. Since Elvis had placed no singles on the trade magazine's "Top 100 Records of 1964" list, the *Roustabout* triumph was doubly important.

Furthermore, in April, Elvis would have surprising success with a single he'd recorded five years earlier. For the first time in his career, he had scheduled no regular studio sessions that year, and RCA, running low on material not pulled from the soundtracks, reached back in its vaults and released "Crying in the Chapel," a quasigospel ballad first recorded by Darrell Glenn in 1953 and covered several times since. The song quickly climbed to number three and sold 1,732,000 copies worldwide by the end of the year.

For most of the entourage, however, Elvis's personal mystery train was now a runaway engine, thundering down the track with no one in control.

MARTY LACKER: One night in '65, in Memphis, Elvis had gone upstairs to bed, and Patsy and I were just getting ready to go to sleep, when the phone rang. It was Joe. This was about eight or nine months after he'd left. I said, "Well, you timed it right. We just got home from the movies." He said, "Let me ask you something. Do you think Elvis would take me back?" I said, "Why? What's wrong?" He said he hadn't been working—he was trying to

346 ELVIS AARON PRESLEY

be an extra in the movies—and he was tired of sitting by the phone waiting for Central Casting to call. And he said, "I'm broke. I need to come to work."

One time before, in L.A., Joe had wanted to come back. But Elvis wasn't ready—he pretty much exploded when I asked him—and I had to tell Joe, "I don't think it would be a good idea."

This time, when Joe called Graceland, he sounded desperate. In fact, he said, "Please. I need the job." I knew Elvis hadn't gone to sleep yet, so I put Joe on hold and I buzzed upstairs. I said, "Joe's on the phone." He said, "What does he want?" I said, "He wants to know if you'll take him back." And the first thing Elvis said was, "Do we need him?"

I said, "Well, yeah, Elvis. Quite frankly, I could use the help." I was just saying that because I wanted to get them together again. The next week, he was back.

LAMAR FIKE: It was a difficult world outside of the gates of Graceland, and Joe found that out.

BILLY SMITH: Elvis let you know that you were secure as long as you were with him. You also knew that if anything happened—when it got hard on the outside—you could come back.

LAMAR FIKE: If Elvis wanted you back, he'd make sure he got you back.

MARTY LACKER: I might be wrong, but in Joe's coming back, I see the fine hand of Colonel Parker. Because the Colonel wasn't getting diddly out of me. Goldman's book said I had an opportunity to do Elvis a favor. No Joe, no pipeline to Parker. It kind of shocked me to read it, but I guess that's right.

BILLY SMITH: I'm not discrediting Joe. He did a good job. But Marty did, too. I think Colonel pushed Elvis, and said, "You need to get somebody else back in there."

MARTY LACKER: When Joe came back, we more or less shared the duties, although I kept the checkbook. Not long after, we went to Hawaii to do *Paradise, Hawaiian Style.* Colonel and Vernon insisted that when we went on location, the guys couldn't sign for their meals at the hotel. We had about thirteen guys, and Vernon and Colonel told Elvis, "If you let them do that, they'll eat steaks all the time." So they gave us a per diem—$84 a week, or $12 a day, for food. And every Monday, from wherever we were shooting, I'd have to go back to the hotel when the cashier's office opened and get a check cashed.

This one day, I came back with a big roll of dollar bills because I had to give everybody precisely $84. We were standing on the beach at Hanauma Bay. And I pulled the roll out of my pocket and started giving everybody money. And Parker, who liked to make fools of people when he had an audience like the crew or Hal Wallis, walked over and said, "Whose money is that?" I said, "This is Elvis's money." Parker said, "Let me have $300." I said, "Colonel, I can't do that. It's not my money." And his voice got a little louder so everyone could hear him. He said, "Didn't you just tell me this was Mr. Presley's money?" Or as he used to say, "Mr. Pwezley," because of his Dutch accent. I always noticed his accent, but I never questioned him about it.

I said, "Colonel, this is for the guys' meals." And then he got really loud. "You're telling me that's Mr. Presley's money and I can't have $300 of it?" I knew what he was doing. I said, "Colonel, look. If it was my money, I'd give you all of it."

By then, he was shouting, "Goddamnit, you won't give me $300 of Mr. Presley's money!" I said, "Colonel, go over and ask Elvis. If he comes to me and says to give you three hundred bucks, that's what I'll do." With that, Parker raised his cane in the air and shouted, "Goddamn you, don't you ever come and ask me for anything again!" And I looked him straight in the face and said, "Colonel, I never have asked you for anything, and I never will. And you can count on that."

Elvis heard me. And he came running over and he said, "What the hell is going on here?" Parker said, "I asked him for $300 of your money, and he wouldn't give it to me." I looked at Elvis, and I said, "If you want me to give him this money, I'll give it to him. But it's the guys' money for their food." And I was so pissed, I threw the money on the sand and started walking up the beach.

Well, in a couple of minutes, Elvis came after me. He said, "Let me tell you what the old son of a bitch said." I said, "What's that?" Elvis said, "Parker says to hang on to you because you're looking out for me."

There was a log on the sand, and I sat on it and looked out over the ocean for about an hour and a half. I wouldn't go back and be around that bastard. But he never tried that crap with me again.

LAMAR FIKE: When they brought Joe back in, it took a little time, but he ended up doing the books. And Vernon was on him all the time. Joe told me, "The only reason I can put up with this job is because I have all these things." I said, "Yeah, it must be rough."

MARTY LACKER: One day, Elvis came up to me and said, "The Colonel wants you to take him to Palm Springs." I had never done that before, and I thought it was a very strange request, considering our relationship. I didn't want to be alone with him. Especially for a two-and-a-half-hour drive. But I did it because Elvis asked me to.

Colonel liked to go to Palm Springs on Thursday or Friday for the weekend because that's where his wife was. So that day, I went over to his office. And I remember I had on a black pullover sweater. And Colonel looked at me and said, "You're not dressed right. Let me give you a shirt." I said, "No thanks." But he opened up a closet and pulled out this ugly, old man's yellow-and-white-striped shirt. And it had a cigar burn on the front.

I said, "Colonel, I don't want your shirt." He said, "You sure?" I said, "That's right." And he put it back in the closet.

We started driving, and we got about a half hour or so out of Palm Springs, and we hadn't said a word to each other. He was sitting next to me in the front seat. And all of a sudden, he started chuckling, and he said, "Boy, I showed those goddamn Jews, didn't I?" Just out of the blue. Then he chuckled again, but he didn't say anything. Now, I'm saying to myself, "You no-good bastard. You old son of a bitch. You've got to know I'm Jewish."

I wanted to take that car and head it into a pole. And just when I was trying to figure out how to kill him without hurting myself, he said, "I want to stop up here and get some coffee." He tried to order something for me, but I wouldn't even let him buy me coffee.

We got to his house. And this is a guy worth millions, right? He got out of the car, and he took five dollars out of his pocket and held it out to me through the passenger window. And he said, "Here, go have dinner on me." I looked at him, and I looked at his money, and I said, "Colonel, I don't want your money. You don't have to buy me anything." And he said, "No, no, no. Take this. I want to do this for you." I said, "Colonel, you have a nice evening." And I drove off. I looked back, and he was still standing there with the five bucks in his hand.

BILLY SMITH: In 1965, we were out in California for nine months. We didn't come home until October, in that ol' mobile home. I should have kicked my own ass for ever doing that. Nine months I allowed Elvis to manipulate me. And then, another time, we were out there for about six months. After that, it had to come to an end. I wasn't going to tolerate being gone for long periods and not being with my wife. 'Cause even when we did come home, we were supposed to go to the movies, and the fairgrounds, and skating—whatever Elvis wanted to do.

Now, the wives could go along on that stuff. And Priscilla was starting to come out to California as often as Elvis would let her, which wasn't all that much, really. But Jo still felt Elvis was taking me away from her. It really interfered with our marriage. I put her through hell, and I hate it now.

MARTY LACKER: The upshot was that Elvis allowed Jo to live at the house in California with us in the later years. That's because of Elvis's relationship with Billy. And he cared about Jo, too, but if push came to shove, it was really because of Billy. If anybody else wanted his wife out there, he had to get an apartment.

LAMAR FIKE: I can see why Elvis didn't want the wives out there. He was going to play around, and he didn't want anybody carrying tales.

My wife, Nora, liked Priscilla real well, and she liked Nora. But being with Elvis would put a hell of a strain on a marriage. And on being a family. I was home so infrequently that my kids would see an extra place at the table and wonder who was coming.

Elvis hated the idea of families. You had to fight to get home with your kids. And they suffered quite a bit, or at least mine did.

They've all had some problems of one kind or another. Especially my youngest child, John. He had spinal meningitis when he was a baby, and he's had a lot of difficulties. There were times I had to go back and be with Nora, of course, and Elvis understood that.

But we all treated our wives like an appendage. Sonny's and Red's and Billy's marriages are the only ones that survived.

MARTY LACKER: Billy and Jo were together more than most of us were with our wives. It would always amaze Elvis how close they were.

🏃 🏃 🏃

LAMAR FIKE: One time, Elvis got on this kick where he wanted me to chauffeur. So I got a black suit, and here I went. One day, Elvis and Alan and I were in the black Rolls-Royce. I was driving. And it had been raining. It was one of those fifteen-day California rains, where it just rains 'til Hitler comes back, and then the mudslides start. We were at Sunset and Sunset Plaza, on the way to Paramount, stopped at the traffic light. That intersection is a hill. And it had rained so much that those cantilevered houses were just falling. And there on the left, a garage was literally coming down the street in this flood of water.

I looked to my left, and I looked at the light, and I looked back to the left at the garage, and I said, "Gee, I hope it makes the light." And I was serious. Elvis opened the door and just started screaming with laughter. Fell clean out of the car. And sure to God, that garage came right in front of the car and went down the hill. I said, "Well, hell, it made it!" The light changed to green, and we drove on off.

These things seemed like everyday occurrences to me. But it was insanity is what it was. We were just so encapsulated in our world. The Memphis Mafia was our thing.

MARTY LACKER: Sometimes it got almost surreal. Not just with weird events, but in the way people responded to Elvis. One day, we were coming back from MGM in the Rolls-Royce, and we were driving down Sunset. We'd just gotten past UCLA, when this limo pulled up alongside of us. I was sitting in the front seat, and Elvis was in the back. I had the window down. And I heard this voice yell, and I turned and looked, and there was Judy Garland, hanging out the limo. She knew it was Elvis because of the Tennessee license plate. Plus, at that time, he was the only person in the United States who had that Rolls-Royce limousine, which was really a big, overgrown, ugly piece of shit.

I turned around, and I said, "Elvis, that's Judy Garland, hanging out the window trying to get your attention." So he rolled down the window, and she said, "Hi, Elvis! How are you?" And Elvis said, "Fine, how you doing?"

About then, I noticed that sitting in the back of the limousine with her, in the corner, was Jack Paar. They were good friends. And Paar leaned forward and said, "Oh, by the way, I'm Jack Paar." Like, "Well, what about me?" It was a funny gesture.

God, what an odd trio—Judy Garland, Jack Paar, and Elvis Presley. But that was it. Elvis closed the window, and on we went.

BILLY SMITH: When we were with Elvis, the pressures of the outside world were taken away. We thought, "Nothing can happen to him. If we're with him, we're safe. It's God's way of protecting us." He had that kind of power over us.

Sometimes I wake up in the middle of the night and think, "God, all the crazy things I did!" We'd try anything. In '66, I got on the damn bulldozer with him and we tore down that house in the back of Graceland where my family lived in the fifties. It collapsed around us, and one beam snapped off and damn near pinned both of us. We done some very dangerous things. But it didn't scare me. He would holler, "Let's go!" and I was ready.

🏃 🏃 🏃

LAMAR FIKE: People do funny shit on drugs, you know? Stumbling and falling. We'd take all these pills and sit up and see who could stay up the longest. Elvis and Sonny would be loaded and just reeling. And Alan would be loaded, and I'd be loaded, and it was like everything was slower than slow motion.

MARTY LACKER: When you take drugs as much as we did, you automatically become paranoid. You think everybody is out to get you. And sometimes you hallucinate. Because they dull your senses. That's why Elvis took pain pills. They helped him escape the thoughts about Priscilla, the thoughts about his mother, everything.

We all started with uppers. What they laughingly call "diet pills." It was nothing but speed, amphetamines. Then we got on sleeping pills to counteract the uppers. The sleeping pills felt so good that we started taking them instead of taking speed. We'd walk around in the daytime with sleeping pills in us. And we never thought there was anything wrong with us. Then sometimes we'd switch off and take pain pills.

I think that after a while, I took pain pills so I wouldn't think about my family being at home in Memphis. Today, I realize what a bastard I was, as far as my family was concerned. My first two children basically grew up without me. And even when I was home, I'd be up at Graceland every night. When I was out in California, I would call home every night or every other night. And sometimes I felt bad about not being there, and I'd want to be with them. And other times, I couldn't wait to get off the phone.

Probably the lowest thing I ever did was right after my youngest daughter, Angie, was born. I'd just gone to California with Elvis. We'd been there about a week, when Patsy started bleeding a lot. She called and wanted me to come home. And I told her I couldn't. The truth is, I could have. She got really upset and called me names and slammed down the phone. And she had to go into the hospital. But I still stayed in California. I didn't want to miss anything with Elvis.

The sad thing is I didn't get any better. When Patsy's mother died, I was in California, and she wanted me to come home and go to Knoxville to the funeral with her. I told her no. And so Priscilla went with her. It was the nicest thing Priscilla ever did. Patsy hated my guts for that, and I don't blame her.

I think Patsy loved me, but she probably stayed with me for the kids. I had a gun under my bed all of the time because I carried anywhere from $150 to $2,000 for Elvis. Fortunately, this was an automatic. One day when Angie was still a little-bitty girl, she walked into the living room holding the gun. My wife had a maid, who was more like a companion, actually, and it scared them both to death. With an automatic, you have to pull back to put a bullet in the chamber. And thank God Angie wasn't strong enough to do that. It makes me shiver to think about that now.

LAMAR FIKE: My thing was Placidyls. You'd take them, and you'd get right in that zone between staying awake and passing out. Which is really wild. It would get the shit off your mind.

We'd take a needle and punch a hole in the back of them. That liquid would ooze in your mouth and you'd just get ripped out. We called them "footballs" because they were shaped sort of like that, and they were green. These were 750 [milligram] Placidyls, the heaviest kahunas you could take. We didn't go to bed 'til eight or nine o'clock in the morning, and I needed something to knock me out so I could sleep. I got to where I was taking ten or eleven of them a night, and I still wouldn't go to sleep.

It really fucks up your system. You can just load and load and load. That's why, when you die, you don't know it. When the mayor of New York, Jimmy Walker, was on his deathbed, his wife came over to him, and she said, "Where are you?" And he said, "I'm halfway across that river." Isn't that a great saying? Well, with that stuff, you'd be halfway across that river, but you wouldn't know it. And all of a sudden you'd be dead. So you had to be careful.

I should be dead, really. I stayed up for five or six days at a time on uppers. Dexedrine. Blackbirds. We took so many uppers, our teeth sounded like Xavier Cugat's rhythm section, man. We just chattered up a storm. This went on for about five, six years in a row, from about '61 to '67.

BILLY SMITH: Back in the sixties, I could have had a drug problem. At times, I know I was right at the point. Because it was so easy to fall into that, trying to keep Elvis's pace. And Elvis had a very cunning way about him. In the sixties, he'd shove it to you like candy. Especially if he thought somebody was not going to be right in the groove of things. He'd say, "Look, we're going to the movies, and we're going to be up most of the night." And you'd think, "Well, God, if I'm going to be able to keep up, I guess I'd better." So I got to the stage where I'd say, "Hey, give me a Dexedrine." And then pretty soon I'd be saying, "Give me a sleeping pill because I've got to have some shut-eye." For a number of years, I might take one Dexedrine a day and maybe one sleeping pill. But then it gradually got to where it was an everyday thing. And then more as I went along. My weight dropped down from about 140 to 116.

I don't buy this stuff that Elvis got anybody on drugs. That was their own choosing. We were leading a fast-paced lifestyle, and hell, when you took that stuff, it was even faster. We were on a dead run and didn't know where we were going. Like that old saying "Live fast, love hard, and die young." We were well on that damn road.

Thank goodness, I reached a point to where I said, "I don't need that. My nerves are shot." I was like a cat, ready to climb the wall. So I shut it off. I'm not a strong individual, but I knew myself.

LAMAR FIKE: Alan used to get so fucked up on pills, he didn't know where he was. Alan truly loved 'em.

MARTY LACKER: Alan should never have done a lot of drugs. His respiratory system wasn't good. He just smoked too much. We used to call him "The Hacker" because he coughed all the time. He used to cough and get choked so bad that it was scary.

One time, Alan and I shared a motel room in Nashville, when Elvis went over there to a recording session. We were at the Albert Pick, on Murfreesboro Road. It's a fleabag, or at least it was then. But it was out of the way and cheap. The Colonel picked it.

Alan was lying flat on his bed asleep. And he started coughing so hard that one cough lifted his whole body—in a prone position, now—two feet off the bed. Like he levitated. Honest to God, he coughed and went straight up, and then fell back down on the bed again. And never woke up. I was on the other bed looking over at him, and I just busted out laughing. And then I started cussing because I was afraid he was going to choke on his own cough.

I said, "Goddamnit, quit smoking all those damn things!" And, of course, he couldn't hear a word I was saying. Because he was not only smoking so bad and taking pills, he was drinking.

LAMAR FIKE: Alan took Seconals, or Tuinals, which are hypnotics. He loved downers. He liked uppers, too, when we were driving cross-country transporting the cars. Of course, I did, too. We'd take a big handful of them, boy, before we'd start out on these trips. Back then, we didn't have CBs. We had walkie-talkies. And we'd stick the aerial out the window and talk to each other, tell each other if we spotted a cop, and tell each other the things you do when you're high.

One time, I was driving the Cadillac limousine, and Alan was driving the Rolls-Royce. I called him and said, "Look over here to the left. Do you see this town?" He said, "Yeah." I said, "Let's stop and look at it."

This was in the middle of the Mojave Desert. Alan and I pulled over, and we saw a whole city together. We stood there and smoked a cigarette and talked about the buildings and stuff. Both of us hallucinated the same thing because we had been driving nearly twenty-four hours. I can still see it. We saw cows in the middle of the road that weren't there. And people who didn't exist got in your car and talked to you for two or three hundred miles.

God, talk about hallucinations! That same trip, we were driving across the desert and all of a sudden, Alan threw on the brakes so fast the car dipped down in front and slid sideways. 'Cause we'd do eighty or one hundred miles per hour—we'd get so damn many tickets that Elvis put a pool of money together just to pay 'em. I said, "What the hell was that?" Alan said, "Damn, all those kids crossing in front of me! I had to stop!" I said, "Alan, we're in the fuckin' Mojave Desert. There are no kids out here!"

Later the same day—because we'd drive straight through to Memphis in thirty-six hours—we pulled into Little Rock, Arkansas. And we came to a school crossing. All these kids were walking across the street in a line, and Alan went right through them. Kids were jumping on trees, just diving and dodging. They scattered like quail. And Alan went right on. I said, "What in the hell are you doing, man? You could have killed those kids!" He said, "Oh, God! You told me there weren't any kids!" He thought he was hallucinating again.

MARTY LACKER: In California, Alan and his wife, Jo, had an apartment on Beverly Glen Boulevard. She used to call me all the time. I'd have to go over and search for the damn pills and flush them down the toilet. Red did it a couple of times, too. We had to haul Alan over to UCLA Medical Center in '65. He had thirty-five yellow jackets [phenobarbital] in him. Tried to kill himself over this tug-of-war between Elvis and his wife. Alan had six, seven, maybe eight real good scares when he wasn't trying to kill himself. That's a lot.

One time in Memphis, he and Jo were staying at his mother's house. And he was in really bad shape. When I got there, he was slobbering all over himself and couldn't talk. All this goop was coming out of his mouth, and he was choking. Strictly from drugs. I got him up and walked him around, and they called the doctor. And then they turned the damn bed upside down and got all the bottles and threw them away. Because he had pills stashed under the mattress. He had them behind the night tables. He had them everywhere.

Alan just got caught up in all that stuff, which you can easily do. And he was combining too many things. When he took pills and drank at the same time, he'd get stupid drunk—he'd look at you and just grin.

One night, Jo called up at the house and said Alan was messed up and she didn't know where he was. Richard and I headed straight for the Red Velvet nightclub and found him there, out of his mind. We took him home, and got out of the car, and just as we were taking him into the house, Jo came out, holding this .25 automatic. She was screaming, "I'm gonna kill you, you son of a bitch!"

It was sort of comical because Richard and I had to lean Alan against the car so he could stand upright while we went after her. I grabbed her wrist with the gun, and Richard grabbed her other arm. And I said, "Goddamnit, Jo, drop this gun! Don't be stupid!"

Jo's a little-bitty hyper woman, but she was so angry that she was strong. And she said, "I'm not dropping anything!" And finally, I just got up in her ear, and I said, "Jo, much as I hate to, if you don't drop this gun, I'm going to break your fuckin' arm." And I grabbed the gun from underneath, and I felt there was no clip in it. I said, "Richard, there ain't no clip in this gun." And then I called Jo a nasty name because she'd scared the pee out of me.

I don't think Alan was ever really happy, except in the early days. There was just always something missing.

LAMAR FIKE: Alan was a very stoic individual, and he hid behind this happy-go-lucky facade. But he was always sad. Alan cried all the time. You just didn't know it.

Nothing ever really worked for Alan. And if you want to

know the truth, nothing ain't really worked for any of us. But not because of the drugs. Our psychological scars are worse than that.

BILLY ·SMITH: I assume Priscilla was taking stuff, too. She says in her book that she took diet pills and sleeping pills to keep up with Elvis. Everybody around Elvis was at one time or another.

MARTY LACKER: About '65, Priscilla began playing a bigger role in things. And part of it had to do with Joe coming back. There always was a little clique in the group, especially when Joe came into it. But when Joe came back, the group really began to splinter into separate camps. Jerry started gravitating more to Joe, and Joe would make sure Jerry got this and that. Schilling sort of rode on Joe's coattails. Joe and Jerry just thought they were better than everybody else.

LAMAR FIKE: That's where that whole thing tilted, when Jerry went with Joe. That caste system got really strong. With the couples, it was Joe and Joanie Esposito and everybody beneath them. It just galled Billy and Marty. I wouldn't put up with it. I just told them all to go fuck themselves. Joe started it, and everybody hated him for it. But Elvis let it happen. It became like the First and Second Family routine.

BILLY SMITH: People always say to me, "I guess you took a lot of pictures of Elvis that nobody's ever seen." No, I didn't. Only a couple of people were allowed to take pictures—Joe and Priscilla. And then, after they took them, you couldn't even get a copy of them. Same with the home movies.

MARTY LACKER: All those years, the only two people Priscilla really paid any attention to were Jerry and Joe. Joe's wife, Joanie, was like Priscilla's shadow. Priscilla was always pushing Elvis to be with Joe.

LAMAR FIKE: Elvis had so much shit goin' down that it's kind of amazing he had the presence of mind to even make those godforsaken movies. In the spring of '65, he did *Frankie and Johnny* at MGM, with Donna Douglas. She was Elly May from *The Beverly Hillbillies*. She was a former Miss New Orleans, but this was one costar he didn't try to date. Because Donna was a smart cookie. Elvis laid that religious stuff on her, and she knew about as much as he did, so they talked books and religion. Nothing like what he did with Deborah Walley in '66 on *Spinout*, though. Whew! He spun her head around like Linda Blair in *The Exorcist*.

MARTY LACKER: The movies were pretty much a blur during this time. *Paradise, Hawaiian Style* was supposed to be a sequel to *Blue Hawaii*, but it fizzled in comparison. Elvis was steamed about this picture, because *Blue Hawaii* had grossed all those millions, and the talk in Hollywood was that Hal Wallis used the profits to finance *Becket*, with Peter O'Toole and Richard Burton. Meanwhile, Elvis kept getting stuck in these crappy beach-and-bikini pictures.

There was a lot of tension on the set. The director, Mickey Moore, was unhappy with Elvis because he thought he looked fat. This was the first time a director had ever actually said anything about it. His face might have looked a little fuller, but I didn't think he looked fat. But if he did, it might have been because he'd started experimenting with downers. Seconals. Yellow jackets.

Every once in a while, when we'd go to a new doctor, Elvis would say to Richard and me, "Would you check out the offices?" That meant he wanted the latest edition of the *Physician's Desk Reference*, with all the pills listed in it. So we'd walk around the hallway and look in the offices. One time, we spotted one at a clinic, and Richard looked at me and grinned. I went in and I grabbed it, and we went out the backdoor.

LAMAR FIKE: In our camp, the *PDR* was like a Bible. Elvis thought hotel rooms came equipped with them, like the Gideon Bible. He read the *PDR* like I do a damn motor magazine.

MARTY LACKER: In '64, when the Beatles first came to the United States, they wanted to meet Elvis. But it couldn't be arranged. Then in '65, the Colonel said Brian Epstein called, and the Beatles were going to be in California, and they really, really wanted to see Elvis.

Colonel knew what he was doing. He said to Elvis, "If you'd like, you could go to their house." And Elvis said, "No, no. Let them come over to Perugia Way." Elvis told us we could bring our wives and kids over to meet them if we wanted.

BILLY SMITH: Jo couldn't believe the Beatles were coming to meet us. We were all real excited. We'd say, "The Beatles, hell, they're hot! This is a big thing!" But around Elvis, we knew not to let on too much because he'd get really pissed.

MARTY LACKER: Somehow, the word got out about the meeting. And it caused a problem because Perugia Way is a very small circle. Before the Beatles even got there, the entire cove was packed with people hoping to see Elvis and the Beatles. The Bel Air police had to come so the Beatles could get their limousine in the courtyard.

When they came in the house, Elvis and some of the guys waited for them in the den. He wasn't going to go to the door because he didn't want to make a big deal out of it. So they came in the den, and when they met him, it was like they were in a trance, just looking up at him and shaking his hand. On TV, they were so boisterous, and here they were real quiet. After they said, "It's such a pleasure to meet you," they didn't know what to say. So Elvis said, "Let's go sit down." He had on a red shirt and gray slacks, and he sat in his usual place on the couch in front of the TV. And the Beatles sat on chairs around the room, as did our families.

BILLY SMITH: At first, they didn't know what to do. They were just sittin' around staring at Elvis. Everybody was looking at each other like "What the hell's going on here? Who's going to do something?"

MARTY LACKER: Finally, Elvis looked at one of them, and he said, "Hey, I didn't mean for this to be like the subjects coming to the king." And then he said, "Quite frankly, if you guys are going to stare at me all night, I'm going to bed. I thought we'd talk a while and maybe jam a little." And when he said that, they went nuts. They all went to the piano, and Elvis handed out a couple of guitars. And they just started singing—Elvis songs, Beatles songs, Chuck Berry songs. Elvis played Paul's bass part on "I Feel Fine," and Paul said something like "You're coming along quite promising on the bass there, Elvis." I remember thinking later, "Man, if we'd only had a tape recorder."

BILLY SMITH: We tried to join in the fun as casually as we could, without paying too much attention to 'em. Ringo wanted to shoot some pool, so we did that. Alveena, this heavy maid, brought some drinks and little hors d'oeuvres, and she stepped on Ringo's foot. He screwed up his face like he was in all kinds of pain, and he said, "I think she's broke my bloody toe." He was funny. He'd get up there with Elvis and impersonate him with a cue stick for a guitar. Then he'd shoot the ball. It turned into a real good night. Seemed like everybody had fun.

MARTY LACKER: In a little while, Colonel Parker walked in. Which meant it was casino time. Because we had this coffee table that could be converted into a gambling table. You reversed it and turned it into a roulette wheel. So Joe and Alan and Colonel opened up the casino in what we called the "round den" because it used to be an outside courtyard. Alan said Colonel was throwing money around like crazy. And I remember Colonel and Joe bragging that they took Brian Epstein to the cleaners, that he owed 'em about two or three thousand dollars.

They didn't leave until about two o'clock in the morning. Colonel used to have a thing about covered wagons. He used one as a kind of logo for his company—he had one on his stationery, I remember. And as souvenirs, he gave the Beatles these little covered wagons that lit up on the inside.

BILLY SMITH: Jo was pregnant with our second child, and, of course, she was wearing maternity clothes, and her stomach was sticking out. We were all standing outside when the Beatles were leaving in their limousine, and somebody took a picture of Jo, and Patsy Lacker, and Jo Fortas, and Joanie Esposito. And it turned up in some magazine, with the headline THE NIGHT ELVIS

SHARED HIS WOMEN WITH THE BEATLES! Jo laughed like crazy, man. She saved that magazine for a long, long time.

MARTY LACKER: As they were saying goodbye, John and Paul said, "We're staying at this house on Mulholland Drive, and we'd like to invite you all to come up tomorrow." And Paul looked at Elvis and said, "I hope you'll be able to come." And then he looked at us and said, "But if he can't come, you fellows are welcome."

When they left, Elvis said, "I'm not going up there." He said, "I did my duty. I met them, and that's it."

LAMAR FIKE: The day after the Beatles visited Elvis at the house, reporters asked Paul what kind of time he had—what he thought of Elvis. He had a one-word reply: "Odd."

MARTY LACKER: The next afternoon, Jerry, and Richard, and Billy, and I went up to where they were staying. And they were overjoyed to see us. They really were. John pulled me over by the picture window, and he said, "Last night was the greatest night of my life."

In subsequent years, the guys visited the Beatles three or four times when they came over here. Of course, Elvis never went. In the summer of '66, we saw Brian Epstein lying out on the chaise lounge by the pool. He was zonked out of his brain. And Paul and the other guys were sitting by the pool, and there were people all over the place—girls running around naked, people dropping acid.

About twenty minutes later, the Mamas and the Papas showed up. All four of them—Mama Cass, John, Denny, and Michelle—came marching in a row, like soldiers. And John and George immediately got up and went into the house with them. I was talking with this guy, Mal Evans, who was the Beatles' road manager and bodyguard. Big guy. And I said, "Where are they going? Are they talking business?" He said, "No, no, they're just going to get blown out of their skulls." It was party time.

From '66 on, the Beatles really changed. They were smashed out of their heads all the time and into their Maharishi trip. And they weren't nearly as friendly. Just before we left during one of those visits—I can't remember if it was '66 or '67—I went in this side room, where Paul was singing songs and playing piano. He looked up at me and he said, "Do you think Elvis would ever cut one of my songs?" The Beatles were the biggest thing in the universe right then. But that goes to show you, they still thought Elvis was bigger.

BILLY SMITH: By late '65, Priscilla was getting more and more restless. She wanted to be with us out in California. And she wanted to get married. At the end of '65, we moved to another house in Bel Air, on Rocca Place. Priscilla pretty much insisted she was going to be there.

Priscilla was a pretty nice person in the beginning. But she changed a hell of a lot when she went to California. She had been secluded at Graceland. And now she saw a whole new world. Hollywood and Elvis changed her.

LAMAR FIKE: Elvis always controlled the guys, but starting about late '65, early '66, Priscilla started lording it over the wives.

BILLY SMITH: Elvis basically told her to exert more control over the wives *and* the guys. He said, "They work for me, so if you tell one of the guys to do something, he'd better do it." She thought it was easy. She'd tell somebody to get her something, and if he didn't, she'd tell Elvis, and Elvis would blow up. The majority of the guys went along with it, but they left a lot of things unsaid.

MARTY LACKER: Priscilla didn't want anyone around who didn't kiss her ass.

BILLY SMITH: Priscilla wanted to use Jo's credit card one time. Jo said, "I don't loan my credit card. You've got access to more money than I have. You need to bring your own credit card." And I didn't blame her. Elvis would have given her anything she needed. But that's the kind of crap that Priscilla would do. We were just struggling to get by, and she was borrowing from us? It was ridiculous.

Priscilla's a very materialistic person. But Priscilla is also a very stingy woman. She had a history of borrowing clothes from the wives and never giving them back. She always thought, "If I can get somebody else to pay for it, that's fine." That's always been her way. Hell, she went to a hairdresser one time and left a fifty-cent tip. My God! If you're the girlfriend of Elvis Presley, you don't do that.

MARTY LACKER: In the mid-sixties, Elvis started getting interested in pornography. And I don't mean just looking at people through the two-way mirror that we had on Perugia Way and Bellagio Road.

BILLY SMITH: I don't remember how he got onto these, but Elvis liked these Danish porno films about women having sex with animals. Now, it wasn't an everyday thing, but he liked them sometimes. And he liked to watch two girls wrestle in those 8mm films. He had Alan go down on Santa Monica Boulevard in Hollywood and have films like that made. And of two women making love. Why, I don't know.

Elvis liked to look at certain things. He had certain sexual fantasies. He didn't like to see women totally nude. That turned him off more then it turned him on. He preferred they wear white cotton panties and a white bra. Even with the two women wrestling or making love. He wanted the bra and the panties on.

MARTY LACKER: About the white panties . . . I remember he fell in love with Peggy Fleming, the ice skater, on television. He loved to watch her skate because she always wore these white skating outfits. Every time she was on TV, he'd turn the volume up loud and tell everybody to shut up. And then he'd start talking. He'd say, "Man, she's gorgeous. Man, she turns me on. Look at those white panties, man."

LAMAR FIKE: Sometimes, he'd masturbate to movies. But I've been in the room when he watched sex movies, and he just watched them. I mean, he didn't masturbate in front of me. Quite frankly, if he'd started, I probably would have started, too. Like I said, Elvis was a great voyeur. He loved to watch.

MARTY LACKER: After a while of watching movies like that, Elvis transferred his interest from 8mm films to real people. In other words, he wanted live girls to do it in front of him.

LAMAR FIKE: Nothing was sacred. Nora, my wife, bent over one time feeding one of the kids and Elvis looked up her dress. I said, "What the hell are you doing?" And he said, "Well, she's bent over. What do you want me to do?" He was so funny about it, I couldn't get mad.

I mean, look, he had his hang-ups. He liked to watch girls wrestle with panties on. And he taught Priscilla to do all of that stuff with other women. That was his thing. Like I said, he molded her.

MARTY LACKER: This talk about Elvis having Priscilla engage in lesbian sex . . . Priscilla befriended this girl. She used to come up to Graceland a lot, maybe once every two weeks. And from time to time she would have the girl go upstairs. Most times, Elvis didn't like any strange women up there, but we noticed that this girl went up time after time.

Actually, this girl used to screw a lot of guys. She was more or less a groupie because she made the rounds at some of the Memphis recording studios. But I saw a Polaroid picture of Priscilla sitting on top of her, and both of them had on nothing but a bra and panties. Now the story goes—and I never saw the other pictures—that Elvis had pictures of Priscilla giving the girl oral sex. And not just pretending, from what I heard from the other guys who saw these.

Elvis took these pictures, and I'm sure he had Priscilla do this. I don't think she did it on her own. Maybe that was Elvis's turn-on, but, God, the woman who's probably going to be your wife?

BILLY SMITH: I think that happened only one time. Let me rephrase it—with one person. They were wrestling, and I don't know what else. The question is why Priscilla done this. But Elvis could talk you into damn near anything. She wanted to please him because she was hoping he'd marry her.

MARTY LACKER: Towards the end of the year, Elvis started spending more time out in Palm Springs. You might wonder why, especially since it meant he'd be closer to Colonel, the bane of his existence. He did it because Parker suggested it. Colonel said, "You can rest here and get away from Hollywood." Which was a button to push because Elvis didn't like Hollywood. In Palm Springs, he could get away without having to go all the way home to Memphis, and he could relax in the sun. Eventually, he found a doctor out there, George Kaplan, who'd give him prescriptions, and that made him happy.

Before he found Kaplan, though, we went to Palm Springs one time and stayed there, and Elvis needed some stuff. He'd go to great lengths to get pills, of course. This time he dug a hole in his foot under the guise of taking out an ingrown toenail. I'm not exaggerating, now, the hole was the size of a quarter. On his big toe. We were sitting in the waiting room, and he took his shoe and sock off, and he said, "Look." And I looked down at this gaping, oozing, bloody pus hole. I said, "God Almighty, Elvis, what have you done?" And he said, "Bet I get some good stuff now."

He mutilated himself on three or four other occasions. He always said that he had an ingrown toenail. But the hole he made was in the middle of his toe, way behind the nail. He knew he could always get what he wanted.

LAMAR FIKE: Elvis liked Palm Springs because he could go up there and screw around and get away from what he thought were the pressures of Hollywood. So he'd go and have his girls meet him up there. The one thing Elvis didn't have there was servants. He was afraid they would see something and it would get back to Colonel.

MARTY LACKER: By Thanksgiving of '65, it was pretty obvious that things were changing in a big way. Usually, we came home for Thanksgiving. But this year, we were in Palm Springs, and the Colonel and Priscilla, along with Esposito and his wife, talked Elvis into spending Thanksgiving there. Well, the rest of us bitched and moaned because we wanted to go home. Elvis got in a little huddle with Priscilla and them, and he said, "Look, you guys fly home from here, and then you can come back. Me, and Joe and Joanie, and Priscilla are going to have Thanksgiving with the Colonel."

BILLY SMITH: I'm sure Priscilla was tickled pink about that. She wanted the two couples to be a foursome, and she was in cahoots, of sorts, with Colonel. We just didn't know it then.

MARTY LACKER: That Christmas, Elvis was even more generous than usual. He bought an old black lady a motorized wheelchair and took it to her house himself. It was more like a shack, really. It got to him to see how poor she was, how she lived. It took him back to his Tupelo years.

That year, he gave me a white Cadillac because I wouldn't take a motorcycle when he bought 'em for everybody. It was a 1960 model—not a new car, but compared to the old Ford I was driving, it was like a Rolls-Royce. I got tears in my eyes because that was the first time anybody had ever given me anything like that.

LAMAR FIKE: In '65, Elvis bought me a house in Madison, Tennessee, just outside Nashville. A pretty big house, $150,000 worth. Actually, he just gave me the money to do it. And he never expected that money to be paid back. How the hell was I going to pay back $150,000?

MARTY LACKER: Elvis didn't buy houses for everyone. But at the time Lamar came and asked Elvis if he would loan him the money, or let him have the money for his house, I was wanting to buy the property where I built my house at the end of '66. My family and I lived at Graceland 'til the middle of '65, and then we moved into these little apartments nearby. We needed some privacy. At Graceland, Elvis wanted us to leave the intercom on in our apartment all night long, so he could talk to me and hear whatever I was doing. Patsy thought that was sort of kinky. We told him there was no way we were going to do that. But in some ways, when we moved, we still weren't getting away from it all because Joe, Larry Geller, and Mike Keaton and their families lived in the same complex.

My sister's husband, Bernie Grenadier, who was an interior designer, said he would draw the plans and build a house for me at cost. And the property that I wanted was a piece of undeveloped land in Whitehaven. I had been talking to somebody about it, and evidently one of the guys told Elvis. So when he told me to write out Lamar's check for the house, he said, "While you're at it, how much is that property you want?" I looked at him kind of strange because I hadn't said anything to him about it, and I hadn't put anybody else up to it through that old third-party trick.

I said, "What do you mean?" He said, "I know you want to buy this piece of property out here and build you and Patsy a house." And I said, "Yeah. I hate to let it go. It's pretty cheap, $3,200 an acre." And he said, "Well, write a check out to yourself for $3,200." And I said, "Elvis, I don't want you to do that." He said, "I don't care what you want me to do. Write it out."

LAMAR FIKE: If Elvis gave you stuff, he didn't care what you did with it afterwards. Like if he gave you a car and you sold it. He figured that was his way of giving you money without really giving it to you. A lot of us sold the cars and made extra money. He would buy us these cars that were so expensive we couldn't afford them. We had to sell them.

The last car he gave me, in the seventies sometime, was a pale blue 600 Mercedes, a four-door sedan, that had actually been his—it had his name on the title. One time, I had to replace one part on it and it was something like $1,000. And you know, at $365 a week and a few bonuses, you can't do that too many times. I sold that car for nearly $35,000, which at the time was a lot of money. An airplane captain bought it. I heard he sold it for half a million, and then I saw it for sale the other day for $2.3 million. I said, "Boy, that's pretty good." But I made a profit. I gave Elvis a dollar for it.

Elvis was always giving me stuff. Jewelry, expensive watches. He liked to give, and he liked to watch people's reactions. But the elaborate gift giving was also a Band-Aid for the abuse he heaped on you the rest of the time. That was the blessing and the curse of Elvis.

CHAPTER 33

FLYING HIGH

By 1966, most of Elvis's singles were either leftover tracks from old Nashville recording sessions or songs pulled off of mediocre movie albums. Despite his spurt of success in '65, by the following year, both his singles and albums had slipped to a new low on the charts. And Elvis seemed too numbed out to care.

That same year, Elvis met a man whose fate would forever be linked with his. Dr. George C. Nichopoulos, a Pennsylvania-born son of Greek immigrants, grew up in Anniston, Alabama, where his parents ran a restaurant. He received his medical degree from Vanderbilt University at age thirty-two, but not without an interruption for academic probation.

MARTY LACKER: Early in '66, Elvis got a bad cold. He thought he'd just tough it out, but it didn't get any better. He was talking to George Klein one day, and he said, "Man, this cold is getting me down." So George said he'd talk to his girlfriend, Barbara Little. Barbara worked for this doctors' partnership called the Medical Group, and she asked one of the doctors if he'd pay a house call. That was Dr. Nick.

Dr. Nick was personable, and Elvis charmed him the way he charmed everybody else. Pretty soon, Elvis was getting what he wanted out of him—which was pills—and Dr. Nick was flattered to be Elvis's personal physician.

Drugwise, Dr. Nick didn't really play that big a role until about 1971, although he was around off and on for a long time before that. He's supposed to be the bad guy in all of this, but Dr. Nick just got in over his head. He was swayed by the glamour, when he should have stuck to being a doctor.

BILLY SMITH: So many people blame Dr. Nick. But Dr. Nick did as much as he could, right from the beginning. I'm sure at times he thought, "To hell with it, let him have it." Because Dr. Nick fought a losing battle.

LAMAR FIKE: When Dr. Nick came into the picture, Joe and Jerry glommed onto him right away. Now Dr. Nick and Joe and Jerry became the elite part of the group, always looking down their noses at people.

MARTY LACKER: In the spring of '66, Elvis got one of the early Sony video recorders. It was huge. The day it came, Elvis was making *Spinout*, which was one of Norman Taurog's pictures.

Elvis showed it to Mr. Taurog, and he really liked it. He said, "This would be great to have because we could play back the scenes right after we shoot them." So Elvis looked at me and said, "I want to give this to Mr. Taurog. Can you get another one?" These things were very scarce at the time, and Sony had a waiting list a mile long. But I called the factory and talked the guy into selling Elvis a second one.

LAMAR FIKE: I remember hauling that nine-ton son of a bitch around. It liked to have killed me.

BILLY SMITH: When Elvis first got that video machine, he started filming a few things here and there, and then it dawned on him, "Hey, this sucker can be used for other things. I can direct my own [sex] movie." So when he was having the intercom installed at the house, it presented the perfect time to have a camera mounted. He even filmed Priscilla with that thing.

MARTY LACKER: I've seen those videotapes of Priscilla with another girl in bed. They're wrestling. In panties and bra. They certainly exist. Or did.

BILLY SMITH: Don't think Priscilla was the only one Elvis taped because she wasn't. He taped a couple of girls that he was going with. He was producer, director, and star, all at once.

MARTY LACKER: In '66, we were coming home from California, and every time we'd stop, Elvis would have the video recorder taken off the bus and carried up to his room. He'd sit up there and watch sex tapes.

One of our regular stops was the Western Skies Motel in Albuquerque, New Mexico. We checked in there, and Elvis called me and said, "Have someone go out to the airport and meet this girl." She was from L.A. I said, "What's she doing here?" And Elvis said, "I called her before I left and told her to meet me here." This was one of the girls he had taped before.

We had to stay four damn days while they played around with the video in the room. I remember we were all pissed off because we wanted to get home to our families.

LAMAR FIKE: These were explicit, graphic, sexual videotapes. The kind popularly referred to as "down and dirty."

MARTY LACKER: One time, everybody went to Palm Springs except me and Joe. And Joe said, "Let's go see if we can find those videotapes."

We went in Elvis's bedroom and looked in the closet, and there was the machine. We pulled it out, and Joe found three videotape boxes. He looked inside, and he said, "Bingo."

We were practically frothing at the mouth because Elvis was very secretive about stuff like this. We got the machine down and took the cover off. And we discovered that Elvis thought he was going to be clever because he either took the power cord with him or hid it somewhere so that no one else could use the machine. Joe was cussing, and I was cussing, and then I said, "Wait a minute." And I called Westwood Camera Shop. They had one cord left. I told the guy if he sold it to anyone else I was going to kill him.

I got the cord, and Joe and I set the machine down on the floor in Elvis's room and watched those videos. We were so spooked we locked the doors. Even though Elvis was supposed to be in Palm Springs, you never knew when he was going to walk in.

Except for the tapes of Priscilla and this other girl, all of these were tapes of girls he had dated. In bed. He was never on there doing anything himself. But he made one mistake—he walked through the frame in one of them while the girl was in bed playing with herself. She was nude, except for the white panties.

Goldman wrote that there were copies of these on the black market in L.A. after Elvis died, and that in one of them, Elvis stepped in front of the camera with a full erection and masturbated. I never saw anything like that. Elvis wasn't dumb. He knew better than that.

BILLY SMITH: You know, this stuff is tame by today's standards. But Marty and Joe weren't the only ones with access to the tapes. While everybody was off touring in the seventies, all those things were left at Graceland. And they definitely missed one. It shows Elvis and the girl on the bed. But they're not really doing anything other than going through the motions. It was a side view, when he had the camera on a tripod. It was easy to see what they were doing, although it wasn't real close.

MARTY LACKER: The tapes I saw weren't particularly raunchy. They were sensual and erotic. Because they were silent. With the ones of just two girls, or of Priscilla and the girl, I had the feeling Elvis was off in the corner telling them what to do.

BILLY SMITH: I heard that story about the tapes being on the black market, but I don't think that's true. As best I remember, I told Priscilla where they were in 1979. They were still upstairs in his room. I imagine she had 'em destroyed.

MARTY LACKER: I think the tapes were just one example of how Priscilla was changing, but it's probably inaccurate to suggest that she had turned into some kind of wild sex addict. One time when Elvis was living on Rocca Place, she came back to the house and said that she'd gone over to visit Larry Geller and his wife, Stevie, and they were trying to talk her into sunbathing in the nude.

Larry was bad news. In '66, we were at Graceland one night. Geller was staying at the Admiral Benbow Inn, near the airport, but he was up at the house. I was out of cigarettes, and I got in the pink Cadillac and started down the driveway to go to the store.

Just before I got to the guardhouse, I saw a bunch of guys in suits up against the gates, trying to see who was coming down the drive. I don't know what made me do it, but I got out of the car. And just when I did, these guys took off running to each side.

I went in the guardhouse, and I said, "Vester, who are those guys out there?" And Vester said they told him they were out-of-town detectives visiting Memphis on vacation and they wanted to see Graceland. Well, that would have been fine, except why did they run? I called up at the house and told whoever answered what had happened, and then I said, "Tell Elvis not to come down to the gate." Of course, that was the worst thing I could have said. Because he and a bunch of the guys came down in two cars.

Elvis got to the gate, and he told Vester to open it. Then he went out and he said, "What the hell's going on here?" These guys were all lined up around the walls, and there was a car setting away from the gate. The door opened, and here came Bill Morris, the sheriff of Shelby County and supposedly a friend of Elvis.

Elvis said, "Hey, Bill, what are you guys doing out here? Why'd you run when Marty came down?" And Morris said, "We're investigating a call from California." And Elvis said, "So what's that got to do with me?" Morris said, "Is Larry Geller up there?" And Elvis said, "He may be. Why?" And Morris said, "The Los Angeles Police Department is investigating a shipment of marijuana and other drugs sent to Larry Geller, addressed to Elvis Presley at Graceland."

Geller was stupid to have a package sent to Graceland. But he had a friend who sent him "gifts," and he probably thought nobody would question Elvis getting a package. But either they were investigating his friend, or they got a tip from L.A. And they immediately called the Memphis police. Elvis said, "Bill, I don't know anything about this." And he motioned for Geller to come to the gate. Geller said he didn't know anything about it, either. Morris said, "Well, we're going to have to take you in anyway, Larry."

Before they put him in the car, and without them hearing, I said to Geller, "Do you have anything else coming to Graceland, Larry?" He said, "Well, I don't know. It depends on what was in that package."

After the guys went back up to the house, I told Elvis I was going to call Larry's friend in L.A. and tell him if he had anything else, not to send it. But I was paranoid. I thought, "Maybe they've got his line bugged. Maybe they think he's a dealer." So when I got him on the phone, instead of coming right out with it, I said, "Hey, look. You know those beauty supplies you sent?" He said, "What beauty supplies?" I said, "That stuff you sent to Larry." And he said, "Oh, yeah!" I said, "He wanted me to let you know he doesn't need anymore." He said, "Oh, okay."

One time in Palm Springs, Geller talked Elvis into seeing this woman who was supposedly clairvoyant. A part-time psychic, part-time masseuse. One day, she came up to this place we rented called the Alexander House and went upstairs. Elvis's suite looked like a huge space capsule, with big windows and a giant bed.

About fifteen minutes after she got there, she came walking down the steps, all upset. She said, "I can't take him anymore." I said, "What are you talking about, lady?" And she said, "Somebody better go look in on him." I went upstairs real quick. Elvis was lying across the bed on his back, and his eyes were closed, and he looked like he was asleep. All he had on was a bathing suit.

I said, "Elvis?" and he didn't answer. I said it again, and he still didn't answer. So I grabbed his arm, and it just fell limp. Then I put my ear down like I'd seen in the movies, to try to hear his heart, and I couldn't hear anything, and I tried to shake his body, but he didn't move.

I thought, "Goddamn!" And I slapped him across his face and said, "Elvis, get up!" And he went, "Ahhhhhh." So I was relieved, because I knew he was alive. And I shook him again. I said, "Damnit, Elvis, get up!" He said, "Ahhh, go on, leave me alone." I left him to sleep it off.

LAMAR FIKE: Elvis tried to act macho, but he was really a sensitive soul. If something happened to me, he would cry. When my son, who had spinal meningitis, got real sick, Elvis cried about that. He really cared for me. But, of course, that didn't mean he wouldn't zing me real good once in a while.

MARTY LACKER: Elvis really never wanted anybody to be able to read him. Even though we knew he loved us, he didn't want us to feel too confident about it.

In '66, on Rocca Place, Elvis was up early one afternoon. Joe and I were the only other ones up. And Elvis said, "Y'all come with me. I've got to meet the Colonel at his apartment."

That was the first and only time I was at Colonel's apartment. It was in the Beverly Comstock Apartments, at Comstock and Wilshire. These were hotel apartments. And his wasn't that big, which surprised me. It had a nice-sized living room, but his bedroom was small. And most of it was taken up by a hospital bed, which is what he always slept in, supposedly for his back. He had an office in the bedroom, and he'd conduct business from bed. Mrs. Parker was in Palm Springs.

When we first got there, Elvis went in Colonel's bedroom and talked, and Joe and I waited in the living room. Then Elvis came out and said, "Y'all come in here."

I forget what they were talking about, but Colonel said to Elvis, "Remember what I told you." Elvis was sitting on the couch. And without looking at me or Joe, Elvis said, "Well, these guys don't mean nothing to me." It took me aback, but I didn't say anything. And Joe just sat there, too.

Elvis and the Colonel talked a few more minutes, and then we left. We got out to the car, and I looked back at Elvis. And he smiled that all-knowing smile. I always meant to ask him about it, but I left it alone. I know he cared for me. A few years ago, Billy and I were talking about what Elvis said to him in that last year. Billy said, "There's a lot of guys who would be totally shocked to learn how Elvis really felt about them."

LAMAR FIKE: Now that I look back on it, I see how stressful it was to be with him. We never realized it at the time—like a guy who works in a damn rivet factory or runs a jackhammer and never hears it.

MARTY LACKER: Elvis would bounce back between being incredibly insecure and amazingly confident. And between being selfish and magnanimous. By '66, he'd outgrown the Dodge motor home, and it was getting some age on it. So Elvis bought a big double-decker Greyhound to get us back and forth to California and had George Barris renovate it for about $50,000. Then he gave the Dodge mobile home to Lorne Greene, the actor, who had a center for underprivileged kids in Canada.

Another time, in the seventies, Elvis was out driving in Mississippi, and he passed this little black kid, sitting at a watermelon stand on the side of the highway. He was maybe ten years old, just dirty and dusty from the cars, and all by himself. Elvis thought about it for a second, and then turned around, and the whole five-car entourage stopped to buy a watermelon. By the time they left, Elvis bought the entire stand, just to see the look on the kid's face.

BILLY SMITH: On one of the last bus trips we made from Memphis to L.A. before Elvis started flying, he invited all the wives. The trip took a week or ten days because we stopped to sightsee along the way. One night, we started playing Yahtzee. Elvis said that anybody who threw the dice out got hit on the hand. By the time it was over, we were all beating each other to death, but I think I got the worst of it.

A day or two later, everybody come in my room to see the bruises on my arms. Elvis was giving me all this sympathy, and then all of a sudden, he hauled off and hit me again. I just laid on the bed 'cause I was hurting too bad to get up. Elvis laid on the floor laughing because I couldn't get up and do anything. He was a kid, you know, very spoiled.

One time in the seventies, it was about four in the morning, and Elvis wanted me to hear this song that he was getting ready to record. We'd been up all night, and I was just pooped. Elvis made Charlie get up out of bed and come upstairs, and Charlie sat down at the organ and started playing and harmonizing with him. I sat there calling out song titles.

About seven-thirty, I couldn't take it no more. There wasn't anything I liked more than hearing Elvis sing, but my eyelids were getting heavier and heavier. I called out another song title, and, boy, Elvis was putting his heart into it. And then I leaned back in the chair, closed my eyes, and started patting my foot. I just fell asleep on him is what I did. In a minute, I felt something mashing down on my leg, just digging in.

Elvis said, "Wake up!" He said, "Goddamnit, you're going to listen to this! It's your special request!" I said, "I'm not sleeping, I'm just resting my eyes." But in a couple bars, I was dozing off again. And he come down on my leg the second time, and said, "Open those marble eyes!" Then he turned to Charlie and said,

"Here I am giving a million-dollar performance, and this son of a bitch just wants to go to sleep!" I broke up laughing, even if he did call me a son of a bitch.

LAMAR FIKE: When Elvis moved to Rocca Place, Cliff Gleaves came back for one of his visits. He'd show up every few years and stay a while, and then take off as quick as he came. Cliff always had something going on. He always wanted to be an actor, but he couldn't cut it. And in the sixties, I think he wanted to give it one last shot.

MARTY LACKER: When Cliff wanted something, he'd just worry you until he got it. So back in the fifties, he kept bugging Elvis, "Man, can't you get me a bit part in your movie?" And Cliff drove Elvis nuts until he finally arranged it. So Cliff walked around popping his fingers and saying, "Yeaaah, I'm gonna be a movie star. I'm gonna be a big movie star." He only had two lines, but he was studying his script. And pretty soon, they put makeup on him, and fixed the little tissue around his neck.

It came time for Cliff's big scene, and he was saying, "This is a piece of cake." The assistant director called him, and they positioned Cliff in front of the camera. But when the director said, "Action," Cliff froze. He couldn't utter one word. And from that time on, Elvis told him, "Don't you ever—ever—ask me again."

It didn't phase him, though. In the mid-sixties, Cliff would come out to California every once in a while to see what he could get. And all he'd have with him was this little flight bag that the airlines used to give out. He'd have all his sole possessions in there, and one of them was a Water Pik, believe it or not.

What always amazed me about him was that he had no shame about bumming stuff. I smoked a lot back then, and I bought cigarettes by the carton. One time Cliff came out, and the first morning, before we left the house to go to the studio, he said, "Hey, man, let me borrow a cigarette." Like he was really going to pay me back. I gave it to him. And about ten minutes later, he said, "Hey, man, let me borrow another cigarette." I gave him another one. Five or six cigarettes later, I said, "Cliff, I ain't the only one that smokes around here." And he said, "Oh, well, don't worry about it. I'll ask somebody else. But just let me borrow one more." And that night, he asked me for another one. I said, "Cliff, go to somebody else." So he said, "Oh, okay."

The next morning, this started again. I said, "Wait a minute, Cliff." I went in my room and got a full pack and gave it to him. And I said, "Here, now don't ask me for any more cigarettes today." Cliff said, "Oh, man, great!" I gave him a pack for four days in a row. By the fifth day, I was out of cigarettes. I just had the pack in my pocket. And that morning, going to the studio, Cliff said, "Got a cigarette?" I said, "No, Cliff, I'm all out." He said, "You ain't got another pack?" I said, "Nope." He said, "You cheap son of a bitch!"

BILLY SMITH: Cliff could talk just like Walter Brennan. Everything he said was funny. He'd say, "That's right, mister." All the time. And he'd say, "You bet your life, and someday you may have to."

One time, Cliff and an actor named Billy Murphy crashed a party in Texas with all these big multimillionaire oil men. Murphy was in *The Sands of Iwo Jima*. Played Richard Jaeckel's brother. Anyway, they were at this party, and they sat around listening to all these guys talk about how much money they made and lost in oil. Well, they got up and went to the bathroom, and all they heard was the same thing. And they couldn't get over it. They went back to the table and got to thinking about it, and they got drunker and drunker, and finally they couldn't stand it no longer. Cliff jumped up in the middle of the table and said, "Gentlemen!" Just as loud as he could. He threw his arm up, and he said, "We're talking in millions!" And they throwed their asses out.

MARTY LACKER: By '66 or '67, Cliff was wearing thin with Elvis. One night on Rocca Place, he was there, and Elvis got hooked on listening to a record of "Cool, Clear Water." And Cliff, just to play along with Elvis, started singing the song. Cliff had made a few records. His "biggie," as he called it, was a song called "Hold Back the Dawn." And he would sing it for you at the drop of a hat. That's what he's been doing all these years, down in Florida. He played at piano bars for these rich old women.

The night he got on "Cool, Clear Water," about three or four of us went to the Red Velvet. When we got back, we heard "Cool, Clear Water" up real loud.

I said, "Elvis must still be up." Which surprised us because he had to be at the studio the next morning. We went in the house, and Cliff was by the sliding door to the pool, sitting at the round table and chairs. He had a fedora on his head and a bottle of vodka. And the stereo was just blaring.

We said, "Cliff, where's Elvis?" He said, "Ah, shit—" He was drunk. He said, "He's in the back sleeping." I said, "Cliff, what the hell are you doing playing music this loud?" He said, "Well, I wanted to hear the record. 'Cool, clear—'" And he started singing. Somebody went over to the stereo and turned the damn thing off. I said, "Cliff, you can either go to bed, or somewhere else, but this ain't gonna happen." And the next morning, Cliff was gone. That's the last anybody saw of him for years and years.

LAMAR FIKE: Trying to get Elvis out to a nightclub was like pulling teeth. Part of it was that he didn't want the hassle of people coming up and asking for autographs. And part of it was that certain performers just made him uneasy. When he did go, it was a rare occasion.

MARTY LACKER: We used to go see Fats Domino a lot in Vegas in the early to mid-sixties. He used to play at the Flamingo. Fats supposedly owed the hotel so much in gambling debts that he played for nothing.

One night, we were sitting at the table and Fats was taking a break between shows. Elvis went up to the bar where he was, which was unusual. He'd usually wait for somebody to come to the table to him. But Elvis admired Fats, so he didn't think anything of it. We noticed they were having this animated conversation. Fats used to drink straight scotch or vodka, and he kept pouring drinks and knocking them down.

I remember he wore this star tiepin. It was huge and encrusted with diamonds. Same thing with his cuff links. Elvis came back to the table and said, "Poor old guy. I guess he's broke. He asked me to buy his tie tack and cuff links for $5,000."

BILLY SMITH: Elvis liked black artists. He liked the way Jackie Wilson sang and the way he moved. He kept up with how he was doing, even after Jackie had a stroke, I believe, in '75 and went into a coma. Now, he didn't like James Brown. He didn't like his attitude, and he didn't like his singing. He thought he was a screamer. He liked Jackie Wilson, and Clyde McPhatter, and Billy Ward and His Dominoes, all those guys.

MARTY LACKER: We used to go to a club called The Trip, in the Playboy Building in L.A. We got Elvis to go there one night when Jackie Wilson was there. That was the first time they met. Jackie kidded him, saying, "People call me 'the black Elvis Presley'" because he always wore his hair in a pompadour.

Jackie was a fantastic guy and a gentleman. So Elvis invited him to the set of *Double Trouble*, which, again, was unusual because he just didn't invite people to the studio. We had a great time with him.

That night, Elvis went back to The Trip. It was the last night of Jackie's engagement there, and James Brown was opening the next day. When Jackie came offstage, the owner of the club, who was a friend of ours, brought over four bottles of champagne. Elvis didn't usually drink like that, but he wanted to toast Jackie, and he was having a good time.

In a little while, James Brown came over. He just barged in. And Elvis didn't like it. James didn't know Elvis, and he was loud and trying to be the center of attention. Well, it killed the atmosphere. But Elvis was polite. And James looked at Elvis and said, "You know, I'm opening tomorrow night. I'm sure you'll be here." Well, the next day was a weekday, and Elvis had to get up at four-thirty in the morning. But Elvis looked at James, and he said, "I'll do my best." And James pushed himself on Elvis. He said, "I know you'll be here."

The next night, me and Richard and Alan were going to go see James perform. Elvis wasn't about to go, so I asked him what I should tell James. Elvis said, "You got one of those watches?" I said, "Yeah."

Elvis had these watches made, where the Star of David and the cross intertwined on the face every thirty seconds. I designed it. And I kept all the extras in my room. So Elvis said, "Give me some paper," and he wrote James a note that said, "Sorry I can't be there. I have to be up in the morning, and I hope you'll accept this gift. I wish you well on your show." And he signed it. That was the first time I ever saw him go to that kind of trouble.

James had two other people in his dressing room after his show, and when he saw us, he said, in this really abrasive tone, "Why didn't Elvis come?" I said, "He has to be up early in the morning." And James said, "Goddamn, he came to see Jackie Wilson, and he won't come to see me!" I said, "He asked me if I would give this to you and tell you he's really sorry."

James opened up the box, and he said, "Oh, yeah, that's nice." Like it was no big deal. And he read the note, and he put it back in the box and closed it, and he slammed the box on his dressing-room table. And he said, "What's this watch?" I said, "Well, James, it's a unique watch, and only the guys have them. Elvis wanted you to have one." I said, "If you'll take it out —" And I had one on my wrist, and Richard and Alan had theirs on. And James looked over at me and said, "Well, it's nice you gave me a watch, but where's theirs?" Meaning the two other guys who were in the room, both white guys. One was the pilot of his plane.

He was trying to minimize Elvis's gesture and make a fool out of me at the same time. So without blinking an eye, I looked over at Alan and Richard. I said, "One of you, let me have your watch, and I'll replace it later." And I took mine off, too, and I gave the watches to the pilot and the other guy.

James didn't know what to do then. So he looked over at Alan, and he said, "How come Elvis still travels in a bus? I got my own airplane." I said, "Maybe he's just a little bit more comfortable in the bus. Some people like to fly, some people don't." And James said, "Well, if you want to be classy, and you're supposed to be number one, you fly. Here I am, flying around, and Elvis is riding the bus."

Just then, somebody brought in this little black kid. It was, like, midnight, and this kid, only ten or eleven years old, was in a nightclub. James started talking to him, and he said, "You go to school? You don't get in any trouble, do you?" And the kid said, "No, sir." James said, "You got a knife on you?" And the kid looked down at the floor, and he said, "Yes, I do." And James said, "I'll tell you what. You give me that knife, and I'll give you some money." And out of goodwill, I said, "And I'll give you something, too," because I couldn't see this little kid carrying a knife.

And James looked up at me and said, "He don't need your damn money." And I said, "What?" He said, "I got money. I can take care of it." I said, "Fine."

We sat and talked for a while longer, and then we decided to go upstairs. Alan was going to get something to eat with James, and Richard and I were going back to the house. We were walking up this circular stairway, and James was right behind me. I turned around and said, "James, it's really a pleasure to meet you. I enjoyed it, and I always love your music." And I was being sincere. He looked at me, and he said, "I don't want you to be that way, man. You know, all that shit was two hundred years ago." I looked at him, and I was just dumbfounded.

I said, "James, what are you talking about?" He said, "You know what I'm talking about." He meant slavery. Now, he had no idea whether I was prejudiced or not. He automatically assumed it because I'm white and because I lived in Tennessee. But that's James Brown. I told Elvis the next day. And he just said, "Fuck him."

LAMAR FIKE: James Brown might have been ticked off that Elvis didn't come to his show. Or Marty might have rubbed him the wrong way. But James loved Elvis. He was the first guy who came to Elvis's wake. I answered the door. I said, "James, how are you doing?" He said, "Man, I've come to see him." And he sat down.

🏃 🏃 🏃

MARTY LACKER: In the middle of all this negative stuff, a bright spot appeared in May of '66. That's when Felton Jarvis took over as Elvis's producer at RCA. Elvis really liked Felton because he was a lot of fun. But Felton still didn't call the shots in the recording sessions. Nobody from RCA ever did. Elvis was still his own producer.

LAMAR FIKE: I found Felton Jarvis in Nashville and brought him into the whole situation. Because for three years, Elvis had just done those soundtrack sessions in Hollywood and no regular sessions in Nashville. I said to Elvis, "You need a really hip producer. And this guy is that." Felton was just different. He used to keep a live snake—a viper—in his office in a burlap bag.

Felton had been at ABC-Paramount. He'd produced Gladys Knight and the Pips, and Fats Domino, and he'd produced "Sheila," that Tommy Roe hit. One reason Elvis liked Felton right off is because Felton let him do several gospel tracks on their first session, which led to that [second] sacred album, *How Great Thou Art.* Elvis ended up getting his first Grammy for it. They laid down eighteen tracks in four nights on that first session. And Felton brought in a couple of bright musicians, like David Briggs on organ. "Love Letters" came out of that session. Felton even got Elvis doing a Bob Dylan song, "Tomorrow Is a Long Time."

Felton was the one who found out that Colonel controlled the mixes on Elvis's records—that he ordered Elvis's voice out so far, which Elvis hated. Felton went to the engineer who did it, and he said, "What are you doing?" The engineer said, "This is the way Colonel wants it done." Elvis went nuts. He made Felton go to New York and follow the mix all the way through so that the engineer couldn't get to it.

MARTY LACKER: Felton used to jump up and down and imitate Elvis while Elvis was recording. And Elvis loved that because it got him up. He always liked to have somebody moving, especially on a fast song. Sonny West was a hell of a good dancer. So Sonny would be out there dancing by himself, and I'd shadowbox and sway back and forth.

BILLY SMITH: Recording with Felton energized Elvis quite a bit. He started taking it serious again. In some sessions, Elvis would know that the first and second take wasn't going to be worth a shit, and he would warm up. He would never sing anything high right off. He'd save his voice.

LAMAR FIKE: Elvis used his voice like a muscle. He'd warm it up, and get it into position, and do it.

MARTY LACKER: The second session Elvis did with Felton was in June of '66. We went back to Nashville to cut material for the singles, not the movies. This was the session where Elvis did "Indescribably Blue," a really pretty song. The first day, Elvis was in a pissy mood. So he faked one of his illnesses. Said his voice was hurting. But nothing was really wrong.

He said, "Just tell them to go ahead and do the tracks." And even though he liked Felton, he said, "As a matter of fact, I want Red to handle the session, and Marty can help him." And he said to us, "Be sure they do what I want them to do," because we talked about how he wanted the songs laid out. He liked the high part that Millie Kirkham, the background singer, did in this particular song, and it really did give the song a fantastic effect. So we said, "Okay," and me and Red went over.

Now, Red doesn't have a bad voice. He can almost sound like Elvis. So Red filled in as the voice while the musicians cut the track. At first, the musicians were a little ticked that Elvis wasn't there. But Red did a really great job of putting this together. We laid down "Indescribably Blue," and "I'll Remember You," and "If Every Day Was Like Christmas." And we got them to cut the acetates, so we could take them back to the motel. Elvis had a stereo set up in his room so he could listen to them.

That afternoon, Elvis got up. We went in his room, and he was playing the dubs, and he said, "Boy, that sounds good. I'll probably go to the studio tonight." And in talking to him, I mentioned that the studio guys weren't too happy about Red and me coming over and telling them what he wanted done.

Something else must have been bothering him because Elvis flew totally off the handle. He said, "What do you mean you told them?" He said, "Who the fuck do you think you are telling those guys what to do?" I said, "Wait a minute, Elvis."

He said, "Wait a minute, hell! These guys have been playing all their lives, and you go over there and tell them how to do it?" I said, "No, I just did exactly what you asked me to do." I said, "Matter of fact, Red was the one handling most of it."

"Goddamnit," he said. "You've got a lot of nerve doing that!" He said, "I don't want anybody going with me tonight except Red. The rest of you fuckin' guys just stay back here at the motel!"

I was really pissed. But we just stayed back and played cards—me, Billy, Alan, Richard, and the others. And Billy got me out of my mood. He lost some money playing cards, so he called Jo and said, "I need you to send me some money." And it was so funny the way he said it because he was drunk, and he was giving her the address, and he said, "And send it to me, Billy Smith . . . "

BILLY SMITH: When I was with Elvis, I wasn't afraid of anything. Even when we first started flying. And I normally would have been scared to death over that.

MARTY LACKER: All of a sudden, Elvis decided he wanted to start flying. I don't know if that James Brown story got back to him or what, but right before we went to Nashville, Elvis said, "I don't want to take a bus. I want to fly up there, and I want to fly up there real quick." I was surprised because up until then, he was really afraid to fly. And he got airsick, too. Even the few times we'd fly to L.A., he'd throw up. He always had to have two barf bags in his seat.

I said, "Elvis, we don't have any reservations, and we don't know the flights." And he said, "No, I want you to get me a private jet. See if you can get Kemmons Wilson's Lear jet."

Kemmons Wilson was the chairman of Holiday Inn. He founded the chain, which started in Memphis. So I called, and we got the Holiday Inn jet. And from Memphis to Nashville, all a Lear jet does is go straight up and come straight down, it's such a short flight. But I said, "Elvis, I'm not going on a Lear jet." I'd never been on a private plane before, and I didn't like to fly anyway. And Elvis said, "No, you're flying with us." I said, "Look, you can't get all these guys on the Lear jet, plus all the baggage, because it will overweight the plane."

I said, "Let me call the airlines and see if I can get on the next jet to Nashville." Elvis said okay, and I got to Nashville before he did. Lamar met me, and we loaded all the stuff in his car, and took the baggage to the Albert Pick, and then waited for Elvis to land. Here he was staying at this old dump, and taking a Lear jet to get there.

LAMAR FIKE: We had a pact, an agreement, that whenever we'd fly somewhere we'd take out flight insurance. A $100,000 policy. They had those insurance machines at the airports back in the sixties. So we'd all make a beeline for them and take out the biggest policy we could. We figured if somebody got killed, the rest of us would buy a Chris-Craft and name the boat after him.

MARTY LACKER: The night before we left Nashville to go home, Elvis was all peaches and cream. He came in and said, "What's going on?" We said, "Nothing. We've been playing cards." And he said to me, "I want you on that Lear jet in the morning, and I don't want to hear any shit about it."

The next day, he sat across the aisle from me, and he just smiled and smiled. He said, "See, I told you they'd take those bags." He was thrilled to be on that jet. And when we landed, Priscilla and the wives were there, and Elvis spent another hour taking people for rides. He was fascinated by it. That's when he got in his mind that he wanted his own plane.

CHAPTER 34

SHOWDOWN

MARTY LACKER: You know the waterfall that's in the den, now the Jungle Room, at Graceland? My brother-in-law, Bernie Grenadier, did that. Actually, he redid it, in '66. Vernon got this cheap-ass plumber—some $4-an-hour guy—to do it originally, and the guy botched the job. That whole wall leaked, and the water would flood the backyard. So Elvis asked Bernie to fix it. He was an interior designer, and my sister, Anne, was an interior decorator. They worked together.

Elvis was so pleased with what Bernie did with the waterfall that after that he said, "I'd really like to have the gardens done." Because there was nothing out there but an old broken-down birdbath and some columns that had fallen down and rotted out.

And Elvis said, "It would be great to have someplace where I could go just to meditate, someplace that's really pretty and peaceful where I could think and be by myself." He wanted something like the Self-Realization Park in California.

So Elvis went to California to do a movie. And Bernie worked day and night. He went to Italy to get the stained-glass windows and the statues. He got the brick for the wall from Mexico. He redid the arches, and planted the bushes, and built that huge fountain with all the different sprays and light formations. When he finished, he'd transformed a 100-by-140-foot eyesore into the Meditation Garden.

Vernon didn't like it that my sister and brother-in-law were Jewish. By this time, I was living in the apartments while Bernie was building my house. But when I was living at Graceland with my family, my mother and father used to come see me and my family on the weekends. Elvis didn't mind. Elvis liked my parents.

One time, Elvis was there when they came, and my mother

brought me this big jar of homemade chicken soup. Elvis saw it and asked if he could have some, and he loved it. To the point where he said to her, "Hey, do me a favor, forget about Marty, just bring this for me." So not too long after that, while Anne was there working on the garden, Daisy, the cook, asked Anne for the recipe. And Anne brought up the Molly Goldberg cookbook. And a couple of days later, Vernon came out with the book in his hand and threw it at Anne and yelled, "I don't want no Jew book in this house!"

It got worse. When my mother used to come up, she'd go in and talk to Elvis's grandmother. Grandma was always nice to me and my whole family, especially my son. When we lived there, he was just a little kid, and she got him hooked on biscuits and molasses, and she'd sit out in the kitchen with him. After we moved, she'd sit in her room all the time by herself. So my sister would go in to see her every day when she was there working on the garden. Anne liked her a lot.

Elvis really appreciated it because he cared a lot about his grandmother and he knew she was lonely. But one day, Vernon went out to the garden and got mad about something, and told Anne, "And another thing—I want you to quit going in there and bugging my mother!" My sister was really hurt over that.

When we came back from California, Elvis said he wanted to go outside by himself. He wanted to be the first one to see the garden at night all lit up. So he went out, and when he came back in, he cried, he thought it was so beautiful.

After all that, the really sad thing is that Vernon questioned Bernie's bills for labor. The Meditation Garden cost $22,000. Anybody else would have charged them $50,000 or $100,000. Vernon and Elvis called me into the dining room one night, and Vernon started this crap, and I just blew up. I told them Bernie was barely making a profit, which was true. I said, "All of this stuff he's done, including the waterfall, has been for the sheer pleasure of doing it here at Graceland for you." And I said, "If you think Bernie's trying to cheat you, you take it up with him." And I turned around and walked out. As I did, I heard Elvis tell his father, "Write the check."

LAMAR FIKE: Elvis was the kind of guy who could give away a Cadillac at the drop of a hat, but I don't think he really shared much of himself.

BILLY SMITH: Elvis felt that women were more trustworthy than men. But he never found exactly what he was looking for in a woman. He probably should have been a bachelor.

MARTY LACKER: Elvis never saw any reason to stop looking at pretty girls. In '66, he had a couple of dates with Cybill Shepherd. He was thirty-one, and she was seventeen. She says it was later, when she was twenty-two. Either way, she'd already been named Miss Teenage America, and he always had a weakness for beauty queens. He thought that was a big deal.

BILLY SMITH: About getting married . . . Elvis used to have a saying about that: "Why buy a cow when you can steal the milk through the fence?" Or sometimes, we'd be going somewhere where there were a lot of women. And we'd say, "Elvis, you got a date tonight?" He'd smile kind of funny and say, "Why take a sandwich to a banquet?"

MARTY LACKER: In '66, Elvis started getting heavier into downers— Seconals, yellow jackets. They made him groggy sometimes. Made his footing unsure, and his equilibrium wasn't good, anyway. One reason he took them was because he was under a lot of pressure to get married.

LAMAR FIKE: At Christmas of '66, Elvis officially proposed to Priscilla and gave her a diamond ring big enough to choke Marilyn Chambers.

The way that whole thing went down is that Elvis had markers called in on him, pure and simple. Priscilla was twenty-one years old now, and Captain Beaulieu figured it was time Elvis fulfilled his obligation.

MARTY LACKER: I guess Elvis could have just said, "No, I'm not going to marry her." But I think Colonel made it clear that's what he should do. And I think her father made it clear that's what he should do. Plus I'm sure Elvis talked to his father about it. They were worried about Elvis ruining his career, à la Jerry Lee Lewis.

BILLY SMITH: Elvis had been with Priscilla about five years. If anything, he thought it was time to get away from her. But Priscilla presented him with a couple of problems. Colonel was laying down the law. And Priscilla was spilling her guts to the only people she could, her mama and daddy. If Elvis dropped her, and Priscilla was asked why she was let out of his life, she was going to tell her story. Or at least that's the way Elvis put it to me. And I think Elvis was also worried about it becoming a common-law marriage.

LAMAR FIKE: Elvis sat down and talked to me one night. He said, "What do you know about common law?" I said, "I'm not a fuckin' attorney, Elvis, but a common-law attorney told me it starts one day after she moves in. It don't mean that seven-year shit." I said, "So you're guilty of it, no matter what."

Vernon might have mentioned that to him. Priscilla couldn't stand Vernon. But I think they colluded on this marriage deal. Vernon figured if Elvis got married, he'd stay at home more and stop running around the country with all these guys. And the size of his payroll would go down.

But what finally got Elvis to the altar was he wanted a kid. A son. And he wanted to name him John Barron Presley. He got on this "J. B. Presley" thing.

BILLY SMITH: From '64, '65 on, Elvis obsessed about having this child. He wanted a woman with dark hair to be the mother. She had to resemble him, and she had to be beautiful, so they could produce the perfect child. Which had to be a male. And I think he thought Priscilla would be the one he'd have it with. But she made it dang well clear that she didn't like the name John Barron, so even if Lisa Marie hadn't been a girl, Priscilla never would have named the baby that. Finally, my wife got a Great Dane, and Elvis named *it* "Barron." Priscilla thought that was real funny.

🕺 🕺 🕺

MARTY LACKER: Sometime in the summer, after my brother-in-law did the Meditation Garden, Elvis had him build the slot-car room. Then he said he'd like for him to redecorate the whole upstairs. He said, "We're going to go do another movie," which was really probably two movies, *Double Trouble* and *Easy Come, Easy Go*, because he did them back-to-back, with just a week off. Anyway, he told Bernie, "You can do it then. Keep in contact with Marty. He'll tell me if you need anything."

That sounded fine, except it meant that it was more or less taken out of Vernon's hands. While we were gone, they worked upstairs. And Vernon would come up and say things that were different from what I told them to do, based on my conversations with Elvis. But Vernon had started getting the bills, and what Elvis wanted probably cost a little more than what Vernon wanted. So they argued back and forth. Then Vernon and my sister got into it full force one day.

Finally, she said, "Mr. Presley, I'm not trying to be disrespectful. I'm just doing what Marty said Elvis wanted. I suggest you go back and talk to Elvis."

In a nice way, she told him to stay the hell out. And he told her she had the same foul mouth as her brother, and he said, "Neither one of you is going to be around Graceland much longer!"

After that, Vernon just manufactured things to get back at her. One day, Daisy, the cook, saw one of the workers carrying out garbage bags with scraps of the black velvet and white padding. She thought they were part of Elvis's teddy bear collection, which was stored upstairs. Daisy mentioned this to Vernon, and he went nuts.

By the time we got back to Memphis, it was the end of November and the renovation was finished. We all went upstairs to see it. When Elvis opened the two double doors and looked at his room, he said, "Man, I ain't seen nothing like this before."

And for his taste, it was beautiful. They upholstered the walls in pleated black-and-red velvet and put green leather, or Naugahyde, on the ceiling, where they'd installed two television sets so he could watch from bed. He was so overjoyed that he cried, like with the Meditation Garden. Vernon was standing there, and seeing Elvis so thrilled over what they'd done made him even madder.

The next afternoon, I came back over, feeling good because I thought Elvis was happy. Elvis and his father were sitting in the den, and when Elvis saw me, I thought maybe he'd compliment my family for doing a great job. But instead, in front of a couple of the other guys, Elvis started screaming, calling my whole family names, from my mother to my sister and brother-in-law.

That's the way he was. He would be supernice one minute and totally different the next. Vernon had fed him a bunch of lies about Bernie and Anne. Like that they'd stolen his teddy bears.

At first, I was going to let it slide. But then he started getting really nasty. And it burnt a hole in me. I got up and I said, "Hey, fuck you! And fuck your father, and fuck your whole goddamn family! You don't talk about my family that way! They haven't done anything but good here. And you can kiss my damn ass." And I left.

If that had been anybody else, I probably would have killed him. And I mean that literally. I was so upset that I took three sleeping pills and stayed in bed for three days.

BILLY SMITH: There's not really an excuse for the way Elvis lit into Marty that day. But how can you think when you're constantly being fed this line by the two people you look up to most in life? Vernon and Colonel tried to poison him about us. The guys were just a bunch of leeches, or hangers-on, in their opinion. And Elvis listened to all this bullshit from both sides, and at some time or another, he had to think that maybe that was true.

MARTY LACKER: I never thought of myself or most of the guys as vultures. Never. And I knew my family wasn't like that. I laid in bed thinking about what it all meant. And on the fourth day, I got up. I figured the way I talked to him, especially in front of other people, I'd ended our friendship. But I thought, "I'll find out. I'll just go up there and see if I get in." Because if Elvis didn't want to see you, he'd have somebody call down to the gate and tell Vester not to let you in.

I got up to the house, and everybody was downstairs in the basement. Richard and Mike were sitting at the soda fountain. They said, "Hey, Marty, how you doing?" and acted like nothing was wrong. And Elvis was sitting on the couch with his father, watching a 16mm print of one of his movies, which he almost never did.

When Elvis heard my name, he got up. I didn't know whether he was going to tell me to hit the road or what. And I was still groggy from the pills and still pissed off. But he said, "Hey, how you doing?" I said, "I'm all right." And then he said something that I'd never heard him say to me or anybody else. And that was, "I'm sorry."

Vernon got up and stood behind Elvis, and he had a half-scared, half-mad look on his face. I don't think he knew what Elvis was going to do, either. I said, "I'm glad you're sorry, Elvis, but that really doesn't excuse it." And I told him, "Don't ever do that to me again." I'd never been that forceful with him, but then we'd never had an argument that harsh before.

Elvis looked at me real intently for a second, and he said, "Come here, I want to talk to you." And we went and sat on the concrete steps that led from the basement to the den. He said, "Look, I've got something to tell you. One of the reasons I acted that way is that I'm under a hell of a lot of pressure." This was early December, before he'd announced his engagement. I figured he was bullshitting. I said, "Yeah, what kind of pressure?" And he said, "I'm under a lot of pressure to marry Priscilla." I said, "Who's doing that?" And he said, "It's coming from her family." And he told me Colonel was worried about a lawsuit. And then he said, "So, Priscilla and I are going to be married. And we've talked it over, and I want you to be my best man."

Well, I was totally shocked. I couldn't think about being mad anymore. My first thought was, "Why me?" I thought of Billy, I thought of Red, and I thought of Joe, and I instinctively knew that Esposito was going to be really pissed because he was such a status seeker. But I really thought of Billy. He should have been the best man. But I said, "That makes me happy."

BILLY SMITH: What's really interesting here is the way Elvis dealt with Ann-Margret during all this. I've always said it was a toss-up between Priscilla and Ann.

MARTY LACKER: I knew Elvis had to make a decision between them. And I thought if push came to shove, he would choose Ann. But once he gave in to the pressure from Priscilla's parents and the Colonel, that was it. He just abruptly stopped seeing Ann.

Esposito and I ran into her on Sunset Boulevard one day while she was riding her motorcycle. We blew the horn, and she saw us, and she pulled over to the side. And the first words out of her mouth were, "What the hell is wrong with your boss?" She said, "One minute we're in love, and the next minute I don't hear from him again. He won't even take my calls."

That's the way Elvis did things. It was part of his weakness. And none of us had the guts to say, "You ought to give the girl a call."

LAMAR FIKE: The truth of the matter is that Ann shut Elvis down. She knew he had this commitment to Priscilla. That's why she started going with Roger Smith. Elvis got real upset about it. But Ann was not going to marry Elvis.

BILLY SMITH: My personal desire was for Elvis to marry Ann. She made his life a little easier because she understood him and didn't make any demands on him. She even understood his need for us. Priscilla never understood that.

MARTY LACKER: The same month Elvis married Priscilla, Ann married Roger Smith. I read in her book [Ann-Margret: My Story] that she and Roger announced their engagement in '66. But she also said they split up in March of '66, and they got back together after that. I think that only happened because she didn't know what to do about Elvis. She was really, really in love with him.

LAMAR FIKE: When Elvis started playing Vegas regularly, in the seventies, he used to go see Ann's shows all the time. He'd send her flowers on opening night—always red roses in the shape of a guitar. And then he'd go to see her backstage, and she'd have on that big diamond that Roger gave her, and Roger would be right there. One time, when she used the motorcycles onstage, we went, and she introduced Elvis from the audience. She says in her book that he came onstage and performed with her—slid across the floor or something. I don't think that's true. I don't remember it. But he went, when he could, and always went backstage. In February of '73, she opened at the Hilton, and he went twice in three days. He still cared.

BILLY SMITH: Ann still cared about him, too. She had a slot machine made for him. Instead of cherries or jokers, it had three guitars that lined up for the jackpot. They've got it in the basement at Graceland.

I'm sure he made the first move to get back in touch. I'd heard he'd even proposed to her, after she was already married to Roger. But in her book, she doesn't exactly say that. She just says he come backstage and got down on one knee and told her he still felt the same way he always had.

MARTY LACKER: Other than Priscilla bitching when she'd read something about Ann and Elvis, I don't ever recall any negative times associated with Ann, except when we'd go back to Memphis and Elvis was away from her. She used to write him letters and sign them "Bunny," or "Thumper." And she'd call Graceland and use the same code.

If Elvis had ended up with Thumper, this whole story might have wound up differently.

CHAPTER 35

"RIDE 'EM, COWBOY!"

In the midst of the squabble about Bernie Grenadier's bills and the pressure to marry Priscilla, Elvis found respite on 150 rolling acres of land across the Tennessee border in Walls, Mississippi. The original owner had given it the quaint, and slightly fairyland, name of Twinkletown Farm—something Elvis would change to the Circle G (for Graceland) Ranch and eventually to the Flying G when he learned the name was already taken by a rancher in Texas.

Almost immediately, the Circle G became a symbol of Presley's increasing spending sprees, which he was now using, like drugs, for escape. The tremendous expenditure, which grew daily with Elvis's improvements on the land, may have spurred Vernon to bond with the parsimonious Priscilla in hurrying up the wedding, in hopes that Elvis would quickly abandon his folly.

"The happiest we ever saw Elvis was when he first bought that ranch," remembers Ray Walker, of the Jordanaires. "He had some horses down there, and he was exercising, and he looked great, and he felt great. As I remember, he even let his hair go back to its natural color for a while. He walked in one day, and he had a tan, and we couldn't get over how good he looked. We just stood there and stared at him. Finally, he broke into a smile and said, 'Shall we dance?'"

MARTY LACKER: The ranch was a natural evolution, you might say, of other things that were going on at Graceland in '66. It started when Elvis bought Priscilla a four-year-old black quarter horse, Domino. But she complained that she didn't have anybody to ride with, so Elvis bought himself a palomino, Rising Sun, which Jerry found for him somewhere. One day, he saw everybody standing around watching them ride, so he went wild and bought everybody a horse, even Vernon. I didn't want a horse.

But he outfitted all the guys, and their wives or girlfriends, in chaps, and boots, and hats. Billy says it was like a Roy Rogers–Dale Evans look-alike contest when everybody got together, and I guess it was.

Elvis would go out in the barn every day and every night. This barn, which he called House of the Rising Sun, a pun on the name of his horse, hadn't been used in years. He fixed up a little office for himself and wrote the names of the horses on the stalls with a big red marking pen. He'd write notes to himself like "What I'm Going to Buy Tomorrow" and "What I'm Going to Do Tomorrow." And he would clean up the barn and buy new tack. He just loved it.

BILLY SMITH: Elvis would go at everything in a big way. And when he got the horses, it was no different. That's why we bull-dozed the house back of Graceland, to make a little riding area.

MARTY LACKER: Graceland was only thirteen and three-quarter acres, and the neighbors complained. It really was too small for all those horses. Red accidentally ran Elvis down one day on horseback and dislocated some cartilage in his chest.

BILLY SMITH: Elvis didn't just stop at horses. He also got into all this farm equipment. One night he was in the mood to go shopping, and he decided to go to Sears. We loaded up the car and went to the Southland Mall. People just fell over, you know, to see Elvis Presley in the hardware department at Sears, gathering up hammers and nails and hinges for the pasture gates.

On the way out, Elvis spotted a little twelve-horsepower lawn tractor with a small loading wagon. It was the display model, but he had to have it, and when we got home, Elvis wanted to take everybody for a ride. That wagon wasn't big enough to fool with, but Priscilla, and my wife, and Jerry's new wife, Sandy, and Alan's wife, and another girl, and even Chief, big as he was—Elvis hadn't fired him yet—got in that thing. And Elvis drove. I tried standing on the wagon bar behind him, but it was too small and I couldn't hold on. Elvis said, "Try the front of this thing, Billy. See if you can stay up there." So I mounted the hood and held on to the gas cap.

Of course, since the tractor was new, there wasn't much gas

in it, so Elvis headed out the front gate and went right across the street to a service station. You should have seen the look on the attendant's face when he seen Elvis driving. And me on the hood and a wagon full of people behind. Elvis liked to startle people, so on the way back, he drove through the subdivision behind Graceland, all of us just a-singin' "Old MacDonald Had a Farm." There were some people having a party, so he just pulled the tractor up to their window and we serenaded the whole bunch. Then Elvis tipped his hat, and we drove off. All those people just stood there with their mouths open.

MARTY LACKER: They got back to Graceland, and Elvis started riding the back pasture like it was the Wild West.

BILLY SMITH: He almost threw me off the front of the tractor a couple of times. I was yelling, "Ride 'em, cowboy!" And the more I yelled, the faster he went, trying to throw me off. We went down this one dip and up a hill, and everybody in the wagon let out a scream. Elvis stopped and looked back, and there they all were, piled up. The wagon had done broke loose and tipped up, and all the girls were on the ground yelling, 'cause Chief was on top and he had 'em trapped. All 350 or 400 pounds of him. He was laughing so hard, he couldn't get up. We had to just pull him off.

The next day, we went shopping for a bigger tractor. Elvis bought a Case. But he didn't think it was fast enough, so pretty soon he went to International Harvester and got a really big one. Elvis said, "If this big son of a gun don't do it, we might as well give up."

He had some of the workmen there at Graceland build a trailer out of a truck bed and fill it with hay so he could carry everybody around. But he still wanted me to ride the front. I said, "Wait a minute." And I went to the barn and come back with my saddle. Elvis said, "What in the hell are you going to do with that?" I threw the saddle over the hood and cinched it up. I said, "I'm going to ride this big bucking son of a bitch, that's what."

🕺 🕺 🕺

MARTY LACKER: One day in the fall of '66, Elvis was out riding in the car with Alan and Priscilla when he saw this big ranch for sale on the corner of Highway 301 and Goodman Road in Walls, Mississippi. He liked it, and that night, he went back to look at it again. What he didn't see in the day, but which was really beautiful at night, was a lighted bridge that spanned a fourteen-acre lake. And better yet, a fifty-foot lighted cross behind it. Well, of course, with all this religious stuff in his head, Elvis looked at the cross, and he thought it was a sign from God that he was supposed to have the place.

BILLY SMITH: The way he told it, he just stood there a few minutes without saying anything. Then he said, "This is the most beautiful sight. It's so peaceful. I think it's a good omen." Elvis met the owner, Jack Adams, and told him he was interested. Adams was smart. He invited Elvis to come spend the weekend in the ranch house, to see how he liked it. Of course, we all went.

MARTY LACKER: I said, "Elvis, what are you going to do about beds? There's only one bedroom in this damn place." He said, "Well, me and Priscilla will be in the bedroom. The rest of you can stay in here. We'll get some blankets, and sleeping bags, and stuff."

LAMAR FIKE: Oh, that was horrible! I looked at that house. I said, "Where am I going to sleep, man?" But he loved everybody together.

BILLY SMITH: Lamar got the couch, and the rest of us started scratching for chairs and, finally, just a vacant spot on the floor. To get up for a glass of water was like going through an obstacle course. And there were only two bathrooms. Elvis and Priscilla got one, so the rest of us stood in line the next morning.

MARTY LACKER: Jack Adams also owned an airstrip, which was about ten miles away from the ranch, and Elvis sent me and Alan down to his office to talk to him. The ranch was 150 acres, with another thirteen acres across the road, but the price was inflated: $375,000, or $535,000, if you believe the [Memphis] *Commercial Appeal.* Two days earlier, my brother-in-law, Bernie, had a Mississippi surveyor come out. Adams was asking $2,300 an acre, and the surveyor said it was only worth $1,200. So we were going to try to get the price down because Adams was really trying to take Elvis.

Alan and I started dickering with him, and I brought up the cattle. There were eighteen head of Santa Gertrudis on the ranch. I knew damn well Elvis didn't need the cattle, and they cost too much to take care of, and we weren't going to be at the ranch that much, anyway.

I asked Adams how much the cattle were worth. He said, "They're worth $75,000 easy, but they're in the price." I said, "I'll tell you what. You keep the cattle and knock the seventy-five grand off." He said, "I can't do that. What am I going to do with them? The auction is three months away." I said, "We'll keep them for you for three months if you'll come off the price."

Just when I thought I had him talked into it, the phone rang. I heard him tell Elvis, "I thought we had a deal. You shook my hand." Then he said, "Elvis wants to talk to you, Marty." I got on the phone, and Elvis said, "Don't say another word. I'll pay him the money."

I said, "Elvis, you don't have to." He said, "Don't say anything else. Just come on back here." So I slammed the phone down, and Alan and I went back to the house. Elvis was sitting in the den with his father. He said, "Daddy wants the cattle, and I want the place. We'll pay the price."

It was okay for Vernon to use Elvis's money, but not for Elvis to use Elvis's money. Vernon wanted to be the gentleman farmer because he never amounted to anything on his own. Here was a guy, in charge of all of Elvis's personal business, who could barely read and write, and who prided himself on being a big horse trader. But he couldn't trade anything. I think they even put Graceland up for collateral.

The day before we went to talk to Adams, Alan and I called Elvis's attorney, Charles Davis. We told him we were going to try to negotiate with the owner, and we wanted him to go with us. And Davis said, "What do you want me for? I'm just his attorney." That's the kind of person Vernon chose to represent Elvis.

It ended up being a quick deal. We first went down there in the fall of '66. And we were practically down there every day after that when Elvis was home.

LAMAR FIKE: Elvis was so funny when he bought that ranch. He said, "Good God, I've moved back to Mississippi!"

MARTY LACKER: There were guys to take care of the horses and the cattle. But they didn't know how to take care of the office, and they didn't know Elvis's likes and dislikes. So Elvis made Alan the overseer, which solved two problems. Alan wanted his wife, Jo, around all the time, and Alan was really wanting to come home.

Alan didn't know anything about running a ranch, but there was nothing much to do, just be sure the grass was cut. Elvis liked everything manicured like a golf course. And he wanted the cattle to be fed—he didn't want them to graze. So Alan took care of all of that. But he was always full of pills down there. Alan had a different personality when he had too many pills in him.

One time, Bill Leaptrott, a photographer from one of the Memphis papers, went down there, and Alan almost got in a damn fight with him.

BILLY SMITH: Alan used to have this little-bitty riding mower, a tractor. He was bad about taking sleeping pills, and one day he took a bunch of them and got on the tractor and went plumb to sleep. Fell right off that sucker.

MARTY LACKER: Not too long after he got the ranch, Elvis got on this kick that everybody should have a truck. Not just a pickup truck, but these miniature Ford Rancheros and Chevy El Caminos.

LAMAR FIKE: He bought twenty-two trucks in one day. And three one other day. He was just overspending. He was giving trucks to everybody—even the carpenters and electricians who were working on the place. And a bunch of us had trucks. He gave me a Ford Ranchero and gave Alan one. Tried to give Alan two. This truck salesman from Hernando, Mississippi, had all these things lined up, and Elvis said to Alan, "Pick one out, man." And Alan said, "I already have one, Elvis." So Elvis was kind of exasperated, and he pointed to the truck salesman and said, "Well, give it to him." And Alan said, "He's got one, too." So Elvis was just completely undone. He said, "Hell, find somebody to give the son of a bitch to." He's probably the only guy in the world who tried to give a truck to a truck salesman.

MARTY LACKER: The truck spree happened after we'd come back from California and Bernie had redone the upstairs at Graceland. Elvis had a couple of months before he had to go do his next picture, which was *Clambake,* and he spent almost every day down at the ranch. It was winter. We had a little office by the stable, and I remember, at two o'clock in the morning, we were standing outside there. It was snowing, and Elvis was on a small tractor, pushing the snow and mud out of the way.

Some of us were just standing there, watching him do this. And Vernon walked out of the office and came up to me with an adding machine tape in one hand and a flashlight in the other. He was, like, whining. He said, "Marty, look at this! He's spent $98,000 on trucks and given them away." I said, "What do you want me to do? He's your son."

LAMAR FIKE: Elvis was a freewheeling spender. If he overspent, he'd just say, "Get a ninety-day note and cover it." It meant nothing to him, he had such a cash flow. But it scared Vernon to death.

Elvis was also pouring a fortune—anywhere from $50,000 to $100,000—into that ranch. And it wasn't a working ranch, so it wasn't producing any income. He built a barn, and got all these graders, put roads in, and put in a gasoline tank. That damn wooden fence he put up at the front of the house against the cyclone fence cost God knows what. And he gave three of those carpenters a truck!

MARTY LACKER: The fence went up when the neighbors began complaining that Elvis was making all these changes and causing a lot of racket. A woman across the street started bitching, and she tried to come over to walk around and see what was going on. And Elvis said, "There ain't nobody coming on here. Matter of fact, we're going to build a wall around this friggin' place." It was about eight or ten feet high. You couldn't see over it.

Then the woman started complaining that the fence was an eyesore. So Elvis said, "Goddamnit. If she doesn't like it, and the rest of them don't like it, I'll buy all their damn properties so they can't say anything." But these people figured they could soak him. Some wanted six figures for their property, when everything they owned was worth about twenty thousand bucks.

LAMAR FIKE: Elvis got depressed about shit like that, but not enough to let anything spoil his fun. He'd get out there every day and play cowboy, wear all that western crap, the chaps, the hat, the boots, the rancher coat. He had a vivid imagination. My mother used to call it "being dressed for the part." Elvis dressed for every occasion. When he flew, he'd put a scarf around his neck and fly the plane. At Graceland, we'd joke about it. I'd say, "Alan, where's Elvis?" And Alan would say, "He's upstairs. He's in the middle of the bed with his helmet and shoulder pads on, watching *Monday Night Football*."

MARTY LACKER: In early December of '66, Elvis was at the ranch. This was when it was snowing, and he'd really gone nuts, buying all these trucks and giving them away. One day, he asked me to call Dr. Max Shapiro. I got on the phone, and I said, "We need this, we need that, and we need a prescription for Demerol." And Shapiro said, "Well, I'm not going to mail it to you. You're going to have to come get it. This week, I'll be in Vegas."

Elvis said, "Well, I want you to go." I said, "You want me to fly all the way out there for one little-bitty bottle of Demerol?" And he said, "No, tell him to give you three prescriptions." I said, "Elvis, it's a Nevada prescription. If I have three prescriptions filled in my name in one day, and they check on that, what do you think that's going to look like?" He said, "Then just get two." So I flew all the way out to Las Vegas, and took the prescriptions to two different drugstores, and I flew home. I was full of sleeping pills because I don't like to fly.

By the time I got off the plane, I was pretty well shot. But I went right out to the ranch and gave him the stuff, and then I went home.

About three hours later, the phone rang. Elvis said, "Look, you didn't get me exactly what I need. I want you to go back out to Vegas." I said, "Elvis, I just got home!" He said, "I need you to go out again. Call Dr. Max and tell him what I need." It wasn't my fault. Elvis just decided he wanted something else. But I went back out. And both times, I was just flying out, getting the stuff, and coming back home.

So after the second trip—the same afternoon I came back—Elvis said, "Guess what?" I said, "No, no. I'm not going back out again." Elvis thought a second, and he said, "Find somebody to go with you and have Max put the prescriptions in both names. That way you can switch off."

At the time, Sonny was in California working in the movies. I flew to L.A., met Sonny, got him a ticket, and we flew over to Vegas to meet Shapiro.

Shapiro gave us five prescriptions, three in Sonny's name and two in mine. We got a cab, and Sonny went to the drugstores I had gone to before, and I found two others.

When we finished, we needed a place to stay for a couple of hours until the plane left. So we went over to the Sahara, and Eddie Warren, the head of security, got us a room to sit in for two or three hours. We didn't want to go anywhere because we had pockets full of pills, and a whole briefcaseful. I worried about going through the airport with them, even though they were legal.

I flew back to L.A. with Sonny, and then I went home to Memphis. By this time, I was really dead tired. I gave Elvis the pills, and then I said, "I'm going home. *Do not* call me again."

I went home and got in bed and went to sleep, and about two hours later, I heard this incredible banging at my front door. I said, "Who the hell is it? What do you want?" It was Elvis. He said, "It's me. Open up!" I said, "Hell, no! I'm not opening this door."

He said, "Open the damn door or I'll bust it in!" I said, "I'm not going nowhere, if that's what you're here for." He said, "Just open the damn door." I opened the door, and all I had on was my underwear and a pair of house slippers. Elvis was standing there with Red. I said, "I ain't going to do it!" And they burst out laughing. Elvis said, "No, come outside for a minute." I said, "I'm not dressed. There's snow on the ground, it's freezing out there." He said, "Just come out for a second."

I followed them downstairs and went outside and stood there shivering in my underwear. There was this Ford Ranchero parked next to Elvis's Cadillac. Elvis threw me the keys to it, and he said, "Here. I want to give you this for what you did the last three days."

I said, "You've got to be crazy." And I opened the door, and it had Priscilla's initials in it. He'd given me Priscilla's truck, the same way he'd given Alan her Corvair.

LAMAR FIKE: Not too long after he found the ranch, Elvis got it in his mind to sell Graceland and relocate. He said, "Lamar, I'm tired of all this. I want to move out."

BILLY SMITH: It wasn't that he didn't love Graceland. He just wanted a more modern place.

MARTY LACKER: The house at the ranch was too small. But Elvis liked it so much there that he decided he'd just build a new community, starting with a home for him and Priscilla near the cross and the big lake.

At first, he wanted to build a replica of Graceland. But then he remembered this house in Trousdale Estates in L.A. that was owned by Jim Nicholson, who was one of the partners in American International Pictures. Nicholson had built this beautiful custom house way up in the hills, but he'd never lived in it because by the time it was finished, he and his wife had decided to divorce. It was really gorgeous. It had columns on the walls. And it was so well planned that the dining room had pin lights in the ceiling that shone directly on each place setting.

Elvis really liked that house, and one day just before Christmas of '66, he said to me, "Why don't you take Bernie out to California and show him the Nicholson house?" So we went out, and Bernie said, "No problem. We can duplicate it." This was a $550,000 house, and Bernie thought he could build it for $175,000 to $200,000.

Right after that, Elvis and I and Joe and Joanie went for a little ride on the property, down to Goodman Road. We started walking around, and Elvis said to Joe and Joanie, "You know, I'm going to build a house down here." And then he said, "Wouldn't it be great if we had our own community here?"

I said, "Elvis, for Christmas, why don't you give each of the guys an acre of land and the down payment to build a house right here?" Because that's essentially what he'd done for me. I'd just moved into my new house.

Well, Elvis loved that idea. His face just lit up. He said, "Man, that's fantastic! Let's do it!" And Joe and Joanie were ecstatic, just jumping up and down. Because nobody in the group had a home of his own except Lamar and me.

We started talking about exactly how it would work, and I said, "What you do, Elvis, is have a contract drawn that stipulates that if anybody leaves, he has to sell the house back to you. That way, you'll hold on to your land and keep the outsiders out."

The next day, Elvis told the guys, and then he told Vernon what he was going to do. I could see Vernon's face tighten up, and I knew he was going to try to throw a wrench in it.

About two days later, I said, "Elvis, Bernie's starting to draw the plans on your house." He said, real low-key, "Well, let him go slow." And then he said, "By the way, I can't give the guys the land." I said, "Really? Why not?" He said, "Daddy doesn't think it's a good idea. He says it will mess us up." I said, "How's that?" And I mentioned the agreement about making the guys sell the house back to Elvis if they left.

Elvis said, "Marty, you don't know how much I want to do this, but I can't." I said, "Because of what your father says?" He said, "That's it in a nutshell."

A couple weeks went by, and I said, "Elvis, Bernie's really coming along on the plans for your house." And he said, "You've got to tell him to stop." I said, "Elvis, it's all you've been talking about. You like it so much down here." And he said, low and slow, just emphasizing every word, "Marty, I can't build the house. Just let it be."

LAMAR FIKE: That's when it all stopped. God, just like BOOM! But you couldn't say anything. If you bad-mouthed Vernon, you had your hands full. God Almighty! Vernon would do stuff beyond reality.

BILLY SMITH: Vernon used the excuse that he'd talked to a lawyer and an accountant, and they said the zoning laws and other restrictions wouldn't let him do it. But it would have been so easy to do that.

LAMAR FIKE: Vernon saw that we were going to get something decent, and he didn't want anybody getting anything except himself.

BILLY SMITH: No, Vernon saw that these houses were going to cost the hell out of Elvis. That's what the greedy old sucker saw.

MARTY LACKER: I asked Elvis, "How are you going to break it to the guys?" He said, "I'm not. You are. I can't tell them."

LAMAR FIKE: Right after all that fell through, Elvis got this idea that "If I can't give 'em houses, I'll give 'em trailers."

MARTY LACKER: I said, "Elvis, if you buy house trailers, you've got to pour concrete pads and put in connections and sewer systems and all of that stuff." He said, "I don't give a shit."

He went out the first day and bought one for Billy. It looked like a cabin. Then he saw one he liked, a three-bedroom, and he bought it for himself and Priscilla and let Alan have the house. Vernon liked the trailer so much he decided it was okay if he had one.

LAMAR FIKE: I guess I started all that trailer shit. We were driving by a trailer park one time, and I said, "God, wouldn't it be neat to have a trailer?" Well, it was the worst thing I ever said. Elvis pulled into this place called Green Acres, and by the time he was through, he'd bought twelve trailers at about $140,000. Man, they had them coming down that highway to the farm all lined up. It was just trailers everywhere.

I went into a panic. I said, "Boy, the day ain't come when my ass is going to live in a trailer!" He said, "Why?" I said, "They shake. And it's all one direction! You never turn."

He said, "Then we'll move every trailer around the lake." And the neighbors raised Cain again and complained to the Hernando County building department that an unlicensed trailer park was going in. And that was hell again for a while, until Bernie got the temporary permits to hook up the trailers. Then Bernie's electricians and plumbers worked through the night.

Elvis created his world and lived in his world. I always predicted that Graceland would be 150 buildings because he kept adding on. I said, "Pretty soon it's going to be like a fuckin' town here, for Christ's sake. There'll be buildings everywhere." That's pretty much true now. They're just across the street.

🕺 🕺 🕺

MARTY LACKER: A number of times, we'd be down at the ranch, and Elvis would run out of pills. One night in early '67 that happened, so he and I and Richard got in the car. I was driving, and Elvis was sitting there eating hot dog buns out of a plastic bag. That was one of his new kicks. He said, "Let's go over to Walgreens." There was this pharmacist at the Walgreens drugstore at Whitehaven Plaza who filled a lot of our prescriptions, so we knew him. But this was a Sunday. And I said, "Elvis, they're not open."

We pulled into the shopping center, and sure as hell, the store was closed. Right across the street was the little Whitehaven Pharmacy. And they were closed, too. But they had a transom at the top of their door. Elvis looked at me and Richard, and he said, "You know, it'd probably be easy for you guys to get in that store." But I just kept on driving. There was no way I was going to stop.

Elvis said, "Wait a minute. Does anybody know where the Walgreens pharmacist lives? He's like a doctor. He's probably got all kinds of shit at his house."

I said, "What are you going to do, Elvis? Go to his house, knock on his door, and say, 'Hi there, I need some stuff'?" And Elvis said, "Well, hell, that's a good idea. Stop at that phone booth. He probably lives right around here, since he works out here." And sure enough, the man did live out in Whitehaven.

Elvis said, "Do you know where the street is?" I said, "Yeah." And Elvis just pointed his finger like "Go on."

The guy opened the door, and there stood Elvis Presley, with this big sheepskin coat on and a cowboy hat. Of course, the man was absolutely stunned. And Elvis relied on that. He used to do that with doctors, too. The pharmacist said, "Elvis! What are you doing here?"

Elvis said, "Uh, I just was wondering if I could talk to you for a while." So we went into the man's kitchen and sat down at the table.

Because he knew the *PDR* so well, Elvis knew exactly what symptoms he needed to fake to get his pills. He said to the pharmacist, "You know, I've had these bad aches, and I've had trouble sleeping. That's why my doctor prescribes," and he named the sleeping pills and uppers he wanted—Tuinals, Placidyls, Dexamil, Dexedrine, Escatrol, and Desbutal. He said, "Except I can't get ahold of my doctor, and I haven't slept in three nights."

Elvis said, "I know your store is closed today. And I really do apologize for bothering you at home. But I figured that maybe you had some medication here that I could have."

And the pharmacist said, "Well, sure." And he got up to go to his medicine chest. Well, instead of sitting there waiting for him, Elvis followed to see what he had. Even if it wasn't something he'd asked for, he was going to take it.

We all got up and followed the guy into his bathroom—four people, now, in this little room, standing in front of the medicine cabinet. And it was just full of bottles. The pharmacist pulled one off, and then he thought about it, and he said, "Well, Elvis, the store will be open tomorrow." And Elvis said, "Yeah, but I might need this, and this . . . " And he started picking through the bottles.

The guy was a nice old man, really, and he looked at Elvis and he said, "I really shouldn't be doing this." And Elvis said, "Hey, if you don't tell anybody, we won't tell anybody. And whatever you give me, I'll get a prescription to cover it." The guy said, "Well, okay." And Elvis walked out of that house with a bag full of stuff.

BILLY SMITH: The hot dog and hamburger bun kick was a strange one. He would tie that wrapper around the horn of the damn saddle and ride along eating those things.

A lot of times, he'd take two or three sleeping pills, and he couldn't sleep 'em off. Because you can't sleep when you've taken five hundred milligrams of something else beforehand. Hell, he'd just get up after two hours and go on about his normal day. Let me tell you, Lee Marvin in *Cat Ballou* didn't have anything on Elvis. Because he'd get up on the horse just about the time the sleeping pills took effect, and the faster he rode, the more he leaned.

MARTY LACKER: He'd walk around the ranch blown out of his skull, with his cowboy hat on, gloves, cowboy boots, jeans, and this big, padded pile coat that made him look even bigger. He'd be so stuffed in that jacket that his walk was almost like a waddle. And in his hand he'd have that plastic, see-through bag of hot dog buns. He looked like a little kid, walking around with a sack in his hand.

He'd talk to you, and he'd be slurring his words, and he'd take a bite of the bun, sort of ripping it off. And then you couldn't understand what he was saying, for sure. It was just this muffled noise, somebody talking through bread.

LAMAR FIKE: He had something in his hand all the time. Billy says it was from nerves. I don't know. But I do know that when he was down there at the ranch, he ate whatever he wanted—hamburgers, steaks, and all kinds of stuff that put weight on him. But he started blowing up in January and February of '67, and he had this movie, *Clambake*, to do in March. I couldn't believe how big he got.

MARTY LACKER: One reason he started gaining so much weight was because he was depressed about his career and depressed about his father killing his plans for the commune. He was depressed about not having a big house down there at the ranch. And he might have been depressed about having to marry Priscilla.

I still had it in the back of my mind that he was going to find some way out of it. In fact, the wedding was supposed to have been right after the first of the year, in '67. But it was already early '67, and he kept postponing it.

LAMAR FIKE: After a while, Elvis lost interest in the ranch. He was tired of hearing Vernon bitch about how it was losing money, and Priscilla didn't like it when he went down there because he was playing with the guys and not spending enough time alone with her. It broke his spirit, in a way. Eventually, Elvis had Alan just auction stuff off.

BILLY SMITH: The ranch was a bad deal to start with, but it turned out to be a good one. They put it up for sale in '68, and a guy named D. L. "Lou" McClellan bought it for $440,000 in May of '69. He was going to put a recreational club on it. Vernon carried the note. McClellan made three initial payments of $50,000, plus he built a swimming pool and another building. But he lost it, and it come back to Vernon and Elvis. They sold it again, in '73, to the Boyle Investment Company, which paid more because of the additional building and the pool. So Elvis made another $75,000. That was about a $200,000 profit from the original cost.

MARTY LACKER: After Elvis died, it was sold again, or maybe a couple of times. The new owner, a guy named Montesi, started charging people $2 a head to walk over the same ground Elvis walked. Now it's a cattle farm again.

CHAPTER 36

THE FALL

When Elvis arrived in California in March of '67 for wardrobe fittings on *Clambake*, his twenty-fifth film, Colonel Parker and director Arthur Nadel were astonished to discover that Elvis's weight had ballooned from 170 to 200 pounds during his vacation on the ranch. Furious, Nadel ordered wardrobe to redesign Elvis's costumes to try to disguise his bulk. For his part, Elvis started gulping diet pills.

Clambake, which drew on *The Prince and the Pauper* for its plot, would be among the most forgettable of Elvis's pictures, if not for an incident that occurred shortly before filming began—an accident that led directly to Colonel's boldest claim on Elvis's earnings and to the beginning of the end of the group as they had known it.

LAMAR FIKE: When he had pills in him, Elvis would get dizzy. And he got up in the middle of the night to use the toilet, and he slipped or fell over the TV cord and hit his head on the bathtub. And boy, all hell broke loose.

BILLY SMITH: About eight o'clock in the morning, some of the guys were in the den, and Elvis come out and said, "I fell and hit my head. I think I need to see a doctor." He was holding the back of his head, and he had a pretty good bump on it.

MARTY LACKER: My first reaction was, "I wonder if he did it on purpose, to postpone the wedding?" But we got him into bed and Esposito phoned the Colonel, and somebody else called this doctor that Elvis had used for prescriptions. He brought portable X-ray equipment to the house, and I held Elvis's head straight because he could barely hold it up. The doctor checked him and said,

"You've got a mild concussion. You can't start the movie right now." And then he told Colonel they'd have to hold off shooting for about two weeks.

Colonel was just beside himself. Out in the hall, he said, "Goddamn you guys, why do you let him get this way? He's going to mess up everything! They'll tear up the contract!" He said, "I want one of you with Elvis twenty-four hours a day, sitting by his bed in his room. If he has to go to the bathroom, one of you walk with him. Do not let him walk on his own."

Then Colonel went back in and talked to Elvis, and he flat laid it down to him. At the time, the Colonel was getting 25 percent. And he said, "Here's the way it is. From now on, you're going to listen to everything I say. I'm going to set down these guidelines, and you'd better follow them. Otherwise, I'm going to leave you, and that will ruin your career. And because I'm going to do all this extra work for you, I want 50 percent of your contract." And Elvis meekly—*meekly*—said yes.

Colonel also said, "From now on, I'm changing these guys of yours. If they don't like it, they can get the hell out. When you get better, we're calling a meeting with all of them and I'm going to tell them exactly how it's going to be. I'm going to say I'm speaking for you. And if you open up your mouth, I'm gone."

BILLY SMITH: Elvis asked me to stay in his room with him and sleep on the cot. He wanted somebody to watch him, and I was a fairly light sleeper. I stayed for about ten days, got his food for him, and never left the room. I knew he was pissed at Colonel about something, but he never would really come out and say what it was. He mentioned he had to redo his contract with Colonel, but he showed no outward emotion. But I could tell that inside, he was just eat up with it.

I had no idea that Colonel had told him he was taking 50 percent. I heard it on the news like everybody else, after Elvis passed away. The afternoon of the second meeting, I had to leave the room. Colonel was coming up. They were going to sign the new contract, and he didn't want me to know what it said.

Best I can remember, we all thought Colonel was taking 25 percent, but one time back in the early sixties, Elvis slipped and said, "That old son of a bitch is paid more than any other manager now. He gets 35 percent." It was rare of him to have even mentioned that much about business. And it shocked me. I thought, "Well, God, what's happening?" I have no idea why it went to 35 percent. But 50 percent? God Almighty!

LAMAR FIKE: Why the uproar? Back then, deals were made like that every day. A friend of mine managed [country singer] David Houston, and they had a fifty-fifty deal forever. I'm talking 50 percent of the net, or after expenses. That's not done anymore, of course. Most contracts are 25 percent of the gross, but 10 percent is paid toward the agent.

I'm sure the Colonel padded some things, but I don't think he ever intentionally ripped Elvis off. Give the devil his due. Elvis at his best was not the easiest artist to manage.

MARTY LACKER: Lamar seems to have difficulty realizing what the Colonel did. Colonel took his 50 percent before the damn net. He took expenses out of *Elvis's* 50 percent.

LAMAR FIKE: Dee Presley told me that Colonel had 35 percent, and Vernon had 15 percent of the management contract. Because Colonel knew the key to Elvis financially was Vernon. Later on, in '74, Colonel talked to Vernon when they set up Boxcar Enterprises. That was a merchandising operation only, but it changed Colonel's overall percentage of Elvis a little bit. Colonel was already looking ahead, see.

MARTY LACKER: When it came time for that second meeting, Colonel told all the guys to be there. Colonel got to the house, and he and Joe went into Elvis's bedroom. About thirty minutes later, the intercom buzzed in my room, and Esposito told me to come in. Elvis was sitting on this little lounge seat, staring at the floor. He wouldn't look at me. Colonel was sitting next to him, and Joe was sitting across from them.

Parker did all the talking. He said, "We're making a few changes around here. Mr. Presley and I have discussed it, and from now on, you won't have to be concerned with being foreman. Mr. Esposito will be the foreman. And no one is to come to Elvis with any problems. They'll deal with Mr. Esposito."

And he said, "Especially, nobody is to come to Elvis to talk about religion." He meant Geller, of course. He said, "I want all the books that were brought up here taken out and burned," which Elvis and Priscilla did together, according to her book. And Colonel said he didn't want Geller coming around anymore.

Then he said, "Mr. Lacker, you will handle special projects for Mr. Presley. That's the way he wants it." I looked at Elvis and he still wouldn't look at me. To see Elvis acting that way, and to hear this old, fat bastard spewing edicts like he was Elvis's ruler, just made me sick. In fact, it destroyed my desire to be part of the group.

Colonel said to me, "The first project you are going to handle is the wedding." I thought it was a joke because the Colonel and Joe had already planned the wedding.

Then Colonel said, "Okay, let's go out and talk to the boys." Everybody was in the living room. And Elvis just kept staring at the floor.

Colonel said, "From now on, you guys will not go to Mr. Presley with your personal needs and concerns. Because you're causing him problems, and you're not taking care of him. You go to Mr. Esposito, and he'll take care of it." Then he looked around the room, and he said, "Also from now on, you guys are going to really work. In addition, we're going to cut back on some of the expenses and the salaries that people are being paid around here." Of course, nobody was paid anything, really. And he said, "If you guys don't like it, you know where the door is."

BILLY SMITH: I remember that afternoon real well. And I especially remember that before Colonel started talking, Elvis said, "Fellas, the Colonel has got some things to say. And he's speaking for both of us. What he's going to tell you is coming straight from me." Colonel told us that Joe would be the foreman. And then he said, "Right now you will continue out this picture with Elvis. But due to expenses, after you get back home, some of you will probably be let go." He said, "It's nothing that anybody's done wrong. It's just business. We have to cut back."

We all kind of looked at each other in disbelief. Elvis was getting a million dollars a movie. I think I was getting $200 a week.

I thought I was going to be one of the ones terminated. Or if not terminated, I knew I'd have to quit. Because me and Jo were getting an apartment in California. Colonel made it clear that when Elvis and Priscilla got married, the guys wouldn't be living at the house, and with cutting down on expenses, there wouldn't be any rent money paid for the ones who wanted to stay out in California. So right after the Colonel's little speech, I went to Elvis and said, "Look, I'll have to be one of the ones that has to go." He said, "Why?" I said, "Because I can't afford to keep a home in Memphis and an apartment out here." Elvis said, "That doesn't apply to you. You'll get your apartment out here, and it'll be paid for."

MARTY LACKER: As it turned out, there were no pay cuts, and nobody was actually let go. The idea was to get people to leave voluntarily.

BILLY SMITH: When you look at this, you see Elvis had a hell of a lot thrown on him at one time. He had a head injury. The studio was coming down on him. He was being forced to sign this new contract. Colonel was now maneuvering the guys. And pressure was being put on him by Priscilla and her parents to marry.

And, of course, on top of it, he was taking drugs. Which I know damn well the Colonel knew. But instead of getting help for Elvis, Colonel took advantage of his weakness.

MARTY LACKER: A big question here is why Vernon didn't do something to get Elvis's drug use under control. But to the very end, and even after Elvis died, Vernon denied that Elvis used any kind of drugs. You'd have to be a blooming idiot not to know.

BILLY SMITH: I wonder if Vernon convinced himself that Elvis needed all that "medication." Otherwise, if he loved him that much, why didn't he do something? There were two people who could have legally helped Elvis—Vernon and, after the wedding, Priscilla. And both of them turned their back. They just ignored it.

I heard Vernon and Elvis argue about it a little. Elvis would say, "Look, goddamnit, I don't want to hear no more! Get the hell out." And Vernon would buckle under.

MARTY LACKER: Vernon couldn't do anything about Elvis because Elvis was the man of the house. And Vernon was afraid if he upset him too much, Elvis would kick him out. It's as simple as that.

🕺 🕺 🕺

LAMAR FIKE: Right after the *Clambake* incident, every relationship Elvis had was strained. With the Colonel, with his father, with Priscilla, with the guys. Colonel empowered himself and put his hand into the group really strong. That was the beginning of the end of the group. And Elvis started getting angrier. And stranger.

🕺 🕺 🕺

MARTY LACKER: During those weeks in March that Elvis was recuperating before he went to work on *Clambake,* he came back to Memphis and went over to Nashville to record. That session didn't amount to much. I think he only got one song down, "Suppose." He was too scattered, for one thing.

On the way back from Hollywood, we got about forty-five miles out of Memphis, in Forrest City, Arkansas, and we started picking up WHBQ, which was George Klein's station. George was on the air that night, and he played "Green, Green Grass of Home," which Tom Jones had just brought out. Elvis liked it, but it put him in a real sad mood. He was driving the big Greyhound, and he stopped at a pay phone and had me call George and make him play it again. Pretty soon, he was stopping at *every* pay phone. George played that thing three or four times in a row. Which he wasn't supposed to do. He was risking his job. But Elvis wanted to hear it because he was just wallowing in how blue it made him feel. He was crying a little.

I was sitting in that tall seat up front that lets you look over the top windows of the bus. And I had tears in my eyes myself because I was thinking of all my family. You know the song. It talks about going home and seeing all the familiar things and faces: "And there to meet me is my mama and papa." It's a real homesick song. And it just hit us all, I guess because things were so bleak for us right then.

We got to Graceland, and we were getting everything unloaded, and I was getting ready to go home. I said to Patsy, "Let me see if Elvis needs anything." I went in the hallway, and I saw Elvis near the front door, next to where his mother and father's room was. He was kneeling on one knee, and he had his head in his hands. And he was sobbing. Geller was standing over him. I said, "Elvis, what's wrong?" He was totally shaken. He said, "Marty, I saw my mama." I said, "What do you mean?" I knew it was just the song. But he said, "I walked in the door, and I saw her standing here. I saw her, man."

Elvis went upstairs to his quarters. We didn't see him for about a week.

LAMAR FIKE: Shelley Fabares was in *Clambake*. She'd already been in *Girl Happy* and *Spinout*. She was another one Elvis was in love with. But she basically held him off. She was married to [record producer] Lou Adler.

MARTY LACKER: Shelley was just a downright nice, sweet girl. We used to have a lot of fun with her. And Elvis really took a liking to her. They used to talk a lot, alone in his trailer or in the dressing room. But I think that was it. One day, she and Elvis came walking out of the dressing room, and Elvis looked at me and said, "I told her." I said, "You told her?" He said, "Yeah, I told her about the wedding." No one outside the group knew about it. He didn't want to tell anybody.

LAMAR FIKE: I was *in* the group, and he didn't tell me.

BILLY SMITH: Elvis didn't even tell me about the wedding until we were going back out to California to do the picture. And he said he was going to get married right *after* the picture. It kind of hurt my feelings. I said, "So? I went down to the justice of the peace and got married. It's quicker." And then I said, "You didn't come to mine, so what's the big deal?" And he said, "I'm Elvis Presley, that's the big deal."

LAMAR FIKE: There for about two years, '66 to '68, Elvis got hit by a lot of tragic family stuff. It started when Gladys's brother, Tracy, who had the mind of an eight-year-old, died of kidney failure at forty-nine.

BILLY SMITH: Uncle Tracy caught some disease when he was lit-tle—scarlet fever or rheumatic fever. He was real slow, but not really mentally unbalanced. And he was partially deaf. He was real easygoing. He loved kids. And he generally liked to be around people. He only weighed about 165 pounds. But I don't think he knew his own strength. He was so strong he could hurt you with-out even meaning to. Especially when he got mad.

MARTY LACKER: One time in the early sixties, Tracy came in the Jungle Room where we all were, and something set him off. He was standing there, grinning about something, and all of a sud-den he just started gritting his teeth and looking around. Elvis said, "Watch him." Elvis loved him, but I think Tracy was also a source of amusement for him. I looked over, and Tracy was clenching his fists at his sides and making sounds like he was getting ready to explode. Elvis said, "There he goes."

BILLY SMITH: Gladys took care of Tracy until she died, and then my daddy looked after him. They were really the only ones who could handle him. Sometimes Tracy would stay down there at the gate with Daddy and pretend he was a gate guard, too. He lived with us up there in that house behind Graceland. Somebody came to see me one time, and Tracy told him nobody was home because he thought the guy meant he was coming to see Elvis.

Well, the guy jumped the fence and come in our house and sat down on the couch. Tracy found him in there and asked him for a cigarette. The guy gave it to him, and Tracy took it, and then he just knocked the hell out of him. He said, "Don't never jump the fence. Elvis wouldn't like it. You ask Tracy." The guy said, "I did ask you, Tracy!" And Tracy said, "You didn't say you were coming to see Billy."

LAMAR FIKE: When Tracy got down-and-out, he'd say to Elvis, "I got my nerves in the dirt." The first time Elvis heard that, he laughed like hell. He thought that was great. And then he gave Tracy some money. That's what he wanted, anyhow.

BILLY SMITH: Tracy used to come up to Graceland and tell Elvis he'd come for what he owed him. Of course, Elvis didn't owe him anything. He meant he needed some money. As soon as Elvis got home from California, Tracy would appear and say, "I come up to get what you owe me." And Elvis would say, "Uncle Tracy, how much you figure I owe you?" And Tracy would say, "Well, I need $5 for tobacco, and I might get some socks—that'd be about $5. And maybe $10 for groceries." And then he'd say, "And I got to have $20 for my woman." Meaning he was going to hire a prosti- , tute. So he figured up $40. That's what Elvis owed him. Every time it was the same amount, $40.

LAMAR FIKE: The same year Tracy died, Elvis's uncle, Pat Biggs, died. He was married to Delta Mae, Vernon's sister.

MARTY LACKER: One night in '66, just before Elvis bought the ranch, he was out in the barn at Graceland with the horses. I happened to be out there, too. The phone rang—the intercom—and he picked it up, which he usually didn't do. He said, "Yeah?" like that. And he said, "Okay," and he punched the line.

It was Delta calling from Montgomery, Alabama, saying Pat had just died. She was all alone in a sleazy motel, and she didn't know what to do. They'd taken Pat's body over to the funeral home, and she needed some help. I could see tears in Elvis's eyes because he really cared for Pat. I heard him say to Delta, "Don't worry. You can stay here for a while. We'll get you back here some way."

I saw how it was affecting him, so I tapped him on the shoulder, and I mouthed the words, "Tell her I'll come get her." So he said, "Aunt Delta, I'm going to send Marty Lacker to bring you up here."

Her car was down there, and Elvis told me to fly down and drive her back in her car. I said, "If you don't mind, I'd like to take Richard." He said, "No problem. I appreciate you doing this." So Richard and I flew to Birmingham and drove to Montgomery in a rented Cadillac.

We got to the motel, and we put her in the backseat of the Cadillac, and she didn't say one word all the way to Memphis. Not even when we got to Graceland. We pulled up to the house and opened the car door for her and still, not a word of thanks, nothing. Not even when Vernon came over and said, "Well, I hope you're okay, Delta." Now, granted, I'm sure she was grieving, and depressed, and maybe in shock from Pat's death. But she was also just not a very nice woman.

BILLY SMITH: When it come to her personality, Aunt Delta was a whole lot like Vernon. She hated everybody. Pat had been a big-time gambler. At times, he had hundreds of thousands of dollars. But when he died, he was completely broke. Elvis paid for his funeral. Pat was the one who instilled the desire in Elvis to own something of his own, like a nice car or a nice house. So when Pat died, Elvis felt like he needed to take Delta in, give her a place to live. He loved her, but he took her in mostly out of loyalty, same way he did Grandma. Delta had a horrible temper, and she drank too much. And, of course, Elvis didn't want any whiskey around Graceland.

LAMAR FIKE: Elvis created places for people, so Delta would go to the grocery, run household errands, and pitch in with the kitchen help.

BILLY SMITH: I think Delta Mae done a lot, from keeping up with all the car keys, to making sure everything was in its place. She kept Elvis's room immaculate. And she made sure he had all the stuff he liked to eat and looked after all the little things, like putting water in his refrigerator upstairs and the current *TV Guide* in his room.

MARTY LACKER: Sometimes Delta shared a room with Grandma, but other times she slept in a room off the kitchen. After Grandma died, in '80, she moved into Grandma's room, which was off the front hall. Delta lived there until she died in '93. All those tours would come through Graceland, and she was right there—a kind of living relic. But you never saw her. They said she was real sick. I'm sure she was still drinking.

After Elvis became famous, his family started hounding him for money. It made him feel they didn't really love him. He said to me, "I'm going to make sure that Billy doesn't turn out like the rest of them."

One day, Elvis was really agitated. He said, "When I get home,

I can't even come downstairs because there's all this family sitting around waiting to get money off me. That's the only time they come up here."

It got to a point where he had closed-circuit television installed, with monitors upstairs in his bedroom, so that he could check before he'd come down. A lot of times, he stayed in his room rather than face them.

LAMAR FIKE: Did you see *Zorba the Greek*? Remember the second after the death, when all those women rush in like vultures and snatch everything in the room, just pick it bare? Elvis's relatives were sort of like that. They'd turn your stomach, man.

MARTY LACKER: Dealing with Elvis's family—on top of this new stuff with the Colonel and Joe—was really more than most people could take. They disliked me and Joe, in particular, because we were ethnic and because we carried the money and wrote the checks. And they thought, "Elvis has given you stuff, and he ain't given us nothin'." And they especially didn't like it when my family lived at Graceland. Three of them tried to kill me—literally. Two in the sixties and one in the seventies.

Elvis's uncle Johnny was all screwed up in the head from that fight he had when he was young, when those five guys jumped him and Travis. And when we lived at Graceland, Johnny came up there one night in about '64 or '65, when Jerry Schilling first started. Jerry and I were sitting up talking, and there was nobody else around. Elvis was upstairs, and the maid, Hattie, was in the kitchen. Somebody banged on the front door, and Hattie answered it, and there was this strange man standing there. He'd climbed over the fence or something. She screamed and slammed the door, and the guy ran away.

I went in my room and got my gun and stuck it in my waistband, under my shirt. Jerry was getting ready to leave, but I said, "You'd better hang around for a while," in case the guy showed up again. Well, just then, Johnny came through the backdoor. He was shuffling and holding his side. And he was bleeding pretty bad. On top of it, he was drunk out of his mind. I said, "Johnny, what's wrong with you?" He looked at me funny, and he said, "You son of a bitch! You're the one that stabbed me, and I'm going to get you!"

I said, "Johnny, what the hell are you talking about?" I was standing at the foot of the steps that led into the Jungle Room from the kitchen. And Jerry was standing right behind me.

Johnny said, "I'm going to take care of you once and for all. You were in that bar, and you stabbed me." And he reached in his pocket and pulled out this knife, and he started coming towards me. I said, "Johnny, I want to tell you something. You take one more step . . . " And I lifted my shirt up, and I took my gun out of my pants. I said, "I'm going to blow your fuckin' head off." And then I told him he'd better get out because if Elvis found out he was there, he was going to have a problem."

Well, he still wouldn't leave. So I told Schilling to call upstairs and let Elvis know what was going on. Elvis said, "You tell that son of a bitch he can either get out of my house now or he'd better never come back again." Jerry told him, and Johnny froze in his tracks. They were all afraid of that because that would cut them off from the money.

Then Jerry said, "Marty, Elvis wants to talk to you." I got on the phone, and Elvis said, "What's wrong with that crazy son of a bitch?" I told him Johnny had been stabbed, that there was blood coming out of his side, and he thought I was the one who did it. I said, "Elvis, I know he's your uncle. But if he keeps coming, I'm going to have to shoot his ass."

Elvis said, "You tell that bastard to go to a hospital. No, you *take* him." I said, "Elvis, I ain't taking him nowhere." I said, "I'll call a damn cab and tell the driver to take him to the hospital, but I'm not getting in the car with this crazy bastard." Elvis said, "Well, yeah, you're right." He said, "Be sure to tell him if he doesn't get in the cab, I'll never see him again." So Johnny agreed.

When the cab came, the driver took one look at Johnny and said, "What do you want me to do with him?" I said, "Take him to the nearest hospital." I gave the driver a fifty-dollar bill, and I told him he didn't have to wait for him. Because I didn't give a shit whether he ever came back or not. Johnny died in '68, and I can't say I was sorry.

LAMAR FIKE: Between all the pills and all his confrontations with that family, Marty should be dead, really. They kept threatening to put him in the ground.

MARTY LACKER: Another night, I was downstairs in the basement where the three TVs are, filling out expense reports. And here came Elvis's Aunt Clettes down the steps, drunk. She saw me there, and she stood by the doorway with this big purse in her hand. If looks could kill, I would have been deader than a doornail. She said, "I don't like you, you no good son of a bitch. I'm going to get rid of you right now." And she put her hand in her purse and came out with the biggest damn butcher knife you ever saw in your life.

There's only one door out of that room, and she was in front of it. And she started coming towards me. I said, "Clettes, let me tell you something. If Elvis comes walking down those steps, or if he ever finds out what you're doing, he's never going to let you in this house again. You won't be able to get near him."

She stopped, and she looked at me with her drunken head bobbing, and *just then*, thank God, somebody—and I've forgotten who it was—came to the top of the steps and hollered, "Marty, are you down there?" I yelled, "Yeah, I am! You better come on down!" He said, "Well, no. You come on up. Elvis wants to see you." And when Clettes heard that, she put the knife back in her bag.

When Delta moved in, I was afraid we were going to have more episodes like that. And I was right. It just took a while.

BILLY SMITH: When we went back to California to finish *Clambake*, Elvis finally started showing his anger about everything. Since the early sixties, he'd had this tendency to destroy an entire room when he got upset. But he'd usually disguise *why* he was mad.

Anyway, this day on Rocca Place, he was going to play this record. There were several of us in the room—Red, and Richard, and Jerry and Sandy, and me and my wife, and Priscilla. Well, the record kept skipping, and Elvis tried to play it over and over. And he was acting like he was patient about it. But when we come into the room that morning, before we ever started playing the record, you could tell he was upset about something. Elvis had a hard time hiding it if something was bothering him.

Finally, he said, "If this son of a bitch jumps one more time . . . "
Well, it did. And he took a cane and beat that record, and then he
broke just stacks and stacks of records. And then he started in
on the record player—the speakers and everything. He threw it
across the room, and he started cussing up a storm at Joe's
brother, Frank, who give him the thing. This was shortly after the
50 percent contract with Colonel episode. So it wasn't about the
skipping of the record.

Elvis was swinging that cane every which way—even broke
the little windows out of the side of the door and started clearing
the shelves. And his hair fell in his face, and he looked like some
kind of lunatic. Me and Red just fell out. We were dying laughing
on the floor. But Jo was afraid Elvis would get mad at us because
we were laughing at him. And it did set him off to doing other
things—he beat the piano and destroyed these feathers that
Priscilla had. Just tore 'em up. Then he said, real angry-like,
"What in the hell are you all laughing at?" And we said, "We're
laughing at you. You look like some damn wild man who just
swung out of the tree limbs."

He got to thinking about it, and he got tickled, and then he
started laughing. We tried not to let things bother him. But we
had our work cut out for us. And it got to be more than most of
us could handle.

CHAPTER 37

"LOVE, HONOR, CHERISH, AND COMFORT"

After months of inventive stall-and-delay tactics, Elvis finally agreed to a spring wedding, shortly after the completion of *Clambake.*

MARTY LACKER: When Colonel put me in charge of special projects, he gave me the title of Special Chief Aide to Elvis. A throwaway title. But Elvis continued to rely on me as he always had. The difference was I didn't write the checks anymore and I didn't have to deal with Parker.

Almost everything about the wedding had already been done. But one night we were talking, and Elvis said, "I'm going to need a tuxedo, and I'd really like something different." So the next night, when I was blown out of my skull, I sat down and started drawing.

I'd designed some of his clothes before—costumes for *Spinout* and *Double Trouble.* He was tired of the wardrobe that they were making him wear. For example, he said, "I'd like to have a bolero jacket with straps instead of buttons."

So we sat in his office upstairs at Graceland one night, and although I'm not an artist, I just started drawing. He told me a couple of other things he wanted, like piping on a jacket and a vest.

The next day, when the Colonel called, Elvis asked him to talk to MGM about using the sketches. And Colonel said he'd try. The call came back that they'd take our suggestions if I sent the instructions with the drawings. And they told me to work with Lambert Marks, in wardrobe, who was a great guy.

I sent all the stuff out to Lambert, and he called me and said, "Have you ever done this before?" I said, "No." He said, "Well, it's fairly good." He said, "We're going to go ahead and start making it up, and when Elvis comes out to do wardrobe, we'll fit it on him."

I told him that was great and that I'd go to some of the stores where we shopped to get his shirts and boots. The studios used to buy these $10 shirts at the stores and put them down on the budget as $65 custom-made shirts. That's part of how they make their money in Hollywood.

There used to be a cheap shoe store called Hardy's Shoes. That was the only store in Memphis that sold Italian dress boots that zipped and came up over the ankle. They cost $10.95. Those are the black dress boots that Elvis used to wear. They'd last maybe six months, a year. When they discontinued the style Elvis liked, he bought the pattern.

Anyway, about three weeks into filming, an assistant director came over to me one day and said someone in wardrobe wanted to see me in his office. I thought maybe he was going to tell me how much he liked my designs. But when I got there, I could tell that wasn't what he had in mind. He was one of those old Hollywood barracudas, and he was sitting with another guy.

He started out by saying, "It sure was nice of you to help us on this wardrobe." And then he said, "But there are some things you don't understand about our business." He started telling me how they structure their budgets, and what they write off, and what they count as expenses. He said, "We have to do certain things." I said, "What are you getting at?" And he said, "The bottom line is, I'd appreciate it if you wouldn't do it anymore."

I said, "Why don't you tell Elvis all this and see what he's got to say, since he's getting 10 percent of this fuckin' picture? Because in other words, what you're telling me, sir, is that you're stealing money out of his pocket."

So when Elvis mentioned this tuxedo for the wedding, I thought, "Well, okay." And I came up with that brocaded paisley material. And he loved it. That kind of inspired me, so I designed a wedding gown for Priscilla. And Elvis loved that, too. He said, "Man, that's beautiful!" I gave him a copy of it, and he showed it to Priscilla.

The next day, she came up to me and said, "I'd appreciate it if you'd mind your own business." I said, "No problem." And she bought a cheap gown off the rack in L.A. and sewed her own train on it.

🕺 🕺 🕺

LAMAR FIKE: In 1990, Albert Goldman wrote an article for *Life*. He said he'd rethought his biography and come to the "inescapable conclusion" that Elvis had killed himself. He talked to David Stanley, who supposedly told him that Elvis had tried to kill himself in '67, at Graceland, just before the wedding. Goldman said Elvis and Priscilla got into a whopper of a fight, and Elvis took a big handful of downers.

A couple of hours went by, and Vernon supposedly answered the phone and turned to David and the others and said, "My son tried to kill himself!" The story goes that they got in the car and raced over there, and Vernon hurried up the steps crying, "Son, please don't die! Don't die!" Elvis was comatose on the bed, with all these paramedics giving him oxygen and trying to revive him.

But I'll tell you, I never heard that. And David and I are thick as thieves. Elvis was just not the suicidal type. If he committed suicide, he'd want fifteen or twenty people around. It would have been the hemlock routine—just as dramatic as anything you'd want to see. By the way, *Life* apologized for running that article earlier this year.

MARTY LACKER: Elvis never tried to commit suicide. To begin with, he believed in God too much. Besides, he wasn't even in Memphis. He didn't finish shooting *Clambake* until April 27, and the wedding was May 1.

I think Elvis tried to psych himself up for the wedding. But one minute, he'd cut Priscilla down, and the next he'd take up for her. The big mistake Priscilla made was trying to *control.* Elvis had her trying to control his personal life, and the Colonel trying to control the business end, and Vernon trying to keep him from having any fun at all.

In some ways, Priscilla's agenda was the worst. She wanted to keep him from going places and leaving her at home—keep him from spending time with the guys. She wanted Elvis to be a normal husband. It shows how little she understood him, and his life. There's no way in the world that Priscilla, or any other woman, could have gotten rid of all the guys. She worked on them, and, eventually, one or two got fired, and a couple left. But I knew that Elvis wasn't going to brush all the guys off because he knew he needed them. Nobody could change Elvis Presley. Not really.

When we went out to California for *Clambake*, Priscilla came along, and she and I were going to fix up the Rocca Place house. Elvis wanted his room changed, for example.

From day one, Priscilla and I had arguments. I was taking sleeping pills, and if I didn't have to be at the studio, I didn't see any reason to get up at four-thirty or five o'clock in the morning. So I'd sleep until nine. Well, Priscilla would start banging on my door real early. I'd say, "The stores aren't open yet!" And she'd say, "We need to figure out what we should get." I'd tell her to get away from my damn door. And I'd go back to sleep.

When Elvis started bringing Priscilla around, his whole attitude changed. He always loved to shock people. He'd say nasty stuff in the company of people who were very prim and proper, just for shock value. And before this attitude change, he'd put Priscilla up to say all kinds of things to the guys. Like one time, when she was about eighteen or nineteen, we were riding in the car, just Elvis, Priscilla, and myself. I heard whispers in the back, and all of a sudden Priscilla said, "You know, it's colder than a gravedigger's dick."

And Elvis cussed like a sailor. He'd say anything in front of the wives. Like, "That no good cocksucker . . . "

Well, in this period just before the wedding, Priscilla got up on her high horse, and she had the nerve to say to Elvis, "I wish you'd talk to Marty about using bad language in front of me." So he came over to me one day, and Priscilla was standing there. He said, "Look, I need to ask you to quit using that filthy language in front of Priscilla." I said, "What?" And he repeated it.

I said, "What do you think you do in front of my wife?" I told him, "I'll make you a deal, cocksucker. When you stop, I will." I had a sort of sly grin on my face, but I wasn't sure how he was going to take it. But he burst out laughing. And Priscilla stamped her foot and walked away.

LAMAR FIKE: I'm not sure when it started, but I think Priscilla made a silent vow to get rid of Marty. She had it in for him.

MARTY LACKER: On one of these weekend trips to Palm Springs that Elvis and Priscilla and Joe and Joanie took, Vernon and Dee went. Most of us didn't want to go, and we didn't go even though we were invited. We knew Priscilla was trying to arrange it where it was nobody but Joe and Joanie. It was so much petty bullshit.

On top of all that, Palm Springs was such a boring place. Elvis would be stoned on sleeping pills, and he'd just go out and lay by the pool. Everybody really started pulling apart.

This one Sunday, they came back, and Joe called me. He said, "Elvis wanted me to talk to you about something. Now don't get mad, but he wants to know if you'd mind if I'm the best man along with you."

I said, "Wait a minute, Joe. I've been talking to Elvis half the night. Why in the hell didn't he say that to me?" Joe said, "Well, you know how he is. He couldn't bring himself to do it." I said, "I'll tell you what, Joe, you call him back and tell him you'll be the best man. I don't need to be the best man."

Joe said, "No, no. Now don't start that. That'll make him mad. He wants both of us." I said, "Do whatever you want. But I know how all this came about." Priscilla was pulling the strings, and the Colonel, too.

BILLY SMITH: A day or so before the wedding, Elvis and Priscilla, and Joe and Joanie, and George Klein flew to Palm Springs. Vernon and Dee had rode the train from Memphis to San Bernardino, and Marty and Jerry and his wife picked 'em up and drove 'em to Palm Springs. I think they did that so the press wouldn't get wind of what was up. Then Priscilla's mother and stepfather come the next day. Colonel put the word out that there would be a press conference at the Aladdin Hotel the following day, May 1.

About three A.M., Elvis and Priscilla and Joe and Joanie and George flew to Las Vegas on a chartered Lear jet. The rest of us come later. Colonel wanted Elvis and Priscilla to be at the city clerk's office at seven A.M. to get the marriage license. They were going to get married in Milton Prell's suite at the Aladdin later that morning and then get the hell out of Dodge before anybody noticed.

I spent the morning with Elvis, helping him get his stuff ready. He had two pairs of shoes with him. One was patent leather, and the other was his regular boots, and he wanted them shined. He said, "Don't forget these." I said, "I'll try not to." He said, "This is my wedding day. If you forget these I'm going to fire you."

A Nevada supreme court justice by the name of David Zenoff married them. He was a friend of the Colonel's, somehow. Elvis and Priscilla promised to "love, honor, cherish, and comfort." But they didn't say anything about "obey." That wasn't in there. Priscilla's sister, Michelle, was the maid of honor, and both Marty and Joe were best men. And you know who the guests were? Priscilla's mother and stepfather and brother, Vernon and Dee, Patsy Presley and her husband, Gee Gee Gambill, George Klein, Harry Levitch, the jeweler—he sold Elvis the rings—Colonel, and me, and Jo. That was it. And boy, that left a lot of guys with red faces. They were steamed, man.

MARTY LACKER: I didn't know that the guys weren't going to be invited to the ceremony until we got ready to go downstairs. But Joe knew all along. And that really ticked me off. But I didn't raise a stink because I didn't want to ruin it for Elvis. I went down and told the guys because nobody else had the nerve to do it. When I walked in, the guys said, "I guess it's time to go." And I said, "I've got something to tell you." Everybody was mad at me.

Red had already found out. He'd gone and knocked on Joe's door and said, "What time should we get ready?" And Joe said, "Nobody's going to the ceremony but me and Marty. You can all come to the breakfast reception afterwards." And that crushed Red. He went back to his room and packed, and he and his wife got out of there. Went right to the airport and flew home.

This was all Parker's doing. He didn't care about anybody. I don't think he even cared about Elvis anymore. Elvis was so damn nervous, I don't think he knew who was in the room. In fact, that's what he told Red when they finally talked about it in '76. Elvis said, "I had nothing to do with that. That was rail-roaded through." But Elvis trusted people to do stuff. I think if he had been told they weren't coming, he would have said, "The wedding isn't going on."

BILLY SMITH: The excuse Colonel give for not inviting all the guys was that the room was too small for everybody and their wives. God, everybody's feelings were hurt. Red's, the most, I think. Because Red not only left. He quit. He went to work doing stunts on Robert Conrad's TV show *The Wild, Wild West*. And he worked as a songwriter for a while. He come back on the payroll later, but I don't think he ever got over it.

Me and Jo went down to the wedding reception, but we didn't stay but a minute. We went out to the casino to gamble. Because it didn't make much sense to me. Like, Redd Foxx, the comedian, was there as a guest. I guess Colonel had invited him.

MARTY LACKER: The truth is, the suite the ceremony was in was big enough for the rest of the guys to be there. But the Colonel invited who he wanted, and in essence told the others to go fuck themselves.

LAMAR FIKE: I was at my house in Madison [Tennessee], and I picked up the paper the next morning, and it read, ELVIS PRESLEY MARRIES IN VEGAS. I said, "Son of a bitch!" God, I was pissed off!

BILLY SMITH: For a honeymoon, Elvis figured him and Priscilla would go to Palm Springs and spend a few days. He thought it would be enough for them to be together. But Vernon and Dee were there, and Priscilla's family, too.

Now, Priscilla wanted the whole place to themselves. But Elvis didn't. And rather than either one of 'em giving in, they had big arguments about it. He wanted one of the guys with him at all times because he was used to people getting him whatever he wanted. He thought, "I'm wealthy, let other people do it." I think he figured he had the loyalty of these guys, and he didn't know if a woman was going to give him that or not.

As it turned out, the day after the wedding, he had to go back to the studio to do some last-minute dubbing on *Clambake*. He come back to Palm Springs that night, but then two days later Elvis and Priscilla flew back to Memphis with Vernon and Dee and Jo and me. Elvis wanted to finish up his honeymoon on the ranch.

LAMAR FIKE: Elvis called me and said, "I'm going to have a second reception at Graceland for everybody who couldn't come to the wedding, and I want you there." And he said, "Before that, though, I'm going down to the ranch. Come on down."

I guess you could say I went on their honeymoon with them. Because the first night they were there, I was there. We stayed in the trailer. All three of us. I didn't have anywhere else to sleep. And it was a forty- or sixty-foot trailer, so it wasn't like we were right on top of each other. I was in the front of the damn thing, and Priscilla and Elvis were in the back in the master bedroom. I'd been with him since the beginning, so nothing had changed, really.

After that, Elvis and Priscilla went to the Bahamas for a few days. But Elvis didn't like it, and they came back. He thought it was a pretty tense place, racially.

Priscilla got pregnant on the honeymoon. We figured she conceived down at the ranch. We tried to pin it down. They were laughing about how I spent their honeymoon night with them, and Elvis said, "When do you think it happened?" I said, "When do *I* think?!"

BILLY SMITH: Believe me, Elvis didn't know that Lisa was coming along. During the time he was on the ranch, he was stoned every day. He didn't know where in the hell he was half the time. So there's no telling when Lisa's conception occurred. I can promise you that deep down in his mind Elvis couldn't tell you what night it happened. He just liked to attach significance to things like that, the way he did with that bullshit about there being a blue light around the moon the night he was born.

MARTY LACKER: In June, Elvis had to go out to California to make *Speedway* with Nancy Sinatra. And Priscilla talked him into taking her out to the coast.

LAMAR FIKE: Elvis was on the set of *Speedway* in July when Priscilla called him from Palm Springs and told him she was pregnant. I imagine she wasn't too happy to be pregnant so soon. She wanted a baby, but not that quick. Except it made the strap that much tighter around Elvis.

It wasn't a comfortable situation for him. When she was seven months along, he told her he wanted a trial separation. He panicked about being a father. I think the separation only lasted two days, though.

MARTY LACKER: I don't know what Priscilla's motives were. She could have taken advantage of the condition Elvis was in out on the ranch to make sure she did become pregnant. But I think Elvis was really happy about the baby. I remember when he told everybody. We were on the set. He'd just talked to Priscilla on the phone in the dressing room, and he opened up the door, and he said, "Priscilla just called! She got back from the doctor, and guess what? I'm gonna be a happy pappy!"

Of course, he was putting the moves on Nancy Sinatra at the same time. I guess you could say they had a flirtatious romance on the movie. Priscilla heard about it from people, but Elvis denied it. She got mad and cried, and Elvis told her she was just overly sensitive because she was pregnant. I don't think he saw anything wrong with fooling around. Just because Elvis was a newlywed and getting ready to become a daddy didn't mean he wasn't going to continue being Elvis. Nancy was a pretty nice girl. She's the one who gave Priscilla her Hollywood baby shower, by the way.

BILLY SMITH: Once Priscilla got that ring on her finger—and pregnant—things got worse.

MARTY LACKER: She's an ice-cold person, but I guess she had some real feelings for Elvis. I think she also thought she caught the brass ring. She thought she was going to get rid of anything that got in her way. But she wasn't alone. The Colonel had something to do with it, Esposito and his wife had something to do with it, and Vernon definitely had something to do with it. Vernon figured the fewer people around, the fewer checks going out.

Priscilla and Vernon bonded with two goals in mind. They could use each other financially because she was as much of a penny-pincher as he was. And together, they were going to stop Elvis from spending.

Charlie used to fawn over Priscilla, but Charlie was phony. Priscilla took a liking to Jerry because Jerry was a good-looking guy, and Elvis said he thought she had the hots for him. At times it caused a little animosity. One time he came down to the kitchen in the middle of the night, and there was Priscilla and Jerry. They were just talking, but they were talking maybe a little too intimately for Elvis's taste.

Elvis was on those back steps, and he stopped midway and watched them for a while. And then he came walking in and said, "What the hell's goin' on here?" They said nothing was going on. But I know that Elvis used to worry that something might happen between them.

Since Priscilla couldn't have cared less about anybody other than Joe and Jerry, she and Vernon and Colonel started a campaign to edge almost everybody out. And one or two guys in the group were always trying to get rid of people, too, and at every opportunity they'd bad-mouth somebody and stab 'em in the back. It started getting really terrible. The old camaraderie was in shambles.

At one point, somebody left because he'd had his fill, and Charlie made the statement, "Who gives a shit? That's more gravy for us." Elvis wasn't there, but it pissed the rest of us off so much that when we were all in the room with Elvis, and the conversation got around to the guy who left, one of us said, "Charlie, why don't you tell Elvis what you said?" And Charlie just grinned because he didn't think anybody would do it. So they said, "Come on, Charlie, tell Elvis how you said that would be that much more gravy for us." And Elvis just looked at Charlie with this mix of anger and disbelief.

In July of '67, two months after the wedding, Vernon and Dee came out to L.A. one weekend, and they trotted down to Palm Springs with Elvis and Priscilla and Joe and Joanie.

The morning of the day they were coming back, I got a phone call from Joe. He said, "Elvis wants his dad and Dee to stay out in L.A. for a while, and he wants them to stay at the house." And then he said, "But the house is getting too crowded. So Elvis wants to give you a choice. You can either go back home and work on the ranch with Alan, or you'll have to go get an apartment out here."

I said, "Well, Joe, you don't really need an answer from me, do you? You know exactly what I'm going to do, and so does he." I said, "You all have a good time." And I hung up.

Before they got back, I moved down to the Bel Air Sands Hotel, on the San Diego Freeway on the way to the airport. And everybody who hadn't gone to Palm Springs came over to the motel with their wives. They were all saying how dirty it was. I said, "No, don't worry about it. That's the way they want to handle it." I was disappointed that Elvis hadn't told me himself. But I said, "They're poisoning his mind, and he's letting them get away with it."

When I went back to the ranch, all I really did was sleep. I wasn't interested in becoming a rancher or even being down at the ranch. And in September, I figured it was just time to move on.

The day I told Elvis I was quitting, he said, "Well, what if I need you?" I said, "I'm not going anywhere. If you need me, call. You know where I am." I remember we were sitting in the dining room, and then we moved into the living room, which he hardly ever used. He said, "You know you'll always be welcome here." I said, "Well, I appreciate that. I didn't think it would be any other way." And really, things didn't change. I was with him about every day he was in Memphis, just out of friendship. I went on some of the tours, and to Las Vegas, and on the *Aloha* special, in Hawaii. And I did a lot of projects for him, gratis. I just didn't have to travel every day anymore, or put up with all the bullshit of working for him, and dealing with Colonel, and Priscilla, and Vernon, and Joe. If they'd had their way, everybody would have been gone. The fact of the matter is that if Elvis hadn't had the guys around, he probably would have died fifteen years before he did.

Vernon filed a separation notice for me, to make himself feel good, I guess. I ran across it just the other day. It's from the Tennessee Department of Employment Security, and it's dated September 22, 1967. It says I'd been employed since November 15, 1963—which was my second stint with Elvis—as a bookkeeper and purchasing agent. At the point I left, my take-home pay was $181.80 a week. And remember, I had three children.

It's signed by Vernon, as manager, and states that my employer was E. A. Presley. And here's my favorite part. Where it says, "Reason for separation," Vernon put down, "Lack of work."

CHAPTER 38

NEW BEGINNINGS

Late in '67, in a rare move, Elvis acquiesced to Priscilla's request to accompany him on location for a film, in this case, to Arizona for *Stay Away, Joe*. While there, Priscilla read an ad in *Variety* for a house at 1174 Hillcrest Drive in L.A.'s exclusive Trousdale Estates. To Priscilla, it must have sounded ideal: a completely furnished, split-level, French Regency–style home, with three bedrooms, security, an Olympic-sized swimming pool, and guest cottage.

Part of Priscilla's thinking was to move Elvis to an environment he had not shared with the entourage—a fresh start for a new life together. The couple moved in at the end of the year.

Only six years old, the $400,000 house was the first residence Elvis owned in California. When he and Priscilla moved away three years later, Elvis left the house intact, allegedly saying, "This home is so perfect that not even an ashtray should be moved." The subsequent owner sold the furnishings at auction.

BILLY SMITH: In September of '67, Elvis took me, and Joe, and Charlie to Nashville to record. He cut "Guitar Man," "Big Boss Man," "Hi-Heel Sneakers," and a few other songs that had some teeth to them—some blues or country blues. "Big Boss Man" and "Hi-Heel Sneakers" had been recorded before, but Elvis's versions didn't sound like nobody else's. He put his own stamp to 'em. I guess this recording session laid the groundwork for the Memphis Sessions in '69. Elvis was just hungering for that kind of release.

"Guitar Man" was a Jerry Reed song. Jerry had put it out himself just a couple of months before, and it started his singing career. Well, when Elvis was doing it in the studio, the musicians couldn't really get the groove. Particularly the guitar sound, which was double important on this song. They had three guitar players on that session—Scotty Moore, Harold Bradley, and Chip Young, but Elvis wasn't satisfied. He told somebody, "Call Jerry Reed. Maybe he could tell one of these guys how he gets that sound." Jerry was on a fishing trip, but somebody found him. And Jerry said, "Better yet, I'll come on over there." So he played on the session and got that hot-wired sound on the track.

That's how Elvis was in the studio in the old days. He kept on until he got it. I remember him talking to Bob Moore on this session, saying, "Bring the bass out, Bob." Or he'd say, "Let's don't use a bass guitar. Let's use an upright [bass]. I want to hear that slapping noise." And, "I need a saxophone. Boots [Randolph], give me this sound here."

That next January, he recorded in Nashville again. He brought Jerry Reed back to play on "Too Much Monkey Business," the Chuck Berry song. And he recorded another one of Jerry's tunes, "U.S. Male." That one got him back into the Top 30 again. And, boy, that had to feel good.

MARTY LACKER: When *Clambake* came out in November of '67, *The Hollywood Reporter* said, "Elvis can't continue for long to rely on the same scripts and songs which have become anachronistic in the increasingly sophisticated and ever-changing world of pop music and pulp films." Everybody saw the handwriting on the wall.

BILLY SMITH: In '68, Elvis's [five-year contract] with MGM was up, and Colonel started reevaluating things. In the early years, when Elvis was hot, Colonel told him, "You're Elvis Presley. You'll get $1 million a picture and sometimes a percentage. All you got to do is show up on time and take the money and run." Even the studio heads said, "Good ol' Elvis. He'll ride a damn hog through a blizzard if that's what the script calls for."

There's an old saying in California: "If you don't make a profit, you don't work." The problem for Elvis was that even the worst pictures made damn good money. Some of 'em more than others. I couldn't understand *Kissin' Cousins* making as much money as it did. But by '68, the pictures weren't making so much money anymore. Elvis's fans had outgrown 'em.

The Colonel saw two things. One, that the pictures had worn out their welcome and Elvis was getting hard to sell. And two, that Elvis was flat refusing to do any more. He told Colonel he'd quit the business before he'd sign another movie contract. And the Colonel saw that he was dead serious. Elvis said, "I want to go back and do concerts and personal appearances." He wanted to see if he still had what it took because he hadn't been on a live stage since that *U.S.S. Arizona* benefit in '61.

So Colonel started to look elsewhere for places to take him. Elvis had three more movies to do in '68—*Live a Little, Love a Little, Charro!,* and *The Trouble with Girls,* but he'd only contracted for one in '69, *Change of Habit.* So Colonel quickly wrapped everything up, and he started looking to television. That's how *The Singer Special* was born. Colonel announced it in January. That was probably the most important performance of Elvis's life.

LAMAR FIKE: Boy, there was a lot of excitement going around about that time. Elvis had the TV special coming up, and then Lisa Marie was born on February 1, which was exactly nine months to the day after the wedding. I don't care what anybody says—Elvis didn't like the idea of Priscilla being pregnant so soon. He told Billy, "I made a mistake and didn't pull out in time."

But then, as the delivery date got near, he started playing the big "Get her to the hospital," macho-Daddy role. He called me in Nashville the day before the baby was born, and he said, "You get your ass up here." I said, "Why do I need to be there?" He said, "We've all got to be here for this thing." I said, "Priscilla's having a baby. It's not the Second Coming of Christ!" But for weeks before Lisa was born, Elvis put the guys through these damn practice drills to get Priscilla to the hospital.

The plan included a couple of decoy cars that would speed out of Graceland and go to Methodist Hospital. Then another car would take Priscilla and Elvis to Baptist. Well, they changed it a couple of times, and by the morning Priscilla woke up with labor pains, Jerry was confused.

Joe and I took off and led everybody to Methodist. Jerry

and Charlie were supposed to take Priscilla and Elvis to Baptist, but Jerry headed for Methodist, too. Priscilla was in labor, and the son of a bitch was taking her to the wrong place! Charlie finally convinced him Baptist was right, and they got on over there.

Lisa was born at five o'clock in the afternoon. She was a pretty little baby. Looked mostly like Elvis. She had that real black hair. Real black. Elvis was happy about that, see, because his "perfect child" had to have black hair. He gave her that middle name, "Marie," for Colonel's wife.

MARTY LACKER: I see that in books all the time, but "Marie" was a name Elvis always liked—"Marie," "Maria"—because it was prominent in one of the Amigos' songs, and he loved the way they pronounced it. When I named my daughter Maria Angela, it pissed Elvis off. He said, "You cocksucker, you stole my name!"

The moment Lisa was born, oh, Elvis was so excited. Everybody except Billy, I think, went to the hospital and waited for the birth. Elvis was talking that baby talk big-time.

In the beginning, the baby changed him some. He settled down a little. He loved Lisa, and he loved having a baby and being a father and part of a family. But then the newness wore off, and he was back to being the old Elvis again.

LAMAR FIKE: Lisa was just another trophy for him. Parenthood didn't change Elvis at all.

About a month after Lisa was born, Elvis turned to me and said, "You know, I really don't like Priscilla anymore." I said, "You're going back to that original thing, aren't you?" He said, "What are you talking about?" I said, "You know what I'm talking about. You never liked a woman who'd had a baby." That was a total turnoff to him.

Priscilla wrote in her book that for months after Lisa was born, she couldn't get Elvis to touch her. At first, he said he just wanted to make sure she'd healed. But after that, she says she wore a black negligee and snuggled up to him while he read, and tried everything, but he just let his sleeping pills kick in. She also says they'd had a pretty passionate sex life until the last six weeks of her pregnancy. Which, actually, I doubt.

But anyway, once that kid got here, Elvis didn't want any more to do with Priscilla. He didn't even want to sleep in the same bed with her. Elvis slept with his mama when she was sick, but he didn't want to lie near his wife once she became a mother. You figure it out.

MARTY LACKER: Elvis told everybody he never wanted to have sex with a woman who'd had a child. He always said, "For some reason I can't do that." He never said why. Everybody theorizes because of his mother. I don't buy that shit. It was just one of his quirks.

BILLY SMITH: Let me tell you something. If it had been a woman he'd been really attracted to, he wouldn't have cared if she had a litter. He'd make a pass in a minute. Elvis lost interest in Priscilla because it was not in his nature to be married. It was over with, and he didn't want any more kids. Not with her.

LAMAR FIKE: Priscilla says [in her book] that she wrote in her diary, "I am beginning to doubt my own sexuality as a woman. My physical and emotional needs were unfulfilled." So she started a life of her own, and part of that was taking dance lessons. Pretty soon, she started jumping the dance instructor. She had an affair while Elvis was making *Live a Little, Love a Little*, in '68. She didn't waste any time after the baby was born.

BILLY SMITH: That was a short affair, I think. She calls him "Mark" in her book. That wasn't his real name.

LAMAR FIKE: Do you know who Priscilla flirted with? That black singer, Little Anthony, of the Imperials.

MARTY LACKER: That supposedly happened when Priscilla went up to New York with Joanie Esposito and Schilling. Jerry came back and told me. Quite frankly, I think Elvis sent Schilling up to New York to see if something would happen between them.

I heard Elvis say, "Well, I'm going to give 'em enough rope." And it so happened that Little Anthony was up in New York at the time, and they met at a disco and danced together.

BILLY SMITH: Priscilla had this desire to see somebody in New York. She was looking at other people, just like Elvis was. I remember she got pretty involved with somebody in the entertainment field.

LAMAR FIKE: Priscilla came back from that trip, and Elvis found out about her dancing with Little Anthony. And, boy, that started a bunch of shit! Because Elvis already thought she had something going with Schilling, and I guess the idea of her flirting with Little Anthony put him over the edge. That night he caught Jerry and Priscilla [talking] in the kitchen, Schilling panicked like you don't know what panic is. Elvis walked up the steps, and he came by me, and he said, "I wouldn't put it past the son of a bitch." I said, "Well, then, what's your problem? You know what to do."

Priscilla really preferred dark-skinned, black-headed guys. Still does. In a *Vanity Fair* interview, she said, "There is a certain strength I feel with dark men. They're very virile." Like the guy she's living with now [screenwriter-turned-computer-programmer Marco Garibaldi]. He's Brazilian, of Italian heritage. That's her thing.

MARTY LACKER: In May of '68, after *Live a Little, Love a Little* wrapped, Elvis and Priscilla went to Hawaii with Esposito and Schilling and their wives for a little vacation. Elvis used the time to get in shape for the TV special. He lost that weight he'd gained on the ranch, and he got a good tan, and I heard he even slacked off on his drug use a little bit. He knew what he had to do.

The next day after they got to Hawaii, by the way, they went to the Karate Tournament of Champions. That's where Priscilla saw her first karate studs. One of them was Mike Stone, who was just her type. He's Hawaiian, but he's dark. He even wore an Afro hairstyle for a while.

LAMAR FIKE: The day that Robert Kennedy got shot—June 5, 1968—my phone rang about midnight. Elvis said, "Turn on your television set." We both sat there watching television with a phone in our hands for four hours. Finally, I said, "Elvis, it's four o'clock in the morning! I'm ready to pass out." But he just had to talk about it.

Towards the latter part of the conversation, he got back on the Jack Kennedy tear. He talked about what it would feel like to actually take somebody out like that—to both give the order and pull the trigger. But he was also freaked about somebody killing him, and that just fed it. By the time we hung up, he was sure that the guy who killed Kennedy was somebody close to him. The Judas theory.

BILLY SMITH: One night we were sitting around talking about gangsters. Elvis used to say the Perugia Way house was the one where Bugsy Siegel got killed. Marty says that wasn't true, that Bugsy Siegel was killed in [girlfriend] Virginia Hill's house, which was on North Linden Drive. But Elvis would say, "Man, I'm telling you. He got blown away with a shotgun, right here." Now, he believed this because he used to go see a doctor who was supposedly Bugsy Siegel's brother. Elvis said Dr. Siegel told him that the Perugia Way house was where it happened.

Anyway, this particular time, Elvis said, "You guys are here to protect me, and you do. But how far would you go? It would be easy for somebody to walk up and shoot me, especially onstage. If you saw somebody getting ready to blow my head off, what would you do?" And a couple of 'em said, "I'd step in front of you, man, if it come to that."

I think this was one of them loyalty tests. Because he turned to me and said, "What about you?" I said, "Hey, my life's important to me, too. I ain't stopping no damn bullet for nobody." He said, "You little son of a bitch!" And then Elvis died laughing. He said, "I didn't figure you would, you dirty little bastard!"

MARTY LACKER: The funny part was that Billy turned the tables on him. He said to Elvis, "Let me ask you this. If somebody was shooting at me, would you stand in front of me?" And Elvis said, "Oh, hell no! It might hit me in the face."

BILLY SMITH: In April or May, just before *The Singer Special*, I quit working for Elvis. There were a lot of reasons. The way things had changed. And my kids were getting ready to start school, and I didn't want 'em to have to spend three or four months in Memphis and then three or four months in California. So I had to make a decision. And I chose Memphis because my daddy was real sick with liver trouble from all those years of drinking.

Elvis had retired him. He worked down at the ranch for about three months, and after that, all Daddy done was just come down there and fish every once in a while. But all my family drank home brew and rotgut. And they took pills.

To tell you the truth, I wasn't sure how I was going to make it financially. But I had to live my own life.

I went to work for Thurston Motor Line, and I worked there just about a year. Then I got on at the railroad [Illinois Central], and I worked for them until sometime in '70.

Once, Elvis was trying to get me to come back with him and I wouldn't do it because I didn't want to travel no more. And he tore the whole damn kitchen up at Graceland. He was mad at me, and he was mad at his daddy, too. He threw dishes, and beat the refrigerator, and jerked the curtains down over the sink. He was unhappy, boy.

LAMAR FIKE: People were just bailing out because of the caste system. Joe was a pretty arrogant asshole.

MARTY LACKER: Just before I quit working at the ranch, I was offered a pretty good position, the opportunity to start Pepper Records. And with that, I started getting involved in the music industry in Memphis. During that time I discovered Rita Coolidge. She was singing background and doing jingles. We cut her first records.

I was also doing a lot of record production with [producer] Chips Moman over at his American Sound Studio. Back then, you could cut an album for $12,000. We were cutting records on a little eight-track tube board, using Chips's rhythm section. They were all white guys, but to hear them play, you'd swear they were black. They worked with the biggest names and cut some of the biggest hits. All those guys are up in Nashville now: Reggie Young, who plays the shit out of a lead guitar, Bobby Emmons and Bobby Wood on organ and piano, Gene Chrisman on drums, and Tommy Cogbill and Mike Leech on bass. Tommy's dead now.

He was one of the best session players there ever was. He was on a lot of the original Aretha Franklin hits, playing both guitar and bass.

Chips had a hell of a run, cutting 122 chart records in three years. And fifty-three of them were million sellers. Like "The Letter" by the Box Tops.

I watched Chips in the studio, and I saw what a vast difference it was from the way Elvis worked. Chips's way of working was to lay the rhythm track down, do a rough demo vocal with the rhythm track, and overdub the final vocal, the background voices and horns and strings. It gave him so much more control over the sound levels and the final mix. Elvis was still recording the old way, having the whole band in the room while he stood in the middle singing. When I saw how things were being done, I was amazed and embarrassed that Elvis was so behind the times.

It really irked me because Elvis never should have had a slump. And the only reason he did was because of the terrible songs and the production, both in Hollywood and Nashville. Today, Nashville is a different ball game. But back in the sixties, it was still real down-home country, and they played what I call "shit-kickin' music." That might have been perfect for the *Kissin' Cousins* soundtrack, but it was not Elvis Presley. Elvis could sing good country songs when he was allowed to, and he did later. But the crap that he'd been given to record so far was terrible.

That's one reason I was keeping my fingers crossed for this television special. Because with a string of shitty movies, and records that didn't really satisfy anybody, a flop with the TV special might have finished off his career. This was his moment of truth, and it could have gone either way.

CHAPTER 39

THE COMEBACK SPECIAL

In June of '68, Elvis went before the NBC cameras in Burbank to tape his first television special, *Elvis*, now best remembered for the sleek, black-leather outfit he wore and the raw, stark energy of the performance. For Elvis, the special was his ultimate test: His last live concert had been seven years earlier, and he hadn't appeared on television since *Welcome Home, Elvis,* with Frank Sinatra, in 1960. On top of it, he hadn't scored a number one record since 1962.

Understandably, he was nervous. At thirty-three, trim and tan after his Hawaiian vacation, he was at his physical peak. But he was no longer the rebellious, hip-thrusting rocker. Recognizing that he now had more in common with Sinatra and Dean Martin than with his earlier incarnation as the "Hillbilly Cat," Elvis confided to the young and visionary producer-director Steve Binder that he was terrified the public might not like him anymore.

Binder, while wrestling with Colonel Parker, who wanted his boy to do a traditional Christmas special (or to sing only songs for which Colonel controlled the publishing), easily convinced Elvis that this performance was the crossroads of his career. He could either recapture the magnificent essence he once was or return to the Hollywood treadmill. In kinder terms, Binder spelled out that Elvis was in danger of becoming a joke, an anachronism as irrelevant to the music of the sixties as Bing Crosby.

With enough footage shot for three one-hour shows, the highlight of *The Singer Special,* as it came to be known (because of the $400,000 sponsorship by the Singer Sewing Machine Company), was the live, and seemingly unrehearsed, Elvis-in-the-round performance segment. Looking like a mythological god in his leather suit—designed by Bill Belew, who would go on to fashion all of Presley's stage costumes—Elvis carried his electric guitar onstage before a 328-member audience. There, he was informally backed by his longtime friends, Scotty Moore on guitar, D. J. Fontana, from his "Louisiana Hayride" days, on drums, and by Charlie Hodge and Alan Fortas, who were there mostly to get Elvis to relax and cut up the way he did offstage ("My boy, my boy"). Between songs, in which he recounted vignettes from his past—such as when the Jacksonville, Florida, police showed up to make sure he didn't violate the decency code—Elvis displayed the humor and vulnerability that characterized his private life but which few fans ever got to see.

Although visibly rattled (his hand shook at the start), Elvis joked and chatted and eventually ripped it up as he hadn't done in a decade, proving that he still had the mettle and the grit to do it right. The show's basic story line, augmented in a lengthy choreographed production number with the Claude Thompson dancers, traces a struggling young guitar player setting out to make his mark in the world. An innocent awash in corruption (Colonel insisted that a bordello scene be cut from the final broadcast), he finds success, only to realize that he sacrificed himself along the way. Eventually, he returns to his roots. It was Elvis's own story in 4/4 time.

For the finale, choral director W. Earl Brown wrote "If I Can Dream," a big, soaring, humanistic ballad with gospel and rhythm-and-blues undertones that Elvis immediately embraced. The song afforded him an opportunity to sing something of depth and to show off his range beyond the three-note span of the movie soundtracks. But it also stirred his evangelistic zeal. One day during rehearsal, Elvis turned out the lights and sang the song to a tape of the band. The startled crew looked out from the control booth to see him literally writhing on the floor, caught up in overwhelming emotion and passion and baring his soul. Later released as a single, the song became Elvis's first gold record in years.

"There is something magical about watching a man who has lost himself find his way back home," critic Jon Landau wrote of the show in the now defunct *Eye* magazine. It was undoubtedly Elvis's finest hour, a breathtaking melding of snarling fifties fire and sixties polish, the culmination of the best of everything he had worked for and learned. In the end, it changed almost everything in his life. The King was back. So was his artistry—and his dignity.

LAMAR FIKE: The way Colonel structured the original deal with NBC was for the TV special and a movie. He did it over the phone. Afterwards, he got a telegram from Tom Sarnoff, at NBC Burbank, which read, "Confirming our phone conversation, we have a deal for production of one Elvis feature and one TV special according to terms discussed between us during last couple of days. Congratulations to both of us . . . "

Colonel sent a copy off to Elvis in Memphis, and Elvis fired a telegram back: "Dear Colonel: Is that the best you could do? Respectfully yours, Elvis."

BILLY SMITH: Elvis said one time, "I was scared to death when I done the special. I didn't know what the heck was going to take place. But the one thing that was always there was my music. I was just wanting to get back to that."

He could have done it so much earlier. But he had to be shoved into a corner and almost kicked before he would bite.

MARTY LACKER: The best part of the '68 *Comeback Special* was the other live performance segment—the one where Elvis paced back and forth in a sort of boxing ring in the middle of the audience wearing the leather suit. That may be the best performance he ever gave. They pretaped the orchestra, but then they brought in these hip young guys to play over it—Tommy Tedesco, of the Fireballs, and Mike Deasy on guitar; Don Randi, who'd done session work with the Buffalo Springfield, on piano; Larry Knechtel, who'd go on to be part of Bread, on bass; Hal Blaine, who was a session drummer for Phil Spector; and the Blossoms, with Darlene Love, also from the Spector sessions, on background vocals. This was just a magic combination.

In the [Jerry] Hopkins book [*Elvis*], Billy Goldenberg, who was the musical director, made a very interesting observation. He said, "The one thing I've always felt about Elvis is that . . . there's a cruelty involved, a meanness . . . a basic sadistic quality about what he does, which is attractive . . . He's excited by certain kinds of violent things. I thought, 'If there was a way we could get this feeling in the music . . . '" And they did.

BILLY SMITH: It could just have been another Christmas special, but Binder flat put his foot down, and that helped Elvis go up against the Colonel. Elvis was really all for it, even though he was saying, "Yes, sir, Colonel," and "No, sir, Colonel." But then when they got off to themselves, he'd say, "Look, Colonel, Steve's more right than you think. That's basically what I want to do." But he didn't say it to Colonel in front of Binder because he wouldn't do the Colonel that way. And at the same time, I guarantee you he was talking to Binder, saying, "Don't budge, man. That's what I want to do."

LAMAR FIKE: Steve Binder's a fascinating person. He always had an original approach to things, and he didn't care a lot about parameters. He did that Petula Clark special where Harry Belafonte touched her on the arm and the whole country went bonkers.

He came up with good ideas for Elvis, like having him sit there with that leather outfit on, although Elvis liked to died under the lights. And putting Alan and them onstage for that jam session.

One thing I want to get straight, though. Marty talks about that Hopkins book. Well, Hopkins wrote that Steve took Elvis and Joe outside on Sunset Boulevard, just to show Elvis he could go out in public and not be mobbed. The idea, I think, was to show him he wasn't such a big damn star anymore. Hopkins said Steve took 'em out in front of a topless bar at four in the afternoon, and kids were knocking into 'em, man, and still not recognizing him.

That's total bullshit. He took Elvis out on Sunset, all right. But phew! It was a mess. We had to fight to get him back in.

Steve Binder and his arrogant fucking ways . . . Elvis liked Steve all right, but Elvis had total artistic control of that show. The only thing he didn't like were the segments with all those dancers. He thought there was too much going on.

Actually, I'm not sure he was all that nervous about the special, like people say. When he was into his gig, you'd better look out. Because the ego would just get monumental.

By the way, you'll notice during that so-called living-room

segment, where Elvis sits around with Alan, and Scotty, and D.J. and Charlie, they keep saying, "My boy, my boy." That came from me. I always liked W. C. Fields, and he used to say, "My boy, my boy." So I would say that, and Elvis would copy me. We'd find a saying we liked and bury it within six weeks.

BILLY SMITH: Alan said that him and Joe brought women back to the dressing room like they were on a conveyer belt. That was to feed his ego. Hell, Priscilla was mostly to feed his ego.

LAMAR FIKE: Elvis met Goldie Hawn during that special. She was going with one of the dancers, Gus Trikonis. Elvis thought she was coming to see him, and he'd kid her—call her "Chicken Head" because of her haircut.

BILLY SMITH: I think the marriage dropped off nearly for good during *The Comeback Special.* Elvis was preoccupied with the show, and Priscilla was hurt and put more time into other interests. She had a new dance instructor by then—she'd broken off that affair. And Elvis realized, "I'm Elvis Presley, and God, it's all here in front of me."

LAMAR FIKE: At the end of July, Elvis went to Apache Junction, Arizona, near Phoenix, to start filming *Charro!,* which was a western, for National General Productions. This was the first picture where he didn't sing or play a guitar, except over the opening credits. The whole picture got away from the formula—no girls in bikinis, no classy wardrobe. In fact, I think he wore the same pair of dirty leather pants for the whole thing. And he grew a beard and wore a hat down over his eyes. The fans didn't like it much.

Alan went out there for that picture because they'd shut down the ranch. His days were numbered, though. I'm not sure he knew that. Priscilla always liked Alan, but she never let sentiment get in the way of her pocketbook.

BILLY SMITH: In September, while Elvis was in Arizona making *Charro!*, my brother, Bobby, died. Then in early October, Uncle Johnny. Then in '69, right before Elvis opened in Vegas, my daddy become bedridden. He had a stroke. I took him to the doctor that morning, and he was talking, and then, just after they run some tests on him, he never spoke again. Yet he lived almost four years. But the family was getting smaller, right quick.

LAMAR FIKE: Six weeks before *The Singer Special* aired [on December 3], RCA released "If I Can Dream" as a single. In late November, it entered the *Billboard* "Hot 100" chart and went to number twelve. That was the highest any of Elvis's singles had gone in three years. Son of a gun sold a million copies.

MARTY LACKER: The night NBC broadcast *The Singer Special,* I saw it on TV before Elvis did because of the time difference.

At first, I wasn't totally blown away until he did that impromptu set in the leather suit—the part where he paced back and forth like a panther. That was just raw, animal magnetism. I remember saying to myself, "That's what Elvis is really about."

As soon as the show was over, I called the house out in Los Angeles. Joe answered, and Elvis grabbed the phone because he wanted to hear somebody's opinion. I said, "Man, let me tell you something. If nothing else, you did one thing." He said, "What's that?" I said, "You finally showed them the real Elvis Presley instead of the guy in those movies." And he said, "Man, I'm glad you said that."

LAMAR FIKE: *The Singer Special* was brilliant. No doubt about it. Bob Finkel, the executive producer, won a Peabody Award for it. It was the highest-rated show of the week, and the most-watched special of the year by women eighteen to forty-nine. Had a damn Nielsen rating of thirty-two, with a forty-two share. Later in the month, the soundtrack went on the *Billboard* chart at 166, and it parked at eight and stayed thirty-two weeks. That was his first Top 10 album since '65.

MARTY LACKER: In August of '69, Singer paid $275,000 to rebroadcast the show. They took out "Blue Christmas" and replaced it with "Tiger Man." By that time, it had already been shown in Great Britain, where it ran without commercials. The Brits named Elvis the "Outstanding Male Singer" of the year in a "New Musical Express" poll. They know their music over there.

LAMAR FIKE: Sometime after *The Singer Special*, we flew into Vegas on Hughes Air West, and the Colonel picked us up and took us to the Aladdin [Hotel]. Elvis wanted to see the shows and stuff, and Colonel wanted to gamble. We were riding in the car, and the Colonel said, "You know, you can do the show that you did for *The Singer Special* here in Vegas."

I looked at Elvis, and he looked at me, and when we got out of the car, he said, "Looks like I'm getting ready to do Vegas."

And he thought that was fine. So he told Colonel, "Yeah, let's do it. And when we finish Vegas, we'll go on tour." So that's how it all started. For pretty much the rest of his life, he'd do his shows in Vegas, then go out on the road. That was the next step, right after the recording sessions he had lined up for the first part of the year.

CHAPTER 40

THE MEMPHIS SESSIONS

While *The Singer Special* earned Elvis new respectability, most of the rock critics who'd sneered at his records for the better part of the sixties still doubted he could turn out an artistically viable—and socially aware—album in the age of the Woodstock generation.

In the middle of January '69, Elvis walked into Chips Moman's American Sound Studio and proved them wrong. It was the first time since the mid-fifties that Elvis had recorded in Memphis, then in the halcyon days of the Memphis Sound—the soulful records on Stax and the other independent R & B labels in the area and the music that poured from the soul-funk studios of Muscle Shoals, Alabama.

Moman's house band played a more commercial and countrified style than its counterpart at Stax, but the sessions Elvis cut with them at American drew on the roots of his primal genius—a seamless integration of black and white music. After so many years of stupefying movie filler, Elvis was ecstatic about recording real songs again, and his performance throbs with startling self-assurance.

From the hits "In the Ghetto," "Suspicious Minds," "Don't Cry Daddy," and "Kentucky Rain" to the less-lauded, but extraordinary "Stranger in My Own Home Town" and "Long Black Limousine," Elvis handed RCA enough material for a year and a half of releases. The profits allegedly accounted for a third of the label's income the following year, precisely because Elvis gave his audience exactly what they most wanted to hear: a brilliant, bold, and passionate return to his legacy, an artist reclaiming, and rebaptizing, himself.

Whether this was a magic coming together of music and man that Elvis would never be able to re-create, his voice darted and flew in perfect response to all that was being asked of him, perhaps for the very last time.

MARTY LACKER: If you just looked at the building, this tiny place at 827 Thomas Street in a mostly black, run-down part of Memphis, you'd never think the American Sound Studio, along with the [black] Stax Studios, were the center of the Memphis music scene. But they were. Or, I should say, Chips Moman and that house band were. Chips was the owner and founder of American, and he was also the chief engineer, cook, and bottle washer. He wrote songs and played occasional guitar on the sessions. Everybody respected him. Neil Diamond had just been in there to record "Brother Love's Traveling Salvation Show" and "Holly Holy" And Dusty Springfield had come all the way from England to get the Memphis Sound on her records.

I'd go up to Graceland and Elvis would start playing demos of sessions that he did, and the stuff was just terrible. He hadn't had a Top 5 record since 1965, and that was "Crying in the Chapel," which was basically a gospel song.

I told him about Chips and the stuff he was cutting, and I told him I thought they'd be great together. He said, "Well, I'll think about it." That was it.

One day when I was working with Chips, he said, "Hey, you know, I'd love to cut some records with Elvis." Well, he kept saying it: "When are you going to tell Elvis to let me produce a record?" I didn't want to say that I already had. So I just told him I'd talk to Elvis about it.

One evening in January of '69, right around Elvis's birthday, I went up to Graceland. Elvis had a sore throat, and he was sitting on the couch in the Jungle Room. And it so happened that Felton Jarvis was sitting in front of him on an ottoman. And George Klein and somebody else was in the room.

Felton started talking to Elvis about the next recording session, which was supposed to be in Nashville the following week. The truth is that Felton didn't pick any songs, and he didn't pick the musicians. Usually, the names were submitted to Colonel Parker's office, and the Colonel and Tom Diskin would pick the musicians, which was the biggest joke of all. Felton's official duty was to coordinate everything with the Colonel's office. His name was never on a record as the real producer. On the *Moody Blue* album, for example, it says, "Executive producer: Elvis Presley. Associate producer: Felton Jarvis."

Anyway, Felton was sitting in front of Elvis, and I heard Felton say, "Okay, we'll start next Monday. Who do you want at the session?" And Elvis didn't know anybody except the same old guys he used. He had no idea of the really good musicians out there.

I was leaning my head up against the wall, and unconsciously, I was shaking it, "No." Elvis looked over at me and he said, "What the hell's wrong with you?" I said, "Damnit, Elvis. I just wish that for once you'd record here in Memphis. I wish you'd try Chips and American." And he said, "Well, maybe someday I will." And he went back to talking to Felton.

Then everybody got up to go in the dining room, but I just sat there. I didn't want to go sit at the table and hear them talk about the Nashville session.

Elvis said, "C'mon, let's go eat." And I said, "No, I'm not hungry." But he knew I never passed up a meal. I just sat there and stared at the TV screen, thinking of all this stuff.

Well, it wasn't two minutes before Felton came out and said, "Elvis wants to see you."

I said, "Felton, I don't want to go in there. With all due respect to you and Nashville, I really don't want to hear about it." And he said, "No, he wants to talk to you about cutting in Memphis." Well, I was out of that chair in a flash.

I had only four days to set it up, 'til Monday. And I knew that Chips had Roy Hamilton, who was one of Elvis's idols, scheduled to record that day and Neil Diamond scheduled for Monday night.

I went out in the hall and phoned Chips at home. I said, "Lincoln," which is his real name. "I'm up at Graceland. Would you still like to cut Elvis?" And he said, "Don't be playing games with me. You know how bad I want to do that." I said, "I'm not joking. He wants to cut here in Memphis, and he wants to cut with you." I said, "But you got one little problem. He's got to start Monday night, and that's when Neil Diamond's in there." Chips's exact words were, "Fuck Neil Diamond. Neil Diamond will just have to be postponed. Tell Elvis he's on."

I told him this would have to be a closed session, with security, so he needed to tell the musicians they couldn't invite any-body. And he said, "No problem." And then I put Felton on to work out the details with him on behalf of RCA.

I had one more thing to do, which was the hardest part. And I phrased it in a way where I knew Elvis wouldn't get upset. I said, "I need to ask you to do me a favor. You're going to have six of the best musicians in the recording business. The studio is great, the producer's great. And we all know you can sing. So please, would you get some good songs." Elvis said, "Well, I was going to play you some stuff that I got out in California. It's from this really odd guy."

When Elvis was doing *Speedway*, Nancy Sinatra introduced him to Billy Strange, who ended up cowriting several songs with Mac Davis that Elvis recorded, like "Memories" and "Nothingville," on the *Singer Special* soundtrack. Billy was also the musical director on *Live a Little, Love a Little*, and *The Trouble with Girls*. He told Elvis he had a great songwriter he wanted him to meet.

Elvis told me he walked into the room, and this guy was sit-ting in the corner on the floor, playing guitar and singing these songs. And that there was no damn furniture in the room. The guy's name was Scott Davis, but he went by "Mac." And Mac Davis played Elvis "In the Ghetto" and "Don't Cry Daddy."

That first night at American, Elvis cut "Long Black Limousine," "This Is the Story," and "Wearin' That Loved on Look." And Chips was totally in control. Elvis wanted this album to be a hit so bad. And he'd never really worked with a producer before. Elvis would be the one to say, "No, I don't like this take. Let's do it again." But Chips would stop him in the middle and say, "Hey, that didn't sound right, Elvis. You need to do it again. You can do it better than that."

A lot of people thought Elvis was going to blow up and say, "Let's get the hell out of here." But Elvis listened, and Chips got him to do a lot of things because Elvis was receptive at that point. And the musicians were really getting into it, and Elvis was loving it. The really big hits that Elvis cut during the Memphis Sessions—"Don't Cry Daddy," "In the Ghetto," "Suspicious Minds"—were all created in that studio by Elvis, Chips, and the musicians, by the way, as opposed to aping what was on the demo.

When we got in the car to go home that morning, Sonny was

driving, Elvis was sitting up front, and I was in the back with Joe and Lamar. Elvis turned around and looked at me, and it had been a long time since I had seen that look of happiness and satisfaction on his face. He said, "Man, that felt really great. I can't tell you how good I feel." And then he said, "I really just want to see if I can have a number one record one more time."

He recorded every day, but during the night of the sixteenth, the sore throat he'd had earlier in the month came back with a vengeance. He had a one-hundred-degree temperature and tonsillitis. So he stayed off four days and went back into the studio on the twentieth and recorded every day through the twenty-third.

The day before he went back in the studio, Red, and George, and Lamar, and Elvis and I were up in his office listening to some songs the Colonel's office sent. Almost all of them were terrible. When we finished, I think there was only one demo in the "yes" stack. Of course, I knew that since Lamar was with Hill and Range, whatever was said in that room about the demos would go back to Freddy Bienstock as soon as Lamar got away from there. And Freddy would then tell the Colonel.

Elvis was sitting behind his desk. He said, "Man, I don't know what I'm going to do. We don't have any more good songs. I don't know why they keep sending me all of this crap."

I decided I might as well go for broke. I said, "Elvis, you may not like what I'm about to say to you, but I know why you don't hear the good demos."

He said, "Why?" And I said, "Let me preface this by saying there isn't a songwriter in the world who wouldn't like Elvis Presley to cut one of his songs." And then I looked him straight in the face and I said, "The reason is, they don't need you anymore." And the whole room was just dead silent. No one had ever said anything like this to him before.

Red had a faint smile on his face because he knew what I was doing, and I knew he agreed. I half expected Elvis to pick something up and throw it at me. Instead, he said, "What do you mean, 'They don't need me'?" I said, "There was a time when you were the only person to have a million seller every time out of the box. And at that point, the Colonel was smart enough, and Hill and Range was smart enough, to get a piece of the publishing."

Elvis said, "Well, you know, that's business."

I said, "Yeah, but that was then, and this is now. There are a lot of people out there today with million-selling records. And there are a lot of singer-songwriters who don't need other people to do their songs. So when they do try to bring a good song to you, they get hit over the head with this thing about giving up 25 percent of their publishing. And they're just not going to do that anymore."

He didn't say anything, so I said, "But you know what else? The real crime is that you don't hear but a fraction of what you get. Someone's picking your fucking music for you. There's no reason in the world why you shouldn't have been the first person to hear the demo of every hit record that's been cut in the last five years. Writers come to us, but all we can say is, 'Send it to the Colonel.'"

I looked at Elvis, and he was sitting there with his hand over his mouth, like he was thinking it over. Lamar was gritting his teeth because I was taking money out of his pocket. And Red's grin was bigger. Even George agreed with me, but he's such a wimp, he wouldn't say a peep to Elvis. They all just let me take the risk.

Elvis straightened up in his chair, and he was kicking his foot a mile a minute, which was his habit when he was nervous. He looked around, and he said, very firmly, "Well, here's the way it is. I want everybody to know this, and I don't give a fuck who they are. You tell them that I'll pick my own goddamn music from now on. I want to hear every song I can get my hands on, and if I've got a piece of the publishing, that's fine. But if I don't have a piece of it and I want to do the song, I'm going to do it."

Then he pointed his finger at me, and he said, "I want you to get me some songs." And he looked at Red and he said, "I want you to get me some good songs, too. I want every one of you, if you know somebody, to get me some songs." He was talking to George on that one because George knew a lot of artists through this TV show he had. So Klein immediately got on the phone and called Neil Diamond. That's how Elvis got "And the Grass Won't Pay No Mind," which he recorded during the third stage of the sessions, in February, along with "Kentucky Rain."

LAMAR FIKE: Eddie Rabbitt was one of my writers then. He was a young unknown. And he'd written this thing called "Kentucky

Rain." Elvis wasn't exactly knocked out with it. But I just insisted
he cut it. I said, "You've got to do it. It's just that good."

MARTY LACKER: When we went back into the studio on January
20, everybody was mumbling under his breath. Elvis had already
recorded "Don't Cry Daddy," the Mac Davis song—Ronnie Milsap
played piano and sang a little background on that, by the way—
and now Elvis took "In the Ghetto" in with him. They were getting
ready to record it, and all of a sudden Elvis came into the control
room and said, "I don't know if I should do this song or not."

Because it had always been drummed into him by Colonel
Parker, "Don't get involved in messages or politics." He looked
over at me, and I said, "Elvis, this song is fantastic. This song
ain't going to hurt you. If you're ever going to do a song like this,
this is the time."

And Chips popped up and said, "Elvis, I've got to tell you,
man, this is a hit song. You should cut this."

Elvis just stood there, thinking about it, with his face knitted
up. And Chips said, "Elvis, let me ask you a question. If you don't
do it, can I have the song?" Because at that time, Chips was also
recording Joe Tex and Joe Simon, these two hit black artists. And
Elvis said, "No, I'll do it."

So Elvis put the demo track down, and then he came back
into the control room. There was a little vestibule in the studio, up
in front of the control board. And Tom Diskin, Colonel Parker's
man, and Lamar, and Joe, and Harry Jenkins, the vice president
of RCA, and maybe a couple other people sat there during all of
this. Probably half of them were hoping this session wouldn't fly
because it interfered with their agendas. None of them had as
much control here, and that included Felton and RCA.

In the beginning, before they started doing takes, Chips and
Elvis and Felton talked. And, actually on this record, their working relationship was fantastic. But Felton's contribution on this
record, other than some overdubs, was just to nod his head. And
Diskin and Bienstock and Lamar weren't happy because Elvis
and Chips were beginning to look at outside songs that Hill and
Range didn't have the publishing on.

LAMAR FIKE: Elvis had never recorded a social commentary song
like "[In the] Ghetto." I mean, "Ghetto" was not for him. "Ghetto"

was supposed to have been given to Rosey Grier, the black football player. And Elvis said, "Hey, I want this song. I don't want
Rosey Grier to have it."

But you talk about the success of this album . . . I remember
a funny thing that happened there. They spent $75,000 on that
album. They spend a half-million dollars on an album today, but
at the time, it was more money than had ever been spent on a
record, or certainly an Elvis record.

MARTY LACKER: After they did "In the Ghetto," they were pretty
much out of really good songs. And during the January 22 session, Chips turned to Elvis and said, "I've got this song that Mark
James wrote. We had a little record out on it, and nothing ever
happened with it, but I really think it's a hit song." And he played
him "Suspicious Minds."

Elvis listened to it, and he wasn't too sure of it, but Joe
Esposito talked him into recording it. Elvis said, "Well, we'll put
the track down at least." Because they were recording the modern way, where he did a rough voice track with the rhythm section, and then they did the sweetening and overdubs with the
horns or strings or background singers, and then Elvis came
back and sang the final vocal track. He wasn't crazy about that
method, but he realized it let the producer get a better balance on
the sounds.

"Suspicious Minds" was spliced together from three different
takes. And, of course, it became a million seller and one of the
biggest hits Elvis ever had. In fact, it was his last number one hit
on the Billboard "Hot 100" chart. Two years after he recorded it,
the local music industry named it the "Outstanding Single"
recorded in Memphis.

There was just this one little problem, see. Chips had the publishing on it. And when they were doing the overdubs on it, Chips
walked out into the hallway. Freddy Bienstock was at this session.
And him and Diskin cornered Chips in the hall. Chips was leaning
up against the wall, and both of them were on either side of him,
trying to get a piece of the song. I was standing next to them, listening, and hoping they wouldn't screw up the session.

Chips doesn't take any shit from anybody, and after a little
bit of this, he decided he'd had enough. He looked at both of
them and he said, "Gentlemen, I thought we were here to cut

some hit records. Now, if that's not the case, let me tell you what you can do. You can take your fucking tapes, and you and your whole group can get the hell out of here. Don't ask me for something that belongs to me. I'm not going to give it to you."

Well, Harry Jenkins, the RCA vice president, spoke up and said he agreed with Chips. And Chips went in the control room and put his feet up on the board and pulled out a pack of unfiltered Camels. He was just hotter than hell.

Diskin said, "I'll go talk to Mr. Presley about this." So I thought, "I'll go listen to what he tells him because there's no need for this session to be sabotaged." I wanted Elvis to know the truth, not some version of the truth that Diskin wanted him to hear. I was standing right behind him, and Diskin never saw me, not even when I followed him into the studio.

Elvis and Felton were still working on something with the musicians, and when Diskin said he'd like a word with them, they came over. Diskin said, "Elvis, we're trying to get this piece of 'Suspicious Minds,' and Chips is being belligerent about it." Elvis saw the look on my face, which said, "This is bullshit." And he said, "Mr. Diskin, I appreciate that you're trying to do your job, but leave the session to me and Felton and Chips."

That's the first time Elvis ever did anything like that. Diskin got so pissed off, he went back up to the front and picked up the telephone and called Colonel Parker in L.A. One of the guys was sitting up there, and he heard them talking, and he told me the whole thing. Diskin told Colonel, "Elvis wants to handle this himself. We don't have any control here. What are we going to do?" And then he said, "Well, okay, if you say so." He put the phone down, walked out the front door, got in his car, went back to the hotel, packed his bag, and left for California.

I later found out what Parker said: "He doesn't want any of us around? Then you leave there, you come back here right now, and let him fall on his ass."

So Elvis fell on his ass, all right. In twelve days, he cut thirty-six sides. Four of them were singles—"In the Ghetto," "Suspicious Minds," "Don't Cry Daddy," and "Kentucky Rain," and all but the last were gold, even though "Kentucky Rain" was a substantial hit. And the two albums that came out of it [*From Elvis in Memphis* and *From Memphis to Vegas/From Vegas to Memphis*] went platinum. That's some falling on your ass.

It was the first, and I might add the only, time in Elvis Presley's [RCA] career that someone from the Colonel's office was *not* at the session.

LAMAR FIKE: What happened there was that Hill and Range was starting to lose control because Elvis was not selling records, and he couldn't demand the fees like he used to. In a way, it was the end of an era. But he still recorded our songs.

BILLY SMITH: Elvis had bucked the Colonel. If he could have only kept that up . . .

MARTY LACKER: The first single to be released out of the Memphis Sessions was "In the Ghetto." It hit *Billboard* real fast, the fastest any of Elvis's records had hit in five years. The *Billboard* charts list the producers of the records. And I looked in there, and for the producer, it said, "Felton Jarvis." Chips's name wasn't mentioned.

I said, "Bullshit." I called *Billboard,* and I said, "Look, you got a mistake here on these charts. On 'In the Ghetto,' you have 'Produced by Felton Jarvis.' When in actuality, it was produced by Chips Moman." Well, the next week the *Billboard* chart came out and it said, "Produced by Chips Moman," and Felton's name was nowhere to be seen.

The third week, I looked, and there was no producer listed. By this time the record was going into the Top 10. So I called *Billboard* again. I didn't use my name. I told them I was some-body from RCA. I acted real indignant, and I said, "What is wrong with you people?"

The guy said, "Did you say you're from RCA?" I said, "Yeah." He said, "Well, I wish you guys would make up your mind. You called a week ago, screaming and hollering, and wanting to know why we had Chips Moman's name in there. And then you had the Colonel's office call and say, 'No producer.'"

I said, "Put Chips Moman back on there." And he said, "We'll have to have this in writing." I said, "I'll get back to you."

BILLY SMITH: The Colonel might have been outsmarted that one time, but he had a way of coming back and goosing you when you least expected it. Like with "Suspicious Minds."

MARTY LACKER: When "Suspicious Minds" came out in September, it had a surprise on it. Because after Chips turned over the master tapes to RCA, somebody took "Suspicious Minds" back to Nashville or to California and remixed it. They put all these other voices on it—Millie Kirkham, for instance—and went back to that Nashville crap. And then they stuck a phony fade-and-bump ending on it, where it drops down and then pops back up.

That's a technique that works well onstage. It's visual, with the dimming of the lights and the dramatic comeback. But on a record, it ain't worth a shit. And radio stations don't like it because they time their music so closely and it screws up their program. Bill Gavin, of "The Gavin Report," talked to me about it. His report was bigger than *Billboard*. He said, "Why did they do that? It was a great record, but I can't tell you how many program directors said they wouldn't play it unless they cut it off themselves. It almost killed that record."

CHAPTER 41

SIN CITY

After the creative exhilaration of the Memphis Sessions, Elvis found it suffocating to return to Hollywood for his last dramatic picture, *Change of Habit*, in which he played a ghetto physician who unwittingly falls in love with a Catholic nun (Mary Tyler Moore) sent out into the lay community.

When the movie wrapped on May 2, Elvis and Priscilla flew to Hawaii on vacation. On their return, Elvis threw himself into fretting over his engagement at the new International Hotel, later the Las Vegas Hilton, for four weeks beginning the end of July.

Believing he still had something to prove to the Beatles, and most certainly to Tom Jones, a Vegas staple who knew how to make the over-forty matrons react the way Elvis had once affected young girls, Elvis paid close attention to certain of Jones's stage moves when he saw him perform during his Hawaiian stay—an irony, since Jones had learned how to move onstage from watching Elvis. In preparation for the opening, Elvis again slacked off on his pill use and toned his body with regular karate workouts.

The challenge deeply frightened and aroused him at the same time. Elvis was now thirty-four years old. He had legitimate concerns about his voice as he had asked little of it since his touring days, and to attempt a long engagement under such pressure could certainly prove problematic. He also worried about his ability to pull crowds to the massive hotel, which, with 1,500 rooms, was two and a half times the size of Caesars Palace.

To Elvis's genuine surprise, he sold out every show, drawing exuberant fans to Vegas from literally all over the world—a feat which amazed Elvis's longtime friend, Sammy Davis, Jr., who knew Vegas as well as any performer alive. Even hardened pit workers admitted they'd never seen such excitement generated over an engagement—it practically crackled the air. During his first four-week engagement, Elvis would set a Vegas record, with 101,509 paid customers and a gross take of $1.5 million.

After the success of opening night, Colonel negotiated a five-year contract at the International, with Elvis playing two thirty-day engagements a year, one in January and another in August. His fee: $1 million, the highest fee ever paid in Vegas. Immediately, Colonel began arranging tour dates to take advantage of Elvis's commercial rebirth.

For Elvis, the victory must have tasted particularly sweet. The last time he'd played the town was in 1956, when his lame jokes and amateurish between-song prattle sank his engagement with Freddy Martin and Shecky Greene at the New Frontier.

In contrast, *Variety* now reported that "the Elvis Presley who was a freakish kid curiosity when he was third feature on a New Frontier showbill is no more. He has become 'ELVIS,' not only in huge electric letters on the International's marquee, but also in more publicized and verbalized affirmations of his superstar status."

LAMAR FIKE: In those months before he opened in Vegas, Elvis was as nervous as Hitler at a packed Bar Mitzvah. The slightest little thing just frayed his nerves. And for a while, Elvis had been tired of putting up with Alan's doping and having to deal with Alan's wife.

MARTY LACKER: The straw that broke the camel's back was that ski trip to Aspen. That was right after the Memphis Sessions in February. They all went out to L.A. first, and Elvis took everybody down to Kerr's Sporting Goods on Wilshire Boulevard, and they picked out ski equipment and clothes for themselves and their wives. And Alan questioned the fact that he had to pay for it.

LAMAR FIKE: I was there when the whole deal popped loose. We were at the outfitters. Elvis said, "Everybody pick out what you want." But then all of a sudden, he decided he was spending too much money. I don't know what triggered it. Maybe Priscilla. And he said, "Okay, you all pay for yourself."

Well, Alan got pissed off. By the time he picked out what he and Jo needed, he had about $500 or $600 worth of stuff. It was equipment they'd never use again, and probably couldn't afford, because Alan was keeping two apartments on $200 a week.

I wasn't two feet away from Elvis. And Alan blew up sideways. He said, "Well, he can stick this stuff up his ass." And Elvis heard him. And he turned around to Esposito and he said, "I set up a party for everybody, and the cocksucker is too cheap to buy his own damn equipment? Fuck him! I don't want to talk to him. Just keep him out of my sight." And then he said, "Better yet, get rid of the son of a bitch. I don't want to see him."

BILLY SMITH: At the time, Elvis had foot the bill for a lot of things, and he was beginning to feel like some of the guys were taking advantage of him. But Elvis would get mad at you and then blow up for something else. Another instance was with Jerry when they went to Colorado. Elvis's commode stopped up, so he was going to take Jerry's condo. Well, Jerry got aggravated about it and blew up at Elvis. And Elvis blew back. Got right up in his face. And so it wasn't too long after that when Jerry left. He decided he wanted to be a film editor. Went to work for Paramount.

LAMAR FIKE: If you set Elvis up, he'd come at you. So you never set him up. The thing with Alan was, he couldn't take it. In May of '69, a couple months after Elvis let him go, Alan tried to commit suicide again. He always denied it, but it's the truth. We were in Hawaii on vacation. We got this call from his wife at three o'clock in the morning. He loaded up on Tuinals or Placidyls, one, because he was losing her and he was losing his grip. And he was facing a fact that all of us had to face after Elvis died—he wasn't Elvis. When he went back into the mundane, day-to-day life, Alan never again had the fun that he had with us.

MARTY LACKER: After Alan got fired, he stayed in California for a while and worked as an extra in pictures. But that was a dead end, and he eventually came back to Memphis. He filed for divorce almost the day he got home. Then he went to work as the manager and bartender at this club, TJ's, which was owned by a friend of ours, Herbie O'Mell. Ronnie Milsap led the house band there. Later, Alan got into the bond business.

He married a second time, around '70, to this woman named

Marian Stokes. The only good thing that came out of that marriage was Miles, Alan's son. He became Alan's whole life.

LAMAR FIKE: I wasn't around Alan a lot in the latter years. But I had the feeling he continued to do drugs. He kept using Dr. Nick.

MARTY LACKER: The fact that Elvis didn't call Alan after the firing really hurt him. He said, "You know, as much as I loved Elvis, I'll never forget that." Yet he never said a bad word about him, not even after Elvis died.

LAMAR FIKE: Sometime in '69, Dick Grob came into the entourage as a security man. He'd been a fighter pilot in the air force and then he became a sergeant in the Palm Springs Police Department. He rubbed a lot of people the wrong way because he's a tough, know-it-all kind of guy. Elvis was getting more and more into all that police stuff, so I think Dick was just a connection.

When Elvis went to Vegas, he mostly wanted the old gang around him because he was scared. So he brought me out to run lights for him. Putting that show together was orchestrated chaos.

MARTY LACKER: When Elvis did the Memphis Sessions, he asked Chips and the American group to be his band in Vegas. I thought, "There ain't no way that Chips is going to do it because he'd have to close the studio, and he's not going to do that." And I knew those guys hadn't played onstage in a while. But I'll be damned if Chips didn't say, "Yeah, man, we'd love to."

In the end, they didn't do it. My guess is that Colonel decided he didn't want Elvis to be exposed to Chips anymore. So they started making up lies about Chips. They fed Elvis some crap about Chips trying to steal "In the Ghetto." But that was part of Parker's game. He'd cut his nose off to spite his face.

Elvis ended up with a good band, though. He had James Burton and John Wilkinson on guitar, Larry Muhoberac—he was later replaced by Glen D Hardin—on piano, Jerry Scheff on bass, and Ronnie Tutt on drums. And then Charlie Hodge stood up there and played guitar and sang harmony vocals. But he was mainly there to hand Elvis his water and, later, his scarves. His microphone wasn't usually connected, except for a couple of songs where he actually sang harmony, and his guitar wasn't hooked up to an amplifier. I thought he was terrible. But he thought he was big-time because he was up there on the stage with Elvis.

LAMAR FIKE: Christ, Elvis interviewed musicians for weeks. He must have gone through two hundred players before he found the ones he wanted. Then they rehearsed at RCA Sound Studios for ten days. Learned two hundred songs or so. And then spent another week putting it together in Vegas.

MARTY LACKER: For his backup singers, Elvis wanted the Jordanaires, but they had other commitments in Nashville, so he chose the Imperials, the gospel group with Jake Hess, who had always been one of his idols. But he also wanted that soul sound. So he hired the Sweet Inspirations, which was a black, female group. They'd sung behind Aretha Franklin.

I was the one who suggested them. I knew they'd cut a hit ["Sweet Inspiration"] with Chips, and I'd heard a lot about them from Dionne Warwick, who'd recorded at Chips's studio. So I told him about them at the movies one night, and he said, "Remind me when I get home, and I'll write that down."

LAMAR FIKE: We went in there in '69 not knowing a damn thing. He didn't even have an act, much less a Vegas act. We literally designed that show from scratch—made it up as we went along. Hugo Granada, one of the greatest light men in Las Vegas, had taught me a lot about lights when I was with Brenda Lee. We had a light man we worked with, but the light show that Elvis used 'til the day he died was the one I designed and developed.

It was pretty impromptu, even during the performances. I'd do something wrong with the lights, and Elvis would holler up at me in the balcony, and I'd holler back, "Hey, it's hard to follow you sometimes." The audience thought it was funny.

We had it planned that when he'd do "Tiger Man," I'd throw a strobe and he would move sideways. But one night, for some reason, he complained about it. So I put a lobster scope on a light. A lobster scope is a round apparatus with a hole in it. You spin it up to speed. And the light hits that one spot, and it causes a strobe effect.

Well, he didn't know what it was, and it liked to blind him. He stopped everything, and said, "What in God's name . . . ?" I said, "It's a lobster scope." He said, "What does that thing do?" I said, "What it just did." And he said, "Well, I can't see!" I said, "Well, I won't use it again." He said, "No, use it." And he cranked back into "Tiger Man" and did it.

MARTY LACKER: The deal that Colonel struck with the hotel was that Elvis would play two shows a day, seven days a week, for a month, starting with the first engagement. And for that he got $100,000 a week, or $400,000 for the month.

Now, $400,000 for a month's work was very, very good money. But you've got to understand something about Vegas. Before Elvis started performing there, every entertainer had one night a week off—Monday or Tuesday. And Elvis said, "I'm going to work seven nights a week." He was so up and excited the first time. He said, "Man, I love this. I'd go stark raving mad if I had to sit around one night, just twiddling my thumbs." So that was a first for Vegas. And the hotels started saying to other entertainers, "If Elvis can work seven nights a week, so can you."

Elvis was also the first artist to have just his first name up on a marquee. The International ran this gargantuan "ELVIS" up there, with the names of the comedian Sammy Shore, and the Imperials, and the Sweet Inspirations in much smaller letters. After that, all the other hotels just followed suit.

The International had just been built. Actually, parts of it weren't quite finished. And they had this 1,500-seat showroom that they could really pack two thousand people into. Alex Shoofey, the general manager, asked Colonel if Elvis wanted to open it. And Colonel said, "Not on your life," because it was risky. The room was a tough place to play because it's sort of like an auditorium—real spread out and not very intimate. So they put Barbra Streisand in it, and then Elvis followed after her run.

We did an interview with Sammy Davis, Jr., for that documentary we made after Elvis died. He said, "Man, I've been performing in Vegas almost since Vegas was opened. And I have never, ever seen somebody fill a two-thousand-seat room." But Elvis's whole engagement was sold out ahead of time.

LAMAR FIKE: Nobody goes to Vegas and plays four weeks any-more—they do five days, tops. Do you realize what kind of hell four weeks is? That's a marathon—nearly sixty performances. And Elvis had such a high-energy show that when he would do an honest hour and fifteen minutes twice a night, he was so tired he was cross-eyed. That's why he took all that stuff [drugs] to keep him going.

MARTY LACKER: You know one reason Colonel booked Elvis to a schedule like that? The Colonel got really into debt out there, gambling. And when he struck his deal with the International, he probably had his gambling debts cut back.

Elvis might have made unprecedented money in Vegas, but he was worth a lot more than he got. Because when the hotel realized that Elvis was going to sell out every show, they immedi-ately signed him to a five-year deal of two monthlong engage-ments a year. But with an increase in fee of only $25,000 a week—$125,000, for a total of $1 million for the two months. That's the key, see. Colonel allowed it.

Just look at the figures: They had a $15 minimum, at two thousand people, for $30,000 a show. At two shows a night, for twenty-eight consecutive nights, that's $1,680,000. But it was really more because 50 percent of the shows were dinner shows, and sometimes they got even more people in that room. So the hotel was taking in more than $2 million a month on Elvis—twice a year for five years. Now, Vegas knows that most shows lose money, but they book entertainment to get people into the casi-nos. Elvis was the first act in Vegas history to make a hotel a profit on the show. Plus, he was bringing the type of people to Vegas who didn't normally come there, like families. They were coming from all over the world.

It's pretty clear what was going on: Colonel was supporting his gambling habit. Shoofey used to work for Milton Prell, by the way—Colonel's old buddy at the Sahara. I think that's what Colonel held out for in the deal at the International—that the hotel would give him perks and forgive at least a portion of his casino debts if he and Elvis signed the deal.

LAMAR FIKE: Now, is that exactly how it went down? Who knows for sure except the Colonel, and Shoofey, and Kirk Kerkorian, the owner of the hotel? You never could pierce that veil. I think that they had the Colonel in an uncomfortable position, and they said, "Okay, you can get out of it if you do this." That's what we've heard.

MARTY LACKER: They supposedly wrote that contract on a table-cloth in the restaurant at the hotel. Colonel says it's true. But you can bet your house that it was written on paper later.

LAMAR FIKE: Colonel had living quarters at the hotel. Now, why would the International let Colonel Parker have a suite of rooms? Because Colonel lost a fortune at the International on blackjack, craps, and roulette. Alex Shoofey confirmed that. He said, "The Colonel was one of the best customers we had. He was good for a million dollars a year."

Back in '75, '76, somebody told me that Colonel was one of the top five rollers in Las Vegas. But you almost never knew what his money was worth because he played with colored chips, and you couldn't tell what the denomination of the chips were. Only the hotel knew.

When Barron Hilton bought the hotel from Kerkorian in '71, he bought Colonel's markers, too. That's how the whole thing stayed in a lock.

A few years after he opened, Elvis and I were sitting in the living room one day, and Elvis said, "Look, damnit, I'll play this town 'til I die. That old son of a bitch owes so much money that they own him, and they're trying to own me." I said, "Are you kidding me?" He said, "Lamar, I'm talking all the way back to 1957 at the Sahara Hotel with his buddy Milton Prell. Colonel was gambling when he had Eddy Arnold, and it carried into me. The markers were moved from there, to there, to here." So Colonel had Elvis where he wanted him, and Elvis knew it.

BILLY SMITH: Colonel would gamble on anything. It's like one time with a picture, Colonel and Hal Wallis got into a little tiff about the girls who were up in Elvis's suite until three A.M. Wallis complained that they looked tired, and that they yawned all the time. Colonel picked up a pair of dice and said, "I'll tell you what, Wallis. I'll shoot you double or nothing for the movie. If I win, you pay double. If you win, we'll do it free. One roll of the dice." Wallis stared a hole through him, and then he said, "You're crazy, Parker."

LAMAR FIKE: A high roller is treated royally in Vegas. That's why Colonel would leave with all those sandwiches and other food, and that's why he had a whole wing of the hotel for his use. If you own a hotel and casino, you make the high roller happy. And if your high roller happens to own an artist, especially your biggest-selling star, you've got a guy that's stronger than Tarzan's armpits.

But Colonel stayed in debt, and the debt got bigger. The tragedy for Elvis was that Colonel apparently never had to pay it back in real money.

I was up, like $40,000 or $50,000 one night, and Colonel came up and took my $50,000 and bet it on the line, and I lost it in one pop. I said, "You can't do that to me!" But he did.

MARTY LACKER: Colonel is the only guy I've ever seen in Vegas that they'd let use two balls on the roulette wheel. I was standing right next to him when he did it. They didn't care what Colonel did in the casino. They just wanted his marker.

LAMAR FIKE: The same night he lost my $50,000, I saw him lose a quarter of a million dollars in one roll of the dice. I know because this time he was betting stacks of $100 chips. And he played what they call "Around the Horn," the center of the table. Those were all the long-shot bets. And your money's not worth anything on those long-shot bets. He would always bet against the guy passing, and the guy started passing and beat his brains out. On roulette, Colonel would play every number on the table. And I promise you there weren't any dollar chips.

MARTY LACKER: When Milton Prell owned the Aladdin Hotel, and before Elvis got married there, we went to Vegas to mess around one time. Colonel wouldn't let anybody on a table he played on, if he could help it.

This was one of the few times I got involved in one of his little games. We were standing at the table, and he was smoking a cigar. This old drunken woman came by and said, "Well, what have we got here?" She staggered around, and she bumped into Parker. And that pissed him off.

After that, she inched her way into the table and said, "I think I'm going to play some roulette," just slurring her words, you know. And the guy working the table looked at the Colonel like "Hey, I can't turn anybody away. This is a casino." So the Colonel looked around, and he pulled a bunch of cigars out of his pocket. And he said, "Pass these out to all the guys." There were about five or six of us around the table. And he said, "All right, boys, let's smoke her out of here." He was standing next to her, and he puffed on his cigar, and he blew a big mouthful of smoke right in her face. And so did everybody else, repeatedly. We made this woman so sick she passed out. That was Parker's way of getting rid of her.

LAMAR FIKE: The night before Elvis opened, we went down and saw Barbra Streisand. Elvis listened for a while, and he didn't really get her. Especially when she went into her Jewish shtick. A little ways into it, he turned to me and he said, "She sucks."

He'd been drinking Bloody Marys, and when we went backstage, instead of telling Barbra how great she was, Elvis said, "Man, what did you ever see in Elliott Gould? I can't stand the guy." And Streisand gathered herself up into this indignant huff and said, "What do you mean? He's the father of my son!" Hardly an auspicious meeting.

MARTY LACKER: As soon as Streisand was out of there, Parker went to work turning the International into the House of Presley. And he continued to handle Elvis like he was some carnival freak. The day Elvis opened, Colonel walked around in a white coat that said "Elvis—International—In Person" and put posters and banners all over the place. And then he sold straw hats, and canes, and teddy bears.

Well, he made money, I'm sure, from the Elvis fanatics. But I can tell you right now, Elvis would have had two thousand people in that showroom, anyway.

LAMAR FIKE: Christ, everybody turned out that night: Ann-Margret, Dick Clark, Angie Dickinson and Burt Bacharach, George Hamilton, Carol Channing, Wayne Newton, Fats Domino, Pat Boone, Shirley Bassey, Paul Anka, Petula Clark. On and on. I think they got 2,500 people in that room. The fire marshal would have shit a brick.

MARTY LACKER: The opening in Vegas in '69 was fantastic. George Klein and I went out for it. I called Esposito and told him we were coming, and he said, "Elvis would like you to do him a favor." I said, "What's that?" He said, "He'd like you to come the second night, not the first night." I said, "Really, why?" He said, "Well, I'll tell you the truth. He knows there'll be all kinds of people there the first night. But he's real nervous that everybody'll leave, and there won't be anybody out in the audience for the second night, or the third or the fourth. So he'd really like you and George to be there the second night, so he'll know he has someone to give him a good reception."

We drove out and arrived the afternoon of the second day. Elvis was on the twenty-ninth floor, the high rollers' floor—later, they built the thirtieth-floor penthouse suite for him. Anyway, I called up there, and Joe answered, and I said, "We're coming up. What's your suite number?" And Joe said, "No, he doesn't want you up here." I said, "What do you mean? I drove eleven hundred damn miles to get here!" Joe said, "He doesn't want to see you until after the show. He wants you to tell him what you think." I thought Joe was joking, but he wasn't. So we just waited.

That was the first time in many, many years that I had seen him perform live, and the performance was absolutely electrifying. He opened with "Blue Suede Shoes," and you could tell he was nervous. Then he went into a lot of the old stuff, "I Got a Woman," "That's All Right (Mama)," "Love Me Tender," "Jailhouse Rock," "Don't Be Cruel," and a couple others. And then he said, "This is the first time I've worked in front of people in nine [sic] years, and it may be my last, I don't know."

But he didn't have to worry. They liked the old stuff, and they liked the newer stuff—"Memories," "In the Ghetto," "Suspicious Minds," "Tiger Man," and, interestingly enough, a couple of Beatles tunes, "Hey, Jude," and "Yesterday." The last song was "What'd I Say," the Ray Charles hit, and then he got this just thunderous standing ovation. He left the stage, and when he came back out, he did "Can't Help Falling in Love" for an encore.

Afterwards, people were filing out, and Joe or somebody came up to get us. We went downstairs to the dressing room, and Elvis was waiting outside the door. He still had his stage costume on—a dark blue karate-style outfit, tapered and belled. He looked at my face to see my reaction, and all I could say was, "My boy, my boy."

It was funny because he just opened his arms, and we hugged. We didn't say any more until we got in the dressing room because we were very emotional. I finally said, "Elvis, that was unbelievable." And he said, "Man, that's the greatest feeling I've had in years. It's fantastic."

There were only one or two occasions when I saw the Colonel and Elvis hug, and that was one of them. Colonel actually looked like he had tears in his eyes because everything went so well. Now, those tears might have been motivated by dollar signs because he realized they were back in business again. But they were tears nonetheless.

CHAPTER 42

THE FINAL DECADE

Badges and Badmen

LAMAR FIKE: In 1970, I went back with Elvis full-time. He'd entered the second stage of his drug use then. He was getting a little bolder about stuff he'd take, especially when he wasn't in Vegas, because he was bored.

In '70, he looked great. God, he was trim, and his cheekbones showed when he smiled. He was damn near gorgeous. But downers will put weight back on you pretty quick. Elvis loved downers, and he loved getting totally fucked up.

BILLY SMITH: Elvis wasn't bombed all the time. I'd say maybe 40 percent of the time in the sixties. It got worse in the seventies— probably 60 percent of the time. He always had pills in him, but he didn't get really bad until the last four years of his life. That's when you actually had to watch him.

MARTY LACKER: In January of '70, Elvis opened his second Vegas engagement. Everybody came, again from all over the world, and they continued to come for as long as he played the hotel. He played 837 sold-out shows in eight years. In fact, Elvis held the record for the number of consecutive sold-out performances in the Pavilion Room until 1991, when George Strait broke it. After the '69 opening, when Elvis first broke all the Las Vegas attendance records, the hotel gave him that big gold belt as a kind of award.

LAMAR FIKE: It's funny about that belt. When they gave it to him, he hated that damn thing. Then, later on, we couldn't get the son of a bitch off him.

MARTY LACKER: It was gold over sterling silver, with this huge, four-by-six-inch buckle, and individual blocks linked together, with animal designs—sort of like the signs of the zodiac. Elvis decided to make it even more gaudy—added diamonds, rubies, and sapphires.

When he went back to Vegas in '70, he started wearing the jumpsuits with the high pointed collars. Bill Belew, the guy who came up with the black leather suit for *The Singer Special,* designed them. And they made an impact on the audience.

Most of them were white, and they were all flared in big bells at the bottom, which was the style of the time. The first one, in '70, was cut down to the breastbone to accentuate his shoulders. He wore a lot of pearls with this first one. Not on the suit, but around his neck in big bunches, and on the belt. The belt was kind of karate style, and it made a rope effect with strands of gold and strands of pearls. He tied it like a sash on his hip so one end hung down and swept his knee.

When you see the jumpsuits on display at Graceland or wherever, they look like polyester. But all of them were made of Italian wool gabardine, which is what ice skaters' costumes are made of. Belew said the fabric would move with the body but still hold its shape. He used metal on some of them, usually silver or brass. And most of them had stones sewn onto them.

Albert Goldman made a big deal of saying that Elvis wore what he called "thin white dancer's briefs, no different from a pair of women's panties," under his jumpsuit. Well, he wore them under the jumpsuit because they didn't leave any lines. It wasn't such a big deal. Goldman just wanted to make Elvis seem weirder.

LAMAR FIKE: The dancer's briefs? They were more like the tights that a male dancer would wear. It's not like he wore them in everyday life, for Christ's sake.

MARTY LACKER: A question nobody seems to ask about Elvis and Las Vegas is how Colonel kept him away from the real Mafia. But it's a good question because they were always around, both in Vegas and in the entertainment business on the whole.

One weekend, I went out to Vegas on business, and I went over to visit this guy we liked who started out as a bellhop at the Sahara, a guy who took care of us sometimes. By now, he'd moved up and over to the Flamingo as the maître d' at the Thunderbird Lounge. He was a supernice guy.

We were sitting in the coffee shop, and this elderly gentleman came up with a couple of guys, and he said hello to my friend. I had seen him around. He'd been introduced to me as "Sonny." He looked like a typical Mafioso.

He sat down and had a cup of coffee, and my buddy told him that I was real close to Elvis. Sonny said, "He's a good boy." And he said, "How's he doin'?" I said, "Oh, he's fine." Then he looked at me, and he said, "Listen, you tell him if he ever needs a favor—or anytime I can be of service to him—just get in touch with me through your pal here." I never mentioned it to Elvis.

That's the only contact that I know of. Later on, in '75, just before Elvis bought the Convair 880, the *Lisa Marie*, there was a situation where he was going to buy Robert Vesco's Boeing 707 jetliner. He made a $75,000 down payment on it. Vesco was that fugitive, or exiled, financier. He was rumored to be in the mob, and bogus as hell. Either way, Vesco's agents sternly advised Elvis to back out. They said the plane would be seized if it ever touched down out of the country. And Elvis and Vernon had a hell of a time getting their down payment back.

There's a book out now, *Elvis: The Secret Files* by John Parker, that says that a guy named Frederick Pro, who was supposed to be linked with Mafia types, ripped Elvis off over another plane, the Lockheed Jetstar. Parker's got this theory that the Cosa Nostra murdered Elvis over that deal.

This Parker guy says that the FBI was so worried about protecting Elvis's life that they were going to have undercover agents in his entourage on what was to be his last tour. Well, Lamar did the advance work for the tour with the Colonel. And he didn't notice anything different.

I don't know how the Colonel kept the real Mafia away from

Elvis. To my knowledge, he was never approached. Although Albert Goldman says that Colonel's friend, Milton Prell, was the front man for the Detroit mob, so maybe that's the answer.

LAMAR FIKE: As much fun as playing Las Vegas was, by the second time, it got to be kind of old. Vegas is a very boring town. So we'd gamble.

I gambled a lot. And that's a habit that, unfortunately, stuck with me. When I did that book with Albert, I made two or three hundred thousand dollars on it and just gambled it away.

We all gambled. Your paycheck would be gone the next day. We'd run through our per diem, and we'd sign room service checks, and then we had to pay at the end if we had the money. Everybody but Esposito. He could do whatever he wanted. He was a big shot.

MARTY LACKER: "Flashy Diamond Joe from Chicago" had this air. It was his job to okay comp tickets, so a lot of people came to him. And he liked that authority.

One day, Elvis had just finished breakfast, and we were sitting around talking. Joe picked up the telephone to call downstairs. We always thought the operators could tell which suite the call was coming from. So Esposito said, "Hey, this is Joe."

Elvis looked over at me, and I looked over at Elvis. It was funny to us. Like "Here's big-time Joe." When Joe said something like that, Elvis would mouth it right after him: "Hey, this is Joe."

Anyway, we just heard silence. Followed by "Esposito." Well, Elvis started to chuckle, and so did I.

Elvis said, "What's the matter, Joe, having a problem?" Joe was still on the phone, and there was more silence, and Joe said, "I'm calling from the thirtieth floor, in the suite." Well, that still didn't cut it, and he said, real emphatically, "Joe Esposito, with Elvis."

Finally, Joe got so frustrated he hung up the phone. And Elvis said, "What's the matter, Joe, didn't they know who you were?" And Elvis burst out laughing. Joe said, "Yeah, that stupid bitch didn't know who I was." And Elvis said, "Well, who are you?" I said, "He's Joe Esposito with Elvis Presley. That's who."

LAMAR FIKE: With so much downtime, it was inevitable that Elvis would have a lot of women up to the suite. And since Elvis liked to watch girls wrestle on those 8mm films, so in Vegas we'd get girls to wrestle in the flesh.

Elvis would hire two girls, or sometimes more than two, to come up and put on a show. And everybody would sit around and watch. In their book, Red and Sonny talk about how Elvis would give his date a sleeping pill, and while she was out, he'd go watch the two women make it with each other, and then he'd get all fired up and go back to his date and wake her up. That actually happened. Dear God! Elvis could promote things.

MARTY LACKER: Elvis's main doctor in Vegas was Thomas R. "Flash" Newman because he was the hotel doctor. He used to give Elvis a shot of B-12 before his performances, and prescriptions, too. There were all kinds of doctors. Max Shapiro had an office in Vegas, too.

BILLY SMITH: The Landmark Pharmacy was the drugstore Elvis used in Vegas. It was right up from the hotel. He also used the pharmacy at Sunrise Hospital. I remember a couple of guys going over there to pick up a prescription.

LAMAR FIKE: Elvis still wanted to buy a pharmacy in Memphis. And I heard he tried to buy one in California at one point. That was still his dream, to have his own pharmacy.

MARTY LACKER: The date that's usually given for the start of the TCB jewelry is '72, but my recollection is that it started around '70.

"Take care of business" was a black expression. Elvis would say it in a sort of ethnic way, with a black accent. It was just a hip saying. Aretha Franklin sang, "Take Care/TCB," on her version of "Respect," for example.

Elvis came up with the jewelry after he met this young guy named Paul, who was a stone-cold killer. He was a bodyguard for Mayor [Sam] Yorty of Los Angeles, and he worked undercover on drugs. He broke the Hollywood High School drug ring years ago, and the Mafia put out a contract on him.

Shortly after that, he met this girl. He started liking her a lot, and he went to bed with her. And in the middle of the passion, he looked down, and he saw she was wearing the lightning bolt around her neck. And he said he froze.

The lightning bolt has two meanings. One is "in a flash." In other words, "Whatever you need to do, do it quick." But the lightning bolt was also the insignia for the West Coast Mafia.

The girl's father was the head of the West Coast Mafia. And that was the guy who had the contract out on Paul. He said that after the initial shock, he just played it cool. He took the girl home because he thought she was planted by her father.

Well, Paul told that story to Elvis, and he loved it. That's why he put the lightning bolt in the design for the jewelry, in addition to the idea of doing things "in a flash." He liked the idea that the West Coast Mafia used it.

LAMAR FIKE: I don't think Elvis ever cared about the "in a flash." He used the lightning bolt *solely* because it was the symbol of the West Coast Mafia. It excited him.

BILLY SMITH: Nah. The lightning bolt come from Elvis's army days. It was the insignia for his battalion. Or maybe in the back of his mind, he identified it with Captain Marvel, Jr. That's where he got the idea for the capes. From the comic books.

LAMAR FIKE: Whoever came up with it, Sol Schwartz, the jeweler in Beverly Hills, made the first ones. They were fourteen-karat-gold pendants, and they hung on a twenty-four-inch rope chain. Elvis gave them to the entourage and to his other close friends and family. And then he came up with "TLC"—"Tender Lovin' Care"—for the women. Shit, he put that logo on everything—on rings, on the plane when he got it, everywhere. It's even on his tombstone. He came up with the "TCB Oath," too. He wrote it out, and Red's wife, Pat, typed it up.

It said, "More self-respect, more respect for fellow man, respect for fellow students and instructors. Respect for all styles and techniques. Body conditioning, mental conditioning, meditation for calming and stilling of the mind and body. Sharpen your skills, increase mental awareness, for all those who might choose a new outlook and personal philosophy." And get this. It also said, "Freedom from constipation." Then it said, "T.C.B. all techniques into one." And he signed it "Elvis Presley 8th." The "8th" was a reference to his eighth-degree black belt. He must have been higher than a kite when he wrote that.

I've still got my TCB necklace. I see 'em duplicated now as cheap shit sold by the gross in souvenir stores.

MARTY LACKER: In 1970, Elvis hired this guy named James Caughley. He used to come to the movies. When we went to the Memphian, we'd want hamburgers, and no one wanted to go get them. Well, James was easy to con. One night, Joe walked up to him and said, "James, do you want to do Elvis a favor?" James said, "Oh, yeah." So Joe said, "Go down to the Krystal [hamburger stand]."

The Krystal was, like, nine thousand blocks from the theater. But James did it. So then it got to the point where we'd say, "James— Hamburgers!" Finally, we just started calling him "Hamburger James."

LAMAR FIKE: Hamburger wasn't all that important, except that he kept a diary. He was a valet, a gofer, not part of the Mafia. But he was a good person, and he was good at what he did.

BILLY SMITH: James thought he was on *I Spy*. He snuck around a lot, always had something going on. If something was real secret, he'd whisper, "Hey, man, come here! I've got something to tell you!" The most ridiculous stuff just totally fascinated him.

LAMAR FIKE: Really, Hamburger was like a Saint Bernard dog. Very loyal. He was funny. But he didn't know he was funny. His face was red most of the time, and he had funny hair—slicked back. And he was short and stocky, and he had real heavy eyebrows. When we didn't call him "Hamburger," we called him "The Brow." But he was a misfit. He was a square peg in a round hole.

When Elvis hired him, we all went nuts. That was the begin-

ning of Elvis changing the group. But then everything was changing. Elvis was getting ready to go back on tour—Vegas on the road.

MARTY LACKER: That February, four days after Elvis closed in
Vegas, he played six shows in three days at the Houston
Astrodome. For $1 million. The first show was on a Friday after-
noon. On the whole, Colonel would pretty much keep him out of
large arenas because he was afraid Elvis wouldn't sell them out.
The Astrodome holds something like fifty thousand people. It's
the length of a football field. And at the afternoon show, only sixteen thousand people came, and four thousand were handicapped children who got in free.

Gee Gee Gambill, Patsy Presley's husband, had come into the
fringe of the group as a valet and chauffeur in '67. He said that
after the show, Elvis went back to the hotel and laid down on the
bed and said, "Well, that's it. I guess I just don't have it anymore." Then Elvis took a little nap.

They were staying at the Astroworld Hotel, which is right by
the freeway. Gee Gee said he went over to the window and looked
out, and the cars were lined up for about three or four miles. He
called Elvis over and told him all those cars were going to his
show. And they were. A total of 208,000 people saw the six
shows. Elvis said, "Well, I'll be damned. I guess I've still got it
after all."

LAMAR FIKE: In March, after he got home from Houston, Elvis
spent three days at Baptist Memorial Hospital for secondary
glaucoma in his left eye. I don't know if it was caused by the
drugs or not. We'd have to ask his ophthalmologist, David Meyer.

BILLY SMITH: Elvis's glaucoma was recurrent, and it got pretty
bad. He wore a patch on his eye for it. One time in Nashville,
Elvis was recording, and his eye got so bad, David had to come
over and stick a needle in it to relieve the pressure. While that
needle was going in, it hurt so dang bad that Elvis bent a metal
tray in half.

MARTY LACKER: Beginning about '70, Elvis started wearing tinted glasses night and day. He had reading glasses, but he'd only wear them upstairs where no one could see him. Then he saw some glasses at Optique Boutique, and he thought they were really sharp.

LAMAR FIKE: The silver-toned sunglasses with the holes on the sides became one of his trademarks. The estate sells replicas for $15. Well, it all started with me. I bought the original ones at a gas station for $3.50. Elvis grabbed 'em right off my face. He said, "I want these. Let me have 'em." Then he had Optique Boutique copy them and build "EP" into the nose bridge.

BILLY SMITH: When I quit working for Elvis in '68, I became my own self. I was going to night school and holding down two jobs. A lot of times, I felt like I couldn't make the kind of money that I could with Elvis, and I didn't like that feeling. Yet I didn't like total dependency, either.

But in '70, I got laid off at the railroad. Somebody told Elvis I was out of work, and he asked me if I wanted a job. I said, "If it's traveling, I don't." Elvis said, "No." So I went back.

I hadn't been back long when he called me a son of a bitch. This was over his date. Her name was Barbara Leigh. She was the girlfriend of Jim Aubrey, the president of MGM. Elvis and Priscilla were either just getting ready to move to this new $400,000 house in Holmby Hills [at 144 Monovale Drive], or just had, but that didn't mean he'd made any kind of commitment to his marriage.

Anyway, I didn't know this girl, and she was talking to me. Elvis looked at her and said, "Look, you need to be over here with me. You don't need to be talking to that son of a bitch." I thought, "God Almighty! I don't need this shit. Even laid off, I don't need it."

Well, he apologized later. That's the only thing that saved it. But within a year, I got hired back at the railroad.

LAMAR FIKE: In August of '70, Elvis went back into Las Vegas. And while he was there, MGM did a documentary on him called *Elvis: That's the Way It Is*. Not a bad movie—for its time. It's mostly studio and stage stuff and talking to fans. RCA taped the shows and put out a live recording with the same title. Felton took the tapes back to Nashville and sweetened 'em a little bit, added some voices in the background. But for the most part, he left the flaws and all. And Elvis liked that. You really got the energy of those live shows. Boy, he could still move—he was still fluid. And he was thirty-five years old.

That was the same year Felton left RCA to spend all his time with Elvis. He worked on his records *and* his live performances. It was also the same year Felton had a kidney transplant. Elvis helped get him a kidney and then paid for the operation.

MARTY LACKER: The record's better than the documentary. It's a Las Vegas record, but a good record. He sang his ass off. It was astonishing how good he was. They went back to using a lot of songs they had the publishing on, and a couple of them, "How the Web Was Woven" and "I've Lost You," were pretty good songs. But Elvis also snuck in some covers of stuff that Chips cut at American—"You Don't Have to Say You Love Me," the Dusty Springfield hit, and "I Just Can't Help Believing," that B.J. Thomas song. He was also doing Neil Diamond's "Sweet Caroline" in the shows. Whenever he did live recordings, he tried to cover songs out of American. Because he knew that sound was right for him.

That second year in Vegas, Joe Guercio took over as the orchestra conductor and arranger. Joe sometimes gets credit for Elvis using *Also Sprach Zarathustra*, the theme from *2001: A Space Odyssey*, which was based on the Richard Strauss tone poem. But Elvis came up with that.

LAMAR FIKE: It sounded like God commanding Moses to part the Red Sea, you know? "BOM, BOM, BOMMMMMMMMM!" Elvis did it one night in rehearsal, and I said, "I've got a great idea for the opening." He said, "What?" I said, "Why don't we put you on a cable and stick some wings on your back, and after that intro, we'll say, 'Now, here's the Second Son.'" He said, "That's not funny." I said, "Well, it's just damn near." But the music became such a trademark for him. He used it on all the tours.

Guercio had a tremendous amount of input. Joe was like talking to eight different comedians at once because when you're an orchestra leader you play behind every comedian there is. He would come up with different arrangements on stuff, and he came up with a really great horn section that Elvis liked. Guercio used to call him "Elvis the Brass Killer," because Elvis hit these high C's and the trumpet players had to go up above that. And they'd have to sustain some of these notes for about two weeks because Elvis would just go, "Uhhhhhhh!" and keep on. You'd see these trumpet players falling like flies.

One night, Guercio coined a saying. He said, "Following Elvis is kind of like following a marble—you never know where it's going to go." Because you didn't know where Elvis would end the song or when he was going to flip into another one. I don't think Elvis knew himself. He would keep some sort of semblance, but then he would up and change the song—just throw everybody off. And, man, you could see the whole damn twenty-six-piece orchestra tearing through sheet music, just flying through the pages, trying to get to the song! You had all these musicians going, "Shit, where is he now?"

BILLY SMITH: Right in the middle of the taping of that documentary, Elvis got a durn paternity suit slapped on him. There was a couple of women through the years who claimed he'd gotten them pregnant. This one was a Hollywood waitress named Pat Parker. She said it happened when he was in Vegas earlier in the year, but all she had for proof was one picture that she had took with him backstage. She gave birth to a son in October. But it wasn't Elvis's. He was careful. He was scared of that anyway.

LAMAR FIKE: Boy, Elvis was hot about that paternity suit. When he was finally served the papers in November, he was getting ready to go onstage in L.A. and he went into this long monologue, telling the audience every good thing he'd ever done. It was an odd reaction, really. She wanted $1,000-a-month child support. And Elvis filed a cross complaint. The court ruled in his favor. The blood tests didn't match.

MARTY LACKER: Colonel got Ed Hookstratten to handle that whole thing. And Hookstratten hired a private detective in L.A. named John O'Grady. In the fifties, O'Grady was a sergeant in the L.A. Police Department. He headed up the narcotics unit, and he'd busted something like 2,500 drug cases. He got to know Elvis pretty well, and he tried to use him.

BILLY SMITH: O'Grady had a sort of forced personality. Too goody-goody. He was there doing a job, but it was like he had to play the game to get in the group.

MARTY LACKER: I was out there one time, and Elvis had invited O'Grady and his wife to dinner. O'Grady drank a lot. And he started talking to Elvis about being the spokesman for a drug crusade. Now, I read that O'Grady did polygraph tests on Elvis because of the lawsuit, and he saw that Elvis's pulse and breathing rates were below normal, and he suspected Elvis was doing downers. So you might say that he was trying to help Elvis. But I think O'Grady just saw a place for himself. I remember he said, "I can set it up where you can do TV spots." And Elvis just sat there and smiled at him.

Everybody could see that O'Grady was just trying to ingratiate himself into the situation. At times out in California, and at Graceland, O'Grady tried to put the make on some of the wives. One of the reasons Elvis kept him around was so he could hear all of O'Grady's cops-and-robbers stories. Elvis had started collecting police badges. And for a while, he'd been obsessed with getting a federal narcotics agent's badge. He wanted to be a narc. And not just an honorary one. So he began asking O'Grady how to do it.

One night, they went to dinner in a restaurant out in California, and O'Grady saw an actor named Paul Frees. He did voice-overs for TV commercials and Walt Disney cartoons. Frees was a police buff like Elvis, but he was also an undercover federal agent. A narc. I assume O'Grady told Elvis this while he was drinking because you don't expose somebody. And Frees carried the badge and ID that said he was an agent-at-large for the Bureau of Narcotics and Dangerous Drugs.

Well, Elvis was impressed, but he got pissed off. He said, "Hey, man, if a fucking guy like that can get a badge, why can't I?" Elvis found out that if he was a federal agent, he could carry a gun across state lines. And that excited him because it represented ultimate power. So he went to work on O'Grady. O'Grady said, "Well, I may be able to get you an introduction to John Finlator, the deputy director of the Narcotics Bureau. We'll apply through him."

🕺 🕺 🕺

LAMAR FIKE: In the third week of his August run in Vegas, Elvis got a death threat. He'd gotten them before, but this one was serious as a six-car pileup.

It started out with a security guard at the hotel getting a phone call on a Wednesday from a guy who said Elvis would be kidnapped that night by two men. Elvis had supposedly met them at a party in California before he left for Vegas. The caller said he wasn't involved, but he knew it was for real because he'd been approached to take part in the deal. The next day, Colonel got a call from a man with a Southern accent who said he had it on good authority that Elvis would be kidnapped over the weekend.

Then on Friday, at six-fifteen in the morning, Joanie Esposito got a call in L.A. That really freaked everybody. How would some crackpot have her unlisted number? This guy also had a Southern accent. He said he had to get in touch with Joe, that Elvis would be shot onstage Saturday night. He called back later and said the shooter would use a silencer, that he was a "madman," somebody Elvis had done wrong about a year before. The guy said he'd provide information like the killer's name and license number, but he wanted $50,000 in small bills.

Ed Hookstratten thought it might be somebody tied in with the paternity suit. But then somebody sent Elvis a hotel menu that had Elvis's picture on the front. They'd scribbled through his face and drawn a gun pointed at his head. At the bottom it said, "Guess who, and where?" And it was written backwards. You had to hold it up to a mirror to read it.

We turned it over to the FBI. They ran a check on it and couldn't find any fingerprints, so they thought they were dealing with a certifiable sicko. They ordered protection for Priscilla and Lisa Marie—the whole nine yards. The place was just swarming with FBI and security men.

This was right after the Manson murders, and Elvis had gotten sort of spooked about those. So he called John O'Grady, and then he just started calling fuckin' everybody—Jerry in L.A. and Red in Memphis. Elvis had them come out, and Red said he just fell in his arms when he got there. Elvis worked out this plan with Sonny and Red that they'd jump in front of him if they saw any unusual movement. I guess they were really going to take the damn bullet.

The hotel wanted him to cancel, but he said if he did that, every blackmailer in the country would be after him. So he just had the hotel call in a couple of ambulances and a complete medical team with plenty of Elvis's blood type. He played it to the hilt.

The night it was supposed to go down, the FBI asked me to keep the houselights up halfway. I said, "It destroys the mood." They said, "Please, help us on this." Well, in the middle of the show, Elvis said, "Stop everything." He looked up at me, and he said, for everybody to hear, "Lamar, why are these damn houselights up?" I thought, "What am I going to say? 'Because you've got a death threat?'" I don't know what I actually said, but we went back and forth, and he said, "Turn the lights down." I said, "You don't understand." And he said, "No, I don't. Turn 'em down." I shut 'em off, and the whole room cracked up.

MARTY LACKER: Elvis always started out "You've Lost That Lovin' Feelin'" with his back to the audience, with just a small spotlight on his back. He thought that was when they'd pop him. He said he was standing there with the mike, looking at Ronnie Tutt, the drummer. And he told me later he was thinking, "Ronnie, you poor son of a bitch. If they miss me, they'll get you."

BILLY SMITH: The funny part of all this was that he kept saying, "I hope they don't hit me in the face." Well, nothing happened for the first few songs. Then this man's voice cried out, "Elvis!" And Elvis dropped down to one knee and reached for the derringer in his boot. And the voice said, "Would you sing 'Don't Be Cruel'?"

MARTY LACKER: After nothing happened, Elvis was so overjoyed that he went to Sol Schwartz at Schwartz and Ableser's Fine Jewelry in Beverly Hills and had him make a bracelet for all the guys. He said, "I'm just so damn happy to still be alive that I wanted to do something for everybody."

🕴 🕴 🕴

BILLY SMITH: After I left Elvis again, he tried to bribe me to come back to work. One day, we were coming back from Tupelo. He'd gone down there to see about getting a sheriff's badge. And he said, "That's a good-looking car there." It was a Ford Cyclone. I said, "Yeah, it is." He said, "If you come back to work for me, you can have one like it." He was very shrewd about that shit.

Right after the death threat, Elvis got real obsessed with cop stuff. I think being in the military stirred his interest, but he didn't get into it heavy until about '69 or '70. Wherever he was, he wanted a police badge for that city, and hell, he'd get to know somebody and get it. He eventually had hundreds of them suckers. I think it started in Memphis, with one from [Sheriff] Bill Morris. So it went all the way from that little badge to a narcotic's badge from the president.

MARTY LACKER: Bill Morris's father and Vernon had known each other in Mississippi. But Elvis and Bill didn't get well acquainted until the late sixties, and then in '70 they got real tight. Elvis gave Bill a $9,000 Mercedes for Christmas that year. It caused a little uproar when Bill ran for mayor the next year. But Elvis was looking to get a few things out of Bill, and he genuinely liked him, too.

This thing about the guns and badges, though . . . see, most of us had guns. After the death threat, Elvis wanted everybody to carry one. Or even two. Because we had to protect him. In Tennessee, at least, we had badges, so we were able to do it legally.

BILLY SMITH: Some of this fascination with the police might have started with Captain Woodward. Elvis liked Captain Woodward a lot. He liked being on the side of law and order, or at least having friends there. If Elvis needed something, Captain Woodward knew who to get in touch with.

When Captain Woodward died, Elvis went to watch him be embalmed. Or at least, that's what Red and Sonny say.

MARTY LACKER: I think Elvis always had a fascination with being armed to the teeth, with being a spy, or a sleuth, starting in childhood. There are several childhood pictures of him with toy guns. Then, when he got older, he always had a gun, and not just the derringer in the boot. He kept a gun in his pocket. And then, for a long time he had this little .25 silver automatic with a pearl handle. He didn't carry it all the time, and he gave it to me. Then one day in the seventies, we were out back at Graceland doing some target practice against the office wall, and he wanted it back. He said, "I like this gun. I'll get you another one." But he never did.

By then, he'd gotten obsessive because of the pills, and the paranoia, and the death threats. He kept saying he wasn't going to let somebody kill him, and he wouldn't go anywhere without a .45—not even to the bathroom or the breakfast table. Sometimes he had two of them, one on each side.

LAMAR FIKE: It wasn't a .45. It was a .22 automatic. He always had it with him. When he sat down, it was uncomfortable, so he put it on the table. But he wasn't the only one who'd wear a gun to the table. Red had a shoulder weapon on. Sonny, too.

BILLY SMITH: See, the seventies is when he got crazy. Of course, that was what we always called him, "Crazy."

LAMAR FIKE: I think the gun obsession might have had a little bit to do with the fact that I collected guns. I would come up with different guns, and I'd show them to Elvis. We went into Kerr's Sporting Goods one time and he saw a .22. It was engraved, and he bought it. Then in '70, he went in there on a spree and bought thirty-two handguns, a shotgun, and a rifle. That included a .44 Ruger Blackhawk gold-plated revolver, which cost $1,850, and a .357 Colt Python revolver, which set him back $1,950. The total bill came to $19,792. Sonny's still got the receipt.

BILLY SMITH: By the time he died, man, Elvis had every gun there was, from a Thompson submachine gun, to an M16 fully automatic assault rifle, to a high-powered assassin's rifle with a telescopic sight. He had his own private arsenal. Some of 'em had the TCB logo or his initials on 'em. But then he'd give 'em away sometimes. He give me an M101 Duramatic pistol and a Belgian Browning twenty-gauge shotgun and a couple more. Hell, he give 'em to everybody.

LAMAR FIKE: The worst thing that ever happened was when Clint Eastwood made those *Dirty Harry* movies with that .357. Because Elvis got on this tear. He said, "Everybody's going to have to wear a .357." And those things weigh about six hundred pounds. They're like cannons. He had one with a barrel on it, and it ran from here to New York. I said, "I can't carry that, Elvis. It's too heavy." And he had Sonny carry a nine-millimeter, a .357, and a .25.

Sonny practiced fast-draw, and he got faster than lightning. He had one of those upside-down holsters, and he was really like a flash. When we went on tour, Elvis liked to put Sonny up against the cops in various cities because he made it a point to meet 'em all. And Sonny was so fast, he had that gun out before those guys ever got to their holsters. Elvis loved it. This one cop told Sonny, "If you could shoot straight, this town would be in trouble." And Sonny said, "I don't know. I've never shot it."

One night, on tour in Dallas—probably in '71—Elvis got off the plane with just a coat on over his pajamas, and he had one of those big-mother magnums stuck in his pajama bottoms. Well, the pajamas weren't sturdy enough to hold that big gun. He was zonked on sleeping pills, and that gun fell out in front of a zillion cops and this big crowd waiting for him. Nobody uttered a word. Same thing happened in Vegas. One night that derringer was bothering his ankle. He took it out in front of the whole show-room and laid it over next to Charlie. Charlie swept it up and put it in his pocket. And nobody said a thing.

🕴 🕴 🕴

BILLY SMITH: Elvis had an active fantasy life. Sometimes I think he wanted to present this image of the ultragood Elvis, and some-times he wanted to present the image of the badass Elvis. Towards the end of '70, he started dressing like a gangster. He'd wear black shirts, and white ties, and he had a black suede suit, and his hair was longer than it had ever been in his life, with these big, bushy sideburns. He looked like a cross between an Italian gangster and a supercop. Sometimes he even wore a wide-brimmed hat.

MARTY LACKER: Part of it came from the movies, like *Shaft*. We'd go to the Memphian and see the black exploitation films with the guys with the "Superfly" overcoats and the hats. Well, I'll be damned if we didn't go to Lansky's and Elvis started buying them. And he'd wear them out in public. He also wore those high-collar shirts. He liked the style, and he wanted to cover up his neck, too. He thought it was too long and thin. But I also think he just had an affinity for the costume because, basically, that was his taste in clothes. This was just an evolution from the wild Beale Street clothes he wore when he was a teenager.

LAMAR FIKE: He liked the way the black entertainers dressed. But he also liked to dress like nobody else, or at least no other white person.

When *Shaft* came out, he loved the white Lincoln limousine they had in there. He said he had to have it. Not one like it—*that* limousine. And he got it.

MARTY LACKER: Sammy Davis, Jr., used to come to Elvis's Vegas shows. You can see him in the audience in that MGM documentary, *Elvis: That's the Way It Is*. Elvis told me he gave Sammy his big black star sapphire ring. He said it was only right—Sammy was the biggest black star in the world.

In the mid-seventies, Elvis invited Sammy and his wife, Altovise, to go riding around Beverly Hills and West L.A. in Elvis's Mercedes limousine. The chief of police of Beverly Hills was in the car, too. Elvis used to run around with him and his wife every once in a while. They were talking, and Elvis got on his biblical kick, talking about when Jesus got up and said, "Woe, you Scribes and Pharisees."

He got in a big way talking, and out of the clear blue, Elvis opened the sunroof, stood up, started shaking this long cane over his head and spouting off bastardized Bible verse. They proceeded to drive through Beverly Hills with Elvis yelling at the top of his lungs, "O, ye motherfuckers! Beware! Straighten your asses up!"

LAMAR FIKE: Elvis shot at a car in Beverly Hills one time, too. The guy gave Elvis the finger. So Elvis just stood up in the sunroof and started shooting at the guy with a .22 automatic. He missed him, thank God.

The drugs made him mean, and you never knew what he was going to do. He got pissed off at me about something one day, and I mouthed back at him, and he drew this short-barreled .44 magnum and stuck it right in my nose. He said, "You talk to me that way again and I'll blow your brains out." When a gun is cocked, and you see a shell in the hole there, you're not going to take chances. I just stayed very still.

He was like a benevolent dictator at times. So I'd say, "Look, mein Führer, if you've got some more suggestions instead of orders . . . " And it would make him so mad.

BILLY SMITH: Elvis really talked down to Lamar sometimes. Called him "Lard-ass" and a "fat fuck." But here's the difference. Lamar loved Elvis. He cared for him. But over the years, when Elvis said some harsh things to him, Lamar fired back every once in a while. But Lamar's a very intelligent person, so he knew how far to go. Lamar was like a bitching old woman, griping all the time. That was his way. And so Elvis would laugh it off.

I hear Lamar and Marty talking sometime about how they told Elvis to do this and do that, like they made a lot of big decisions for him. And that's irritating. It's almost like, "He didn't have any mind of his own." Nobody would have had the nerve to talk to Elvis like that. The truth is, we all feared him.

MARTY LACKER: Well, that's right. You didn't *tell* Elvis to do anything. You chose your words, and you used a calm tone. You never knew how he would react to what you said.

BILLY SMITH: You especially had to be careful of what you said in the seventies. Because he was like a caged animal. He was coming out any way he could. You didn't embarrass him, and you didn't scare him. And you certainly didn't ever humiliate him. Most of the time we just let him rant and rave.

🕺 🕺 🕺

MARTY LACKER: In September, Elvis went back on tour for the first time since the fifties. This tour wasn't very organized. They traveled on a plane that was sort of like "Greyhound Airlines." They didn't have any idea how much equipment they needed, and they were picking up new horn and string players in every town. Concerts West, which was Jerry Weintraub and Tom Hulett, handled it. They made a name for themselves promoting tours for Cream and Jimi Hendrix, and they handled all of Elvis's tours until he died.

This was kind of a test run for Elvis. And he loved it. Tickets sold out a couple of hours after they went on sale, and he was on top of the world again. He couldn't wait until next year to do another one.

It gave him the confidence to do all kinds of things. Like, in late November, he met Vice President [Spiro] Agnew in Palm Springs, and he gave Agnew these gold-plated .45s as a gift. He tried to give him a .357 magnum. But Agnew wouldn't take it. I'd love to have seen Agnew's face when Elvis pulled that out.

LAMAR FIKE: Once Elvis went on tour and met all those cops, he became more fixated on becoming a narc. But Mr. Finlator had turned Elvis down cold on getting his badge. He said Elvis wasn't the type of person that they wanted. It really upset him. He said, "Well, screw Finlator. I'm going to go over his head." So he went to Washington to get him a narcotics badge, which was hypocrisy with a bigger "H" than the Hollywood Hills sign.

MARTY LACKER: One night in the middle of December—this was '70—Sonny told us that he and his girlfriend, Judy Jordan, were getting married December 28.

He'd apparently already told Elvis, and Elvis told Sonny he'd give them the wedding as a gift. Elvis was going to be best man, Priscilla was matron of honor, and some of the guys were going to be ushers. Sonny said, "Elvis, can I ask you another favor?" Elvis said, "What is it?" Sonny said, "Can I let Marty handle all the arrangements?"

We talked for a while, and then we went to a movie. And the next day, which was December 19, I came back up because I wanted to ask Elvis how much I could spend on Sonny's arrangements.

Well, I'd pretty much gotten there when Vernon walked in and said, "Anybody seen Elvis? He ain't up in his room." This was about four or five in the afternoon. Vernon said, "No one has seen him."

We couldn't figure out where the hell he was because all the guys were there. Since then, I've heard that Elvis and Vernon had this terrific argument sometime after everybody left that night, probably about Elvis paying for the wedding and for all the guns and Christmas presents he'd bought—ten Mercedes alone, at something like $85,000. Priscilla says it was over Colonel—that Elvis wanted to fire him and Vernon said no.

Whatever, about an hour later, the phone rang. The maid said, "Mr. Sonny, telephone." Sonny went to the phone, and he came back and said, "You won't fuckin' believe this. Elvis is in Washington, D.C., with Jerry Schilling. He went over there to see President Nixon."

Elvis had gone to the airport in Memphis by himself. This was the first time he had ever done anything like this, without at least one of the other guys with him. And it must have spooked him, because instead of flying directly to Washington, he called Schilling in L.A. and asked him to meet him at LAX. And he told him to get $500 cash because he didn't have a penny in his pocket. This was big, secretive superspy shit, see?

At some point—I don't know how many hours later—Elvis and Jerry flew from L.A. to Washington. On the plane, Elvis wrote a letter to President Nixon declaring himself a concerned American. He talked about how deplorable the country had gotten, with the hippies, and the drug culture, and the Black Panthers, and the SDS [Students for a Democratic Society], and he said he wanted Nixon to make him a federal agent at large. He said he didn't want an appointment, just to be named a federal agent. Because he said the people he mentioned didn't consider him an enemy, and he could be of service to the country. And he said he'd met Vice President Agnew three weeks before and told him how concerned he was about the state of the country.

It just so happened that George Murphy, the former actor and at that time a California senator, was on the plane. And he and Elvis started talking about all this. Elvis put that in his letter as a sort of recommendation. He also told Nixon he was about to be named one of the Ten Outstanding Young Men of America and reminded Nixon that he'd once been named one, too. And he told him he'd be staying at the Washington Hotel under the name of Jon Burrows and he'd be in town as long as it took to get his credentials. Then he asked Nixon to have one of his staff call him to set up an appointment so they could meet.

The irony is that it was pretty obvious from his handwriting that Elvis was stoned when he wrote the letter. And who knows what else was going on in his head? Some heavy-duty patriot shit, that's for sure. Because Elvis also met some soldier on the plane who was coming back from Vietnam. The guy didn't have any money, and Elvis told Schilling to give the guy the five hundred bucks.

Schilling said, "Elvis, that's all the money we got." And Elvis said, "Jerry, I said give the man the money." So they gave him the five hundred bucks, and Elvis gave him either a watch or a ring he had on, and told him how proud he was of what the guy had been doing over there in Vietnam. He said, "I want you to enjoy yourself while you're home." And then he and Jerry were flat broke again.

Schilling had arranged for a limousine to pick them up in Washington, and on the way to the hotel, Elvis stopped at the gates of the White House and gave his letter to the guard.

When Elvis and Jerry got to the hotel, they called Sonny. Elvis decided he wanted another guy with him for security. Of course, Sonny was getting married the next week. But Sonny told us, "What can I do? He said he wants me up there." Turns out Elvis had already put Sonny's name in the letter to Nixon as one of his two point men at the hotel. So Sonny went.

Elvis left Jerry back at the hotel and got in a cab to go see John Finlator, the deputy director of the Bureau of Narcotics and Dangerous Drugs, who was O'Grady's contact. This was another attempt to get the narcotics agent badge, see. And he apparently went in there under his pseudonym of Jon Burrows although there's an FBI memo that says Senator Murphy arranged an appointment for Elvis with John Ingersoll, the head. But I think Elvis saw Finlator, who, of course, knew who he was. And to butter him up, Elvis told him he'd be happy to donate $5,000 to the Federal Drug Enforcement Bureau for their antidrug campaign.

Finlator told Elvis they didn't accept donations. So then Elvis showed him some of his other badges and came right out and asked if he could have one from the Narcotics Bureau. Finlator said only an honorary one. Elvis said he had to have a real one. And Finlator refused. So Elvis thanked him, but he was ticked. He was getting ready to leave when Jerry called him at Finlator's office. Elvis told Jerry he didn't get the badge, and Jerry said he had tears in his voice.

The White House, in the meantime, had read the letter. And when they found out it was on the level, Egil "Bud" Krogh, who was later one of the Watergate indictees, called Jerry at the hotel and told him he'd like to meet with Elvis in half an hour.

About ten A.M., they went over to Krogh's office in the Old Executive Office Building. Krogh sort of preinterviewed him. They left about ten-fifteen, and Krogh typed up his memo, and H. R. Haldeman approved it. Then Krogh called Jerry and said, "The president will see Mr. Presley for twenty minutes."

By that time, Sonny had gotten there. And about twelve-thirty in the afternoon, they went back to Krogh's office. Have you seen the pictures of Nixon and Elvis? Elvis had on his black suede suit, a white shirt with high collars that was open to below his chest, that big belt from the International Hotel with the gigantic gold buckle, and a lot of gold jewelry around his neck. And he topped the whole outfit off with this dark purple velvet cloak, and a cane, and amber-tinted sunglasses. Jerry said he looked like Dracula. His hair was down over his collar in the back, and his eyes looked like he was wearing heavy shadow and mascara. And he probably was. Above all, he looked completely stoned.

Elvis went in the Oval Office, and he showed Nixon some pictures of Priscilla and Lisa Marie and some of his badges, and he told Nixon how much he supported the police. Then the White House photographer came in and took some pictures. Then they got down to business. Nixon told him he knew Elvis could influence young people in a way nobody in government could, and he sort of suggested that he not tell anybody about this meeting—that they needed to keep it secret. Which Elvis loved, I'm sure. He said, "I do my thing just by singing, Mr. President. I don't make any speeches onstage. I just try to reach them in my own way."

And then Elvis said a strange thing, or something we hadn't heard him say before. He said, "I think the Beatles are kind of anti-American. They came over here and made a lot of money, and then they went back to England and said some anti-

American things." Krogh's written a book now, *The Day Elvis Met Nixon*, and he said that comment came out of left field. He didn't know what the shit Elvis was talking about, unless he was just jealous of the Beatles.

But Elvis went on. He babbled a lot of stuff he thought Nixon would like to hear, like "I want to help get people to respect the flag because that's getting lost."

Then, when he really got rolling, he said, "Mr. President, can you get me a badge from the Narcotics Bureau? I've been trying to get a badge from them for my collection." Nixon knew he was there for something because he'd said in his letter that he wanted federal credentials. But this must have caught him completely by surprise. He didn't know how to answer, so he turned to Krogh and said, "Bud, can we get him a badge?" And Krogh, who grew up on Elvis and was really a fan, said, "Well, sir, if you want to give him a badge, I think we can get him one." And Nixon nodded and said, "I'd like to do that. See that he gets one."

Well, Elvis was so overjoyed, he did the unthinkable. He *hugged* Nixon! Just like Sammy Davis, Jr. You know how Nixon's shoulders went way up when he was nervous? Well, they must have gone through the White House roof. But he patted Elvis on the shoulder and said, "Well, I appreciate your willingness to help us out, Mr. Presley."

When they were getting ready to take the formal pictures—and the White House photographer took twenty-eight separate shots—to kind of break the ice of standing there all stiff and posed, Nixon looked at Elvis and said, "You dress kind of strange, don't you?" And Elvis told me he said, "Well, Mr. President, you got your show, and I got mine."

They talked a few minutes more, and Nixon went to the bottom left-hand drawer of his desk, which is where he kept the gifts for visitors. He pulled out some tie clasps with the presidential seal on them, and he gave them to Elvis and Jerry and Sonny. Elvis was feeling so comfortable by this time that he started rooting around in Nixon's drawer! And he looked over at the president, and he said, "Remember, Mr. President, they've got wives." So Nixon gave them some pendants. Here he was, getting the president of the United States to do whatever he wanted. He was so proud that he got to see the president at the drop of a hat, without having an appointment months ahead.

By the time Elvis left, he had his badge, much to the consternation of John Finlator, who presented it to Elvis himself after lunch. And Elvis had given Nixon a chrome-plated World War II Commemorative Colt .45 with a wood handle, a fancy automatic, and seven silver bullets in a display case—even though he had to leave it at the gate when he came in. He couldn't take it into the Oval Office.

Sonny told me that when they got out of there, Elvis looked at him and Jerry and said, "Who said something can't be done?"

When Watergate happened, Elvis refused to believe Nixon was involved. But the funny thing is, when Agnew got in all that trouble for income tax evasion and had to step down as vice president, Elvis said, "I want my goddamn guns back."

LAMAR FIKE: Nixon met with Elvis because he thought it would lighten up his image with the kids in this country and give him an avenue to them. Even though Elvis's real fans were older than that. Krogh had this idea they could get him to record an antidrug record with a "Get High on Life" theme at the federal narcotic rehabilitation and research facility in Lexington, Kentucky. Christ!

By the way, Nixon spoke well of Elvis after that. Said he thought he was sincere. But I don't think it was an easy meeting. When Nixon didn't immediately offer stuff for the guys' wives, Elvis said to him, "Now I know why they call you 'Tricky Dick.'" And Nixon said, "I know why they call you 'Elvis the Pelvis.'"

MARTY LACKER: After Elvis got his narcotics badge, he never let up on the superspy thing for a second. The night of Sonny's wedding, I picked up Elvis and Sonny, and we holed up in the preacher's office, waiting for everybody to come into the sanctuary. Elvis was standing there, and he was dressed all in black, except for a white tie and those amber glasses. He had on a suit made out of crushed velvet, with bell bottom pants. His hair curled up in the back, it was so long. And he had gold on everywhere—his sheriff's badge belt with diamonds, this second belt with gold eagles and chains, and some kind of chain around his neck. And he had his guns on, and he carried this fifteen-inch long, Kel-Lite police flashlight, black metal.

The preacher came in and said, "Sonny, it's time to go." And then he said, "Mr. Presley, if you'll come with us, also." So Elvis started walking out of the office to go into the sanctuary.

When he did, I took hold of the flashlight. I was going to take it out of his hand so he wouldn't walk out there with it in front of everybody. Well, he pulled the damn flashlight back. He wouldn't let me take it. I said, "Elvis, this is a wedding. You don't need this flashlight." He said, "If I'm not taking my damn flashlight, I'm not going." I started to laugh, and Sonny was looking at him like "God, man, are you nuts?"

I said, "Elvis, you can't take this flashlight up on the altar with you. It's not right, and it won't look good. It's going to mess up the wedding." I was laughing, hoping to joke him out of it.

He thought a minute, and he said, "Goddamn, I hate to give this up." And I just took it out of his hand. So he went up there without it, but he still had his guns on. He had two gold guns in his shoulder holster, a pearl-handled pistol in the waist of his pants, and another one in the back of his pants. And the derringer in his boot. I'll bet he was the only best man in the history of Memphis to go to the altar with five guns on him, just to stand up for a groom.

After the wedding, we went back in the party room of the church for the reception. Everybody was milling around—all of Sonny's family and friends and the guys with their wives. We were there about forty-five minutes, when Elvis came over and said, "Let's go." He said, "Tell all the guys to bring their wives up to the house."

I said, "Elvis, this is Sonny and Judy's wedding reception." He said, "Well, I'm getting tired of this place. Let's just move the party to Graceland."

I went over to Sonny and Judy and I told them what Elvis wanted. And Sonny just shook his head. He started laughing, and he said, "That crazy son of a bitch." But we went to Graceland, and the family came, too.

That was the night the picture was taken of all the guys with their badges—the one with Bill Morris, the former Shelby County sheriff and later the county mayor, and Roy Nixon, then the present sheriff. Dr. Nick was there, too. Roy Nixon had just deputized all of us in one fell swoop and given Elvis a new badge. When it started getting late, Elvis said, "I want to go to the Memphian to see a movie." Well, nobody else was in the mood. But Elvis said, "No, I want to go to the movie. Set the Memphian up."

I told all the guys, and Sonny and Judy got ready to leave. Elvis said, "Where are y'all going?" And Sonny said, "We're going to change our clothes." Elvis said, "Okay, I'll meet you at the Memphian." Sonny and Judy looked at each other, and one of the guys said, "Hey, Elvis, this is their honeymoon night." Elvis said, "I don't give a damn. They've been together for a good while. I expect to see them at the Memphian."

LAMAR FIKE: Two days later, on December 30, Elvis decided he wanted to meet J. Edgar Hoover and tour FBI headquarters. So he and Bill Morris and six of the guys flew up to Washington on a private jet.

When we got there, Bill called Assistant Director Casper from the hotel and told him he was there with Elvis and six other people. He said he'd like a tour of the FBI building and a meeting with Hoover the next day. Casper told him Hoover was out of the city, but he'd see about arranging a tour, which he did. And then Bill took us by the National Sheriffs Association, and Elvis paid for each of us to join. You could join if you had a badge, see. The membership carried a life insurance policy, and Elvis wanted to make sure we all had one.

The next day, we went for our FBI tour. You aren't allowed to bring weapons in there, so the guys who were carrying took 'em off. But Elvis wasn't about to do it, and when he leaned over to get a drink of water, a derringer fell out of his pocket. The agent told him he knew he had it all along. Then when he went in the bathroom, he went in the stall and a .25 automatic tumbled out onto the floor. Elvis just reached down and picked it up and put it back in his belt. When he came out of the stall, these FBI agents were looking down at him, and Elvis smiled at them, and they sort of smiled back.

There wasn't a whole lot to do at the FBI. We went in and

watched 'em shoot those machine guns and perused their big gun collection. That was about it.

By the way, we found out later that Hoover was there all along. We just didn't get to see him. He was probably in there giving head to Clyde Tolson.

MARTY LACKER: When Elvis went to the FBI building and wanted to see J. Edgar Hoover, the agent who met him, M. A. Jones, sent a memo to a Mr. Bishop in the bureau that said, "Presley's sincerity and good intentions notwithstanding, he is certainly not the type of individual whom the Director would wish to meet. It is noted at the present time he is wearing his hair down to his shoulders and indulges in the wearing of all sorts of exotic dress." He attached a photograph of him from Sonny's wedding that was in that day's *Washington Post*. And then he alluded to the paternity suit and to all the previous entries in the bureau's file, mostly about Elvis's gyrations on stage in the fifties.

But there was a second memo from Jones to Bishop, after Elvis visited the building. And this one's more interesting. Elvis told the FBI he considered Hoover the "greatest living American" and that he'd read his stuff: *Masters of Deceit, A Study of Communism*, and *J. Edgar Hoover on Communism*.

The memo also said that Elvis "indicated that he is of the opinion that the Beatles laid the groundwork for many of the problems we are having with young people by their filthy unkempt appearances and suggestive music while entertaining in this country during the early and middle 1960s. He advised that the Smothers Brothers, Jane Fonda and other persons in the entertainment industry of their ilk have a lot to answer for in the hereafter for the way they have poisoned young minds by disparaging the United States in their public statements and unsavory activities."

Then the memo said, "Presley advised that he wished the Director to be aware that he, Presley, from time to time is approached by individuals and groups in and outside of the entertainment business, whose motive and goals he is convinced are not in the best interests of this country, and who seek to have him lend his name to their questionable activities. In this regard, he volunteered to make such information available to the Bureau on a confidential basis whenever it came to his attention."

In other words, Elvis offered to be a stoolie. In the name of his country. But I really think he wanted to meet Hoover to get an FBI badge.

CHAPTER 43

"THE WRECKING CREW"

MARTY LACKER: In January of '71, the Junior Chamber of Commerce named Elvis one of the Ten Outstanding Young Men in America. It was the only award Elvis ever received in person in front of a group. Normally, he didn't go for stuff like that. But Bill Morris explained that the Jaycees took strong political positions in countries threatened by Communist movements. And he told Elvis no other entertainer had received the award before. The year Elvis got it, [Nixon aide] Ron Ziegler was named, for example. So that appealed to Elvis.

He told me he wanted me to handle everything. He said, "Find out where I go and where all the entrances are." He was just going to fly in the night before, from Vegas.

Then he said, "I don't want to stay at Graceland. I'd rather be somewhere close to the auditorium." So I arranged for him to have the whole top floor of the Rivermont Hotel. And then he did something completely out of character. He said, "I'd like to do something for the other honorees."

So we came up with the idea of doing a dinner. I said, "Let's have a big cocktail party at Graceland and then go to the Four Flames," which was this terrific restaurant. He said, "Great, but I want to do it first-class." And I repeated one of his old sayings: "That's the only way to go."

We had Graceland done real sharp, and we decided that one of the guys would meet each honoree at the door with his wife and take them on a personal tour.

Elvis was really happy. Except for one thing. In the middle of dinner, the side door opened, and in walked Al Capp, the cartoonist who drew "Li'l Abner." Well, nobody had invited him. And the sheriff's deputy at the door said, "I'm sorry, sir. This is a private party. You can't come in."

In a loud voice, Capp said, "I'm part of this ceremony, and I should be here." It turned out that Capp was going to be one of the speakers at the awards. But we didn't know that. And Capp was drunk, and he started yelling, in a raspy, obnoxious voice, "I don't know why I wasn't invited. I'm Al Capp . . . "

Finally, one of the big-shot Jaycees told him he was going to have to leave. Capp yelled all the way out the door. And he didn't even go to the ceremony. Elvis said, "Who gives a shit?" But it hurt him, and it put a damper on his evening.

BILLY SMITH: The part of Elvis's speech everybody remembers is, "I learned very early in life that without a song, the day would never end. Without a song, a man ain't got a friend. Without a song, the road would never bend—without a song. So I'll keep singing the song." That was the last part. In the first part, he said, "When I was a child, ladies and gentlemen, I read comic books, and I was the hero of the comic book. I saw movies, and I was the hero in the movie. So every dream that I ever dreamed has come true a hundred times."

Well, one of the comics he read when he was a kid was *Captain Marvel, Jr.* And if you go back and look at a drawing of Captain Marvel, Jr., it looks a whole lot like the seventies Elvis—one-piece jumpsuit, wide belt, boots, cape, lightning bolt and all. Even the hair is the same. Elvis just had bigger sideburns.

Captain Marvel, Jr., was "the most powerful boy in the world." He went after Captain Nazi during World War II. And he had this dual image—normal, everyday guy and super crime fighter. Sounds like Elvis, don't it?

LAMAR FIKE: Elvis always believed you acted the part. You didn't see Hopalong Cassidy walk around in slacks and a sport shirt, for Christ's sake.

The first time he put that cape on, I said, "Man, we ought to put a wire on you so you can fly over the audience."

🥋 🥋 🥋

MARTY LACKER: When Elvis would open in Vegas, a lot of celebrities would come. Some were old friends, like Sammy Davis, Jr., and Juliet Prowse. There were times when B. B. King would be playing in the lounge, and Elvis would be playing in the big room, and Elvis would invite B.B. up to the suite after the shows. He liked B.B. And B.B. liked him. During Elvis's early years, he'd go down to Beale Street and see B.B. perform.

Cary Grant used to come to some of the shows, too. I think the hotels had a list of celebrities, and every time somebody opened in the big showroom, they'd bring them in. Because people like Grant were always there for openings. And Ernest Borgnine came a number of times. He was a really nice guy.

Not everybody in Vegas was nice. Karen and Richard Carpenter came backstage to the dressing room one time in the early seventies. She was totally domineering. Elvis came out, and she had this stuffed animal, and the first thing she said to him was, "Sign this," real haughty and demanding. Elvis said, "Well, I'll be more than happy to, if you ask me in a different way."

Elvis had a similar experience with one of Johnny Carson's sons, also in the early seventies. Carson had one of his people call to get his son a table and arrange for him to meet Elvis backstage. When he came back, he was completely obnoxious. Later, Johnny called Elvis and apologized for his kid's behavior.

BILLY SMITH: Elvis was always crazy about Johnny Carson. But then a few years later, Johnny was doing his monologue one night, and Elvis was watching him, and Johnny said something about Elvis being "fat and forty."

And, boy, Elvis turned against him after that. He wouldn't hardly watch him anymore. Elvis took stuff like that hard. That's why we kept the bad reviews from him. Joe would cut that page out of the paper. If Elvis saw it anyway, he'd stay mad the whole damn day.

MARTY LACKER: About '71, Elvis told Priscilla he thought she should stay away from Vegas except for the openings and closings. He didn't want her there because he had other company. Sometimes he'd go seven weeks without seeing her.

His excuse was that he was still worried about security. And a couple of times, Red and Sonny hit some people who tried to get into Elvis's room. That's what they were paid for—not to hurt people, but to protect Elvis.

But these people sued. And, of course, they didn't sue Red and Sonny. They sued Elvis. After I quit working for Elvis, he rented Jack Warner's house in Palm Springs, instead of the Alexander House. One time during this period, Priscilla and some of the wives went out to Palm Springs while Elvis was in Vegas. And when she looked in the mailbox, there were all these letters from girls who'd obviously had a wild time there.

Well, Priscilla hit the ceiling. But Elvis had his explanation together. He said they were just big fans with bigger imaginations.

LAMAR FIKE: Elvis would move people around like chess pawns. The girls would come, and we'd play and party. And they would come by later on, after we left for L.A., and slip notes in the mailbox. And some of those notes were pretty hot. One of the girls called Sonny "Lizard Tongue."

I was standing there when Priscilla read one of the notes to Elvis on the phone, and I could see the blood drain from his face. Then he started hollering and ranting and raving. But Priscilla kept right on.

He got off the phone, and he said in this real serious voice, "Lamar, the end is near." I said, "'The end is near'—my ass! We're all doomed. Let's just get one divorce attorney, and let him handle the whole thing and give us a group rate."

That little liaison eventually cost Joe his wife, cost me my wife, and cost Elvis his.

$$ \text{🏃 🏃 🏃} $$

MARTY LACKER: In March, Elvis's glaucoma flared up while he was in Nashville doing a recording session. He had to wear a black patch for a while, and it meant he couldn't tour that spring. When he felt better again, in May, he went out and chartered a Bach 111 twin-engine jet and a full-time pilot. For $470,000 a year. He decided he had to get over his fear of flying and travel like a superstar.

BILLY SMITH: That plane seated twelve people. The pilot was young and didn't always make the wisest decisions. Like, he'd stayed up most of the night partying and drinking the night before he flew Elvis somewhere one time, and when he got ready to land, he misjudged the length of the runway, and the control tower began to shout over the radio, "Abort, abort!" The pilot panicked and set the plane down so hard that he threw it back into the air on its side. Shook everybody up, and Elvis was scared to death it was going to crash. Elvis decided then and there he was going to buy his own damn plane and get a crew he knew and trusted.

MARTY LACKER: For a long time, I'd been thinking that the city ought to name something in honor of Elvis. In the summer of '71, there was a big brouhaha about whether to name what's now known as the Mid-South Coliseum after him. And it was embarrassing the hell out of Elvis because it got to be a public debate. People were writing in, "No, you shouldn't" and "Yes, you should." We were watching the news one night, and he said, "I wish they'd cut this out, because I'm not asking them to name anything after me."

Well, I did a lot of maneuvering behind the scenes, and I finally got the city to act on my suggestion, which was to change the name of Highway 51/Bellevue Boulevard to Elvis Presley Boulevard. That was the street in front of Graceland. I said, "If it wasn't for him, there wouldn't be anybody out there anyway."

It didn't become official until January of '72. The area they renamed is a twelve-mile stretch, and it took a while to get all the signs up. The problem was, people would steal them the same day. They had to keep replacing them, and finally they put them up over the intersections on wires instead of poles. That was the only way to keep people from snatching them as souvenirs.

BILLY SMITH: Between '69 and '71, when he was at Graceland, Elvis used to go down to the gate quite a bit and cut up with the fans. Sometimes he'd even let 'em come inside. When Harold [Loyd] was on duty, he'd time it to about an hour and fifteen minutes, and then Elvis would go back up to the house. But he'd have a ball with everybody, and, of course, they would with him.

Now, when Vester was working the gate, all this made him nervous. There used to be a little stump down there where Elvis would stand for the fans to take pictures. And he'd sign autographs for two or three hours. But it would cause the traffic to get so bad, they'd have to call the cops. In fact, there was a lot of wrecks while Elvis was down at the gate. So he had to stop because the people around there complained. I think '71 was the last year he did it.

One time, this really pretty lady was standing there looking at Elvis, and he walked over and kissed her. Well, when he done that, she run right out into traffic. Vester had to go catch her. She just went crazy.

$$\text{💃 💃 💃}$$

MARTY LACKER: In July of '71, Elvis played his first engagement at the Sahara Tahoe Hotel. This was in Stateline, Nevada. He played twenty-eight shows and set a new attendance record. After that, he went back almost every year. He liked it there. Of course, Tahoe's a lot smaller than Vegas and not as glitzy. But Colonel got just about as many people in the showroom as he did in Vegas—just under two thousand—by putting eight people at a table that normally seats four.

LAMAR FIKE: Tahoe's an interesting place. Used to be so loose there the waiters would get tipped with vials of cocaine.

Elvis was sitting down in the living room of the suite one time eating. And we both looked out at the mountains and the pine trees at the same time, and he said, "If you say one more fuckin' time how pretty those goddamn pine trees and that lake are, I'll throw this chair through the window."

But that place is really rough, with the altitude. It's 6,200 feet at the lake. Shit, water won't even boil, it's so high. It just beat him up to sing.

MARTY LACKER: That year, '71, was when the overdoses started. The worst one happened after a show at Tahoe. Sonny told me about it. Elvis saw this girl in the second row, and he was really taken with her. She was a teenager. Real innocent. A nondrinker, nonsmoker. Didn't even wear makeup. And she was crazy about Elvis Presley. She and her mother would drive to Vegas to see him. And her mother was with her at the Tahoe show.

Elvis waved to her from the stage, and after the show, he told

Sonny to bring her backstage. She sent her mother home, and she stayed with Elvis that night and, actually, for quite a bit of his engagement. He'd give her pills so she could keep up his hours.

One night after the show, they went to Palm Springs. Elvis was taking Hycodan, which is a narcotic, analgesic cough syrup. In large doses, that stuff's dangerous. Elvis and this girl were drinking it out of champagne glasses. They didn't go to bed until about four A.M., and when they did, they took their Hycodan with them.

By one o'clock the next day, Elvis wasn't up. Sonny banged on the door. And when Elvis didn't answer, he went inside. It was like a meat locker in there, Elvis kept the temperature so low. Sonny said Elvis was sprawled across the bed lengthways, and his breathing was real erratic.

Well, Sonny freaked out and went and got Hamburger James. And it took a while, but they eventually got Elvis up, and slapped him back to consciousness. Then he took some Ritalin and came out of it.

The girl was another story. She was in much worse shape. They couldn't slap her awake, and she barely had a pulse. Sonny said she was dying right there in front of them.

They phoned Dr. Kaplan and he came up there and called an ambulance. He was shocked at how far gone she was, and he warned them that she probably wouldn't make it. She was already turning blue. Elvis was telling him what to do, you know, "Just give her a shot of Ritalin and she'll pop out of it." I think everybody was pretty disgusted by that. But he used to just hand out Ritalin tablets to all of us in the late sixties. Elvis was just Ritalin nuts. He always thought no matter how bad you got, that's all you needed. He also thought it was a good way to wake up.

Charlie was there, and he and Sonny followed the ambulance to the hospital. They pumped the girl's stomach and hooked her up to life support, but Dr. Kaplan was still saying he didn't think she'd live. But Elvis just waved it off. He said, "I told her not to drink so much of that." And he went in the bedroom and called Colonel Parker and John O'Grady, I think, and Dick Grob, to make sure the Palm Springs police stayed out of it and that it didn't hit the papers. And then they came up with this plan that if she did die, Charlie would take the rap. He'd say she was his date, and he'd given her the stuff.

Well, something like seventeen hours later, the girl came to. Charlie and Sonny went to the hospital, and Sonny said when he touched her arm, she came halfway off the bed and started hissing at him like a wild animal. It scared the shit out of him. The doctor said she was suffering from oxygen deprivation to the brain. Elvis paid her hospital bill, and he had Joe get in touch with her mother and offer her some money. But the mother wouldn't take anything. She said they'd never sue. They didn't want to hurt his image.

The thing is, Elvis never got in touch with that girl. Didn't go to the hospital and didn't call her when she got out.

Later on, Joe ran into her and her mother again in Vegas. They were there for the show, sleeping in their car. He got a room for them at the hotel, and Elvis paid for it. Sonny went to see her, and she told him she didn't hold Elvis responsible. But Sonny said her whole personality had changed.

LAMAR FIKE: I think this thing with the girl in Palm Springs got really close to Elvis, and the fact that she almost died scared the water out of him. And I think he thought, "Holy shit! I really got off lucky here! So let's not bring this up anymore. I don't want to think about it."

But pretty soon he was back to his old ways. Elvis could pick out a girl in the third row, six chairs over, and say, "She's going to go down tonight." And he'd be right.

BILLY SMITH: He had a lot of fear there. At first, it was fear that "God, if she had died!" And then it was, "That dumb bitch! She could have jerked me down right with her and ruined my career!" He totally denied the fact that he was the cause of it.

MARTY LACKER: Elvis was a very selfish person in some regards. He did what he wanted to do, and he didn't give a shit the way it affected anybody else.

BILLY SMITH: I think to some extent Elvis lost touch with the feelings of other people. He changed from humble to hard. Deep down, Elvis was a good person. He was just a victim of a lot of things that changed him and made him the way he was. He got more depressed in later years. The drugs enhanced the pressures, made them seem a lot worse. But he didn't deal with them directly. Instead, he chose to take more drugs.

There were a lot of times I hoped he would snap out of it and become the strong individual that I'd seen in the earlier days. When he really wanted to, he could still focus and say, "Hold it. This is the way it's going to be." But he did that less in the later years.

$$\text{\textit{\&}} \quad \text{\textit{\&}} \quad \text{\textit{\&}}$$

MARTY LACKER: When Elvis went back to Vegas in August of '71, they had him playing three shows a day because of the overflow crowds. When he finished his engagement, he'd broken his own attendance record.

By '71, I was a partner in a company called Mempro, Inc., which was a general service company for the recording and publishing industry. And I'd also become one of the founding members of the Memphis chapter of NARAS, the National Academy of Recording Arts and Sciences. That's the group that awards the Grammys. Eventually, I became an alternate trustee to the national board of governors.

I was talking with Esposito one day, and he mentioned that Colonel had said that NARAS had called. They wanted to give Elvis a Lifetime Achievement Award, which is a living legend honor. I think Sinatra had gotten one, and the Beatles. And as big as Elvis was, he hadn't won any Grammy Awards except for his gospel records.

Joe said that Colonel told NARAS, "That's very nice of you." And they said, "We wanted to ask how many numbers he'd like to perform on TV at the awards." And Colonel said, "What do you mean, 'perform'?" They said, "Since he's going to be there to accept the award, we thought it would be great if he'd be on the show."

Colonel said, "How much are you paying?" And they said, "Well, we don't pay for performances." And Colonel said, "Elvis don't appear without being paid. I don't know that he'll appear anyway." So they went round and round, and NARAS really showed their ass. They said, "Well, if he's not going to be here, we're not going to give him the award."

When I heard that, I really got fuckin' upset. Because if you're going to give somebody an award on merit, you give it to him whether he's there or not. Here's Elvis Presley, the guy who made the whole rock 'n' roll movement what it was, and fifteen years later they weren't willing to give him a Lifetime Achievement Award.

One night, my partner, Don Burt, and I took Ron Alexenburg, the vice president of CBS/Epic Records, to catch a plane back to New York. Ron knew that I had been with Elvis, and he asked me how he was doing. I said, "Fine." And then I told him the story about NARAS and the Lifetime Achievement Award. Ron said, "That's the worst thing I've ever heard." And he said he'd see what he could do.

About six months later, in the fall of '71, I opened *Billboard*, and I saw a picture of Bobby Vinton and [music industry executive] Allen Klein presenting Elvis the Lifetime Achievement Award in his dressing room in Vegas. They still wouldn't do it at the award show.

All the time I was running my business, by the way, I was stoned. I was still taking about ten or more pills a day, which is what I was doing when I worked for Elvis. But I always functioned, even taking sleeping pills during the day. At the time they were a nice sensation. I look back now, and I thank God I got through all of that without doing real damage.

LAMAR FIKE: Those shows in Vegas in August of '71 . . . that's when you saw the first signs that things were starting to fall apart. Elvis would be so ripped his tongue would be thick, and he'd tell the audience, "I'm sorry, folks, I just got up. I'm not really awake yet." Or he'd walk funny—he'd spread his legs out to keep his balance until he got into it.

One time his show was just real bad. He was so fucked up. He went onstage, and he'd start a song and he wouldn't finish it. He was doing about fifteen bars of a song and stopping, then doing another song.

And he'd go into this karate demonstration instead of singing. He was just entertaining himself, and entertaining the people onstage, and not the audience. Well, about eight hundred to one thousand people walked out. I was sitting by the soundboard in the middle of the place, calling the lights, and people were walking out in droves. He did a thirty-five-minute show. He was supposed to do an hour and a half. The maître d' came up to me and said, "Lamar, we got all kind of complaints." I said, "I know it."

He came off that stage, and, boy, I flew back in the dressing room and I lit into him like a circular saw. In front of everybody. All these people were saying, "Oh, you did a good show," and this and that. And I said, "That's the worst show I've ever seen in my life. You ought to be shot for what you did." And, boy, he got mad. He said, "I want to see you in the back." And I said, "Fine."

We got back there, and I said, "You're probably the best show-man that ever walked the face of this earth. But you ought to be ashamed of yourself for what you did tonight."

He said, "I knew that was coming, you son of a bitch!" And then he went crazy.

I stormed out and went upstairs and threatened to fly home. But Elvis made sure I came back down for the second show, and he did a great second show. He ran thirty minutes over—he did a full two hours—which drives the casino crazy because the people won't come out and gamble.

I went backstage and he said, "How was that, Lamar?" I said, "God Almighty! But you're not doing it for me, are you?" He was trying to prove to me he could do it when he wanted to. I said, "You've got two thousand people out there. Prove it to them." So we'd fight and make up.

Later on, we were talking, and I said to him, "Look, this thing is a trick bag here. You're doing two shows a night, sometimes three, for four weeks." I said, "I don't think Superman could do that, but you've got to make the best of it." And he said, "Well, I just got giddy." I said, "Everybody does. You get tired."

I think Elvis had planned on firing me just before he died. Charlie told me he was going to fire me after that ['77] tour because we were always fighting and arguing. But Elvis would say that every day about somebody, and it never came to pass. He was rough on Charlie, too. Elvis liked to beat Charlie to death. Just figuratively, of course. Onstage, he would correct him real hard and embarrass him in front of everybody. It wouldn't be Charlie's fault, but Elvis would slam-dunk him. You see, with me, I would set myself up for an argument. He'd start something with me, and I'd just rot 'til I got it finished. I wouldn't just lay down and let him walk on me. He wasn't right all the time. I never saw him walk across Lake Mead, you know.

MARTY LACKER: When Elvis incorporated karate into his moves onstage, he was the first to do it. He did more for karate than anyone in this country.

BILLY SMITH: He took his karate real serious. In '74, he started producing this karate movie. Supposed to be called *The New Gladiators*. It was never finished. But that was Elvis's dream—to do an educational karate documentary.

LAMAR FIKE: Somebody asked me the other day, "Was he actually any good at karate?" I think Elvis was an honest second- or third-degree black belt. Anything else he got was just awarded. I remember one time in Vegas, we were sitting downstairs in the dressing room, and Elvis had gotten a red-and-white belt, which is a very high honorary degree.

He put it on and walked over and showed it to me. And he flipped the top down and it had a bunch of Chinese writing on it. He said, "Do you know what that means?"

I said, "Yeah, with six you get egg roll." It looked like a damn Chinese menu to me. He got so mad he wouldn't speak to me the rest of the afternoon. It was a good line. I couldn't pass it up.

BILLY SMITH: In November of '71, Elvis went on tour and did fourteen shows in twelve days. He'd done twenty-eight shows in fourteen days at Tahoe and fifty-seven performances in twenty-nine days at Vegas. He'd had some time off before this tour, but he was tired. And I'm sure he was taking a lot of downers.

Of course, things were so different then. I was gone, Marty was gone, Alan was gone, and Richard was gone. Vernon fired him sometime in '71. Elvis hated to lose an older person in the group. It hurt him. But the group, the original Memphis Mafia, was pretty much dead. It didn't finally die until a few years later, but it was pretty darn sick in '71.

LAMAR FIKE: It became so tedious with Elvis because of his drug problem. But then, once you got away from him, you missed it, so you went back. He had such control. Some of those guys had been with him for twelve years. Shit, if you were selling Fuller brushes for twelve years, and you weren't selling them anymore, you'd miss it. But anyway, they were gone. That's why Elvis brought those new kids in.

MARTY LACKER: When Richard left, Elvis brought Ricky Stanley into the entourage. He was seventeen and still in high school. Elvis made him his personal aide. Not out of love, but convenience. And because Vernon asked him to do it—Ricky was getting in so much trouble that Vernon wanted him out of his way.

Dee had a fit when Ricky joined the group. She wanted him to go to college and become a doctor. Elvis told her he'd get tutors and teachers for him on the road, if you can believe that. But Dee knew that if Ricky joined, then Billy and David wouldn't be far behind. And Dee knew what Elvis's lifestyle was like. Even Joe and Red argued against bringing Ricky into the group. That's probably because they knew what was in the back of Elvis's mind. The Stanleys would be his drug runners.

Billy Stanley tells this story, that as soon as Ricky got on the plane for the first tour, Elvis, who was still talking about tutors for him, sat down, put his arm around Ricky, and said, "I might as well tell you now. I'm the teacher."

LAMAR FIKE: We called the younger guys "The Wrecking Crew." We'd say, "Wrecking Crew! Get up here." And they would come and pack Elvis up and get everything together. Eventually, it was Ricky and David Stanley, and Hamburger James, and starting in '74, Dean Nichopoulos, Dr. Nick's son. They were a real contrast to the rest of us.

BILLY SMITH: In the earlier days, we were a real tight-knit group. We didn't leak things to the press. Then, as people filtered in and out of the group, things changed. The new group wasn't as reliable. The emotional ties weren't as strong.

MARTY LACKER: In the last years, the guys didn't hang out at Graceland much, except on the eve of a tour. Elvis started getting tired of everything and everybody. And also he was paranoid.

LAMAR FIKE: As a rule, we hung out during the day, but not at night. I'd drive that trip from Nashville to Memphis like I was blindfolded. But the camaraderie had changed dramatically. The guys from the original group had families. And of course, Elvis hated that. That's one reason he went on tour—to forget about how things had changed.

BILLY SMITH: The routine on tour was this. Dick Grob worked security. He'd fly ahead, and he'd look at the route going in and out, and the stage area, and whatever surrounded it. He saw what needed to be done, and who needed to be placed where, including the hotel. This was a bigger job than it sounded because a little later on, Elvis would go out for twenty days at a time. They tried to keep the cities no more than three hundred miles apart, but they couldn't always do that.

That first night, they'd all get to town, do the show, grab a little sleep, and then go on to the next town in the morning. And you're talking about moving one hundred people here. There were three truckloads of stage and sound equipment, and the roadies traveled with that. They went on ahead with Colonel. Then the musicians went on ahead, too, to set up and do a sound check in the afternoon. Then Elvis and the entourage left. He usually got there in the late afternoon, and then he slept until time to get ready for the show.

MARTY LACKER: Colonel played the advance man on the tours. He could have stayed in L.A. But the Colonel wasn't going to let anything go on without him being there. If the checks weren't sent to his office before the show, he picked them up from the promoters, or from the venue. One of the guys, usually Sonny or Lamar, went with him to set up security, transportation—which was two limos and a bus—and the rooms.

The Colonel actually got the hotels, but Sonny would tell the hotel staff, "We need half the floor, and you have to have somebody man the elevator, so nobody can get off." By the time Elvis and everybody else got there, the group was assigned a room, and the room assignment sheet was hanging out with all the room numbers.

LAMAR FIKE: The preparation began the day before we left. Usually, they took as many concert suits as possible. They always had eight or nine carrying cases for Elvis's stage wardrobe. Once all that shit was packed, we had two pickup trucks to carry all the luggage. Two or three of the guys would go with the trucks to load the plane.

When it came time for Elvis to go, they had two cars ready and waiting at the front door of Graceland. Elvis went in a car with two or three security guys. But before he came out, he'd say goodbye to his father, if Vernon wasn't going on the tour, and Aunt Delta, and to Grandma. He always spent a few minutes alone with her. Then he'd come out and say, "Let's roll 'em, boys!" And it was off to the airport. Once he got the airplane, the *Lisa Marie*, he'd walk on, go back to his bedroom, and put on his pajamas.

MARTY LACKER: Hamburger James would get to the hotel before Elvis and prepare his bedroom and bathroom. Albert Goldman says he had the instructions written down in three notebooks. But that's bullshit, quite frankly.

I do know that Hamburger and Ricky, or one of the other younger guys, would put aluminum foil on the windows, so it would always be dark, and Elvis could sleep. And they fixed his bed, and got all his stuff unpacked, and turned the thermostat down to sixty degrees, so it would be like a tomb in there, dark and freezing.

BILLY SMITH: About the three notebooks . . . it wasn't that complicated. You knew what Elvis had to have—everything from aspirin to Fleet's enemas. On his bedstand, you had a jug of ice water. And in his refrigerator, some Pepsis. The costumes were kept in a whole separate room. Elvis didn't call for those until he got ready to go to the coliseum. So that's it. Except he always had his books with him—*Cheiro's Book of Numbers*, you know, numerology. And *The Scientific Search for the Face of Jesus*. See, he didn't really give up all that stuff.

LAMAR FIKE: You had to haul those damn books around. They weighed twelve tons. It was like carrying an anvil. He wanted them put beside his bed. Everything had its place—even his toothpaste. See, his rooms were created, whether they were on an airplane or a hotel. Once he got the plane the way he wanted it, Elvis did not go from place to place in a seat, he went in a virtual bedroom. He never had to get out of his comfort zone.

By the way, you know what else he took on tour? That Jaycees trophy.

MARTY LACKER: That was kind of funny. He carried it everywhere. With a ribbon around it. Showed it to everybody.

LAMAR FIKE: In '71, Dr. Nick started going on the tours with us. He was really eaten up with the whole celebrity thing. Nick loved that. He used to use Jerry Lee Lewis's plane. It was the whole "Golden Greek" routine. Nick's a high roller. He loved to be on the high side of it. Although you wouldn't know it from the way he dresses. He's "The Polyester Kid."

BILLY SMITH: About '70 or '71 was when Elvis started seeing Dr. Nick on a continual basis. He'd go on the tours and give Elvis his medication. He'd have to have medication to get up for a show, and to come down after the show, so he could sleep. Then the next morning, he'd have to have medication to get up. And he'd get medication on the plane, then more to take a nap before the show, and then it would start again before and after the show.

But Dr. Nick was real limited in certain areas to what he could do. People don't understand—he tried to control what Elvis got. He really was trying to help him, I think. But Elvis outsmarted him. Like Dr. Nick said in an interview, at the time Elvis died, he was prescribing four different things that Elvis was taking, yet there was fourteen drugs found in Elvis's body.

LAMAR FIKE: I've seen Dr. Nick come in before we went on tour with a brown grocery sack full of stuff. Now, that was drugs, but it was also shit like first-aid supplies and corn plasters and eyedrops, the works. He was a walking drugstore. Mainly for Elvis, but for whoever else needed it.

Dr. Nick was in practice with a bunch of other doctors. And at first, Elvis just paid Dr. Nick to go on the tour, but then the other doctors got pissed because they were having to see his patients. So then Elvis had to pay the group $800 a day for Dr. Nick's services while he was gone.

Dr. Nick would go on those tours to do two things—hand out pills, because he was the proverbial pill roller, and chase women. He'd hang out with Joe—Joe and Dr. Nick were big buddies. And he wouldn't hang around with the rest of the guys. At the time Elvis died, Joe was making $40,000, plus bonuses and cars. And he made sure you knew it.

BILLY SMITH: Everybody wanted to be number one with Elvis. And when Dr. Nick come in, it just got worse. Where Elvis went, Joe went, and he took Joanie, and they went in the Rolls-Royce, no matter if they were playing a game, or going to a movie, or going to the fairgrounds. Priscilla and Elvis were number one, and Joe and Joanie were number two, and everybody else was behind them. Patsy Lacker says Elvis thought "wife" was a four-letter word. But he didn't think everybody's wife was. That's the class separation. That's why I hated it.

MARTY LACKER: Dr. Nick got caught up in that life. And he got himself into a situation with his partners where he needed a great deal of money, and he was also greedy. Dr. Nick was in terrible financial shape. And Elvis knew it and took advantage of it.

Every time Dr. Nick got in trouble, Elvis was the one to bail him out, either with big gifts like a new gold Cadillac and a gold Mercedes or loans. At one point, in '75, Dr. Nick went to Elvis and asked him to loan him $200,000 to build his house. And Elvis did it. Two years later, he borrowed another $55,000 from him.

When we found out about it, we were just astonished. It was nothing for Elvis to give somebody $5,000 or $10,000, but to loan somebody a quarter of a million dollars—and to give him expensive cars and jewelry—was totally shocking to us. I'm sure Elvis did it because he felt he'd have Dr. Nick in his pocket.

522 ELVIS AARON PRESLEY

LAMAR FIKE: Dr. Nick looked for the easiest route and took it. He's a grabber-on-er. He gets what he needs. The Greek community, of course, rallies around him, but he's as guilty [of overprescribing narcotics] as sin. There's a band in Nashville called "Dr. Nick." They've got bumper stickers that say, "If you're feeling sick, call Dr. Nick." It's hilarious.

I'd say that Dr. Nick's professional judgment got clouded. How many doctors do you know who "borrow" six-figure amounts from their patients?

Right after Elvis died, Nick said he was never financially dependent on Elvis, that he was paying the money back to the estate. I don't know if he was or not, but Vernon made him sign an agreement to repay more than a thousand dollars a month. But let me give you some hard figures. From the beginning of '70 to the middle of '77, Elvis made personal loans to Dr. Nick of $275,000. And Elvis paid him $76,000 for professional services, and he paid the Medical Group $147,000 on top of that to compensate for Dr. Nick's time while he was away on Elvis's tour. Not bad, huh?

BILLY SMITH: Colonel didn't like Dr. Nick. He saw what was happening—he had to know. And Vernon liked him even less because Elvis bought Dr. Nick a house and cars. Vernon was afraid Elvis was going to give away the mansion.

I don't mean to totally run Vernon down. The man had some good to him. But Elvis's fame created one person who couldn't handle a lot of pressure—Elvis—who deep down had a heart of gold. And then it turned the other one, Vernon, into a greedy Scrooge that cared about nobody but himself and his son.

MARTY LACKER: When Elvis went back on tour in November, George Klein and I went out for a few shows—in Cleveland, Louisville, Cincinnati, and maybe a few other places. We were going to leave Elvis in Houston and go to a disc jockey convention in New Orleans.

About two minutes before each show, Colonel Parker would walk out in the arena and go into his routine. He'd always be sure he had two or three suckers standing around. And he'd pick one out, and say, "I'm going to tell you how many people are in this house right now because the Colonel is all-knowing." He'd say, "It's 11,492. Remember that number. The Colonel knows."

He'd come back later with the tally. Colonel would hold up the paper, and he'd say to the guy, "How many people did I say were in here?" And the guy would read off, "11,492." Well, of course, Colonel knew that before he ever walked in the damn place. But he still loved to pull that carny crap.

Sometimes Vernon went on the tours, and part of the reason he went was to screw around. Matter of fact, I happened to catch him in the act in a hotel room in Cincinnati. The woman was, to put it nicely, servicing him. Vernon didn't know I saw him, and I never told him. I just happened to open the door to the room, and his back was turned because Vernon was standing up.

One night after that, Elvis, and Red, and I were out riding around in Memphis. I was in the backseat. We were talking about stuff in general and being kind of raunchy, actually. And I said, "Yeah, your father ain't too old yet!" And Elvis and Red both looked back at me. Red said, "Marty, he don't want to hear that about his father." And Elvis sort of cringed. So I dropped the subject. But he knew what Vernon was like.

$$ \text{🕺 🕺 🕺} $$

LAMAR FIKE: Elvis had plenty of company on the tours. One of the women was Joyce Bova. She says she's been a staff member of the Armed Services Committee of the U.S. House of Representatives for twenty-five years. But that doesn't necessarily mean anything. I think she worked for some big shot in the government, some senator in Washington. She was a secretary. She had a twin sister who worked for the government, too. Joyce was a very attractive girl. She had that long black hair and the heavy eyebrows. I think she was Italian.

Joyce was an interesting person, but there was no torrid love affair there. He met her at the hotel in '69, and she came out to Vegas a few times more on her own. And then Elvis dated her when he was in Washington, like when he went to see Nixon, and again, I think, when he went to the FBI building. He was in Washington about two or three times after that, and he flew her to Vegas once or twice for a few days. She claims she was with him about three years, but from what I saw, she was about two short.

MARTY LACKER: This woman, Joyce Bova, has written a book [*Don't Ask Forever: My Love Affair with Elvis*]. She says she saw Elvis off and on in the seventies—from '69 to '72—and that Elvis kept it secret. Well, Elvis dated her, but I don't believe it was that long.

Elvis did buy her a car, but he bought cars for girls he saw for only two days. Now she's saying she was pregnant, and she aborted. She also says he got her hooked on drugs, sleeping pills mostly. Maybe she was predisposed. I didn't see her around him that much.

I will say this—Joyce was one of the best-looking girls he ever dated. She was sweet and nice, and she got along with everybody.

But you almost need a calculator to keep these women straight because they didn't last very long. Or he'd have one date with them in '70 and another in '73. They'd call one of the guys, like Joe, in Vegas, and say they'd like to talk to Elvis or say, "Tell Elvis I said hello." And Elvis would say to Joe, "Why don't you call and see if she wants to come out here?"

They were all kinds, too. One girl was a dancer in one of the shows in Vegas. Another one was a radio promotion girl in Philadelphia. He had that one travel with him to two or three different shows on the tour, and he flew her out to Vegas when Priscilla wasn't around. What he didn't find out 'til later was that she was posing for pornographic pictures. And, boy, he dropped her quick. Later, we found out that some of his girls were hooking on the side.

🕺 🕺 🕺

LAMAR FIKE: The most money I ever made with Elvis was $365 a week, and that was when he died. I guess I was making $250 a week in '71. But at the end of a tour he would give us a bonus—a big amount of cash and maybe a car that would be too expensive for us to maintain. The estate says Elvis always paid the insurance on any car he gave you. I don't remember that. But when it was cash, it would be a thousand here, ten thousand here, twenty here. So you never knew what you were going to have. But Elvis was very generous after a tour. And Vernon liked to shit.

MARTY LACKER: In '71, Elvis bought his first Stutz Blackhawk. He eventually had two or three of them. This was the first one made for the trade after the prototype car. The story goes that it was originally ordered for Frank Sinatra, but that Elvis talked the dealership out of it so he could have the first one, and Sinatra got the second. Elvis sent it out to be washed one day, and it ended up in a wreck. After that, he just put it in storage. The estate finally restored it.

He loved that car, and he'd go for rides down Sunset Boulevard in it, sometimes by himself. In California, the times he went riding around were really the only times he was out of the house, except when he was making movies or doing concerts. Sometimes he'd say to one of the guys, "C'mon and go with me." But with the Stutz, a lot of times he'd go out on his own. I think he just liked the kick of driving around in that unusual car and showing it off. Especially with the horn. He used to come back and say everybody recognized him in that car because the horn played "Never on Sunday." And he'd ride down Sunset and blow the horn at girls. He never stopped being a flirt, not 'til the day he died. Except with black girls. He never flirted with blacks.

I was visiting Elvis out in California at the Monovale house in late '71, and this one day, I was sitting in the den with a couple of the guys. It was late afternoon, and Elvis had gone out riding in the Stutz by himself.

He came back in a little while, and he said, "Guess what happened? I was driving down Sunset, coming back to the house, and a limousine pulled up alongside me, and the window rolled down." He said, "It was Diana Ross." He'd never met her before, just seen her on TV. This was when she had that real skinny look, skinnier even than when she was with the Supremes.

The way Elvis told it, Diana said, "Hi! How you doin'?" He said, "Oh, fine." And she said, "Where are you going?" He told her, "I'm just on my way back home." And she said, "Why don't we go somewhere together?" I can't remember if he said she wanted to go in the Stutz, or if she wanted him to come in the limo, but she wanted them in the same car. And he said, "I just thought real quick and told her I had a meeting at the house." And then he said he sped off.

One of the other guys said, "Why did you do that?" And Elvis said, "Man, she's too damn skinny and ugly for me."

LAMAR FIKE: When we came off that tour in the middle of November ['71], it was pretty obvious that Elvis and Priscilla were nearly finished. She says touring was the beginning of the end of the marriage, although I'd put it a lot earlier than that. He discouraged her modeling career and whatever she wanted to do in dance and acting, but he did encourage her to take up karate.

That's how she had that affair with Mike Stone. Priscilla first saw him in Hawaii, when she and Elvis went to Ed Parker's karate tournament in '68. And she remembered him. And then in '71 or so, Stone was a bodyguard for Phil Spector. Phil had come backstage somewhere and Mike was there. And Priscilla used the phrase "their eyes met," and that was it. She was starting to come out of her shell. And Mike became a big thing.

Everybody knew about the affair before Elvis did. Henrietta, the maid at the Holmby Hills house [on Monovale], told Red that Mike was spending too much time at the house. Or more than he should have been if he was just teaching Priscilla karate. And Lisa Marie told Hamburger James that Mike took them camping. She said, "I saw Mommy and Mike wrestling in their sleeping bag on the beach. They wrestled all night." Hamburger told Ricky Stanley, and Ricky told Billy Stanley and the whole crowd. So Priscilla was done in by a three-year-old.

The way we finally knew for sure was that Sonny caught them in the shower together. Elvis was in Vegas, and Sonny went to the Monovale house to pick up something, and he heard singing in the bathroom. He turned the corner down that hall to Elvis's bedroom, and he looked to the right, and there was Mike and Priscilla in the shower. They never saw him.

Sonny came back to Vegas and told me. I said, "You better go to Elvis now, and tell him." And Sonny went in and talked to Elvis and told him about it. And a few days after they came back, Sonny told Priscilla, too.

Elvis came over to me, and he said, "You son of a bitch, why didn't you tell me?" I said, "I didn't want to go through that shit. I just counted on watching this one fly." And Elvis went berserk. It got *real* bad.

It wasn't a case of him losing her, see. And it wasn't jealousy. What bothered him was that she had the effrontery to screw around on *him*. He said, "How can she do this to me?"

BILLY SMITH: It hurt his ego more than anything else. He couldn't understand why any woman would leave him for another guy.

MARTY LACKER: At Christmas of '71, there was a lot of tension in the house. Priscilla was cooler to everybody than usual, more aloof. Elvis had told her earlier that he was giving her a car for Christmas, and she told him to keep it—she didn't want it. So he gave her ten $1,000 bills. Those she kept. And she left for L.A. the next day.

Usually at Christmas, Elvis gave us all something real nice. That year, I remember, Bill Morris was there, and so was George Klein. Elvis handed us all these envelopes, and George said, "Thank you, E. You shouldn't have done that." He thought he was getting big money, see. And Elvis said, "Oh, it's nothing. You deserve it." Everybody opened his envelope, and inside was a gift certificate. It was from McDonald's, for fifty cents.

SPIRAL

MARTY LACKER: In '72, when Elvis turned thirty-seven, we went out to Graceland for a little birthday celebration. Somebody asked him about Priscilla and Lisa, and he said Priscilla had decided to stay out in California for a while. He made it sound kind of offhand, but it was obvious they were separated. She wasn't even staying in the Monovale house. Turned out she and Mike Stone were living together.

LAMAR FIKE: Elvis went back into Vegas at the end of January with a new male backup group—J. D. Sumner and the Stamps Quartet, a gospel act. J.D. had one of those real low bass voices—like a guy with five balls, you know? Elvis used to say he could go down four keys off the piano. He used to sing with the Blackwood Brothers Quartet. Elvis had known him since he was sixteen. J.D. used to let him in the backdoor of the gospel sings at Ellis Auditorium. At the time, Elvis thought he was God.

MARTY LACKER: The gospel singers, just like the evangelists, present themselves as Goody Two-shoes, and some of them are anything but. J.D. and the Stamps Quartet were no different. When I went on tour with Elvis to Cincinnati, J.D. had his little gospel groupies visit him.

Since Elvis died, J.D. acts like he was around Elvis all the time. The truth is, he was there when Elvis went on tour, and that was it. And even then, the two camps were separate.

LAMAR FIKE: After a few shows out in Vegas, Elvis started cutting 'em short again. He'd barely wait for the applause to end before he'd start another song. Or he'd get on these long, rambling jags where he'd just talk.

After one of those, we got in another fight. He did forty-five minutes and left the stage, and I roared into that dressing room. I said, "Well, you topped yourself. You did the lousiest show I've ever seen you do in your life!" He turned around real quick and said, "I'll fucking kill you for that! You're fired, Lard-ass!" I said, "Fuck it! That's fine with me!" So I went upstairs and started packing.

In a little while, Elvis came up to the penthouse. He yelled, "Lamar!" I said, "What is it?"

Joe came around the corner and said, "Elvis is in the foyer and wants to talk to you." I said, "Fuck him! I don't give a shit. I don't want to talk to him."

Elvis was around the corner, listening to all this. And he yelled, "Look, you son of a bitch, we need to talk this over!" And I yelled back, "I don't need to talk to you! I've already quit. What are you going to do, whip me?"

He said, "Will you meet me at the end of the hall? I'll come down to the end of the hall and meet you halfway." I said, "No, I'm up to here with this shit!"

I turned around and went back in the bedroom and closed the door. And I heard him scream, "I'm down at the end of the hall. What are you going to do about it?" I screamed back, "Just stay at the end of the hall!" Joe was in the middle, saying, "Will one of you guys give in?" I said, "I'm staying here in the fucking room. I ain't coming out." Well, Elvis kept on yelling until I had to come out. It was so funny. We met literally halfway and hugged, and Elvis said, "Look, I love you, Lamar." So we made back up.

But this stuff went on all the time. One night—this was a few years later, probably '75—we'd been arguing about something, and he really got me mad. I said, "I'm going to tell you something, buddy. I call the lights, and you're going to have a bad problem tonight. You're going to have to find the light."

Well, I ran him all over that stage, chasing the spotlight. He'd walk into the light and I'd move it. He was from one side of that place to the other. He screamed, "Do you mind?" It was like a routine.

He was standing in the dark one time, and he said, in front of everybody, "Lamar, would you mind putting the light on me?" I was in the balcony, shouting to him on the stage, see. I said, "Nope." He said, "Nope, you're not going to put the light on me, or nope, you don't mind doing it?" I said, "I'm not going to do it." People were in stitches.

There were a couple of instances like that. It got so we left it in the show for a while. We would yell back and forth at each other, and people didn't know what to think.

MARTY LACKER: About '72, Elvis started getting more erratic. One day in Vegas, he got mad at Joanie Esposito and threw a butter knife at her.

Elvis's routine in Vegas would be to get up about five or five-thirty P.M. and have breakfast. He'd eat it out in the den. There was a big, long coffee table out there in front of the television, and he knew when he got up that his breakfast would be there waiting for him. He'd eat and watch the news or flick stations.

This day, a few of the guys were sitting up in the suite. Joanie said something in a joking way, but Elvis was in no mood for games.

Elvis said, "Goddamnit," and flung that butter knife in her direction. It was heading straight for her face. Sonny happened to be sitting right in front of her. And luckily, he reached out and caught that knife in midair. Otherwise, it would have hit Joanie in the face and gone clean through her head. Elvis paid absolutely no attention to it.

LAMAR FIKE: In the early seventies, and up to the end, Elvis got really mean. The drugs made him that way. I also think he felt a lot of his fame slipping, and he didn't like it. He started hating Vegas so bad, and eventually, he just detested the business. But nobody bothered him when he went onstage. That's where he controlled it all. And that's the only place he felt he could control who he was.

In '72 or so, Wolfman Jack came backstage one night. We were sitting in the dressing room, and Wolfman just offhandedly said to him, "What's it like to be Elvis Presley?" And Elvis said,

"I'll tell you what, Jack, it's very, very uncomfortable."

Bored. That's what he was. Bored to tears: Getting a group around and talking to them. Getting loaded and going to bed. Waking up. Doing two shows a night. Felton Jarvis went looking for him one time when they were recording in Memphis. He couldn't find him in the studio, so he went outside. Elvis was there in the dark. And Felton said, "Why are you sitting out here, Elvis?" And he said, "I'm just so tired of being Elvis Presley."

Those last five years, he was close to being somebody else. He was just a tormented person. He couldn't get his shit together. He didn't know how to stop the drugs. And he didn't want to.

The one thing that might have made a difference was playing Europe. In the first part of '72, it was heavily rumored he was going to go over and play London and Paris. Tom Diskin always denied there was any truth to it, but we were hoping there was. We thought maybe Elvis would get himself back together again. And I think he thought it would turn him back into what he was in the fifties.

He didn't talk about it in those terms, of course. He wouldn't have acknowledged it. But I think a tour abroad would have completely revitalized him. Elvis was a person who, if he had a real challenge, would face it and meet it. The last great frontier for him was the world outside the United States and Canada. But the Colonel would always talk him out of it.

BILLY SMITH: After the threats on Elvis's life, Colonel would say, "Our security just won't be good, and we don't want something to happen over there. Besides, I can make you just as much money here. Let's just increase the tours in the States."

LAMAR FIKE: In February, when Elvis was getting ready to close the engagement, Priscilla came to Vegas. In between shows, she told Elvis about Mike Stone and said she wanted a divorce. Elvis knew why she'd come, and he told Red to go down to the restaurant and get her, that he wanted to talk to her.

She says in her book that he told her she was out of her mind, that she had everything a woman could want. But she didn't back down. And she told Red's wife, Pat, that Elvis forced her to have sex. She writes that in her book, too. I think she uses the term "very forcefully." She said it was uncomfortable and she cried. Now, she never uses the word "rape," but she pretty well suggests he raped her.

I think that's a crock. It wasn't in his nature. Maybe she just thought it was rape. I don't know. It's just so abhorrent to me that it's hard for me to think Elvis would ever resort to that. But maybe he did, out of anger.

He called us all in after the second show and told us, "Another man has taken my wife." Somebody said something to the effect of "I thought you wanted to get rid of her." And he said, "Not that way, man."

MARTY LACKER: I remember when Elvis told me she was going to divorce him. I went out to California on business, and I went up to the house. Elvis was outside. I got out of the car, and we hugged. And he said, "Marty, I've got a problem. Priscilla's leaving me. She wants a divorce." And he said, "Man, it hurts."

I told him I was sorry. And he said, "What am I going to do?" I said, "Let me ask you a question: Are you going to change?" And he said, "Hell, no. I ain't doing that for nobody." I said, "Well, much as it hurts, Elvis, you're just going to have to live with it. Because if you change just to make her happy, you're not going to be happy. So you're going to have to accept it." He said, "Yeah, I guess you're right. But it's kind of hard to take."

This whole conversation surprised me because usually he didn't talk a whole lot about things like that. And this was the first thing out of his mouth. But then this might have been right after he got to the Monovale house and saw that she'd moved out. That shakes anybody up.

I'll tell you how much he cared about Priscilla—he never remembered her birthday. The day before it rolled around, one of us would say, "Elvis, tomorrow is Priscilla's birthday." And he'd say, "It is? Well, you know what to do." And we'd send flowers for him. So with the divorce, he wasn't upset because he was losing her. He was upset that something was being taken away from him. And he didn't like the way it looked to his fans.

BILLY SMITH: In one of these TV movies, they've got Elvis chasing after Priscilla, begging her to come back. He looked like an idiot in this thing: "Don't say anything in front of the guys . . . " That would be typical of Elvis, except for one thing. When Elvis got to that point, he was bitter. He hated as much as he loved.

Now, I imagine he may have said at one time or another, "Why don't you come back to me?" Because they stayed pretty close in touch about Lisa Marie and even done some things together. But I have a hard time believing that he would go as far as she said, then or any other time. She said in *Glamour* magazine that Elvis hoped they'd get back together again when he was fifty and she was forty, and that it wasn't out of the question.

I never heard him say that. Elvis was not one to cross the same road twice.

MARTY LACKER: Priscilla says he came over to her house one time and talked to her about coming back. Now, knowing Elvis, he might have been screwed up, and he might have looked at her and thought, "Well, maybe I want a little [sex] tonight." So he might have talked to her about coming back. But I think that if he got her in bed, he wouldn't have done anything. Because the thought of her being with someone else would have turned him off.

It was devastating to him that a woman—especially his wife— would leave him, and especially leave him for somebody who had nothing. Elvis felt, "I'm giving you everything, and we have this family." I think that was the only divorce in his family, other than his grandfather, Jessie. And he would have thought of that.

BILLY SMITH: I think Priscilla would have been more willing to give it another chance than Elvis because he wouldn't give up the women. But there was still something there on both their parts. She says they were best friends after the divorce, after the strain was out of the relationship. She tells this story about him even calling her about his girlfriend troubles. She says, "You aren't going to believe this, but sometimes he would hand the telephone to a girl and ask me to tell her how to handle him."

But their marriage just couldn't work. Not with their different thoughts and attitudes. Elvis would have liked to keep Priscilla like a bird. Elvis's attitude towards all of us was like "Keep them there, take them out and play with them when you get ready, and then throw them back in the cage."

🕺 🕺 🕺

MARTY LACKER: Ed Hookstratten handled the divorce. He represented Elvis and then picked Priscilla's attorney for her. Somehow, Vernon got Priscilla to accept a lump sum of $100,000, plus $1,000 a month for her own expenses and $5,000 a month in child support. Which is amazing. They told her, "Well, you won't have to pay a lot to your lawyer because Hookstratten will draw up the papers." That's pretty stupid. But she was so tight with her money that she wanted to hang on to every penny she got. And she later said that her lawyer—the one Hookstratten got for her—asked her to sign a letter saying she hadn't hired him to advise her about Elvis's assets or income.

Elvis actually filed for the divorce, in August. Supposedly, he filed as a favor to her. Whoever files has to have his address on the public document. And Priscilla didn't want her address out. She might have been afraid of the fans.

🕺 🕺 🕺

LAMAR FIKE: I think the divorce weakened his resolve. When all this brewed up, Elvis got more into downers and started gaining weight.

The seventies were when he started getting really bad, see. Because he got into sleeping pills in a big way. Elvis loved downers. It was nothing for him to have all this stuff in his system at one time, like a Valium, a Placidyl, a Valmid, some Butabarb, phenobarbital—all of which are downers, sedatives—and some form of codeine. So he started looking to other things—things past Percodan and liquid Demerol, even.

Later on, in the mid-seventies, he started using Dilaudid, which is synthetic heroin, drugstore heroin. You're talking about extremely strong shit here—five times stronger than morphine and two and a half times stronger than heroin. Doctors prescribe it for terminal cancer patients.

It was in pill or liquid form. Elvis would inject it. But he wouldn't inject it himself because that's what a junkie did. And he made a great distinction between himself and a junkie. A junkie did heroin. Not Dilaudid. And a junkie mainlined. So he seldom shot himself up. He'd have one of us do it. And he wouldn't have us shoot into the vein, or into his arm, because he didn't want needle tracks. He wanted intramuscular injections. He'd make us shoot into his hip. Dilaudid became his favorite drug.

BILLY SMITH: Elvis was scared of heroin. And, of course, it wasn't prescription. As long as things were prescription, it was okay. He had his own doctor, so that made it all right. Elvis would be the first to tell you, "I don't want street drugs, or even marijuana, around me. And I don't want to hear about anybody in the group that's bein' it, either."

LAMAR FIKE: I sat down and talked to him one night. I said, "Elvis, what the hell do you think Dilaudid is? Who are you fooling? Do you understand what's happening to you?"

He said, "You don't understand—I need this stuff." It was a total psychological dependence. I said, "Nobody needs the stuff you take except advanced cancer patients." And he said, "I'll tell you what. I don't want to talk about it anymore. And if you say anything more, I'll knock the shit out of you and fire you at the same time."

BILLY SMITH: Elvis never admitted that he had a problem or that he needed to get off of anything. I look back at him now, and I think, "God, how did he make it at times?"

LAMAR FIKE: One time, I looked at him and I said, "Elvis, you know who's going to get the blame in the end? We'll get the blame." And, of course, we did.

But shit, we all liked it. When we went to Vegas, I started right back taking stuff with him. But I couldn't handle the hangover the next day, so I quit.

I had a scare or two out there. The worst one was in '70 or '71. I had taken about six or seven pills. Well, right before you pass out, you get really hungry. You basically eat the refrigerator 'til it gets light. So I ordered a cheeseburger and French fries to the room.

This was about five-thirty or six o'clock in the morning, which was our normal time to go to bed. And I took two big bites of cheeseburger, and it stuck in my throat. I couldn't get it out, and I couldn't breathe.

Really, I was dying. I was turning blue. I thought, "What can I do?" And I had the presence of mind to get up and walk towards the end of the bed and run as hard as I could backwards into the wall. I must have been doing five miles an hour. And when I hit the wall, BOOM! The hamburger shot out of my mouth and flew clean across the room. I looked over there, and it was a hunk of meat about the size of a golf ball. I went, "Holy shit!"

It scared the hell out of me. I called everybody and I said, "Well, I liked to died last night!" And they said, "Okay," and they hung up. I said, "Well, you motherfuckers . . . "

MARTY LACKER: In May, after a bunch of road dates in April [1972], Elvis and some of the guys went to Hawaii on vacation. He wanted to attend a karate demonstration, and he wanted a tan.

Early in June, he was set to play four shows in three days at Madison Square Garden. Elvis never had felt comfortable in New York, going back to when he auditioned for Arthur Godfrey and didn't get on the show. So he was nervous about it. And this was a big event, with a press conference and a live album coming out of the shows.

Well, that place seats twenty thousand people. And all four shows sold out in a day. All kind of rock legends were in the audience—Bob Dylan, John Lennon, George Harrison, David Bowie, Art Garfunkel.

LAMAR FIKE: I wasn't there. But I read the review in the *New York Times.* He slayed 'em up there. The reviewer for the *Times,* Chris Chase, said he "looked like a prince from another planet." She compared him to Joe Louis and Joe DiMaggio. She said he was the kind of champion "in whose hands the way a thing is done becomes more important than the thing itself."

MARTY LACKER: I remember that review, too, and it made him out to be more of a nostalgia act than anything else. You know, language like, "It was 1956 again." And "Time stopped, and everyone in the place was 17 again." But he did contemporary songs at those performances, like "Proud Mary" and "Never Been to Spain." They were covers of other people's hits, but they were recent songs.

He also did a press conference there at the New York Hilton. That's where you saw how with-it Elvis was. He skirted the questions about politics, but some woman asked him about being a shy country boy, and he had that comeback with "Oh, I don't know, I've got this gold belt," and he stood up and opened his jacket and showed off that monstrosity the International gave him.

BILLY SMITH: He was pretty high there, but he wasn't stoned. His wit was real sharp that day.

LAMAR FIKE: Let me tell you where Elvis's humor was at its best. Watch the outtakes of his press conferences. I have never heard anybody deflect as quick and as good as he could, except maybe John Kennedy. Elvis was very intuitive. He picked up on stuff quick as a flash—almost like he plucked it out of the air. His humor was so unusual, and so hip and inside, that few people caught it. He would do things, and people would walk off saying, "What the fuck was that?" And we'd be on the floor laughing because we knew what it was.

MARTY LACKER: Elvis and Priscilla didn't formally separate until late July, but by late June, everybody in Memphis knew they were getting a divorce. And since they both had the same lawyer, and this wasn't going to be a prolonged fight, they were both pretty open about doing what they wanted. Mike Stone was married, with two kids, see. His wife sued him for divorce that same year, '72, and got the house and kids.

One of the girls Elvis dated during all this was Barbara Leigh. He'd seen her off and on for a little while. He more or less stole her from Jim Aubrey, who was the president of MGM. Jim was supposed to have been the model for the Robin Stone character— the great lover—in Jacqueline Susann's *The Love Machine*. Barbara was a would-be actress, and Jim brought her backstage to meet Elvis in Vegas after a show in '70. Elvis figured he had to see her again and asked her for her phone number right under Jim's nose.

He had her to Graceland a couple of times. I went over there one day, and I saw this woman standing at the dining-room table with her back to me. She was wearing this sheer, almost see-through, yellow gown. She turned around, and Elvis introduced us. She was a beautiful girl. But the gown surprised me because nobody dressed that way at Graceland. It stopped just above her breasts so that her shoulders were bare. That relationship didn't last long. He gave her a Mercedes-Benz, and I don't know what else. Then she was gone. There was just a parade of girls. And none of them meant anything.

LAMAR FIKE: In July, Elvis went to the midnight movies, and George Klein introduced him to the current Miss Tennessee, Linda Thompson. Linda was making the most of this beauty queen stuff. She'd been Miss Memphis State and Miss Liberty Bowl. Elvis liked her, and it wasn't any time until she moved into Graceland.

When Elvis first started seeing her, we didn't think she could chew gum and walk at the same time. It was amazing when we found out she could. She had a real good spirit. But she also had that beauty queen mentality. She was the kind of girl who put Vaseline on her mouth so her lips would slide easy over her teeth. You know, the beauty queen smile. I said to Elvis, "That's interesting." Elvis said, "Yes, it is." And we laughed like hell. But she turned out to be the best one of the group.

Linda's a good lady. A lot of fun. Scattered, but smart as they come. She was a speech and drama major at MSU [Memphis State University]. I guess she was the only one of Elvis's women who was educated. She'd play the dumb role, and be subservient to a degree, but she'd get what she wanted. And she's done very well in everything she's done, from acting to writing songs.

Elvis only went with two strong women. Ann-Margret was the other. And Linda might have been stronger than Ann. Linda was very motherly. And from that standpoint, I think she was very good for Elvis. Now, as to what he gave her as a person . . . I think once everything had boiled down to a good thick broth, he probably would have been able to give more of himself later on. Maybe. But not as he was. After a little while, Linda didn't think

he was all that hot a lover, either. She said, "Once in a year . . . "
But Linda was quite happy being there.

MARTY LACKER: When Linda came on the scene, she was with
Elvis everywhere he went. That tells you that if Elvis wanted
Priscilla with him, she would have been there. Linda started trav-
eling with him from the very beginning.

The difference in Priscilla and Linda was the same as the difference between Priscilla and Ann-Margret—neither one of them
felt threatened by anybody or anything. And neither one was trying to change him. Linda, to a certain extent, tried to change him
in regards to the pills. She hated to see what they were doing to
him and what he was doing to himself. But she wasn't trying to
change him as a person.

She spent four years basically taking care of Elvis—and I
mean taking care of him. She was like a mother, a sister, a wife, a
lover, and a nurse. She understood that he saw other girls when
she wasn't around. But from the last part of '72, when Linda
started, to '75, he didn't fool around that much on the road.
Because she was with him all the time.

It hurt her when he did that, but her attitude was "What am I
going to do about it? Say, 'Hey, Elvis, you can't do that or I'm
going to leave?' He would have said, 'Adios.'"

BILLY SMITH: Linda wasn't the usual type of woman Elvis liked.
She was kind of thin, but she was tall—5'9". And she was pretty,
but her personality made her beautiful.

LAMAR FIKE: Linda babied him. She'd do that whole baby-talk
routine, use the same secret language as Gladys did with him.
Pretty soon, she was using it with Foxhugh, her poodle. She sent
Elvis a Mailgram when he was in Beverly Hills one time. Becky
Yancey, who worked in the office with Vernon, saved it because it
was all in that baby talk. It's amazing. Becky wrote a book right
after Elvis died [*My Life with Elvis* by Becky Yancey and Cliff
Linedecker], and she put it in there:

Baby gullion, you are just a little fella. Little fellas need
lots of butch, ducklin', and ittytream, sure. Sure I said it.
Iddytream. Iddytream? Grit. Chock. Chock. Shake. Rattle.

Roll. Hmmmmm . . . Grit. Roll again. Hit. Hit. Pinch. Bite.
Bite. Bite. Hurt. Grit. Whew. My baby don't care for rings,
da, da, etc. etc. Pablum lullion (in or out of the hospital).
P.S. Foxhugh will bite sooties if you say iddytream again.
Grit. Grit.

Ariadne Pennington (3 years old)

You know what's funny about this? I recognize some of the
words. "Iddytream" was ice cream. "Butch" was milk. "Ducklin'"
was water. "Sooties" was feet. And Ariadne Pennington was
the name of a character, a little girl, in *Follow That Dream*.
Elvis just had Linda adopt that persona, I guess, for their little
games.

MARTY LACKER: I think we all liked Linda. She was nice to
everybody, including my wife, and she helped Patsy finally understand Elvis. When Linda came around, Patsy's resentment disappeared, and Patsy and Elvis got to be good friends. As a matter of
fact, she and Linda used to sing background with him in the car
and in the house.

After Elvis died and Priscilla took over Graceland, she started
bad-mouthing Linda and her taste. Elvis redecorated Graceland
in '74. He and Linda looked at stuff, and she said, "Oh, yeah.
That's pretty. Let me show you this, let me show you that."

But it was always Elvis's choice. The original color scheme
was blue, white, and gold, and most of the furniture on the first
floor had been custom-made in the fifties. And in '74, Elvis
bought a lot of faux French Provincial furniture and changed the
color scheme to red—it was red crushed-velvet everything, and
red satin drapes, and red shag carpet. Real kitschy. It looked like
a French bordello.

Well, Elvis liked it. But when Priscilla started redoing
Graceland, she said she was going "to put it back the way it was
when I was there." And she and [Graceland manager] Jack Soden
started doing a little campaign on Linda, which I personally
resented, only because I knew how good Linda was for Elvis.

LAMAR FIKE: Let's face it—Elvis's taste sucked. But you couldn't
come right out and tell him that.

Linda tried to teach him that red shag carpeting wasn't

befitting a man of his income bracket, but she wasn't success-ful. He got what he wanted.

One time, we were at the Century Plaza Hotel, and Elvis walked in his room, and he said, "Lamar, all this furniture—it's really cheap." I went, "Holy shit! This is the Presidential Suite." He was used to such overblown opulence that this was not up to his standard.

Elvis and Liberace had two things in common, other than the fact that they were both musicians. They were both twins who lost their brothers at birth, and they both loved opulence. So if some-thing wasn't overdone, it was abnormal to Elvis. He never under-stood the concept that less is more. We were riding in the car one day, and Elvis said, "I hope they keep making the cars smaller and smaller because I'll start buying them bigger and bigger."

MARTY LACKER: When Elvis went back into Vegas in August of '72, the hotel had been bought by Barron Hilton, and it was now called the Las Vegas Hilton. And Elvis got another death threat. This time the maître d' told Joe he'd gotten word that some crazy woman in the audience had a gun and was going to shoot Elvis during the performance. Red and Sonny positioned themselves in front of the stage the whole time Elvis was on.

Elvis stood way at the back to perform, in this sort of side-ways pose so he'd make himself a smaller target. But nothing happened. He'd gotten a bomb threat when he played Roanoke, Virginia, a couple of months before, too. Nothing happened there, either. But with this second Vegas threat, Elvis got kind of cocky. He liked to brag that the guys were so loyal they'd take a bullet for him. He'd say, "That's the kind of loyalty I can get."

LAMAR FIKE: When there were celebrities in the audience at Vegas, usually we'd write their names down and hand them to Elvis so he could acknowledge them from the stage. But he didn't know who half of them were.

He'd do a false exit and come offstage, and he'd say to either Joe or me, "Who's out there?" One night, Elvis said, "There's a name here, Arnold Palmer. What does he do?" I said, "He's a golfer." He said, "How do I introduce him?" I said, "Call him the Babe Ruth of golf."

Elvis went out there and said, "I'd like to introduce you to the Babe Ruth of baseball, Mr. Arnold Palmer."

MARTY LACKER: Once Elvis started performing out there, he didn't go to as many shows. But he loved to go see Joan Rivers. He thought she was just crazy. Because she would say anything about anybody, and that's what he liked. He loved her humor. He'd go backstage and see her. But mostly he'd go to see singers.

Elvis never stopped attracting celebrities. One night, Jim Nabors came down to the dressing room. Actually, he came down two or three times. There were other people there, too.

Elvis received people in the living area. There was a bar there, and a huge round table in the center, and couches against the wall. Jim came in after Elvis had already changed clothes. Elvis was sitting at the round table, and Jim sat down next to him. And in talking with him, Jim put his hand on Elvis's knee.

When he did that, Elvis sort of flinched. Because first of all, Elvis didn't like any man putting his hand on him, period. But he'd also heard rumors about Jim. And Jim didn't take his hand off Elvis's knee. He just left it there.

Well, Elvis quickly made an excuse to get up. He said, "Uh, I'll be right back. I've got to get something," and he went in his dressing area. And when he came back out, instead of sitting back down at the table, he sat on the couch.

About fifteen or twenty minutes later, Elvis got up and said, "Well, it's time for me to go on upstairs. Thank you for coming." Which was always the cue for visitors to get the hell out. So everybody left, and as soon as he was sure that Nabors was upstairs, boy, he started screaming. He yelled, "That no-good fuckin' fag! Putting his hand on me!" He looked at all of us, and he said, "Goddamnit! I don't know if I'm ever going to let him back down here! But if somehow he does get back down here, and the chairs on either side of me are vacant, I want one of your asses in those chairs! I don't ever want to be embarrassed like that again!"

Well, something like two weeks went by, and Elvis saw Jim Nabors on television. He was on a variety show, performing with

his big, booming singing voice. Elvis picked up his glass of water
and threw it right at the TV set. He said, "That phony son of a
bitch!" Because both of his voices are put on, see—the high,
Gomer Pyle voice and the big virile singing voice. Every time Elvis
saw Nabors singing on television after that, he threw something
at the TV.

🕺 🕺 🕺

LAMAR FIKE: The drugs would get him on all kinds of tangents.
He wouldn't go to sleep. He'd get up and want to keep everybody
awake. You'd be walking around like a zombie, trying to stay
awake, and he was just wired to the wall. He fought insomnia
until he died—a combination of nightmares and his day-for-night
schedule. And then he still walked in his sleep.

MARTY LACKER: If he really didn't have a whole lot of pills in
him, and he was sleeping, a mouse could walk across the thick
carpet and he'd wake up. And because he always kept a gun on
him, it got tense a couple of times.

BILLY SMITH: He could take three or four sleeping pills, and if he
was wired up, two hours later, he could be leaving to go somewhere.

LAMAR FIKE: When Elvis did a lot of downers, and especially
when he started doing Dilaudid, he would eat big plates of
Popsicles. At four o'clock in the morning, he'd send Hamburger
James out to buy $100 worth of Popsicles, Fudgsicles, and
Dreamsicles. And then he'd get constipated. We should have
bought stock in Fleet's enemas. We'd have made a killing.
    People on Class A narcotics can't hold anything solid on their
stomachs. It makes them throw up. But the body accepts sweets.
That's why they drink a lot of Kool-Aid and eat a lot of sugary
things. So we'd keep maybe one hundred cartons of yogurt in the
suite in Vegas because Elvis would eat twenty to thirty at a time.
    The suite at the Hilton was enormous, and it had this big
kitchen. Elvis would wake up and go out his door, walk across
the foyer, and go into the kitchen and get some yogurt. He liked it
with fruit, so we kept a big bowl of fruit in there, and we kept
some fruit in his room.

One day, he called us into his bedroom, and he said, "I've got a gash in my foot." And he did. He'd cut a big slit in it. I said, "How did you do that?" He figured out that he was walking over to the kitchen to get some yogurt, and he was eating a peach, and he finished it, and he just dropped the pit. Who else could cut the shit out of his foot on a peach pit in a $3,000-a-day suite with three-inch carpet?

So odd things would happen. But they became normal.

At first, I'm not sure Nora, my wife, knew what to make of it. Elvis would call at ten o'clock at night and say, "There's a plane on the way to pick you up." I'd say, "God Almighty, I just got home!" But I'd have to go. If I'd said no, he would have fired me again.

Nora would say, "You're going again?" I'd say, "Yeah." It just sort of got out of hand because Elvis became more clingy the older he got. So I began taking Nora out to Vegas some.

But in Vegas, see, Elvis would wander around the halls at night and go visiting in the suite. Nora and I would be in bed asleep, and Elvis would unlock the door and come in and get in bed with us. I'd look over and go, "Holy shit, Elvis! Give me a break here!" He'd say, "I want to talk about something." He'd be lying there, and he'd get into these rambling dissertations. I'd say, "Look up in the mirror. Isn't that a picture? All three of us in bed. This is really great here." But he'd fall asleep talking. Then he'd wake up and leave and go back to his room. Or if he got mad at me, he'd say, "Well, you ain't no fun to talk to." And then he'd go get in bed with Joe and Joanie. He was like a bat. He would flit around at night at the Hilton.

One time in Vegas, I was asleep, and I had my door open, and Elvis came in the room. It was about two o'clock in the afternoon. I woke up and Elvis was in the bed with Nora and me again. I raised up and said, "Is this the start of something?" He said, "Good idea. We might could do that."

I said, "You know what? Let me tell you the bad thing about you." He said, "What?" He knew I was nailing him. I said, "You want this to happen so bad, but you ain't figured a way to push the button." He said, "Have you got any suggestions?" I just got mad and shut up. There wasn't anything I could do. Then later on, he came up and said, "What do you think about that?" I said, "Well, everybody can be bought." His mind went on more different tacks than anybody I ever met. You never knew what was going to come out of his mouth.

It's like when he bought the ranch and wanted to start a commune. I said, "I know what's in the back of your mind." He said, "Oh, no," real innocent. And he walked off saying, "Um-hum." He was devious, man. He said to me one time, "You have no idea what I think about." I said, "No, don't you start that crap! I *know* what you're thinking!"

MARTY LACKER: In September of '72, Elvis brought Linda out to Vegas for the first time. He was still seeing three or four girls at once, but I think he knew she was special. This was apparently the first time they'd spent the night together. Linda hadn't been around addicts before, and she hadn't been around people who took a lot of sleeping medicine. She saw him taking fifteen to twenty pills every night and powerful narcotics on top of it. And she saw who gave it to him—Flash Newman, the Hilton doctor, and another doctor that the Hilton used, Elias Ghanem, and Dr. Nick, although she never did blame Dr. Nick for anything. I believe the very first time she was there, Elvis passed out with food in his mouth and started to choke. She had to clear it out of his throat and turn him on his side to get him breathing again.

Since Elvis's death, Linda has said that she went to Dr. Nick and told him how concerned she was and asked him how they could get Elvis to stop taking all that stuff. Dr. Nick told her the best thing would just be to leave. But she cared enough about him to stay.

LAMAR FIKE: Elias Ghanem became as big a player in Elvis's life as Dr. Nick. Elias was a good person, but as slick as they come. He's Lebanese. I think he was about thirty-seven years old when Elvis met him. He was boyish-looking, but also swarthy. Very intelligent. He always aligned himself with the right people.

Consequently, Elias has a great practice in Las Vegas. He's a very wealthy man. He has medical centers and emergency-room franchises all over, or he did. And he had an interest in an air service, Jet Avia, with a heart surgeon out there. They had a $300,000-a-year contract with one of the casinos to bring gamblers into town. In one day, in '76, Ghanem lost two aircraft. Frank Sinatra's mother got killed when her plane went into a mountain, and that afternoon, another of his planes got caught in a wind shear and cartwheeled down a runway in Detroit.

Elias liked Elvis a lot, but he got caught up with Elvis like Dr. Nick and everybody else. I don't know where the line starts and where it ends for a doctor, or where it crosses over. I'll tell you one thing—Elvis couldn't buy Elias the way he could Dr. Nick.

But Elvis knew how to manipulate Ghanem. He gave him a Stutz, and a Mercedes, and some other stuff.

BILLY SMITH: It was like everybody blamed Dr. Nick. Hell, he was a contributor. But he was not the only one that done Elvis in. I mean, let's get all them suckers, if that's the case, and take 'em all right down the tubes. Don't just blame one doctor.

LAMAR FIKE: Elias was there to the end. But it got really difficult for him. His contacts were very, very wealthy individuals, like Adnan and Esam Khashoggi. Adnan's the Saudi billionaire businessman who's been in the news lately. He's an arms dealer who collected funds for the new Palestinian Authority and helped Libyan pilgrims visit Israel. So with friends like that, Elias really didn't have to rely on Elvis's wealth to get him by.

I think Elias got off in pretty good shape. Most people it would have hurt. But Nevada operates by another set of rules.

MARTY LACKER: Ghanem later became the Las Vegas boxing commissioner. He's tied in with all those people in the World Boxing Association. And he's a smooth operator. He's a Palestinian Arab. He was born in Haifa, Israel, but he had passports from both Israel and Lebanon.

Ghanem was also a reserve policeman. That's another reason Elvis liked him.

LAMAR FIKE: Elvis started getting prescriptions in my name, and Joe's name, and Charlie's—even in Lisa Marie's name. Elias would do it, and so would Nick. And I put a stop to it. They had me with thirty-five different prescriptions. I said, "Fuck that!" I told Elvis, "You just quit it. I don't want my name used on all this stuff."

Sonny did the same thing. He said that Max Shapiro sent
Elvis a bottle of liquid Demerol in Sonny's name, and that he
took it back to the drugstore and said, "Don't you ever put any
prescription in my name again." They wrote 'em in Judy West's
name, too. And even in Sonny's kid's name, Brian. Nobody was
immune.

MARTY LACKER: It started getting more out of control. Sonny
said that Dr. Nick was up at Graceland one night, and Elvis told
him he'd tried to get some stuff out of Dr. Nick's medical bag, but
it was locked. Elvis told him that from now on, whenever he came
up, he wanted him to leave his bag open. And Dr. Nick said he
wasn't going to do that. Sonny said Elvis looked at Nick and told
him, "If that's the way you want it, next time you're up here, I'll
just blow that son of a bitch apart and get what I want."

LAMAR FIKE: One fuckin' day, at Graceland, Vernon was
upstairs, and Elvis called me. He said, "Get your ass up here!" As
I was going up the stairs, Vernon was coming down. Vernon said,
"I just got fired."

I said, "Oh, shit!" And I went in, and Elvis fired me, too. He
called me up an hour later, and he said, "Fire Dr. Nick while
you're at it." I said, "How do you fire a doctor?" He said, "You just
do what I tell you to do, goddamnit, and fire him." I called Nick
up. I said, "You're fired." Nick had no reaction. He knew it wasn't
over. Elvis fired him about three times, usually when Nick would
tell him to cut back on the drugs or complain about the packages
coming in from Vegas. To get back in, Elvis would make him
apologize. Then he'd tell him to get back to work.

BILLY SMITH: Dr. Nick shut Elvis off many a time. And when he
did that, bang! Elvis was gone. Dr. Nick was standing over there a
damn outcast.

MARTY LACKER: They went 'round and 'round at times. Nick
told him at one point, "I'm not going to give you anything anymore." And Elvis told Nick, "Fuck, I don't need you! I'll get it from
somewhere else." He always knew he could get what he wanted.
Dr. Nick came back to try to control the situation.

The fact is, even with Nick's control, Elvis was still getting stuff from other people. Linda Thompson has said that Ghanem used to ship amphetamines back to Memphis to him. And Elvis would get drugs from Max Shapiro. And other doctors in Palm Springs.

You know the incongruity of all this? Elvis also took vitamins. Especially vitamin E, because he'd heard it retarded aging. Here he was poisoning his system with this other stuff and then taking handfuls of vitamins.

LAMAR FIKE: The same month Elvis filed for divorce—August— he opened again in Vegas. People were surprised that Priscilla and Lisa came to several of his shows. But Elvis and Priscilla were trying to be civilized about this, and Elvis wanted Lisa there.

Elvis had a big hit on the charts then, "Burning Love." That was his highest charting record since "Suspicious Minds," in '69. "Burning Love" got to number two. People always remember that song, for the "hunka, hunka" part, I guess. The Elvis impersonators have a field day with it.

MARTY LACKER: In September of '72, the morning after Elvis closed in Vegas, Colonel held a press conference at the Hilton to announce that Elvis would do a big concert on January 14, 1973. They were calling it *Aloha from Hawaii*. This was the big satellite show—everybody in the world was going to be able to see it, although not exactly at the same time. Colonel was smart enough to have Elvis be the first entertainer to take advantage of the new technology. And he was also smart enough to find a way to let him "tour" Europe and Asia without ever leaving the U.S.

LAMAR FIKE: As soon as Colonel announced that satellite special, Elvis said he was going to get in shape. He went home for a week, and then he flew to L.A. and went out to Ed Parker's karate studio in Santa Monica. That's where he met Dave Hebler. Dave was a karate champion, and he became another karate connection for Elvis. And in '74, he became a bodyguard in the truest sense.

MARTY LACKER: Dave was blind in his right eye. Somebody shot him with a BB gun when he was a kid. But he was deadly as far as the martial arts are concerned. He could kill you in a second, but he was also a supernice guy. Elvis liked that combination.

It's funny—Dave was the third author on Red and Sonny's book. He wrote in there that when he first met Elvis, he was surprised at how little Elvis actually knew about karate. At first, he tried to make Elvis look better than he was because Linda and the whole entourage were standing there. Elvis was so doped up that he was moving slow and kind of stumbling around.

Right after that, Elvis officiated a little tournament, and since he'd never done it before, Dave whispered to him how to call it. That same day, Elvis showed up at Dave's own studio in Glendora [California]. Dave was astonished because it was seventy-four degrees out and Elvis had on a big, fat black overcoat and, of all things, a turban.

Two weeks later—the third time he saw him—Elvis gave Dave a Mercedes 280SL. Ten thousand dollars' worth of car.

LAMAR FIKE: One reason Colonel probably set up the satellite show was that he knew Elvis was tired of Vegas. In November, the Vegas paper said that there was a rumor going around that Elvis would be moving from the Hilton to the new MGM Grand but that it wasn't true. Colonel was quoted as saying the MGM's showroom seated six hundred fewer than the Hilton. And he said, "Besides, what hotel could match the Hilton's generous offer?" Elvis would get so mad.

MARTY LACKER: For Christmas that year, Lisa Marie came to Graceland. Elvis loved to buy things for her. He even bought her a big, round bed, the same as he did for Ann-Margret. A lot of times, he slept in that bed when Lisa was out in California. It was one of those fake fur things, with a round mirror on top and a built-in radio and stereo. It was tacky. But he'd sleep in it because it was unusual.

BILLY SMITH: I think, on the whole, Elvis tried to give Lisa all the stuff he wanted himself. For example, he bought her a golf cart for Christmas, and by the time he got through, he'd spent probably around $2,500 on a $1,200 golf cart. Because he had it painted special, with a little rose put on the side and all.

He gave her everything. But Priscilla was right the opposite. If Lisa got anything, it was very, very minimum. Lisa used to tell her mother, "Let me go to Graceland because I'll get anything I want there." She must have been a very pulled child.

One time, Lisa lost a tooth while she was visiting her daddy in Memphis. She told her mama about it on the phone, and she said, "The tooth fairy brought me five dollars." So Priscilla asked Elvis, "How come you give her five dollars for her tooth?" Elvis said, "Well, that's what the tooth fairy left her." Priscilla said, "But five dollars! Fifty cents would have been fine."

Elvis said, "Look, goddamnit, I don't know the going rates for the tooth fairy nowadays! I give her five dollars. So what?" That shows the difference between the two of them.

Albert Goldman said that in the later years, Elvis got all weepy and cried, "I wish I could be a better father." Bullshit. He thought he was a good father.

MARTY LACKER: There were quite a few times when Elvis said to Lisa, "Go back to your mama." That's not saying he didn't love Lisa. He loved her a great deal. But if he was doing something, or talking, or wanted to go somewhere, and Lisa said something like "Daddy, I want you to stay here tonight," he'd go do what he wanted.

BILLY SMITH: As much as Elvis loved Lisa, he didn't want to share the attention. Elvis would say, "Now, Daddy's talking, Lisa, you go on and play." He didn't want her to upstage him.

One night, she was at Graceland, and Elvis had taken three or four sleeping pills. There was only two or three of us in the room, and Elvis said, "Let's go put Lisa to bed." We all went in her room, and he was going to kiss her good night. Well, he leaned over, and when he did, [his penis] fell out of his pajamas. Elvis didn't notice it, see. He was telling us, "Oh, ain't she sweet. She's my teddy bear." And Lisa said, "Daddy, your goober is hanging out."

Elvis said, "Lisa, you don't say things like that, goddamnit!" Well, we broke up. We couldn't help it. And it really angered him, the fact that we laughed. But only for a moment. Then he realized he might as well laugh about it because it was the truth.

LAMAR FIKE: Sure, Elvis loved her. But his daughter was still an object. He bought her a mink coat, same as he did Linda Thompson.

MARTY LACKER: When Elvis gave Linda a mink coat that first Christmas, and all this other stuff for everybody else, Vernon got shook. Of course, they argued about money all the time, but there was one argument that really stood out.

Elvis was sitting in the dining room eating breakfast. This was late one afternoon, at Graceland, in the early seventies. There were four of us sitting with him. Vernon knew that Elvis had to have his second cup of coffee before you hit him with any serious business. But he didn't pay enough attention.

Elvis was still eating, and his father came in and stood against the wall of the dining room. Vernon started talking about a business problem. He rolled out a lot of negative talk, and then he said, "Elvis, we've got to do something about this because it's costing us money." And when Vernon first said it, Elvis just glanced up at his father and went back to his plate and started eating again. Well, his father said it again, and Elvis looked over at me and the other guys.

You could tell when he was starting to bubble. He'd grit his teeth, and the side of his jaw would tighten up. A lot of times you could see it in his eyes, too. And he mumbled, "I don't want to talk about it now." And his father kept going. It was like he was never going to stop.

Elvis had a biscuit in his hand, and, finally, he just threw the damn biscuit across the room. He said, "Listen, goddamnit, how many times do I have to say it? You know better than to bring this negative shit up to me when I just got up!"

Vernon yelled, "Well, goddamn, Elvis, you got to!" And Elvis just exploded. He said, "This is my goddamn house, and you work for *me*, and I'm the fucking boss around here!" And Vernon looked at Elvis and said, "You'll never be the man I am."

Boy, that really got Elvis. He jumped up in his seat and took his plate of food and just threw it across the room against the wall. Then he picked up his chair and threw it, too. And he said, "Let me tell you something. You wish you were half the man I am."

And then, rather than get into it with his father any further, he said to us, "I'll see you all later." And he went upstairs and stayed for a while.

People could look at that as Elvis being spoiled and petulant. But he just wanted some time to be normal, which was almost impossible for him. Especially in the seventies. And it just got worse and worse.

CHAPTER 45

MELTDOWN, 1973

For the *Elvis: Aloha from Hawaii via Satellite* television special, Elvis decided he wanted an unusual jumpsuit that both reflected his patriotism and set him apart as a symbol of America. Designer Bill Belew picked up his sketch pad and came back with a white suit emblazoned with an American eagle stenciled in gold and appointed with red-and-blue stones—one of the most handsome stage costumes of Elvis's career.

The event marked the first time in the history of television that a one-man performance would be beamed all over the globe and seen by a quarter of the world's population. Some time before, Elvis wrote down his Philosophy for a Happy Life for his friend, Pat Parry. The first requirement was someone to love. The second was something to look forward to. And the third was something to do.

The *Aloha* special was Elvis's final appearance as a certified superstar and his last glorious moment.

MARTY LACKER: Right after New Year's of '73, we were sitting in the den when Colonel phoned. Elvis took the call in private. When he came back in, he had this big smile on his face. He said, "Colonel's made the final arrangements for the satellite TV special in Hawaii. We leave next week." That ended up being one of the best times we'd all had together in a long, long time.

LAMAR FIKE: We did it at the Honolulu International Center Arena. Even though it was a television show, the live audience was asked to donate what they could. Elvis wanted every cent—even from the merchandising—to go to the Kui Lee Cancer Fund. Kui Lee had written "I'll Remember You," which was one of Elvis's favorite songs. They raised $75,000—three times what they expected.

The reason Colonel picked Hawaii was because of the time zone. Elvis went on at twelve-thirty A.M. Hawaiian time, so the show could air at prime time in Australia, Korea, South Vietnam, Japan, Thailand, and the Philippines. Today, the estate says he got 38 percent of the viewers in Japan, 70 to 80 percent of the viewers in Hong Kong and Korea, and 92 percent in the Philippines. We read in the Honolulu paper the next day—and Colonel also told Elvis—that they got 98 percent of the viewers in Japan. I don't know.

But that was live, see. And then thirty European countries saw it on a delayed basis. That was the sixty-minute version. For the U.S. market, they added thirty minutes of Hawaiian scenery and some extra songs. It didn't run over here until April, and he got 51 percent of the audience, which is pretty amazing. All in all, something like a billion and a half people saw it, by satellite, in forty countries. Shit, not that many people watched the moon landing.

MARTY LACKER: Elvis looked so great for that special. After he looked at a tape of the rehearsal, he said, "I don't like the way my hair looks," and he had somebody cut and style it a little different. Around '72, Elvis started gaining a lot of weight. He'd tried all kinds of regular diets, but they worked too slow for him. So before the satellite show, he went on this kind of crazy diet, which was based on injections of the urine of a pregnant woman. A doctor in Vegas put him on it. Buddy Hackett popularized it, and his daughter worked for the doctor.

Elvis got Sonny and Lamar and Red on it with him. The doctor supplied the food, little-bitty pieces of meat that you'd either boil in the package or take out and eat dry. They'd be in the kitchen up in the suite in Vegas, boiling these bags. They started giving the shots to themselves. I remember sitting there one day in the kitchen, and Lamar popped himself in the fatty part of the leg—right behind the knee—with one of those needles.

LAMAR FIKE: We found out it was just vitamins. We only ate five hundred or six hundred calories a day. My God, anybody could lose weight on that. Elvis got down to 175 or 180 pounds.

MARTY LACKER: Musically, Elvis was back to doing not so great songs, the exception being "American Trilogy," which he started doing in '72. But his performance was so terrific that we were mesmerized by it. Almost at the end of the show, he did something completely unexpected. In one fluid movement, he removed that big jeweled cape from his shoulders and slung it into the audience. And the thing was worth $5,000. The amazing thing about the way he prepared for this show was that he stayed off the pills. He was straight for two weeks.

Most of us stayed over in Hawaii an extra day. And the night after the show, we all gathered in his suite. Elvis was so happy. He said, "Everybody was really a big help to me. I want to do something not just for the guys, but the wives, too. I want to buy them all a fur coat." And he wanted me to go get them.

I said, "Elvis, you're in Hawaii. I don't even know if they have fur coats here, it's so hot." He said, "No, you can get 'em." So I made some calls to the stores, and they sort of laughed at me.

I went back and said, "Elvis, there ain't no fur coats available, but there's a nice jewelry shop off the hotel lobby." So Elvis gave all the wives beautiful diamond and emerald rings, and he gave each of the guys a check for $1,000.

The next morning, we were all supposed to go to the Arizona Memorial because Elvis had given that benefit concert in 1961 to help get it built. We banged on his door, and nobody answered. Finally, Linda came, and we said, "Are you all ready?" And she just made a face at us and shook her head. She said, "He can't go." We went in, and Elvis was sitting on the balcony, on the top floor of the hotel, stoned out of his gourd. He was sweating profusely, with a towel around his neck, and he could hardly talk. He'd gone right back into it.

LAMAR FIKE: Elvis wasn't as straight during that time as everybody thought. David Stanley went on the trip, and when Elvis couldn't find Dr. Nick, he asked David to give him a shot of B_{12} mixed with amphetamines straight in the hip before he went onstage. David didn't want to—he got Hamburger James to do it.

MARTY LACKER: Elvis did a promo for that show. I've seen a clip of it recently, and it's obvious he was drugged. He was slurring his words—a dead giveaway of sleeping pills, and he just looked dazed. But on the show, he looked 100 percent. He hit all his high notes. And he was so pumped up he could have hit the ceiling.

The *Elvis: Aloha from Hawaii* album entered the *Billboard* chart at number 99, stayed for thirty-five weeks, and went all the way to number one. That was his first number one album in nine years. It was also his last.

A couple of days after the satellite show, after Elvis went back to taking pills again, he and Linda went to [actor] Jack Lord's house for dinner there in Hawaii. Jack used to visit Elvis on the movie set.

You know who else used to come see Elvis? Muhammad Ali. There's a picture of them together in Vegas, where Elvis is wearing a Hawaiian pendant around his neck from the *Aloha from Hawaii* show. Elvis liked to watch Ali's fights, and he liked his sense of humor, too. Ali gave Elvis an autographed pair of boxing gloves that said, "Elvis, you are the greatest." And Elvis had a special robe made up for Ali to wear in his fight with Ken Norton. Ali was real proud of it, and he wore it in the ring. But then he lost the fight, so he said he'd never wear it again.

BILLY SMITH: At the end of January, Elvis went back into Vegas. By now, especially after the satellite show, he was really tired of it. And it showed. In one of his reviews, they [*Variety*] called him "The Colonel's mechanized doll, at least onstage." I think Joe made sure he didn't see that.

LAMAR FIKE: Sometimes he would pretend to get sick and not want to do a second show. But not until the end did he ever say to Colonel, "Look, I don't want to do this shit. I hate this fuckin' place, man." He hated it worse than hell.

I think Vegas was the erosion of Colonel. The last two or three years of Elvis's life, that relationship changed drastically.

MARTY LACKER: Elvis got to where he would conveniently develop Vegas throat. He didn't really have it. But he'd say he had these symptoms and he wanted to see a throat doctor.

The first time Elvis saw one, in February of '73, it was late at night. All of a sudden, he said, "I've got Vegas throat." And he opened up the phone book and picked Dr. Sidney Boyers. The guy was Jewish, so Elvis figured he was good. And his office was in a nice area of Las Vegas, so Elvis liked that. We all piled in the car, and Elvis just walked up and knocked on the doctor's door. Boyers happened to be there, and he opened the door and there stood Elvis Presley. He was completely overwhelmed. Elvis talked to him for two hours in his office. And he started telling the doctor all his symptoms and he came out with three prescriptions and a big smile on his face. Within a week, he and the doctor had developed a relationship, and Elvis kept going back.

About the fourth time he went up there, Elvis knocked on the door and said, "Doctor, are you through for the day?" Boyers said he was. And Elvis said, "Well, come outside. I want to show you something." He'd bought the doctor a brand-new white Lincoln Continental so he'd feel indebted to him.

BILLY SMITH: There were more death threats in the later years. Like those guys who came up onstage in '73.

MARTY LACKER: A group of foreign-looking men came in with some of the local hookers. The leader had on a cape, and a hat, and he carried a cane. And they all sat at this long table right by the stage.

Well, during the show, one of them jumped up on the stage. He had a jacket over his arm, like maybe he had a gun in his hand, and he was heading towards Elvis. Red rushed him, and a security guard grabbed him and searched him for weapons. Then one of his friends came up onstage to help him. And Jerry Schilling happened to be there, and he literally threw the guy off the stage so that he landed on his back on a table. And then the strange-looking leader came up, and Elvis started doing his karate moves. He didn't hit him, though. He just sort of gave a demonstration. People just kept coming up, and Sonny and Jerry and Red took care of them. It was nuts. The stage was filled with people, most of 'em trying to help Elvis, I think. But Elvis was screaming, "Let me at him! Let me at him!" He was really out of control.

Sonny took a look at him and went over and gave him a bear hug to try to calm him down. But Elvis got so upset that Vernon had to come out and pull him offstage.

Finally, the security men got the guys and took them to the

office and photographed them. Turned out they just wanted autographs. But one of them had tape on his knuckles, and Elvis thought he was a Hawaiian karate killer. He told the cops he wanted rap sheets on all of them. But they weren't killers. They were South American porno dealers. And the guy with the tape on his hand had just injured himself in an altercation with a slot machine.

LAMAR FIKE: The first guy just wanted to give Elvis the jacket as a present. They were a little drunk, and they weren't thinking. By the time Elvis got through telling the story, he was Mr. Bruce Lee—he whipped all three of 'em. But it wasn't that serious.

BILLY SMITH: I don't think it was all that innocent. I always believed that those guys had something else on their mind. After so many death threats, Elvis started saying that if he was shot onstage, the guys should put him in a wheelchair and bring him home. Dick Grob might have had a more detailed plan than that. At one time, Grob told me he had a plan about what to do if Elvis died on the road and about how they would get him back to Memphis.

MARTY LACKER: Elvis started getting angry about everything, including the fact that he was older, because he'd just turned thirty-eight. He felt like he was losing everything. Mostly, he couldn't stop brooding about the incident with the South Americans. He was convinced they were really Hawaiian killers, and in his fury about Priscilla leaving him, he got it in his mind that Mike Stone was behind the guys coming up onstage.

The very next night, he called Lamar and Red and Sonny in from the living room. He had worked himself up into a blind rage. This was about three o'clock in the morning.

LAMAR FIKE: Elvis was sweating like he had some kind of jungle fever. He was really out of it. He had this massive platform bed up in the suite, and he was propped up in it, in his pajamas. Linda looked plenty worried. Elvis called Sonny over, and he told him to look deep in his eyes, like he was going to hypnotize him. He was slurring his words, and he said, "Mike Stone has to die,

Sonny. That son of a bitch has to go, and you know it. He's caused me too much pain. Do it for me, Sonny. I know I can count on you." He was saying this over and over, like a mantra.

Elvis was literally going to have Mike Stone killed. Sonny was pretty dumbfounded. He said, "Let's forget that kind of talk, boss. I know he's caused you a lot of pain, but that's not right." Sonny kept trying to calm him down, but Elvis jumped out of that bed and went over to the closet and pulled out an M16 [rifle]. Sonny started backing away, and Elvis went after him and put the gun in his hand. Sonny said something like "I don't want to do this, Elvis." And Elvis said, "Why doesn't anybody understand this man has to die?"

Hell, we didn't know what to do. We looked at each other like "What the shit now?" And then Elvis started climbing the fuckin' wall. He really did. He jumped back on the bed and tried to dig his fingernails into the wall and tried to get a toehold. He was going up that mother if he could. He was saying, "He's hurt me so much. He's broken up my family and destroyed everything, and nobody cares." It really got us. He was just a madman. Sonny left the room. I followed him out in the living room, and he had tears in his eyes. I said, "Delbert, it's going to be an awful long night." Linda called Elias Ghanem to come give Elvis a shot.

MARTY LACKER: Elvis started this same business with Red. At first, Red stalled him, but Elvis kept after him for several days. And Red loved Elvis so much that for a little while, he thought maybe it was right, that it would bring Elvis out of his depression. So he made some calls, and he set it up. I think the going rate was $25,000, but because it was for Elvis, some guy was going to take Mike Stone out for $10,000.

LAMAR FIKE: An intermediary in Hollywood was taking care of it. About a week after all this started, we told Elvis, "Hey, man, it's getting ready to go down. Are you sure you want this to happen?" And Elvis chickened out. He said, "Well, let's just leave it for now." But Mike was within hours of getting his head blown off.

MARTY LACKER: Elvis would never have had anybody killed. He couldn't fire somebody, so how in the hell could he have someone killed? And I don't think Red would have done it, either.

BILLY SMITH: For Elvis? Maybe. Elvis would tell people, "Well, these hangers-on of mine . . . " But the things we did for him, he knew we wouldn't do for nobody else.

LAMAR FIKE: I sat down with Elvis after that. We were back at Graceland. I said, "Elvis, you have to see that you're not the same person." He said, "Lamar, we all change." I said, "Yes, but you aren't Elvis anymore."

He stewed on it overnight. And then he came down the next day and sat at the table and said, "Motherfucking Lamar sat up there last night and gave me a damn speech about who I'm not." I was waiting for somebody to help me, and everybody just got real still because I had stepped over the line.

I guess he was getting heat from every direction. Because even though the *Aloha from Hawaii* album sold real well, in early '73, Vernon told Elvis, "You've spent us in the ground. There's no more money."

I don't know exactly how it came down, but I'm sure that Vernon went to Colonel and said, "We're broke. Find some way to get some money." So Colonel went to RCA and negotiated a buy-out deal, effective March 1. He did it for Elvis, but he also did it for himself. That RCA buyout was not the best of deals, but Elvis needed the money.

MARTY LACKER: Between the percentage that Colonel took out of everything and the way Elvis spent money, there were times when Elvis was that far from being broke. And this was one of them. He needed money for a couple of things, one of which was for Graceland. They were going to have to mortgage it.

Colonel went to RCA and signed an agreement that allowed them to buy back the royalty rights on all the records Elvis made prior to '73. That's something like seven hundred recordings. In other words, they gave RCA the future royalties on his whole catalog, the best records he ever made. For $5.4 million and a seven-year guarantee of $500,000 a year. Against royalties. But All-Star Shows got 50 percent of the $5 million, and 25 percent of the $400,000. So Colonel got $2.6 million and Elvis got $2.8. That means that after taxes, Elvis only got $1.4 million. For probably the most valuable records in the history of popular music.

But listen to the rest of this deal. Parker argued later that the old songs weren't selling that well in the seventies. But Elvis had to give RCA two albums and four singles a year—for seven years—for a royalty of ten cents a single and fifty cents an album. That might have been high for some recording artists—I think most artists got a 7 percent royalty, and Elvis would have gotten 8.4 percent—but that was low for an artist of Elvis's stature. And, again, half of that went to Elvis, and half to Colonel, or All Star Shows, as he was incorporated. Then RCA agreed to give Elvis and All Star $100,000 each when the seven-year contract expired. But RCA also said it would give All Star $675,000 over those seven years, with a matching amount from RCA Records Tours! And Colonel would get 10 percent of the tours, for what they called "planning, promotion, and merchandising." Colonel already had one-third commission on the profits of the tours as of February '72. So add it up.

It doesn't stop there, though. RCA also said they'd give Colonel a $50,000 consultant's fee, payable over a five-year period. And then All Star got yet another $350,000 over seven years for "planning, promotion, and merchandising in connection with the operation of the tour agreement."

That gives you some idea of Colonel's side deals. And it probably explains why he didn't insist on a better sliding royalty rate. At least there were periodic supplements to the '73 agreement. In '74, RCA gave Elvis sixty cents an album and twelve cents a single, and there were regular adjustments to keep Elvis's royalty at about 8 percent. But Parker was mostly interested in front money for himself. In the end, he got $6,200,000. And Elvis got $4,650,000. Colonel made a million and a half more dollars off that deal than Elvis did.

LAMAR FIKE: I don't know that what the Colonel did was so bad. As far as RCA is concerned, Colonel got a lot of money out of them. But RCA made a lot of money, too. It was one of those situations where one was scared, and the other one was glad of it.

MARTY LACKER: After both Elvis and Vernon died, and Lisa Marie inherited the estate, the court appointed an attorney named Blanchard E. Tual as a guardian-*ad-litem* to look after her interest. Among other things, Tual investigated Colonel's deal with RCA. He delivered his original report in September of 1980

562   ELVIS AARON PRESLEY

and an amended report in July of '81. Tual wrote that "there is evidence that both Colonel Parker and RCA are guilty of collusion, conspiracy, fraud, misrepresentation, bad faith, and over-reaching." And he called for a full accounting.

I read both those reports. And when I got through, I realized just how ignorant Elvis and Vernon were about the entertainment business.

🕺 🕺 🕺

BILLY SMITH: I didn't see Elvis during this time. I was taking care of my family. My daddy was real, real bad off, close to death. And he did die in August. But I'd talk to Elvis on the phone every once in a while, and he didn't always seem himself.

🕺 🕺 🕺

LAMAR FIKE: Elvis knew that a lot of people just looked at him as a dollar sign. Peggy Lipton, the actress, tried to get him into Scientology in '73 or '74. He dated her on and off for about a month. He sent his plane to bring her up to Tahoe one night when he was playing there. But she wanted to talk to him about Scientology more than anything else. And she stayed on him.

In Scientology, they do a process called "auditing." They hook you up to a machine that's kind of like a lie detector. And they ask you questions about your personal life, and this machine records the electrical changes that take place in your body as you answer. Then they analyze that and have you cleanse your soul to get all these negative thoughts and painful experiences—they call them "engrams"—behind you.

One day, in L.A., we got in the limousine and went down to the Scientology center on Sunset, and Elvis went in and talked to them. We waited in the car, but apparently, they started doing all these charts and crap for him.

Elvis came out and he said, "Fuck those people! There's no way I'll ever get involved with that son-of-a-bitchin' group. All they want is my money." Well, Peggy still kept on about it, so Elvis didn't date her anymore. And he stayed away from Scientology like it was a cobra. He'd shit a brick to see how far Lisa's gotten into it.

MARTY LACKER: In May of '73, I went to Tahoe with Elvis. He was performing at the Sahara. We were up in the suite, and he was in perfectly good health. About an hour later, he came out of his room and said, "I'm sick, man. I can't eat. We've got to leave and go to the hospital in Memphis. Tell Colonel to cancel."

He wasn't sick. He was just tired of all that shit. We flew home, and he was fine. Elvis was a very good actor.

LAMAR FIKE: In May, Priscilla pulled a good one. If brains were dynamite, Priscilla couldn't blow up a goddamn gnat. But someone started telling her about the law out in California, telling her what she could have gotten in the divorce. So she filed a motion in Santa Monica Superior Court to set aside her original property settlement. She found her a sharp attorney who called the original settlement "extrinsic fraud." He was out for blood.

MARTY LACKER: Priscilla's new lawyer, Arthur Toll, claimed she needed $11,800 a month. I was there when Elvis found out. We were standing out in the back of Graceland, laughing about something. And Vernon came up cussing, just madder than hell. He was white as a sheet. Elvis said, "What's wrong, Daddy?" He said, "It's that damn Priscilla. Her lawyer just called. She's suing you for more money."

And Elvis's words were, "That no-good, greedy fuckin' bitch! Damnit, I gave her enough!" I remember in the early years, long before he was married, when Elvis would hear about divorces and women taking their husbands to the cleaners, he'd always say, "That'll never happen to me. I'll kill the bitch first."

LAMAR FIKE: When she switched attorneys, that's when it all changed. Boy, I mean, son! Vernon liked to blow a gasket. Elvis looked at his father and he said, "I thought you had the deal done, Daddy."

Toll got her a lump sum of $2 million—$6,000 a month for ten years. Plus $4,200-a-month alimony for a year, and $4,000-a-month child support, and $250,000 from the sale of the

Monovale house, although Elvis didn't sell it right away. On top of it, she got 5 percent of two of Elvis's music publishing companies.

Do you know where the money came from? Most of it came from the RCA buyout, in March.

MARTY LACKER: Somewhere around June or July of '73, Dr. Nick told the guys, "I don't think Elvis is just a medical addict anymore. I think he's a hard addict."

Hamburger James used to tell this story about being out in the kitchen on Monovale when Elvis first got up one day. James was about to drop a saccharine tablet in his coffee, and Elvis came in and saw it and thought it was something else, and snatched it right out of his hand. He said, "Give me that!" and grabbed it and popped it down his throat before James could say, "Hey, man, it's just sweetener!" James left the room and fell over on the pool table laughing.

The sad part is, Elvis was already beginning to have trouble controlling his bladder and bowels. Not all the time, but a lot of the times. You get that way when you're so far out of it, you're half asleep most of the time. And you really have no control. On tour, James would have to check Elvis's bed before they left the hotel. It would have been embarrassing if it had gotten out.

LAMAR FIKE: In June, another Elvis documentary came out. This one was *Elvis on Tour.* It was supposed to be a behind-the-scenes look, "as he really was," you know. You read the reviews on that thing, and you see how well we fooled everybody for so long. The *New York Times* said, "The film strips away the storybook myth to find underneath a private person who is indistinguishable from the public one, except for the fact he dresses with somewhat less flamboyance."

MARTY LACKER: Even though Elvis said he never wanted to talk to Gene [Smith] again after that incident over the jewelry in the early sixties, every once in a while, Gene would come up to

Graceland. In July of '73, I was up there one afternoon, and Elvis and Linda were out by the pool, and Sonny was in the water. It was just the three of them. And I had my swimsuit with me.

Elvis was laying on the chaise lounge, and he was pissed off about something. I knew it from his tone, and then he was gritting his teeth and pumping his cheekbone, the way he would when he was getting ready to blow. I said, "Hey, what's wrong with you?" And then I remembered that when I drove up the driveway, there was this strangely painted motorcycle that I'd never seen before. I said, "Whose chopper is that? Did you buy it?"

Elvis said, "No, goddamnit. That fuckin' Gene came up here with that motorcycle, and he was whining, 'Oh, Elvis, would you buy it for me? I really would like to have it.'"

I think it not only angered Elvis, but it hurt him. Because he still cared about Gene. If Gene had come to him and said, "Hey, I'm sorry," even after all those years, Elvis might have even asked him to come back to work.

I put on my swim trunks and jumped in the pool, and I started talking to Sonny. Well, anytime Elvis saw two people talking and he wasn't included, he wanted to know what the hell was going on. So he yelled, "What are you guys talking about?" In this abrupt tone, see. I said, "Nothing." He said, "No, damnit, what are you talking about?" And, in a flash, I decided to try to joke him out of his bad mood.

I said, "I was saying I really do like that motorcycle, and I wish you'd buy it for me." Elvis looked at me, and then it dawned on him that I hate motorcycles because I refused the first one he tried to give me. He smiled and said, "You no-good son of a bitch."

And then he said, "Well, now I'm going to have to buy you something."

I'd gotten him out of thinking about Gene, but I inadvertently started him on a tremendous shopping binge. He started out buying a Pontiac Grand Prix for Patsy, my wife, and then another one for Billy's wife, Jo. And within a week and a half, Elvis bought twenty-nine cars, and a motorcycle for Sonny. And just gave them all away. Vernon probably came close to having a heart attack. But that's the way Elvis would get himself out of a funk.

And Gene Smith never did get his motorcycle.

LAMAR FIKE: That little spree cost over $200,000—Pontiacs, Cadillacs, and Lincolns. He was giving cars away like you wouldn't believe. If somebody on the floor wanted one, he'd say, "You take that one." He didn't care. He would have given one to Hitler.

MARTY LACKER: After the American [Sound Studio] sessions with Chips, Colonel's camp, which included Felton Jarvis, in addition to Joe and Charlie, started not telling me when the recording sessions were. I just happened to stumble into one of them in L.A., in '72. "Burning Love" came out of that session. And I brought in a real left-field song by Paul Williams, "Where Do I Go from Here?"

I had my own company at the time, representing music publishers who wanted to get songs cut in Memphis. From time to time, I would come across songs that I thought were right for Elvis. I was really good friends with Alan Ryder, who handled a lot of songs and a lot of good writers. Peter Allen was one of them. I was out in L.A. on business and Alan said, "Listen, I got this song for you. I think it would be a hell of a good song for Elvis."

We went in his office and he played the demo for me, and it was "I Honestly Love You." I said, "Yeah, maybe Elvis could use that." I knew he had a session coming up soon, but they purposely didn't tell me when so I wouldn't bring Elvis any songs. So Olivia Newton-John did "I Honestly Love You," and it made her career. I also had "Moody Blue," that Ira Jaffe gave me from Screen Gems. Felton happened to get "Moody Blue" from Mark James later on, and that's how it ended up on Elvis's session in '76, but I got it first.

More than anything, I wanted to see Elvis have another hit record. And I knew Chips could do that for him, but Elvis wouldn't go back to Chips. Colonel and them had fed him all those evil lies.

Elvis and I had an argument about Chips about a year after he did the session there. We were up in the suite in Vegas. He mentioned it to me because at the time I was running Chips's studio. The whole group was around, and I looked Elvis straight in the face and said, "Elvis, let me tell you something. Whoever told you that stuff is nothing but a fucking liar. They're trying to ruin it for you, and they're trying to ruin it for Chips. Because they want your ass back in Nashville, doing the same old crap with the same old people, with the same old fucking songs."

And he took it the wrong way. He said, "Oh, what do you think you're going to do, whip my ass?" That really surprised me. And just as I predicted, for the most part, he went to cutting crappy songs again and recording them the same old way. Freddy Bienstock would come to every session, and the Colonel would still send him music. And they started cutting more out in L.A.

By the summer of '73, Elvis was getting really lazy. He didn't want to leave Memphis to record, and, in fact, he'd pretty much lost interest in recording. He had lost all enthusiasm, really. He looked at the records now like he looked at the movies. He was tired, but he didn't want to fight about it.

I went up to Graceland one afternoon. We were out by the pool, and Elvis said, "I want to record in Memphis again, but I don't want to record at American with Chips." So he said, "Moon, find me a studio that I can use here in town." Well, the only one that was secure at the time was Stax. And Stax was pretty famous because they'd had all kinds of hits out of there with Booker T. and the MGs, and Otis Redding, and Isaac Hayes. I said, "What about the musicians, Elvis?" He said, "Oh, I don't know. What do you think?" I said, "Well, what about the guys from American?" He said, "Get Reggie Young, and see who else you come up with. But I don't want you to make a big deal out of it." Because he just wanted to fulfill the obligation. But I got Reggie, and Tommy Cogbill, and Bobby Wood and Bobby Emmons, and then I asked Donald "Duck" Dunn, and Al Jackson, who were half of Booker T. and the MGs. And he went into Stax for four days in late July, and he went back in for a week in December.

Well, RCA and the people from Nashville didn't like this. Felton had a lot of buddies in Nashville because he lived there. Plus, recording in Memphis took money away from Nashville, too, especially with the musicians. To show you the politics, RCA pulled a remote truck out back, and they ran the soundboard through the truck. They said they wanted eighteen to twenty-four tracks, and Stax didn't have that at the time.

Jim Stewart, one of the owners of Stax, let Elvis use his office. Elvis would go in there and sit at the desk and listen to demos. This first day, Red and I were sitting over by the bar, and on the couch were Vernon Presley, Tom Diskin, Freddy Bienstock, Lamar Fike, and a couple of other people. We kept everybody else out, except Isaac Hayes came by a couple of times.

Naturally, Bienstock was playing this crap for him. And Elvis didn't like any of it, but he picked about two songs just to appease him.

When he finished, Elvis looked around and said, "Does anybody else have any songs?" He did that because he wanted Red and me to speak up. I said, "Yeah, I do." And Red said, "Yeah, I do, too." And Elvis said, "Well, let me hear what you've got." So I played him a couple of songs, and one of them was "Raised on Rock," a Mark James song. "Raised on Rock" was no earth-shattering record. But it was better than what Bienstock had.

So Elvis said, "I'm going to do this one now." We got up, and we were walking towards the studio, and he said, "Bear with me, I've got to put up with this shit from them to make it look good." I said, "No problem." So he went in the studio, and Red went in with him. I went back to the office, and I sat in the chair in front of the desk.

Well, Diskin and crew thought they were going to be like the Colonel and use fear tactics. Bienstock walked over to me, and he said, "Say, Mr. Lacker." And he used "Mr. Lacker" sarcastically. "I noticed that some of these songs you're playing for Elvis are all from this same company." They were from Screen Gems, which is no lightweight publishing company. He said, "Are you getting a little piece out of this, Marty?"

I said, "Yes, Freddy, as a matter of fact, I am making money— off of Screen Gems." And he got this little smirk on his face, and he said, "Do you think maybe Elvis would be a little upset with you if he knew that?" I looked him square in the face and I said, "Freddy, I think you ought to go in the studio there and tell him, don't you?" And he got this surprised look.

My relationship with Elvis was straight up. I had already told Elvis about this at the house. And he said, "Oh, I don't have any problem with that. Don't worry about it." So I told Bienstock, and he got red in the face and said, "Well, I don't want to bother him while he's recording."

I talked to Elvis about it later, and he said, "Man, just leave them alone. This fuckin' session don't mean nothin' to me anyway." And he really was at that point.

At the end of the year, when he cut again at Stax, the session was even more of a joke. After the first session, the musicians were really disappointed. Duck Dunn had asked me, "Man, what's going on here?" And Elvis got upset. So he said, "I don't want those guys again." And he had Felton bring in James Burton on guitar, Norbert Putnam on bass, and David Briggs on keyboards. But Felton would use the same old guys that were entrenched in Nashville fifty years ago. Except for people like David Briggs, who was a hell of a piano player and songwriter and who eventually built a fantastic publishing company.

Elvis had the studio for a week, and the first day, we started listening to Bienstock's crappy demos again, and Elvis hated every song.

Well, I had two new songs, and two others that had already been out before, but they were such great songs that I figured if he did either one, he might have a hit. One was "Loving Arms," that Dobie Gray had out, and the other one was "We Had It All," which was on a Dobie Gray album.

It so happened that David Briggs and Norbert Putnam had the publishing on "We Had It All," along with Irving Almo [Music Publishing]. Elvis listened to both songs, and after he heard "Loving Arms," he went in and did it. Then he came back out, and he said, "Let me hear 'We Had It All' again." He loved the song. He listened to it over and over again. If he listened to it once, he listened to it forty times. All the musicians were sitting around, scratching their heads, and saying, "If he likes it that much, let's cut it." But then he came to me and he said, "Marty, I can't cut that." I said, "Why not?" He said, "If I do this, people will think I'm singing about me and Priscilla."

He was really screwed up that night. The pills put you in so many different moods. Sometimes you get depressed and start feeling sorry for yourself.

David and Norbert both came to me and said, "Man, we thought he was going to cut it!" And I said, "No, he just decided he didn't want to, for personal reasons."

After the Stax sessions, Joe and the Colonel kept all the other sessions secret from me again.

LAMAR FIKE: In early August, Elvis went back into Vegas. The reviews were starting to get bad. I looked at the *Variety* notice the other day. It used words like "somnolent," and "lackadaisical," and "sleepwalking." He just didn't give a shit.

He had a fight with Colonel about a couple of things. For example, when he did the Stax sessions, he used this group called Voice. It was Donnie Sumner, J.D.'s stepson, and Tim Baty, and Sherrill Nielsen, the tenor, who'd been with [gospel groups] the Statesmen and the Imperials. And they liked to use Tony Brown, who's now a big record producer and the president of MCA Records/Nashville, as their piano player. Tony's on that session Elvis did at his house in Palm Springs [in September '73].

Well, after Elvis used Voice on the sessions, he wanted to hire them to sing behind him in Vegas, and on the road, and on records, and give them $100,000. This was on top of the Stamps and the Sweet Inspirations, mind you. He introduced them in Vegas—brought 'em out and let 'em do one number one night when he was fucked up. And then he wrote out a contract for them on toilet paper. Now, there's no way they were worth $100,000. Colonel told him $50,000 would be too much, and Elvis got pissed. He got 'em, though. Used 'em for two years or so.

MARTY LACKER: Elvis was just going to get them started. See, Elvis liked certain kinds of voices—real deep voices and real high voices. And Sherrill Nielsen—he calls himself "Shaun" instead of "Sherrill" now—had this real high voice, and Elvis really liked it. And Nielsen sang with some friends. Elvis always said he found them working in an upholstery shop in Nashville, that they were covering seat cushions in the daytime and singing at night. I don't know. But Elvis made them a group, and he called them "Voice" because of Sherrill's tenor and because of this spiritual book, *The Voice of Silence,* that Larry Geller got him into. And they talked Elvis into giving them money.

Nielsen and his friends said, "The only problem is we can't get started. We don't have the backing. Boy, if we just had this . . . " So they ingratiated themselves into Elvis's life simply by singing gospel music around him. So Elvis got the idea, "I'm going to help you." And pretty soon, Elvis said, "I'm going to give you guys a break. I'm going to be your manager."

All he really wanted was for them to sing gospel music with

him, but he signed them to an impromptu agreement where he was going to guarantee them that $100,000 a year. And when Colonel and Vernon heard that, they fuckin' blew the roof off. But in this instance, it didn't stop Elvis. Elvis just said, "Fuck them. I want you guys around, and that's what's going to happen."

It didn't last very long, though. Because as a group, they weren't that talented.

LAMAR FIKE: One night, Elvis had taken so many pills that he was out onstage and his throat just closed up. Dr. Boyers, the throat doctor, used some kind of special equipment and got up all manner of mucus and congestion. They thought Elvis might be getting pneumonia. But he went back out onstage and finished his show.

He was getting more erratic. One morning, he woke Red up and told him he had to go see Dr. Boyers and he wanted Red to take him. Red kind of grumbled about it, and when he got over to Elvis's room, Elvis pulled out that M16 and told him he was going to shoot his head off. Red called his bluff, and Elvis winked at Sonny like it was all a big joke.

He was just so unpredictable. He pulled a gun on Jimmy Dean, the singer, one night. Jimmy came down to the dressing room after a show, and Elvis kept him waiting for an hour, and when he came out, Jimmy joked with him and said, "I ought to rip a yard out of your ass, making me wait like that." And quick as a cat, Elvis pulled out a .357 magnum and jammed it under Jimmy's chin and said, "And I ought to blow your head off, talking to me like that." He did that at the Memphian one night, too, to some guy who wanted to get in the washroom.

He would go on these tangents. He was always wanting to kill somebody, and he was getting so paranoid it was unbelievable. One time in Vegas, he got real mad at some guy, a stranger, and got up in his face. He thought the guy had said something, and the guy hadn't said a word. It was just Elvis's paranoia. He went up to him and threatened to kill him. Things like that would never get out, though, because he was so well protected.

Hell, he threatened all of us all the time. And he became increasingly maniacal and insane, really. It would have been easy to leave, but we stayed out of love and loyalty. Those are pretty priceless commodities. But I guess we were also masochistic. It was kind of like being in love with a woman you know you've got to get away from. You put up with all the bad shit for one hour of good. We built our whole lives around that one hour. That became our whole focal point, to get that glimpse every once in a while that he could be normal and straight.

It was really a love/hate relationship. We used to walk off just shaking our heads, saying, "What the fuck are we doing?" And we'd go, "Well, we'll see how he is tomorrow." We pushed it one more day. And it became so difficult. So difficult. We were addicted to it, but God, it was rough. It was intolerable.

BILLY SMITH: After my daddy died in August of '73, Elvis tried again to get me to come back to work for him. And I wouldn't do it. He said, "A lot of these guys don't understand me. I need you here." I said, "I can't, Elvis, not now." We were living in this little house on St. Margaret's Place. And I said, "I've got my mama livin' with me, and Daddy just passed away." I said, "When you're at home, I'll be there. But right now, I can't find my way clear to come back with you."

We talked about a lot of things, including Priscilla. I said, "I heard you were going to have Mike Stone done in." He kind of laughed. I said, "You don't have to stoop to their level. I know it hurts. But you're a lot stronger than that. Don't even think about something along that line."

MARTY LACKER: You know, this supercop shit of his never let up. Sometime around July or August, before he went to Vegas, he was out in California. And he was driving down the street and he saw these two guys fighting. One was a gas station attendant. And one was bigger than the other. Elvis stopped the car, which was a limousine, so you can imagine what these guys thought. And he got out and told the bigger one to leave the other one alone. Well, the guy mouthed off to him and took a stance like he was going to hit Elvis.

Elvis had these guns on him, and he was reaching behind his back to get one of them. Elvis wouldn't have shot the guy, I don't think. But Hamburger James, of all people, stepped behind Elvis's back and said, "Let me have that pistol," and took it out of Elvis's hand.

On the whole, see, James was a real dimwit. In '73, after Elvis closed in Vegas, James was going home to Memphis on vacation to see his parents. His dad was a retired cop, so Elvis liked that. Elvis had given James a $500 bonus at the end of the engagement, and I think he gambled it away. But he said somebody stole it. So Elvis gave him another $500.

At the same time, Elvis also suspected that James had taken a couple of rings from him. He couldn't find his big thirty-karat sapphire that the Sahara Tahoe had given him for breaking the attendance record. And James came up with it—said he'd put it in his briefcase for safekeeping and forgotten about it. But Elvis still couldn't find his karate ring, and he was really pissed about that. He bitched and moaned about it, and the next day, it showed up lying inside a bunch of pipes next to the laundry chute.

Then, worst of all, two or three of those Polaroids of Priscilla in a compromising position with that girl were missing. Elvis figured James fingered 'em.

Sure enough, James had gone to the airport with at least one of them, and fortunately Elvis had discovered they were missing in time to do something. James's plane was leaving at, like, eleven in the morning, and at ten Elvis and the guys raced out to the airport there in Vegas. The airport is pretty close to the Hilton, and Hamburger was already on the plane, but it hadn't left yet.

So Elvis, in this big, dramatic move, ran out on the tarmac and flashed his narcotics badge that Nixon got him and stopped the damn plane. They pushed the steps back up to it and opened the door, and Elvis marched into the cockpit and told the pilot he couldn't take off until he surrendered the suspect. And Elvis dragged James off that plane by the back of the neck.

He got him out to the car, and he started reading him his rights. He said, "James, you have the right to remain silent, you have the right to an attorney . . . " And then he couldn't remember any more of the Miranda, so he just said, "And you have the right to all the rest of that shit. Get the fuck in the car."

They took James back to the hotel and slapped the shit out of him—really slapped him around some. Red and I were laughing about that just the other day. Because that was such an incredible scene. James was almost bald, and he usually combed his few remaining strands over. And when they slapped him on top of his head, his hair flew up in the air.

He was a pathetic bastard, really. A couple of the guys had their guns drawn, and James thought they might really shoot him. First he smarted off that his father, being a cop, would hunt Elvis down and kill him. And then he pleaded for mercy.

Elvis said, "Okay, James, go on back to Memphis. I won't bother you anymore, as long as you keep your mouth shut." Elvis felt bad about it later.

I don't know what happened to James after that. I heard he was pumping gas for a while.

LAMAR FIKE: What Elvis really wanted was the picture of Priscilla and that girl. That's why we chased him out to the airport. Hamburger was basically a loyal guy. But I think he felt that he was mistreated about something, and that's why he took the photograph.

BILLY SMITH: I don't think James was the only one that stole the pictures. There was more than one missing. Elvis confiscated the one from him, but I don't know what's happened to the others. I keep thinking somebody'll sell them to the tabloids. And hoping they don't.

LAMAR FIKE: We had our work cut out for us in the seventies. But we kept that shroud around him. And I mean, *nobody* penetrated it. Or if they did, they had a hell of a time getting out.

Like this one guy who worked at one of the hotels—a guy Elvis routinely gave a $100 tip to—was shooting off his mouth that Elvis was a druggie. Jackie Wilson's people told Sonny about it, as a favor. And they sent a guy from the real Mafia to Sonny, and he volunteered to take care of the guy. Sonny said, "Thanks, but no thanks." But Sonny called the guy up anonymously and told him he'd better stop talking or he was history.

Towards the end, there were too many holes in the dike to plug. You could stick everything you had into it, including your dick, and it wouldn't be enough. It was getting that bad. Stories would appear in different trades [newspapers] of Elvis being fucked up onstage or in public somewhere. And people could tell. Back in the early days, you could hide stuff because there were still Teletypes and telephones, not this fucking satellite in the skies. We still did an awfully good job, but we couldn't outrun the electronic media.

MARTY LACKER: After Elvis got rid of Hamburger James, Al Strada went on the road as Elvis's wardrobe manager. He prepared his stage costumes and his bedroom, along with Ricky Stanley. Elvis hired Al in '72 as a sort of night watchman. He guarded the Monovale house while Priscilla and Lisa were there and Elvis was in Vegas or on the road. He was a Mexican guy, Mexican American. Elvis liked him a lot.

LAMAR FIKE: When Elvis hired him, it got everybody mad again. The guys said, "What are you hiring him for?" The reason was really just to worry everybody.

BILLY SMITH: Al was a pretty straight person, a nice guy. Of course, he was Mexican, and he had, I think, a kind of a built-in inferiority complex. We always kidded him, but he took it well.

MARTY LACKER: It was Hamburger's job to pick up and destroy the empty pill bottles and used syringes Elvis left around, so I guess Al inherited that chore, too.

LAMAR FIKE: You'd see two or three syringes all the time during the last five or six years of Elvis's life.

BILLY SMITH: You didn't see them laying around very often, unless it would be in his bathroom upstairs. On one or two occasions, syringes were left at hotels, and that never should have happened. There was a few asses tore up about it, to put it mildly. So they started double-checking his room. They'd even take the garbage and put it on the plane and dump it later. It was Joe's job to make sure everything was kept under wraps.

MARTY LACKER: In October, Elvis and Priscilla's divorce became final. You can tell by those photos of them leaving the courthouse that Elvis was puffy and that he'd put on weight. Priscilla says in her book that she was shocked at how he looked. They went into the judge's chambers and held hands while the judge checked off the formalities, and then they went outside. Priscilla walked to her car with her sister, and Elvis walked over to his limo with Vernon, and his attorney, and some of the guys. Priscilla waved goodbye, and Elvis winked at her. That was it. Except they still had Lisa to talk about on the phone.

BILLY SMITH: Elvis changed a lot after he was married and after Lisa was born. But I think he changed the most after his divorce.

MARTY LACKER: Six days after the divorce, Elvis ended up in Baptist Hospital in Memphis. At the time, they said it was for recurring pneumonia and pleurisy, with the additional symptoms of toxic hepatitis and an enlarged colon. They did all these tests under the phony name of "Aaron Sivle," which was his middle name and his first name spelled backwards. He was really in there for detox. He stayed two weeks—until November 1.

Dr. Nick told Rose Clayton and Dick Heard [*Elvis Up Close*] that they had to keep his chart locked up, even away from other people who worked in the hospital. He said, "The lab technicians were selling his blood and urine. It was crazy."

Elvis had three overdoses in '73. One was near fatal, in St. Louis, the end of June. Vernon witnessed that one.

BILLY SMITH: If that had been my son, we would have had one hellacious knockdown, drag-out. And then if need be, I would have said, "Look, we may lose it all tomorrow, but either you get help or I'll get it for you."

LAMAR FIKE: I don't know if that overdose was near fatal, but he got pretty screwed up. We had to throw him under the shower. He was in bad shape. No circulation, little heartbeat, just out of it. He wouldn't respond to anything—shaking, slapping, or any-thing else the guys would do.

Dr. Nick would bring him around when something like that happened. We started calling him "Needle Nick, in the nick of time." Elvis was in the hospital five times in the last seven years. It was always for detox, but it was under the guise of other things.

That first hospitalization came about after he went for acupuncture in L.A. for bad sinuses and a strained back. I was there when he did that. The acupuncturist used steroids, and those on top of his usual Demerol blew him up like crazy. He looked pretty bad. And Linda and Dr. Nick got him in the hospital. Dr. Nick cut off the Demerol and gave him Methadone, like any other addict.

BILLY SMITH: In the beginning, I tried to justify his taking drugs. He did need them for a colon problem, and he had a liver disease, which I believe was hereditary and came down from his mama. Because I remember Dr. Nick asking me what kind of liver prob-lem Daddy had. Dr. Nick said Elvis had this condition where a portion of your liver diseases and dies off.

MARTY LACKER: While Elvis was in the hospital for this first detox, he got a drug shipment from Las Vegas from one of his doctors. Jerry Schilling was in Memphis—he wasn't working as a film editor anymore—and he intercepted the package and took it to Dr. Nick.

Jerry told Nick he thought Elvis was really trying to dry out and get straight. And Nick decided to test Elvis on it. He told Jerry to take it to Elvis, to see if Elvis was serious about getting better. Two days went by, and Elvis never mentioned it to Nick. Dr. Nick searched Elvis's medicine cabinet and found all the stuff hidden in the back.

BILLY SMITH: Elvis had been taking a lot of cortisone in Las Vegas. Just heavy doses. That's why he was so puffy.

MARTY LACKER: His colon was distended. And I've heard, and read, that he had little control over his bladder function during this time. And he'd taken so many drugs that he'd aggravated his digestive system something fierce. Dr. Nick got him to see a Memphis gastroenterologist, Dr. Lawrence Wruble. Wruble helped him with his symptoms, but when he tried to counsel him, Elvis told him he needed drugs to get up for his shows and more drugs to come down afterwards. Wruble told him, "Either you've got to quit doing two shows a night or nobody will need to take care of you any longer."

But Elvis couldn't do that. Not with the deal Colonel cut with the Hilton.

BILLY SMITH: I don't think the colon trouble was entirely related to drugs, but I think it had a whole hell of a lot to do with it. They just throw your natural cycle off. He'd always had a little bit of difficulty. But it increased as years went on.

Being on the road lends itself to constipation, too. That and his eating habits. It wasn't just the junk food. He didn't have a real routine. It was just whenever the hell he got up. It could be twelve o'clock noon, or three o'clock in the morning, and that's when he ate. So it's not surprising that his colon bothered him.

MARTY LACKER: During this first detox, Dr. Nick called in two psychiatrists, Dr. David Knott and Dr. Robert Fink. They put Elvis on methadone treatments. Dr. Knott came in the room all the time when Elvis was in the hospital. He was a consultant at Baptist, but he was also the head of the Tennessee psychiatric hospital. He's well known in Memphis as an alcohol and drug abuse doctor. He used to treat Jerry Lee Lewis. But Elvis dumped both their asses. He didn't want anything to do with a psychiatrist.

BILLY SMITH: Elvis would have thought it wasn't macho to see a psychiatrist. Besides, Elvis thought he was in control of everything.

LAMAR FIKE: In the years since Elvis died, there's been a story floating around that Vernon hired John O'Grady to track Elvis's drug use in '73, after he blew off the Tahoe engagement.

MARTY LACKER: Vernon hired O'Grady? I don't think so. O'Grady was gotten through Ed Hookstratten, who was taking his directions from Colonel Parker, not Vernon. Now, Parker might have talked Vernon into doing that. But Vernon knew what was going on. He was on some of the tours when Elvis couldn't sing a lick up onstage.

Vernon wasn't going to say anything because Vernon didn't want to lose the money. If Vernon was that concerned with Elvis's reputation, he would have given back the money for that CBS special [Elvis in Concert] that ran after Elvis's death and told them not to air it. Elvis is so fat and drugged there, you just wish the television would blow up. It's a disgrace to his memory. And it's a big reason comedians have cracked jokes about Elvis's size since he died. That's the image that sticks in a lot of people's minds.

BILLY SMITH: Hookstratten may have been Elvis's lawyer, but he was closer to Colonel than he was to Elvis. And it wouldn't surprise me if I found out Colonel had nonchalantly asked Hookstratten to work John O'Grady into being around Elvis a lot, to see what he could find out.

I've heard that Hookstratten hired O'Grady and another detective named Jack Kelly to find out where Elvis got his drugs. O'Grady says he give Vernon a copy of his investigative report, and they supposedly went to 'em and put pressure on them to stop giving Elvis all that stuff. You see how much good it done.

LAMAR FIKE: I've read that after Elvis and Priscilla divorced, she went to Elvis and asked him to go into the Scripps Medical Clinic. This was supposed to have been at the suggestion of Hookstratten and O'Grady. That didn't happen that I know of. Mother Teresa she's not. And I don't think O'Grady had enough fuckin' intelligence to do it.

BILLY SMITH: That's possible, but none of us knew about it, if she did. First of all, why in the hell didn't Priscilla do that when she was married to him? Or make the suggestion herself? Or talk to some of the guys in the group? I've never heard one person mention that Priscilla was worried about Elvis's drug problem.

And I don't know of any conversation she had with Elvis or anybody else about it.

Instead, she went her separate way and let him go. Priscilla's feelings were, "Give me a quarter, and I'm gone." I don't think she cared a damn about helping him. Nobody who was in a position to legally do something seemed to give a shit.

CHAPTER 46

THE TURNING POINT

LAMAR FIKE: At the end of January '74, when Elvis opened in Vegas, it was only a two-week engagement. Colonel's contract with the Hilton expired in '73, and when they renegotiated, a bunch of the other hotels—the Aladdin, the MGM Grand, where Kirk Kerkorian had gone—came calling. Henri Lewin, who was a Hilton vice president, finally got Colonel to commit to staying for two more years. And Lewin gave Elvis the option of playing only two weeks at a stretch, twice a year.

Boy, Elvis snapped at that. At $150,000 a week. And $150,000 was still more than anybody else was getting out there. Plus, by the time Elvis got his suite and anything else he wanted free, it added up to about a $25,000 perk. He was doing all right.

He brought Linda Thompson out there for that gig, but he also had two or three girls stashed in different rooms at the same time. Then Linda wanted to go off to do a little modeling. And Elvis said, "Sure, go on! Have a good time!" Because then he could bring in these other women. Elvis squired Sheila Ryan around for a while. She'd just been on the cover of *Playboy*. He saw Sheila off and on for eighteen months or so. And Linda knew it.

MARTY LACKER: Linda was the best woman he had ever been with. He called her "Mommy," and she called him "Little Baby Buntin'." She cared about him. She wouldn't fall asleep at night until after Elvis did. If something happened while he was sleeping, she'd be up in a minute. She even cleaned Elvis up when he got nasty. He would get so bad at times that Linda had to take him to the bathroom. But the way Elvis saw it, there was no more challenge with her.

BILLY SMITH: Like we said, from the time Elvis Presley became famous, he never stopped seeing other women. And they were always young. He was almost forty now, and he needed to prove to everybody around him that he was still capable of getting a young woman. And it was easy until the seventies. But from about '74 on, he started getting heavy, and he didn't feel good.

He also didn't think he could have a life with somebody and still be Elvis Presley.

MARTY LACKER: In '74, while he was living with Linda, Elvis dated Ann Pennington. Her sister, Janice Pennington, is one of the models on *The Price Is Right*.

Elvis used to fly Ann into different places on tour. I remember picking her up at the airport in Monroe, Louisiana, one time. Someone else took Sheila Ryan to the airport while I was picking up Ann. He had women in revolving doors. They could run into each other at the airport and not know it.

After Ann stopped dating Elvis, she posed for a centerfold for *Playboy*, just like Sheila Ryan. Then she went on to marry Shaun Cassidy.

🏃 🏃 🏃

LAMAR FIKE: During that Vegas engagement, Elvis was pretty trigger-happy. One night while Linda was there, Elvis had his .22-caliber Savage revolver out and decided to pick off a statue of an owl up in the suite. He had a bunch of pills in him, and his aim was off. Linda was sitting in the bathroom, and out of nowhere, a bullet ripped through the wall and grazed the toilet paper roll right next to her knee. Then it zinged on and shattered the mirror on the back of the door.

BILLY SMITH: I think that bathroom incident scared the fool out of Linda. But nobody said a whole lot to him about it. They just kind of fluffed it off, and said, "Man, you got to be a little more careful with that thing." The way he was with guns, it would have been damn easy for him to have made a mistake and shot somebody. But he'd always grumble, "Oh, goddamn, I know how to handle a gun."

LAMAR FIKE: The Savage revolver had a long barrel on it. Serious gun. He hauled it out after Red one time. I don't know which was tougher—Red or that gun—but we nearly had us a showdown.

BILLY SMITH: Elvis pulled a gun on Red two or three times. Red told him one time if he ever pulled it on him again, he'd better use it.

MARTY LACKER: One afternoon in '74, when Elvis was eating breakfast, he turned on the TV and there was Robert Goulet. He'd never forgotten that letter Goulet had written him in Germany about Anita Wood. So Elvis just put down his knife and fork, pulled out his .22, and blew the television to kingdom come. Then he calmly picked up his utensils and said, "That'll be enough of that shit."

Another time, at Graceland, he was sitting in bed watching TV—that big RCA series 2000 console. He was eating a cheeseburger and drinking milk. And this hemorrhoid cream commercial came on. Elvis had a really weak stomach about things like that, so he threw the rest of his cheeseburger and milk at the screen, and yelled, "Rub that on your ass, you son of a bitch!" And then he reached over on his nightstand and picked up his turquoise-handled Colt .45 automatic and blasted the whole screen out.

BILLY SMITH: Lisa was there at the time, and Elvis didn't want her to see the blown-up television, so he threw his robe over it. And then he called [his uncle] Earl Pritchett [the head groundskeeper] and told him his TV didn't work anymore and asked him to get rid of it. Earl come in the bedroom and, without looking at it, said, "I know what's wrong with that TV, Elvis. I had the same trouble with mine. It's a high-voltage tube." Elvis said, "Does yours have a hole in it?"

Earl carted it out and later asked if he could have it. Jimmy Velvet, the Elvis collector, sold it at auction in '94. It brung all kinds of money.

🕺 🕺 🕺

LAMAR FIKE: The paranoia really got bad in the mid-seventies. We'd be asleep, and Elvis would get up and raise hell with everybody, wanting to kill somebody.

One night he got on a table and started shooting because he couldn't find Dr. Ghanem to get his drugs. Elias was on Adnan Khashoggi's yacht somewhere in the Caribbean. And Elvis went into this maniacal raving, and he pulled his gun out and started firing at everything he saw. Boy, we were diving under the chairs during that one. Bad, bad.

He started that self-mutilation stuff again, too. He had a hole in his hand that he would pick at. It started off as some small injury, and by the time he finished, you could have parked a truck in it. Really, you could see the bones. Had Elias not gotten to it when he did, Elvis could have lost his hand.

You know why he did it? Same reason he dug a hole in his foot that time. To get more medicine.

BILLY SMITH: Elvis hurt himself on purpose like that another time, too. He beat his hand into the wall. Then he said some fan scratched it with her fingernail, and it got infected while he was shaking hands onstage.

LAMAR FIKE: It got to where he had to cut that shit out because his recuperative powers were gone. He didn't heal like he should have. That was another indication of how sick he was getting.

If it hadn't been for Elvis's group, he would have died three years earlier, at the very least. Because being with him was like living in a firehouse. You never knew when the alarm was going to go off. But we literally kept that man alive.

I guess there were a good five or six times that he got so fucked up that he almost died. Dr. Nick would shoot him full of Ritalin and bring him around. That happened three or four times. He'd be damn near comatose, and we'd get Dr. Nick in, and he'd bring him back.

The first time happened in Vegas, probably '74. Dr. Nick had to give him a shot of Ritalin straight in his heart. We thought we'd lost him. He was going down for the count, man. And Elvis popped out of it just like that. Talk about the gnashing of teeth and wringing of hands, we did it.

Another time, at a Howard Johnson Motel somewhere on the road, he had the opposite problem. He was so wired that Nick had to go in through his neck and shoot him to knock him out.

MARTY LACKER: Aside from just overdoses, you had to watch him when he ate because he'd get a load of stuff in him, and then he'd choke on his food. Drugs numb the nerves in the throat that control the swallowing reflex, and then food goes down the wrong way. Elvis had to be rescued all the time.

LAMAR FIKE: One time, in Vegas, Elvis was eating a peach and swallowed the pit, and it stuck down his fucking throat. Linda called Joe, and he went rushing in there, and Elvis had already started turning blue. Joe had to stick his finger down Elvis's throat and pop that pit out. Later, Elvis swore up and down it never happened. The last five years were so difficult, it was unbelievable. God, it was horrendous.

MARTY LACKER: You might think that every time something like this happened, Elvis would repent or at least say something. But no. Nothing. Deep down inside, he knew what he was doing was wrong, and dangerous, but he got to the point where he didn't think anything would happen.

LAMAR FIKE: There would be moments of contrition. But they wouldn't last long. People say, "Oh, he was so unassuming." He was not unassuming. He knew exactly who he was. He was the King.

MARTY LACKER: You can't possibly control drug use like that unless you really set your mind to it. And Elvis was an escape artist.

Elvis wanted to be happy. He just didn't know how to do it. He felt it was too late for him to find happiness. He could have found it with Linda. But instead of concentrating on that, he looked back at Priscilla and thought, "Maybe I'm not cut out to be married." He dealt with it the only way he knew how—by getting wasted.

LAMAR FIKE: If we're dealing with psyches, I think Elvis did not want to be what he was, but he didn't want to give it up. We were talking one time, and I said, "Let's go to Hawaii—get your act together." He said, "I just can't do it." I said, "Well, I guess not."

His tours were getting so bad that I would just fly a day ahead with Colonel and work advance. That way, I wouldn't have to see the shows. He was losing his beauty—just all gut and chin. And he was forgetting lyrics, and preaching onstage, for God's sake, and going into these interminable monologues. He was so drugged up, it was really embarrassing.

The worst performance I witnessed was in Houston, Texas. That morning, he was so loaded that we had to throw him in a cold shower to try to bring him around. He had damned near overdosed. When the cold water hit him, he didn't even know it. He was that screwed up.

When he went out onstage that night, he did twenty-two minutes and forgot all the songs. Then he walked offstage and got in the bus. He wouldn't have even done the twenty-two minutes if we hadn't thrown him in the shower. He didn't remember doing the show. He didn't even remember where he was. He came by me and said, "Where the fuck were we?" I said, "Well, I can promise you it wasn't Secaucus, New Jersey." He said, "Don't get funny." I said, "We were in Houston," which was one of his big towns. I said, "You've got to watch what you're doing because you don't know what's going on out there."

It didn't register. He didn't pay any attention to it. They were booing and everything. I think they even asked us not to come back. That was in '74. But he didn't care. He would cancel a show at the drop of a hat. If he was straight, that would never happen in a thousand years.

You know, people say to me, "What was the problem? Colonel? Priscilla?" Elvis was the problem—his own worst enemy.

I think Elvis wanted to be like Frank Sinatra. One night, I said to him, "You know, Elvis, no matter how pissed off you get at Frank Sinatra, you know what he is?" He said, "What?" I said, "He's his own man. He took the risk, and he went out there and did it. He's been through the bramble bushes, and he's been scarred up. Do you know the difference between Frank and you?" He said, "You give me a smart answer, and you're a dead man." I said, "I'll give you a true one. He did it. But you wouldn't."

BILLY SMITH: Those last years, Lamar was the advance man for a reason. A lot of times, especially in the later years, Elvis would get tired of people being around him. He told Jo and me that. And I've said this to Marty—there were times when Elvis didn't want Marty around him. He said he depressed him. Marty was Elvis's dark cloud. Elvis didn't like what Lamar and Marty had to say.

MARTY LACKER: In April of '74, everybody got real excited again because Elvis got a $1 million offer to tour Australia. But, of course, nothing happened. According to the *Commercial Appeal*, Parker pulled out standard line number 101: "That's plenty for me, but what about the boy?"

BILLY SMITH: That May, they went back into Tahoe. Elvis was supposed to do two shows a day for eleven days. But he canceled two shows—said he had the darn flu.

MARTY LACKER: Elvis had Lisa with him out there. She'd just turned six. The guys went into Tahoe a few days early to rehearse, and the Jackson family was finishing their run there. Jerry took Lisa down after the show one night. That's where she first met Michael Jackson, her husband-to-be. Schilling actually did it, but you might say that Elvis introduced them.

BILLY SMITH: That was the same time in Tahoe that Red, and Sonny, and David Stanley, and Dick Grob roughed up a real estate developer outside the suite there on the fourteenth floor. He claimed he'd given one of the guys $60 to get into a party there after the show one night, and when he come up, they wouldn't let him in. So he found the breaker switches and turned the lights off on 'em.

Everybody come running out of the suite, and the guy said they beat the livin' daylights out of him. I don't know what really happened. But the guy filed a $6.3 million lawsuit. It took a while, but I think Elvis settled.

🕺 🕺 🕺

LAMAR FIKE: When we went back to Vegas in August, Elvis got the word that Barbra Streisand and Jon Peters wanted to come meet him. So they came down after a show.

They wanted to talk to him about taking the male lead in her remake of *A Star Is Born*. Peters was going to coproduce. And they went back into Elvis's private room and talked to him about it. He told me about it afterwards, and he was real excited. He really wanted to do it. But Colonel said no.

Actually, I think it was a mutual decision. Elvis would not have subjugated himself to Jon's and Barbra's decisions. And both Elvis and Barbra would have wanted to see how late the other one would get to the set.

It would have been a great role for him. Very, very different from what he had been playing. But in a way, he would have been playing Elvis. And he realized he would have dropped into [playing] a pathetic character. He let everybody think he wanted to, but deep down he just didn't want to push that button.

In the end, I don't know what Colonel really said to him. You hear that it's because Colonel wanted $1 million and Barbra balked. But I don't think Colonel had to do much nudging. Colonel says Elvis told him to make the contract stiff enough where they would turn it down 'cause he didn't want to do it.

BILLY SMITH: Elvis wouldn't have done it without the Colonel, no sir. And he wanted to do that picture so bad. But it's true Elvis had to be the most important person.

He'd been offered other real good roles that either him or Colonel turned down. Like the Jon Voight role [Joe Buck] in *Midnight Cowboy*. And before that, the Paul Newman part [Chance Wayne] in *Sweet Bird of Youth*. But if he'd ever put his foot down, he could have been some hellacious actor. Heck, he *was* a good actor. He acted every day.

MARTY LACKER: Elvis told me, and Red, and everybody else, that he wanted to do *A Star Is Born*. And the guys who were there told me that he was really enthused after Streisand and Peters left because he thought he was finally going to get an opportunity to act in a quality production.

Colonel gave the excuse that Streisand wanted top billing, and that's why Elvis wouldn't do it. But I think Parker wouldn't do it for several reasons, including he didn't want Elvis to be exposed to the "business" of show business with someone like Streisand.

And there's another reason he might not have done it. Elvis might have been intimidated by Streisand. They were two very strong people.

BILLY SMITH: Colonel should have presented Elvis with an ultimatum of "Get yourself straightened out because I've got a couple of challenges for you and you can't meet them in the shape you're in." He should have said, "Let's find you a decent movie and do a worldwide tour. But you've got to get in shape first." But there was no way in hell Elvis was going to do anything on his own, because the Colonel had so much control that he would have thrown a block in front of everybody.

LAMAR FIKE: During this engagement in Vegas in August, Elvis had a big showdown with Colonel. Not over the Streisand thing. Over stuff a lot bigger than that. It started with an incident with the maître d'. But it went back a lot farther.

Elvis had been on this kick that he could heal the sick and dying. Right around Christmas '66, Alan's father was in the hospital, dying of cancer. Elvis had never met him, and he felt bad for Alan, so he wanted to do something. So he gave Mr. Fortas a gold pocket watch that the Aberbachs had given him. In retrospect, it wasn't the best gift because Mr. Fortas didn't have much time, you know? The man was, like, right at the point of death.

Elvis went to the hospital to give him the watch himself. A bunch of us were there—Alan, Marty, and I don't know who else. Mr. Fortas was drugged into unconsciousness. And Elvis got right down in his ear, and he whispered, "You can overcome this."

When we got out of there, I said, "Elvis! What were you doing?" And he said, "Right before people die, they can remember everything that's been said."

Well, from there, Elvis decided he could move bushes, and twigs and shit, just by moving his hands over them. And he thought he could heal with the laying on of hands.

BILLY SMITH: In Self-Realization, they teach you that some people have the gift of healing. And of course, a lot of people say it's fraud, but who's to say whether it's real or not? All I know is, sometimes we had these readings and studies on people, like Rasputin, who were supposedly capable of doing these things. And Elvis got to believing, "Hey, maybe it's possible." So he got to experimenting.

LAMAR FIKE: In '73, Sonny and Judy's little boy, Brian, got a real high fever. He was, like, a year old, and they were worried.

Well, Elvis decided he'd do the laying-on-of-hands trip and rip that fever right out of the kid. He went over to Sonny's house with this big green scarf because he said green was a healing color. And he put on this damn turban, if you can believe it, with some kind of fake jewel on it. Looked like Ali Baba.

Elvis laid Brian down on the cloth, and then he went into the fucking lotus position and meditated. And he said all this mumbo jumbo and told Brian to concentrate on letting his fever pass into Elvis's hands. The kid's a year old, right? Elvis started working on him, and Brian got fixated on that fake stone and reached up to snatch it off the turban. Elvis snapped, "Don't do that, Brian!" The kid was ruining the show! It was hilarious.

Well, Elvis put his hands on both sides of Brian's head, and his solar plexus, and mumbled all this crap about the fever traveling through his arms and out. Then he said, "I think the fever's starting to break." Sonny put his hand on Brian's forehead, and he was as hot as ever. But Sonny said, "Yeah, I think you're right."

The next day, Brian was a lot better. His fever was down, but hell, they'd been giving him all kinds of medicine. Sonny called Elvis and gave him the news. And Elvis said, "Good, that pleases me. Call me if there's any change."

MARTY LACKER: Geller's influence lingered on.

In August, in Vegas, Elvis was talking to Mario, who used to bring and serve Elvis's dinner in the suite. Elvis asked how his family was, and Mario told him that his wife was dying of cancer. And because Elvis thought he could heal the world, he said, "Look, don't worry about it. I'll take care of it."

He asked Mario where he lived. And a whole bunch of us got in two or three cars and went out to Mario's house. We all went in, and Elvis started talking in this real hushed tone. He asked Mario, "Where is your wife?" Mario said, "She's in the bedroom."

Elvis said, "I'd like to go in there and make her feel better." He was going to put his hands on her [to heal her] and all this other stuff. He looked around the room, and he said to two or three people, "Come on, go with me." He glanced over at me, but he didn't bother to ask me because I had just given him a look like "I ain't going in there," and he knew I thought it was all hokum.

Well, somehow the hotel got wind of Elvis going out to Mario's house. And they made it seem like Mario was taking advantage of his position. So one night, somebody else brought the food up. And since Elvis insisted on having Mario all the time, he said, "Where's Mario?" And the other waiter said, "Mario doesn't work here anymore." Elvis asked why, and the guy told him he'd been fired. And Elvis blew up.

That night, he went onstage and lambasted Barron Hilton. He said, "I think you people ought to know that the big shots at the Hilton are an unfeeling, uncaring group. They're rotten. A man's wife was dying of cancer, and just because I went out there to try to help her, they fired him. Barron Hilton's behind this. He's not worth a damn." He just berated him. The pills were screwing him up so much that he didn't care what he did.

LAMAR FIKE: Elvis went to the Colonel about it before he went onstage. And the Colonel tore into him. He said, "You don't need to interfere with the hotel's business!" And that's what tilted Elvis. He said, "Fuck the hotel's business!" He said, "Mario's a friend of mine, and Barron shouldn't have fired him." And Colonel said, "This is hotel policy. You're involving yourself in something that isn't any of your business, and you're setting yourself up for trouble."

MARTY LACKER: I think Elvis was making a statement, which was, "I don't want to play here anymore." He told me, "I'll see that the old son of a bitch doesn't book me in Vegas again!"

LAMAR FIKE: Colonel came charging out and walked up to me and said, "This is going to cause us a lot of problems." I said, "Well, Colonel, you go on in and tell Elvis what he did wrong because ain't nobody here going to tell him."

Elvis left the stage and went downstairs to the dressing room. And Parker went down there just screaming and yelling. You could hear them through the doors in the back. Colonel said, "What the hell are you doing? Who gives you the right to say those things about Barron Hilton?"

Elvis said, "Look, if you don't like it, that's tough shit." And Parker said, "Well, I don't like it, and I don't know if I'll take this anymore." And Elvis said, "Well, goddamnit, if you don't like it, just get the fuck out! We're through. Finished."

MARTY LACKER: Parker said, "Okay, I'll call a press conference in the morning, and I'll announce that I am no longer your manager because of the weird, stupid things you do."

And Elvis snapped back, "Well, then, I'll tell you what *I'll* do. I'll call a damn press conference tonight and tell them I fired your ass." Parker said, "You do what you want. I'll get my bill together and present it to your father in the next couple of days. And when you pay it, I'm finished."

Now, there shouldn't have been a bill because of the way that money was split up. And all that night, Elvis just screamed and hollered, "That old rotten son of a bitch! Fuck him! I don't need him anymore."

One of the other guys told me that when Colonel left, Esposito spoke up and said, "Good. Now we can handle this ourselves. We can run things because the tours are laid out anyway." But Joe was way over his head. He was road manager on the tours, and Joe was good at what he did, but he was no manager. And no disrespect to Joe, but Elvis was down on his case bad, too. He wanted to weed him out.

LAMAR FIKE: I told Elvis, "Joe wants to manage you." I said, "You can write it down. Joe and maybe Jerry Schilling." And I think they'd scouted around for somebody like Jerry Weintraub to help them, although I don't think Weintraub ever approached Elvis about it. Weintraub handled Sinatra and John Denver. But I told Elvis, "Something's going on. I don't know what it is, but you'd better watch your ass."

That whole thing with Colonel lasted for days. It started with a big buildup, and it all came to a big, screaming explosion.

The day Elvis really blew up, he was in his bedroom in the

THE TURNING POINT 593

suite. He told me to get Colonel up there, and I went downstairs and got him. We went in the bedroom, and I walked over and sat by the Exercycle. Esposito was there. And Elvis just ripped into Colonel all over again. He said, "You're through. You're fired." The Colonel said, "You can't fire me." Elvis said, "I just did." The Colonel said, "You're going to have to pay me off."

That was the first time I'd seen Colonel get really ballistic. He said, "I'm going to call a conference, and I'm going to lay it all out." And Elvis said, "You get your ass out of here!" And the Colonel stormed out of the room.

About ten minutes later, I went downstairs. And Colonel said, "Tell Elvis such and such." So I did. And then Elvis said, "Go back and tell the Colonel . . . " They had me in the middle, and I was like a Ping-Pong ball, bouncing around.

BILLY SMITH: From there on, Elvis despised Colonel. Didn't even like to be around him.

MARTY LACKER: Two or three days later, Vernon went out there and said, "Son, I think we have to make up with the Colonel."

Elvis said, "What are you talking about?" Vernon said, "He just presented us with his bill for $2 million. He says we owe it to him." Which was bullshit. And Elvis said, "What do you mean, $2 million?" Vernon said, "Well, he's got it listed here. And he says once we pay him, he'll give up the contract."

Elvis and his father talked for a while, and Elvis came out and said to Joe, "I guess we're going to have to go down there and make up with the old bastard."

BILLY SMITH: That was Elvis's big chance to get away from Colonel. And he missed it.

MARTY LACKER: Vernon had no idea that somebody else could put up the $2 million, and they could have told the Colonel to go to hell. There were so many managers in the entertainment business who would have given their right arm to have Elvis. Record companies, too.

There's a book called *The Death of Elvis* [by Charles C. Thompson II and James P. Cole] that concentrates on the last year. But it also has a brief interview with Colonel Parker by Larry Hutchinson, chief criminal investigator for the attorney general of Tennessee. Parker told Hutchinson that in '74, when Elvis was playing Vegas, Elvis came out to Palm Springs and went over to Parker's house.

Parker told Hutchinson, "He didn't look well. I said, 'Do you want to take a rest? There's something wrong. I don't know what it is, but you don't look well.' That's when Elvis told me, 'I do drugs. I don't tell you what to do with your life. I don't interfere with it. I don't want you to get involved in my personal life. I know what I'm doing, Colonel, no disrespect, but I know what I'm doing, and I'm fine.'"

Colonel said that later he got concerned about Elvis's weight gain, and he said to Elvis, "You've gained so much weight." And Elvis supposedly repeated, "I know what I'm doing, Colonel. Please don't interfere."

So Hutchinson said to Colonel, "You never did interfere into his personal life?" And Colonel said, "I never had from the start."

Now, I don't know if that conversation between Elvis and Parker ever really happened. But if it did, it's unconscionable. I know that Parker said to Elvis once, "If you don't straighten out, no one's going to want to book you." But Parker wasn't concerned about Elvis's welfare—he was afraid he wouldn't be able to make money off him anymore.

Elvis didn't care what anybody said. Parker waited too long, and said too little.

By the way, it's interesting to note that 1974 was also the year that Colonel set up Boxcar Enterprises to oversee the merchandising of Elvis products. Souvenirs, for example. And there was a short-lived Boxcar Records. They put out an all-talk album, *Having Fun with Elvis on Stage*. Basically, it was just comments Elvis made in concert. Parker used to sell it at the souvenir stands in Vegas and on the road.

Appropriately enough, "boxcar" is a gambling term. It means double sixes on the dice. Colonel set up Boxcar for two reasons. Most of Elvis's income was from live performances. And Colonel saw that Elvis couldn't go on all that much longer. His health was deteriorating so fast. And Colonel also wanted to give his faithful pals another break. Because here's how the stock of Boxcar broke down: Parker, 40 percent. Tom Diskin, 15 percent. George Parkhill, 15 percent. Freddy Bienstock, 15 percent. And Elvis Presley, 15 percent. So Parker and his cronies got 85 percent of the stock.

Now, Elvis got a salary, too. In '74, it was $2,750. But the others also got a salary. In '74, Colonel got $27,650—almost $25,000 more than Elvis! And by '76, Colonel would get $36,000, Elvis would get $10,500, and Diskin, who was president, would get $46,448.

LAMAR FIKE: Boxcar was set up for merchandising and merchandising only. And consequently, the merchandising at times made more than Elvis did.

Colonel earned 50 percent, and Elvis earned 50 percent. Well, maybe Colonel had 56 percent. Colonel could have charged a 6 percent administration fee over and above it, for running it.

But compare that with merchandising today. The artist gets X amount of dollars up front. The merchandiser puts up all the money, and it's a 70/30 deal.

BILLY SMITH: The thing is, Colonel put all these other people in the Boxcar deal. And when he done that, Elvis come out on the short end of the stick.

MARTY LACKER: On September 2, Elvis closed his second two-week engagement at the Hilton. Sheila Ryan was his date that night. She shared Elvis's booth with Priscilla and Lisa Marie. And Elvis was still going with Linda.

Sonny says Elvis introduced Sheila to his audience as his "new girlfriend" and asked her to show off a diamond ring he gave her. Then he introduced Priscilla and said, "We get along fine. There's no trouble." But then he turned around to the band and said, "But Mike Stone ain't got no balls. Mike is a stud, my ass."

And the audience heard it. I'm sure both Sheila and Priscilla were embarrassed as hell. I'll say one thing for Sheila—she didn't pump him for cars and gifts like so many of the other girls.

BILLY SMITH: In late '74, I saw Elvis for the first time in a couple of years. And I was shocked to see the condition he was in. He was overweight, naturally—up one time to, well, about 250 pounds. And he was just drugged out. I wondered how he was going to keep going because now that he'd cut his Vegas dates in half, he was trying to increase his tours. He needed the money, and he wanted the world to know he was still great.

He had this one more tour to do in late '74, which was his fourth tour that year. After that, he took five months off. And he pretty well begged me to come back to work for him. When I made that decision to stay home and go to work in the late sixties, that changed a whole lot between us. And he knew it.

In fact, he made a promise to my wife that if I'd just come back, he wouldn't take me on the road. He wanted us to move back to Graceland and have a trailer out back. He swore to Jo that wherever I went, she would be able to go. Because he saw that to get one of us, he had to take two. And he swore on the Bible that he wasn't going to try to separate us.

When I did come back, the group of guys was pretty different. It had all these new people now, like Al Strada, and Dick Grob, and David and Ricky Stanley, and Dave Hebler, and Sam Thompson, Linda's brother. Sam didn't come to work for Elvis until '76, but he was around a lot before that.

LAMAR FIKE: Dave Hebler didn't really play that big a part. He was hired in '74 as a bodyguard. Dave would do karate exhibitions with him.

And Dick Grob was a bodyguard in the strictest sense of the word. Jerry Schilling sometimes worked security, too, though he was too afraid of hurting his looks. Jerry was kind of a peacock. The only thing he didn't do is fly on top of a roof.

MARTY LACKER: Sam Thompson was all right. He had been a Shelby County sheriff's deputy for about four years before he came to work for Elvis. And he made $350 a week, which was a lot more than some of the other guys got.

LAMAR FIKE: I'd say Sam was a Tonto Straight Arrow. Not a terrific personality. Sort of a dour person, just an average, big, tall guy.

BILLY SMITH: Sam met Elvis through Linda. He was going to law school when we first met him. He's a real nice person. Very intelligent and, like Linda, down-to-earth. He really looked up to Elvis.

We had a pretty good group, but there was changes that had to be made. Everybody was fighting to get somebody else's position. Back-stabbing, in a sense.

When I went back to work for Elvis, we sat down and had a long talk. Me, him, and my wife. 'Cause, see, I give up a damn good job at the railroad. I said, "I'm not being nasty, but you have no kind of retirement fund. All you can offer is Social Security. And I really hate to give up my benefits."

And he said, "God, if you'll just come back to me, I'll make sure that you get more than what you're making down there. And you know the benefits with me are more than they ever could be at the railroad." And he presented a beautiful package.

We also talked about some of the problems around him. I told him I wouldn't come back if things were still the same. And by that, I meant the class separation, the gap between a lot of the guys.

I said, "Elvis, you allow certain things to go on around you that force some people away. Especially your older group." Because he asked me. He said, "Why do you think so many of 'em left me? Why did you leave?" And I broke down and told him. I said, "Well, it was true about my daddy and my kids gettin' ready to go to school. But I also resented the way I was treated. I was family, but I was more an employee. And to me, you were my family, number one, not number two. I thought I ought to have some privileges."

And from there on, I stayed with him. I was trying to help him. And, of course, I liked being around him. He was not drugged-out all the time, but his moods would swing like a pendulum. And his life was exciting. 'Course at times it was total hell. And he would get irrational. But at first, when I went back with him, I think he tried not to let that show too much. Maybe because he didn't want to scare me into thinking I'd made a mistake, I don't know.

In September, when he come home from Vegas, and before he started his tour, Elvis went down to Schilling Lincoln-Mercury on Union Avenue and bought their whole stock of '74 Continental Mark IVs. He give one to Linda, and one to Red, and Marty, and Richard Davis, who didn't even work for him anymore, and one to me. He'd gained a whole lot of weight just in the three weeks since he'd been back—really just ballooned—and I'm sure that made him unhappy. And when he got unhappy, he liked to go buy cars.

Well, I didn't want another car. He'd just bought me a car a short time before. So I said I wasn't going to take this one. And he said he was going to shoot me in the leg if I didn't accept it. We were down at the Lincoln dealer's.

And I said, "Well, then you might as well pull the trigger because I don't want the son of a bitch!" And he pulled a gun out, his World War I Commemorative Colt .45 with the turquoise handle, which was one of his favorites. The grip has "E" on one side and "P" on the other. But I knew he wasn't going to do anything. So anyway, a salesman, Percy Kidd, come over, and Elvis said he wanted the car we were looking at. But Percy was going to charge Elvis full price. And that pissed me off no end. I said, "You're not going to knock anything off?" He said, "No, you're buying a Lincoln Continental."

I said, "I don't give a damn if it's a Rolls-Royce. You've got a hell of a range here that you can knock off." And he said no again, and I said, "Well, we don't want it then."

Well, Elvis bought the car anyway. He bought all those cars that afternoon. And by the time we got home, it was late—about ten P.M. The car lot was already closed. But I was still ranting and raving. I just couldn't see it. Because after we left Schilling [Motors], we went down to Madison Cadillac and Elvis bought five Cadillacs. And they'd give him $1,200 off.

So the more I thought about the guy at Schilling, the madder I got. Elvis said, "What in the hell is bothering you?" I said, "Look, I don't care who you are. It makes no difference." I said, "If I went in there and bought that car, I could have gotten a discount. There's no reason why you can't."

So Elvis called his daddy and told him the whole story, and

he said, "How come I can't get a discount?" Well, his daddy called
Percy Kidd. And Percy told Vernon, "He's already bought the cars,
now, Mr. Presley. It's not like Elvis can't afford it. After all, you're
buying a Lincoln."

Vernon said, "Well, let me put it this way, Mr. Kidd. Either
discount it or we'll have the cars back up there." Percy kind of
hemmed and hawed, and Vernon said, "It won't look good if I call
the paper tomorrow and tell them that Elvis Presley was probably
the only person in Memphis who never got a discount from
Schilling Motors."

And Percy still didn't offer to make it right. So Vernon held
his own, and we took them damn cars back at three o'clock in
the morning, and parked them, and left them. Halfway up there,
we even got a police escort. Boy, I was still fuming. I didn't get
over it that whole night.

Well, everybody had pretty much fallen in love with the car
Elvis had bought them. So Elvis told us, "I want the same color,
the same make car, with the same stuff [options] on it for each
person. And I want them here by tomorrow afternoon."

I called all over the place, but I couldn't get them. Finally, we
called Foxgate Lincoln, which is also in Memphis. And I never will
forget it. The boy's name was Dewayne Curtis. He had just been
made sales manager. He didn't have the cars, either. And he
called Mississippi, and he called Arkansas. He said, "Man, I can't
do it. But what if I give Elvis the discount, and I get the same
cars from Schilling [Motors]? Just don't tell him."

So we got the same damn cars we already had and got a
$1,400 discount. Now, ain't that something? The funny thing is,
Schilling also owned Foxgate. Elvis didn't know that, either.

MARTY LACKER: At the end of September, Sonny, who'd been
working advance with Colonel, saw Elvis in College Park,
Maryland, for the first time in about a month. Sonny was so
shaken by how he looked that he cried. He said that he and Red
and Dave Hebler went in their motel room and said a prayer.

Some of the guys in the band said they hardly recognized
Elvis. When he got out of the limousine at the show, he fell out
on his knees. People flocked around to help, and Elvis just

pushed them away. Then he went onstage and held on to the microphone stand like it was the only thing that was holding him up. He slurred his words, and he cut the show short, the way he did in Vegas. Joe Guercio, his old conductor in Vegas, was there. And he cried, too.

After that, Elvis straightened out for a few dates. Vernon took Linda to Abilene to see the show. He had Tony Brown playing piano for him in his band by that time. Tony replaced David Briggs, who'd joined Elvis's band at $3,000 a week. Linda had begun to have some interest in David. I think "interest" was all it was at that time, though. David dropped out of the band to go to Nashville, where he could earn more money.

Vernon was so upset at how Elvis looked that he had Dr. Nick come out from Memphis. I heard Elvis got all right for a few shows, and then he went to Detroit and fell back into the pattern. Pretty soon, he went to Tahoe to make up for the cancellation the year before. After that, he took five months off.

🕴 🕴 🕴

LAMAR FIKE: Everything was starting to fall apart. Sometime in September, Vernon and Dee formally separated. I guess that had been coming for some time. Vernon had cheated on her for years and with pretty much anything. When Elvis played El Paso in '72, Vernon took the Stanley brothers to a whorehouse, picked out the best hookers there, and paid for the whole party. And Dee started having more of a social life, although to what extent, I don't really know. I do know she and Vernon threatened each other with divorce a few times. Billy Stanley says Vernon told her he'd smash every bone in her face if she didn't keep her ass at home.

MARTY LACKER: What finally led to the split was the fact that Vernon had a girlfriend, Sandy Miller. He met her on the road, in Denver, I think, and took a shine to her. Pretty soon, she was writing him letters, and he moved her to Memphis and rented an apartment for her. But he had to find an excuse to have her around. He'd had a mild heart attack in '73 or '74, so they hired Sandy, who was a nurse, a thirty-three-year-old divorcée with a couple of kids. One day, Dee came home and Vernon and Sandy looked too cozy—they were decorating something together. And

Dee snooped around and found out they were having an affair. I think she even confronted Sandy about it. Anyway, Dee moved out, and Sandy moved in, and Dee eventually filed for divorce.

BILLY SMITH: In the fall, like October or November, a rumor went around that Elvis had showered Priscilla with all these gifts and asked her to marry him again. Well, I don't believe that for a second. But one night, he was talking about her with all the wives. He said, "When I was married, Priscilla wouldn't let me give good presents. She only wanted me to give small things."

And he said, "I hate her. I don't know why I married that bitch." He kept up the ranting and raving. And when he stopped for a minute, I said, "You still love her, don't you?" And he paused, and bowed his head, and all of a sudden he was just like a wall crumbling. He said, "Yeah, I do." And he looked over at me and said, "I never could fool you, could I?"

LAMAR FIKE: By the end of the year, the press was having a field day with Elvis's weight and the unevenness of his shows and records. Everybody was pointing out that he'd be forty in January.

He was more depressed about everything, and he was pretty much broke. In '77, that lawsuit with the guy in Tahoe required Elvis to produce a record of his earnings in '74. His income for '74 was $7,273,622. More than $6 million of it came from Vegas, Tahoe, and the road shows, and the rest of it was from records, publishing royalties, and motion picture rentals. But his accountants put his operating expenses at $4,295,372, and his personal expenses at more than $3 million. Goldman says Colonel took only 25 percent that year.

BILLY SMITH: In the early seventies, when Elvis played Denver, he dropped in on the cops out there. He took a liking to two of them—Captain Jerry Kennedy and Ron Pietrofeso, who was in charge of the Colorado Strike Force Against Crime.

He stayed in touch, and he went out to see them a couple of

times. And after he got a badge out of them, he conned them right out of a captain's uniform. He'd put it on and parade around, just to show he had it.

At some point—I don't remember exactly when—one of the policemen on the Denver force got killed. And Elvis attended the funeral and actually wore the uniform. He loved playing cop.

LAMAR FIKE: Oh, Lord, that was it! Going to the funeral of a cop, dressed in a cop's uniform. David Stanley went with him. The dead cop was a brother of one of Elvis's friends there, I think. He said he wore the uniform out of respect.

When they got back from Denver, I went up to the house. And Elvis came down the steps in that thing—with the hat on, even— and I didn't recognize him. I said, "Damn!" He thought that was neat.

The pathetic part about Elvis is that from a dramatic standpoint, his life was equal to Greek tragedy. There's sadness in pathos and exhilaration in pathos. But his life was almost surrealistic. I used to look at him when he was acting strange, or when he was so out of it, and think, "You couldn't dream up a situation like this if you tried." And I'd remember Elvis when he was so straight and happy-go-lucky, sitting over on Audubon Drive, playing "Name That Tune" on the piano.

CHAPTER 47

BILLY AND JO

JO SMITH: I grew up in a family that didn't show much affection. We were close, but it had always been hard for me to express my feelings until I met Billy. That was when I was thirteen or fourteen. I knew from the first time I saw him that I would be with him as long as we both lived. Mama and Daddy were always very protective of me and my two sisters, so I didn't *go* with Billy. He came to see me. My daddy was so strict that Billy and I just married real young. I was fifteen, and he was eighteen.

I was never an Elvis fan. My sister was. When Billy and I were dating, I didn't even want to meet Elvis. I think I was afraid of him. Maybe I had a premonition that this was going to change my life. Because I've known from the time I could walk that I wouldn't be just an ordinary person flipping eggs on a gas stove. I guess I was destined for what was ahead. I think about it sometimes and still wonder if it all really happened.

Being with Elvis was Billy's way of life. It was like a religion. He grew up that way. And once I married Billy, that's all I ever knew, just Elvis, Elvis, Elvis. I grew up fast, and I still don't know how I handled all the stress. I never wanted to be without Billy, but he was always leaving.

Elvis could be downright cruel when he wanted to be, and in the early years, he wanted to be. I lived by myself in Memphis, while Billy lived in California. And I was miserable. But Elvis would take him away on purpose. Because he wanted Billy. He couldn't live without him. Billy's mother said Elvis was always protective of Billy. Elvis loved him, and he trusted him. And Billy loved him.

So Elvis really didn't want Billy to get married. And I hated Elvis for that. When he took Billy on trips, it was like he was taking him *from* me.

Sometimes Elvis was like the devil to me. I pitied him, but I also feared him. I knew the power he had over everybody who worked for him, and I lived in fear that Elvis would win and take Billy away forever.

I had both my children by the time I was nineteen. I was only sixteen when I had my first son, Danny. Elvis named him: Danny Mac Smith. Yet when Danny was born, Elvis wouldn't let Billy come home. About the time I went into labor, they were coming home from L.A. by bus, and Elvis stalled as long as possible. So I had the baby alone, except for my mama and sister and grandmother. And then Elvis got as far as West Memphis [Arkansas] and stopped to wash the bus. And then they stayed overnight. Only to punish Billy for wanting to get home and be with me. I was just across the bridge—not even ten miles away—so Billy could have gotten a cab, but he didn't.

Billy was special to him, but he didn't want Billy to be special to me. And he didn't put him in the same category as Joe and Jerry because Billy was Elvis's own personal property. He didn't want him to be independent.

God, I think of all the pain and tears that we've gone through, and I have so much bitterness still. Patsy Lacker, Marty's wife, was my best friend then. Patsy used to say Elvis made her a hateful person, even to herself.

Elvis used to comment on how close Billy and I were. I think he wanted a similar lifestyle. But he wanted the closeness to be just on the wife's part.

In later years, Linda Thompson would tell Elvis what a good relationship Billy and I had and Elvis would get irritated. He'd say, "Okay, that's fine. To hell with that." Because he didn't want Linda to hold him that way.

I think Elvis made exceptions for us. I know he made exceptions for me. Even though Patsy and I were close, we didn't agree on a couple of things. I wanted to go where Billy went. I wanted to go to the movies. I wanted to ride the motorcycles. Patsy didn't. She stayed home. So for a long time it was just the guys, and then all of a sudden, it was me. Elvis let me do things with them, and he let me live in the house in L.A. in the mid-sixties. Lamar says I was one of the guys. But that didn't mean I got special privileges.

When I was pregnant with our second son, Joey, in '66, I thought I was having labor pains in the movie one night. Billy said, "I'm sorry, we can't go right now. I can't leave." And he couldn't because Elvis wouldn't let him. Thank God, they were false labor pains. I just sat there like a fool 'til they passed. But I pushed myself to the limit to spend every minute with him.

When Joey was finally born, Elvis let Billy stay back for two days. But when I got out of the hospital, Billy had to leave for L.A. the next morning. I didn't see him again for three months. Once, it was nine months before he came home. And Elvis did it for spite.

One time, Billy called and said, "We'll be home in two weeks." Then after two weeks, he called and said, "Well, we're not going to get to leave yet. It'll be about three more weeks." It turned into three more months. The only way I got through it was to pretend Billy was dead.

It was awful to be that young and lonely. Yet I didn't feel that I could ask anyone for help, so I lived by myself with our babies until I started to travel cross-country with Billy and Elvis and the group. That was only after Priscilla started to go out to L.A.

But I wised up about something. I picked up Billy's check at home. Because all the guys used to have their checks sent to Bel Air. I thought, "If I'm going to be sitting here with these two kids, I'm picking it up, and I'll send Billy what he needs." And Vernon didn't bitch about it. He probably liked it. That way, he didn't have to pay postage. He was so tight. He was terrible. He saved Coke bottles. Billy says Vernon would have used candles instead of light bulbs, if he could have.

That's another thing. I grew up poor. And then to be thrown into this . . . I was so unprepared for any of it. I was alone out there [in California in '65] in the Watts riots. The guys were in Hawaii, making a movie. I was there at the house with my son Danny—I was pregnant with Joey—and Patsy Lacker and her three children. And that was my first time in California. I'd never been anywhere before. Patsy and I depended on each other. We even had our own little lingo that only we understood.

When Elvis and everybody took that trip cross-country in '67, Patsy and I were the only wives who didn't go. Because anybody who had children, Elvis and Priscilla didn't want. So Patsy and I threw rocks at the bus. And we wished them all dead. We always thought the only relief we could get was if Elvis died. We thought, "Just die, and leave us alone."

Marty says Patsy had a nervous breakdown. Hell, I probably

had fifty. I was just too stupid to know what they were. If you get like you're a zombie, you know you're in trouble.

I begged, and pleaded, and thought of blowing my brains out many times. I remember once I was driving along the road in the country where we lived. There was an S curve, and I had a great urge to floor the gas pedal and keep going straight. I started not to care if I lived or died.

It was an awful life. I didn't hear from Billy for three or four weeks when they went to Las Vegas. So I didn't even know how they were. All I knew was what I saw in the paper. I would call there, and sometimes a girl would answer the phone. It was horrible. And especially during the Ann-Margret period. I was with Priscilla, and she was going crazy. I understood how she felt. Can you imagine being married to Elvis? Priscilla was a victim, in a way. We may not like her, but she was.

We all were, really. I've held a gun in Billy's back, with the trigger pulled, thinking about killing him. Just because he was leaving the next day. I thought, "I can't take anymore." I was seventeen, and I figured if I killed him, I wouldn't have to pretend he was dead. He would be dead, and I could move on.

In your wildest dreams, you can't imagine what that life was like. But as bad as it was, it could be just that good.

I grew up in those years. And in '74, '75, I began to see exactly what Billy saw in Elvis. I used to think, "How could you leave me and go with him?" But then Elvis had to have Billy back, and to get him, he put the charm on me. And when he did that, I understood. He promised me everything in the world.

We were living in Whitehaven. Billy's daddy had passed away. And we sold our house and moved into a town house so his mother could live with us. And Elvis wanted us to move to Graceland and live in a trailer out back. I said, "If we move up here, you have to promise me that you will not try to take Billy away. Because I swear I will never live like that again."

And he promised me that if I would just move to Graceland, Danny and Joey could have the run of the place. They would be safe inside the gates, and they could do anything they wanted. Anything. And *I* could do anything. There were no limits. He said, "Just name it—cars, jewelry, money, anything." And he said we would never have to worry. Because of his love for us, we would be well taken care of forever.

So I had to make a choice. I had sworn that if we ever got away, I would never go back. Never! And the whole time I was saying, "Never," I was sitting there taking it all in. Then Elvis got my Bible out and swore, "I'll never take Billy away again. Not even on tour. I only want to make sure he's at Graceland. I have to have him here. I can't trust anybody else." And he was crying.

I told Billy, "I've got to get all this out in the open." Because I was always afraid to say anything before. I'd try to get Billy to tell him things. But Billy wouldn't do it, either. And then, finally, we grew up. I think that's the main thing that really hit Elvis. Because Elvis always said he raised us. And in a way, he did. But all of a sudden, we had minds of our own.

I said to Elvis, "What about your daddy? And your aunt Delta?" Because I would not put my children through being around them when their behavior was bad. We're real close to our kids. I drug my babies cross-country during the movie days. Everywhere we went, they went. I was so young and naive and dumb about everything, but I fought tooth and nail to hold on to them.

So I put this question to Elvis point-blank. His exact words were, "Jo, my daddy works for me. Not the other way around. And Aunt Delta's up here by the grace of Elvis. Her ass can go at any given time." And I will say, many times Elvis asked me if they had been rude to us or hurt my feelings in any way.

The whole time he was promising me this, I was scared to death. I was thinking, "I'm really stepping into it." And then I thought, "To hell with it. I'll just join 'em." And the very next day, Elvis said, "We're going to Nashville, Billy." And I said to myself, "You dumb bitch."

BILLY SMITH: I went to Jo first and said, "He wants me to go to Nashville. He's filed a flight plan." He'd bought what they call a G-1, which is a four-engine Rolls-Royce engine prop plane, as a present for the Colonel.

Me and Jo talked it over about me going, and since it was just for the day, we said I'd go. Well, we got up in the air with the thing, and Elvis said, "Let's just go on and take it up to the Colonel [in Vegas]." I said, "Well, Colonel's probably not there. He's in California." He said, "Well, we'll fly on up there anyway." I said, "Look, I'm supposed to be back home in a little while. You just promised Jo that we weren't going to do this." And he said,

"Well, let's go on out to Palm Springs and take Colonel the plane."
I said, "That's even worse."

He said, "We'll fly back and get Jo and the kids." And by that
time, Jerry and all of 'em were begging me. They said, "Say no. If
you don't go, he won't go." So I had to put my foot down. I said, "I
can't. You all drop me back in Memphis, and go on ahead." So we
got back to Memphis, and we stayed home that particular time.

JO SMITH: That's when his whole strategy changed. He saw that
Billy wasn't as easy to manipulate as in the past. And Billy
gained Elvis's respect. But from then on, Elvis worked on me.
And God, I felt so good!

But I fell for every bit of it. Every damn bit of it! He just had a
way about him. He wanted us to go on tour with him, and the
whole time I was saying, "No, no, no," I'll be damned if I wasn't
packing my suitcase. I was saying, "No, I can't do that. I don't
like to fly." And Elvis was saying, "Nothing can happen to you if
you're with me." And I believed it. I was right on that plane, and
still saying, "No, I'm not going to do it."

And when Billy would say, "We'd better not go," I was saying,
"Why not? We need to go. He needs us to go." I couldn't believe it
was me saying that.

BILLY SMITH: I remember at one point, Elvis wanted to go to
Palm Springs. He said, "We could have the plane ready in just a
little while." And I said, "No, I can't. We got the kids, and I'm
pretty sure Jo don't want to go. I think we'll pass."

He said, "Oh, man, you'll have fun. The kids can go. We'll
take Lisa." I said, "I can't because Danny's up here [in Memphis],
and Joey's in Mississippi." Elvis said, "That's no problem. We'll fly
a helicopter down there and get him." He said, "If Jo goes, will
you go?" I said, "Yeah, but she's not going to go."

JO SMITH: Elvis called me and said, "You know, I haven't been
feeling well lately. And I really need you to go. I can't trust anybody else. We'll take the kids. Danny and Joey can play, and I'll
take Lisa. Because I need Billy to go. You don't know how bad I
need Billy to go. Will you go?" And I said, "I don't know." And he
went, "Jo, I'm really depending on you." And then he repeated it.
And I said, "Okay, we'll go."

People ask me, "Why did he need Billy so badly?" He loved him—so much so that he couldn't be away from him for even two days. I really think Elvis wanted Billy with him around the clock. I know he wanted Billy to be out of the trailer the minute he woke up. He'd call and say, "Is 'Marble Eyes' up?" That's what he called Billy because he has such big eyes. And on tour, Elvis would say, "I don't want anybody but Billy to wake me." That started as soon as Billy went back to work for him, and it went on almost until he died.

When we lived at Graceland, and my kids would go to my mother's in the summer, Elvis would have us come spend the night in Lisa's room. Or sometimes he'd just want Billy. He called me one night out at the trailer, and he said, "Jo, I want you to hear this song." He made Charlie hold the telephone, and he sang "Danny Boy." The whole song. Because he knew I loved it.

And then he started the baby talk. He said, "I don't really feel very good tonight." I said, "You don't?" Billy was over there with him. And he said, "Could Billy spend the night with me?" And I said, "Yes." He never grew up. He was so strong in so many ways. And if you were with him, you felt so safe. But in other ways, he was like a little kid.

BILLY SMITH: Elvis needed me because I was family. And at that time, I was the person closest to him. And from this period on, a lot of times it would just be me and him.

JO SMITH: Billy was always like Elvis's own personal, private companion. A brother, maybe a son. It might go deeper than that. Part of it is the connection to Gladys, I guess. Because Billy was close to her. It was like "You're my life before. You're what it was like back then." Billy was a connection to Elvis's past. He brought Billy with him from the slums. He said it a million times: "I saved you." And by having Billy around, he could relate to what that life was like. And to their parents.

Part of it also is that Elvis's father and Billy's father were in prison together. There was nothing that Elvis had to be ashamed of with him. And Billy's parents thought if he was with Elvis, he was with God.

Another thing is that Elvis could talk any way he wanted around Billy. You know how Southern and country we talk? So did Elvis when we were alone. Instead of saying something like "the only one," he'd say "onliest." You couldn't tell him and Billy apart. When he was out in public, it was different, but he had to work at it.

After we'd been back with him a little while, my feelings about Elvis changed. He called me Josephine. That's not my name. But every single time he came down the steps, he sang that Fats Domino song to me, "Hello, Josephine" ["My Girl Josephine"]. And he'd give me a big bear hug. He told me, "I'm going to make up for all the pain I put you through." But he could never make up for that. I didn't keep blaming him, but nothing could change that. And nothing could take it out of my memory. It's like I tell Billy now and then, "Nobody will ever, *ever*, make me feel that way or do that again."

It sounds like it was all bad, but it wasn't. Elvis took care of us. He protected us. We went everywhere, saw everything, and we were right with him. And he made sure my children were cared for. He used to say he'd bring me out of my shell, make me more involved. And he did.

I came to love him very much, and I tell Billy to this day, I *think* Elvis loved me. But I'm not sure. He told me he did. But I still look back and think, "He loved *Billy*. Maybe he *used* me."

BILLY SMITH: He may have loved Jo. Most of the time there's no doubt in my mind that the man loved me. But at times, I wonder if he loved anybody.

JO SMITH: You have to be realistic about him. If he wanted a lollipop, and it took ten cars, he thought nothing of it. He got what he wanted. We were suckered. But I truly loved him.

There was never any romance between us, of course. That's not how we were connected. Part of it was that he had to have a female around, somebody to do the little things that needed to be done. He just liked a woman doing things for him. In Palm Springs, where there wasn't a maid, I washed his pajamas and his sweat suits. He wanted a woman to baby him, and take up for him, and defend him.

After he accepted me, and we were close, he told me, "You're deaf, dumb, and blind when it comes to anything that I do." And I never told on him. That's why he allowed me to go on tour or anywhere they went. If Billy went, I could go. If he went to a girl's motel room, I went, too.

BILLY SMITH: Elvis tested Jo in a lot of ways. He'd been with Linda for over a year now, and Jo and Linda were close. Jo loved her. Well, one night, Elvis convinced Linda that she was sick. He said, "You need to stay home and wrap up and get your throat better. We're going to go out riding. Billy and Jo's going, and if Jo's going, it's going to be okay."

He used her, see. And right on down the highway we went, to the Admiral Benbow [Motel]. He was seeing some young lady up there. And we just waited, like we were supposed to. Now, if that had ever gotten back to Linda, Jo would have been the outcast.

JO SMITH: Larry Geller wrote a book. And in it, Larry says that Elvis asked him to keep a personal diary. That's not the Elvis Presley that I knew. I believe Elvis would have killed him if he thought he was writing something down about him. You didn't even whisper around him.

He was very strict about all kinds of things. For example, in the last half of '76, once Marty didn't come around anymore, Elvis would not let me accept a call from Patsy at Graceland. I couldn't talk to her. In our circle, we only had friends in the group. And if they left the group, and Elvis shut 'em off, you shut 'em off.

All these people say, "Oh, God, you got to *be* with *Elvis!*" Well, it wasn't their life. And it wasn't a job. It was a way of life.

I don't want to make it sound like I thought he was evil. Because no matter what, Elvis had a good heart. And he believed in God. He knew that he was beneath God, and he never put himself above Him.

BILLY SMITH: He had some faults, and the drugs caused him to be certain ways. He could reach the depths of sheer misery and take it out on everybody around him. But eventually, he was going to come back to being that good-hearted person.

JO SMITH: He wanted everybody around him to be happy. And he wanted to be happy. But he just couldn't be.

In '75, we were going out for the day with Elvis and Linda in

Memphis. Lisa was there, and she begged to go. And Elvis finally said okay. He had promised to buy her a puppy. Well, Elvis didn't want to get the puppy first because he was a bigger kid than Lisa.

So Lisa kept saying, "Daddy, when am I going to get my puppy?" And he said, "We're going to go to this place, and then we're going to go to that place, and then we'll get your puppy." We were in the Stutz Bearcat, and Lisa was sitting in the middle, between Elvis and Linda. And Billy and I were in the back. And Lisa would interrupt us and say, "But when are we going to get the puppy?"

Elvis would get perturbed and say, through sort of clenched teeth, "Lisa, Daddy is going to do what Daddy wants to do first. Don't make me shoot you." Well, Linda gave him one of these "Aren't you ashamed?" looks. And he shot back one of those pouty, little-boy looks. Then he said, "Just relax, kid. We'll get the dog. But we're doing what Daddy wants to do first because I said it first."

So, we went several places, like the dentist. Elvis wanted us to watch while the dentist worked on his teeth. And then we went by the karate school. A class was going on, so Elvis just thought he'd do a demonstration. Well, time was running out, and Lisa kept asking about her puppy. So Elvis had Linda call the pet store over at the mall in Whitehaven, and they kept it open for him.

We finally got over there, and when we went in, Elvis said, "Look at all the dogs. They're saying, 'Oh, God, that's Elvis Presley! Pick me! Pick me!' They can already see themselves at Graceland, all reared back and taking it easy." And then he started talking to the dogs. He said, "Yeah, that's right. Here I am, it's me, Elvis." It was so funny.

I saw this little chow that I loved. He was just a bundle of fur. Looked like a little lion. So Elvis picked him for himself. That was Get-Low, who ended up dying of kidney disease when he was about a year old. Elvis tried everything to save him—even flew him up to a hospital in Boston for three months. And he got Lisa a little toy poodle, and I got a Great Dane. And he got three sheepdogs for Graceland, and Laura, Sandy Miller's little girl, got a pug. God knows, we came home with about eight dogs in the car. Dogs were clawing and climbing at all angles. The whole back end was dogs. And he had four more on order.

The next day, Elvis sent everybody back up. All the guys' girl-friends had to go get a dog, to clear out the pet store. Because he thought the animals looked pitiful. He said, "We can't disappoint all those dogs."

He could be very compassionate. Once, when he came back from a tour, he gave me a $5,000 bonus. And just because my dog—the one he'd given me—died. Linda told him I was upset. And Elvis couldn't stand for anybody to be in pain. If anybody in the group had a problem, he had to solve it. And he meant it.

It's like a lot of guys made fun of his interest in religion. But he was totally sincere. It was like a search—it wasn't just a kick. Elvis liked to say, "God's the Head Honcho."

We spent hours and hours in his room, just me and Billy and Elvis and Linda. I grew up with the notion of hell, fire, and brim-stone. And I feared it. But Elvis made religion feel good. He didn't like it to be scary.

In '74, we started this chant we'd read about. We'd dim the lights. And then we'd sit in the middle of Elvis's bed and hold hands and picture our loved ones. Say somebody was going on a trip. We imagined them as they were the last time we saw them. If they were getting on an airplane, we pictured a white aura around that plane. Then we said, "Christ's love, Christ's light, and Christ's peace." To protect it. And we kept saying it, with our eyes closed. We did it every night for months. Billy and I still do the chant today. I do it every time he leaves for work or my chil-dren leave.

BILLY SMITH: During the Larry Geller period, Elvis even studied witchcraft. He was fascinated by the idea of getting away from somebody who might be wishing you evil. It's a simple thing. You say, "I deny you. You have no control over me. You're beneath me, and I deny you." But he didn't stay with it very long.

JO SMITH: He could twist 180 degrees. And a lot of people would have been offended. But there was nobody who knew the Bible better than Elvis. He didn't go to church. But there were very few Sundays when he didn't wake up and watch programs about gospel music and preaching. He liked Oris Mays, a black preacher.

He never got away from his religion, even though he said all those filthy things the guys said he did about Moses when he'd jump up on a table and preach. He had a big plaque in his room that said, "Yeah, though I walk through the valley of the shadow of death, I will fear no evil, because I'm the meanest son of a bitch in the valley." And it set right at the end of his bed. He loved it. I think J. D. Sumner, the gospel singer, got that for him.

Elvis was such a contradiction. As selfless as he was in religion, he always had to be number one in everything else. One time, everybody wanted to go bowling. So Elvis rented Bowlhaven Lanes, right down the street from Graceland, in the Whitehaven Plaza. I don't guess he'd ever been bowling. And he couldn't bowl. He guttered, and he tried to throw the ball too hard. But Billy had been on a team, and Red and Pat, and Richard, and several of the other guys had gone bowling in California. So they were pretty good. And Elvis wasn't good at all. So that's the last time we ever went bowling. If he couldn't be the best at whatever we did, we didn't do it anymore.

I think a lot of what drove Elvis was fear. Elvis couldn't fail at anything. You might as well kill him. And he didn't understand why everybody didn't love him. If there was anyone that he knew of, he went after him until he won him over.

Lisa asked him one time, "Does everybody in the world know you?" And he said, "Probably so." She said, "Do they know me?" And he said, "Yeah, they probably know you, too." He loved that.

Even if we attended an outside affair, our group always stuck together. We were Elvis's security, and we were also his security blanket. We knew his language, his feelings, his needs. And we knew his eyes. Those eyes showed it all. And they could change in a split second.

If his feelings were hurt, he expected you to hurt just like he did. And we did. We went to the movie one night, and an old woman was rude to him, and oh, God, I wanted to kill her. I just couldn't stand for him to be hurt. And she hurt him so bad.

BILLY SMITH: This was in '75. Elvis had rented the Memphian, and this woman's daughter worked the concession stand.

It had been in the paper about Elvis giving a lot of people cars, including a black woman—a total stranger—an $11,000 gold-and-white Cadillac. Elvis had gone down to the automobile agency, and a lady by the name of Minnie Person was in there looking at cars, and it was pretty obvious that she was only looking, you know. And he walked over to her and said, "Do you like that car?" She said, "I sure do." And he said, "Would you like to have it?" And she said, "Shoot, yeah, but there ain't no way." And he said, "Yeah, there is. 'Cause I just bought it for you." That was the time he bought fourteen Cadillacs at a whack.

Anyway, during the movie, Elvis got up and went to get something to drink. I don't even know what the woman was doing there, unless'n she was just waiting for her daughter to get off work. But when Elvis got up there, she said, "She hasn't been paid yet." Elvis said, "What do you mean?" She said, "The renting of the theater, and the concession stand. She hasn't been paid yet." And boy, that's one thing Elvis wanted promptness on.

He turned to Al Strada and said, "How come she hasn't been paid?" Al said, "I beg her pardon. She was paid for yesterday. And I've got her money ready for tonight. But we don't pay for the night until we leave." Elvis said, "Everything before tonight has been paid?" Al said, "Yeah." And the woman said, "Oh, no. That's not right."

JO SMITH: She said, "Y'all don't appreciate this girl. She works up here every night, and she doesn't have a way to get back and forth to work, and you give away cars to total strangers." And then she said to Elvis, "It wouldn't hurt you to do a little walking yourself, you're so fat." Well, I couldn't believe it. And I thought he was going to slap the woman.

BILLY SMITH: When she said that, the blood just drained from his face. I thought, "Ohhhh, God." And when his jaw started flexing and bulging out, I said, "Uh-oh." I knew what that meant. He was on the verge of striking. So I just eased over and barely touched him. I said, "She's not worth it."

Everybody else flew mad. But I was trying to keep my composure. Because I thought, "If I don't, he'll hit this woman, and there'll be a lawsuit." I said, "Elvis, she's nothing but a big blowoff. Look at her. She's calling you fat?" And she heard me. She said, "Well, he is fat. Not only that, he's selfish as hell." And then she said to him, "And look how you're dressed."

He lowered his head. And he said, "Yes, ma'am, I guess you're right. I am. But as far as your daughter being paid, I assure you she'll be paid." And then he said, "I'm sorry she doesn't have a way to work." By that time, I was saying, "Let's go. There's no sense in arguing."

JO SMITH: She was trying to get a car out of him. She figured he gave away all these cars, so they should have one.

BILLY SMITH: I could tell she'd really wounded him. And when we got out to the car, he broke down. He just fell across the car and cried. And he turned to me and said, "When we get home, take this car back up there and give it to her."

I said, "Like hell I will. Get someone else. I wouldn't give that bitch the time of day. If you go back and give that woman that car, it'll be the worst thing you've ever done in your life. Because she won't respect it, and she won't have no respect for you."

Jo and Linda tried to talk him out of it, too. But Elvis just cried and cried. Then he went wild. The more he thought about it, the madder he got.

JO SMITH: He was the most filthy-talking human I've ever known. There's nothing he wouldn't say. And at the same time, you'd think he'd just stepped out of church. He'd go from "Yes, sir," "No, sir," to "son of a bitch, mother . . . " And just on and on.

When we got home, he went straight upstairs and got up in the middle of his bed and walked and pranced and cussed and raved and thought of what all he could do. He called her all kinds of names, starting with "slut" and then every filthy thing you can possibly think of. And he came up with all these horrible acts to mutilate and torture her.

He was spitting, practically, and stuff was coming out of his nose because he was like a wild stallion, just snorting and stomping. And the whole time he was walking on the bed, he was looking at himself in the mirror. We were sitting on the floor and looking up at him, and all of a sudden, he stopped and said, "Goddamn, I'm a handsome son of a bitch!" And then he died laughing. We all fell out. And then it was over.

When he was strong, nobody could outdo him. Because in a real fight, I assure you, he always came out on top. But then something like this could just bring him to his knees.

Lamar says that Elvis got bored being Elvis. I will never believe that. He loved it.

For example, in '75, when Louise, Sam Thompson's wife, went into labor, Elvis went to the hospital about one A.M. He went in the back entrance and caused a minor riot. He didn't even think about how it would look, but he just barged into the labor room. He thought, "Well, they'll be glad to see me. I'm Elvis Presley."

And I guess they were. Some woman asked him to autograph her stomach! Here she was lyin' there having a baby, and she wanted her stomach autographed. Elvis said she went, "Oh, Elvis!" And some other woman was screaming in pain, and he went right over and laid his hands on her abdomen and started his psychic healing stuff. He said, "Now, now, it won't hurt anymore. You'll be fine." And she told him he was right.

He came out, and he had to explain everything. He said, "Man, she had one foot here and one foot here . . . " In the stirrups, you know. And he said he turned to the fathers sitting around and got real accusatory, in this low tone. And he said, "Someone in here is a motherfucker." Then he laughed like crazy. He said, "Well, it stands to reason. Just think about it!" I said, "Oh, my God."

His world was so unreal. We were like vampires. We only lived at night. And eventually, his reality became ours. If he'd lived, we'd probably all be dead by now.

One time, everybody was going to Palm Springs. Danny and Joey were going, and Lisa, of course, and Sandy Miller's two children, Rory and Laura.

In Palm Springs, we always stayed at the house with Elvis. Especially with the kids because Elvis wanted somebody to keep Lisa occupied.

Billy, and Elvis, and several of the guys were going to drive to Los Angeles to a motorcycle place. So Elvis asked me if I would watch Lisa while he was gone. And he gave me $500 to spend on toys. Then he gave me a pistol to take with me, just in case.

I didn't even think about it. Later I thought, "God, if I'd gotten stopped with no permit or license . . . " But I took the gun, and we went to a toy store and a 7-Eleven because Lisa loved Slurpees.

When we got back to the house, nobody was there. And the dadgum gate was locked, so we couldn't get in. I had to shove

618 ELVIS AARON PRESLEY

Danny and Joey over the wrought-iron fence and then hand Lisa and Rory and Laura over. I had this other girl, Pam Smith, with me. She was the girlfriend of one of the boys. And we finally got up to the door, and they had changed the locks. We got into the house through a window.

That was some day. There I was with all these children to look after. And one of them was Elvis Presley's daughter. As concerned as he was about somebody killing him, you'd think he would have been paranoid about somebody kidnapping Lisa. But he wasn't. I think he gave me the gun to protect myself. I was more worried about Lisa than he was.

BILLY SMITH: In the last years, after Linda, his interest in sex went way down. The drugs were starting to affect his desire, if you know what I mean. Now, he didn't come right out and say this, but a man has ways of knowing things like this.

He said he didn't try to make love too much when he was getting ready for a tour, or if he was on tour, because he had to preserve his strength. He'd say, "I need to have all my bodily fluids to heal myself."

There was nobody like him, boy. You had to tune into his world and know what to say next. If he had a date for the movies, and that was going to be it for the night, he would use a line like "We're going on tour, and I've got to save my bodily fluids." We'd be standing there, and, naturally, we weren't going to say, "What the hell are you saving 'em for? Go ahead!" Instead, we were expected to say, "Yeah, that's right. He always saves his bodily fluids before a tour."

JO SMITH: There at the end, he got stranger. We had to take care of him and cater to him like a small child. I did things I never thought I'd do. Like, when it came time for him to go to sleep, he liked to be put to bed. And he liked to be told good night—the whole send-off. Sometimes, even if he had a girl with him, Billy had to sit in there with them, which I resented. Elvis would be in bed with the girl, and he'd have Billy come in there and pull up a chair close to the bed, or sometimes sit on the foot of the bed, and talk and talk. Like she wasn't there.

BILLY SMITH: A lot of times I thought, "Well, what the hell does the girl think?" But we'd talk about whatever he wanted to talk about—maybe a movie or some book. And sometimes the girl would talk, although usually not.

JO SMITH: I'd say to Billy, "What do you do? Sit there and watch?" But later on, I had to do it, too. The girls would just lay there and smile, with their little negligees on.

BILLY SMITH: It didn't dawn on me that Jo would be upset. Not that the girls weren't pretty. It didn't make any difference. My mind is not geared that way. I was only thinking of Elvis's needs. And if you'd get up to leave the room, he'd say, "Where you going? Come on back here." I'd have to stay until he fell asleep. A lot of times, I talked baby talk to him.

JO SMITH: I had to talk baby talk to him, too. One time, I'd started into the kitchen, and Elvis called me and said, "Come in here and sit with us." I thought, "Billy's in there asleep—everybody had been up for days—and he's calling me back there to sit with 'em." So I went into his room, and he was in bed with a girl. They were sitting up.

We talked for a while, and I got ready to go. He said to me, "Tell her all about the lamps." So I started telling her about these lamps that he had bought to go in my trailer. And he was almost asleep. He nodded off. So I started to get up again, and he revived and said, "And tell her about the . . . " and named something else.

Before I got out of there, he said, "Tell her that I have to have this medication because I'm getting ready for a tour." He said, "I've got to get my rest." He had this scratch on his hand. And he held it up, and he said, "This has to heal, and I need all my bodily fluids for it to get better."

I said, "That's exactly right." Because I thought I could leave. But every time he'd almost go to sleep, and I'd get up and start to go out, he'd grab me and say, "Wait! Tell her about the . . . " So I told about, and told about, and told about. Finally, he fell asleep.

There were times when Elvis had me screen the girls for him. This was at Graceland. George Klein would send a girl up to the house, and she'd wait downstairs in the living room. Elvis would have me go down and check her out, like she was a car or something.

He'd say, "You know if I'd like her or not. If her fingernails are dirty, or if her toenails are dirty, she's a definite out." So I would go down and meet her.

I didn't ever ask any of them to take off their shoes, but in the summertime they wore sandals a lot. So I'd look at 'em, and I'd go back upstairs and say, "She's this, that, and the other." And he'd say, "Well, how do you think she'd . . . " I'd say, "I think she's real nice. I think you'd like her."

So he'd say, "Well, go down. And in about ten minutes, send her up." So I'd go in and talk. I'd say, "How you doing?" And then in a few minutes, I'd say, "Step this way." Like, "Here we go. The spider's upstairs." And then I'd have to sit because he wouldn't want to be alone. These girls had to think it was nutty.

When we were in Vegas, he would give me money to go down to the shops in the hotel and buy the girls outfits. Why he didn't give the money to them, I don't know. But he would give me money and say, "Go down and make sure they buy something. Let 'em try on something out of the ordinary—something really unusual that would look good with what I wear."

So we'd go down and buy the whole works. And always white underclothes. Always. He insisted on that. Except for Linda. She could wear whatever she wanted. I remember she had a peach-color outfit, and when she wore it, he would bite at her. He would be talking, and as she passed by, he'd go, "And so and so . . . gnaw-gnaw-gnaw-hhhhnnnnhhhhh." Like a shark or something.

At the end, he would have given me anything. But I could never ask for material things. Because I'd fallen right into what Billy was into. And then the roles were reversed. Billy saw what I went through all the years. We both learned a good lesson.

BILLY SMITH: Jo and me have always been close. But we're closer from all we've been through together. Like right now, I know if something's bothering her and basically what it is. It can be something she's rehashed—thinking about Elvis or her daddy passing away. A lot of times, I even know what she's going to say. And sometimes I'll come out with it, and she does me the same way. And with Elvis, sometimes I knew what he wanted. I'd go on and do it before he even said it. But he fooled me sometimes, and I couldn't do nothing about what happened.

JO SMITH: In '75 or '76, we were getting ready to go to the movie one night. Elvis had this new Italian sports car that only two people could ride in, this yellow Pantera [Didamasa Pantera 265]. He'd left it in the drive in front of Graceland. And Billy and I were parked right behind him in this new Lincoln that he had given us.

Billy always said, "You'd better keep the keys in the cars because you never know which one he's going to want." Elvis wanted the keys left in the cars at all times, so he could go out and leave whenever he wanted. But Vernon couldn't stand it if there were keys in the cars. Probably, he just didn't want any of the guys driving them. So Vernon had Delta start taking the keys out of the cars. And Elvis would pitch a fit.

This particular night, they didn't think he'd want to go in the Pantera. So Delta had put the keys up. I think he overheard them talking about it because he would do something like this on purpose. He was ornery like that. And he and Linda got ready to leave, and he came down the steps and realized that he didn't have the keys to the Pantera, so he went straight to it.

They looked and looked, but they couldn't find the keys. Finally, they had to wake Delta up. It was about one o'clock in the morning, and he just said, "Get her up. I want my keys."

Well, she couldn't find the keys, either. And she was looking and looking because she had this big keyboard hung in the closet.

Finally, Elvis got real mad, and he went out to the Pantera and he pulled his gun. Billy followed him out, and he said, "Wait, wait, don't shoot!" And Elvis said, "Why not?" Billy said, "'Cause I'm parked right behind you! The bullet might ricochet and hit my new car!" And Elvis said, "To hell with you!"

I was already sitting in the Lincoln, and when I saw Elvis pull that gun, I just laid down flat in the seat. He could have killed me. Or the bullet could have bounced back and hit him. And Billy was still yelling, "Wait! Let me move my car!" And Elvis just, Bam! Bam! Shot that Pantera up. And then he opened the door and shot all inside it. He said he was trying to shoot the ignition. Then he ran out of bullets, and he and Linda went and got in another car and went to the movie like nothing ever happened.

BILLY SMITH: It could be pure pleasure or total disaster. But on the whole, I think all those experiences made us better people.

JO SMITH: Right now, I'd give anything if Elvis were here. I wish that we could go back to being twenty and have it all over again. And have it normal. When I say that, Billy always says, "Elvis couldn't have been who he was if he'd been normal." And I guess he's right. Elvis could never change.

You know, I loved him more than anything. And it broke my heart when he died. But if I hadn't known him, my life would be so different today. I don't think I would be so paranoid. I can't even watch a movie where somebody leaves. If I know ahead of time that they're going to leave, even for overnight, I won't watch it. I hate it. Anything like that just throws me into a state. It's more than abandonment. It's like death.

I get panic attacks sometimes. I still have dreams that Billy and the guys are getting packed to leave with Elvis. I wake up sobbing. It's crazy, but I have all these phobias. I see couples where one of them goes away for maybe just a night. And I think, "How can you waste time apart? You're soulmates." At least, Billy and I are. We do just about everything together.

BILLY SMITH: We spent a lot of time apart. And what time we've got left, we try to spend together. Because we have that fear that if it can happen to Elvis Presley, hell, it can happen to us, maybe tomorrow. We cling to one another.

JO SMITH: I feel like Billy and I are the same person. I regret a lot of things, though. Because when Billy would come home, I wanted all his time. He spent as much time as he could with the kids. But it wasn't very much. Then his brother died. And I felt guilty about that. And I feel guilty that he didn't get to spend as much time with his daddy and mother.

I look back at this experience, and I don't know how we didn't go the easy way and just pill out. For relief. We did some. But not like some of the others. And it didn't solve anything. But I don't blame Elvis so much anymore. The bottom line is, we were with Elvis because we wanted to be.

CHAPTER 48

"AN EMOTIONALLY UNSTABLE BOY"

LAMAR FIKE: Early in January of '75, Elvis canceled his Vegas engagement for later in the month. He was going to work on his weight and try to feel better. Really, he just didn't want to be there.

Just when Elvis was trying to figure out how to quit Vegas altogether, the Hilton was trying to figure out how to get him to play to more people. Barron Hilton came up with the idea of building that big room [the Hilton Center] off to the side of the son-of-a-bitchin' hotel. That was so Elvis could do one show a night and play to four thousand or five thousand people.

When he canceled in January, the hotel released a statement that the cancellation was just a postponement until March. And they announced their plans to build the big showroom.

Shit, that showroom wasn't finished until after Elvis died. He never played it. They had to turn it into a convention center.

BILLY SMITH: At the end of January, Linda woke up real early in the morning and heard Elvis breathing kind of strange. He'd overdosed, and he was having respiratory problems.

I think that was a pretty close call. When they brought him down to the fire department ambulance, Patsy Presley was there, and she said he looked like he was dead.

Dr. Nick took him to Baptist [Hospital], and he stayed more than two weeks. They said it was for a general medical workup, but he was there to be detoxified. While he was in there, they did a biopsy on his liver. It was enlarged, and somewhat fatty, because of the drug abuse. The medical term for it is "hepatomegaly," I think.

The shame of this, see, is that pretty much each time he went in the hospital, people would still smuggle [drugs] in to him. In '75, I stayed with him some. And one of the guys was on duty at all times, and Linda stayed the whole time. But he still got stuff. I'm pretty sure he got some from the nurses. Elvis was a very persuasive person. But if he didn't get the stuff in the hospital, he'd go right back to taking drugs the minute he got out.

None of these attempts to detox really worked. This one in '75 was the longest "cure," so to speak. Boy, he lost weight, and he looked good. And he started doing some tremendous shows.

LAMAR FIKE: People blamed us for him being like he was. But you can't keep me from eating, and you can't stop a drunk from drinking. Unless he wants to do it himself.

MARTY LACKER: Linda mentioned that Elvis would ask for tranquilizers or sleeping pills, and he would save them up. They were supposed to be mild, but when you save them up and take them all at once, you get a buzz.

I went to see him in the hospital. He had a suite at the end of the hall. I walked in, and he was lying there, and he was coherent, and he looked pretty good. He was in great spirits. At one point, he shifted in the bed, and the top sheet sort of tilted up on an angle, and I could see under the bed. There were all these hoses coming out. It scared the hell out of me. It was like they had him punctured everywhere, and all this gook was just draining out of his body.

When he'd come back out on the road, Colonel would send him back to the same old shitty-ass towns. Over and over and over. I'm sure Elvis thought, "I'm supposed to be the most famous guy the entertainment business ever saw. And there ain't nothing new out here for me to do."

BILLY SMITH: On February 5, when Elvis was still in the hospital, Vernon had a major heart attack. They took him to Baptist, too. And Elvis went to see him. They got to talking, and Vernon made Elvis feel bad. He said, "This is all your fault. I can thank you for this." And Vernon blamed him for Aunt Gladys, too.

He said, "You worried your mama right into the grave." Elvis broke down and cried. It about killed him.

MARTY LACKER: The middle to the end of '75, Elvis started getting really bad. He was popping more than the prescribed amount of sleeping pills.

After Elvis died, and the state of Tennessee went after Nichopoulos, they got a year-by-year breakdown of the prescriptions Nick had written for him. In '75, Nick prescribed 1,296 amphetamines, 1,891 sedatives, and 910 narcotics. In '76, it was 2,372 amphetamines, 2,680 sedatives, and 1,059 narcotics. And in '77, until the day Elvis died on August 16, he prescribed 1,790 amphetamines, 4,996 sedatives, and 2,019 narcotics.

And you've got to remember—this is what Elvis was getting from Dr. Nick alone. He had all those other sources, too.

LAMAR FIKE: That March, Elvis got two offers to play England. One was for a million pounds, and the other was for two million pounds. And a pound was worth an average of $2.20 back then. When Colonel turned the first offer down, he said the ticket prices were too high. And then on the second one, which was to appear at Wembley Stadium, Colonel said Elvis didn't like to play ballparks.

God, the times Elvis got cranked up to go over there and then have it fall through. One time, we thought we were going to go over to Saudi Arabia because Adnan and Esam Khashoggi wanted to make a deal with Elvis. Esam came backstage. And they wanted Elvis to do the thing that Frank Sinatra eventually did at the pyramids, at Gaza. And Khashoggi was going to pay Elvis a truckload. I forget what it was, but the amount of money was unbelievable! And all of a sudden, the Colonel stopped the deal.

BILLY SMITH: The best I remember, Colonel presented the Khashoggis with a number, which he didn't think they'd meet. But Colonel forgot who he was dealing with. And they met his price. Which I believe was $5 million.

The Colonel said, "Well, I'll get back with you." And he

thought, "They didn't even hesitate. Now what am I going to do?" So he jumped the price from $5 million to $10 million. And you know something? They met that, too!

LAMAR FIKE: Elvis came out to the bus, and he said, "Lamar, it's this now." And he held up ten fingers. And he said, "You'll all get a lot of stuff out of this."

BILLY SMITH: Elvis was really worked up. And then, bang! It just slapped him in the face. I never did find out how Colonel crawfished out of that one. You could almost see the blood drain out of Elvis's face when the deal fell through.

LAMAR FIKE: In April, Elvis bought a Delta Airlines Convair 880 jet. That's the one he later named the *Lisa Marie*. At the time, Elvis was the only entertainer who owned his own private four-engine jet.

He bought it out of Florida for $250,000. And then he spent close to $1 million customizing it. It had a front lounge, where we all hung out, a conference room, and a big bedroom in the back. He put a queen-size bed in there, with a seat belt on it. And gold washbasins. And closed-circuit TV, a sky phone, and an intercom.

It wasn't ready until November. So he bought a bunch of airplanes in between. Like the Lockheed JetStar, which was a little smaller. You know the name of the pilot on the JetStar? Milo High. Believe it or not.

Elvis ended up buying about eight planes in all, four in one day. He had airplanes out the ass.

The money he spent! He had eight pilots and copilots on the payroll at one time! And everything was in Elvis's name, not in a corporate name. That's why Vernon had a heart attack! Hell, the fuel costs were staggering.

One time, we had the [Convair] 880, and we set down in El Paso because we'd get fuel cheaper there. And Joe went to pay for it, and he discovered he didn't have a thing. No cards, nothing.

Elvis called me back in the room, and he said, "Do you have an Exxon credit card?" I said, "Yeah." He said, "Give it to [the pilot] Elwood for the fuel." It was right at $5,000. They brought me that slip to sign, and I said, "Good God Almighty! I don't know if this will even go through!"

I signed the bill, and we started taxiing, and I got on that phone. I was practically rotating. I called Vernon and said, "I have just used my credit card to fill this damn thing up, and I don't know if it's going to clear. Can you help me?"

Vernon said, "I'll meet you at the airport." Not only did Vernon meet me, but two executives from Exxon were with him to make sure they got paid.

BILLY SMITH: When it come to those airplanes, Elvis was like a kid with new toys. The *Lisa Marie* used to really thrill him. He'd say, "Do you believe anything this pretty can actually fly?"

LAMAR FIKE: I don't know how pretty it was, but eventually the estate made money on it. They charge admission to go through it now.

When he was buying all those damn planes, Elvis was frequently broke. He had a lot of money going out and, when he wouldn't work for three or four months, very little coming in. And with his lifestyle, boy, you had to pump money through the well.

BILLY SMITH: In '75, Elvis mortgaged Graceland to meet his payroll. But he wasn't really broke. He always had $1 million in the bank. And he wouldn't go below that because he had one thing in mind: "I always want to be a millionaire." So he mortgaged Graceland to keep his money in the bank.

LAMAR FIKE: Elvis never ever missed paying the guys on time, every week.

Let me get my figures right. It cost $40,000 a month to run Graceland. With the payroll, a little over $100,000 a month. My God! He had twenty people working on the grounds alone at Graceland. That place was a monster to maintain.

BILLY SMITH: Elvis thought, "Once the tour is over, I'll pay that back." And he did. He hated the grind of being at a certain place at a certain time, but he enjoyed the shows. Sometimes they were just mediocre. And other times, they were good. It depended on how he felt that day. But he had to be out there on the road, and

I believe wholeheartedly that the reason was financial in the later years.

MARTY LACKER: As much as Elvis grossed, he didn't make much money. Because Colonel always lowballed the tickets. He wanted the arenas sold out.

BILLY SMITH: You know one other reason Elvis liked to go on the road? The tours were a way to get drugs. Because Dr. Nick, and sometimes Dr. Ghanem, went with him. Elvis would say, "I've got to have this, man. I've got to be up." And it was easier to play that scene on tour than when he was just home relaxing.

That's why Elvis took a lot of quick trips to Palm Springs or Las Vegas. Somewhere around this time, Elvis took out a life insurance policy, and the company required a urine test. Well, he just got somebody else to pee in a bottle.

MARTY LACKER: At the end of April, Elvis went on his first tour of the year. The reviews were full of comments about how over-weight and tired he looked. He said, "I keep hearing that shit about being fat and forty." And he wanted to do something about it. He couldn't take seventy-five pounds off overnight, but he could do something about looking tired. So he scheduled a face-lift for June, to take the bags from his eyes and to tighten his facial tone.

He showed it to me after he came home. He was in bed, and I was standing by the side of it. He tilted his face up, and he said, "Do you see anything different?"

I looked around his room, and I said, "No, everything looks the same." He said, "No, no," and he held his face up even higher and put his fingers up around his eyes and his cheekbones, like he was pointing things out. He said, "Now do you see any difference?"

I said, "Elvis, you look the same to me." And that's when he told me he had plastic surgery. Dr. Asghar Koleyni did it.

LAMAR FIKE: It was a minilift. Any performer worth his salt will stretch his skin to about a B-flat to look good. It's like he said, "As long as there's doctors out there, I'll still look a certain way."

BILLY SMITH: Me and Jo went to the hospital with him. They blocked off the second floor, so there weren't any other patients there. We put aluminum foil on the window for him, and we took a room across the hall. Stayed up there with him the whole time.

He needed a face-lift like he needed a new rear end. I tried to tell him. But, of course, he didn't listen. Even Dr. Koleyni told him, "You don't need it. It's hard to improve on a face that's almost perfect." And Elvis said, "Well, I want it done. I want this excess skin taken out of my eyelids." So he had the lids pulled up somewhat and some of the fatty tissue taken out of the jowls in his cheeks and his throat.

I could have kicked his rear. He never looked the same again. To me, it ruined his eyes. He always had those sleepy, sexy eyes. And they took the droop out. The droop was part of his mystique. Gladys had it. And that's how Lisa looks.

He hated that he was getting older. His hair was thinning somewhat. And if he hadn't dyed it, he would have been real gray. His beard was a giveaway. If he'd let his beard grow out, it would have been damn near white. He was a very vain person. Elvis would think, "Give me some hair color, man. As long as I've got hair color, I'm in good shape."

MARTY LACKER: It wasn't too long after he had this plastic surgery that Elvis started talking about possibly switching identities with someone. He wanted to get out from under it all. So it had to be someone who was about to die. Because if the person lived, he would have been found out immediately.

Whoever he would have gotten to take his place had to have plastic surgery to at least come close to looking like him. That way, even his father, or one of the guys, could look down in the coffin and see the [surgery] marks and be satisfied it was Elvis. He already had the surgeon picked out.

BILLY SMITH: We were talking and carrying on one day. He was in a good mood, one of his joke-pulling moods. And he said, "You know something? At the time I had my plastic surgery, another guy was there having plastic surgery, too." I wasn't following him. I said, "Who's that?"

He said, "Well, this guy was having plastic surgery to look like me." I tried to pin him down who it was, and he came up with some crazy name. I knew dang well he was making it up. And then he said, "I think I'm going to swap places with him. He can have this shit, and I'll just take the everyday, normal life."

Well, I knew better. That right there give it away. But anyway, a minute later, he said, "It could be done. They can do wonders with plastic surgery now. They could make *him* look just like *me*."

I said, "Elvis, where would you go? There would be two Elvis Presleys. People would think you're the traveling-est person that ever was." And Elvis said, "Oh, I'd get secluded somewhere. They wouldn't know where I was."

Well, a few days later, Elvis had somebody call me in the wee hours of the morning. The guy told me he was terminally ill, and for the right amount, he was going to swap places with Elvis."

I asked where he was from. He said, "Up north." I said, "Why would you want to do this? You got a family?" He said, "Yeah, I've got a family. I'd do it to get the money for them."

I didn't believe any of it. So I said, "Let me ask you this. How is Elvis going to get away from here?" He said, "Oh, he's met this woman." I said, "He has? Who is she?" He said, "Maria." I said, "Is that right? Who in the hell is Maria? I don't know her." He said, "And you ain't going to know her."

After a few minutes more, I got bored with it. And I think he did, too. I said, "Well, maybe you're on the level, but I think I'll ask Elvis." So I went over to the house, and Elvis carried it on right on down the line. He said, "Man, I'm telling you now, that's what I want to do. I'm tired of living like this." Then he said, "Mind you, though, I'm going to take most of my money with me."

I said, "In other words, you're not going to give up a lot!" And he said, "Well, I *am* giving up a lot. I'm giving up being Elvis Presley."

A little later, he wanted to go somewhere, so we got in the car, and we went out the gate. And he went out so quick, not a damn soul recognized him. We went up to the Whitehaven Plaza, which is about a quarter of a mile up the road, and he said, "Let's go back. I forgot something. Go back through the gate." He couldn't stand it, see. And when he went back in, he waved at everybody. To make sure they knew it was him. I said, "You really want to get away from it all, don't you?" He said, "Aw, shut up, you son of a bitch!" He never brought it up thereafter. And I have no idea who called me.

LAMAR FIKE: You know, Elvis thought a pill cured everything. Dr. Nick says he got psychologically hooked on some kind of Swedish herb he took to cleanse the body so he wouldn't have to take a bath. What I remember best is some kind of chlorophyll pill.

He showed it to me one time. I said, "What the fuck is this?" He told me, "You take a couple of these three times a day, and you never have to take a bath. It cleans your whole body."

I said, "Elvis, there ain't such a damn pill. What happens, you take it, and you break out in lather and wash yourself off? What the hell are you talking about?" He got so goddamn mad. But it made no sense. He said, "You ought to try it." I said, "Shit, no."

BILLY SMITH: They're called Nullo deodorant tablets. A little company down in Jacksonville [Florida] still makes 'em. Linda introduced him to them, and he pursued it thereafter. Linda took them to keep down menstrual odor. But Elvis took 'em because he thought they'd take care of his body odor. Actually, the box says they're for "Control of body odors including odor due to problems of bowel control and colostomy."

They're sold over the counter, but Linda used to fly to New York to get them. They look like candy pills, real dark green. And you take 'em by mouth. Elvis thought they'd kill any type of body odor, from bad breath to butt. Even underarm. Hell, he ordered bottles of 'em. And that was his bath.

I'd say Elvis got bad about bathing about '74 on. You never smelled him—never—until the later years.

MARTY LACKER: When Elvis went out on his third tour of '75, it was pretty obvious he was getting even more erratic. On July 20, in Norfolk, Virginia, he started one of those long, rambling monologues. He introduced the Sweet Inspirations, who are black. He started out by saying he could feel all 11,000 members of the audience breathing on him. Then he said he smelled green peppers and onions, and he said, "The Sweet Inspirations' breath smells like they've been eating catfish."

Well, they took it as a racist put-down. And they were hurt by it. And he made a disparaging remark about [high soprano singer] Kathy Westmoreland. On a couple of shows, he'd said, "She doesn't care where she gets her fun." Or, "She'll take affection from anybody, anytime, anyplace. In fact, she gets it from the whole band." Which was a rough thing to say, because Elvis had dated Kathy a little. Well, she'd told Joe to ask Elvis to stop saying that because she said she was getting ugly phone calls. So this night, Elvis said, "This is Kathy Westmoreland. She's our soprano singer who doesn't like the way I introduce her. If she doesn't like it, she can get the hell off the stage." And the audience went silent.

Well, two of the Sweet Inspirations started to cry. And they left the stage. Kathy did, too. So Elvis walked over and gave a ring to [the Sweet Inspirations'] Myrna Smith. She happened to be going with Jerry Schilling, who'd gotten divorced from his Hawaiian wife, Sandy. I guess Elvis gave Myrna the ring for staying onstage.

This was the same date he started giving away rings to the audience. He had two shows in Norfolk. The first show, he had a pretty sedate crowd. So he told Lowell Hays, the Memphis jeweler, to bring in about $30,000 worth of rings. And this wasn't costume jewelry—it was real diamonds and precious stones. Well, the audience went nuts, grabbing for this stuff. And Elvis got what he wanted—a screaming crowd. He later apologized to everybody onstage and gave them all rings. But he was clearly more peculiar than he had been.

LAMAR FIKE: Giving away rings onstage meant nothing to Elvis. He was always giving J. D. Sumner big diamond rings. J.D. had what he called his "Elvis Presley hand." Every ring on it came from Elvis. About $100,000 worth.

MARTY LACKER: Two days after the Norfolk show, Elvis performed in Asheville, North Carolina. In the middle of the act, Elvis took a $40,000 ring off his finger and gave it to J.D. He was just wild that night. Before the show, they were at the Rodeway Inn, and Elvis went to put his arm around his father, and his pistol went off.

Well, this time the bullet ricocheted, and it whizzed past Vernon's head and hit a chair and went on to hit Dr. Nick in the chest, just under his heart. Luckily, it was pretty well spent. It gave him a little burn, and that was it.

LAMAR FIKE: I never heard that until recently, and I thought it was bullshit. But apparently it's true. I'd tell Elvis to try again. He should have shot the son of a bitch between the eyes.

BILLY SMITH: In the seventies, he had a lot more periods of violence. I'm talking about when he wasn't drugged. Violence out of frustration. It's funny . . . at one point in '75, there was a little story in the paper that said "an emotionally unstable boy" got into Graceland and shot up one of the rooms. Well, you know who that was.

He was angered about something that was taken out of the show tour. And the more he talked about it, the madder he got. He reached over and grabbed a .45, and he started shooting, just willy-nilly.

I said, "Elvis, you'll destroy the house!" He said, "I don't give a fuck! I'll build another one!"

He shot the commode one time. I laughed 'til I couldn't see straight. It was the funniest damn thing I have ever seen. I got a call out at the trailer. It was pretty late at night. Whoever it was said, "You need to come over here. Elvis is mad and shooting his gun off." I said, "All right. I'll be out there in just a minute."

Well, water was just pouring off the chandelier in the entry hall. I said, "God Almighty, damn! What in the hell has he done now?" It was beautiful—water just glistening off that glass and off the lights, too.

I went on upstairs, and I went in his room, and I said, "What in the world has happened?" He said, "I need a new goddamn commode." I said, "What do you mean?" He said, "I never did like that black motherfucker." His toilet was black, see. The lever would stick, and the commode would run. He had told 'em several times to get it fixed, and they didn't do it. And the water kept running. And it drove him crazy. Anyway, that sucker was all to pieces, and water was still going everywhere.

He shot the ice maker in Lisa's room one time because it kept making noise when he was trying to talk. Jo and me were in there, and he was telling a story, and every time he'd get to the punch line, the ice maker would make this big "Rrrrrhhhh" and drop the ice. And he got pissed about it, 'til he just pulled a gun and said, "One more time, and I'm shootin' it." And it did it. Well, he shot the hell out of it. With a .45! That bullet could have went anywhere.

LAMAR FIKE: He'd shoot up all kinds of shit. But the television remained his favorite target. Elvis was connected to the outside world through the TV. He loved to watch the news.

We had quite a collection of TVs. We'd come back off a trip with eight or nine sets. Joe would go to the desk and tell them that Elvis liked the TV and wanted to buy it. Well, shoot, he'd already blown it up. So Joe would buy it, and we'd put it in the cargo hold of the airplane, and bring it back and throw it away. If we'd left it there, it would have been in the news the next day.

BILLY SMITH: It's kind of amazing that nobody ever saw us carrying out a busted TV. But we'd wrap a sheet or a bedspread around it so they wouldn't know what it was. And nobody ever asked. Elvis had better security than the president.

That's why we always did a general inspection on the road. Joe would say, "Anything out of the ordinary, clean it up. Whatever needs to be done." He might drop a pill on the floor. Well, these housekeeping people know who stayed in the room. You had to be real careful with stuff like that.

If it was a sheet, and he had messed it up, we took it with us. We just paid for the sheets. That way, the hotel didn't know what happened to them. One of the fans could have come in afterwards and got 'em. You never knew. But after we left those hypodermic needles, we didn't want anything else embarrassing to happen.

LAMAR FIKE: This guy was so pampered. He certainly had the best drugs, I'll tell you that. The grass, the acid, and whatever else he got into later on was always primo.

I've said this before, but I want to say it again. I know Marty and Billy see this differently. Marty thinks he had no alternative to turn to, nothing new to do, so he just continued to take stuff to escape. I think Elvis did mega amounts of stuff not so much to get away from things, but because he liked to get fucked up. He loved it! It wasn't because "Well, I've got these burdens." It was nothing that sophisticated. He just liked to get fucked up!

None of this stuff was really to escape any kind of reality. Shit, there was no reality in the first place, so how can you escape it? Where was there reality in that group? Jesus Christ! We're not talking about a sword of Damocles hanging over Elvis's head all the time. He just said, "Shit, I liked the way that made me feel. Let me do it again."

About '75, when he got into really high-grade dope, he entered his third and final stage of drug use. That was cocaine, Dilaudid, and morphine, in addition to the Demerol and codeine he was already doing. That's when it really became very, very serious.

With the cocaine, we did regular dust, Peruvian gold flake. Elvis wasn't all that crazy about it.

BILLY SMITH: I think Elvis only tried the powder cocaine a couple of times. We finally cut that supply off. Somebody—it might have been Sonny—talked to Elvis and said, "Look, you're talking about street drugs now." And I think he finally convinced him.

LAMAR FIKE: After that, maybe late '76, Elvis got into liquid cocaine. Ghanem prescribed it for him to use with sleeping pills and amphetamines. Ghanem would always say it was Lidocaine, which is a local anesthetic. Elvis wouldn't shoot it. He'd put that on cotton swabs and stick it up his nose.

I used to do it, too. We'd take square strips of cotton—about three or four inches long—and soak 'em in that liquid cocaine and stuff 'em up our nostrils. Man, you'd stay high forever. If you'd take a line of coke, you'd stay up for twelve, fifteen, twenty,

twenty-five minutes. If you stuck that liquid cocaine in your nose, you'd stay high for three or four hours.

$$\text{♣ ♣ ♣}$$

MARTY LACKER: In August, Ricky Stanley got arrested for trying to get Demerol from the Methodist Hospital pharmacy with a forged prescription. Elvis bailed him out of the Shelby County jail that night, and he got the charges reduced to malicious mischief, with a fine of fifty bucks and a six-month suspended sentence.

You know, at some point, Linda got Ricky fired. Ricky smarted off and said something bad about her, and she overheard him and told Elvis. But he hired him back again later. Elvis would have been better off if he hadn't. Of all the Stanleys, Ricky, in particular, was really into drugs, and I mean heavy street drugs—cocaine, hallucinogenics, in addition to marijuana and downers. And he washed it all down with tequila and bourbon. Ricky was an alcoholic by the age of nineteen. Billy Smith says all three of the Stanleys—Ricky, David, and Billy—drank quite a bit. I do know that Ricky had been busted two or three times, and by the time Elvis died, it was up to five.

Elvis never referred to the Stanleys as anything but "Dee's kids." When they were younger it was "Dee's brats." Since Elvis died, they keep referring to him as "brother." They never did that while Elvis was alive. He probably would have slapped the hell out of them. He hired a couple of them to appease his father while he was still living with Dee.

Towards the end, the Stanleys were there for three reasons: One, to procure drugs for him. Two, they would listen to him. Because most of us got tired of hearing the same stories over and over again. And three, Elvis would preach to them and think he was teaching them stuff.

LAMAR FIKE: Oh, listen. Ricky was "The Whitehaven Raven." He had all kinds of script [prescriptions]. He was always going down and getting stuff. But a lot of that was Elvis's stuff. Ricky just took the fall.

We were in Vegas one time, and I got a call. Whoever it was said, "Ricky's been arrested for presenting a falsified prescription." Ricky was getting it for Elvis, and he got caught. I turned around to Elvis and said, "What's this about?" And Elvis said, "Well, he shouldn't have been doing it." I said, "Oh, okay." It was like "If the trapdoor's open, and you fall, adios and adieu, motherfucker."

That particular arrest was written up in the newspaper. It was a bad situation. Elvis called up one of his cop pals and got Ricky off. But Ricky had frequent run-ins with the law. He just stayed screwed up. Ricky was really a heroin addict. And I think you have to blame Elvis for that. He exposed him to all that stuff. Of course, at the same time, Elvis was hoping all three of the Stanley boys would become narcs.

BILLY SMITH: Ricky and David both could have been drug addicts. But then a lot of times when we were on tour, they were straitlaced. Because I didn't allow drugs, to start with. Not that I'm a saint, but I had been down that road, and I knew how easy it was to get on that shit.

One time, I made Ricky flush his marijuana down the commode. He was hollering, "That's my Colombian gold!" I said, "I don't give a damn what it is! Either you can go back to Memphis without a job or you can pour it in the toilet here and flush it." And his sleeping pills, too. It liked to killed him.

MARTY LACKER: When Ricky started bringing cocaine to Elvis in Vegas, the sparks started flying. He got it from some of the guys in the vocal group. I think they got it from some pusher in Nashville. And Red and Sonny found out about it, and they told Dave Hebler. Dave went to Ricky and said, "If you bring it to Elvis one more time, I'm going to break both your fuckin' legs." And Red went in and said the same thing to the guys in the vocal group. So what did Ricky do? He went back and told Elvis.

The next day, Red tried to talk to Elvis about trying to get off pills. This was up in the suite. Red was sitting up at the bar. Elvis was at the bar, too, and somehow the conversation got on that. Red said, "Elvis, this stuff is really bad for you. I wish you'd stop doing it and go get cured. I can tell it's really getting to you."

Elvis sat there, and he said, "Yeah, yeah. I know what you're saying. But don't worry about it." He was real calm. Well, a few minutes later, Elvis went to bed. And brooded about it all night long.

When he got up the next afternoon, Elvis came out of that

room screaming. He just went nuts. If I'm not mistaken, he pulled an AK–47 [automatic weapon] on Red and threatened to shoot him. Sonny was there, too, standing right next to him. Elvis screamed, "Goddamn, Red, mind your own fuckin' business! Telling me how to run my life!" Everybody always says, "If you guys really cared about him, you could have done something about him." These people have no idea what went on. They have no idea of how Elvis was.

BILLY SMITH: You had to pick and choose your times. Like a couple of occasions, I said to Elvis, "Why do you need so much? Why don't you let up on it some and see if you don't feel better? Or maybe quit taking this one medication altogether? Maybe you don't need as much." And Elvis said the same thing each time: "You don't know what all is wrong with me. I need it, man. I know what I'm doing." I later found out that's every addict's excuse. But at the time, who was I to say that he didn't need it?

$$ \text{辰} \quad \text{辰} \quad \text{辰} $$

MARTY LACKER: One night in '75, he was sitting in the middle of the bed, higher than a kite. He had all these karate certificates in front of him from the Kang Rhee Institute [of Self Defense], and they were all phony. He had them for all three of the Stanleys, and some for the other young guys. They were up in the room, too. None of them earned them.

That kind of stuff never did impress me, so sometimes I'd just antagonize the hell out of him. Well, this was not a good time.

He had a gold-plated .45, which is in the Trophy Room at Graceland now. And he was so out of it that he was patting these certificates and talking to these guys, just slurring his words. He said, "Now, I want you to put these in frames. I got these special for you."

Elvis looked at me, and he was so drugged that he was weaving. He said, "I'm going to get you one of these, too." I said, "Elvis, that don't mean nothing to me. It ain't real. I haven't earned it." And he looked at me, and he was gritting his teeth.

He said it again, and I said, "No, Elvis, it's worthless." And just real quick, he whipped out that .45 and stuck it straight in my face. That gun barrel was no more than two inches from my nose. I was looking straight down the hole. And he said, "You son of a bitch! You know I love you, but if you don't shut up, I'm going to blow your fuckin' head off!"

So I just sat there, and I looked straight ahead for a minute. He put the gun down, and he said, "Okay, that's better." Then he said, "And by God, I'm going to get you one of these." I said, "Yeah, okay, Elvis. Okay." After all these years, it still scares me to think what could have happened, by accident. When a guy puts a gun in your face, you remember it forever.

LAMAR FIKE: At the end of the summer, Elvis went back out to Vegas to begin his gig there. He took the Jet Commander. And all of a sudden, he couldn't breathe. He got down on the damn floor to the air vent, and he said, "Land this plane right away! I'm suffocating!" They clamped an oxygen mask on him, and Milo High dived down and got on the ground as fast as possible.

I think they landed in Dallas. And he checked into a motel to rest for about five hours. Then he was all right, and they got back in the air again. That was August 16, 1975. And Elvis died on another August 16. Boy, that wasn't a good day for him, was it?

BILLY SMITH: I remember the incident, but I don't know if it was just from the cabin pressure or from drugs. Red and Linda were on the plane, and they said he'd been taking his pills.

There were just so many frightening situations. In Vegas, he would order his food, and then he would take his sleeping pills on an empty stomach because he had to get that feeling. And then, by the time the food got up there, he would be just groggy as hell, and he would try to eat.

One time, Linda said he was eating some soup, or some chili, and he just fell face over, right into the damn bowl. He could have smothered slap to death. Another time, he got choked on his dinner because he'd fallen asleep. Just sitting up. Once again, Linda opened his mouth and reached in there and dug the food out of his throat. She saved his life at least three times.

LAMAR FIKE: It wasn't like every day at four o'clock he passed out in his mashed potatoes. But it happened more than a couple of times. The load [of drugs] would hit him, and he'd have no control. He'd keel over wherever he happened to be.

BILLY SMITH: For a long time, I didn't see that he was killing himself. I always imagined that Elvis would die in a plane crash and all of us would be with him. We even talked about it. But never once did I think about him dying from drugs.

MARTY LACKER: If I've said it once, I've said it a thousand times—we thought we'd die before he would. We thought he was invincible. I'd get up in a plane with Elvis, and I didn't think the plane would go down as long as he was on it. I didn't think God would do that.

BILLY SMITH: I could see Elvis overdosing back in the early years, maybe mixing two drugs that interacted with each other. But not in the seventies. I guess over the years, the drugs just took their toll. Now that I look back on it, I see it could have happened anytime.

CHAPTER 49

"SLOW ROAD TO DEATH"

LAMAR FIKE: Two days after that experience on the airplane, Elvis opened in Vegas. Halfway through, he got tired, and he had to sit down a lot and let the Stamps and the Sweet Inspirations take over. He was heavy again, and *Variety* pointed it out:

> Presley may be suffering from a continuing physical disability. His overweight condition, lack of stamina, and poor vocal projection may spring from such a malady. It is difficult for him to maintain any credible vocal lines . . . In addition, he lumbers around in travesties of his earlier karate moves.

That's pretty devastating. It also talks about him spending more time diddling with the women in the front rows than anything else.

But on the second night, boy, he shocked everybody. He stayed out onstage after the show and told everybody that he didn't do drugs. He said, "Last night, I had a real bad case of the flu, and somebody started the rumor that I was strung out on drugs. If I ever find out who did that, I'll knock his goddamn head off. Because I've never been strung out on drugs in my life."

Well, Colonel flipped out. He told Elvis to get the hell out of Vegas if he was sick and just cancel the rest of the gig. So he did. He canceled after about five shows.

Colonel would check Elvis out before the shows, but I never remember him telling Elvis he was too screwed up to go onstage. Colonel was kind of like Elvis. He hoped it would go away. As long as Elvis got there and did the show, and we got the money, everything was okay.

MARTY LACKER: Henri Lewin, who was a Hilton executive vice president overseeing the Nevada operations, wrote an article for *Las Vegas Style* in 1994. He said, "I was there when Colonel Parker pleaded with Vernon Presley, and then they both pleaded with Elvis to understand the importance of taking care of his personal life."

Well, it seems highly unlikely that Colonel would do something like that in front of a Hilton official. I don't buy it.

LAMAR FIKE: A couple of days after Elvis ranted and raved onstage in Vegas, he started having breathing problems again, and Joe called an ambulance for him.

BILLY SMITH: They brought him back to Memphis and put him in Baptist [Hospital] for two weeks. Dr. Nick told everybody he was suffering from severe fatigue.

You'd think he was doing so good, and then you'd walk in and see him out of it on the bed. You'd realize, "Uh-oh. He's done had more than a required amount of sleeping medication."

Anytime he went into the hospital like that, the guys would come visit. But this time, Dr. Nick let him go home to Graceland for four or five hours each day. Which was just an opportunity for him to get into his secret stash.

MARTY LACKER: Dr. Nick released Elvis from the hospital the first week in September. When he got out, Elvis hired this nurse, Marian Cocke, at the urging of Dr. Nick. She was nice enough, but she looked like an army sergeant. Elvis gave her a car and a mink.

She was only there from September until January, and yet she had the gall to write a book, *I Called Him Babe: Elvis Presley's Nurse Remembers*. She may have called him "Babe," but that's not what Elvis called her when she wasn't around.

BILLY SMITH: After he got out of the hospital, Elvis didn't work for almost three months. So he put the Jet Commander and one of the Lockheed airplanes up for sale. He just wanted to rest and play. He bought some of these supercycles, the three-wheeled jobs, and him and Linda rode around the neighborhood a little bit. And he was having the racquetball building built. Dr. Nick was a real enthusiast, and he got Elvis interested because he thought it might help him take off some weight.

Before the racquetball building was finished, we used to go to Memphis State [University] to play. There for a time, we were playing almost every night for three or four hours, and then we'd go on to the movies for maybe another four hours. That kind of stuff was exactly what he needed. He started getting like his old self again, sort of silly, just having a good time.

Since he had all that time off, we had a lot of talks. I was still getting adjusted to being back with him, and I had some things to work out. Especially about the way people thought of me around there. And that included the Colonel.

In the early days, I admired Colonel. I really did. He had a very strong look and piercing blue eyes. You knew he was in control. Hell, for a fourteen- or fifteen-year-old, anybody like that would have impressed you. But he was likable, and he seemed to take an interest in the family.

Then in the mid-sixties, I was getting older, and I started seeing things that weren't really gee-hawing between Colonel and Elvis. And Colonel started that stuff of picking the guys, including me, for information.

After I went back to work for Elvis, Colonel tried that again. He called one time and demanded this and that, and I told him, "Look, I'm not that kid coming up that I used to be. I don't quack like a goddamn duck no more."

Elvis got a little mad, but he understood. At the time, I was very, very independent. So I thought about Colonel, "You've got millions, you old son of a bitch. But I'm as good as you are. And I don't quack, and I don't bark for you no more. If you've got a question, you ask me like a man, or you don't get an answer."

Now, as for Joe, Elvis still cared about him, but he thought Joe was licking Colonel's rear end and telling Colonel every move he made. Which I'm sure he was. And a lot of times, Joe wouldn't stay in Memphis with Elvis. After a tour, he went back to California. And Elvis got kind of upset about that a few times.

So we talked about that. And I wanted to get a couple of things out in the open. Like, when we went on tour, Joe was road manager. But I was supposed to have the same authority. So why was he and his girlfriend—Joanie had divorced him by that time—getting to ride in the limousine with Elvis, and Jo and me not? Boy, that pissed me off. I knew that not everybody could ride in the limousine. But I damn sure intended to ride in the limousine, and I did. I wouldn't take second seat to nobody—not anymore.

When we landed the plane someplace, Joe would say, "We've got to get the luggage off." Well, one day, he come back to where I was with Elvis, and he said, "We're unloading the plane. Do you want to come out here and help us?"

I said, "No, I'm helping Elvis." And Elvis said, "Tell you what, Joe. You go help them. Billy's with me right now."

Just because Joe was in a position of authority didn't mean he could just bark an order. We didn't mind taking it from Elvis. But we didn't have to take it from anybody else.

There was a lot of dissatisfaction. A lot of the guys were losing their enthusiasm. They felt like "Hey, I'm going nowhere. All I do is run and get this and get that." So I had a talk with Elvis, and he give David, Ricky, and Dean Nichopoulos a raise. Because all of it had to work.

MARTY LACKER: There seemed to be a lot more concern about somebody maybe getting a little bit more than the next guy.

In August of '75, Patsy left me and took the kids. She went up to her brother's [house] in Ohio. Mostly because of my drug use. She hated Dr. Nick, and she blamed him for a lot of it because he'd write prescriptions for whatever I wanted. At one point, Patsy went over to Graceland to confront him and to tell him he was ruining our lives. She ended up threatening him. She told him if he didn't stop giving me drugs, she was going to report everybody to the authorities. Dr. Nick didn't say a word. He just turned and walked away. I think he pretty much laughed at her.

After Elvis died, we got certified copies of the prescriptions Dr. Nick wrote for me through Kessler's Pharmacy in Memphis. This was over a forty-six-month period, from January 24, 1973, through October 28, 1976. And, of course, I took every pill: 6,464 Placidyl, 3,204 Darvon, 1,508 Hycomine, 708 Empirin with codeine number 3, 500 Dalmane, 400 Valium, 216 Darvocet, 200 Valmid, and 91 other assorted pills, which aren't very important. That's 13,291 pills right there. In 1,300 days. We showed that list to Sonny, and he was just amazed. But, of course, Elvis was taking a lot more than that.

When Patsy left, I was really upset and depressed. I went over to Graceland one day, and Lamar went upstairs and told Elvis. Lamar came back down and said, "Elvis wants to see you." I went up to his room, and Elvis asked me what was wrong, and I told him.

He said, "Well, let's see if we can't make this better." And then he said he was going to give me $10,000, buy me a new car, and send me and Patsy and the kids to Hawaii. Which was incredible, of course. This time I didn't argue with him. I thought the trip would help our marriage, and it did.

But when Elvis gave stuff to people, he'd get in the mood, and he'd just keep on giving. What happened next was typical. He looked at me and he said, "Is there anybody else down there who's got a problem?" And he did the same thing for Richard Davis.

Well, when Esposito and Schilling heard about this, Joe called Elvis and typically said, "Where's mine and Jerry's?" And Elvis ended up giving both of them $10,000 to keep peace.

BILLY SMITH: Believe it or not, when I went back to work for Elvis, for about the first few months, I fell right back into that same situation of taking pills. I'd take a Dexedrine and a sleeping pill. Because Elvis would say, "Look, man, we're going to do this and that all night. And you look tired already." It was his way of getting you high with him.

Sometimes there would be days when I wouldn't take anything at all, but he'd always try to give me something. He would put it under my tongue, and he'd get pissed if I didn't take it. Elvis would say, "It's not going to hurt you. I've got my own doctor."

When I resisted, sometimes he'd get angry. But a lot of times, I'd get dog-sick. So when he'd walk out—Pooh!—I'd spit it out in the commode. I even got good at pushing a pill under my tongue. I could talk pretty good like that, and even drink, and make him think I swallowed it. Then I'd spit it out later.

In the seventies, a lot of us come to our wits. Some of us

thought, "Hey, I'm on a slow road to death here. Why can't Elvis slow down some?" But we couldn't end that road for him.

MARTY LACKER: When Elvis went back out to Vegas in early December, he looked and sounded a whole lot better. And he only had to do one show a night during the week and two on Saturdays. The group, Voice, had disbanded, but Sherrill Nielsen stayed on.

BILLY SMITH: While he was at the Hilton, Elvis had Lisa Marie come out for about a week. Usually, she was just there for opening night or so. But this year, she wasn't coming to Memphis for Christmas. And it was just as well that he visited with her out there because when she'd come to Graceland, Elvis didn't give her all that much time. Funny, she was real blond as a kid, like he was. And now she's got real, real dark hair. I guess she works at it like Elvis did.

Once, Lisa was visiting in Memphis, and her golf cart had a flat tire. We were sitting on the patio off to the side of the house, talking. And Lisa come running up. She said, "Daddy, my golf cart's got a flat on it, and I can't ride it anymore." And Elvis said, "Okay, Lisa, Daddy's talking right now."

She said, "But, Daddy, won't you fix it for me so I can ride?" And she just kept on and on. And finally, Elvis said, "Goddamnit, Lisa! Go get Earl." She said, "But, Daddy, I want you to fix it." And he said, "Daddy don't fix flats, Lisa. Daddy's rich. He has people to do that for him."

Lisa could be an irritating little girl, but I think she was just starved for his attention, really. She was up early in the morning, and we were up late at night. And Elvis slept most of the day.

So the only time he was with her much at all was when he'd first get up. Which was just before she'd have to go to bed. And a lot of times he had things planned that she couldn't do. We couldn't take her to the movie, for example. And he wouldn't want to do a lot of the things she wanted to do. If it was riding the golf cart, Elvis might ride the kids around once and then say, "Y'all take the golf cart. Daddy's going to go in and talk." She would have loved it a whole lot more if Daddy hadda rode her on the cart himself.

The sad thing was that to Lisa, her daddy was it. Sometimes she'd even go wake him up. It would make him mad, but she would. And every chance she got, she'd get up in his lap and put her arm around his neck, especially if she wanted something. She was a whole lot like him. She knew how to work him, boy.

And she would do things to get his attention. Some of 'em are funny, but they're kind of naughty, too. Like, she'd go down to the gates and sign autographs for the fans. This was when she was about eight. She'd write, "Fuck you, Lisa Marie Presley." Then she'd get on the golf cart and take off.

She was a pistol. Lamar called her "The Little Führer."

MARTY LACKER: That Christmas '75 is one I'll always remember. Because of Elvis's Aunt Delta.

Elvis was still having trouble with all the relatives congregating at Graceland, looking for a handout. Before he'd come downstairs, he'd look at the TV monitors to see who was sitting there. He'd say to us, "Tell them I'm not here," or, "Tell them I'm not feeling well." But it got to a point where they just kept sitting there. They figured, "I'm going to outsmart him."

Well, the longer they sat, the madder he got. Sometimes, he'd sneak out the front door because they'd be in the den. He'd call down and say, "Bring the car around the front. I'll meet you there in fifteen minutes." If there were three or four of us, we'd all go in different directions, so the relatives wouldn't catch on.

I think Elvis saw it as being kicked out of his own house. And that's the sort of thing that started taking a toll on him.

LAMAR FIKE: When Elvis would cocoon like that, Billy would go up, and he'd talk to Billy. But that was about it. One time, Elvis had been up there for ten or fifteen days. In that womb situation. Some of it, I think, was self-consciousness over the way he looked, his size. Although he'd get up there and eat like crazy. And some of the withdrawal was just his drug use.

Anyway, I came up to the house. And since he had the [closed-circuit] TV cameras that scanned the rooms, I knew he was up there punching buttons and watching what we were doing.

I was fuckin' mad because we couldn't get any answers out of him. So I made a bunch of signs, like "The weather today is hazy. But it's clear in Denver . . . " And I put them in front of the camera, like a newscast. And then I held up a newspaper.

All of a sudden, the phone buzzed, and Elvis told whoever answered, "Get Lamar on the goddamn phone!" I got on, and he said, "What the fuck are you doing?" I said, "Well, I figured you'd want to know what's going on outside, so I thought I'd televise it."

He said, "I can read a fucking paper. I get it every day." I said, "Well, I didn't know. You stay up there, and nobody sees you."

MARTY LACKER: One time, Elvis's Aunt Clettes came up to the house with her husband, Vester. We were all in the den, and she was drunk. It was sometime around Christmas, so all the relatives were thinking about the cash Elvis always gave them.

With absolutely no conversation leading up to it, she looked at Elvis and said, "I want mine now." Elvis said, "What?" And she repeated it.

Then she pointed over at Vester, and she said, "Don't give that old son of a bitch nothing! But I want what's coming to me now."

Elvis knew what she was saying, but he was trying to feign bewilderment because he was so damn hurt. He said, "Aunt Clettes, what in the world are you talking about?" She said, "You know what I'm talking about. I want what's mine now. But don't give that son of a bitch nothing because he don't deserve nothing. He's worthless."

Elvis looked at her, and I could see tears coming to his eyes. And he got up and he went upstairs. And he wouldn't come down.

When Elvis first got the *Lisa Marie*, he used to take people up for little trips. He'd show 'em the plane and just fly around Memphis a little. On Christmas Eve—this was '75 now—country singer T. G. Sheppard and his wife, Diana, showed up. We knew him as Bill Browder, which was his real name. He used to work for RCA records as a promotion man. And he was always trying to get around Elvis.

Browder had four singles out by this time, and two of them, "Devil in the Bottle" and "Tryin' to Beat the Morning Home," had gone to number one on the country chart. I didn't like him. I thought he was a phony, so I continued to call him Browder, which used to piss him off.

We went for a ride, and we landed back down at the Memphis airport. But we didn't get off the plane right away. We had to wait for some reason. And we were all up in the front lounge.

Elvis had Lowell Hays, the jeweler, come on this trip. And Lowell had brought his case full of jewelry. Elvis gave stuff out for Christmas on the flight. He'd call everybody back to his compartment one at a time. I was sitting on the floor in the compartment, and he looked at me, and he said, "I ain't giving you shit." And I said, "Good, 'cause I don't want nothing." And we both laughed.

Elvis's aunt Delta was on the plane. And she was drunk. Either she had a bottle in her purse or she'd gotten loaded before she got on there.

As you looked towards the rear of the plane and Elvis's compartment back there, the first sitting room had two groups of four seats in it and a couch. Linda was sitting by the window, and at this point, Elvis was sitting next to her, by the aisle. And Delta was sitting on the floor, right next to Elvis's seat. I was facing her. And Browder and his wife were right behind me.

I got up from the floor, and I was stretching my knees, and we were talking about something.

All of a sudden, Delta looked at me, and she said, "You're a son of a bitch. I don't like you." Well, this came totally out of the blue, and I was just flabbergasted. It took me a minute, and then I said, "Why, Delta, I've never done anything to you."

I looked over at Elvis, and Elvis was shaking his head, "No," at her. But she turned back to me, and she said, "You ain't no damn friend of his. And I got a good mind to take this .38 I got in my purse and just shoot you dead."

Well, this was basically the same thing that happened with me and Clettes a few years earlier in the basement at Graceland. Except Clettes had a butcher knife.

I couldn't fuckin' believe this was happening again. And I got a little spooked because I knew Delta was capable of using that gun. Just about then she looked over at Browder, and she said, "And you ain't worth a shit, either, you walleyed son of a bitch." And she just kept on. She said, "All you sons of bitches are here for the same thing. You just want his damn money. Here's this goddamn jeweler, and Elvis has to buy you some of his crap."

She reached her hand in her bag, and I could see she was serious. I was standing over her, and her head was right in front of me. Elvis was looking down at her, and I saw he was getting mad because his jaw tightened up. Meanwhile, I was trying to decide what to do because if she came out of her purse with a .38, I was going to kick her square in the face.

I said, "Delta, I really don't understand why you're talking this way." And she just snapped. She screamed, "You shut up 'cause I'm gettin' ready to blow a hole in your damn head!"

With that, Elvis jumped up real quick and said, "You ain't going to do no such goddamn thing!" A lot of people were up in the very front of the plane, where the conference room was. And he yelled, "Some of you guys, get up here! Get this drunken bitch off this plane and take her home!"

He looked over at me and he said, "Man, I'm sorry." And he looked at Browder and said the same thing. I said, "That's all right, Elvis. You know I understand. Don't worry about it."

We got off the plane, and they took Delta home. Some of the other people were going back to Graceland. But I'd had enough. It was one o'clock in the morning. I got in my car and went home.

BILLY SMITH: About two o'clock in the morning, I heard the damnedest racket there ever was. I jumped up and grabbed my gun, and I run to the door. Well, it was Elvis. He had his cane, and he was beating the door on my trailer. His hair was messed up, and he was wild-eyed and red-faced. I said, "What in God's name is wrong?" He was just sputtering. I got him to come in, and I said, "Just settle down, man. You look like you're ready to explode."

He sat down for a second, and he started beating the floor with his cane. Then he went after the couch—just damn near beat the stuffing out of it. He was out of his mind, he was so mad.

He said, "Goddamnit! I'll kill that bitch! I'll sew her cunt up and throw her over that damn wall!" He was just ranting and raving, and when he did that, he always said all kinds of embarrassing things.

I said, "Who?" He said, "That goddamn Aunt Delta. That old whore has got to go!" He said, "She's cussed and abused my friends with her language, and I'm sick of her!" He was just screaming. "How dare she do something like that? Goddamnit! I took her in out of the goodness of my heart, and I'll kick her fat ass out. She would do that to a friend of mine for no reason at all? She embarrassed the shit out of me!"

Well, he kept on ranting and raving, and then he said, "Go

out there and tell the bitch she's got to leave." I said, "You don't mean that." He said, "Yes, I do. Because if you don't, I'm going to wind up doing something I don't want to do."

I said, "Elvis, let's sit down and talk this thing out. This is an old woman you're talking about. You know how she is when she gets to drinking." He said, "That ain't no reason for that bitch to insult my friends and ruin my Christmas."

We talked for a few more minutes, and he settled down some. I said, "Look, what you need to do is go out there and tell her, 'Don't ever do that again.' But you don't want to kick her out. She's got nowhere to go." And he said, "Yeah, I guess you're right." But then he broke down and started crying. He said, "She had no right to do that. Those are my friends. I love her, too, but she's got no right to make me look like that."

I hugged him, and I said, "Just go out and tell her. And mean what you say. If nothing else, you can always rent her a damn apartment, if that's what you want to do. But just think of the things she does around Graceland that's good for you. Weigh the good and the bad, and realize what you're saying."

Well, he cussed a few more times, and then said, "Okay, I guess I will. Come with me." I said, "You don't need me." He said, "Yeah, you and Jo come on with me. I might blow a fuse out there and wind up beating that old woman to death."

So we went along. Delta was in Grandma's room, and Elvis went in to where they were. They started yelling, and that went on for a few minutes, and then I heard him saying something along the lines of "That was my friends! Don't you love me enough not to pull that?" Well, she was all emotional, and she said, "Oh, my God, son, did I do that?" He said, "Yeah, god-damnit, Aunt Delta, you know you did!" She said, "No, I don't remember doin' that at all."

I think they put on an Academy Award–winning performance for each other. 'Cause he broke down with the crying, and he said, "Aunt Delta, I would never have done that to you." And she broke down, too. She said, "I can't believe I did that, son." And Elvis sort of pulled himself together. He said, "Yeah, you did it. And now I'll tell you something else you're going to do. You're going to get the phone numbers, and you're going to call every one of these people and apologize. Either that, Aunt Delta, or you've got to go."

So she called everybody and said she was sorry. It was funny, but he had real intentions of kicking her ass out. He'd gotten that mad.

MARTY LACKER: About T. G. Sheppard and Elvis. He didn't really know Elvis. They were acquaintances. He told Merv Griffin on his TV show once that he went to Graceland for sixteen Christmases. I was at Graceland every Christmas until '76. And I never saw him there. And he told him that when Elvis was on tour, we'd put Elvis in the back of a semitruck trailer and back it up to the stage door of the arena. Then he said we'd open the back doors of the trailer truck, and Elvis would run out, do the show, and then run back into the truck, and we'd ride away to the plane and the next city.

That's bullshit. He wouldn't know what we did. When he went on the Jet Commander that time, if he mentioned it once, he mentioned six times that he needed a bus. He was hoping Elvis would give him one. Where he got the nerve, I don't know.

About the third time he brought up the bus, Elvis looked over at me, like "Oh, fuck, here we go again." Actually, I would have bet money that no way in hell was Browder going to get one because Elvis recognized what he was doing. But when we got off the plane, I saw Elvis was walking a little slower, and he hung back so I could catch up with him because I was the last off.

I got up next to him, and he said out of the side of his mouth, "I'm going to get the motherfucker a bus." He had me arrange it through J. D. Sumner.

BILLY SMITH: In the early days, Elvis made a statement to everybody: "Don't mess with my women, and I won't mess with your girlfriend or your wife." And then he said, "But I'm going to look, just like every one of you all."

LAMAR FIKE: He also said, "Let me tell you, Lamar. Never think I won't try anything." I got mad at him one day, and I said, "You lust after every one of our wives." And he said, "Do you find anything wrong with that?" It was funny. So I said, "No, not really. But I don't know how to follow this up!" We had to watch him like a hawk.

BILLY SMITH: One time in the sixties, we'd been out in California a long time, and I said, "I've got to get home to Jo." Elvis said, "She's that good, huh?" I said, "Yeah, you ought to try it." And he said, "I would if you'd let me." I said, "Well, we'll switch wives." I was just teasing. I had no intention of doin' that. And he said, "Wait a minute, now . . . "

MARTY LACKER: When Priscilla first came over in the sixties, we went to Treasure Island, on McKellar Lake, outside of Memphis. We had the boat, and Elvis pulled it up on the beach. George Klein and I had gotten out, and just Elvis and Priscilla were left in the boat. Well, Priscilla was worried about how she was going to get out without tripping and falling. So she put her hand out to George.

Klein looked at me and he said, "I'm not touching her." I said, "What are you going to do, George, just let the girl fall on her butt?" That's how freaked we were about this rule about the girl-friends.

BILLY SMITH: There are all sorts of funny stories about that. In about '67, after Elvis and Priscilla were married, we were in Palm Springs, and we were going up on the mountain to ride horses. Well, Priscilla borrowed a pair of my jeans to wear. I said, "Oh, that's nice!" I carried on with Elvis about it, you know. And Elvis said, "The sons of bitches will be washed when you get 'em back!"

LAMAR FIKE: We went on a submarine in Hawaii one time in the sixties, when Alan was still with us. Alan jumped down the hole first, and he said, "It's okay, let Priscilla come on." She started to step down, and Alan was looking right up her dress. Elvis realized what was happening, and he said, "You low-life son of a bitch!"

BILLY SMITH: As the years went on, a lot of that propriety went by the wayside. In Vegas, or on tour, hell, there's no telling how many times Elvis come to my room and crawled right in the dang bed with Jo and me. I don't know that he thought anything of it.

This one time, though, he stepped clear over the line where Billy Stanley was concerned. It was the early seventies. Billy was married to this eighteen-year-old girl, Angie. She was pretty well making passes at Elvis, or at least that's what Elvis said. To hear him tell it, she went after him like he was the last piece of cake on the platter. And Billy had this thing for another girl who went to the movies with us. So Elvis set Billy up with her so he could be with Angie.

Now, Billy wrote this book [*Elvis, My Brother*, with George Erikson]. And he says in there that Ricky told him that Elvis and Angie did have a short affair—about a month—and that Elvis felt bad about it. I don't know if he had sex with her or not. At the time—which would have been about '72, when I wasn't there—he led everybody to believe he did. I didn't talk to him about it until maybe '75. I flat-out asked him.

Elvis told me they didn't do anything. He said they just talked, and he preached to her a little bit. He had intentions, but they never did go through with it. He was quite capable of it, though.

MARTY LACKER: Shortly after this supposed affair, Elvis and I were walking down the steps into the den from the kitchen. And Billy Stanley walked past us. I was thinking about Elvis and Angie, and somehow Elvis knew that. He kind of glanced over at Billy, and then he looked at me, and he said, "Well, it ain't like he's my brother."

BILLY SMITH: On New Year's Eve that year, Elvis got a big boost. He did a special concert at the Silverdome in Pontiac, Michigan, that set a world's attendance record for a single performance. They had nearly eighty thousand people there, and Colonel scaled some of those tickets up to $15 for a change. The gate receipts were something like $816,000.

MARTY LACKER: The Colonel didn't want any empty seats, so he only took Elvis into the really big places twice—the Astrodome in Houston, for a rodeo, and the Pontiac Silverdome. And both of them were sellouts. It just shows you what Elvis could have done.

BILLY SMITH: I don't know that Colonel didn't play that right. I don't remember a concert that wasn't sold out. But if he had routinely gone to coliseums that seated sixty thousand instead of twenty thousand, I'm not sure he would have sold out.

A lot of times, I saw sections closed off behind him. I don't know whether it was Elvis's suggestion not to sell those seats, or if they just didn't sell out and the Colonel said, "Let's close that section. It'll look sold out."

Elvis didn't really like those big outdoor places. He liked the sound you got inside a building. But on this Silverdome concert, Elvis put a little bit more into the show than usual. And just as he was ending one song, he heard the sound of cloth ripping. They had a real high stage there, and he said later he could feel a slight draft in the seat of his pants. He backed up to the singers, and he said, "Y'all sing 'Sweet, Sweet Spirit.' I've done tore the hell out of the seat of my suit!"

🕺 🕺 🕺

LAMAR FIKE: Around '75, Miss Miller, Loanne Miller, went to work for the Colonel. She'd been Alex Shoofey's secretary there in Vegas. She'd go to Colonel and tell him everything he had to know. And she'd carry back his story to Shoofey, and pretty soon she knew it all. And Colonel took a shine to her. His wife had such bad Alzheimer's that she didn't know who Colonel was the last ten years of her life. And he and Loanne became friends.

MARTY LACKER: They finally got married after Mrs. Parker died, which I believe was after Elvis's death. Today, you see Colonel, you see Miss Miller. And he just brags on her.

BILLY SMITH: You know what else happened in '75? Priscilla broke up with Mike Stone. He moved to Vegas and went to work as a dealer in one of the casinos. And after that, Priscilla was just as wild as Elvis had always been. She was dating everybody.

MARTY LACKER: Mike Edwards, her first long-term boyfriend after Stone, claimed in his book [Priscilla, Elvis and Me] that Priscilla disappeared one time and came back two days later. He said he point-blank asked her, "Where've you been?" And she told him she'd been down in Miami with Julio Iglesias. It must be true because she told Vanity Fair she and Julio had a fling, but they never consummated it. Whatever that means.

I'm sure that being with Elvis all those years affected her

thinking. I guess she figured, "What's good for the gander is great for the goose." I think anything's possible with her. The front she puts up for people—demure little Priscilla—is bullshit.

BILLY SMITH: Until she had a son with Marco Garibaldi, Priscilla changed men all the time. That's another pattern she got from Elvis. Did you know she's made Garibaldi sign a statement that he won't write a book about her if they break up?

MARTY LACKER: When Priscilla and Mike Stone called it quits, Elvis made no attempt to date her again. But he wasn't paying that much attention to Linda, either. In late '75 and early '76, Linda started seeing David Briggs, who'd been Elvis's keyboard player. She used to flirt with him. I don't think Elvis knew it.

BILLY SMITH: Oh, yes, it got back to Elvis. She said they were just friends. And I choose to believe her. I know after Elvis died, they dated. But when she was going with Elvis, I think her and David pretty much kept it to just talking and playing cards. She needed somebody to talk to because it would almost stifle you to be around Elvis, he demanded so much.

But Linda was aware that Elvis was seeing other women. So the whole situation was getting to the point of blowing up. He bought her a house and got her away from Graceland, which was one of the first signs. He had that pattern. He was never completely true to any woman for any length of time. If he went a year, hell, he was doin' good. Which almost makes him sound like a monster. And at times, I guess he was. He's like that nursery rhyme. When he was good, he was very, very good. And when he was bad, he was horrid.

CHAPTER 50

BROKEN BONDS

MARTY LACKER: Colonel probably had a clearer picture than any of us that the end was near. In January '76, he demanded more money. Instead of a third commission of the net profits of the tours, which he'd been getting since '72, he now took half. And half of all the money from television specials and merchandising, too.

Now, why did he do this at this particular time? Because the Hilton was fed up with Elvis's behavior. He just didn't give a damn anymore, so he'd get up and sing half a song. And after he did that a couple of times, the Hilton wouldn't buy him. In fact, Elvis didn't play the Hilton in January.

LAMAR FIKE: That January, we all went out to Vail, Colorado, for Elvis's forty-first birthday. This was supposed to be a dream vacation, but Elvis was just stoned out of his mind the whole time. He was threatening to kill people right and left.

I guess it's because he was doing a lot of Dilaudid up there. He stayed ripped every day. He flew Dr. Nick in a couple of times to get more prescriptions. He said at least he could control the situation. I say if he could control it, why did Elvis die?

Elvis was doing a lot of uppers, too. And when he did uppers, everything was magnified. Sometimes I think he had a little movie in his head and that he gave stuff away because it was in the script. But he was that way when he was a kid. He would give money away to other kids and buy 'em presents.

When we were out in Vail, he wanted to see his Denver cop friends, Jerry Kennedy and Ron Pietrofeso, who were basically narcs. Elvis was feeling good, so we drove over to Kumpf Lincoln-

Mercury, and before the night was over, Elvis had spent nearly $70,000 on five Lincoln Continental Mark IVs, at $13,000 apiece. One was for Captain Kennedy, and another was for Kennedy's wife. Then Pietrofeso got one. Even the police doctor, Gerald Starkey, and Bob Cantwell, of the Crime Strike Force.

The next day, Elvis told Dave Hebler in these real hush-hush tones that the real reason he went into Denver was to go on a drug raid with the narcs. He said he sneaked up on this guy holding a sawed-off shotgun, and the guy heard him and turned around real quick and was ready to blast him away, and Elvis delivered a karate chop to the neck and killed him.

He told me some other version of this story, and he said, "What do you think about that?" I said, "I think I just sat through an episode of *Dragnet.*"

BILLY SMITH: I don't think he went on a drug raid in Denver. But he wanted to get involved in stuff like that so bad.

MARTY LACKER: Sonny said Elvis went on his own little drug bust in Memphis after that. Dave Hebler supposedly went with him. Elvis had his .22 Savage, and his holster, and his flashlight, and his badges. And it was like "All right, let's get me a criminal." He even put on a ski mask. And a jumpsuit, with a parka and gloves over that, even though it was something like 73 degrees out. And he topped it all off with a hat and a cigar. Because he said, "I'm going incognito." Like nobody would notice him like that.

He supposedly had this all worked out with the Memphis cops. But when they got there, the bust had already gone down and the suspects were in custody. Elvis was real disappointed. Dave said they just sat around the police station, talking to the cops. And every once in a while, Elvis would give the suspects a dirty look.

LAMAR FIKE: One of the classic Elvis stories about how whimsical, or extravagant, he was is the one about him taking the [Convair] 880 [the *Lisa Marie*] to Denver to get a peanut butter sandwich. I put that deal together. It was February of '76, right after he got the jet.

I said, "Man, let's do something. Let's go somewhere and just kind of get away." He said, "What have you got in mind?" I said, "I don't know. Let's go to Denver, for lunch. There's that great place out there [the Colorado Gold Mine Company] that has those big peanut butter and jelly sandwiches on Italian bread loaves." I said, "They'll cater the plane and everything." Elvis said, "Sounds like a good idea. Let's do it.".

So eight of us got on the plane, and we called in our order, and we flew to Stapleton Airport and parked. And sure enough, they catered the airplane with twenty-two loaves. We had Moët champagne and Perrier water, the whole works. And all the narcotics guys—Kennedy and Pietrofeso and their pals—came on board. We stayed there about three or four hours and flew back.

Let's see . . . it's a four-engine jet, and he had two pilots, an engineer, and a flight attendant. I'd say that trip cost anywhere from $20,000 to $40,000. Elvis got a kick out of that.

BILLY SMITH: I didn't go. But Elvis went there more than once, and neither time was it just to get a damn peanut butter sandwich. Best I remember, he wanted a badge from the Denver police.

LAMAR FIKE: On one of these trips, Elvis was on Dilaudid. And he pulled his ingrown toenail stunt again. I think it was like the other self-mutilations—it became this gross, infected thing. So Elvis called the Denver police doctor, Dr. Starkey. I guess he asked him for more Dilaudid and showed him his prescription.

Whatever happened, Starkey figured Elvis was using, and he showed the prescription to his undercover friends. I'm sure Kennedy and Pietrofeso had already guessed that by the way Elvis looked and acted, but it was a tough spot for everybody.

They were prescription drugs, so they couldn't really do anything. But they tried to talk to him about it, in a Denver hotel. They wanted Elvis to go in and dry out someplace and told him nobody had to know about it. They were concerned about him, and they were embarrassed that he was flaunting his [drug] use right in front of them. When Elvis realized they were onto him, he checked out of that hotel in a heartbeat. He didn't want to hear about it.

MARTY LACKER: Just a couple days after that, Elvis was making the *From Elvis Presley Boulevard, Memphis, Tennessee* album at Graceland. And he got it in his head that he was going to kill all the drug pushers. He called Red up to his bedroom, and Red said he had this big arsenal spread out on the floor. Just everything, from automatic weapons to rockets.

Red said he gave him a list of names and even some police file pictures—some head-and-shoulder shots of guys he said were pushers. And I'm sure it's true because Elvis had shown me part of the list in the lobby of the Memphian Theatre a couple of nights before. Elvis said, "These sons of bitches need to be wiped out." He wanted Red, and Dick Grob, and Dave Hebler to lure them all back to Graceland. And then he was going to kill them.

He told Red he would sneak out the back and make the hit and then sneak back in. That way, it wouldn't be traced back to him.

BILLY SMITH: The cop stuff lasted a good while. But mostly, he'd stick to the little stuff. Like, he'd put on his uniform and go out and stop traffic—pull a guy over, tell him he was driving too fast, and give him a safety lecture.

I can imagine what the person thought. Like he goes home and says, "You are not going to believe this, but Elvis Presley stopped me for speeding." Elvis would wind up giving them an autograph, since he couldn't write a ticket. But he got so wrapped up in it that we all had to have the special blue police lights.

LAMAR FIKE: He and I would get in the light blue Mercedes, and Elvis would say, "Here we go, Lamar. Out to serve law and order." And he'd put his blue light up on top of the Benz and chase people down the interstate—stop 'em, pull 'em over, and tell 'em to watch their speed. I'd just slink down in the seat and go, "Oh, dear."

BILLY SMITH: He never left Graceland without his blue police light, his long flashlight, a billy club, and at least two guns.

LAMAR FIKE: You remember that segment of *Laugh-In* where the Keystone Kop came out and hit somebody over the head with his club? Elvis thought that was a mockery of law enforcement. He told Bill Morris he got that taken off the show. Morris also says Elvis helped get a couple of drug abuse centers opened, one in Denver and one in Los Angeles.

MARTY LACKER: At the end of '75, and all through January of '76, RCA tried to get Elvis to record another album. But he just didn't want to fool with it. Finally, somebody suggested bringing the portable recording truck to Graceland. The first week of February, the truck rolled in, and Billy, and Earl Pritchett, and Mike McGregor, and Ricky Stanley turned the den into a recording studio.

BILLY SMITH: I remember those sessions. They put up a partition because Elvis didn't want anybody to watch him on certain songs. He'd just tear up something awful.

MARTY LACKER: There were two groups of sessions, one in February and another in October. RCA pulled two albums out of them—the *From Elvis Presley Boulevard, Memphis, Tennessee* album and the *Moody Blue* album, although Felton pieced the *Moody Blue* album together from various recordings, because Elvis wouldn't give him any more studio time.

The song "Moody Blue" came from the February sessions. And "Way Down," where J.D. hits that really low note, came from the October sessions. From listening, it's obvious how sick Elvis was. And how tired.

BILLY SMITH: For some reason, Elvis played bass guitar on "Blue Eyes Crying in the Rain." Felton bragged on him, I remember.

He had fun on those sessions. When J.D. hit that real low note on "Way Down," Elvis just fell out laughing. He walked over to J.D. and put his arm on his shoulder and said, "J.D., that's lower than whale shit."

MARTY LACKER: Elvis sounds so bad on "I'll Never Fall in Love Again." They never should have released it. The four songs they got in October—"Way Down," "It's Easy for You," "Pledging My

Love," and "He'll Have to Go"—are better than what they got in February. But it still hurts to listen to it.

BILLY SMITH: During the first sessions, they took a break, and Elvis and Joe went upstairs and put on these big wide-brim hats and black coats and sunglasses. And Elvis had two submachine guns that had been plugged up—you couldn't actually fire 'em. And they come down lookin' like mobsters. Elvis yelled, "I'll stop all this damn stuff! I didn't want to do any recording in the first place! I'll give you five seconds to clear out of here, and then we're going to shoot up all this equipment!"

Well, we all knew it was a joke. But the guy out in the sound truck didn't. And the next day, it was all over Memphis and Nashville that Elvis went plumb crazy and shot up the place and all the recording equipment, too. This was one time he didn't.

MARTY LACKER: When Elvis went back on tour in March, he had to read some of the words from a cue sheet. He also started wearing a corset. He didn't get really, really heavy until the middle of '76. But when he gained weight, he had to get in those jumpsuits some way.

LAMAR FIKE: He came on tour, and it was horrendous. I told the Colonel, "My God, are you blind as a bat? Look at him! He weighs 250 pounds!" One time I told Elvis, "If that damn metal starts flying off your outfit, you'll kill the first five rows from shrapnel." And he laughed himself into a spasm. He thought it was hilarious.

I blame his fans for a lot of this. Because they accepted him, even seventy pounds overweight.

MARTY LACKER: In the last year or so, Sherrill Nielsen hit a lot of Elvis's high notes for him, the notes he couldn't sustain anymore. And Larry Strickland [of the Stamps] sang a lot of his low notes. Not every night, because Elvis still had a tremendous voice.

But on "It's Now or Never" and "American Trilogy," Nielsen doubled him. Elvis would hit it to a certain point, and Nielsen took over. And then Elvis would start singing again, and the audience never knew the difference. On [the record of] "Unchained Melody," the last four notes are Nielsen's. Felton just dubbed Sherrill over Elvis.

LAMAR FIKE: I don't think Elvis understood why he was bloated like a sow. We were talking one day, and I said, "Elvis, your mother went through the same thing you're going through. You realize that, don't you?" And he said, "Sometimes I think about that." He looked so much like her, like the way she looked when she died. It was like he missed her so much, he just became her. And I said, "Well, man, I'm telling you, you need to do something about this." The physical deterioration was just horrible.

I don't think Elvis knew he was dying. Just like all of us think we ain't going to die. You think, "Shit. I'll make it." Until you wake up and go, "Holy shit, I'm dying here!"

BILLY SMITH: The drugs didn't help a bit, but Elvis was a strange eater. At times he would eat, and you'd think he wasn't ever going to stop—maybe three cheeseburgers and several banana splits at a time. But then he would go for days and not eat that much. And when he started eating again, he'd eat so much junk food that he'd put on weight just quick.

He always thought he'd take it off before tour time. And now that I look back, I see how hard he tried to get it off. But he just wasn't physically able. He was so tired that just anything exhausted him. By '76, he'd just abused his body beyond its limit.

MARTY LACKER: Elvis liked sweet stuff, and he loved to eat, which is one reason he put on weight. But in the final years, it was more illness than food. The food contributed, of course. But since he had that intestinal blockage, they were shooting him with cortisone because his colon was two or three times its normal diameter and it had lost its elasticity. He even had to lie in a tub of hot water to take that Fleet's enema. The cortisone was one of the big reasons he blew up like he did. And he couldn't do anything about it.

LAMAR FIKE: The unraveling was absolutely astonishing. His system was really fucked up. He would go from enormous bouts of diarrhea to bouts of constipation.

BILLY SMITH: When we'd get ready to go on tour, in addition to all the scarves and things that Elvis needed, they had to pack just trunks of Fleet's enema. Tons of 'em. Because he had to have 'em. He had that bowel problem with a twisted colon, or a paralyzed colon, which kept him from going to the bathroom.

Albert Goldman wrote that a lot of times Elvis lost control of his bowels in the last couple years. He makes it sound like he was practically in diapers.

Most of the time, Elvis could control it. He was still quite proud, and he was cautious about things like that. When it did happen, it was almost like he broke down. He was embarrassed, and it was best you didn't talk about it. Sometimes, Elvis would say, "Look, I couldn't help it." Usually the excuse was "I took Ex-Lax before I went to bed."

LAMAR FIKE: I think the diapers have been exaggerated. But that's not a lie. They put towels down to keep him from defecating in bed. He would be so damn drugged up, he couldn't make it to the bathroom.

That's a clue to a person losing it. By late '75, early '76, it became a real problem. Everybody just tried to ignore it. But I would tell Colonel and Dr. Nick, "God Almighty, this guy is really, really sick. He's going on us!"

BILLY SMITH: One time, he messed in the bed at Graceland, and one of the maids cleaned it up. And she suggested, just in case it happened again, to put a towel under him. But Elvis would never have been wrapped in a diaper or had a towel put around him. From then on, he always walked to the bathroom. But even that was dangerous. Because it was not unusual for him to fall asleep in the bathroom. He would take sleeping pills and get up and go to the bathroom, and the first thing you knew they'd hit him, and he never would make it back to the bed. He'd fall right there in the floor and go sound to sleep. If there was nobody there to help him, he would just lay there until somebody found him. But many times, they'd buzz me, and I'd have to come out and help get him up.

Goldman said we used a fireman's lift to carry him to the bathroom. That's the biggest crock of shit. The only lift I know was a 5'6", 145-pound lift, and that was me. And it was hell at times, when I was the only one there. I'd have to drag him. But I never would call anybody 'cause I didn't like for them to see him that way and make fun. Like "What's he done, passed out again on the damn bathroom floor?"

I couldn't stand the thought of anybody degrading him. That was his home. And it was his right to do whatever he wanted to do in his home, without somebody else criticizing him for it. So I'd just get him up myself and not comment on it. Linda was a lot like that. That's the reason I thought so much of her.

LAMAR FIKE: It was really bad. You've been around people who are dying. You know it. We all knew it. But we wouldn't say it, even though it was just tearing us up, ripping us to shreds.

And now that I think about it again, I think he knew it, too. Because it was a thread that permeated everything he did. He was getting rid of money like it was going out of season at sundown. He would always talk about his mother's death at forty-two—even though she was actually forty-six—and the lifeline on her side being very short.

One time, we were having a very philosophical conversation, and I said, "Can I give you a very blank statement?" He said, "What's that?" I said, "I can never see you old." He said, "You're saying that you don't think that I'll be around a long time." I said, "Yeah, I think that's it." And he said, "Lamar, I'll never be an old man."

BILLY SMITH: When we went back out on the road in '76, Elvis would come to my room a lot of times on tour. He had a list of where everybody was, and I was in the room next to his. Well, after a while, Joe started putting me way down the hall. I guess because he had to have a suite, just like Elvis did.

Well, one morning, Elvis got up about three o'clock and looked on his sheet and saw my room number. But he couldn't find the room. He was wandering up and down the hall about half drugged, and he had to ask Dick Grob where it was.

There was this pounding on the door. Me and Jo was in bed, and he come in, and he sat down on the edge of the bed and started talkin'. He said, "Man, something unbelievable just happened. I dreamed I saw the face of God."

He said it was just a white light, so bright he almost couldn't look at it. And it startled him. He had to get up and walk around to get it off his mind.

Well, the next thing I knew, he was on the other side of me, laid down in the dadgum bed with us. Of course, I didn't say nothin' about him barging in on us. I was more interested in what was bothering him.

He talked for about an hour and a half. And then in the next minute, he was sound asleep. I looked at Jo, and she looked at me, and I said, "I guess I'd better take him back down to the room."

The next day, he said, "What in the hell were you doing way down the hall?" I said, "That's where they put me." He said, "Okay, I'll take care of that." I went back to my room, and I left my door open, and I jumped up real loud and said, "Today, the limousine and tomorrow the damn hotel suites!" And from then on, Elvis made sure I was right next to him, or right across the hall.

🕺 🕺 🕺

MARTY LACKER: That April, when Elvis was on tour, they broke ground for Elvis Presley Center Courts, Inc., in Memphis. This was supposed to be the first of a franchised chain of racquetball courts. Dr. Nick talked Elvis into it. Him and Joe.

Presley Center Courts was going to be fifty courts nationwide. And Elvis was supposed to underwrite it for $1.3 million, which would have taken forever to make back. He was getting 25 percent of the stock.

But, see, Elvis didn't understand that. He thought he was just lending his name to the project, even though he signed the contract. Elvis said later that he did it as a favor to Nichopoulos. He probably figured he could get whatever he wanted from Nick if he did it.

Anyway, Elvis didn't realize he had to put up all this money, and pretty soon, they came asking for $80,000, as a starter. And Elvis backed out of the deal.

LAMAR FIKE: There were all kinds of problems. Number one, Elvis had never endorsed anything in his life, except Southern Made doughnuts in an early radio jingle. You can imagine what Elvis's endorsements would cost. Boy, the Colonel went ballistic! If the Colonel had been a moon shot, he'd have gone to Mars!

That was about July, I think. And we got on the plane and flew to Palm Springs, and Elvis fired everybody. He said, "Fuck the sons of bitches! Get rid of the wop, and get rid of the doctor. I never want to see 'em again in my life. They conned me." I said, "Holy shit, man, calm down." He didn't relent on Nick for a long time. Wouldn't let him go on the tours. He took Ghanem instead. But I talked him into taking Joe back. And I shouldn't have.

MARTY LACKER: As likable as Dr. Nick was, he could take advantage of Elvis. Harry Levitch, the jeweler, told me that Elvis had somebody call him and ask him to bring some rings out to the house one time.

When he got there, he was told to go on up. He knocked softly on Elvis's bedroom door, and then he opened it. And he saw Dr. Nick sitting on the side of the bed with a syringe in his hand. He was sort of holding it away from Elvis, and he was saying, "My wife needs . . . " And when he saw the jeweler, he changed the subject. It was almost like "My wife needs such and such. Now do you want this shot or not?"

BILLY SMITH: Elvis had so many things weighing on him about that time. The pressure was really starting to get to him. At the end of April, he was supposed to go to Lake Tahoe. And when they were loading the plane, he was crying. Vernon was sick—he'd gotten down to about 165 pounds. And Elvis was scared to death something was going to happen to him. You could tell Elvis didn't want to go. He hugged me and Jo, and he said, "I'll see you all in a few days."

He had a full engagement booked, but sure enough, a few days later, he was back in Memphis. He said he got out there and got sick. And this particular time, I think he was just not capable of performing. We could tell when he got back home that he was drugged and exhausted.

LAMAR FIKE: When we were in Tahoe, Elvis had an oxygen tank beside the stage. Every entertainer does, not only him. They'll do a false exit and take two or three shots of it. That picks 'em back up again, and they'll come back out.

Well, Elvis had done it about eight or nine times. He kept coming back and forth. Finally, I said, "Why don't you just take the damn cart and bottle back out there with you?" I was only kidding. But he said, "Okay." And he just grabbed hold of the handle, spun it around, and walked back onstage. Then he put the mask on his face and pulled that son-of-a-bitchin' tank behind him.

And everybody just cracked up. He was talking through that clear plastic tube, and he said, "You always wondered how I keep my strength up at this altitude. Here it is." That was the last time he was ever out there.

🐾 🐾 🐾

MARTY LACKER: In July, everything blew apart. Elvis went out to Palm Springs for what was supposed to be a three-week rest. He fired Joe over the racquetball deal then, but, of course, he took him back. But after that, he did something we didn't think we'd ever see in this lifetime—he had his daddy fire Red, Sonny, and Dave Hebler.

It started on July 5, which was Sonny's birthday. Elvis finished a tour by doing his last show in Memphis. He drove to the Coliseum with Red and Esposito. And Elvis was acting kind of weird. He hardly talked to me or anybody else. He got out of the car, and went to the dressing room, and stayed in there until time to do the show. And then he got right back in the car and went home.

Eight days later, I got a call from Sonny. He said, "Man, you won't believe what just happened." He said Vernon called him that morning, and said, "I need you to come up and talk about an important matter." And Sonny said, "Can't we talk about it on the phone?" And Vernon said, "Well, things haven't been going too well lately. Our expenses are getting too high, and we're going to have to cut back. I'm afraid we'll have to let you go."

Well, Sonny was totally stunned. He said to Vernon, "What do you mean, you're going to have to let me go?" Vernon said, "Don't feel bad. You're not alone."

You have to understand how long Red and Sonny had been with Elvis. Red went all the way back to high school with him. He would have given his life for Elvis. And he and Sonny were hurt even more so because Elvis hadn't told them himself.

They were just out in the cold. I felt bad about both of them. All they had to their name was one week's pay. After all those years and all the things they had done.

BILLY SMITH: It surprised the hell out of me. I'm sure a whole lot of it had to do with the fact that Sonny and Red confronted him about the drugs. Red, especially. And a lot of times, they intercepted stuff coming in.

MARTY LACKER: At first, they tried to figure out what to do. They tried calling Elvis. And Elvis wouldn't talk to them.

Vernon's excuse about expenses didn't really hold water. It was Colonel, Vernon, Charlie, Dr. Nick, and Joe saying that Red and Sonny were causing too many lawsuits by hitting people. But Red and Sonny were just trying to protect Elvis. They were just doing their jobs.

LAMAR FIKE: Vernon just didn't want them around. He saw a chance to get rid of them, and he took it.

MARTY LACKER: Elvis had reached the boiling point, and he was just running. And he made it worse by leaving Palm Springs and going to Vegas, where he stayed at Dr. Ghanem's house. Ghanem had a room he'd built for Elvis. He was going to put him on some kind of sleep diet or some rest cure. It might have been to get him off drugs. But it was bullshit, whatever it was. And he'd done that something like five or six times.

When Dave found out Elvis was there, he flew out to Vegas and went to Ghanem's house. Ghanem came to the door, and Dave said, "Elvis is here, isn't he?" And Ghanem said, "Yes, he is." Dave said, "Tell him I'd like to speak with him."

Ghanem went in and came back and said, "I'm sorry, but he doesn't want to see you."

BILLY SMITH: Ghanem might have had a place for Elvis in case he ever come to visit, but I don't think Ghanem could get him off nothing or even help him lose weight. I don't think he cared that much.

LAMAR FIKE: Elias built the room because he wanted to add on to the house, period. He had this Spanish-style hacienda next to the golf greens of the Las Vegas Country Club. And the decor was . . . well, you know the type—shag carpet, a bed on a dais, with mirrors on the headboard and more mirrors overhead. Ghanem put Elvis on a lot of medication and called it "sleep therapy." He said he'd put Elvis to sleep and he could lose weight.

Well, all he did was keep him fucked up, and he didn't eat. He stayed up there three or four days. It was really sad. Elvis would shit all over the bed. God Almighty, if they put you in bed and you don't eat for five fuckin' days and you're asleep, you're going to do something.

MARTY LACKER: One thing that's been lost in all this was Elvis's true intention—to teach Red and Sonny and Dave a lesson—that you can't go around hitting people. He'd told his father to give them $5,000 apiece to tide them over and to tell them that they would be hired back. But Vernon didn't do it.

LAMAR FIKE: When this thing came up with Red and Sonny, Elvis called Frank Sinatra and told him he'd just lost his three bodyguards. Frank said, "I'll take care of it." Elvis said, "No, I'll take care of it. Don't worry about it." But Frank offered to help in any way he could. Which was interesting. Both that Elvis called him and that Frank made the offer.

At the end of July, we were playing Hampton Roads, Virginia, outside of Washington, D.C. And Elton John came backstage before Elvis did the show. He had on a suit with shoulders that came up in an arch. An exaggerated zoot suit. Elton dresses very bizarre anyway. He met Elvis, they talked, and Elton shook hands and left. It wasn't any big parting of the waters.

In 1991, he made a video biography [Two Rooms], and he mentioned this. He said, in essence, "I looked into Elvis's eyes, and there was no one there. He was vacant." Well, that's his opinion. Maybe what Elton saw was a reflection of himself. All these stars think they're psychiatrists. They're just dreaming.

MARTY LACKER: When Elvis and the guys came back from Vegas, about the third week of July, I called the house. I was going to go over that night because Elvis was getting ready to start another tour. Billy said to me, "I'm glad you called. I was getting ready to call you, and George, and Richard, and everybody else. I didn't want you to come to the gate and be turned away."

I said, "Turned away?" He said, "Yeah, Elvis doesn't want anybody around here for a while. He's had enough, Marty. He wants some peace and quiet. He wants to calm down and enjoy the house." And I respected that.

I said, "Hey, okay. How long is this going to last?" He said, "I don't know. Probably a month or two." But it never changed. I never saw Elvis again after that night at the Coliseum in July of '76.

LAMAR FIKE: Basically, what Elvis said to Billy was, "I'm tired of all these people being around. It's not fun anymore." And Billy said, "Look, we don't have to have all the guys here. We can clean the house out."

MARTY LACKER: Elvis said, "Well, Billy, I want you here. I need somebody to talk to." And Billy said, "I'll be here. But as far as the guys, we can have them come in shifts, just one guy at a time on duty." Elvis said, "Yeah, that's what I want." So Billy set up a schedule for the shifts and told everybody else to stay away.

Charlie continued to live in a converted apartment behind Graceland because Charlie didn't have any other place to go. But Elvis got tired of Charlie, mostly because Charlie would get drunk and whine. One night, Elvis lost his patience and yelled, "Take this son of a bitch away! Get him out of here!" He'd gone up to Elvis's room and started crying about something. But Elvis felt sorry for him, even though Charlie had no regard for anybody else. He'd stab somebody in the back and laugh about it.

BILLY SMITH: One night in '76, everybody was out in front of Graceland. Elvis had already gotten to the point where he was ed and upset a lot of the time. This was right after a tour.

apologize. I don't think Elvis had the right to hit Charlie, no matter who he was. And it really surprised Charlie, but he kept telling Elvis, "It's okay. It's not your fault. I know you love me."

LAMAR FIKE: When Elvis really cared about you, you knew it. In '76, I had intestinal bypass surgery. Because I had gotten up to 400 pounds. It was elective surgery, but it was very difficult.

The morning I went into the hospital, Elvis called and kept the line open for forty-some hours, all through the surgery and afterwards. To make sure I was all right. And, of course, he paid all my bills.

MARTY LACKER: About three weeks after Billy told me Elvis didn't want to see anybody for a while, I was in bed one night, and I reached for some pills, and the bottle was empty. I was also broke at the time. And Tuinals and Placidyls are not cheap.

My wife said, "Let me go borrow some money, and I'll get you some." And something just made me say, "No, don't."

Patsy said, "Are you sure?" I said, "Yep. I don't want any

more." I don't know why I said it. But I started thinking, "Hey, I've got to go on and live my life and forget about all this." I'd been on the stuff fifteen years. And I know that if I'd still been around Elvis, I wouldn't have stopped.

It took me six months to withdraw, and I did it by myself, with God's help. I never took another pill. And it's been nineteen years.

BILLY SMITH: Some people say I was Elvis's best friend. I guess if anybody knew him at all, it was me. In the last eighteen months, I was with him eighteen hours a day, at least six days a week, usually seven.

LAMAR FIKE: Billy was the closest to Elvis. He was the one Elvis shot the straightest with.

BILLY SMITH: Part of the reason was that I was family. And he wanted to go over old times. And Elvis didn't feel like the younger guys understood him. He didn't feel like he could talk to them. And he couldn't understand why things had gone wrong with the old group. Mostly, he couldn't understand why they weren't still loyal. He actually thought the guys were changing and that he wasn't. He kept saying, "The loyalty. Where's the loyalty?"

LAMAR FIKE: Elvis would hole up in that damn bedroom for sometimes a week at a time. He'd just lie on that extra-king-size bed. God, what a room that was! It looked like the backseat of a limo. Had a red shag carpet and a padded ceiling. And, of course, the windows were closed and sealed off from the world, which gave it a sense of timelessness. It's that same feeling you get in Vegas. It was like a goddamn cave in there. You expected to see bats in it. And that's pretty much where he spent his last year—his inner sanctum.

MARTY LACKER: When you went up the steps, you saw two black, padded double doors. And as you walked in, you could look into Elvis's bedroom to the right. But what you were really walking into is what he called his office. And as you walked to the left, there was a bathroom that Priscilla, or whatever female he was with, used.

His office, which was more like his study, was done in a tan color. It had an upright piano in it. On the back wall, there was a couch built into the wall, underneath a double window. Then, to the left, was Elvis's desk. And he used to have that console TV in there that RCA gave him for selling his first 50 million records. And he had a little refrigerator where he kept his Popsicles, and Eskimo Pies, and Fudgsicles, and yogurt.

Then, if you walked to the right, you went into his bedroom. A rough guess is that it was twenty by thirty feet. He never changed it after my brother-in-law did it over. It had a sort of a jade green, padded Naugahyde ceiling, with two televisions sunk flat in there, so when you were lying in bed, you could look straight up and watch TV. And he had another TV mounted at an angle up in the ceiling.

The walls were all tufted red velvet, except the wall toward the foot of his bed. That was smoked mirrors. And the top of the walls had black velvet borders around them. Real flashy. The bed was custom-built with a black Naugahyde headboard. It had armrests that came out, so you could sit up. And he had two huge, round, imitation-fur lounge chairs in there, one in each corner. And he had a nightstand next to the door, which you saw as soon as you walked in. Of course, the air conditioner was going all the time. It was just freezing in there.

There was a little hallway that led to the bathroom, with two closets, one on each side. Then, in the bathroom itself, to the right of the doorway, was a twelve-foot-long marble counter, with a purple sink built in it. And then there was a dressing mirror, or a makeup mirror, in back of the counter, with oversized lights. I'd say the bathroom was ten by twelve [feet]. Most of it was done in black and gold tiles.

There was another room on the other side of the bathroom. It used to be Grandma's room. But Elvis broke the wall down and made it into a combination bathroom/dressing area/wardrobe room and he kept all his clothes in there. That room was bigger than the bathroom. He had an Exercycle in there, too, that he used sometimes.

The shower had a circular, curved wall, and it was about seven feet in diameter, done in black, brown, and white tiles. It was in the corner. Oddly enough, he kept a vinyl chair in there. The curved wall was just half a wall, with a shower coming out.

His toilet was black, even after they replaced the one he shot up. It sat close to the floor and had a padded seat. There was a yellow throw rug in front of it. And there were two telephones and an intercom mounted on the wall next to the toilet. And he had another TV he could watch from there.

Everybody hears about this reading chair that he had in there. It wasn't really a reading chair—it was a barber's chair. And it was big, and tall, and comfortable, so he just sat in it and read sometimes. He used it when someone did his hair.

Then across the hall was Lisa's room. It used to be the small conference room. When Elvis had a conference table in it, we used to meet in there a lot and sit and talk. That's where he and I used to do the Christmas list.

It's kind of funny. Elvis started out in two rooms in Tupelo. And he ended up in two rooms in Memphis.

BILLY SMITH: The delusions got pretty bad. In '76, Jimmy Gambill, Patsy Presley's son, was playing guns with our kids. And he got up on the fence. Elvis happened to be looking out, and he saw him, and he thought Jimmy was somebody looking to assassinate him.

Elvis got a machine gun and went outside and yelled, "Where's the son of a bitch? I'll kill him!" And the kids broke running. We had to explain to Elvis that it was just Jimmy. And boy, he pitched a fit. He said, "They don't need to be playin' like that!" He was about half out of it on medication.

He didn't shoot the gun that time, but he did another time. It was probably about seven or eight o'clock in the morning. Al Strada saw this snake goin' up a tree there at Graceland. He went in and started tellin' Elvis about it. And Elvis had already taken his sleeping pills, but now he was ready to snake-hunt.

In a few minutes, somebody called me and told me he was out there. I went out, and he was shootin'. And about half the time, he couldn't even see the snake. I never did see it myself. Anyway, he looked like some kind of drunk. He'd say, "I see it," and he'd rear back and let fire. And when he'd shoot, he'd go about two steps back, and about ten forward, with the gun just wavin'.

Finally, I got him to sit down on the curb. And when I did, well, he just knew he saw it again. He cocked the gun again, and he shot it, and the old shotgun kicked so hard that Elvis just went right on over in the drive.

I said, "Uh, Elvis, we might ought to go in. There's some people down at the gate." And he looked, and he said, "Yeah, maybe I ought to."

I staggered him on in and got him in the bed. And I told Al, "Man, you're crazy! Don't never get him out there with a gun." The pellets had to be sprayin' all over the road 'cause that's the way he was shootin', just straight towards the road.

MARTY LACKER: I don't know how long Elvis went before he had somebody call Dr. Nick again, but it wasn't all that long. And at some point, I think in early '76, after Marian Cocke left, Dr. Nick had a nurse who worked for him, Tish Henley, move into a trailer there at Graceland with her husband so Nick could keep a closer eye on what Elvis took. He didn't want him waking up and taking whatever was on his nightstand and maybe miscalculating.

Tish picked up the prescriptions at the Prescription House, which was a pharmacy across the street from Dr. Nick's office. She also went on the tours with Ghanem when Nick couldn't go or Elvis wouldn't let him. She kept all that stuff in an overnight bag under lock and key in her trailer. But Elvis knew how to get what he wanted.

BILLY SMITH: I guess you could say that Elvis had his own pharmacy in the backyard. I don't know how much of a supply of anything Dr. Nick give her, but he give her enough. So that the Stanleys, or Aunt Delta, or whoever, could go out there to the trailer and pick up Elvis's stuff and bring it back to him.

In '76, I went to Dr. Nick and I said, "What in the hell is going on with all the stuff he's getting?" Dr. Nick told me, "We need to get together as a group around him. I can't do it by myself, and if I shut him off completely, he'll just go somewhere else and get it. We can't stop it, but we can reduce it."

So I asked him to set up a plan. And we started draining his drugs and substituting things. We'd take a syringe and actually draw liquid out of a Placidyl in capsule form and then blow it back up. Or if it was a capsule you could break apart, we would put sugar or Sweet'n Low in 'em.

You couldn't hardly do anything with tablets, unless they happened to be the same size as something less harmful. For Demerol tablets, we used phenobarbital about half the time. And with liquid Demerol, we either squirted some of it out or diluted it with saline or just plain water. Or we substituted Talwin—which is a synthetic narcotic and not as powerful—or Elavil, which is a mood elevator, not a narcotic.

You can't imagine the amount of stuff that we substituted. I even guinea-pigged myself one time to make damn sure Elvis couldn't tell what we were doing. But like any drug addict, he caught on to the diluted shots pretty damn quick. At first he'd say, "Hey, bring on some more. This ain't doin' shit for me." And then after that, he figured out what was happening, and he started wanting the tablets instead of the shots.

Mostly, he'd confront Dr. Nick. But he outsmarted us right often. When he could get his hands on a whole bottle of something, he started increasing the dose. That way he got the same amount as the shot. And all the while, us saying, "No, you've had your amount for the night. That's it." That's when Elvis would fly out of here and get all the damn Demerol pills that he wanted.

It was a vicious cycle that most of the time we didn't know how to control. But we tried.

MARTY LACKER: One of the things Billy set up with Nichopoulos was these packets of medication. In other words, they doled out Elvis's drugs to him in little envelopes at certain times of the day and night. And half of that stuff was placebos.

The Stanleys pretty much delivered it. And sometimes Delta Mae. They got the packets from Tish. The Stanleys called them "First Attack," "Second Attack," and "Third Attack." They were real proud of that. They thought that was hip.

BILLY SMITH: With the packets of medication . . . very seldom did it get to three. We tried to keep everything away from him. Usually, we'd put his sleeping medication and whatever else he needed, say, medicine for his blood pressure or his colon, in a little envelope. That was Medication Packet Number One. There might be eleven pills in it at a time. And he'd get that about four A.M.

If the first one didn't put him out, and he asked for more, the second packet was brought out. That was usually a couple more sleeping pills. Because after he took his initial medication, they didn't add anything but sleeping pills. Elvis didn't sleep but about four hours at a time, but I know damn well that a lot of times he fought going to sleep, just to get more. So he might get that about eight A.M. If it got to the third packet, it was maybe a little stronger sleeping medicine, and he got that a few hours later. And, of course, the Demerol and Dilaudid came in between all the pills.

LAMAR FIKE: Ricky, and David, even Linda, would inject him with Demerol or Dilaudid three or four times a night. Used to stick it right in his hip. David said he looked like a pincushion. It was hard to stick a needle in because you couldn't find a clear spot.

BILLY SMITH: Most of the time, the Demerol and Dilaudid was drawn ahead of time. Dr. Nick would give it to him if he was there or Tish Henley, the nurse. When he started, he always wanted somebody else to do it. But now, he'd got to the point that he was desperate enough to give it to himself. He took enough that it disfigured some portions of his hip and his arms.

MARTY LACKER: From the evidence that the state gathered when it went after Dr. Nick, Elvis's drug schedule was a lot different when he went on tour. Nichopoulos wrote out a drug protocol in six stages. He kept it in his medical bag. The bag was stolen from his Mercedes just before Elvis died. But Metro narcotics officers recovered it, and they made copies before they gave it back to Nick. The protocols were in his handwriting, so they're authentic. And the state produced them when they indicted him.

Stage one came at about three P.M., when Elvis got up. Nick gave him a "voice shot" that Ghanem had come up with. In addition, he gave him three appetite suppressants, some medicine for dizziness, a laxative, some vitamins and herbs, and some testosterone.

Stage two came an hour before Elvis went onstage. This was another voice shot, plus a decongestant with codeine, an amphetamine, some kind of treatment for vertigo, and Dilaudid. Stage three, which was timed just a few minutes before Elvis's performance, was made up of Dilaudid, Dexedrine, and some caffeine. And stage four, which came right after Elvis's performance, was all to bring him down—a pill to lower his blood pressure, some watered-down Demerol, a tranquilizer or some other kind of sedative, and an antihistamine.

Later on, just before Elvis went to bed, they gave him stage five. That consisted of Placidyl, a Quaalude, three other kinds of sedatives, an amphetamine—why I don't know, with that many downers—a blood pressure pill, and a laxative. Then, if Elvis couldn't sleep, Nick would give him stage six. That was Amytal, which is a hypnotic sleeping pill, and more Quaaludes.

Dr. Nick gave him 19,000 doses in the last 31½ months of his life. And not just that stuff. Also Percodan, Nembutal, Carbrital, which is a barbiturate, Biphetamine, which is another upper, Parest, which is a methaqualone like Quaalude, Tuinal, Dexamyl, Ionamin, which is an appetite suppressant, Valium, and Leritine, a narcotic used by people allergic to codeine. Apparently, Elvis couldn't take codeine in large doses.

LAMAR FIKE: Dr. Nick says he gave Elvis placebos 80 percent of the time. I don't think that's right. I think there were more of the real drugs than the placebos.

BILLY SMITH: I don't know about 80 percent. I would say more along the lines of half and half. But we were doing any damn thing we could. We'd even steal his drugs—take a lot of 'em when he was asleep. If he knew how much of the drugs I stole from him, I'd have been gone, and we'd probably never seen or spoke to each other again. The amount of stuff I flushed down the toilet was just unbelievable. But we still couldn't stop him.

Maybe I should have been even tougher. But I thought he would fire me. So I had a decision to make. And I chose to stay. I was wrapped up in that world, and I didn't know how the hell to leave.

MARTY LACKER: In October, Elvis started another tour. When he was out in Tahoe in May, people said he was in such bad shape that he had locomotive attacks where he couldn't walk across the stage. And he was forgetting the words to his songs again. He looked awful. But by October, people said he'd lost some weight.

BILLY SMITH: His attitude was worse, though. He wouldn't even rehearse. He'd say, "Hell, I know this. Let's get it over with." He never rehearsed in the last year or so, even after he'd been off three or four weeks. And he wouldn't change the show any, either.

He got around it by saying, "We're going to a different city, and they haven't seen that show. It's different to them." He never stopped to think that a lot of fans traveled from one city to another.

MARTY LACKER: October was also when Elvis found out for sure that Red, and Sonny, and Dave were writing a book [*Elvis: What Happened?*]. Elvis called everybody into his hotel room and cried and asked them what they had on Red and Sonny. Originally, the guys had gone to the *Star*, the tabloid, just for a story. And the *Star* went to Ballantine Books for a paperback deal.

BILLY SMITH: Red took it heavy for the way the book was written. But I don't think anybody had more love for Elvis than Red.

MARTY LACKER: They wrote the book to get back at him, and to make some money, so their families could live. And maybe to help Elvis wake up and see what was happening. That's what they said, and I believe them.

BILLY SMITH: I went up there one day, and he'd done ranted and raved and tore up the damn room, he was so mad. He was in the bed. I went over to him, and I put my arm around him, and I said, "It's all right. They didn't mean no harm. You know you still love 'em. This is the only way they could get back. And it's nothing you haven't heard before." I petted him, and I talked baby talk to him. I said, "It's okay. It's going to be all right."

MARTY LACKER: Elvis thought Red and Sonny had betrayed him. But the main reason the book upset him was because he knew people would find out he spent $1 million a year on drugs and doctors.

A lot of performers have contempt for their audience, believe it or not. But not Elvis. He loved his fans. I've never seen anybody who cared as much for them. He knew that without them, he had nothing. And he was afraid if they found out he was doing drugs, they wouldn't like him anymore. Because his fans were conservative, middle-aged Bible Belters, for the most part. He thought he was about to lose the last thing he had.

LAMAR FIKE: At some point in the fall, Elvis was out in California visiting Linda. He'd gotten her an apartment in Santa Monica so she could go on her acting auditions. And he started thinking about Red, and Sonny, and Dave's book, and he pretty much went nuts. According to David Stanley, Elvis banged on his door in the middle of the night, and when it took him too long to answer, Elvis just kicked it down.

He was wearing a black jumpsuit with a Drug Enforcement Agency patch on it and one of his gladiator show belts with two .45s stuck in it. And he was carrying his Thompson submachine gun. David said he had cotton balls stuffed up his nose, so he was doing liquid coke. And he got David up and said, "We're goin' head-huntin'. We're going to kill those sons of bitches!"—meaning Red and Sonny. They were staying in a motel in Hollywood.

Elvis told David to get his gun, and they went roaring down the Santa Monica Freeway in Elvis's new black Dino Ferrari Spyder. Elvis was just raving on about all he'd done for Red and Sonny, and now they were going to repay him by letting his daughter read he was on drugs.

David said, "Better she read you were a druggie than a killer, Elvis." And David said Elvis slammed on the breaks in the middle of an intersection and broke down crying. David drove him back to Linda's apartment, and they put him to bed.

Elvis carried that stuff on for months, saying he wanted to do them in and this and that. But he would calm down and say, "You know, I guess they did what they needed to do. But I wish they hadn't done it."

He put in another call to Sinatra about it. Elvis made some

remark about wanting to kill 'em, and Frank said, "Who do you need?"

Frank was probably kidding. But I think Elvis got scared. Maybe he thought Frank really could have it done. He thought about it a little more, and he said, "Thanks, but I'll pass." And Frank said, "Again, anything I can do to help you on it, let me know."

MARTY LACKER: Because they were scared, Red and Sonny said they put a statement in a safety deposit box, along with what they called extremely damaging photographs and documents. I don't know what they would have had, unless they were those photos of Priscilla and the girl. Red intimated to me one time that he either saw the pictures or he had a couple of them.

In desperation, Elvis had John O'Grady go to Red and Sonny and offer them $100,000 to stop the book. And they told O'Grady to go to hell. So then Elvis called Red himself. I guess Red taped it because there's a transcript of the conversation in their book. Elvis was kind of incoherent, but he basically said, "I'll do anything you guys need me to do for you. You know I still care a lot about you, and I'll take care of your families or get you a job. Just let me know." Quite frankly, he was just saying that to stop them. And who knows whether Elvis would have kept his word?

BILLY SMITH: Mostly, Elvis called Red to ask why they were doing it and to lay a pity act on him.

LAMAR FIKE: The book came out two weeks before Elvis's death. Bad, bad timing. Or great timing, from a marketing point of view. It sold 3.5 million copies. And it's still in print. I think Red was extremely upset about it. But as he said, they were trying to get Elvis's attention, and they needed money. But Elvis saw it only one way. The [Memphis] Mafia code of silence had been broken.

MARTY LACKER: Everything started collapsing like a house of cards. In early November, Linda left. She wrote Elvis a Dear John letter and had her brother, Sam, deliver it. Elvis had been easing her out slowly but surely. She saw that he wasn't going to marry her, and she also saw that he wasn't going to get off the pills. And she didn't want to see him that way anymore. She was just tired of it. She wanted a life of her own.

BILLY SMITH: There was also a conspiracy to get rid of Linda. Maybe Vernon and some of the others looked at the house and the apartment Elvis got her and thought, "We can't stop his spending, but we can stop hers."

MARTY LACKER: Elvis liked for her to spend money, so she'd be away and he could do what he wanted. Towards the end, he told her, "Just go on and use the credit cards, and buy what you want to buy."

Well, when Vernon started getting the bills, he came to Elvis and said, "Look what she's doing!" I think she ran up something like $30,000 on his MasterCard. Elvis told Vernon, "Don't worry about it." Evidently, Vernon told people like Joe and Charlie. Because they started calling Linda a bitch and a gold digger.

I can tell you that whatever Linda bought, and whatever Elvis gave her, she earned, and then some.

BILLY SMITH: They couldn't see that she was good for him. All they saw was dollar signs. Priscilla had always been leery about asking for money, or maybe felt belittled by having to ask. But Linda was right the opposite. If she needed something, she just flat told him. And she didn't do without anything, and she shouldn't have, as far as I'm concerned. None of them should have. Whatever they got, they deserved. Except maybe the last one.

MARTY LACKER: Two weeks after Linda left, George Klein brought Ginger Alden up to Graceland with her sisters, Terry and Rosemary. Elvis couldn't get away from beauty queens. Terry was the reigning Miss Tennessee. And Ginger had been runner-up. But she held her own titles: Miss Mid-South and Miss Traffic Safety, if you can believe that. The day after he met her, Elvis took Ginger to Vegas for the day. Three weeks later, he was buying her a car.

There's some irony here. Elvis had met Ginger before. When

she was five, he'd patted her on the head and taken her for a ride on the roller coaster at the fairgrounds. Her mother, Jo, was an Elvis nut. The whole family was always hanging around the gates. And Ginger's father, as a sergeant in the army, was in the room when Elvis was inducted into the service.

Ginger was one of the worst choices Elvis ever made. But George is proud he introduced them. He brags about it. He says the only significant woman Elvis ever went with that he didn't introduce him to was Priscilla. See why we call George a glorified pimp?

BILLY SMITH: Ginger was not a petite woman, but she was a pretty woman. And she looked like Priscilla. Dr. Nick thought something about her, maybe her eyes, reminded Elvis of Aunt Gladys. I don't know. She had that dark, teased hair and wore a lot of makeup. Ginger wasn't dumb, but she was kind of shallow and self-centered. She wasn't a caring, nurturing person like Linda.

I think what it all boiled down to was the fact that she was a pretty woman, she was twenty years old, and Elvis still wanted to be seen with a woman with that virginal look. So he could sort of say, "Hey, I can still get it."

One day on tour, Elvis stopped me and said, "Billy, do you think Ginger's a virgin?" Right in front of her! I said, "Well, let me put it this way. What did she tell you?" He said, "She says she is." I said, "Well, if she told you that, I guess she's right then."

I'd say that relationship was more about companionship. In the last year, I don't think the sex mattered one way or the other.

LAMAR FIKE: Dr. Nick wasn't giving Elvis testosterone just to make him more virile onstage. Shit, no. He gave it to him for impotence. You couldn't dope up that much and get a hard-on if Elizabeth Taylor stuck her ass in your face.

BILLY SMITH: I think Elvis was having a problem, yeah. It was caused by the drugs. For about the last year and a half, I think he was incapable of it. And I think he was somewhat limited for a couple years before that. He never told me that, of course. Too macho for that shit.

When he first met Ginger, he put up a front. But from things going around, we knew that he wasn't making it with a lot of the women he was with. Some of his partners said it was kind of a disappointment.

Every once in a while, he'd say little things to get you to believe that he was still functioning full-tilt, like "We had a lot of fun last night," or, "Yeah, I didn't just sleep all damn night, in spite of what you guys might think."

LAMAR FIKE: There was so much weird shit going on. Like when Jerry Lee Lewis got arrested out in front of Graceland. That was November '76.

BILLY SMITH: Harold called up at the house, and I answered the phone. He said Jerry Lee was down there just drunk out of his mind, waving a .38-caliber derringer around. He was demanding to see Elvis.

I went upstairs and told Elvis, "Jerry Lee's down there. He's been drinking, and he's got a gun. And he's saying you called and wanted to see him." Which I knew wasn't true. Elvis didn't want to be around Jerry Lee because of his attitude. He didn't think he knew how to treat his fans or other people. Elvis would always say, "If Jerry Lee would just play the piano and keep his mouth shut, he'd be a hell of a lot better off."

I said, "Elvis, there's a lot of other people down at the gate, too. Harold wants to know what to do." Elvis said, "Tell Harold to either have that drunk son of a bitch locked up, or I'm going down and beat the hell out of him." So Harold called the cops and had Jerry Lee arrested.

MARTY LACKER: Elvis had gnawed on Jerry Lee's nerves for years. He was just so jealous of what Elvis had accomplished. Because Jerry Lee thought he was more talented than Elvis. And he knew that Elvis never liked him. To this day, it still eats at him, even though he sometimes talks nicely about Elvis.

A couple years ago, Jerry Lee was on *The Arsenio Hall Show*, and Arsenio brought that incident up. Jerry Lee looked straight in the camera and said, "It's a bald-faced lie. It never happened. It's just a rumor that someone started spreading. I never did that." All anybody had to do was call the Memphis Police Department and find out that he did.

LAMAR FIKE: Elvis buzzed me in the kitchen and said, "Come up here. I want to show you something." I went up there and sat down beside the bed, and we watched Jerry Lee on the monitors. We'd take that camera and dolly it in on him. Harold must have told him what Elvis said because Jerry Lee got mad, got back in his car, and butted the gate. Elvis said, "That son of a bitch is trying to tear the gate down! He's lost his mind!" Jerry Lee is a real dog. Always has been.

🕺 🕺 🕺

MARTY LACKER: In December, Elvis went back into the Hilton for ten days. The hotel really didn't want him, but Colonel said, "Let us have the room, and we'll take the door." And he jacked the price up to twenty-nine bucks a person. And it was a sellout. From what I heard, Elvis wasn't in great form. He'd sing half songs, and be incoherent some of the time, and forget some of the words. I think he had the Stamps sing a couple numbers. And he sat down for several songs one night because he said he'd sprained his ankle.

People got upset. Some of them asked for a refund and said they wouldn't come back. And Vernon got chest pains and had to be put in the hospital out there.

It was pretty much a disaster. Elvis was too unstable. Like what he pulled with Don Rickles. In the early sixties, Elvis went to see Rickles in the lounge at the Sahara. This was when Rickles was just starting out in Vegas, when he really cut people up just terrible. It didn't matter who you were.

I wasn't there, but Elvis told me that when he went in to see him, Rickles said, "Well, look here. Here's Elvis Presley. Normally, I'd be making fun of him as part of my act. But this is one man I'm not going to say anything about because I know how much he cared for his mother and how good he was to her." He said, "I have nothing but respect for a man like that." Because Rickles was well known for his devotion to his mother.

Well, when Elvis played Vegas in December of '76, he went

over to see Rickles at the Riviera. And Rickles introduced Elvis from the audience. The guys said Elvis came up from the audience and went onstage and instead of just saying "hello" to everybody, he started reading from *The Voice of Silence*, one of his religious books. And Rickles just stood there. He didn't know what to do.

Finally, Rickles looked at Elvis and gave him this big smile and said, "Hey, Elvis, where are we going with this?" And Elvis asked Rickles to read a few passages. He told him it was important. By this time, the audience was really losing patience. And Rickles was, like, dying. Elvis finally let Rickles quit reading, and he left the stage. And the audience applauded, but just politely, you know.

That got around to the other hotels, the same as the quality of Elvis's shows at the Hilton. The word was out that Elvis was unpredictable, an embarrassment, and maybe even unbankable.

After that, Elvis never played Vegas again. It was over.

LAMAR FIKE: When Elvis died, Rex Humbard, the evangelist, told his television audience that he met with Elvis at the Hilton that last time. He said that Elvis told him he knew his time was short, or some such. He also said he was surprised at Elvis's knowledge of the Bible, especially the prophecies of the Old Testament. Elvis supposedly told him, "These are the last days before Jesus comes, aren't they? We've had all of the wars, and we've had the pestilence and starvation. The Lord's coming soon, don't you think, Rex?"

Well, Rex said tears came up in Elvis's eyes, and Rex reached out and clasped both his hands, and he said, "Elvis, I want to pray for you." And Elvis said, "Please do." And they prayed for five minutes or so, and everybody in the room—J.D. [Sumner] and [Humbard's wife] Maude Aimee—started to sob and cry and stuff.

Rex said he thought Elvis was "cramming for the Big Exam."

I don't know how much cramming Elvis did or what else they did in there. But Rex came by, that's true. He went into Elvis's dressing room, and they got back there and had a little prayer session. Rex was a weird dude. He thought I was insane, too. He thought we all were.

BILLY SMITH: I don't remember that meeting at all. But if Lamar says it happened, I guess it did. It's just that now that Elvis is gone, so many people had these little meetings with him.

LAMAR FIKE: A couple of years ago, Wayne Newton bought a note from Sotheby's that Elvis supposedly wrote in Vegas in December of '76. I never saw it, but I read about it, and I've seen pictures of the note. It says, "I feel so alone sometimes. The night is quiet for me. I'd love to be able to sleep. I am glad that everyone is gone now. I'll probably not rest. I have no need for all this. Help me, Lord."

The story goes that Elvis wrote it on the telephone pad by his bed, and that he crumpled it up and threw it away, and that one of the guys saved it. I don't know how it got to Sotheby's. But it's got to be worth a lot of money.

Newton wrote a song about it called "The Letter." And he made a music video on the stage of the Hilton and in Elvis's suite, and he showed the note on camera, and read the whole thing. Good song.

BILLY SMITH: I don't believe Elvis wrote that, and neither does Jo. Because he just didn't write down his feelings like that. Now, he would write down things that he had read in a book, but that's it.

MARTY LACKER: I think it's possible. Elvis was into religion full steam at the end. And my experience is that he didn't write letters, but he used to write a lot of things down. Now, who got it out of the wastepaper basket and sold it, I don't know. Newton says he bought the note because he was so moved by it, and that he wrote the song to make Elvis's death less painful to his fans. He said he wanted them to know Elvis wasn't alone. Give me a break. Newton just saw that he might finally have a hit record for the first time in twenty damn years.

Wayne Newton is sickening. I've seen him in about eighteen different interviews say how he used to sit and talk and run around with Elvis in Vegas. Whoopie Goldberg had him on her interview show, Christmas of '92. She said, "You were a close friend of Elvis Presley, weren't you?" He answered something like "Yes, we used to talk a lot. He was very troubled and depressed, especially in the later years." Then he went on to say that Elvis didn't have any real friends around him, that it was one thing for the guys to "take" his money, but when Red and Sonny revealed his personal life in a book, it was worse.

First of all, Newton was not close to Elvis. They talked briefly a couple of times in Vegas. He had no idea what Elvis was really like. Second, none of us "took" Elvis's money. We earned it. Third, I'd like to see Newton say what he said about Red and Sonny to their face. And last, since he cared so much for Elvis, why didn't he just buy the note Elvis supposedly wrote and keep it as a personal memento instead of trying to get a hit record out of it?

It's tiresome to hear these so-called celebrity friends of Elvis, like Tom Jones and Newton, get on TV and tell the public all this crap. The public doesn't know it's not true. After he died, they all started singing his songs and taking on some of his mannerisms. Why? Because they were trying to get Elvis's fans. They couldn't carry Elvis's bags, much less take his place.

CHAPTER 51

THE SLIDE

BILLY SMITH: At the end of December '76, Elvis started his ninth tour of the year. He was just working too damn much. On New Year's Eve, he played Pittsburgh. And then early that morning, he decided he wanted to fly on back into Memphis. It was snowy, and gall dang, it was cold. And Elvis got a bomb threat.

Some wacko called and said he'd planted a bomb on the *Lisa Marie*. We had to evacuate the plane there in Pittsburgh and wait until they checked it all out. Dick Grob got with the police up there, and they found the guy and locked him up.

One of the reasons Elvis wanted to get back home was because Ginger's grandfather had died, and he said he'd take her to the funeral over in Arkansas.

Elvis made a lot of concessions to Ginger. Normally, he didn't attend funerals because they were such a downer. But he did it for her. And that was the complete reverse of how he acted when Linda's grandfather died. It was the day Elvis was supposed to go on tour, so, naturally, Linda didn't go with him. Elvis said, "Goddamn, he's got bad timing! Don't he know I got a tour?"

LAMAR FIKE: Albert Goldman wrote that when Elvis went to Ginger's grandfather's funeral, he said, "It won't be long before I'm there." Albert uses it as support for his theory that Elvis killed himself. Goldman also says that sometime around this period, Elvis broke down and sobbed, "I wish I'd been a better father." Are you kidding? Elvis was not a person who thought about what he should have done or what he should not have done. None of that poignant bullshit. There was no cry for mercy that I remember.

MARTY LACKER: During the third week of January, Elvis went to Nashville to record at Creative Workshop. But he was ticked off about something, and he just stayed over at the Sheraton South for three days, then flew home without ever singing a note. He'd lost all interest in that, and he was sending a message to Colonel.

From what I understand, he was also mad at Ginger because she wouldn't go with him. Felton Jarvis would go over to the hotel and take him demos to listen to. But Elvis supposedly spent most of his time in the hotel room calling Ginger. And he just let the musicians sit around the studio and wait.

BILLY SMITH: Before we ever went over there, Elvis said to me, "I'm not going to do it. If I have to, I'll say I'm losing my voice." Well, that's what he done. He was getting back at Colonel *and* RCA.

🕴 🕴 🕴

MARTY LACKER: From what Billy and the other guys tell me, Ginger probably added to Elvis's downfall. First of all, she didn't care anything about him. Second, she was too young for him. And third, the way I saw it, she was there for what she could get. She forced her whole family on him. He ended up buying them a house with a swimming pool. And he bought them cars, and he took them on trips.

Ginger was always disappointing him. She didn't love him—she didn't even want to be around him. She wouldn't move into Graceland, she didn't like to spend the night, and she didn't want to go on all the tours. She didn't seem interested in pleasing him much at all. And she certainly didn't watch him until he went to sleep like Linda did or make sure he didn't choke while he ate.

One night, she started to go home, and Elvis fired a pistol over her head. But it didn't stop her. So he started seeing other women. Even a fifteen-year-old schoolgirl, Rise Smith. But he really wanted Ginger. Billy asked him one time, "Why the hell do you put up with her?" And Elvis answered, "I'm just getting too old and tired to train another one."

BILLY SMITH: I think Ginger was the first woman he'd run across other than Priscilla who rejected him. You could tell they were having problems. Sometimes she wouldn't come up for a few days, and he'd get all agitated and sullen and say, "Where is she, man? Why don't she stay here?" And when she did come, she'd get up and go home after Elvis went to sleep. One time, he even told one of the guys, "Let the air out of her tires so she can't leave."

Another time, about six o'clock in the morning, Elvis called me, and he was real upset because Ginger was fixin' to go home. He said, "Don't let her out! Keep the gate closed!"

I said, "Goddamn, Elvis! Open the gate and let the girl go home, man. This is not a prison!"

I said it because I was mad and fed up with it. One night, God, they were into it. She hadn't been up there in two or three days. And he was trying to keep her from leaving. She finally got to go home. And Elvis asked me, "What do you think about Ginger? Do you think I should find somebody else?" I said, "I think she's everything in a woman that you always hated. And you're just tolerating it." Well, I saw his jawbone go to flexing. And I figured, "This is it." I thought he'd fire me. He didn't, but he stayed mad at me for three days.

LAMAR FIKE: Ginger didn't give a rat's ass about him. I'll tell you something else. At the end of January, something like nine weeks after they met, Elvis gave her an eleven-and-a-half-karat diamond. Cost something like $70,000. But when Elvis gave a woman a ring, it didn't mean a damn thing.

BILLY SMITH: Elvis was not going to marry her. But she thought he was. We even took her out window-shopping for wedding dresses once, about midnight. We'd drive by a store, and he'd say, "Hey, there's one." And he would describe what he wanted Ginger to wear on her head—that thing that stands up that the Spanish women wear. And a long train on her dress. And Ginger believed all this. But he'd also say, "Yeah, and when we get married . . . " and then turn to Jo and me and say, real low, "Whenever that is."

The reason he give her an eleven-and-a-half-karat ring isn't what everybody thought. He saw the need to buy her again. She come over one night, and she hadn't been up in a few days, and about one A.M., Elvis wanted to get her an engagement ring.

He got Lowell Hays up there, and nothing Lowell had suited him. Elvis said, "I need a bigger stone." And Lowell said, "I don't have anything over maybe three carats. But why don't I go to New York and buy you one and then make a ring?" Elvis said, "How long will that take?" Lowell said, "About a week." And Elvis said, "That's too long. I got to have it no later than tomorrow."

So Lowell said, "Well, you could just take the stone out of your TCB ring, and I could replace it later." So that's what they done. And Ginger stayed at Graceland for a little while then. But she went right back to the same old pattern. Elvis kept buying her more jewelry just to keep her there.

MARTY LACKER: I don't know that there was any way that that relationship could work. Ginger wanted to go out and party all the time and show Elvis off. And she wanted him to socialize with her group of friends—all sorts of things that Elvis wouldn't do.

BILLY SMITH: I was suspicious of some of the things she done. Like, we'd call and she wouldn't be at home. I'd ask her mother, "Where's Ginger?" And Mrs. Alden would say, "Ginger's spending the night at a girlfriend's house."

I'd say, "Well, has she got a phone there where I can reach her?" Mrs. Alden would say, "Ah, no. I can run over and tell her, though, and she'll get back in touch with you."

It really didn't make any difference whether she was true to Elvis or not. Elvis thought she was faithful, and that was the main thing. But I was afraid Elvis would say, "Find out where her girlfriend lives, and we'll just go over there." And I was leery about what he'd do if it turned out she wasn't there.

To be honest, we had her followed a couple times. If Elvis had ever known that, God, he'd have fired all of us. But she was in a nightclub dancing with a guy.

His relationship with Ginger pointed up a lot of things. To me, Elvis went through four stages. There was the fifties Elvis, which was a happy-go-lucky, I've-got-it-all type of guy. He understood other people's feelings more during that time, I think. Then there was the sixties Elvis. He didn't really care about others. He became harder. He was concerned with what Elvis wanted, and that was it. And then there was the seventies Elvis, when he realized that the people around him needed certain things.

After that came the final stage. That's when he was just reminiscing about the past, about how it had been. And talking about not really having anyplace to go or any new challenges. What Ginger and her friends done to have a good time, we had already experienced so many times. And it wasn't just a problem with Ginger, but with the newer guys in the group.

MARTY LACKER: After Elvis died, Mrs. Alden sued the estate for $40,000. She said Elvis promised to pay off the mortgage on that house he gave them, but that he'd never had it put in their name. And she claimed he was going to pay for home improvements and even for part of her divorce from Ginger's father.

BILLY SMITH: Elvis always had a pet name for a girl he was really involved with. Ginger's was "Gingerbread." Elvis didn't know it, but I always called her "Gingersnatch." And I didn't stop there. I called her sister Rosemary "Poundcake." Which was really crude of me, but I couldn't help it. I was so pissed off at that family.

This one time when we were talking about Ginger, when he asked me if I thought he should stay with her or find somebody else, I said, "There are a lot of nice women your age. Why don't you find somebody like that? Somebody you can talk to and have a real relationship with?" And Elvis said, "What in the hell could a forty-two-year-old woman do for me?"

MARTY LACKER: Early in February, RCA made another attempt to get Elvis to record. This time, they came back to Graceland and set up a recording studio in the racquetball court. Elvis pulled the same stunt he did in Nashville—complained of a sore throat and left everybody holed up in the motel for days. Finally, Felton called it quits. That was the last time they made the effort to record him.

Right after that, I heard all kind of reports about how erratic his shows were. In Charlotte, North Carolina, at the end of February, he tried to sing "Moody Blue" a couple of times, but he gave up on it. Said the note was too high. He really just didn't know the song well enough to perform it. He was reading it off the lyric sheet. Finally, he just ripped the lyric sheet in half. But the next night, he got it.

LAMAR FIKE: That was the tour up through North and South Carolina. Elvis was mad at Dr. Nick again and refused to let him go. So Tish Henley went, and Elias Ghanem.

Somewhere in South Carolina, Elias had to put Elvis in a tub and wash him down in ice to bring him back around. Then we almost lost him somewhere in North Carolina. God, it was just so bad. This one time, I saw him, and I said, "Are you all right?" And he said, "Yeah, I'm fine." I said, "Man, you can't keep putting yourself through this." He said, "Aw, Lamar, I'll watch them lower your big ass into the ground." I said, "I doubt that seriously."

Elvis always thought he would outlive me because of my size. But now that I'd had that intestinal bypass, I was down to 185 pounds, from four hundred. I was losing weight, and Elvis was gaining. I weighed about seventy pounds less than he did.

We came off that Carolina tour, and landed the 880, and he got mad at me about something. And he called me "Lard-ass," the same way he'd done for years when he got angry. I left him alone for a few minutes, and then when it was time to get off the plane, I walked back in the bedroom and said, "Let's go, Lard-ass."

He said, "You son of a bitch, you've been waiting twenty years for this." I said, "You're right." And this time he didn't get mad.

🏃 🏃 🏃

MARTY LACKER: The day Elvis came off that winter tour, George Klein got indicted. He was still working as a deejay. They nailed him for one count of conspiracy to commit mail fraud, plus three counts of possession of stolen mail, and aiding and abetting a crime. It had to do with, shall we say, "acquiring" Arbitron Radio Research reports and doctoring the listener ratings to make them higher than they were. That was to boost the advertising revenue.

Klein called Elvis and asked him if there was anything he could do to help him out because he was looking at a sixty-day federal sentence in the Shelby County jail.

Elvis tried his usual contacts, and nothing happened. So he decided to go to Jimmy Carter, who'd just been elected president. Elvis liked Carter. He used to come to the shows a lot. The first time Elvis played the Omni, in Atlanta, Carter came back to see him, and then when he was running for president, he came back to see Elvis twice. So Elvis felt like he was a friend.

BILLY SMITH: Elvis didn't know how to contact President Carter. So he asked me, "Do you think you could get in touch with him?" I said, "I don't know, but I'll give it my best shot."

First, I called a friend who was an FBI agent in Memphis. And he give me a number to the White House. That just got me to a secretary. But I said, "This is Elvis Presley's cousin calling. I'm calling for him. And it's not a joke. Would you tell the president that Elvis Presley wants to talk to him the first chance he gets. In the next day or two, if possible." I said, "In a few hours, Elvis'll be gettin' up, so late afternoon is the best time to get him."

Well, they passed on the information, and Elvis got a call one afternoon about five o'clock. It was Chip Carter, the president's son. Elvis answered, and Chip asked for me. Elvis said, "He's not here, but this is Elvis Presley. Can I help you?" Which I thought was kind of funny. Anyway, I don't know what good it done. George had to do that jail time after all.

LAMAR FIKE: George was guilty of falsifying the WHBQ Radio logs—changing the numbers—but in this situation, I think George was a dupe. He probably didn't know what the term "mail fraud" was.

MARTY LACKER: In March of '77, I moved to California and went to work as a salesman for a food company. I'd been off the drugs five months, and I wanted to get away from everything.

Just before I left, I sent Elvis a letter, through Billy. I explained that I'd been off drugs all these months and that I hadn't felt that good in years. I was hoping two things would happen: that he'd be happy for me and that he'd think about getting off drugs himself.

I heard later from a friend of my nephew who worked for Malco's Theatres that the night Elvis got the letter, he started screaming about me in the Memphian. He said Elvis got up and said, "Goddamn Marty, trying to reform me!"

Billy says it never happened, but maybe he was trying to spare my feelings. Because I was selling everything I had, including my house, and for only the second time in all those years, I asked Elvis if he'd loan me some money to start over in California. And he didn't give it to me. This kid said Elvis was yelling about that, too. I never heard back from him about it. Not a word.

BILLY SMITH: That winter, Elvis got it in his mind to have his will updated. He was fixin' to go on vacation to Hawaii in March, and he had the tours coming up right after that. So February was his only chance to do it. He'd say to me, "Get Daddy on the phone. I need to talk to him about my will." This went on for a couple weeks.

I never heard their conversations, but Elvis told me and a couple other people, "You're in the will, so if anything happens to me, you can be assured you'll be taken care of." Which is what he promised me when I give up my job at the railroad. Of course, Aunt Delta and Grandma were in it, also.

Well, on the night of March third, they brought the will up to him to sign. I was upstairs in his room. We were going out motorcycle riding a little later, and I was getting his stuff ready.

I forget who all was there—Vernon, and Beecher Smith, the lawyer, and his wife, Ann, I know. And the witnesses, which were Ginger and Charlie. Anyway, they stayed about six or seven minutes—hardly any time. They didn't read it to him. He was just briefly told that they had done everything he'd requested and all they needed was the signature.

When everybody left, Elvis handed the will to me, and he said, "Put this in a safe place. And remember where it is." And then he said, "If you want, you can read it." I said, "I don't want to read it." He said, "Well, you might ought'a read it—you're in it." And I said, "I don't like to think about wills. They're morbid to me. So I'll just put it up." And I did.

A couple of nights later, he got it out and showed me a section of it. He said, "This is what I'm leaving everybody." I remember it mentioned the sum of $50,000 for two or three people and cars to certain people, like Aunt Delta. I don't know what all to

Grandma. And then it mentioned five or six of the guys. He was providing for everybody, and he was proud of it. That's why he was showing it. I only saw it quickly and only one section of one page.

MARTY LACKER: The truth is, there were two wills at the time. Joe Esposito never told this to anybody except some of the guys, but Elvis had another will. It was handwritten. And Joe always carried it around in his briefcase. Vernon knew about it, but he couldn't get it out of the briefcase. So he pretended it didn't exist.

BILLY SMITH: When it was just me and Elvis up there in his room, we talked about a lot of things he never told anybody else.

I was spending twelve to eighteen hours a day, every day, up there, unless Ginger come over. Elvis was kind of withdrawn because of all that had happened, and he was leery about who he could trust.

At times, I knew that something was bothering him. He'd hint around at things without talking about them. He talked about the future, things he wanted to do. He had his heart set on touring worldwide. I don't know how he thought he was going to get around Colonel, but it didn't stop him from talking about it.

One of the things he came back to a lot was how much he wanted a male child. He was obsessed with it. He loved Lisa to death. But he still wanted a boy.

He got into a lot of detail. He said, "He'll have my eyes and, of course, my face." With his ego, Elvis thought he was the most handsome man in the world. So it just had to be a beautiful kid. He'd say, "Can you imagine what he'd be like? He's got to be an entertainer, and my gosh, if I have him with the right woman, he'll be the best-looking and the most perfect kid in the world."

He had about five types of women in mind. Each one was a model of some of the women he had been with. But he hadn't really picked the woman yet.

He didn't want to get married again. Or, at least, not right away. So he even thought about frozen embryos. He talked about that a lot and about freezing the sperm. That was in case he didn't find the perfect woman before he died. Immortality fascinated him. He was real intrigued with cloning, and he was fascinated by how far medicine had come. He'd read that somebody had invented an artificial heart. So he was automatically going to have two put aside—one for him and one for his daddy. But it was just all talk. I guess he was thinking, "I'll do it when I need it."

Mostly, he talked about the olden days. People who had died. You know the one thing we didn't talk about? Him growing old.

LAMAR FIKE: Elvis had this dream one time. He was apparently on trial for his life. He saw the whole courtroom. Colonel was the prosecuting attorney. And Red and Priscilla were the witnesses for the prosecution. Elvis said nobody would defend him, not me, not any of the guys. The only people who were sympathetic to him were two members of the jury, Sol Schwartz and Lee Ableser, the jewelers out in Beverly Hills who made his TCB stuff. I don't know who the judge was, but he didn't wear a black robe—he wore a white one. And he had a little black medical bag with him all the time. Elvis told me and a couple of the other guys about it. I said, "What the shit does that mean?" Elvis said, "It means the end is near."

It got so the guards—the guys who looked in on him—started calling themselves "The Lifers" because they were always rescuing him. They pretty much held his life in their hands.

MARTY LACKER: Right around the time I left for California, in March, Vernon had another heart attack. I'm sure Elvis was real freaked out about it because all the foundations were crumbling.

BILLY SMITH: I think one reason Elvis wanted me with him all the time had to do with my brother, Bobby. Elvis still had some guilt about that. Also, in '76, he lost another cousin that he had been close to growing up—Bobbie Jane Wren. Her parents were Lillian Smith, who was Gladys's and my daddy's sister, and Charles Mann.

Anyway, Bobbie Jane committed suicide, at thirty-eight.

It hurt to have to tell Elvis. We were on tour. I waited 'til after the show that night. By then, so many of the relatives had died. Elvis took it hard. He said, "I'd just as soon go myself as to have to see anybody else in the family die."

MARTY LACKER: When Elvis went back out on tour the third week of March, the reviews made a big point of saying that he'd lost a lot of weight compared to how he looked in the summer of '76. It got so they talked more about how he looked than anything else.

I'm a little thin-skinned about all these fat jokes about Elvis. The people who talked about how fat he was never would have said it had they been around him. They would have been awestruck, just like everybody else was. Even when he was heavy, no celebrity liked to be in his presence because it made them seem so much less charismatic.

The man was ill. Not with bone cancer, like Dick Grob and Charlie Hodge told everybody. And not with serious heart trouble. The blockage of his arteries was mild, and the blockage of the aorta was minimal. But he was sick, absolutely.

BILLY SMITH: Jo says Elvis started looking exactly like my daddy did right before he died. And she's right. Elvis would always sit in his bed, slumped, with his feet crossed. And his stomach was swollen. My daddy had the same problem with his liver and all, and his stomach just all of a sudden puffed out there. Same thing with Elvis's mother. There were times you wondered how he could function. But he pulled off some unbelievable acts.

We were getting ready to go on tour that March, and he didn't look like he could make it. He had a bunch of shows, starting in Tempe, Arizona. He was at Graceland, and we were supposed to leave late that night. Tish was talking to us outside. She said, "There's no way he's going to make it. If he was my son, I'd have him in the hospital." Vernon said, "Well, do what you can. He's got to make this." So Dr. Nick put all these IVs in him, trying to get him built up. Tish said, "I can't believe they're doing this."

All the way to the airport, Elvis sat slumped with his hat over his eyes. He didn't say anything. Then when he got on the plane, he was just groggy, slurring his words. We thought, "This is one time he really won't make it." All the way there, we thought the same thing. And when we got to the dressing room there at the Coliseum, I said to Jo, "There ain't no way." Then right before he stepped out on the stage, he stopped and looked at us and said, "You didn't think I'd make it, did you?" And he put on a hell of a show.

He did that another time, too. We were getting ready to go on tour, and he was so out of it that he couldn't find his hand in front of him. I was wondering if we should go ahead and cancel. And what little Elvis could speak, he said, "Just get me to the damn city, and I'll take care of the rest of it." And that night, when he come out of that damn dressing room, you would have thought he was a whole new person. When it come to his performances, he could reach down and pull it out of himself. I don't know how he did it.

LAMAR FIKE: At the end of March, he canceled four dates—in Baton Rouge, Louisiana; Mobile, Alabama; Macon, Georgia; and Jacksonville, Florida. We had to add them onto the next tour. But he wasn't really incapacitated. He was in a fight with Ginger, and he just didn't want to do the shows. We flew him back home to the hospital to give him an excuse because we'd have had the shit sued out of us.

MARTY LACKER: Once they got him into Baptist, they said it was for gastroenteritis, mild anemia, and a problem with his back. And he did have some gastroenteritis, from what Billy said. But they also tried to detox him again, drain some of that shit out of him.

BILLY SMITH: I believe Dr. Nick talked him into going back in the hospital to run some tests on his colon. Because I remember they took X rays of his stomach area. He always had dark spots on the X rays, and he was concerned. He said, "Well, what is this?" The doctor give him some long explanation. And Elvis said, "What does that mean?" And the doctor said, "Well, you might refer to it as an unborn fart—trapped gas." And we all had a big laugh.

He stayed for four days, and then he'd just had enough. I

went up there, and he said, "Get my stuff together, and let's go." I said, "Has Dr. Nick released you?" He said, "I don't need his damn release. I'm releasing myself." Well, I tried a couple of things to get him to stay, but finally, out the door we went.

It was funny. Elvis walked right by my car because he thought I was in my Lincoln, and I was in the little red Corvair. I said, "Here's the car." We started down the expressway, and he said, "I don't like this little son of a bitch. It feels like my ass is scootin' on the pavement."

I laughed, and he said, "Would you give this car to me?" I said, "Why would you want it if you don't like it?" He said, "I'm going to burn this little bastard. It looks like a tomato can."

We made it to Graceland, and I said, "To show you how nice a guy I am, I'll pull in the front gate." And Elvis said, "Not in this son of a bitch, you won't. I'll kill you first. You go to the back."

I wish I could have gotten him to stay in the hospital that time. That was probably the last real chance we had to do something.

LAMAR FIKE: The sad thing about this whole situation is that none of us could do a fucking thing. We went through such hell and frustration that it was unbelievable. The self-recrimination . . . Nobody in the world could have heaped on us what we felt. It was like watching a goddamn runaway Peterbilt truck. We'd all look at each other and just shake our heads. So we sort of made a vow. We said, "We've got to keep him going as long as we can."

I made a speech to him one time. I said, "You know, you're doing the worst thing on this earth." Elvis said, "What's that?" I said, "You're abusing talent. God gives very few what you've got, and you're blowing it out the window."

He looked at me, and he said, "I can't help it." I walked away shaking my head. I said, "Jesus Christ." I told Marty later, "How do you fight that?"

BILLY SMITH: Nothing was going to stop him from taking the stuff. And he didn't care who it hurt. In '77, me and Jo were in the limousine, going to the airport to leave on tour. We started to get out, and he said, "Jo, bring this sack right here." She said, "Okay." He said, "Don't even stop. Just come straight back to my room [on the plane] and bring it." Of course, it was a sack full of drugs. Jo asked me later, "Why would he do that to me?" And I said, "To get past Dr. Nick. Because you would have had the sack, and Dr. Nick would have been looking for Elvis to get on the plane with it."

MARTY LACKER: From what Billy told me, Elvis would promise Ginger the world just to keep her there, but he was seeing other women at the same time.

BILLY SMITH: About the second week of April, Elvis met this girl named Alicia Kerwin. She was a bank teller in Memphis. Alicia was twenty-one, I think. George Klein told Elvis about her. He'd just had another fight with Ginger, and he told George to send her. She come over by herself, about ten o'clock.

That first night, Elvis wanted Jo to talk to her a little bit, make sure he'd like her and all, before she went up. Jo would always go up to the room with him and the new girl for a little while, 'til they got acquainted. She had to back up his stories. And he could show a girl, "Look, I've got everybody at my beck and call."

Elvis liked Alicia. She was a really nice girl. Jo liked her a lot, too. A few days after she first come up, Elvis invited her to go to Las Vegas and Palm Springs with him. It was Elvis and Alicia and me and Jo. The real reason he was going out to Las Vegas was to get more prescriptions from Ghanem. I remember Elvis wanted Alicia to be dressed up so Dr. Ghanem could see how beautiful she looked. This was one of the times Elvis was hacked at Dr. Nick. So we flew out there, and Elvis got what he wanted from Ghanem, and we flew on to Palm Springs.

Everybody was just beat by the time we got there. So Elvis went to bed with Alicia, but he wasn't sleeping right. He just kept waking up and breathing funny. Alicia came and got Jo, and she went in there—I don't know where the heck I'd gone—and it shook her up. Jo couldn't see him breathe. Alicia was scared to death, and so was Jo. And Jo come and got me, and shit, he was totally out of it, man.

I thought he had overdosed. It scared me real bad 'cause you couldn't have stirred him with a stick. Jo thought he was going to die. We called Dr. Kaplan there in Palm Springs, and he come over. I'll never forget him sneaking in. He didn't want to be seen there.

What happened was, Ghanem give Elvis these Placidyls, and hell, Elvis would take two or three at one time. He felt like "Aw, that's nothing," but usually, they would wipe him out. And when he'd get that way, he'd talk 'til he fell asleep. And when he fell asleep, he breathed so shallow it scared the hell out of you.

We called Ghanem in Las Vegas to find out what the hell he'd prescribed. And even he got scared. He flew on out there. He checked him out, and he said, "No, he's all right. He's just got too many sleeping pills in him."

It turned out that Elvis had been hiding a lot of stuff out there. He had him a nice little stash. And he was mixing it. He'd taken some muscle relaxer along with sleeping pills, and God, that's a damn no-no. And he must have taken 'em all at one time.

Another time, he was with Alicia, and he was eating red Jell-O squares. And he took his sleeping pills, and the Jell-O squares melted in his mouth, and she thought he was hemorrhaging. It scared the fool out of her. When Elvis got out of it and just babbled on, it had to be a shocker to see him like that. And young girls just couldn't understand it. It upset them.

Elvis could have cared about Alicia, I think. He bought her a new Cadillac in Palm Springs, and somebody drove it back for her. But that didn't win her over. She told Albert Goldman she was never intimate with him; and I imagine that's true. She said to Jo, "I really like him, and I care a lot about him, but I can't handle that lifestyle. I'd rather just be a friend."

🕺 🕺 🕺

MARTY LACKER: At the end of April, the *Nashville Banner* ran a story saying Colonel was putting Elvis's contract up for sale. The reason—Colonel was supposedly in bad health with his heart, and had been for a while, and he also needed money. The paper said he'd gambled away $1 million just in December. Supposedly a group of "West Coast businessmen" were interested in the contract.

Sam Thompson says Colonel told him, "Elvis is getting to be more trouble than he's worth." Sam says Colonel specifically mentioned Elvis's drug abuse—even named the doctors who supplied him. And he talked about Elvis's erratic performances. But he wouldn't say who the prospective buyers were. That kind of candor was pretty rare for the Colonel. Now he denies ever saying it.

LAMAR FIKE: It was flying apart like a two-dollar watch. And Colonel just got to the point where he was paranoid about the whole deal. I mean, you don't walk away from a multimillion-dollar income very easily. Colonel didn't want to walk away at all. But he didn't know how to handle it.

BILLY SMITH: The Colonel may have been trying to get rid of Elvis, but I think Elvis was trying to get rid of the Colonel, too. He told me so. But he died before he ever got around to it.

MARTY LACKER: It wasn't just Colonel Elvis wanted rid of. The last year, Billy arranged the schedule because Joe didn't want to come to Memphis anymore. He stayed in L.A. So unbeknownst to Joe, Elvis was about to fire him and let Billy run everything. Elvis asked Billy one night, "Do you think you can run this show?" And Billy said, "Yeah, if that's what you want." And Elvis said, "Well, I've had enough of Joe. I'm going to tell him to stay home." Joe was on his way out.

There were really no big emotional ties, except with Billy and Lamar, and Elvis didn't see Lamar all that much because he was working advance for the tours and then he would go back to Nashville afterwards to be with his family. But Elvis really wanted to clean house, from Colonel to Joe.

LAMAR FIKE: Early in May, Joe, Dr. Nick, and Mike McMahon, their other partner in the racquetball court chain, sued Elvis for backing out of the deal. And for refusing to let them use his name. They wanted $100,000 or $150,000 in damages.

Elvis ended up settling with them. And he got stuck with borrowing the $1.3 million from the National Bank of Commerce and putting Graceland up as collateral. He didn't need any more money problems. And Elvis raved about that until the day he died.

MARTY LACKER: Two days after Dr. Nick and the others sued Elvis over the racquetball deal, Vernon filed for divorce from Dee. They'd been married almost seventeen years. Elvis never had accepted her. But three years before, when Dee left after she caught on about Sandy Miller, Elvis offered her $10,000 to come back.

Towards the end, the only reason Elvis was civil to Dee was because Vernon asked him to try to talk her into not demanding a whole lot of money. Elvis could turn on the charm anytime he wanted to, even with Dee. So he called her and said, "Well, I know you've been good, and you don't want to hurt my dad. So if you want to be set up in something, I'll give you the money." But that was strictly to get her to back off. She ended up getting a quarter of a million dollars.

The divorce was final in November. They got it in the Dominican Republic, the same place Lisa Marie [later] went to get a quickie divorce from [musician] Danny Keough and marry Michael Jackson.

🕺 🕺 🕺

LAMAR FIKE: At the end of May, Elvis played Baltimore, and he was in no shape to be performing. He fell onstage during the first half, and then right in the middle of the show, he completely left the stage for thirty minutes. J.D. said he was just having trouble with his colon, but they had a doctor look at him. Boy, the press got all over him. Said he looked high on drugs and everything else.

The next day, some broad who called herself a psychic got on the radio in Boston and said Elvis would die soon. Then another woman said the same thing on TV in L.A. in July. I don't believe in that shit, but this one guy in Philadelphia, Marc Salem, was pretty scary. On August 12, he not only predicted Elvis's death but the exact headlines in all three of the Philadelphia papers. He wrote 'em down and put 'em in an aspirin box and had it baked inside a fuckin' pretzel.

🕺 🕺 🕺

MARTY LACKER: On June 19, CBS started taping Elvis in Omaha for their *Elvis in Concert* TV special. This is the one that was shown in October, after his death. Most of it was shot in Rapid City, South Dakota, a couple days later in June.

That whole thing never should have happened. When I saw what Elvis looked like, tears came to my eyes. And I got angry at the greedy bastards who let that go on the air—Colonel and Vernon—just because CBS waved $750,000 under their nose.

They professed that they loved this man, and then they allowed him to be shown like that—so big and bloated, forgetting the words to songs, slurring his speech. He was like some kind of clown, making fun of himself in this self-mocking way. You look at it, and it's shocking. There's no other word for it.

They made Elvis a laughingstock. I'll give the estate credit— that's the one video they won't license for distribution. But even then, Elvis's voice, like on "How Great Thou Art," was still strong. His talent never faltered.

My daughter, Sheri, is friends with Kathy Westmoreland. She talked to her a couple of days after Elvis died, and Kathy told her that when they were taping the CBS special, Elvis said he was concerned about the way he looked. Then he said, "I'll tell you one thing. I may not look good now, but I'll look good in my coffin."

LAMAR FIKE: On June 26, we were in Indianapolis. That was the last show on the tour. We were on the airplane, on the ground, and Elvis walked off to accept some plaque from RCA. And he was so tired. I said, "Boys, I'm going to give you one of my great speeches. He'll never see the snow fly. I promise you."

BILLY SMITH: He had nearly two months off before the next tour. Basically, all we did was sit up in his room and talk. During those times, it was always just one-on-one. He didn't like to get real emotional around a bunch of people. And usually, something was bothering him. A lot of times we'd get into it heavy, and a lot of times we wouldn't. He'd wait for you to start the conversation.

Sometimes we'd just carry on a bunch of nonsense—just total damn craziness, in a comic way. We were liable to do that for hours, going off on things we'd seen in the Monty Python movies.

You know how nutty they are. We used to do that all the time. People would have thought we were plumb crazy if they'd heard us and hadn't seen the movies. But we knew what we were carrying on about. It made perfect sense to us. That was to relieve his pressure.

When we got talking kind of heavy and all, there were four or five things he focused on a lot. He went back over stuff that he really got into, like the Kennedy assassination and the Vietnam War—things he discussed in private but never discussed in public because Colonel didn't like it.

But Red and Sonny's book was the most important thing on his mind because it was fixin' to come out in August. He was back to talking about having Red and Sonny killed. He said, "As good as I've been to those dirty sons of bitches, how could they do this?" He said, "They don't deserve to live." He'd just go stark raving mad. But that was total malarkey. He never would have followed through with anything like that in a million years.

Knowing how he was, I played off of it, though. You had to. This one time, I said, "Look, they're not worth it. And anyway, you know it wouldn't change anything. It wouldn't even change how you feel about them. You know that deep down you still care about them, and that's what really gets you."

And he broke down and cried. It wasn't just a few tears. He was sobbing. And I cried with him because I couldn't stand to see him in that kind of pain. So I leaned over and hugged him. He said, "You're right." But then he said, "Goddamn them! At times, I get so mad I really want to kill them. And if they hurt my career, I *will* have them killed."

I had read part of the book, so I knew basically what it said. This one day, he said, "I can't wait to read that damn book." I said, "Don't waste your time. You don't want to read it." He asked, "Why?" I said, "It says that you're a drug addict and a son of a bitch. That's all it is."

But I said, "How many things have been written about you over the years?" He said, "I don't know. Millions, I guess." I said, "Right. So it's not going to make any difference. It'll blow up for a short period of time, and then it'll be over." And I think that helped him. Because he did read some excerpts of it, best I remember.

MARTY LACKER: In July of '77, when I was living in Irvine, California, I had to go up to L.A. on business. And while I was there, I went by Esposito's apartment to see him. We sat and talked for a while. And through him and Billy, I exchanged messages with Elvis. My business was going slow, and I mentioned it to Joe. And later, Joe was talking to Billy, and he told Billy to tell Elvis. One day, I opened the mail, and Elvis had sent me a damn check for $1,500. And I sent a message of how much I appreciated it. That's basically the last time we heard from each other.

BILLY SMITH: Close to the end of his life, in the last few months, Elvis was paranoid about everything. By that time, he wanted me there twenty-four hours a day. Sometimes he didn't even want Jo. And he stopped George from coming up to the house, period. The only time he would see anybody was on tour.

He was starting to get like Howard Hughes. Because now he wasn't just paranoid about people—he was paranoid about germs. Yet he still didn't like to bathe. We were playing racquetball one day, and he had this big Jacuzzi upstairs in the racquetball building. I tried to get him to get in it afterwards, mainly because Dr. Nick had said, "Try to get him to take a bath and relax."

I went up to him and said, "If I put the water in the whirlpool, do you think you might want to get in and unwind?" He said, "Sure." So we went upstairs, and I got the water going, and Elvis come in and looked at it. I said, "Looks nice, doesn't it?" And he said, "If you think it looks that damn nice, you get in it. I'm going to my room." So he went on, with a towel wrapped around his head. He wouldn't have taken a bath for anything. But he washed his hair constantly. And brushed his teeth.

On August 8, a week before he died, Elvis rented Libertyland, which was the new name for the fairgrounds. Lisa Marie was there, and Elvis always took her to ride the Fender Bender and the Little Dipper. Well, when it come time to actually go, he didn't want to. Ginger got upset because she was taking her niece, Amber. Elvis told her, "Everybody out there has already gone home."

And Ginger come back at him with "Why, Elvis, you told me one time that you could do anything." So he felt like he had to go. But his enthusiasm was gone, and it showed. And it was depressing to him. First, the spark of the old group had left. And now he didn't feel comfortable around young people anymore.

LAMAR FIKE: I think Elvis had planned to fire me for good after the next tour—the one he never took. According to Charlie Hodge, Elvis said, "I can't face Lamar. Fire him for me." So I guess I was out of there, too. Billy says Elvis was tired of hearing me bitch.

BILLY SMITH: When depression started coming over Elvis, he usually had to get out of it quick. But sometimes he liked to be miserable, and he liked for you to be miserable with him. If you were up, and if he was miserable, he had a way of bringing you right down into his world.

The last day or two before he died, Red and Sonny's book was on his mind more so, I guess because it had been out about two weeks. He was scared of how his fans and the public would react to it. And he couldn't sleep.

At times he would put it aside and be happy. Because he was excited about the tour. And then he'd get right off of that, and all the happiness would drain out of him. And he'd be so depressed he'd just go through hell. He was having a real hard time coping.

He started imagining what people were going to say to him about it when he was onstage. He worried about somebody yelling out things like "Hey, drug addict!" or "Aw, hell, you're wiped out." So he started thinking of things he would say if that happened.

At first, he thought he'd just say that a lot of things had been written about him, good and bad, and that he was not a perfect person. He still wasn't going to admit that he abused drugs or even that he was on pretty heavy medication. And then he thought he'd say, "No, I'm not a drug addict. Sure I take certain things, but I need them. And here's my doctor. He'll tell you." And he was going to introduce Dr. Nick. At first, he thought he'd jot something down. And then he decided to play it by ear and hope that everything went well.

He just anguished over this something awful. And finally, he said that if it was necessary—in other words, if he was confronted by his audience—he'd tell them he had a message he wanted to give them. And he had a little speech ready. He didn't write it down. But he had it in his mind, and he told me about it. He was not going to deny anything. He was going to go ahead and say he had a problem with drugs.

It went something like "I know you've read a lot about me over the years. And after this tour, I'm going to take time to get myself straightened out." Because he finally realized, "The best defense is no defense at all." He was just going to open up and say, "This is what's happening." But only if the audience got hostile—if they started booing and throwing things.

Still, that was a giant step, to say he knew he needed treatment and that he was going to get it. He'd always dealt with things by sticking his head in the sand. But when he realized that the book was real, then he saw, "I'm not beyond striking distance, if somebody really wants to get back at me." And he faced reality for one of the few times in his life. He was just so desperate.

MARTY LACKER: The decision to give that speech was such a turning point for Elvis that it just compounds the tragedy of his death. For the first time, he was going to own up to his problems.

LAMAR FIKE: On August 14, Elvis started a sort of pre-tour fast to lose weight. Of course, he was leaving on the sixteenth, so that didn't give him a hell of a lot of time. But Elvis was the type of person who would go on a diet today and try to lose fifty pounds by one o'clock. At one point, I think he was eating nothing but no-cal Jell-O ten times a day.

BILLY SMITH: This was only a ten-city tour and not to places where he'd get a lot of media attention—Utica, New York; Lexington, Kentucky; Roanoke, Virginia—but he was thinking, "God, maybe I can get the weight off." Knowing he couldn't, but still making an effort. He was just under so much pressure.

At the time he died, he was on a liquid protein diet, which didn't help matters with all those drugs in him. On the fourteenth, he tried on the new jumpsuit he was going to wear on the tour. It was powder blue, with silver trim and studs. And when he put it on, it didn't fit. And boy, he was upset, because now he was going to have to wear one of his old jumpsuits on the tour. At first, he blamed it on the people who made the suit. And then he turned to me and said, "Billy, I'm just too damn fat."

He always got excited before a tour. Got real hyped up. But this time, while he was excited, it was like he was tired, and he was really pushing himself to make it.

LAMAR FIKE: The last time I talked to Elvis was two or three days before he died. I was managing a guy named Little David Wilkins, and I got a deal for him with Playboy Records. And before I flew to Portland, Maine, to meet the Colonel for Elvis's two dates there on the seventeenth and eighteenth, I needed to fly Little David to Los Angeles to sign the Playboy contract. We were going to go out to the [Playboy] mansion to do some stuff with [Hugh] Hefner.

Right before I left, I called Elvis on the hot line. He had a red phone, just like the president, and I think the only people who had the number were Joe and me. He answered, and I said, "How you doing?" He said, "Oh, Lamar . . . hell, you know, I'm tired." He said, "I don't feel good. I'm having trouble with my eye again. I got David Meyer [the ophthalmologist] coming over to check it."

I said, "Elvis, you can cancel a tour twenty-four hours before it starts." And he said, "Lamar, I need the money. I've got to keep everything going." I said, "Well, I know that. But what if everybody just quits? Let's shut it all down and take six months to a year off. Let's go to Hawaii. Do something. Anything. See if we can go to Europe, so you can get it all together."

He said, "Lamar, I'd love to do it, but I've got this obligation." I said, "Well, man, keep yourself together." He said, "Yeah, I will."

I flew on to L.A. And the night before the tour started, I called Joe. I said, "Joe, Elvis is in bad shape. I'm going to tell you flat across the board, we're not going to make this tour." I said, "He's going to die, or something's going to happen. But we are not going to make it." And Joe said, "Lamar, he'll be standing over our graves. He'll see us all dead."

I'm not a clairvoyant, but, boy, when everything starts pointing to something, and it's so blatant that you can't ignore it, you've got to face the inevitable. He was dying by inches, right in front of us.

CHAPTER 52

"BREATHE FOR ME!"

BILLY SMITH: The day before Elvis died, the fifteenth, I went over to the house about seven P.M. Elvis was sitting cross-legged in the middle of the bed, wearing his dark blue silk pajamas and his dark blue robe with the gray stripes.

We sat around and watched a lot of television up in Lisa's room. She was supposed to already be gone, but Elvis wanted her to stay until he left on the sixteenth. We talked a while about the tour and about the fact Elvis wanted to go back to Vail for vacation. He was restless, and he was a little ticked because he was trying to get the Memphian to show *MacArthur* for him, but nobody could find a print. He was also hacked because Ginger didn't really want to go on the tour.

After a while, Elvis asked me to get Ginger on the phone. We were all going motorcycle riding, and then he had a dental appointment at ten-thirty. He had this crown on his back tooth that was giving him a problem. I helped him change into a black sweat suit with a DEA [Drug Enforcement Agency] patch on the back, and a white silk shirt, and a pair of black patent boots, which he couldn't zip because his ankles were swollen. He wore his sunglasses. And he put two .45 automatic pistols in the band of his sweatpants.

LAMAR FIKE: Elvis had this dentist, Lester Hofman, in East Memphis. Elvis had given him a Cadillac, and I don't know what all.

BILLY SMITH: There's this theory that Elvis made up that tooth problem to get some codeine tablets from Dr. Hofman. And I understand Dr. Hofman did give him codeine tablets that night.

When we went over to the office, it was Elvis, Ginger, Charlie, and me. He had to have all these people, just to go to the dentist. For protection and for company. Elvis drove the Stutz.

We come back somewhere about midnight, or maybe a little later. I went to my trailer to get some sleep. And Elvis and Ginger went upstairs. Then about four A.M., Elvis called me on the phone. He said, "Me and Ginger want to play some racquetball. You and Jo want to come out?" I said, "Sure, give us just a few minutes."

It was just the four of us. We went out the backdoor and down the concrete walkway. It had been raining that night, but it stopped, and now it was raining again. Jo said, "Oh, heck, here comes the rain." I said, "Yep, and I'm sick of it, too. I wish it would stop."

It was a light rain, just a few drops. Elvis said, "Ain't no problem, I'll take care of it." And he put out his hands like he was telling it to stop, and, by golly, it did. And he said, "See, I told you. If you've got a little faith, you can stop the rain."

Jo and Ginger started playing first. And then me and Elvis went out to play. But he was just not physically able. A game exhausted him. It lasted maybe ten minutes, and three quarters of that was just standing in one spot, hitting the ball to each other.

He was slow on the court, but he wasn't groggy at all. So we got to clowning around, trying to hit each other with the ball. Every time I'd serve, he'd try to hit me on the return shot. And he hit me two or three times. Then I started dodging the ball. And he got plumb silly. He did work up a little bit of a sweat. And then he said, "That's it. I've had it. Let's go."

We left the court for a while, but then we come back out. And on one serve, he swung his racquet at the ball, and he come all the way around and hit himself on the shin. He said, "Goddamnit! That's it." So we sat down, and he pulled his pants leg up, and he was rubbing it. He said, "Boy, that hurts." I said, "Hell, if it ain't bleedin', it ain't hurtin'." And he threw his racquet at me.

He said, "Hell, yeah, it's hurting! I ought to kill you!" And we carried on a lot of bull until Jo and Ginger come off the court.

The lounge area there on the first floor has a bar, and a jukebox, and a pinball machine, and some exercise equipment, and a piano. Elvis had a big glass of ice water in his hand, and he walked over to the piano and sat down and played several things. "Blue Eyes Crying in the Rain" is the only thing I remember. That was the last song he ever sang.

We went back to the house, and I went upstairs with Elvis because he liked his hair washed and dried before he went to bed. I guess I was up there maybe an hour, and we started talking about Alicia Kerwin because he was still thinking about taking her on the first part of the tour.

And he wanted to talk about Red and Sonny and the book. He had this plan to invite 'em to Graceland. He said he was going to kill 'em himself and dispose of the bodies. He was still thinking his career was all coming to an end because of their book.

He was also talking about how much he wanted to make this a good tour. I was going out the door, and the last thing he said to me was, "Billy . . . Son . . . this is going to be my best tour ever."

That was about seven-thirty or seven-forty-five. I told him I'd see him later. And I went home.

Sometime after that, Charlie, and Larry Geller, who'd just come back to work for Elvis, went up to Elvis's room. And Ginger went on to sleep. Then she woke up when Elvis come in the bedroom in his pajamas to read. He was too hyped up to sleep. So he read for a while, and then, from what she says, he turned to her and said, "Precious, I'm going to go in the bathroom and read for a while." And she said, "Okay, but don't fall asleep." And he said, "Don't worry. I won't."

$$\text{\Large 🕺 🕺 🕺}$$

MARTY LACKER: In 1990, David Stanley teamed up with Albert Goldman to say that Elvis committed suicide. Well, my answer to that is this: If Elvis Presley was going to commit suicide, number one, he wouldn't have had his pajamas on—he would have worn a jumpsuit. Number two, he probably would have had video cameras rolling. And number three, he would have written a note— no, a *book*— to Billy, his father, and Lisa Marie.

BILLY SMITH: Marty's right. If he had taken his own life, the goodbye note would have been real dramatic and gone on forever.

MARTY LACKER: Goldman's biggest "proof" is his claim that Elvis saved up all three of his "attack packets" that morning and took them all at once. He says they found all three envelopes on the bathroom floor, along with used syringes. And he says that's why Elvis refused any food because he knew it would interfere with the drugs. His theories are 100 percent bullshit.

BILLY SMITH: Elvis took all the packets at once? No, he did not. I know because when the first one was brought out, I was still there. I saw him take it around six o'clock in the morning. After a little while, the first pack had some effect, but not a whole lot. So he ordered the second. And the next pack was about seven-forty-five, just before I left. I seen him take it. It wasn't that much, so it didn't alarm me. I don't know about the third packet. I wasn't there.

LAMAR FIKE: Elvis hadn't eaten for fifteen or twenty hours, and I think the load hit him harder than it normally would have. He'd probably forgotten about his empty stomach. When you're filled with chemicals, your body reacts differently at different times. He probably went "Holy shit!" and keeled over and died.

BILLY SMITH: It's funny . . . I didn't think he was going to die, ever. I thought, "It can't happen to him. He's too great. He's the biggest thing in life." And yet the morning he died, and we were with him playing racquetball, it was a weird day. It just didn't feel right. Everything was moving kind of slow. And Jo just had a feeling. She could tell by the way he looked.

The stories that have gone around . . . I heard Ricky on *A Current Affair*, for instance. He was going over the last day, where he was sitting on the bed talking with Elvis when he brought him his medication. He said Elvis held up Red and Sonny's book and said, "How are the fans going to take this? How is Lisa going to feel about her daddy?" And he said Elvis told him to get down on his knees, and they prayed together. And Elvis said, "God, forgive me for my sins. Let the people who read this book have compassion and understanding of the things that I have done. Amen."

David tells a lot of stuff, too. He went to Nashville two days earlier, and he says when he told Elvis goodbye, Elvis hugged his neck and cried and said, "David, I will never see you again. The next time I see you will be in a better place, a higher plane."

MARTY LACKER: David says he was in a position to see a lot of stuff the morning Elvis died. David was not on duty, even though he was supposed to come on at noon. Ricky had been on duty all night, but he was asleep down in the basement.

These kids have written all kinds of books, and their stories aren't always the same. One book was written with their mother. And I told Dee to her face on the Regis Philbin show, "Your kids put themselves in situations and places where they weren't, when in actuality it was two or three of the other guys." And she just shook her head yes.

BILLY SMITH: The shifts were from twelve midnight to twelve noon. Well, at noon on August 16, Ricky was downstairs, passed out. He told *People* magazine in 1989 that the day Elvis died, he had enough Demerol in him to sedate all of Whitehaven. He said instead of going up to Elvis's room to check on him, he went back to his own room and shot up. So he was out of it. And David was supposed to come on at noon and relieve him. But as far as I can figure it, neither Ricky or David seen Elvis from the time I left him at seven-forty-five 'til the time they found the body.

I got me a couple hours' sleep, and about eleven o'clock, I got up and dressed, and I went over to Graceland about eleven-forty-five. And the only person I saw out there was Al Strada. He was packing everything up in those wardrobe cases, getting ready for the tour. I said, "Al, has anybody seen Elvis?" He said, "No." Elvis wasn't supposed to be woken up until about four o'clock in the afternoon.

Then I said, "What about Ricky? Is he still downstairs?" He said he didn't know for sure. I said, "Well, how about David? Has he come in yet to relieve him?" Al said, "No, David's not here yet." I said, "Well, let me know if David doesn't show up in a few minutes or if Ricky's not here. Somebody needs to be here." Then I asked if Ginger was up there with him. And she was.

I started up the stairs to check on Elvis, and then I thought, "No, if they ain't heard from him, God, let him rest. He needs it."

So I just said to Al, "If you hear anything from Elvis, let me know." And then I went on back to my trailer. My sister-in-law was going to keep the kids while we were on tour, and I was putting in an air conditioner for her.

I don't blame Ricky or David. I blame myself. That's one of the hardest things for me to deal with, the fact that I started upstairs and didn't go. Dr. Nick thinks Elvis died somewhere around eleven o'clock. I keep thinking I might have been able to save him, even though Dr. Nick says I couldn't change what happened.

MARTY LACKER: We'll never know exactly what happened because Ginger was asleep when Elvis died. But we can pretty well piece it together.

BILLY SMITH: There's all kind of speculation about what book Elvis was reading when he died. It was *The Scientific Search for the Face of Jesus,* the Shroud of Turin book, by Frank Adams.

Dan Warlick, the investigator for the Shelby County Medical Examiner's Office, says Elvis was reading a raunchy book about astrology and the sexual positions. If he changed books, he changed after I left because I remember it well. He'd bent the page over to mark the picture of the shroud and the outline of how Jesus supposedly looked. He was sitting there reading it while I was washing and drying his hair.

LAMAR FIKE: Elvis had that reading chair in the bathroom, with a Tensor light that he could direct over his book. From what I understand, he was sitting there, and the load hit him, and he fell forward.

Some people say he was on the commode, not in a chair. If he'd fallen forward from the commode, he would have been directly in front of it. But he was in the middle of the room, which means he fell forward, towards the middle of the room.

BILLY SMITH: Lamar means well, and we never really wanted to say this, but Elvis was actually sitting on the toilet, with his pajama bottoms down. His colon was bothering him. And he fell over, and, and, best I understand, he crawled several feet.

So this was not an instantaneous death. Or a painless one. They know that from all these little hemorrhages he had from the waist up, where the blood vessels had burst after he fell. That goes along with a drug death. He must have struggled for a while, too. Because he vomited a little bit and laid there a while before he died.

MARTY LACKER: Ginger says that she woke up about two o'clock in the afternoon, and Elvis wasn't in the bed, but his reading light was still on. Instead of immediately going to look for him, she called one of her friends.

Finally, Ginger got up and went looking for him. She knocked on the bathroom door, and when he didn't answer, she went in and found him slumped on the floor. He was kind of on his left side, with his knees drawn and his hands underneath his face. From what I understand, he was almost in a praying position. He had on his gold pajama bottoms, and they were down past his knees. And his face was in the carpet, with blood in his nostrils. She called to him, and he didn't respond, so she touched him, and he was cold.

She said later that she turned his head, and he seemed to breathe once. But dead people often expire a little air. And his face was all distorted. His eyes were closed, and she opened one of them, and it was real red, and it just stared ahead, empty-like. And his tongue was lolling out of his mouth.

She called downstairs, and said, "Who's on duty?" And Pauline, the maid, said, "Al." He was the first person to go upstairs. Al looked at Elvis, and he pretty much panicked. He called out to the office, and Joe, who'd just flown in from California for the tour, came up there with Patsy Presley right behind him, and they found Elvis all discolored, just purple—almost black—from the waist up, where all the blood had settled.

Al said Joe slapped Elvis a couple of times to try to bring him around. And when that didn't work, he tried to give him mouth-to-mouth resuscitation. But Elvis's jaw was clamped tight, so Joe tried to bust his front teeth out, but he couldn't get his mouth open. Elvis had clamped down on his tongue so bad that he'd just about cut his tongue in half. And it was black.

BILLY SMITH: Joe now denies he knocked Elvis's teeth out, but Patsy told me about it. She said it was a hard thing to see. Joe worked on him a good few minutes.

MARTY LACKER: Joe called Dr. Nick, and when he couldn't get him, he tried Dr. James Campbell, there in Whitehaven, and said Elvis was having trouble breathing.

The doctor told them to bring Elvis into the office. Which they couldn't do. So Joe called the fire department for an ambulance and just said that somebody—he didn't give a name—was having trouble breathing at 3764 Elvis Presley Boulevard. Then he called Colonel, who was in Maine setting up the first stop of the tour, and Vernon, who came up there with Sandy Miller.

When the paramedics got the call, they thought Vernon had probably had another heart attack. Elvis's body was so dark and so overweight that they didn't even recognize him. One of them, Ulysses Jones, told *20/20* later on that he thought the body was a black guy. And he said he couldn't figure out why so many people were working so hard to revive him because he was so obviously dead. He asked Joe and the others, "What happened to him?" And Al said, "We think he OD'd."

At some point, before the paramedics arrived, they were trying to turn Elvis over, and Lisa Marie came up the stairs, wanting to know what all the fuss was about. She said, "What's wrong with Daddy?" Ginger said, "Nothing." She didn't want her to see Elvis like that. But Lisa said, "Something's wrong with Daddy, and I'm going to find out!" And she ran around the hall there so she could get to the bathroom from the dressing room, but Al locked the door to keep her out.

Joe and Al said they finally got Elvis turned over, and when they did, his knees stayed flexed. Rigor mortis had set in. That's about the time the two paramedics got there. Charlie was there, too, and it took all five of them to lift Elvis on the stretcher. By the time they got him downstairs to the ambulance, Dr. Nick arrived.

BILLY SMITH: Some time after two, I got a telephone call from my cousin, Patsy. I knew right off from her voice that something was wrong. She was just wild.

She said, "I think you ought to get to the hospital!" Well, I didn't get real excited because it wasn't the first time. I said, "What's wrong?" She said, "I think he's dead!" I said, "Oh, my God, no. Don't tell me that." I thought he'd probably just over-dosed again. So I said, "He'll be all right." But she said, "No, Billy, I think he's gone this time!" And I started getting scared.

I run out to get my motorcycle to go to the hospital. And that's when David come in. So I just jumped in the car with him. He said, "Where are we going?" I said, "To Baptist Central." All the way there, I was still telling myself he was going to be okay. But then there was another part of me that just knew.

When we got there, "The Harvey Team"—that's what Baptist calls the emergency crew—had Elvis in Trauma Room 2. And all the guys who'd gone in the ambulance—Charlie, Joe, and Al were in Trauma Room 1. I had a hard time getting by security, and finally, Marian Cocke come by. She saw me, and she said, "Let him through. That's his cousin."

I walked in Trauma Room 1, and Joe put his hand on my shoulder and said, "He's gone. I know he is."

You hear all kind of tales now. I never saw Elvis in that room. But in 1992 or so, Dr. Nick come out with that story in the *National Enquirer,* where he said he got a heartbeat on the EKG monitor but the brain was dead.

Now, David told Lamar that when The Harvey Team pumped Elvis's stomach, there were so many pills, it sounded like gravel goin' in the aluminum pan. And he heard this through the closed door, he said.

He also says he caught a glimpse through the door, and he saw Elvis naked on this steel table, and they'd cut him from his neck to his midsection.

I don't know how he could have seen that. David walked in the same time I did, and it was pretty well over. And the only incision they made that day was a smaller one, in his side, when they were trying to massage his heart and get it started.

Anyway, we weren't standing there very long when Dr. Nick walked out. And he looked right at me and Joe, and he shook his head. He said, "We've lost him." And, of course, we all just grabbed one another and broke down and started crying.

Dr. Nick put his arm around me, and he was crying like a baby himself. He said, "He's in the next room here. Do you want to see him?" I thought about it, and then I said, "No, not like that." I made a break for the door, and I said, "You all forgive me, but I got to get the hell out of here."

The only thing I could think was, "God, man, this is not happening. This is not real. It can't be. Get back to Graceland, and he'll be there. Everything will be all right back there." But when we got back to Graceland, it was no better there than it was at the hospital. I walked in my trailer, and my wife said, "Tell me it's not true." I said, "Oh, God, Jo, he's gone." And we broke down.

After that, it was all so blurred I couldn't tell what happened. I thought if I could just take off running, and run 'til I passed out, I'd be all right. And yet, I couldn't. I thought, "Wake the hell up. You're in a dream." It just blasted my world. Shot it all to hell.

MARTY LACKER: Joe was supposed to break the news to the reporters at the hospital, but he was too shook up. So [vice president] Maurice Elliott, the hospital's chief spokesman, made the announcement. It's interesting how people react in a time like that. People heard Vernon on the phone after they took Elvis away. He said, "They've taken him. He's gone. My baby has died." And then he went into this terrible crying. Just buckled in two.

BILLY SMITH: Vernon pretty well collapsed in the bathroom when they were trying to revive Elvis. They said he kept crying, "Don't go, son! You're going to be all right!" And then he started wailing, "My son is dead!" After Dr. Nick told Vernon, they announced it to the world, around three-thirty P.M., CST.

LAMAR FIKE: Joe was the one who called Colonel. We were at the Dunfey Sheraton, in Portland, Maine. I'll remember that hotel 'til the day I die. I had been up all night flying from Los Angeles on the red-eye, and I was worn-out. I got up there, and I set up all the security and the rooms for the tour, and then I went downstairs and ate breakfast.

After that, I told Tom Hulett and the Colonel, "I'm going to lie down for about two hours." Well, I'd just gotten to bed when Tom came banging on my door. He said, "Lamar, the Colonel wants to see you." I said, "Look, tell him that I'll see him—" And he said, "Lamar, answer the door! You need to come down to the room and talk to the Colonel right now."

The way the hotel was built, in the round, you had to walk this circular route to go anywhere. I remember walking it down to Colonel's room. I went in, and he was sitting on the side of the bed, talking to Joe on the phone. Everybody was looking down at the floor.

I said, "What the hell is going on here?" Colonel hung up the phone, and he got up from the bed and walked over to me, and stood probably a foot away from my face. He said, "Lamar, you need to go to Memphis and meet with Mr. Presley. Elvis is dead."

I said, "That's it?" He said, "Yeah, that's it." I said, "Well, it took you a while, but you finally ran him into the ground, didn't you?" I was shattered. I looked around, and I said, "I kept telling you guys, but none of you listened to me."

I had to get a plane out of Portland, and there were two or three heavyweight broadcast reporters on the flight. And they had their cameras set up. But I didn't want to talk to anybody. So the stewardess put me up in the cockpit the whole trip back to Memphis.

When I landed, a couple of the guys met me and took me to the house. I don't really know how to describe that time. It was so stunning. Elvis's death was like some sort of ringing in my ears. It didn't quit for about three years. It really shocked me. Just overwhelming. I kept myself together, but, phew! Bad situation.

MARTY LACKER: I'll never forget it. I was working as a salesman for a food company. And I had just left my office in Irvine, California. I got in the car, and as I turned on the ignition, my radio automatically came on. And all I heard was, "—ley is dead."

The disc jockey followed it with one of Elvis's records. And I kept saying to myself, "No, it can't be. It's got to be a coincidence or a bullshit rumor."

It was the longest two minutes, waiting for that record to be over. Finally, the DJ said, "Ladies and gentlemen, as we told you earlier, Elvis Presley, the King of Rock 'n' Roll, died today."

I got so upset that the car started heading for a light pole. But I pulled the car back on the road, and I started driving real fast to my house because I wanted to call Graceland. My heart was just pumping. The DJ kept playing Elvis's records over and over and saying, "Elvis is dead."

We lived in a planned community. And as I pulled into my street, my wife and daughters could see the car coming. And they ran out in the middle of the road. They were just hysterical. They were screaming, "Is it true? Is it true?" I said, "I don't know. Let me get in the house." I pulled the car in the garage, and I immediately called Graceland. And Larry Geller answered the phone.

I said, "Larry, what is this stuff?" He said, "He's gone, Marty. He's gone."

I can't explain the feeling I had. But I remember I could feel myself shake. I said, "What happened?" He said, "He had a heart attack in the bathroom." And then he said, "I can't talk anymore." So I said, "Put somebody else on the phone." And Lamar got on. By that time, I was crying. And Lamar said, "Cut that shit out, man! We got enough of that here."

It really got to me, what Lamar said. I said, "Well, goddamnit, I loved him." And Lamar said, "Well, we all loved him, but that's not going to bring him back."

I told my wife it was true, that Elvis was dead. And Patsy had another nervous breakdown. Because in the last years, she really cared about him.

After a while, I called back, and I talked to Joe. I said, "I need to be there. I need to be at the funeral." And he said, "All right. We'll have a ticket waiting for you at the airport." But then my wife got so upset that she couldn't be left alone. One minute, she'd say, "It's okay, go on." And then, when I'd start getting ready to go, she'd start screaming.

It hit me that I had neglected her and the kids for too many years. And I said, "No, I can't leave her." And I started thinking that I didn't want to see Elvis lying in that casket, and I didn't need to see him lowered into the ground. It was probably the first time in twenty years that I chose my wife and family over Elvis. So I watched it on TV like everybody else.

🕺 🕺 🕺

BILLY SMITH: Either Vernon or Joe ordered the maids to clean up the bathroom before the investigator for the medical examiner's office got there. But I don't think they tried to cover anything up. In fact, all the syringes and stuff like that weren't gotten out until Elvis went to the hospital. Because the paramedics saw them.

I think Dr. Nick knew Elvis was dead here at Graceland. The guys said he kept pressing on Elvis's chest in the ambulance and saying, "Breathe, Presley! Come on! Breathe for me!" But he didn't pronounce him dead until they got to the hospital, after they worked on him for an hour or so.

They would have had to do an autopsy anyway because Elvis died under what they call "suspicious circumstances." But in

Tennessee, if the family requests an autopsy, it's a private matter, and they don't have to release the findings.

So what did Vernon do? He give his okay for an autopsy to be done, and he told everybody it was going to be made public. He said he wanted to find out what really killed Elvis. And then when it come out that Elvis had all those drugs in his body, Vernon said, "I didn't know he was on drugs."

Hell, he didn't know! Who's he trying to fool? But nobody else would have known if three things hadn't happened: if Vernon hadn't opened his mouth about making the autopsy public, if Red and Sonny's book hadn't come out when it did, and if somebody hadn't leaked the toxicological findings to the *Commercial Appeal*. Because the preliminary autopsy report didn't mention any drugs. You know one reason Vernon wanted that autopsy? He actually thought that somebody might have harmed Elvis, that one of the guys might have poisoned him. And I think he thought Dr. Nick might have killed him. Dr. Nick give Vernon the form, and he signed it.

LAMAR FIKE: Dr. Nick had just prescribed all of Elvis's regular tour drugs, which were different from the drugs he used for his sleeping protocol. He had fourteen different drugs in him when he died.

The list of what they found at autopsy was codeine; morphine; Quaalude; Valium; diazepam metabolite, which is a sedative; Valmid; Placidyl; Amytal; Nembutal; Carbrital; Demerol; Sinutab, the decongestant; and Elavil and Aventyl, which are antidepressants.

They sent a lot of the specimens to this lab in Van Nuys, California [Bio-Science Laboratories], under the name of Ethel Moore. Which Elvis would have gotten a charge out of. The head guy out there [Dr. Norman Weissman, chief toxicologist] said, "I've never seen the number of drugs we found in this case in any other specimen." I guess he thought Ethel was a pretty wild woman.

BILLY SMITH: There at the last, it was almost like Elvis didn't even think about mixing drugs anymore. There was more codeine in his bloodstream than any other drug. I read that the toxic level for codeine is 1.6 micrograms per milliliter of blood, and Elvis had ten times the [therapeutic] level in his blood, sixteen times the level in his liver, and twenty-three times the level in his kidneys. So maybe he took all of the codeine tablets Dr. Hofman give him.

Now, he might have thought he was taking the Dilaudid that Dr. Nick had prescribed for a toothache at two o'clock that morning. Ricky picked up the prescription and took it to the Baptist Hospital pharmacy and delivered the tablets to Elvis about four A.M. Dr. Nick told *20/20* that Elvis never took the Dilaudid—that he saw all the tablets in the bathroom after Elvis died.

I guess the real question is, What did Elvis die of? Was he allergic enough to codeine that he went into [anaphylactic] shock? Linda says Elvis was somewhat allergic—that he would break out in a little rash and get short of breath and go all panicky when he took enough of it. And Marian Cocke says so in her little book.

One of these toxicologists [Dr. Randall C. Baselt] says the codeine alone could have killed him. It was finally too much. It's just like day after day, you kick-start a damn motorcycle, and after a while you kick it to death.

LAMAR FIKE: "Death by codeine" is the theory of these guys Charlie Thompson and Jim Cole [authors of *The Death of Elvis*]. All these guys are letting us in on this enlightening information that Elvis died of a drug overdose, like it's supposed to be the light at the end of a big tunnel. Bullshit, everybody in the world knew what he was. Elvis fell forward and suffocated. Simple as that.

When I came in for the funeral, I didn't have anyplace to stay because all the hotels were taken. There was a damn Shriners convention in town. So I spent the night with Elias Ghanem at the Howard Johnson's. And Elias said, "Lamar, Elvis suffocated." He said, "Anytime a person bites through his tongue, he's suffocating."

MARTY LACKER: We'll probably never know for sure what killed him because they destroyed the contents of his stomach at the hospital. [Shelby County Medical Examiner] Jerry Francisco has come under attack for how he handled it. Francisco is the guy who announced Elvis died of heart failure—of "cardiac arrhythmia due to undetermined causes." When the toxicology report got leaked, and they found all those drugs, Francisco still said Elvis died of heart disease.

And Dr. Nick told the press that Elvis "really didn't have a drug problem." He said it was pretty impossible for him to have overdosed at Graceland because, "I don't think he had anything there to OD on." Then, before the autopsy was even complete, Dr. Nick signed and tried to file a death certificate that listed "cardiac arrhythmia, coronary artery disease, hypertension, and diabetes mellitus" as the cause of death, with "fatty liver" as a contributor.

The state law says he had no legal right to sign a death certificate. And the Department of Health refused to accept it. They sent it to the medical examiner's office, to Francisco, who filed his own death certificate.

Just this past year, the Tennessee Department of Health hired a Florida pathologist [Dr. Joseph Davis] to come in and review the autopsy findings and toxicological reports. That was motivated more by political pressure to get rid of Francisco—to find out if he acted properly—than to find out what really killed Elvis.

The new findings only determined that Francisco did not "willfully and knowingly" lie on the death certificate when he said Elvis died of a heart attack. But according to the *Commercial Appeal,* the pathologist didn't investigate whether Francisco made the right call on the actual cause of death. And the state won't release the new report.

🏃 🏃 🏃

LAMAR FIKE: The funeral was a circus. The day before, Vernon opened up the house to let the fans file by the coffin, the same thing he tried to do with Gladys. I told him, "Vernon, you can't do this." He said, "Well, he belonged to them." I said, "Bullshit, he's dead. He doesn't belong to nobody now but God."

James Brown was the first show business person there. And Sammy [Davis, Jr.] came. And Caroline Kennedy covered it for *Rolling Stone.* Then I looked up, and Ann-Margret walked right into the kitchen and said, "Lamar, I'm here." I said, "Yep, I knew you would be."

BILLY SMITH: Priscilla come back for the funeral, too, of course. I saw her the next day. I said to her, "Elvis loved you. Whether you know it or not, he did." And I didn't get much response.

MARTY LACKER: Everybody said it didn't look like Elvis in the casket. But he'd laid on his face so long that the undertaker had to put all kinds of stuff on him to make him look flesh-colored again. And then he was dressed in clothes nobody expected to see him in—a white business suit Vernon had given him for Christmas. That's how all these rumors got started that it wasn't Elvis in the casket but a wax dummy. Joan Rivers said they didn't bury Elvis at all—they buried a fifty-two-pound candle.

BILLY SMITH: People said he looked so fat in the casket. We'll argue about that forever. Elvis was swollen and sick, and he was overweight, but not to the point they were talking about. But I was worried about how he was going to fit in that suit. And Dr. Nick said, "It won't be any problem. Because there won't be all that there. We can put him in anything."

The funeral was strange. All kinds of weird things ran through my mind. I actually got mad at him for dying. I thought, "Why did you do this? You left us here."

LAMAR FIKE: I looked in the casket, and at first, all I could think of was how bad he looked. And it was such a useless death. A forty-two-year-old man died. My father died when he was forty-two. I thought about that a lot. But Elvis's death was more devastating than my father's.

A very funny thing happened. The month Elvis died, Nora and I started going through a divorce. I'd say 60 percent of it was because of my life with Elvis. I was with him more than I was with her. And she said, "I'm tired of being Mrs. Lamar Fike."

I talked to Elvis about it early in August. I said, "My God, she's wanting a lot of money." He said, "Don't worry about it. I'll raise your salary, and you won't miss it. Go ahead and sign the papers." Ten days later he died, and it cost me a damn fortune.

I said a few words to him in the casket about it. I ripped into him is what I did. I said, "Thanks a lot. You're dead. You're leaving. But I've got to pay for this the rest of my life." It was a funny routine. The minister walked up to me and said, "Have you lost your mind?" And I said, "Almost. I just can't wake him up."

BILLY SMITH: Vernon had sixteen white limousines in the funeral procession. People thought it was like "Mystery Train," that reference to "sixteen coaches long." But that was just all the white and cream-colored limousines they could find. Seemed like it took 'em forever to get out to Forest Hill Cemetery. We put him in a big mausoleum there, with his mama. By the time Vernon got through paying for the police escort, and all the other expenses, that funeral ended up costing just under $50,000.

LAMAR FIKE: A couple of people wrote that Colonel showed up at the funeral in a Hawaiian shirt. A Hawaiian shirt, for Christ's sake! Absolutely no. He had his baseball cap on and a blue short-sleeved shirt. The Colonel wouldn't wear a coat and tie for anybody.

When Elvis was still lying in state there at Graceland, Colonel cut a deal with Vernon for all the Elvis merchandise and souvenirs. Colonel's gotten a lot of criticism for that, and for doing it when he did, within forty-eight hours of Elvis's death. The way I understood it, Elvis had $1,055,173 in his checking account—and that was an interest-free account—but it was a ninety-day loan that had been shifted out of one account into the other. He had the money coming, and the bank advanced a million because they knew a check was coming in from RCA. He had gone through a bunch of money, and he was in more desperate straits than it appeared.

The merchandising deal, which was with a company called Factors, Etc., Inc., has been reported a bunch of different ways. The thing to remember is that it was done through Boxcar, the company Colonel and Elvis set up in 1974. Factors gave Colonel and Vernon a $150,000 advance plus 5 percent of the sales. Right off the top the William Morris Agency got a 10 percent commission for putting Factors and Boxcar together. And Boxcar and Vernon, as executor for the state, agreed to equally divide half of the remaining money between the estate and Parker. The other half stayed in Boxcar Enterprises. And Colonel owned 40 percent, and later 56 percent, of that. Later, after Vernon died, the coexecutors calculated that the Colonel got almost 62 percent of Boxcar.

People think that's terrible. But thank God Colonel did what he did. He's the one who made the estate what it is today. He moved fast and locked that whole deal up. Had he not, you would have had wolves crawling all over the place. The Colonel saved that estate a tremendous amount of money.

You know what he said, don't you? He said, "Elvis isn't dead. Just his body is gone." And he was right.

BILLY SMITH: Right after Elvis died, Vernon made the statement about the guys, "They ain't working on Elvis's chain gang anymore. They're working on mine." And I resented that, boy.

LAMAR FIKE: When we came back from the funeral, Vernon was standing at the end of the dining room. I said, "Vernon, I'm gone. I'm sure as hell not going to tend the flame, and I'm not going to drive a motor scooter around these fourteen acres." He said, "I knew you'd be the first to quit."

It was such an emotional day. I was one of the pallbearers, along with Billy, and Joe, and Charlie, and Jerry Schilling, and George Klein, and Gene Smith, and, of all people, Dr. Nick. That casket was vacuum-sealed. It had a big glass sheet over the top of the body. Same kind of casket his mother had. It was copper-lined. Cost $775 and weighed nine hundred pounds. Jesus, was it heavy.

I grabbed hold of that damn thing, and I said, "God Almighty!" I said, "Boys, he tried to kill us when he was alive, and now that he's dead he's trying to kill us again."

The weird thing is, we were coming out of the house, and the hearse was parked right down in front of the steps. We had just pulled the casket off the rollers to walk it out to the hearse, and we'd got the thing out the door, when this big limb snapped and fell off one of the trees in front.

Now, there was no reason for that limb to snap and fall off. It was just as still as it could be. And hot as hell. Everybody looked at each other, and I said, "We knew you'd be back, Elvis. Just not this soon."

BILLY SMITH: One of the things we couldn't figure out was how the reporters for the *National Enquirer* beat everybody else to the story. Because the *Enquirer* knew Elvis was dead before it was ever announced to the press. And they were here at Graceland, too, before anybody else. Then when they put that photo of Elvis in the coffin on the front page of the paper [September 6, 1977], we started trying to find out who took it and how they got all their other information.

Dick Grob got to nosing around. And during that time, something like forty of the *Enquirer* folks were still here in Memphis, searching for whatever they could get. But we couldn't find out anything. So we set up a deal where we would give the *Enquirer* certain information for a certain price, if they would tell us things that we wanted to know. Well, that didn't work, either.

About a month later, Dick met this girl, a friend of one of the guys who was here to cover the story. And they got to talking. She told Dick that one of the other cousins, Billy Mann, took the picture of Elvis in the coffin. They paid him something like $50,000. And then Dick asked her, "How did they get the news out so quick?" She said, "Well, they were tipped off." And Dick said, "By who?" She said, "Well, I don't know who it was exactly." He said, "Then tell me this. Who did they contact?" She said, "One of our stringers. A guy named Jim Kirk."

So we set up a meeting with Jim Kirk. We brought him to Graceland and put him down in the racquetball court. And we rigged up a tape recorder and a microphone. And Dick started asking him questions. I only heard part of it. I was upstairs, and I couldn't tell a lot of what he was saying because the damn water was dripping down and affecting the microphone. So I really only know what Dick told me.

It seems that when Ginger called downstairs, she might have known Elvis was already dead. We think she may have called her mother first, and they talked about what to do. And then about twelve-thirty—an hour and a half before she called downstairs—she hung up and called this Jim Kirk, who was a freelance writer and a stringer for the *Enquirer*.

We guess she called him twice and struck a deal with him for her story and a page-one fee, for $105,000. Now, both Ginger and her mama deny this. But see, she knew this Jim Kirk. A couple of stories had already come out in the *Enquirer* about Ginger and Elvis. And at the time, we didn't know exactly how they got their information. But now we're pretty sure that's how the *Enquirer* had people flying in here on August 16, taking pictures and making phone calls three hours before the hospital announced Elvis was dead.

We do know for sure that by the time Ginger called Al up there, she was all dressed and made up to perfection. She sure didn't look like she just rolled out of bed, like she said.

If she did deal with the *Enquirer*, she probably figured, "Well, what have I got to lose? He's dead." But then she later talked to the *Commercial Appeal*, too, so I heard that the *Enquirer* cut her fee down to $35,000.

When Dick got Jim Kirk over to Graceland, he told him the truth—that we'd just like to know who made the phone call to him that day. And Kirk said, "Well . . . " At first, he said he didn't recognize the voice. And Dick said, "Well, was it a man or a woman?" And finally, Kirk told him, "Well, it was a woman." And Dick said, "Ginger, right?" And Kirk put his head down and said, "Yes, I think it was."

AFTERMATH

BILLY SMITH: Right after Elvis passed away, Vernon closed off the house. A few days after he did that, Patsy Presley [Gambill] called me, wanting to know where Elvis kept his important papers. I said, "Is Vernon looking for Elvis's copy of the will?" I figured they couldn't find it because I had it hid so well. And stupid me, I told her right where it was.

MARTY LACKER: On August 22, Elvis's will was filed for probate. It was thirteen pages long. And there was nothing in it about Elvis leaving anything to any of the guys. Apparently, Vernon also found the handwritten will, but I heard from a very good source that it was destroyed.

BILLY SMITH: Two or three days after I told Patsy where Elvis's copy of the will was, they burned a lot of papers out behind the office. It still bothers me deeply. When that thing was probated, and I saw it wasn't anything like what I read, it just floored me. Because either Elvis was the biggest liar in the world or somebody altered that will.

MARTY LACKER: There for a while, almost everything was a freak show. At the end of August—right after Elvis was buried—three guys were arrested for trespassing at the cemetery. They were after the ultimate souvenir—Elvis's body. They had a crowbar, some wire cutters, some bolt cutters, a wrench, a screwdriver, and a shotgun.

How they thought they were going to get into the mausoleum,

past the wrought-iron door that separated Elvis from the rest of the crypt, and get a nine-hundred-pound casket and a corpse out of there undetected, I don't know. But supposedly they were going to pry out the marble marker and the concrete slabs sealing the crypt, drill a hole in the casket, screw an eyebolt in there, and use a hand winch to pull the casket out. Then they were going to load the thing in a gold Chrysler New Yorker, and take it to a refrigerator in the Armour meatpacking house. There, some other guy was supposed to pay them $40,000. And then he was going to hold the body for $10 million ransom.

The cops staked out the cemetery for three nights. The first night, they didn't show. The second night, they drove by real slow, but didn't get out of the car. Then the third night, two of the guys got out, came through a hole in the wire fence, and rattled the wrought-iron doors on the back of the mausoleum. But then something spooked 'em, and they took off.

The cops caught 'em at the corner of Person Street and Elvis Presley Boulevard. All they could charge them with was criminal trespass, which is a misdemeanor, because they never got around to actual grave robbing. Bail was fifty bucks apiece. And a couple of days later, the charges were dropped. The main guy, Ronnie Lee Adkins, told *Southern Magazine*, "There's only two people on earth that everybody has heard of, and that's God and Elvis. I was just trying to get at the only one I could."

BILLY SMITH: After that, Vernon applied for a variation in the zoning regulations. He wanted Elvis and Aunt Gladys brought up to Graceland and reburied in the Meditation Garden. They moved them in the middle of the night, early in October [of '77].

By that time, Elvis had been dead about seven weeks. And I was still having a really hard time dealing with it.

I'd be walking out to the gravesite, and something—a click, like—would tell me to look up at his window and I'd be able to see him. And I did see him a couple of times. But not real vividly. And twice I heard him calling me in a loud whisper, like "Billy!" I heard it so plain. But I guess it was just in my mind. Then I started going out to the gravesite in the wee hours of the morning. I was still mad at him for dying, and yet I was hurt so deep. I talked to him a little bit. I said, "All these promises you made to me, man! I moved back up here to Graceland because you wanted me to, and then you kick out on me like this? What the hell do you mean doing that?"

Pretty soon, I started dreaming that Elvis was alive and that he was saying, "I didn't die. I'm not really dead." I'd walk around Graceland and think, "Hey, he's here." It was hell.

In November, I knew it was time to go. My grief was not going to get better as long as I was there. To this day, when I talk about his death, I get teary-eyed. Sometimes I just want to break down and sob.

MARTY LACKER: When Billy and his family decided to leave, they were still living in a twenty-four-by-sixty-foot trailer behind Graceland. Elvis gave them that trailer, and he even went out to the store and bought furniture for it. He told Billy in front of me that he was putting the trailer in his name.

Well, Vernon had kept the title of the trailer in Elvis's name. And when Billy went in to tell him that he wanted to move down to Mississippi, where Jo's family lived, Vernon said, "That trailer doesn't belong to you, Billy."

Billy got really mad, and he said, "Well, by God, just keep the damn thing! But I'm taking my furniture." And Vernon said, "No, that furniture goes with the trailer." Billy said, "I'm taking my furniture, and I'd like to see you try to stop me."

BILLY SMITH: You can turn bitter towards somebody, and I did towards Vernon. I guess I could have fought it in court, but we just went on down to Mississippi. We had nothing to speak of. And to go back into the normal world was a hell of an adjustment.

MARTY LACKER: A year after Elvis died, we had a memorial ceremony at the ranch in Mississippi. Billy asked me to come and talk and sit on the stage with the dignitaries. When it came time for me to speak, I got so emotional that the only thing that would come out of my mouth was, "I hope he's happy and that he finally realizes we all really did love him."

LAMAR FIKE: Essentially, Elvis's death fucked up everybody's life. Most of us weren't trained to do anything but look after him.

MARTY LACKER: In 1978, Charlie got a little taste of his own medicine. He'd continued to live at Graceland, and I guess he thought he was going to stay forever. Because Vernon and Charlie acted like old country buddies. Vernon sold his house on Dolan and moved into the garage apartment there at Graceland. So he and Charlie used to sit around the kitchen and drink coffee and smoke in the mornings, tell all these old country stories and talk about everybody behind his back.

One Friday morning, Vernon was his same old self, patting Charlie on the back and laughing. And then Charlie went out to the office and got his paycheck, and there was a pink slip in the envelope. Charlie was out on the street. He didn't know what to do.

🕺 🕺 🕺

LAMAR FIKE: If I learned anything from Elvis, I learned loyalty. And yet, some people thought I was incredibly disloyal for working on the Goldman book. But it was 1978, and I was dead broke. Elvis didn't leave us any money, but he left us a hell of a legacy.

It bothered me when I saw the galley proofs. The problem was Albert's personality. At first, he liked Elvis. But then, he started disliking him. And by the end of the book, I think he hated him. I said, "Albert, you can't do this." But I couldn't stop him.

I own one third of the copyright on the book, and I did a lot of the research. But Albert requested my name not be on it as coauthor, and it thrilled me to death. Still, a lot of people looked at it as "Lamar's book."

When I finished the research, I left Nashville and moved to Texas. I got down to Waco in early '80, I think, and got married again, to Janice Fadal. Her father was Eddie Fadal, who used to have us over a lot when Elvis was at Fort Hood. I was married for eight or nine months, tops. It just didn't work. My intestinal bypass was starting to go wrong, and I was losing weight so fast, I was beside myself.

I was under so much stress with the book, and the marriage, that I went from 155 pounds to 118 in about a year's time. My shirt size was down to twelve and a half in the neck, and my waist was twenty-three inches. After a while, it got so a meal was through me in two minutes. I was literally dying.

I never had anything scare me as bad in my life. But I still wouldn't have gone for surgery if it hadn't been for a motorcycle accident in '81. I was on a friend's 750 Suzuki, and a gust of wind caught me. The bike started drifting on me, and I couldn't stop it. I was moving into the curb, so I hit both brakes at once, and the bike laid down. I went over the handlebars and landed on my shoulder and crushed the ball joint. They had to put a rod and five pins in there.

When the surgeon opened me up, he called my doctor and said, "This guy's bones are like an eighty-year-old's. They're cracking and coming apart. You better do something quick."

They had to give me four pints of blood to bring up my oxygen level, and then they hooked my intestine back up. I'm all right now. I never could maintain the 155 again, but at least I haven't gotten back up to four hundred pounds.

MARTY LACKER: On June 26, 1979—Colonel's seventieth birthday—Vernon died of heart failure at sixty-three. They buried him in the Meditation Garden, next to Elvis. Then the next year, Grandma died, at eighty-six. And they buried her on the other side of Elvis.

Right after Elvis died, Priscilla tried to get into acting, and for quite a while, she didn't have much success. So a year before Vernon died, she began maneuvering to gain control of the estate.

In early 1978, Priscilla and her sister, Michelle, stopped in to see us in California. They were on their way to the La Costa Spa in San Diego. I'd call Priscilla from time to time and say, "Anytime you need me to do something for you or Lisa, feel free to call me." I did it for Elvis, really. But she would always say, "Oh, thank you. Thank you."

Vernon was still alive, and he was the executor of the estate. And Priscilla sat there and whined to me that Vernon wouldn't name her as his successor. She said she wanted to be sure that Lisa Marie was protected. But that was only half the truth. Priscilla wanted control of the estate for her own sake.

She said, "Marty, what am I going to do? I keep pleading with him, but he won't do it." I said, "Priscilla, you've got to find a way to convince him that you don't want it for any other reason than to look out for Lisa."

Elvis's will said that if Vernon died without naming somebody, the National Bank of Commerce in Memphis would become the executor and/or trustee. So Priscilla was desperate.

During that visit, she told me her father wanted to buy a liquor store in northern California. And she said she had asked Elvis if he would give her father $100,000. I'll never forget this. She said, "Elvis was going to do it, but then he up and died." Just like that. "And there went my father's liquor store because Vernon won't honor what Elvis said he'd do." But that's Little Miss Goody Two-shoes for you.

The fact is, she aced her way into being an executor, even though she wasn't Elvis's widow and she wasn't in his will. Elvis had no intention of Priscilla running the estate.

LAMAR FIKE: Priscilla knew that Vernon was just mean enough to go to his grave without naming her executor. She hated Vernon. She called him a son of a bitch and everything else. And when he died, it was the best thing that ever happened to her because at the last minute, she'd finally talked him into naming her his successor, along with Joe Hanks, who'd been Vernon's accountant since 1969, and the National Bank of Commerce.

I read what she said about what a burden it is to have to run the estate and how she wants to be her own person. She told USA Weekend, "When I was first named executor, I thought it was a curse. Here I was, trying to get my career going and my life in line . . . "

Who's she kidding? Boy, she's milked it for all it's worth! And she hasn't treated family members the way the will stipulates. It provides a trust for any Presley relative in need of emergency assistance for "health, education, support, comfortable maintenance and welfare."

BILLY SMITH: In 1979 or so, Priscilla filed a lawsuit against Marty. Over fifteen or twenty years, Elvis had given the guys a lot of cash. He'd give you $10,000 a pop. And a lot of times, when Joe, or Marty, or Charlie wrote the checks, he'd tell them to mark it "personal loan." But Priscilla knew that Elvis never expected to see that money again. He'd tell you, "Don't worry about paying it back. This is a gift." But after Priscilla became executor, the estate decided to go after that money.

LAMAR FIKE: That brilliant law firm of Priscilla's let it slip to another lawyer—who told Marty's attorney—that they were using Marty as a test case. If she won from him, she was going to go after all of us. So we were all going to testify against her.

Marty went for his deposition, and when it was over, he said to her attorney, "I'd like you to give Priscilla a message for me. Tell her that she knows what she's doing is wrong. And tell her one other thing: She opened up a can of worms, and I'm going to slam it right down on her head." And then he gave him Elvis's variation on General MacArthur's farewell speech: "With that, I bid you a fond, affectionate, fucking farewell."

BILLY SMITH: Marty meant what he said. So when they asked for a second deposition, he was ready. He told his attorney that Elvis had started this karate film, and we were all going to be in it, and Elvis was paying us $50,000, plus a percentage, for either participating in it or helping out. Which was true.

When Priscilla went after Marty, the estate was trying to do something with that film, and none of the guys had been paid. So Marty told his attorney to file a countersuit for $50,000. And two days later, Marty's attorney got a phone call saying, "You drop your suit, and we'll drop ours."

MARTY LACKER: Just before she sued me, she called and said, "I wonder if I could ask a favor of you and Patsy and the kids. I'm making this deal on my home movies." She was involved somehow with [producer] Burt Sugarman, who owned an amusement park. And she said, "Burt wants to run these movies as part of an attraction." Priscilla wanted us to sign a release.

She didn't offer any money, and I didn't expect her to. We did it just to be nice. And one week after we signed it, she filed the lawsuit against me.

I picked up the phone and called Joe Esposito, who was still tight with her. I told him, and he said, "Hey, man, that's the way the game is played."

The irony is that about ten years later, Joe was trying to market the 8mm films of Elvis he'd taken on our trips. He had a big deal for them over in England. But Priscilla filed suit to stop him. When I heard that, I had such an urge to call him and say, "Hey, Joe, that's the way the game is played." I didn't, but Priscilla sure keeps her lawyers busy.

LAMAR FIKE: Priscilla's the chairwoman of Elvis Presley Enterprises. She's the keeper of the flame, the number one Rock 'n' Roll Widow, the way she paints it.

The fans literally cannot stand Priscilla. She gave an interview to *McCall's* last fall, saying she thought the fans realized she wasn't the bad guy anymore and that they're treating her with a little more charity these days. She said, "In the beginning, I was the enemy because I married Elvis, and then, because I left him. A lot of people felt that when I left he started his downward spiral, and that if I had stayed I could have helped." She essentially said she left because there were things she didn't want Lisa to see.

That's neither here nor there. The estate has obviously done something right—it's gone from being worth $4.1 million when Elvis died to something like $100 million today, and it grosses $15 million a year. That's more than Elvis ever made in any one year while he was alive and a hell of a lot more than any dead entertainer takes in.

BILLY SMITH: I understand that she wanted to look after Lisa's interest. But I think Priscilla was gold-digging when she took over the estate. She makes a real good living from it. Lamar thinks it's about 1½ percent of what the estate earns.

She did this video tour of Graceland, where she went through telling this and showing off that. To be honest with you, she couldn't give a damn. It goes back to the root of all evil—money.

MARTY LACKER: I'll tell you how greedy this woman is. After *Elvis Aaron Presley: The Tribute* concert last year, Larry Nager, the pop music critic for the *Commercial Appeal*, wrote that the reason there weren't any stadium-filling names on the bill was because the big names perform only at "pure" benefits. Meaning that all proceeds after expenses go to charity. But the estate set up the concert, and the video, and the album as for-profit ventures. Just a small portion of the money went to Saint Jude's Children's Research Hospital and the T. J. Martell Foundation, which raises money to fight AIDS. Nager wrote, "It was a business venture worthy of that ace dealmaker Colonel Tom Parker himself. But do you think Elvis would have done it that way?"

BILLY SMITH: I'll never really understand why Vernon let Priscilla step in and take over. And now she sits up and complains that the Presley name has hurt her more than it's helped. I'll tell you what—if it's such a disadvantage, why doesn't she call herself "Beaulieu"?

LAMAR FIKE: Elvis's will states that Lisa Marie should inherit everything—including control over the estate—at twenty-five. Well, that birthday came and went on February 1, 1993, and Priscilla is still in charge. The Memphis probate court oversees the executors, and they've decided to leave everything in place until Lisa turns thirty.

Priscilla's shepherding her deal very carefully now because she doesn't want it messed up. If Priscilla knew she could make it without the estate, why did she extend the guardianship of her daughter five years? It's obvious what she's doing. It's not concern over Graceland.

I think Priscilla's a smart business lady. But she's not the brains behind the estate, no matter what you read. The advisers have helped her a lot. She, and Hanks, and Fletcher Haaga, from the Bank of Commerce, set up a management team. It's made up of California businessmen and Memphis lawyers and bankers. Priscilla definitely couldn't handle it all by herself. She had a couple of businesses—a boutique and a line of children's clothing—go under.

MARTY LACKER: Graceland is a cold piece of nothing. None of the people up there have anything to do with Elvis, with the exception of maybe an uncle and a cousin. There are a couple of fanatical fans, but for the most part, these people are just doing a job. All they care about is how many paying customers come through that gate.

BILLY SMITH: After I moved away from Graceland, me and Dick Grob got to talking one day. I said, "Why don't they open Graceland to the public?" He said, "Vernon had talked about that." Except Vernon was so chintzy that rather than pay somebody to run it, he just let it be.

I don't think that Priscilla particularly wanted to open it. But she saw that it cost something like $480,000 a year just to maintain the place, with taxes, and insurance, and twenty-four-hour security for the graves. And the inheritance taxes were something else. In 1981, the government looked at how much money the estate made since Elvis died, and reappraised it at $25 million, instead of $4.1 million. The IRS said they owed an additional $14.6 million, plus $2.3 million in interest.

Back in the mid-seventies, Elvis grossed about $130,000 a concert. And each new album brung in about $250,000 in royalties. But now there wasn't no more concerts or new records. The estate took in about $1 million a year in '79, but it had dropped way down to about $500,000. Expenses were going up, and income was going down.

It was looking like they might lose Graceland. So Priscilla decided to open it to the public. It took the whole $500,000, plus $60,000 more, to get the place ready. Priscilla hired Jack Soden, a stockbroker and investment banker from Kansas City, to be the CEO of Elvis Presley Enterprises. He was a pretty good choice because they made back that $560,000 in thirty-eight days.

When I moved down to Mississippi, I went back to work for the railroad. I was a car inspector for Illinois Central Gulf. But I stepped in a hole in the train yard and twisted my back, and I couldn't work on the railroad no more. Things were pretty tight for us. We had to sell a lot of the things Elvis give us to stay alive.

In early '82, when I found out Priscilla was going to open Graceland, I thought, "What the heck?" And I went up there and applied for a job. I didn't see Priscilla. I saw one of Soden's aides.

At first, they seemed kind of reluctant to hire me, although I never knew why. But after a day or two, I had the job.

Because I knew where Elvis kept everything in the house, and how it looked when he was there, they had me set up certain of the rooms. Mostly I worked on the Trophy Room. I had to coordinate everything, like find all the records and put them in order and catalog everything. And I had some fairly good ideas, which were taken. I thought I did a hell of a job, to be truthful.

When I finished, they stuck me in the position of tour guide. I even had to buy my own uniform. I thought, "My God, what am I doing? This is pretty demeaning." But I needed the job.

Well, one day, Priscilla come to Graceland, and she saw me working as a tour guide. She hugged me, and she said, "It's good to see you again." I thought she might pull me off to the side and say, "You don't need to be a tour guide." But I never got that respect.

A little while after that, they raised my salary. I guess Priscilla thought it didn't look good and said something. And in time, they made me a tour guide supervisor. But after almost two years, I was still making less than what I'd been making with Elvis in '77. And far less than what I made at the railroad.

So I was pretty dissatisfied. And I didn't like it that Priscilla started acting like Elvis. One time, she come into town, and they showed some clips of Elvis down in the racquetball court. Everybody come in, and she sat in the middle, and people gathered around her the way they did Elvis. And she seemed to expect that.

I also didn't like the way she treated Patsy Presley [Gambill]. She yelled at her, and gave her orders. So a lot of bitterness set into me. And in 1983, Jack Soden fired me. He said, "You've got this love/hate relationship with Graceland." And he was right. I loved Graceland, but I hated the suckers that were running it.

After I got fired, I tried to call Priscilla. Lisa answered the phone. But Priscilla never called back.

LAMAR FIKE: Priscilla played favorites. Jerry Schilling worked himself into the estate and made a good living from it for quite a few years out in California. Billy got the shaft.

BILLY SMITH: I don't have much feeling for Priscilla, but I can let bygones be bygones. What I can't comprehend is why she doesn't have much feeling for Elvis. She says now that she understands him better and that she thinks of him in a different way. Maybe so. But when I knew her, she was just like the highway out there, cold and hard.

Since Elvis died, Priscilla's kept Lisa away from the family. It was like she said to her, "They're lower-class. You don't want to associate with them." And that hurts. The last time I saw Lisa was when I worked at Graceland. We talked for about five or ten minutes. She was growing up to be a pretty young lady. But she hasn't made an effort to contact any of us since then.

I think about Lisa, and I miss her, really. She should have an opportunity to judge this side of the family for herself.

MARTY LACKER: You've got to question Priscilla's judgment in a lot of ways. Like how she handled Colonel Parker's relationship with the estate. When Elvis died, Vernon and Colonel agreed they'd split whatever money came in exactly as they had when Elvis was alive. Colonel said, "We're going to treat Elvis's death the same as if he was in the army."

Vernon wrote Colonel a letter on August 23, 1977, which said, "I am deeply grateful that you have offered to carry on in the same old way. As Executor of Elvis's estate, I hereby would appreciate if you will carry on according to the same terms and conditions as stated in the contractual agreement you had with Elvis dated January 22, 1976, and I hereby authorize you to speak and sign for me in all these matters pertaining to this agreement." In other words, Colonel still got the lion's share of everything.

Then in '80, the new coexecutors wrote Parker a letter and said, "We do want things to continue as they have and as set forth in the letter of August 23, 1977, from Vernon Presley as the then executor of the estate." They were going to let him get away with it forever!

But when they went to probate court to get the compensation agreement approved, Judge Joseph Evans got suspicious about Colonel's 50 percent commission. And he appointed Blanchard Tual, this young Memphis lawyer, to be Lisa Marie's guardian-*ad-litem*, since she was a minor.

In September of '80, Tual submitted a report that opened a lot of people's eyes. He was flabbergasted at what he found in Colonel's dealings with RCA, with the William Morris Agency, with the publishing companies, with Boxcar, and the merchandising partners.

Tual came to nineteen conclusions. The most important one was, "All agreements with Elvis Presley terminated on his death." And he chastised both Vernon and the new coexecutors for not obtaining opinions from experts in the entertainment field about the fairness of those agreements.

Essentially, Tual said that Colonel had handled affairs in his own interest. And that he was guilty of self-dealing and over-reaching, and he violated his duty both to Elvis, when Elvis was alive, and to the estate.

Tual recommended that any money that came in go directly to the estate and not to Colonel, and that the court prohibit the estate from paying Parker any more commissions until Tual finished his investigation. Most of all, he asked the judge not to approve Colonel's receiving the 50 percent commission. He said such a figure was "excessive, imprudent, unfair to the estate, and beyond all reasonable bounds of industry standards."

Finally, Tual said Parker had no claim against the estate for the $1,693,125.39 he said Elvis owed him at his death. And Tual wanted Parker to pay back whatever monies he'd retained since Elvis died. Then he called for Colonel and everybody he did business with—including RCA and all the movie companies—to open their books for an audit and complete accounting.

LAMAR FIKE: I don't know why Vernon or the new executors never insisted on an audit. Except that the estate didn't have much money. They probably thought, "Why get into something that could cost $400,000?"

MARTY LACKER: Tual filed a second report on July 31, 1981, in which he specifically singled out the 1973 RCA buyout agreement as "unethical and fraudulently obtained."

Tual said, "These actions against the most popular American folk hero of this century are outrageous." Then he pointed to examples of Parker's poor management and arrangements that were extremely favorable to Colonel but not to Elvis. Like his failure to register Elvis with BMI so he could receive his share of writer's royalties; Elvis's surprisingly low figure for playing Vegas; Colonel's failure to tour Elvis overseas; and his side deals with most of the people Elvis did business with.

Among Tual's recommendations this time was that the court direct the coexecutors to file a complaint against Parker to void his contracts with RCA and the estate. Tual said it should "allege collusion and conspiracy with Colonel Parker in an effort to defraud Elvis of his royalties from such masters." And he suggested the estate should file another complaint against RCA to void the 1973 buyout agreement.

LAMAR FIKE: When all this started, Colonel didn't say a peep. For one thing, he'd had an accident. He was leaving his office in the RCA building in Hollywood one night, and he stumbled as he was getting on the elevator. He fell across the doorway and couldn't get up. The automatic door kept trying to close, and I don't know how long he laid there, but that door just pummeled him and permanently disabled his right shoulder.

When the second report came out, though, Colonel decided to defend himself. He picked up the phone and dialed a couple of newspapers to plead his case.

MARTY LACKER: Colonel told the Memphis *Press-Scimitar,* "You should remember that I was not involved in Elvis's personal financial affairs. If Elvis or Vernon asked my opinion on such matters, I'd give my advice, [but] Elvis wanted to always make the final decision on business matters. He had a mind of his own." As examples, he cited two foolhardy investments Elvis made—the Robert Vesco jet and the racquetball-court chain.

About the RCA buyout, he said, "When [RCA] approached us, I was not interested. I thought it was a stupid idea to even consider it. I knew there wasn't much coming in [from the older songs], but it could change. I said the money wasn't enough . . . Keep in mind that Elvis approved all of the contracts with RCA. He was fully aware of the entire transaction, and it was his decision. I had absolutely nothing to hide from Elvis."

Then he went on about how Elvis was moody and headstrong and that he had little self-motivation. He said, "Sometimes it was such a heartache to keep [Elvis] going. We had to have a way to [do that]." Finally, he complained that Tual hadn't presented the whole picture.

The upshot was that everybody filed a lawsuit. The estate sued Parker and RCA—which, according to Goldman, Elvis's death saved from bankruptcy, they sold so many records. RCA sued Colonel and the estate. And Parker brought a countersuit against the estate.

But Colonel strung it along for a while. He probably wanted to drive the estate into insolvency and then reach a compromise.

At one point, in June of '82, Colonel acted like he thought he was cornered. Because that's when he finally admitted that he was Andreas Cornelis van Kuijk—a man without a country.

Now, why did he admit the very information he'd hoped nobody would find out? Maybe because if he was stateless—he said he'd given up his citizenship in Holland and never was naturalized as a U.S. citizen—he could argue that he couldn't be sued in federal court.

After that, the estate must have realized it had no course but to settle with him. So in November, Colonel gave up all his claim to future income from anything connected to Elvis. But he was still entitled to 50 percent of all royalties before September of '82. And RCA gave him $2 million, paid in installments, for his "right, title, and interest in all Presley-related contracts."

The estate was now entitled to all royalties after September of '82. And RCA agreed to give them $1.1 million. But while the label pays them royalties on the records Elvis made after March of '73— the date of the buyout agreement—it still doesn't pay any royalties on the pre-1973 records. Elvis scored sixty-six Top 20 hits before March of '73. You know how many he had after that? Two.

And here's the kicker: Even though a June '83 settlement outlined that Parker was no longer affiliated with the Presley estate, and he was supposed to cut all connections with them, it didn't end up that way.

LAMAR FIKE: In late 1990, the estate made a deal with Parker to rent a lot of his memorabilia—photographs, letters, documents, and artwork. They hauled it to Memphis in seven semitrucks. It weighed thirty-five tons. The estate sent out a press release that said, "Because of Colonel Parker's fondness for Elvis and Elvis's many fans and friends, Colonel Parker has graciously agreed to furnish a sampling of his collection."

Somebody told me Colonel cleared another $2 million out of that deal. The estate plans to build an "Elvis and the Colonel" museum. When Colonel dies, all the stuff comes back to Loanne, his wife, to sell it.

It's interesting . . . in '93, when the estate sanctioned a coffee-table book about Graceland, they somehow failed to read [music journalist] Chet Flippo's introduction. Flippo essentially said Colonel ripped Elvis off or, at best, mismanaged his finances. When Priscilla found out, she tried to get the publisher to pull the book off the shelves.

MARTY LACKER: Was it part of the settlement not to speak ill of one another? I don't know. But I do know that in '94, the estate kicked off a yearlong tribute, and published an *Elvis and the Colonel* magazine for him. Jack Soden gave a statement to the *Commercial Appeal.* He said, "Elvis and Colonel Parker made history together. They also shared an abiding friendship that is often overlooked and misunderstood by the press and the general public."

LAMAR FIKE: It may simply be a situation of keeping the image intact. No matter how much anybody bitches and moans and groans, Colonel's the one who saved the estate. I don't like him, but that's the way it is.

MARTY LACKER: Priscilla is protective of Parker for some reason. Barron Hilton threw a big eighty-fifth birthday party for Colonel last June [1994] in Las Vegas, and Priscilla went. The newspaper reported that she hugged and kissed him and his wife and that Colonel pointed a finger skyward and said, "I'm still working for you, Elvis."

LAMAR FIKE: I think they just don't want to destroy the myth.

MARTY LACKER: When Elvis died, nobody could foresee how hard the fans were going to cling to his memory or how affected they were going to be by his death.

In 1982, the year Graceland was opened to the public, they held the first Candlelight Vigil. Every August 15, the fans line up at ten P.M., and walk up the long driveway with a lighted candle to pay their respects at the graves.

That first year, I was standing by the gate watching. And I moved up by the guard shack because the crowd started getting heavy.

All of a sudden, I heard this sobbing from inside. I went in there, and this woman was just completely torn up.

I said, "What's wrong?" And her husband started to speak in broken English. They were from France. He said, "The doctors told her eight months ago that she has cancer, and she wasn't supposed to live this long. But she said she wouldn't die until she was able to go to Graceland."

I put my hand on her shoulder and patted her, and I said, "You're here now. You got your wish."

She tried to say something, but I couldn't understand her. Her husband said she was saying, "Yes, but the one thing I want to do is go up to see the grave, but I can't walk."

I said, "Don't cry. Elvis wouldn't want you to cry." And she looked up and said, "How would you know that? Who are you?" I said, "My name is Marty Lacker." And this woman jumped up and grabbed hold of my neck and got almost hysterical. Her husband said, "She knows everything about Elvis, so she knows who you are."

I said, "If you like, your husband and I will help you go up there." And she quit crying, and she let go of my neck, and she said, "I can do this on my own now." And honest to God, with her husband at her side, that woman walked up to Elvis's grave. I'll never forget that as long as I live.

🏃 🏃 🏃

BILLY SMITH: One of the things Blanchard Tual recommended was that the estate not file a wrongful death action against Dr. Nick. In 1979, the Tennessee Board of Medical Examiners went after him for overprescribing. I think that was the same year somebody took a shot at him at a football game here in Memphis.

MARTY LACKER: That was pretty strange. Around the time of the hearing, Dr. Nick took a guest, Dr. Charles Thomas Langford, to the Memphis State–Utah State football game at the Liberty Bowl. Dr. Langford sat directly behind Dr. Nick in the stands. And near the end of the game, Dr. Langford got shot in the shoulder. The police don't know if someone just randomly shot a bullet up in the air or if they just missed the guy they were after.

BILLY SMITH: In January of '80, the board suspended Dr. Nick's license for three months and give him three years' probation. Then a month after he started practicing again, the Shelby County grand jury indicted him—on criminal charges of overprescribing drugs to ten of his patients, including Elvis, Jerry Lee Lewis, Marty, and Alan.

Dr. Nick's attorney was James Neal, the Watergate prosecutor. He presented the defense that Dr. Nick was trying to cure Elvis with what they call "drug maintenance."

LAMAR FIKE: The defense called me to be a witness. And I said, "You don't need me there. He'll go to prison if I come."

MARTY LACKER: When all this first came down, I told everybody, "The only way you're going to get me there is if you subpoena me." So they subpoenaed both me and my wife as witnesses for the prosecution.

When Jim Neal heard that, he asked me to come and talk to them. So I went down to the Pilot Hotel, by the Mississippi River, where they had this huge room set up.

Neal started talking to me, and I noticed that Nick wasn't in the room. I said, "Wait a minute. Where's Nichopoulos?" And Neal said, "He's in the other room." I said, "Well, I'd like for him to hear what I've got to say." So they brought Nick in, and I said, "I want you to know how most of the guys feel about you and what you used to do." And I told him that he and Joe and Jerry walked around like privileged characters and that it caused a lot of dissension in the group.

Then I said, "I'm not going to get up in court and say anything that will hurt you. I think you've suffered enough."

BILLY SMITH: I have to look at both sides. I mean, why not go after Dr. Ghanem? He wrote a hell of a lot of prescriptions. I'd like to see Elvis's bill from him. Or from Dr. Shapiro. How about Dr. Kaplan? Dr. Nick wasn't a damn bit worse than these other guys. If he hadda been, I might have testified against him. The difference I saw was they'd give it all to Elvis at one time and Dr. Nick kept most of it in his bag.

So I testified for the defense.

The assistant district attorney [James D. Wilson] thought he was bein' real cute. I told him about the placebos me and Dr. Nick tried to slip in on Elvis. And about how we drained the Placidyls. But he was trying to catch me.

He said, "How do you drain a tablet?" I said, "You don't. You try to find something close and replace it with that." I said, "Have you ever looked at a morphine tablet? It'll look just like a damn saccharine tablet."

The fans don't understand why I testified for Dr. Nick. I think a lot of them felt ill towards me because of that. It's hard to explain. But the man cared. And I'd hate like hell to have been Dr. Nick and had Elvis Presley for a patient.

Even now, people say, "Why didn't you all help Elvis?" You know how I answer that? I say, "Pick the damn spot I was in, and tell me in a year how you're handling it."

MARTY LACKER: Evidently, the jury believed Billy and that Good Samaritan defense. Dr. Nick got acquitted in November of '81. On all counts.

LAMAR FIKE: It's funny the turns things take. In 1990, Dr. Nick went around saying he thought Elvis was murdered. He hooked up with a writer named Murray Silver, who did that Jerry Lee Lewis book [*Great Balls of Fire*] with Jerry's child bride [Myra Lewis]. They sent a book proposal all around New York saying Elvis probably died from a karate chop to the neck.

Red West saw that and said, "I'm glad I didn't see the son of a bitch [Dr. Nick]." Red would have torn his head off. Nick is tired of being blamed for Elvis's death. But he's also desperate for money.

BILLY SMITH: You know what else Dr. Nick said? He hinted to an editor at one of the tabloids that Elvis was gay. I guess he thought it would sell his story, and he needs money. Because they've done got him again.

MARTY LACKER: The state filed new charges against Dr. Nick in 1992. They've got him on three charges of overprescribing, and "unprofessional, dishonorable or unethical conduct, with gross malpractice, ignorance, negligence or incompetence." They want his license for good this time.

👟 👟 👟

LAMAR FIKE: We've all been through a lot. But there are bright spots, too. Before I married Janice, I was dating a girl named Mary, a flight attendant for one of the major airlines. I was very much in love with her. But I was doing the Goldman book, which was terribly difficult. I worked three solid years on it, and I was just totally burnt out. Mary wanted to get married, and I said, "I'll never get married. You can take that to the bank." So she married another guy, and then I married Janice.

After I divorced Janice, I called Mary, and we've been married now for ten years. Ricky Stanley, who became a minister after Elvis died, married us in Waco.

Mary's been the best thing that's ever happened to me. We laugh a lot, and carry on insane conversations, and just have a lot of fun. She's more than a wife. She's a buddy. When she looks at me, she doesn't see how big I am. She sees me the way she wants to see me. And, at best, I am very hard to live with. I have a difficult time sharing myself with a person. I think we all developed that trait from Elvis.

Down in Waco, I didn't know that I'd ever get back in the music business. I went into the car business, and I had two van-conversion plants. I thought I knew what I was doing. Boy, I learned quick I didn't. The Texas economy did a nosedive, and I lost a little more than $1 million.

That was a very cataclysmic fall. I washed out and bankrupted. Mary said, "Look, I'm moving to Nashville. I think you should go back and work in the publishing and entertainment business." She said, "If you don't go, I'm going without you." So we packed up and left in '83.

I pretty much had to feel my way back. Jimmy Bowen [then president of MCA/Nashville Records] was an old friend, and he put me on as a consultant at $500 a week. Then I went back into publishing, and I've done well these last twelve years.

A lot of other guys never got that lucky. Knowing how to order a limo isn't a strong qualification for anything. With some of the guys, it was like *Death of a Salesman*. And still is. It's really sad.

We all have terribly bad habits that we developed during that time. Lack of discipline for one. In a way, we self-destructed when Elvis self-destructed.

MARTY LACKER: Red's done well. When the furor over his book died down, he got back into acting. He's turned into a very good character actor and done a lot of pictures, like *Road House*, with Patrick Swayze, and a lot of television. Red has an acting school in Memphis now.

Sonny and Judy raised Arabian horses in California for a while. But they wanted to come back to the South, so they moved near Nashville. Sonny was road manager and head of security for the band Alabama. For the past couple of years, he's been trying to write movie scripts. He's a born-again Christian now, and he's real serious about it.

LAMAR FIKE: Joe Esposito was with the estate for a while. He lives in Sacramento. He had a book out last year. After Elvis died, he worked as road manager for some of the rock-pop acts—the Bee Gees and John Denver. After that, he became a partner in a limousine-rental company in L.A. Then he got involved in a celebrity food company. Joe's had a couple of auctions to sell his Elvis memorabilia. And he makes a little money at the fan conventions.

BILLY SMITH: Some of the guys have done real well, and some have done the best they could. I heard Dave Hebler went into real estate in California. Sam Thompson is a judge now. And Gene Smith is still in Memphis. He drove a cookie truck for a while.

Dick Grob became head of security at Graceland after Elvis died, and Al Strada and Dean Nichopoulos worked with him there. Then Dean went into the wholesale liquor business in Memphis, and last I heard, Al was working for Federal Express in Memphis. Dick managed Charlie Hodge for a while.

MARTY LACKER: Charlie sings in a little Elvis show over in Gatlinburg now. He's just perpetuated the same old stories about Elvis for years.

When the state first went after Nichopoulos, Larry Hutchinson, the chief criminal investigator for the attorney general, interviewed Charlie about Elvis's drug abuse. Hutchinson said, "He was in love with Elvis and would tell any lie he could to protect Elvis's image." I don't think it was just Charlie being loyal. He was also trying to jump back on the gravy train. During the first couple fan festivals after Elvis died, he charged people $5 to $10 to have their picture taken with him.

Richard Davis has done some of those Elvis conventions, too. For a long time, he helped George Klein set up DJ booths in nightclubs. Right now, he's working internal security for one of the new gambling casinos in Tunica, Mississippi. Klein picks up a few pennies with the estate, but mostly he works in a casino in Tunica, too.

LAMAR FIKE: Jerry Schilling had that cozy estate job. He managed Lisa Marie's singing career for a while and coproduced the [short-lived] TV series *Elvis.* He had a couple of film editing jobs in Hollywood and then tour-managed Billy Joel when Joel started out. I think he's doing freelance production work now. He was involved with *The History of Rock 'n' Roll,* that syndicated mini-series.

Marty has his own advertising and sales firm. He does marketing and promotion projects for various companies.

MARTY LACKER: The Stanley brothers weren't really part of the Memphis Mafia, but some people thought they were. Ricky got himself into drug rehab and became a born-again Christian and an evangelist.

David was in evangelist work, too, but he's not anymore. He got a degree in communications and traveled the country giving antidrug lectures. He cowrote *The Elvis Encyclopedia* [in 1994] and produced a video on it.

LAMAR FIKE: Billy Smith has a factory job now. He works in maintenance, and he's an apprentice machinist, tool and die. He's blue-collar, but he's done very well. He's kept it together, which is something, considering what he's been through.

MARTY LACKER: Since his death, Elvis has become an even bigger magnet for crackpots and con artists. There are a lot of devoted fans, but a whole array of opportunists have come out of the woodwork. Even Elvis's undertaker was writing a book, but the man died.

A couple of years ago, *Entertainment Tonight* took a poll that showed that somewhere between 6 and 16 percent of all Americans think Elvis is still alive. As late as '94, some crazy group called the Presley Commission issued a "report" that said Elvis was working as a government agent—that threats from organized crime forced him to fake his death. The head of this group, Phil Aitcheson, says the body found in the bathroom was Colonel's cousin. And that what everybody saw in the coffin was a wax dummy. For proof, he says it was sweating, and dead men don't sweat.

What started all this was Gail Brewer-Giorgio's [1988] book, *Is Elvis Alive?* She never actually said Elvis didn't die, but she fed people's hope that he was still around. That's what started all the rumors that Elvis was seen in Michigan and at Burger Kings coast to coast. There's no end to it.

LAMAR FIKE: Somebody said to me, "Lamar, are you sure that Elvis is dead?" I said, "I think a rock's got more life than Elvis."

When you think about how this story continues to evolve, it's really amazing. In '93, Dee Presley had her lawyers look into her divorce from Vernon. She thinks it wasn't binding. The judge in the Dominican Republic supposedly caused some kind of a problem.

Dee's after the estate, and I think she's got 'em cold turkey. If she's still legally married to Vernon, just think what that means. Whoa! That could change everything.

MARTY LACKER: It's interesting to see how the women have gained control of it all. Or tried to. And how they've handled it. Lisa's a high school dropout. For a while there, it looked like she was going to end up like her father, a drug addict. She's talked in an interview with *Life* magazine about going on a three-day coke [cocaine] high when she was fourteen. That was before she decided to go off drugs for good. Priscilla put her in the Church of Scientology's main facility out in L.A., the Celebrity Centre International, which is a kind of detox center. Scientology is pretty antidrug.

Now, of course, Lisa's marriage to Michael Jackson puts everything about the estate into question. In '88, when Lisa married Danny Keough, she seemed to want nothing to do with the estate. But after she married Michael—something Priscilla says she didn't know about ahead of time, by the way—Lisa started making noises about turning Graceland into a private home again. Which must make the estate real nervous. Because Lisa says that's why she extended her mother's executorship to begin with—to quell the rumors that when Lisa took over Graceland she was going to sell it. The investors were freaking out.

When Michael and Lisa got married, Jack Soden put out a statement that said, "I know very well that [Lisa's] very content and secure with the way things are . . . Lisa is very intent in leaving all of Elvis Presley's assets independent and intact." But Lisa's only given them authority to manage the estate through 1998. And then she might just claim what's hers.

LAMAR FIKE: Lisa's marriage to Michael Jackson is the single most shocking event. Hell, it's the most shocking marriage since Jackie Kennedy and Aristotle Onassis. People have gone stark, fucking nuts over this. Did you read what Michael said about proposing? He said, "I made love to Lisa in my Mickey Mouse pajamas. And then I asked her to marry me." Watch. If they move into Graceland, Michael will change its name to Never-Never Land.

MARTY LACKER: I think when the rumors of that marriage first came out, Elvis started doing flips in his grave. And then when it was verified, he probably tried every which way to get back here, to slap the shit out of both of them.

Elvis wouldn't like it for a number of reasons. One, because Michael is black, or used to be. Elvis wouldn't want Lisa to marry out of her race, just as there are black people who don't want their children marrying white people. Two, he wouldn't have liked Michael's weirdness. Elvis would want the best for his daughter, and Jackson ain't the best. And three, with Elvis's ego, there's no way he would want any other entertainer to have a claim on Graceland, although there's supposedly a prenuptial arrangement.

I'm sure Michael has an agenda, but I don't think it's money. I think most people believe he married Lisa as a cover-up, to draw attention away from the charges that he sexually molested a thirteen-year-old boy. The only person I know who says he believes they're actually in love is George Klein.

The really goofy thing is why Lisa did it. Lamar says it's a marriage made in defiance. Lisa and Priscilla were on the outs for a while. And Priscilla's kept her on a short leash. That $100 million is Lisa's, but her mother won't let her have it. She wants to manage it for her. I've heard that Priscilla gives Lisa an allowance of $4,000 a month. And Lisa has supposedly said, "You're no longer going to tell me what I can and can't do. I'm going to show you." That's why she wants to be called Lisa Marie Presley-Jackson.

LAMAR FIKE: Then there's the theory Lisa wants Michael to help her with her singing career, which never got off the ground. I got news for you—she has the talent of an anvil.

MARTY LACKER: There's also a possibility that the Church of Scientology is behind this. "Auditing" is expensive and Michael sure can afford it. I'm sure they'd welcome him with open arms.

It's funny . . . The one religion Elvis put down was Scientology. He couldn't stand it. And then Priscilla brought up his daughter in it. Jo Smith thinks that's why she did it.

LAMAR FIKE: Danny Keough's father is a minister in the Church of Scientology. And Danny's brother, Thomas, and his wife were witnesses at Lisa and Michael's wedding in the Dominican Republic. What does that tell you?

MARTY LACKER: One night, I was sitting in my house all by myself, and I was feeling a little lonely. I started thinking what a friend Red has been for forty years. And then I started thinking about the relationship I had with Elvis and the group as a whole, and how the camaraderie was gone. So in April of '92, I put together a reunion of the Memphis Mafia.

The original six or seven guys have never had any serious arguments. But since Elvis died, three of the guys—George, Jerry, and Joe—don't want to have anything to do with a few of the other guys, especially Lamar because of the Goldman book. So George, Jerry, and Joe turned me down.

I said to them, "Who the hell are you to judge? There wasn't one soul around Elvis who didn't take advantage of him when he was alive or after he died." I said, "We've all been through a lot together. We shared something special. And to try to pull that apart just because you don't like somebody isn't right."

I thought that once everybody got together, there was a good chance that they'd bury the hatchet. But it didn't work.

LAMAR FIKE: I tried to get George and Jerry to come to the reunion myself. Jerry said, "I can't do that." I said, "Why not?" He said, "Well, you know, that book you wrote." And George said the same thing. I said, "What do I have to do, make a cross out of that book and put it on my back and crawl up the Graceland driveway?"

George changed a lot after he got so involved with the estate. He's pretty much of a prick now. When the book came out, Albert [Goldman] was on a radio talk show, and the host said, "George Klein said . . . " And then he rattled off a bunch of accusations. Albert said, "Isn't it amazing that someone would take the word of a convicted felon over a person who has never had a police ticket?"

But George is right—the estate still hates my guts. And that's how the guys split down the middle these days—by those who want to play footsie with the estate and those who don't.

MARTY LACKER: George and I were like intertwined fingers for twenty-five years until he did something that really hurt me. The falling-out was over a book I wrote [*Elvis: Portrait of a Friend*] in '79. It didn't say much of anything. But my wife wrote some things George didn't like.

Later on, I came up with the idea of having an Elvis memorial gathering each August at Memphis State. I mentioned it to some people, and lo and behold, it got under way. But next thing I heard, the person in charge was George Klein.

I called George up and asked him how that happened, and he said, "Well, we thought it best if you weren't there." I said, "Really? Why is that?" He said, "Well, because of your book. We took a vote—me, and Dr. Nick, and Charlie Hodge."

I said, "Klein, go fuck yourself." And I didn't talk to George for twelve years.

Finally, I said something to him at a funeral in '91. I watched a friend of ours being lowered into the ground. They were shoveling dirt on the coffin, and I went over to George and put my hand out. I said, "Hey, life's too short. Let's forget about it." He took my hand. But we're still not friends.

BILLY SMITH: I still have strong feelings for all of them. You can't live with a group of guys that long and not be tuned into their feelings.

LAMAR FIKE: After the reunion in '92, all of us went to see Alan Fortas. He was battling kidney cancer, and he hadn't felt good enough to come up to the hotel.

You know what was odd? Alan was sick for a couple of years. And when Colonel heard Alan had cancer, he called him every Sunday. When Elvis was alive, Colonel didn't particularly like Alan.

Maybe his feelings changed later on. But I also think the Colonel has turned into a rather benign figure. He's got an empty saber—he can't rattle his sword anymore.

MARTY LACKER: You know what else was strange? When Priscilla was back in Memphis making a video, she called Alan and had him picked up in a limo and brought over to Graceland. It was really nice of her, and it meant a lot to Alan. And it shocked a lot of people that she would do that.

When Alan got cancer, he was kind of pitiful. We all pretended he'd get better. But the doctor told him that there was nothing they could do for him. He laid up in the hospital and said, "I wish it would just come on and get me."

He'd alternate between crying and making jokes. The pain was just so bad. He even went to Reno for some kind of quack cure. One day, he said, "There's 50 million cars on the street. Why can't one of 'em just hit me?"

LAMAR FIKE: One morning in September '92, Marty called me at seven A.M. and told me Alan was gone. I was really upset. Alan was the first member of the core group to die. It was just overwhelming. The invincibility of the group was shattered.

The day we buried him, I sat on the side of the bed getting dressed, and I said, "I hate to go to this funeral. I cannot explain how bad I hate this." And I choked up. It was just so shocking. Mary said, "I've never heard you talk like this." But it was unbelievable to me that somebody could fall from the group.

After Alan's funeral, Marty, Red, and David Stanley, and I went to Corky's for barbecue. I turned around to everybody and I said, "Boys, now it begins." They said, "What do you mean?" I said, "It's going to come quicker for all of us. You have no idea what we're getting ready to go through."

MARTY LACKER: We're still feeling so many repercussions from the old life. In '92, Patsy divorced me. After thirty-one years. She waited until all the kids were grown, and then finally, she did it. She said, "One day I just fell out of love with you." My only bewilderment is why she waited so long. I'd been trying to make it up to her for the last fifteen years. Maybe I should have stayed a bastard. Maybe she'd still be with me. But we're still friends.

LAMAR FIKE: There's no doubt that we're all haunted by this experience. Even now, I dream about Elvis three or four times a week. Very vivid dreams. In one, I said, "Where are you?" He said, "It's not anyplace you'd want to be right now." I said, "Well, where is it?" He said, "Son, it's not Cleveland."

Last night, I woke up and heard him call my name. I sat straight up in the bed. It scared the hell out of Mary because she felt Elvis was in the room. I can just be walking down the hall and I'll hear him. His voice is as plain as mine is right now. Usually, we have long, protracted conversations.

After Elvis's death, I went to a psychiatrist for three fucking years. I had two or three hundred hours of psychotherapy, trying to get over it. The doctor said, "You're going to have these dreams for the rest of your life." And he's right. There's not a day that goes by that I don't think of Elvis.

MARTY LACKER: Elvis is in a lot of my dreams. The funny thing is that he's always trying to avoid me or avoid other people. What it means, who knows. I think of him all the time. He's just always in my thoughts. Always will be.

LAMAR FIKE: In 1986, *USA Today* ran a computer-generated portrait of what Elvis would look like at fifty-one "as he left the Betty Ford clinic after kicking drugs." He still looked handsome, but older, of course.

Musically, I think we have a pretty good idea of what he'd be like today. Marty thinks he would have been doing up-tempo stuff. But I think Elvis would have been like Sinatra. When he died, somebody said he looked like a rock Sinatra in Liberace drag. But at sixty, which is what Elvis would have been in 1995, he would have been a personality. He wouldn't have needed a record label or even chart records. He would have done about one big tour a year, and millions of people would have gone to see him.

MARTY LACKER: Sonny says he doesn't listen to Elvis's music much these days. He says, "How can you listen to those songs the same way anymore? They're different songs now. They say something else."

🕴 🕴 🕴

LAMAR FIKE: Every one of us is exactly like Elvis in some way. My cousin said to me one time, "You play a guitar like Elvis." That's because he taught me. And David Stanley tries to act like Elvis, and he doesn't know he's doing it. We all became one bundle, wrapped up with the same string. I know that when I die, Elvis will still get top billing. Like, "Former Elvis Employee Dies."

For better or worse, we are what he left behind. He lives through his music, but he also lives through us.

We all have these carryovers. I'll go to the grocery store and buy fifty pounds of sugar when I don't need but five. In my mind, I'm buying for the whole group. My wife will say, "What are you doing?" I'll say, "I'm doing what I've always done."

We're all handicapped in a way. You can look at every one of us, and we all have the same problems. We try to survive with him not around, and it's not easy. It's even colored the way we interact with people. I don't make friends very easily because I don't know where they're coming from. And Marty is always suspicious of everybody. I think we had the rug pulled out from under us too many times. We carry our insecurities around like a knapsack.

BILLY SMITH: Back in the early days, I would have give anything to have been Elvis Presley. Now, I don't know. I guess it's easy to see somebody else's insecurities and not be able to face your own. But it makes no difference what kind of person he was. It's what he done to change everything. And what he left. Did he leave total bad or total good? Or did he just leave a little bit of both? That's my thought. He had it all, and he misused a portion of his life. He dug his own grave. That's all you can say.

LAMAR FIKE: What's incredible is how Elvis has endured—his popularity eighteen years after his death. Nobody's generated that kind of devotion except Jesus Christ. Elvis is the quintessential American icon—the personification of sex, drugs, and rock 'n' roll. He's an artistic genius. And he's the premier symbol of wretched excess, a guy who had everything and squandered it all. He's both a hero and a joke. The face on a postage stamp.

I was at the Hard Rock Cafe in New York some years ago, and Eric Clapton was there. He and some other rock 'n' rollers sat at the table with us talking. Somebody mentioned a musician who had a pretty heavy drug problem. And I just left-handedly said, "I'm not going to get sanctimonious here, but Elvis died for your sins." And they all passed out from laughter.

Nobody's ever done what he did, and no one ever will. The guy's sold more than a *billion* records! If you put 'em end to end, they'd circle the earth twice. He did what everybody wasn't supposed to do, and he died for it. He's a prototype, a blueprint. And an example of what everybody in the business doesn't want to turn into.

Because of all that, he's become the messiah of rock 'n' roll. We just happened to be the guys who sat on the right and the left of him. It's a permanent label. Whether we like it or not, we wear it.

EPILOGUE
The Pledge

BILLY SMITH: In 1967, when we were out in California, I happened to walk into the room where Elvis and Priscilla were talking one day. And I heard Elvis tell her something personal about me, from when I was little, maybe five or six years old. It wasn't that I got in trouble—it went beyond that. And I wouldn't have discussed it with just anybody because this was a very hurtful and traumatic experience, something I was just devastated about.

I think the fact that it happened is one of the reasons Elvis was so dadgum protective of me—why he had to know where I was at all times, especially as a kid and as a teenager and even after I got grown. I guess he thought he could protect me better than anybody. It could very well be the key to our whole relationship.

When he saw me there in the room, he quit talking about it. But I couldn't believe he done it. It hurt my feelings just so bad. I didn't think he'd ever tell it.

Priscilla left after a minute or two, and I confronted him. I said, "I don't tell stuff on you! Why did you tell on me?" Even to this day, it bothers me. I guess he wasn't thinking. But it upset me so that I was going to quit when we got back to Memphis.

One night a week or two later, we were in his bedroom, and he apologized for what he done, and he said he'd come up with something to strengthen our trust in each other. He said, "We'll make a pledge. That way, you'll know that I'll never say anything to anybody else. We'll embrace, and repeat this to each other, and it will bond us together in friendship. I won't tell anyone about it if you won't."

It shocked the fool out of me because I didn't expect it. But I agreed. Elvis dimmed the lights, and we sat on his bed in total darkness, facing each other, with our legs folded. And we placed our hands on each other's heart and took this oath. I don't know where it come from, whether it was from a book, or if he just made it up. But he knew it from memory, and we went over it several times so I could memorize it, too. Afterwards, we both cried like crazy. I'll remember it as long as I live.

There were two secret parts to it. One was a word, a password. Kind of a nonsense word, combined from parts of two or three other words. Later on—more so in the last years—if we were with other people and there was something he wanted to talk about in private, or if something was personal to him, all he had to do was say that word. Then we would ease off together.

We also had a secret embrace. It was done a certain way so that if you were in complete darkness you would still recognize the other. From then on, every time we were in a crowd, that's the way we embraced. And people never really noticed. None of the guys ever knew it, even. Not in all those years.

I don't know of anyone else who knows either the word or the gesture. Because I never broke our pledge or betrayed Elvis's trust, and I never will. What we pledged, I'll hold forever in my heart. We reached out to each other, from the love we had then, and now. We meant for it to continue, even if one of us should die. I know as well as I know anything that this meant as much to Elvis as it does to me.

I loved him more than anyone can ever understand, and I always will. You could not truly know him, and not love him.

THE PLEDGE

It's just a simple word, you see,
To get inside you need no key.
For we who know, know it well,
And you who don't can never tell.

As I place my hand upon your heart,
And you place yours on mine,
From this day forward, our minds, our souls,
Our hearts will intertwine.

If either one should have a doubt,
Now is the time to back out.
For this pledge together us will tie,
Even if one of us should die.

What we share in confidence now,
Even in death cannot part,
For it comes not from the mind,
But from the heart.

You just hold my words true,
For where I go, you'll be there, too.
I know your inner self, and you know mine.
Honor and keep it for all time.

And when I'm gone,
Every now and then,
Think of this pledge,
For I love you, my friend.

You can confess to me,
And touch my heart,
And I'll know it's you by ["the word"],
Even in the dark.

Elvis Aaron Presley
Billy Wayne Smith

INDEX